Slutsk and Vicinity Memorial Book (Belarus)

Translation of
Pinkas Slutsk u-benoteha

Original Book Edited by:
N. Chinitz, Sh. Nachmani, Yizkor Book Committee

Originally published in Tel Aviv, 1962

Volume I

JewishGen
מרכז עולמי לגנאלוגיה יהודית
The Global Home for Jewish Genealogy

A Publication of JewishGen
Edmond J. Safra Plaza, 36 Battery Place, New York, NY 10280
646.494.2972 | info@JewishGen.org | www.jewishgen.org

MUSEUM OF
JEWISH HERITAGE
A LIVING MEMORIAL
TO THE HOLOCAUST

Slutsk and Vicinity Memorial Book (Belarus)
Translation of *Pinkas Slutsk u benotehu*

Volume I

Copyright © 2025 by JewishGen. All rights reserved.
First Printing: February 2025, Shevat, 5785
Editor of Original Yizkor Book: N. Chinitz, Sh. Nachmani, Yizkor Book Committee
Project Coordinator Emerita: Margot Tutun
Cover Design: Irv Osterer
Layout, formatting and indexing: Jonathan Wind

Library of Congress Control Number (LCCN): 2024949233

ISBN: 978-1-962054-14-0 (hard cover: 538 pages, alk. paper)

About JewishGen.org

JewishGen, is a Genealogical Research Division of the Museum of Jewish Heritage - A Living Memorial to the Holocaust, serves as the global home for Jewish genealogy.

Featuring unparalleled access to 30+ million records, it offers unique search tools, along with opportunities for researchers to connect with others who share similar interests. Award winning resources such as the Family Finder, Discussion Groups, and ViewMate, are relied upon by thousands each day.

In addition, JewishGen's extensive informational, educational and historical offerings, such as the Jewish Communities Database, Yizkor Book translations, InfoFiles, Family Tree of the Jewish People, and KehilaLinks, provide critical insights, first-hand accounts, and context about Jewish communal and familial life throughout the world.

Offered as a free resource, JewishGen.org has facilitated thousands of family connections and success stories, and is currently engaged in an intensive expansion effort that will bring many more records, tools, and resources to its collections.

Please visit https://www.jewishgen.org/ to learn more.

Vice President for JewishGen: Avraham Groll

About the JewishGen Yizkor Book Project

Yizkor Books (Memorial Books) were traditionally written to memorialize the names of departed family and martyrs during holiday services in the synagogue (a practice that still exists in many synagogues today).

Over the centuries, as a result of countless persecutions and horrific atrocities committed against the Jews, Yizkor Books (Sefer Zikaron in Hebrew) were expanded to include more historical information, such as biographical sketches of famous personalities and descriptions of daily town life.

Following the Holocaust, the idea of remembrance and learning took on an urgent and crucial importance. Survivors of the Holocaust sought out other surviving residents of their former towns to memorialize and document the names and way of life of those who were ruthlessly murdered by the Nazis. These remembrances were documented in Yizkor Books, hundreds of which were published in the first decades after the Holocaust.

Most of these books were published privately, or through *Landsmanshaftn* (social organizations comprised of members originating from the same European town or region) that still existed, and were often distributed free of charge. The languages used to document these crucial histories and links to our past were mostly Yiddish and Hebrew. JewishGen has undertaken the sacred responsibility of translating these books into English so that the culture and way of life of these communities will be preserved and transmitted to future generations.

In 1986, a group of farsighted JewishGenners started a project to pool their efforts together in groups based upon their ancestors' towns and donate funds to translate the Yizkor books of their ancestral towns into English. As the translated material became available, it was made accessible for free at https://www.JewishGen.org/Yizkor . Hardcover copies can be purchased by visiting https://www.jewishgen.org/Yizkor/ybip.html (see below).

It is our hope that the translation of these books into English (and other languages) will assist the countless Jewish family researchers who are so desperately seeking to forge a connection with their heritage.

Director of JewishGen Yizkor Book Project: Lance Ackerfeld

About JewishGen Press

JewishGen Press (formerly the Yizkor Books-in-Print Project) is the publishing division of JewishGen.org, and provides a venue for the publication of non-fiction books pertaining to Jewish genealogy, history, culture, and heritage.

In addition to the Yizkor Book category, publications in the Other Non-Fiction category include Shoah memoirs and research, genealogical research, collections of genealogical and historical materials, biographies, diaries and letters, studies of Jewish experience and cultural life in the past, academic theses, and other books of interest to the Jewish community.

Please visit https://www.jewishgen.org/Yizkor/ybip.html to learn more.

Director of JewishGen Press: Joel Alpert
Managing Editor - Jessica Feinstein
Publications Manager - Susan Rosin

Notes to the Reader

The images in the original book were reproduced from photographs from the time of the first edition. These reproductions were already of poor quality, being pre-war and at least 60 or more years old. As a result, the images in the book are the best achievable.

A reader can view the original scans of the book on the websites listed below.

The original book can be seen online at the Yiddish Book Center website:

https://www.yiddishbookcenter.org/collections/yizkor-books/yzk-nybc314001/nachmani-samson-chinitz-pinkas-slutsk-u-venoteha

OR

at the New York Public Library Digital Collections website:

https://digitalcollections.nypl.org/items/f6dfc840-74eb-0133-bf27-00505686d14e

To obtain a list of Shoah victims from **Slutsk (Belarus),** the reader should access the Yad Vashem web site listed below; one can also search for specific family names using family name option. These lists are continually updated by Yad Vashem, so it is worthwhile to periodically search them.

There is more valuable information (including the Pages of Testimony, etc.) available on this website: https://yvng.yadvashem.org/

A list of all books available from JewishGen Press along with prices is available at: https://www.jewishgen.org/Yizkor/ybip.html

Additional Information is available at: https://kehilalinks.jewishgen.org/slutsk/slutsk.html

Cover Photo Credits

Cover Design by: Irv Osterer

Front Cover:

Photograph (retouched and restored) of *The Cold Synagogue in Slutsk* a 1923 watercolor by Jacob Kruger (Jankieĺ Kruhier): https://www.wikidata.org/wiki/Q13033604; Picryl.com Public Domain

Back Cover:

The New Synagogue – [Page 209]
Talmud Torah – [Page 77]
Der Kalte Shul (The Cold Synagogue) – [Page 13]

Geopolitical Information

Map of Belarus showing the location of **Slutsk**

Slutsk

Slutsk, Belarus is located at 53°02' N 27°34' E 60 miles S of Minsk

	Town	District	Province	Country
Before WWI (c. 1900):	Slutsk	Slutsk	Minsk	Russian Empire
Between the wars (c. 1930):	Slutsk	Minsk	Belarus SSR	Soviet Union
After WWII (c. 1950):	Slutsk			Soviet Union
Today (c. 2000):	Slutsk			Belarus

Alternate Names for the Town:

Slutsk [Bel, Rus], Słuck [Pol], Slutzk [Yid], Sluzk [Ger], Słucak

Nearby Jewish Communities:

Gresk 10 miles NNW
Pahost 13 miles SSE
Grozovo 13 miles NW
Lenino 14 miles W
Urechcha 15 miles ESE
Chyrvonaya Slabada 21 miles SW
Kapyl 21 miles WNW
Starobin 21 miles S
Lyuban 24 miles SE
Tsimkavichy 24 miles W
Shatsk 27 miles N
Losha 27 miles NNW
Staryya Darohi 29 miles E

Jewish Population: 10,264 (in 1897), 8,358 (in1926)

Table of Contents

Slutsk and Vicinity Memorial Book, Volume I

Additions

End Volume I

,

Slutsk and Vicinity Memorial Book (Belarus)
Volume I

53°01' / 27°33'

Translation of *Pinkas Slutsk u-benoteha*

Edited by: N. Chinitz, Sh. Nachmani, Yizkor Book Committee

Published in Tel-Aviv, 1962

Acknowledgments

Project Coordinator:

Emerita Coordinator: Margot Tutun

Our sincere appreciation to Chaim I. Waxman for permission
to put this material on the JewishGen web site.

With grateful thanks to Stefanie Holzman for obtaining the pictures appearing in this translation project.

This is a translation from: *Pinkas Slutsk u-benoteha* (Slutsk and vicinity memorial book),
Editors: N. Chinitz, Sh. Nachmani, Tel Aviv, Yizkor-Book Committee, 1962 (H, Y, E, 450 pages).

Note: The original book can be seen online at the NY Public Library site: Slutsk

[Page 2]

Preface

by the Committee

Translated by Jerrold Landau

When we began to collect the material on Slutsk, and to organize and edit it, some things came to our view, whether factual or popular legends, that were hidden in the treasury of ancient literature and in the memories of the elders of the community. Indeed, the annals of this city throughout the latter four centuries testify clearly, according to documents and historical sources, about its greatness in the distant past, and its essence as a Jewish center in the recent past. Slutsk served throughout the generations as a host to Torah, Haskalah, Zionist activity, and the dissemination of Hebrew culture.

Similarly, our city gave forth famous personalities, great rabbis, famous writers and poets, and communal activists of stature. We find many prominent people in the towns around Slutsk as well, and material and spiritual influence existed among them.

Various images from the past stand before our eyes: images of simple folk, various tradespeople, porters, wagon drivers, good for nothings, leaders of parties, and counselors of youth.

Where are they all? Indeed, during the Holocaust, the Nazis wiped out virtually the entire community of Slutsk, as they wiped out all the Jewish communities.

We, the survivors of Slutsk and its environs, found today in Israel and the United States, bear in our hearts the memory of our city, in which we lived during our childhood. Unforgettable images of our brothers and sisters who perished at the hands of the wild beasts in the form of humans flutter before our eyes.

So that the memory of Slutsk will not leave us for generation after generation, we took council and decided to establish a memorial monument in the form of this book, presented in Hebrew, Yiddish and English, for the readers who are natives of Slutsk and its environs, and for their descendants in Israel and the Diaspora.

* * *

Our thanks are extended to all those who helped materially and spiritually to actualize the desire of our souls.

[Page 3]

Editors:
Shimshon Nachmani Nachum Chinitz

Editorial Committee:

Tzvi Hagivati
Rabbi Nisan Wachsman
Tzvi Assaf

Printed in Israel
Etchings: Land of Israel Zincography
Publisher: Achdut Cooperative Co., Tel Aviv

[Pages 4-6]

[Page 7]

[Blank]

[Page 8 - Hebrew] [Page 264 - Yiddish]

Heavenly Slutsk

by Y. D. B.

Translated by Sara Mages

Slutsk, the ancient Jewish city in Raysn [Belarus], which sits on the border of Polesia, surrounded by dense forests and swampy fields, decorated with extensive vegetable gardens and fine fruit gardens. The deep Sluch River, which flows in a narrow channel but in a clear stream, cuts it to its length and breadth. Slutsk is established, its old houses and shops are sturdy although most of them were made of wood. It is praised for its synagogues and schools, big and small yeshivot, which attract young men and boys, who seek education, from the surrounding cities and towns. Its Jewish inhabitants, who are God-fearing and pious, hold on to the old and do not stay away from the new. They are all important homeowners and honest craftsmen, almost all of them are well-versed in the book and even the owners of wagons enter Beit HaMidrash with their whip under their armpit to hear a lesson in the Gemara. The same Slutsk, which was considered to be an important Jewish metropolis, is gone, lost from the world. The beginning of its collapse and destruction took place immediately after the First World War. With the outbreak of the Great Revolution in Russia, gangs of Polish soldiers destroyed the area and abandoned it to all evil and cruel. They attacked cities and towns, carried out pogroms, murdered, robbed and abused their defenseless Jewish inhabitants. Later, the Bolsheviks took control and, apart from bringing distress and hunger to the Jews living in the cities, who were deprived of the means of existence in times of chaos, they also destroyed everything sacred in their lives, everything that exists and lifted their spirit throughout the generations. With brutal malice, under the guise of redeeming the people and repairing the world, it suppressed the Jewish soul and uprooted it with the rage of tyrants. The Jewish population, which was miraculously saved in these places, was destroyed by the beast of horror, the scum of a human race, in the decree of madness of the evil Satan. Slutsk, with all the thousands of Jewish communities in Eastern Europe, was erased from the face of the earth, and no one survived there.

[Page 9]

Therefore, we, the natives of Slutsk and her daughters, the nearby towns, which were bound to it with substance and spirit, need to direct our eyes and our hearts to the Slutsk that once existed, the one that is still in our memory, the nest of our good and warm childhood. It is revealed to us now, out of the fog of the past, as a "Heavenly Slutsk " as a homeland that no longer exists on the earth, but hovering in the heavens, rising sometimes, in moments of solitude, in our thoughts, in our minds, in our longing for what was and is not - the one that we carry within us, without knowing the best of its inheritance, the influence of her nature and spiritual atmosphere.

"Know where you came from" - this command, in its supreme sense, should serve as a great guide for members of a nation as a whole, but also, to a small extent, for members of the private public in a small corner. We should remember, and we will also tell future generations after us, that we weren't collected from the market, that we are the sons of a father and a mother, natives of a homeland excellent in its virtues, that it is good and pleasant to cling to it, that it is better to receive something from it and learn something from it for the future.

[Page 10]

On the Verge of a Legend

by Avraham Epstein

Translated by Mira Eckhaus

I see it from the distance, through a veil of twilight. Years and events have created a mist partition between us. Its realistic image has faded in my memory and once again I can't distinguish between facts and rumors.

However, under the pile of impressions, places and the time that passed, echoes of forgotten memories emerge and rise, echoes of memories of a distant childhood.

My hometown is small and is placed in the lowlands of the border of the Polissia forests. Around it, as far as the eye can see, stretches of low, flat, mound-strewn forests, interrupted here and there by a stretch of stream and marshy lakes. Single, feeble and small groves of birch and linden trees - poor remnants of the glory of forests from ancient times - are visible at dusk as if from pale vapors and cast shadows from the trembling treetops. A remote and forgotten city, far from the flow of life and hidden in the shadow of its gardens-orchards. The livelihood of the residents is from the zucchini and its pride is on its rabbis and its genius. It has been a place of Torah since time immemorial and from the windows of its Beit midrash, the voices of the students, the voices of boys and men, were heard in the streets in an excitement full of longing and devotion. And in the heart of the city - the market square with its shops clustered on both sides of the "road", that divides the city to two - this is the only path that stretches from vanishing distances and receives into it, like a river in its streams, many entrances and alleys dotted with houses and immersed in greenery; It is the main road, on which the minister of interior of the province will come to command his people, the district officials. At such a time, there is a lot of bustle in the city, and battalions of soldiers pass through it during the summer days on their return to their camp from the battle training. Blurred-faced and gray-eyed peasants come from the surrounding area with their merchandise and family to the market days, boil the town with their bargaining, spend out the money they have earned in the wine houses, make a lot of noise until the evening and return home drunk, while speaking in obscene language and singing, and disappear in their villages that are hidden in the forests and the swamps. And then, the town returns to its peaceful and is quiet under the management of its administrators - the great Torah scholars and the wealthy people of the town.

This is how I saw it as a child. The patriarchal orders of life were still solid and the soul of the recent past still overlapped them. The ears heard a lot of rumors, the stories of old men about righteous men, genius rabbis, faithful community leaders, who walked in the sanctuary in the previous generation. Their shadow was still influencing the townspeople and a legend was formed, a near and alive legend, in which imagination and reality are mixed together. The rumor was reliable and its witnesses were alive and kicking: here is the "cold" synagogue with its system of columns and with its tin roof towering above all the buildings of the city; An ancient building, wonderful in its beauty and in its dimensions. Polish nobles developed its form, the Prevoslav church submitted its claims to it and miraculously it became the property of the Jewish congregation... Here is the Beit Midrash of the Governor Isarke, where Rabbi Mendele, a prominent student of Rabbi Chaim of Volozhin, who, through his obedience, avoided the rabbinical service, established a yeshiva. Here is the rabbi's house next to the neighborhood of the synagogues, this house served as an apartment for Rabbi Yosili Peimer and Rabbi Yosef bar Solovitzik - the genius of Lithuania and its glory. Here is the courtyard of Rabbi Yona and Rabbi Shechna Iserlish - the city officers and its wealthy people, whose basements contained legendary treasures. Every Saturday, tables were set up along the yard for hundreds of Jews, the city's poor and its scholars. In the large oven, semolina challahs were baked and poultry soup was cooked for the sick and poor women giving birth, and in the basement, there were barrels of wine for Kiddush and Havdalah for the synagogues and a variety of jams ready for anyone who needed them. Next to the "courtyard" of the lord

Simchowitz, the son-in-law of Reb Shechna, the one who came to us from abroad and brought the smell of Distant lands, separated from the crowd, fortified…

[Page 11]

The City and Its Fullness

by Y. D. Abramsky

Translated by Sara Mages

In the past, a sack of soil from Eretz-Yisrael was brought to a "resting place" in every Jewish city, whereas now, the sons of the Diaspora are awakening to bring a handful of soil from their land in a foreign country to a grave in Eretz-Yisrael, because the soil has turned to ashes.

A fire came out and ate Jewish dwellings.

And there is no survivor.

Only the calamity, the disaster, the memory of destruction survived.

And also Slutsk is nothing but a memory, a story that was…

And Slutsk's hand, which is usually clenched, is now fully open, to spread praises to Slutsk with a wide open hand, to erect a monument for her and thank her for past kindness.

* * *

How is my city from other cities?

Slutsk was specific and recognizable by its own distinguishing features

Slutsk - cities and towns around it - and it wasn't able to subsist without outside help. Slutsk was one of the open cities, open to all four directions, and it took in new forces from there: Kapyl and Timkovits (not only the place of Mendele Mocher Sforim, but also the home of genius rabbis), Uzda (Dvorah Baron), Grozovo and Pohost (Gerzovsky), Viznah (Reuven Valenrod), Strobin and Lyuban (Yitzchak and Zalman Epstein, Rachel Feinberg, HaRav S. Asaf). All were the sons of the city of Slutsk, because each town is like a limb of the city itself, from it, and in it. Slutsk was "*Beit HaMoked*" [The Hearth], the fire of the Torah blazed there and each "*Beit Hanitzutz*" [House of Sparks], from near and far, was lit by its fire.

When it was time to build a "yeshiva," the Ridvaz [Rabbi Yaakov Dovid Wilovsky] set a place for it next to an uncultivated field, outside the city. When he was asked why he wanted to distance the yeshiva from the settlement and its residents, he replied: "If a "*patron*" [ball in Yiddish, and a nickname for a yeshiva student] will fall - it would fall far from a settlement… However, the "*patron*" fell in a settlement. Slutsk became the father and the patron of the Torah, Slutsk was the place of study. It firmly sat there.

Slutsk had an abundance of Batei Midrash and synagogues. Its many craftsmen - tailors, blacksmiths and slaughterers, built synagogues for themselves. Wherever a Jew walked in Slutsk, his feet stood in the confines of a synagogue. Everywhere he turned, he was in a synagogue's courtyard. And when you want to know the number of synagogues in Slutsk, you always come to the wrong number: you always remember one too many synagogues, and you always add it to the first ones that you remembered. In any event, Slutsk's houses of worship and synagogues were in the shape of a "Star of David." At each end, at each angle - a house of worship, and in the center - the heart, the "spiritual center," *Der Shul Hoyf,* the synagogues' courtyard, the houses of worships' square.

The houses of worship were full and stuffed, until they gasped.

Slutsk was a city of *Mitnagdim* [opponents of Hasidim]. *Mitnagdim* and "extreme," but not "Hasidim"... The elders of my generation knew to tell a story about R' Yisrael Baal Shem Tov who came to Slutsk, to the city's abyss, and they wanted to hurt him, tie him to a stone in the chilly synagogue ("*Di Kalt Shul*") and punish him for disobedience. Baal Shem Tov escaped and the city's gates, which were closed, were torn off and lifted up, and to this day they are suspended in the air. The story of this act can be interpreted: this is Slutsk, gates carried themselves there, bore their head to the name of the Torah, and Slutsk's gate was always a high and elevated. "A city full of sages and writers" wrote about it the emissary of Sabbatai Zvi.

And at the same time Baal Shem Tov said: the Messiah will come when there is a *minyan* of Hasidim in Slutsk.

During the First World War a group of Hasidim gathered in Slutsk and had their own *minyan* at the "*Shtiebel*" of the Synagogue of Mishnayot, and the Messiah has not yet arrived. They said: "Baal Shem Tov didn't say what he said, only when all the Hasidim are followers of one rabbi, while those are not of one rabbi and not of one skin"...

[Page 12]

In the days of "*Va'ad Arba' Aratzot*" ["Council of Four Lands"], Slutsk's letters were interpreted to say: *Solet*, **LO**mdim, **T**zadikim, **K**zinim [the finest, study, righteous, leaders]. The community leaders were also among the learners, and from them - great scholars. And when they attended the "fairs," the councils of the lands, their answer was raised to the place of worship, because the home of the city's proprietors was in the synagogues,

* * *

Slutsk was more than a "city of gold," a "crown of gold" was on its head: Slutsk wore a necklace to its neck and each genius rabbi was a necklace. Slutsk strung a necklace of rabbis, one after another: R' Yosef Feimer (the first), R' Yosef Ber, the Ridvaz, R' Isar Zalman Meltzer ("*Even HaEzel*"), R' Yehezkel Abramsky ("*Hazon Yehezkel*"), all of them, the Cedars of Lebanon, the mighty of the Torah.

However, Slutsk didn't conceive and give birth to the "children of this necklace." They only "lowered the light" on Slutsk. And against them you find the "children of the house," Slutskaim, sons-of-Sluts aim: Dr. P. Lifshitz who built the basic law for social sciences in Hebrew, he started out as an economist and sociologist in Hebrew (in his book, " Social Sciences in Hebrew," Mr. Gezel Kressel gives P. Lifshitz credit for this primacy), Y.D. Berkowitz, Yakov Cohen, A. A. Lissitzky and Dr. Y. N. Simchoni praised their birthplace among the gates of Slutsk.

And two of them: Avraham Epstein and Meir Waxman, Baruch Katzenelson and the rest of Slutsk's sons, each gave as much as he could, each according to what he is.

* * *

As mentioned, the largest synagogue in the city was called "*Di Kalt Shul*," to differentiate it from the Great Synagogue ("*Di Grosse Shul*"), and there is something in the name to teach you about: it became cold in the synagogue. A chill entered the hearts towards religion and conventional tradition. Another voice was heard with the voice of the Torah, of "new birds." The letters began to blossom in the Jewish "spring," the new Hebrew was confused, and it seemed that the old "parchments" were burnt or hidden deeper into a corner. The young people were drawn away from the Torah, drawn to the Hebrew language and its literature. They were the first Zionists and teachers of those who aspired to learn Hebrew.

* * *

But the Torah cannot extinguish its past. There was light and fire in Slutsk, but its shadow was also great. There was someone who once said about Slutsk: **Slutsk** - to say: **Slutsk,** **L***eizanim* and [**O**] **TZ***iknim* **K***amzanim* [Slutsk clowns and stingy cowards]. Slutsk was well known for its stinginess, and the city's clowns were telling about Binyamin Avin (who was a rich man, but not a rich man to his brothers. His hand was clenched, as was the case with every man in Slutsk who was fond of his money the way he was fond of his body, and even more than that). Avin asked a carpenter to make him a wooden box and covered it with white cloth. It was always placed on his table and everyone who saw it said: Ah-Ha, the "rich man" eats cheese every day. A loaf of cheese per day…

This and more: there was a yeshiva student in Minsk who was a great spender. His wife's family tried to convince him to change his taste and way of life. He said to them: what can I do that God made me like that, how can I change for the better? They pleaded with him to travel to Slutsk to learn stinginess from Avin. He was moved by their humble request and traveled. Came, entered the best hostel, ate the heartiest meal and went to Avin. Avin was happy that his reputation precedes him, he found a student worthy of learning from him, and invited him to his home for the Sabbath. He would show him the doctrine of stinginess. On the Sabbath, the yeshiva student from Minsk saw black candles burning and thought: a person, who wants to be a miser, should know that black candles are cheaper than white candles. Then he saw that Avin was making a blessing over coarse-bread, not over fine-bread. He pondered: is this all the wisdom of stinginess? It turns out that I didn't have to spend a fortune on this journey. And when he saw herring instead of fish, he said to himself: the expenses I spent were not worth the damage of time because I didn't acquire more wisdom. And so it was the next day. He was uncomfortable with what he saw until it was time for the "cholent." And here he sees: the lady of the house, Mrs. Avin, unties the stuffed intestines and hangs the strings on a hook on the wall. What is the reason for that? - asked the yeshiva student. Avin answered and said: these strings can be used several more times.

[Page 13]

The "Cold" Synagogue (*Di Kalt Shul*)

The yeshiva student was immediately satisfied and his heart was no longer troubled: this thing would not have occurred to me, and if I only came for this thing only - my expenses are justified.

However, Slutsk's stinginess was a fable, kind of tale, but not a real act. Things were exaggerated.

The story of Slutsk, the reality of Slutsk: the moneylenders in it. There were, there were loan sharks in Slutsk.

* * *

The "Community Book" of Slutsk is, in general, the "Community Book" of the entire "community," and other communities in those days. From the description of each community you can learn about Slutsk and, the other way around, from what you discover about Slutsk you are allowed to tap on other Jewish settlements. The history researchers of Slutsk would probably reveal much of what was wrapped in mystery to this day. It is a place for scholars and persons of powerful memory to study and explore.

In the past, Slutsk, like any other Jewish metropolis, it was a "place" and not "time": it was a Jewish settlement and it seemed to stand still, frozen, beyond all time. Whereas now - the place is destroyed and desolate. There's only "time," a memory of the days that were. In the words of one, who observes, looks and sees, and knows what he sees: "geography ended, history has begun again."

* * *

Was Slutsk a rich city with great poverty, or a poor city with great wealth? I catch that last expression: poor and rich in poverty, meager - and proud. There was a lively Jewish life there. Slutsk was rich in power: there was Jewish charm, Jewish friendship, and Jewish brain. The children of the poor had a strong will and, therefore, didn't kneel under the burdens of their lives. They, the porters, who shouldered the suffering, looked up: to education, Zionism, and socialism. The ideal got them to their feet, gave them strength to live. They ate a little bread, bread of poverty, but not bread of nerves. They ate their bread happily and hopefully, a small amount of bread and a lot of vision, a narrow plot of land and vast horizon. The sky over Slutsk was vastly larger than the land of Slutsk. Life and hopes fermented in the depths of poverty.

[Page 14]

Indeed, there was a thing called "the instinct of existence." If not for this instinct of existence, how, how were they able to be enlightened with the light of the living and emerge from this darkness of Slutsk, Slutsk the poor and the dark?

Slutsk was also compared to a king who had thin glasses. The king said: "if I put hot liquid in them - they crack, cold - they collapse." And what did he do? He mixed hot with cold, put it in them, and they stood. Slutsk was a vessel that collapsed and lost its original form. But Slutsk was twisted, "black - and beautiful." This vessel lasted for many years, and for many years this vessel held Judaism and preserved Judaism. Slutsk, which blackened and rotted, wasn't only a virtue of smoke, but also a virtue of grace and beauty…

At the doorstep of *Kiryat Sefer* [republic of letters] sits Efraim E. Lisitzky, a native of Slutsk, son of poverty, and he is tortured and bleeding.

Mendele [Mocher Sfarim] wrote "*Sefer Hakabzanim*" [The Book of Baggers]. Bialik is the "poet of poverty" of a good family (*Shirati, Yatmot, Shivah*), Lisitzky wrote in "The History of Man" that he is not only a man of the poor class, but also from the edge of society, from the most outcasts who have no attribution. His father was a water-drawer, "*Givony*" [woodcutter and water drawer for the entire community]. And he drank the cursed bitter water, the poisoned water.

And they turned in him into living water.

A thorn sat in his heart. Lisitzky turned the crown of thorns into a bouquet of flowers, not the "flowers of evil," but flowers of glory and majesty.

A personal binding, Lisitzky was sacrificed in Slutsk: according to his origin and birth. He's Iyyov [Job] that was and became - for example, to be an example, a sign and a wonder. Even God, so it seems to me, is watching Lisitzky with honor. God examined him carefully and found him worthy to be filled with life experiences.

An autobiography was not written for Shlomo Maimon in Lisitzky's autobiography, "The History of Man." You cannot find many books like this one in any nation and language. In Hebrew literature there's no one more pure and more holy than Lisitzky.

He was born - in the furnace of poverty. He grew up - in purgatory, the purgatory of suffering. Berger was his brother and Lisitzky was greater than him as a man, as the writer of a biography, the history of life. His revelation is nothing more than the events of his life and the circumstances surrounding his life. This is the history of all the poor people of Slutsk who lived in darkness and drew light.

* * *

About the end, about the parting from Slutsk, told me Akivah Barski, my soul mate, and the story, the story of us all:

One day, the place became too narrow for me in Slutsk, as if I was bigger than Slutsk, A city which is actually a town, a big town, a family unit, or a home, with many branches and wings. And I was a stranger in my family, cut off from them. I became alienated and also fell into great terror and darkness. I didn't have a bright and polished perspective, I only saw blackness. I saw an act: a brother rose up against his brother - in the market! - and killed him with a log: two brothers - natives of the place and sons of the sons of Avraham Avinu - one of them was Cain and the other was Abel. The light in my soul darkened, my soul suffered. And I saw more: the arrest of Zionists in Slutsk and their prosecution, their stand in the trial with Jewish dignity and Jewish pride. These two things filled my whole heart, and my soul found no other interest to deal with. I wanted to escape, to escape to the big city. The big city is bigger than me, there's "no end" there, there's serenity there. You see clearly, the city is too big to hold in your arms. Your arms will not contain it, and it will contain you. And there was a vague hope in your heart that you would meet a group of pioneers and cross the border with them in secret. I ran away once, and failed, and ran away for the second time, and failed again. In the end, I came to a large city in Russia. Slutsk dropped from my memory, as if it had fallen to the bottom of my knowledge and lay hidden deep in my soul.

I also didn't find my place in the big city, and in the end, God revived me and I arrived to Eretz-Yisrael.

And I drew Slutsk from of the depths of my soul. I turned back to her.

And behold, it shines in the light of the Torah, illuminates many lights: Torah and enthusiasm, enthusiasm for Hebrew, literature and spiritual renewal. Rich, rich, was Slutsk, and from Slutsk's well, the well of life, the heart will go forth and irrigate the past with the drug of life, and the future with a drink of grace, innocence and hope...

[Page 15]

History of the City

From Encyclopedias

From the Russian Jewish Encyclopedia published by Brockhaus–Efron

Translated by Jerrold Landau

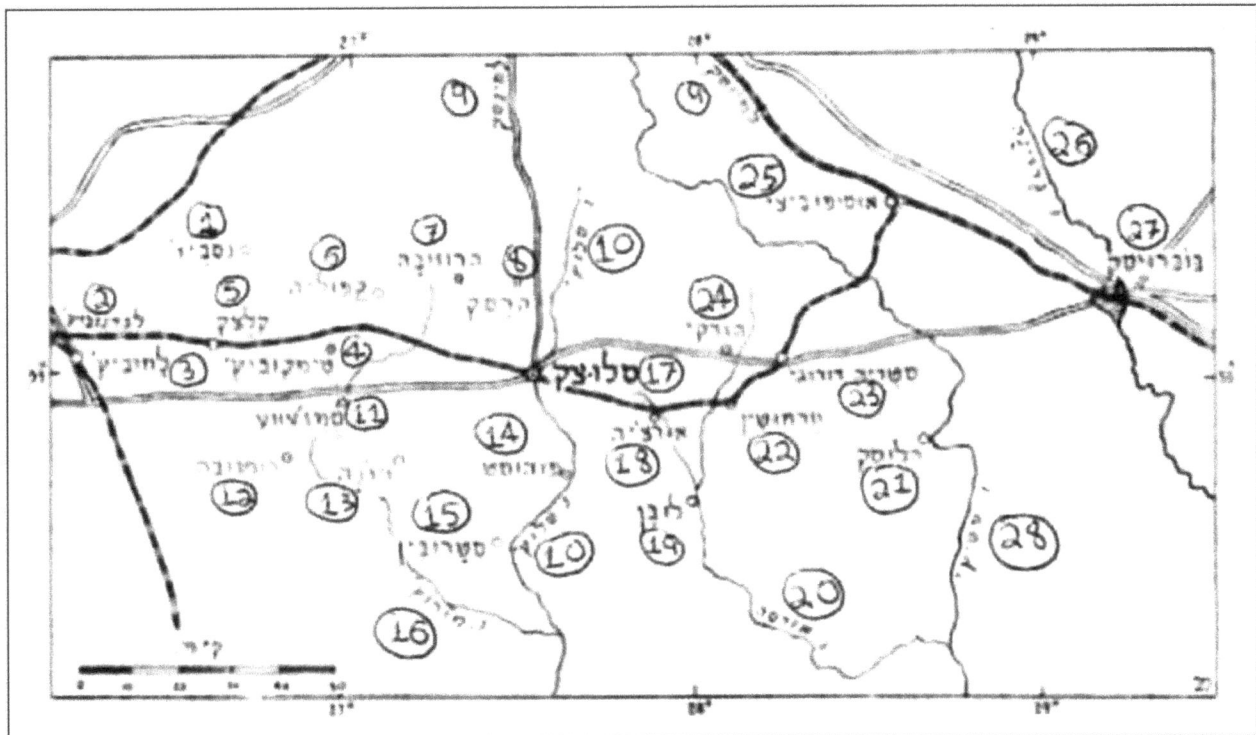

Map key:

1. Nesvizh (Niasviž)
2. to Baranovichi
3. Liachaviču
4. Timkovichi
5. Kletsk
6. Kapyl
7. Hrozava
8. Hresk
9. to Minsk
10. luch River
11. Semezhevo
12. Romanovo
13. Vizhna
14. Pohost
15. Starobin
16. Moroch River
17. Slutsk
18. Urechya
19. Lyuban
20. Uresa River
21. Hlusk
22. Verkhutino
23. Staryya Darhoi
24. Horki
25. Asipovichi
26. Berezina River
27. Babru

The City of Slutsk was the capital city of the Principality of Slutsk in the Region of Novogorodok. The earliest information regarding Jews relates to the year 1583. There was already a Jewish community in Slutsk at the beginning of the 17ᵗʰ century. According to the regulations of the Lithuanian Council of 1623, it was under the influence of the Brisk Council. The heads of the council only included community of Slutsk among the chief communities in 1691, having taken into account the population increase and the Torah greatness therein. From that time, the delegate (head of the state) of Slutsk sat in meetings with the right to vote when they adjudicated matters that affected the Jews of Lithuania. The final meeting of the council took place in Slutsk in 1761. When brigades from Moscow invaded Lithuania in 1655, a commotion took place in Slutsk and the Jews fled to Vilna. At the end of the military disturbances, Slutsk once again became a commercial and information center of Lithuania. The Radziwills, who were the owners of the Principality of Slutsk, assisted greatly in the restoration and expansion of the city. They preferred Jews over other residents. This explains the complaint of the Slutsk Archemandrite to Prince Boguslaw Radziwill in 1660. The Greek Russian Church in Slutsk complained to the commissar of the Principality about this once again in 1754, stating that with the leasing of the meat tax to Jews, all the income of the priesthood had disappeared. In 1776, the number of Jews in the community of Slutsk and its region reached 1,577 (Ledgers of the Communities of Lithuania, according to Bershadski[11]). According to the ledgers of the year 1800, there were 3 Christian merchants, 47 Jewish merchants, 641 Christian citizens, and 1,537 Jewish citizens. According to the revision and inspection of 1847 in the district, the community of Slutsk had a population of 5,897, and Kapyl had 1,824. According to the census of 1897, there were more than 260,000 residents in the district, including 40,906 Jews. This included 14,349 residents of Slutsk, of whom 10,264 were Jews. From among the residents of the district: Vizhna – 1,593 residents of whom 532 were Jews; Hresk – 1,674 residents of whom 207 were Jews; Hrozava – 928 residents of whom 765 were Jews; Kapyl – 4,463 residents of whom 2,671 were Jews; Pohost – 863 Jews of whom 685 were Jews; Romanowa – 1,535 residents of whom 494 were Jews; Semezhevo – 2,538 residents of whom 288 were Jews; Starobin – 2,315 residents of whom 1,494 were Jews; Timkovichi – 2,393 residents of whom 1,523 were Jews.

From information from 1910, there was a two–grade private school in Slutsk for children, a seminary for girls, a Talmud Torah, a Yeshiva, and a private school.

Documents

A royal command to the Slutsk Prince Yury regarding the return of merchandise that had been confiscated in Slutsk to the king's subject, the Jew Shmuel Nochimovich of Kobrin, with the addition of reparations for the merchandise that had been damaged or was missing, in accordance with the list of the aforementioned Shmuel.

In the event of non–fulfilment of his command, the king ordered to repay

[Page 16]

the aforementioned Jew in lieu of the entire sum of 100 kopecks, owned by ten servants from among the subjects of the Prince of Slutsk, up to the complete amount of the damages of the aforementioned Shmuel.

* * *

This command was issued in accordance with the principality, and was adjudicated in court by the commissars of the king. The Prince of Slutsk refused to allow the commissars of the king to be present while the list of the aforementioned Shmuel's confiscated merchandise was being inspected. The merchandise was being guarded in the home of a Polish citizen.

Number 167, October 5, 1537.

From the registry books of events of Lithuania.

"Matters of Judgments" number 21, paragraph 195.

* * *

The command of King Sigismund to Yuri, the Prince of Slutsk, regarding the return of merchandise to Yoska Peiskovich, a Jew of Brisk, that was stolen from him by Werbicki, the director of the estate of the Slutsk Prince in Petrikov, as well as the issue of payment for the missing merchandise in accordance with the price set in Yoska's list regarding the pillaged property.

October 5, 1537, number 166.

From the registry books of events of Lithuania

Paragraph 193, number 21.

* * *

A letter from King Sigismund to Yuri, the Slutsk Prince, in which the king explains that justice demands equal rights for a simple person as well. Therefore, the king sees no possibility to permit the Prince of Slutsk to be a sole judge regarding Werbicki, the director of his estate in Petrikov. Rather, he commands the Prince of Slutsk to provide an accounting to the commissars, the emissaries of the king, regarding the accusation against Werbicki for attacking the Jew Yoske Szajn, a citizen of the king, along a free roadway, pillaging the money (from the income of the district of Mohilov and the district of Bobruisk), that he was bringing to the treasury, and for imprisoning him in the warehouse.

Number 165, June 20, 1537.

From the registry books of events of Lithuania, paragraph, number 21, in 159.

* * *

From the General Russian Encyclopedia published by Brockhaus–Efron

Slutsk is a district city in the Minsk region, on the banks of the Sluch River. It has a population of 14,180, including 6,764 men and 7,416 woman, one monastery for men, eight Christian churches (including Ospansko–Nikolivskaya, built in 1409), one Roman Catholic church, a Calvinist, two synagogues, and several Jewish houses of worship, a gymnasja for males, an Orthodox school, a school of the Pravovlavic Church (Приходское училище – Parish School), a seminary for Jewish girls, a Talmud Torah, private *cheders*, several charitable organizations, civic hospitals next to the prisons, and an infirmary next to the school for priests.

In 1896, the income of the city was 16,264 rubles, the expenditures were 15,986 rubles. There were two flourmills, a beer brewery, and businesses to work and tend to plantations and vegetable gardens. Many of the residents of Slutsk and its region grew fruit that excelled in taste and health. The pears of Slutsk (*beri*) were especially well–known.

Slutsk is first mentioned in the annals of the generations in 1116, when it belonged to the Kievan Prince Vladimir Monomakh, and it was conquered and burnt by the Minsk Prince Gleb. In 1148, Slutsk transferred to the ownership of the Chernigovian Prince Stanislav. Fourteen years later, it transferred to the Kievan Prince Mstislav, and later to the Turovian Prince. At around 2017, Slutsk was owned by the Lithuanian princes. After the unification with Kapyl in 1395, a special area was created where the first prince, Vladimir Olgradovich, ruled. Prince Oleksander (Olelko) was considered as one of the princes of Slutsk, who were called by the name Olelkoviches. Through their direction and rulership, the city was built up and expanded at a quick pace. In the year 1444, it was considered as one of the principal cities in Lithuania. At the end of the 15th century, the city suffered from attacks by the Crimean Tatars. They did not succeed in conquering its fortresses. Slutsk especially suffered from the Tatars during the years 1503–1504, and from Michal Glinski in 1506. At that time, Princess Anastasia, the mother of the young Prince Yuri II, headed the defense of the city. In 1579, Slutsk was divided among three brothers. In the wake of this partition, Old Slutsk, New Slutsk, and Ostrov remain to this day.

Sofia, the last of the Olelkovich dynasty, married Prince Jan Radziwill. After her death, it transferred as a bequest to the Radziwills. They imposed German law and order, and conducted bi–weekly market days there. They also organized effective and strong army brigades. Thanks to them, they were able to stand up to the Moscow army in 1655. From 1673 until 1732, friction and disputes arose between the Radziwills and the Sofiagites, which concluded in favor of the former. From that time, an economic decline began in the city, to the point that, in 1775, the residents of the city had to be freed from various taxes and fees for the period of several consecutive years. After the area was annexed to Russia in 1795, Slutsk was declared as a regional city in the commissionership of Minsk. In 1848, Slutsk was sold by Prince Wittgenstein to the Russian government for the price of 342,821 rubles (lists of information from the district of Minsk, 1878).

The district of Slutsk consists of an area of 18,528 square verst[2], or 713,833 dessiatin[3].

After the census of 1897, the population in the district of Slutsk numbered 261,047, corresponding to 39.1 individuals per square verst. The district of Slutsk was third in the district of Minsk in terms of population density, following the districts of Minsk and Novogorodok. The Pravoslavs formed 73.3% of the population, the Catholics 8.8%, the protestants 0.1%, and the Jews 17.3% (most of them in towns), and the Muslims 0.5%. The farmers formed 65.7% of the population, the city residents 23.5%, the nobility 4.6%, with the remaining 6.1% belonging to other classes.

Commerce was centered in Slutsk, Nesvizh, and other towns. The towns that were prominent in commerce included Kletsk, Kapyl, Lachovichi (which provided approximately a half a million pod of grain), and Starobin. The district of Slutsk included a city (Nesvizh), 12 towns, and 514 villages and other settlements (such as farms and the like). There were 62 Pravoslavic churches, 6 Catholic churches, 4 mosques, and 15 Jewish synagogues and houses of worship. There were 11 postal and telegraph branches (outside of the city ones), 2 village hospitals (with 10 beds), 4 infirmaries, 2 physicians, 7 pharmacies, a teachers seminary in Nesvizh, 31 public schools of various types, 11 church affiliated schools, *cheders*, and yeshivas. In some schools, professional studies were taught, including gardening, planting, and beekeeping. There were many mounds of earth, ruins of settlements and paved roads in the district.

The ancient settlements in the district included Kapyl and Kletsk (which was its own principality).

* * *

The crafted weaving and handworking products in the second half of the 18th and first half of the 18th century were called

[Page 17]

"Slutsk belts." Production of those belts was set up in 1758. They served as a substitute for valuable belts that were imported from the lands of the east for the suits of the wealthy people of White Russia, Poland, Ukraine, and Russia. After some time, these belts were also manufactured in Nesvizh, Warsaw, Krakow, and other places, with the name "Slutsk Belts" being preserved. They also imitated them in the French and Moscow factories. The Slutsk belts were woven of silk, silver, and gold. They were double sided, very long (3–4 meters) and wide (5–30 centimeters). A narrow, marginal adornment was on the perimeter, with wonderful designs copied from the plant world. The first artist and craftsman in Slutsk was Armoni (according to another version: Ungari) Jan Mozeski and his son Leon. The Slutsk belts are found in many current house, and in museums of the U.S.S.R, Poland, and other countries

The Soviet Encyclopedia

Slutsk is a central regional city in the Minsk Region of White Russia. It is situated on the banks of the Sluch River, and is on the Baranovichi–Asipovichi railway line. It has factories for mechanical welding, fixing of engines, sawing lumber, manufacturing of butter and cheese, and others. It has four high schools, two public schools with seven grades, a school for working youth, schools for mechanics, two libraries, a culture house, a theater, and movie theaters.

Surrounding the city are fields of grain, wheat, barley, corn, flax, tobacco, potatoes, and all types of fruits and vegetables, as well as for the care and raising of livestock. There are three stations –for tractor repair, and for machines for the drying and raining of bogs.

The entrance to the agricultural exhibition on Wygoda Street in 1908

Translator's footnotes:

1. See https://en.wikipedia.org/wiki/Sergei_Borohadski
2. An obsolete Russian unit of measure. See https://en.wikipedia.org/wiki/Vaud
3. See https://en.wikipedia.org/wiki/Dessiatin

[Page 18]

From Historical Ledgers

Translated by Jerrold Landau

The aspiration for internal autonomy in preserving economic and spiritual life stands out in the history of Jews in the Diaspora. This aspiration was expressed strongly in ancient times from the Babylonian exile until the Diaspora of Spain. We will not deal extensively with this in this survey, but rather only touch on matters relevant to our enterprise, the memorial book of Slutsk a major Jewish city.

The Council of the Four Lands was founded during the 16th century, in 1580, which is the year 5341 according to our calendar. It included Lesser Poland, Greater Poland, Rus, and Volhynia. In the year 5348 [1588], Lithuania was added, and from the regulations of that year, the "Five Lands" are mentioned (Lesser Poland, Greater Poland, Rus. Volhynia, and Lithuania). The main communities were Poznan, Krakow, Lwow, and Brisk.

For many years, the communities of Lithuania, headed by the community of Brisk, participated in the Council of Four Lands, but in the year 5383 (1623), after the community of Lithuania had developed from an economic and spiritual perspective, the leaders of the communities of Lithuania gathered in Brisk and founded the Council of the State of Lithuania, in which the leaders of Brisk, Horodno, and Pinsk were the first to participate.

At a meeting of the Council of the State in the year 5412 [1652], they decided to include the leaders of Vilna. The community of Slutsk was under the influence of the community of Brisk, and only in the year 5451 (1691) was it granted an equal place with the other communities on the Council of the State.

The meetings of the aforementioned councils took place during the fair days in various central cities, and dealt with question that arose at the times.

> a.   The relationship with the central and local governments.

> b.   Imposition and collection of government taxes.

> c.   The internal order of life in the communities: the election of *parnassim* [administrators], judges, *gabbaim* [trustees], *shamashim* [beadles], etc.

> d.   Matters of religion and education (Yeshivas and Talmud Torahs).

> e.   Economic matters, leasing of property, taxes, etc.

In a meeting of the Council of the State of Lithuania that took place in Brisk in the year 5383 (1623), a charter was composed that covered all orders of life in the Jewish communities.

The charter deals with the obligations of each community to the government, internal relations between the communal members, and intercommunal relations.

The following are the sources. We bring some excerpts of them with omissions.

949 959

Rister Terifa, the assessment of a head tax that as assessed for each person, as we, the tribes of Israel, gather together, that is the captains, leaders and heads of the communities of our country, may it be built up, who were chosen from the primary holy communities to the holy council in the state. The holy community of Slutsk, may it be protected [has been assessed] (6,000) Polish zloty, corresponding to 41 guilder to our mighty, pious master, the great, famous ruler, the renowned, great head of the army of the State of Lithuania, may G–d protect it; as well as the sum of 21 guilder to the flag of the tribunal. This was enacted with the agreement of all the leaders chosen, may G–d protect them, in accordance with our and their regulation. Today, Friday, eve of the holy Sabbath 24 Sivan 5551 [1791]. – – – The holy communities of Slutsk, Hlusk, and Kapyl, T.Ch. Z.P.

951 961

The sum made in the great country of Lithuania, may G–d protect it, in the council of the state in Slutsk, may G–d preserve it, 5551 [1791] a – – – the holy community of Slutsk with the holy community of Kapyl. A.Z. Ch.G.

956

Regarding that which took place in the holy council of the greater state, here in the holy community of Slutsk in the year 5521 [1761], where the holy community of Amdor dealt with the head tariff as it is, and as it never had been previously, for they were evaluated together with the holy community of Horodno and the district a – – – .

957

With the help of the Blessed G–d. The following are the significant enactments that we here, the sages, have enacted, and the strong men and the counts of the country, in a gathering of the nations together and in a gathering of the heads and leaders of the nation, may G–d protect them, the leaders, captains, and heads of the State of Lithuania together with the honorable rabbis and *Gaonim*, the renowned luminaries of the holy council of the greater state, may G–d protect it, in the holy community of Slutsk, may G–d protect it, 5521 [1761].

(All the enactments of the council of Slutsk up to item 1027 are also noted in an arrangement unique to this council, from item 1 until 69.)

1027

All of the previous enactments that were not contradicted through the enactments of this current holy convention remain in force. (And every enactment in the conventions that has been erased, and the leaders of the states have enacted them themselves in accordance with their own will, and not in accordance with the *Gaonim*. All the aforementioned, has come forth from us, the rabbis, *Gaonim*, people of renown, heads of the rabbinical courts, heads of the Yeshivas of the primary communities, in conjunction with the heads of the communities of our country, may G–d protect it. We have signed today, Wednesday 27 Tammuz 5521 [1761], here in the holy community of Slutsk, may G–d protect it, and the holy council of the greater state.)

Regarding the acceptance of the mediator of the state in Vilna 5521 [1761]

– – – We have agreed with complete agreement, and have chosen and accepted the venerable and great scholar, Rabbi Chaim the son of Rabbi Yosef as a mediator, to be the emissary of G–d and of us to intercede and to serve as attorney throughout our country of Lithuania, may G–d protect it. His eyes will be open to all the needs of the state, to defend us before the king, may his honor increase, and the ministers of the kingdom – – – His salary will be paid from all the guilders of the head [tax], the larger half according to the tariffs, in a manner that his residence will be specifically in the holy community of Vilna. – – –

All the aforementioned has come from us, the leaders, captains, and heads of the provinces of the major communities, in conjunction with the honorable rabbis, the great luminaries, heads of the rabbinical courts, heads of Yeshivas, may G–d protect and bless them. At our convention here at the meeting of the great state. Today, Sunday, 24 Tammuz, 5521 [1761], in the holy community of Slutsk.

[Page 10]

Regarding the warning that was sent from the leaders, captains, and heads of the holy community of Vilna, and from the honorable leaders and captains of the holy community of Slutsk; a special emissary was sent to the holy community of Shklov to come to a meeting of the council of our state of Lithuania, may G–d protect it, that will convene in the holy community of Slutsk. They should come with all their complaints and demands to the aforementioned leaders, captains, and heads that come from the holy community of Shklov and the country of Russia, whether regarding debs that are owed by the states of Russia and from the holy community of Shklov to the aforementioned communities, or with regard to the tariffs, or with regard to the rabbinate. –

From the Ledger of the State of Lithuania to Dubnow

The names of the rabbis and communal leaders who signed the enactments of the councils, as well as those mentioned within the edicts (Ledger of the State of Lithuania to Dubnow)

1.   Aryeh Leib, the head of the rabbinical court of Slutsk. 939.

2.   Asher Zelig the son of Yosef Freinkel of Slutsk. 947–48.

3.   Yehuda Yudel the son of the holy Avraham Halevi Horowitz of Slutsk. 947, 948.

4.   Yaakov the son of Yitzchak Izik HaLevi Epstein of Slutsk. 949, 951, 953, 1027, 1028, 1029, 302.

5.   Yitzchak Izik the son of Avigdor of Slutsk 949, 951, 953, 302.

6.   Yitzchak Meir the son of Yona, the head of the rabbinical court of Slutsk (also of Pinsk).

7.   Yissachar Ber, the head of the rabbinical court of Slutsk. 952, 1027, 1029, 1030, 302, 304.

8.   Tzvi Hirsch the son of Moshe, the scribe of the state, from Slutsk. 950, 951, 953, 954, 956, 303, 302.

9.   Shaul the son of Tzvi Hirsh Mezia of Slutsk. 942.

During the time of the head of the rabbinical court, Rabbi Avraham Epstein of blessed memory who served as the head of the rabbinical court in Horodno from the year 5376–5393 [1616–1633], the council of the state of Lithuania separated from the state of Poland, which conducted itself in accordance with the Council of the Four Lands. They set up for themselves a council of three main communities in the year 5393 [1623]: the first was Brisk, the second Horodno, and the third Pinsk. From the year 5430 [1670], Vilna was also a main community, numbered fourth. In the year 5451 [1691], Slutsk became the fifth main community.

Relations Between the Communities

(A compromise between the holy community of Slutsk and three main communities regarding business in several areas)

The leaders of the holy communities of Horodno, Pinsk, and Vilna made a positive compromise with the important leaders of the holy communities of Slutsk regarding the business of those three communities with Slutsk. That is: permission was given for those communities to conduct business in the city of Slutsk to the extent that they please, whether to buy or to sell. However, they can only bring in four individuals at one time, and no more. These four individuals can only remain there for a period of two weeks from when they first arrived. The merchandise that they bring to Slutsk cannot be sold to any gentile during the first three days from the bringing of the merchandise to Slutsk. They cannot make any ruse or trick in this manner, under threat of confiscation. If they cannot sell to Jews within the first three days from bringing in the merchandise, then they have permission to sell all or some of the merchandise to any gentile that they desire. After the end of those three days, no resident of the aforementioned communities can come to Slutsk for business until six weeks after the four individuals leave Slutsk. After the conclusion of the six weeks, residents of those communities are permitted to come to Slutsk for business for a period of two weeks. They can only bring the four aforementioned individuals at one time, and in any case, in accordance with the aforementioned protocol. This is enacted from today and forever as an inviolable law until the end of all generations. The residents of the aforementioned communities cannot keep merchandise in the houses of gentiles in Slutsk, but rather only in the markets and the streets, in accordance with the aforementioned protocols. Enacted on Monday, 18 Elul 5394 [1624]

(Enactments of the council from 5394)

From the Ledger of the Council of Four Lands

It is noted that the Duchess Battenstein announced that the Catholic apostate Jan Serafinowicz libeled the Jews and appeared at the blood libel trial in Kuzmir and testified that Jews require the blood of Christians. He was summoned to trial by the Council of the Four Lands, and escaped. She issued a certificate that his guilt has not been proven.

The apostate was born in Brisk of Lithuania [Brest Litovsk], and received rabbinical ordination in Slutsk and Brisk (according to the words of Father Pikolski in his anti–Semitic work)

506 – 984

As I pass through the holy community of Kostantin in the company of eminent rabbis, great luminaries, the Gaonim of the country who have gathered together from the four lands of the country of Poland, may G–d protect it – – as the spokesman states – – Sunday night 11 Elul 5506 [1746], which actually was on the Sabbath, on Saturday night (*Geulat Ben David*)[1]

Avraham the son of the Gaon Rabbi David Katzenelboigen, of the holy community of Slutsk, may G–d protect it.

Amulets

Blessed is G–d, Sunday 27 Menachem [Av] 5512[2]. My words have already been stated, a statement of love, holy love, to cleanse and purify myself from the travesty that took place in Israel[3] with regard to several amulets – – and a writ was already issued from the leaders of the State of Lithuania, may G–d protect it – – – I was shown several amulets, and we have no clarity regarding who produced them – – – therefore they are banned and forbidden before G–d – – – Anyone who intends to enter the name of Shabtai Tzvi, may his name be blotted out, into the amulets – – these are the words of Avraham, etc.

In *Edut Yaakov*, page 50 (70), the name is written in full: Avraham of the family of Katen Aleh (Elen Bogen), may G–d protect and bless him, who lives in the holy community of Slutsk, may G–d protect it.

In the ledgers of the Council of the Four Lands, page 71, from the year 5424 (from the Gromnitz fair) at a meeting of the elders of the lands, we find the name of Rabbi Yissachar Ber Segal, the head of the rabbinical court of Slutsk, participated in the meeting "to rectify every thing and statement properly in accordance to the good hand of G–d upon them. Only with respect to taxes and communal payments, and anyone who wants to move their place of residence from our community – – "

454

Its pages are seven, sermons from Rabbi Betzalel the son of Rabbi Shlomo, the preacher of Slutsk, Prague, 434. The Council of the State of Lithuania provided significant help to the author to publish his book. Apparently, the Council of the Four

[Page 20]

Lands also helped him to some degree, as the author testifies in his introduction: I found grace in the eyes of the captains, chiefs, heads, and leaders of the State of Lithuania, who generously gave me a large, great gift to publish my book. I also found grace in the eyes of the captains, heads, and chiefs of the State of Poland, who did good and proper for me."

444 – 415

The rabbi and renowned, great luminary, the honorable Rabbi Meir the son of the great luminary Rabbi Yona Teomim (head of the rabbinical court of Zalkovi, and later in Slutsk and Pinsk, died before the year 5463 [1703]), may the memory of the holy be blessed. His kindness was great and wondrous, with vigorous diligence, to publish the fine book, *Ein Yaakov*, with novellae on *aggada* [Talmudic lore] – – – Thus are the words of the leaders, captains, chiefs, and heads of the four lands, may G–d protect them, at the holy convention on the market day, which is a time of gathering every day, Sunday, 13 Tishrei, 5444 [1685], here in the holy community of Jaroslaw.

Signed – – –

376

Regarding matters and disputes that broke out in the fairs of Kapyl and Stolovich [Stalovichy], and there is nobody to function as a mediator, to realize the results of mediation. It arose, and was concluded: at all fairs, there should be a special *shamash* [functionary] who is fitting for mediation. That *shamash* must stand on guard for all needs of mediation during the times of the fair, with all his energy: for the needs of individuals or the public. The income for serving in that capacity at that fair will go to that *shamash*. The acceptance of a *shamash* for the Kapyl fair will be in accordance with the two communities of Slutsk and Nesvizh, in conjunction with the merchants of the community of Brisk. The acceptance of a *shamash* for the Stolovich fair will be in accordance with the merchants of the community of Brisk, and the expenses will be paid as above.

From the Ledger of the State of Lithuania, convention of 5451 [1691]

Today, the case of the leaders, chiefs, and heads of the holy community of Slutsk, may G–d protect it, has come before us, with the presentation of many complaints against the leaders, chiefs and heads of the holy community of Brisk, may G–d protect it, regarding that they have been subordinate to the community of Brisk, may G–d protect it. Today, G–d has made them numerous, and they are as the stars of the heavens in purity. It is a big city, with many political opinions, and we praise them. They have evaluated their situation, and wish that their splendid, praiseworthy community be recognized among the main communities in an honorable fashion We have already seen the strength of what was written already by the *Gaonim* of the land and the rabbis and leaders of the communities of our State of Lithuania, the holy ones of the land, who connected themselves and gave honor to the G–d fearing leaders of the holy community of Slutsk, may G–d protect it. It has already been several years that they were not able to see the conclusion of this, and to set the matter straight. As of this day, after negotiations and great deliberations, when we heard and also saw in the city of

G–d, with a praiseworthy community, scholars of intelligence, of which the walls of the houses of study testify that their wisdom spreads afar, who expound the Torah with proper faith, built like fortresses, with brave people around them, and a double edged sword in their hand to fight the battles of the Torah, pious people of modesty, of whom it is fitting to make use of the crown of freedom[4]. After seeing all this regarding the praiseworthy city, of course, it is established in Heaven, and is declared that they should have a praiseworthy mark and name. Therefore, in accordance with their recommendation, and in accordance with the will of the two leaders of the aforementioned sides, we have issued a verdict, and it should be established. The following is what has emanated from us:

From this day and onward forever, until the advent of the Messiah, the holy community of Slutsk will be an independent community in accordance with their honor. The leaders and heads of the holy community of Brisk will have no authority or governance over the leaders and heads of the holy community of Slutsk in any matter, whether large or small, from anything that the mouth can speak and the heart can think, in any fashion at all. All complaints, disputes, verdicts, written statements, and oral demands that existed between the leaders of the two aforementioned sides up to this day, everything is null and voice, as a broken shard. Neither side can have any complaint against the other. Furthermore, the leaders of the holy community of Slutsk can have settlements, that is, all areas within six parasangs of the holy community of Slutsk, whether a community or individuals, are all considered subordinate to them, and must heed their statements. We have extended this matter only for the holy community of Kapyl until the next convention, when it will be registered in the ledger. Eight weeks prior to that future convention, the leaders of the holy community of Slutsk have permission to deal with the three main communities, may G–d protect them, other than the holy community of Brisk which does not have to be consulted, and to intercede with the three aforementioned communities regarding Kapyl, and it will be established by majority. In any case, judgments regarding the holy community of Kapyl will be adjudicated at the judges of the fairs. Other individuals will belong to the cemetery of the holy community of Slutsk, which is a holy, complete city, even if they are beyond six parasangs from the holy community of Slutsk.[5]

We have seen that the leaders, heads, and chiefs of the holy community of Slutsk, which is the holy city, full of council, a bustling city full of scholars and scribes, dear sons of Zion, who are fitting to be experts and noblemen, all the leaders and heads of the four main holy communities at the gathering of the emissaries of our state (Lithuania), may G–d protect it, were all willing to give over of their honor, and to coronate them with the crown of glory, so that the leaders and heads of the holy community of Slutsk could become the fifth community in Lithuania, may G–d protect it. The division of honor and leadership will apply to their Gaon and rabbi as one of the other main communities, may G–d protect them, from now and forever. This will apply in the following manner: That they have two state heads as of today, and that in the current convention they will have one additional assessor; after the current convention, that is eight weeks prior to the next convention, they leaders and heads of the community of Slutsk have permission to approach the four leaders and heads of the main communities, may G–d protect them, and to present their words regarding the third head of the state, and it will be established according to the will of the majority of those heads of communities; and if the heads of the communities do not agree, then, in any case, after the conclusion of three state conventions that will take place after the current convention, they will have a third head of state. On account of the sitting of the council, the leaders of the community of Slutsk will have a place on the council of the state. Their rabbi, head of the rabbinical court, and Yeshiva head will be the rearguard. They will also have a *parnas* [administrator] for the state council, a scribe, and a *shamash*. They matter will wait until the convention of the council first takes place in the holy community of Vilna, and then it will cycle around in turn. Then, when the time for the holy community of Vilna arrives, the leaders of the holy community of Slutsk will have permission to present their matters regarding the aforementioned distribution of honor. Regarding judgments during the fairs, they will have one judge in all the fairs, with the exception of the Kletzk fair and the Zelwa fair, where they won't have a judge. At the Kapyl fair, the leaders of the holy community of Slutsk will have permission to choose their rabbi and appoint him as judge, for those fairs, or for one judge[6]. Regarding the convention of kinds and ministers,

[Page 21]

the holy community of Slutsk will only send in accordance with the approval of the heads of the main community. However, if the heads of the holy community of Slutsk wish to send to the convention of kings and ministers at their own expense, they are permitted, and it will be required that their emissary be included in all business of the convention like the rest of the heads of the communities, may G–d protect them. If necessary, the heads and leaders of the holy community of Brisk or the heads and leaders of the holy communities of Slutsk can interchange with each other, Brisk with Slutsk or Slutsk with Brisk. If the state gathers for their aforementioned business, they should not sit atop of each other. Only the *Gaonim* and rabbis from the two aforementioned communities are approved to conduct their business. At the end of six years, the leaders of the holy community of Brisk will have the option to not exchange with the holy community of Slutsk, and to not negotiate their busines between the aforementioned conventions. Thus, the holy community of Slutsk should not exchange with the holy community of Brisk, and the only ones who shall conduct their business are the rabbis of the two aforementioned communities, who are authorized to sit. All this is only for twenty years from today. Aside from all the aforementioned details, they are equal to the other heads of communities, may G–d protect them. At the current convention and the upcoming convention, the holy community of Brisk should not interchange with the holy community of Slutsk, and the holy community of Slutsk should not interchange with the holy community of Brisk.[7]

All the aforementioned has been decided upon at a full meeting and with a full, pure table, also with the approval of the sides in any case, and with full force and effective authority. No rabbinical court or community of any state, and no rabbi, even in a convention of the leaders ,shall speak against this or negate any of the aforementioned details stated in good faith. They shall not even change the smallest tittle of any large or small matter. Everything shall remain in full force as an immoveable stake , as words of the wise, and as nails planted firmly from now and forever. If any person, no matter who, whether an individual, a group, or a community, wishes to dispute this decision or to remove even the smallest tittle of the aforementioned, then they will be punished with bans, excommunication, harsh, bitter punishments, and large fines that will be unbearable. All the aforementioned is on paper, written so it can be read currently and for generations, so it will stand for many years until the advent of the Messiah, who will take us to freedom and liberty.

These are the words of the leaders, captains, and heads of the states of our county of Lithuania, may G–d protect it, in conjunction with the honor of the great luminaries, the heads of the rabbinical courts and the heads of the Yeshivas of our country (Lithuania), today on 2 Adar II, 5450 [1690], at the convention of the state in the holy community of Chomsk, may G–d protect it.

The Convention of 5521 [1761] in the Holy Community of Slutsk

It was discussed that several communities and regions are obligated in the head tax. Every community, region, state, and city that does not discharge [the tax] for every head, and pay the expense, is liable to have some merchant from the community or the state sequestered.

957 (967)

It was noted that these are the great edicts that have been discussed here by the wise ones, enacted and formulated by the heads and chiefs of the land, at a convention in which the heads and chief of the nation, may G–d protect them, gathered together – the heads and chiefs of the main communities of the State of Lithuania, in conjunction with the honorable rabbis and *Gaonim*, the luminaries of the Diaspora, people of renown, at the holy convention of the greater state.

The Convention of 5551 [1791], Slutsk

… The following emanated from us, the leaders, chiefs, and heads of the main communities of our country, and we have been charged to sign their orders. Today, Tuesday 4 Av, 5551 [1791], here in the holy community of Nesvizh, at the convention of the greater state, may G–d protect it.

After meetings of the council in Slutsk in the months of Sivan and Tamuz 5521, factors apparently arose that forced us to move its location – at a meeting of all or part of the members – to Nesvizh, and to conclude our work there.

For forty years, from the year 5412 to 5451 [1652–1691], the council of the state was the central governing authority for the union of the four main communities of Brisk, Horodno, Pinsk, and Vilna. In the year 5451 [1651], the community of Slutsk came to requisition a place at the conventions of the council. In the convention of Adar 5454 [1961] that convened in Chomsk, it was decided that "the community of Slutsk shall become a main community in our state of Lithuania" – that is that they would have two heads of states at meetings of the council, and after some time, also a third head of state, a *parnas* of the council, and a scribe (a *shamash*, as in the rest of the main communities). Thus, it became a center for the organization of five communities. It remained in this form for 70 years, from the year 5451 [1691] until 5521 [1761], when the final convention of the state of Lithuania convened in Slutsk.

From the Cemetery Ledgers of Slutsk

(copied by Rabbi Yosef Feimer)

5614 [1854]

On Wednesday, the seventh day of Passover of the year 5614, the renowned scholar and wealthy man, Rabbi Shalom Shachna, the son of the renowned scholar Rabbi Yona Isserlin, died. He is buried on the left of his father, who died on the Sabbath, 2 Av, 5609 [1849] in the row in front of his grandfather, on the south side.

5566 [1805]

On Wednesday, 13 Kislev 5566, the rabbi and renowned, great Gaon Rabbi Chaim the son of Rabbi Aryeh Leib, rabbi and head of the rabbinical court, and teacher of our community, died and was removed from us. He is buried in a new row opposite the Gaonim, headed by Rabbi Yudel the son of Rabbi Alexander, who was also a teacher in our community.

5669 [1909]

On Tuesday, the last day of Passover 5669, the rabbi, renowned in Torah, may G–d bless him, whose mouth never ceased uttering his studies in the *Beis Midrash* , day and night throughout his life – that is the elderly, Rabbi Chaim the son of the scholarly Rabbi Baruch HaKohen, the *shochet* of our community. He rests in honor far from the grave of Rabbi Yehuda Leib Czernichow who died on the 10th of Kislev of that year, in the fifth row on the side of the city. His grave is two graves away from he who died on the 15th of Shvat of that year (Yosef Gincberg).

5620 [1860]

On Wednesday, 12 Nisan, 5620, the young man Rabbi Yisrael (Behmer) the son of the famous rabbi and Gaon Rabbi Yosef, the rabbi of our community, died. He is buried next to he who died on Tuesday, 14 Kislev of that year, in the fifth row on the side of the city.

[Page 22]

He runs like a dear and is mighty like a lion

To do the will of his father in heaven[8]

Yud – A person should look at this monument

Vav – and understand who is lying in the dust

Nun – We will weep together than the closet of our strength has been taken

He – He was a great prince, how did he fall from our people

Beit – The sun of his righteousness appeared at the edges of the earth

Nun – He was called the father of the orphan, and a saving angel to the poor

Aleph – He desired the final day from the beginning of his life

Beit – His soul shall be sated with the pleasantness of the Supreme One

Reish – He did a great deal of good, as if he lived a thousand times

He – He had just reached the age of might [i.e. 80]

Mem – Many days will pass and he will still illuminate

His spirit returned to on high, and his memory will be for generation after generation. He is the wealthy rabbi, Rabbi Yona the son of Rabbi Avraham Iserish, who died on the holy Sabbath, 2 Menachem–Av 5609 [1849]

A Stone Monument[9]

Shin – Shmuel died, and reposes here in the ground,.

Mem – What are you waiting for, raise a wail of desolation,

Vav – and raise a bitter lament for the breach in Israel

Aleph – Woe, for he is no more. Shmuel's place is missing.

Lamed – He fought the wars of G–d as a lion with bravery

Beit – In a sitting of the council of rabbis in the capital city

Nun – He preached the teachings of his Torah to nations and ministers

Tzadi – Right are the words of G–d, pure and upright

Beit – Weep, weep over his passing. The pain is very great

Yud – Days and years will pass, and Shmuel will not return

Shin – Joy set, and behold there is grief, pain, and darkness

Aleph – One thing will comfort us, his name did not die and he did not descend to the depths

The honorable rabbi and Gaon, the wise man who blended Torah and greatness together, Rabbi Shmuel the son of Rabbi Tzvi Simchavich. He died on Monday 3 Adar, 5656 [1896], here in Slutsk.

May his soul be bound in the bonds of eternal life

5495 [1735]

Wednesday, the seventh day of Passover of 5495, two people were found murdered one parasang from Pohost next to the village of Nevlad: Reb Avraham the son of Hirsch Katz and his son Reb Michel, members of the community of Hlusk. They were brought here on the last day of Passover. According to the words of the residents of the village of Pohost, these men were killed on Thursday, 16 Adar 5495, and were buried on Wednesday 27 (24?) Nisan 5595. Their graves are in the area of martyrs. The son is buried on the right side of the father. Next to them on the right is buried Zelig the son of Lipman, who was killed on a route, and was buried on Wednesday 26 Tishrei 5406 [1647]. Next to the aforementioned Reb Avraham is Yitzchak Segal who drowned in the Vyuben River on 26 Cheshvan 5504 [1745].

5521 [1762]

On the second day of Rosh Hashanah, four martyrs were killed. They gave themselves up to death and sanctified the Name of G–d in public, as they extended their necks and withstood the test. They placed their heads under the sword, and their blood was spilled like water in sanctification of the Singular Name. Their souls left them in their blood, as they were all killed together. They are the martyr Reb Noach the son of Reb David of Romanow, the martyr Reb Baruch of Romanow the son of Reb Yaakov, the scholar Shimon Yuda Shamash, the martyr Reb Yaakov of Romanow the son of Reb Shlomo, and the martyr Rabbi Yisrael the son of Reb Chaim of Romanow. The aforementioned martyr Rabbi Yisrael is buried next to Shalom Mastrew, first day of Rosh Chodesh Elul 5518 [1758].

Here is buried

The year Woe for the Ark Has Been Taken 5660 [1900][10].

Reish – See here the splendid memorial stone

Peh – He acted justly, and was holy like the ark

Aleph – His faithfulness to those forlorn aroused the spirit from heaven

Lamed – To teach the way of G–d to all who desire life

Yud – He sat and studied Talmud and decisors for 47 years

Vav – And pursued peace at every opportunity

Samech – He refused gifts, and was satisfied with meager bread

Peh – He prayed for the sick and brought joy to bitter souls

Beit – He left us at the age of 71

Nun – Weeping and wailing is heard from all the people of our city

Yud – Our eyelids drip water and our eyes tears

Tzadi – He was righteous and modest, we have lost, we have lost, who will comfort us

Chet – He loved the early ones, and he always observed his customs[11]

Kuf – The sound of his prayers was heard on high, and his progeny will always inherit the land[12]

He is our teacher, the righteous, pious, modest rabbi, Rabbi Rafael Yosef, may the memory of the holy be blessed, the son of Reb Yitzchak, peace be upon him. Died on Wednesday 23 Sivan 5660 [1900]. May his soul be bound in the bonds of eternal life.

See the Memorial Book of Rabbi Tzvi Hirsch, may his light shine, Maslanski, New York, 5684 [1924], folio 60, and what I noted there in on the pages of the book.

Rabbi Meir, who was a rabbi in Brezin and here in Slutsk, Karelich, and Lyakhovich, served as the rabbi in our community for 35 years. He died on Thursday, 20 Iyar 5671 [1911] in Slutsk. May his soul be bound in the bonds of eternal life.

Translator's footnotes:

1. The dating here is obscure, with two conflicting dates. 11 Elul 5506 was indeed a Saturday. The phrase *Geulat Ben David* literally means "the redemption through the son of David", but is written with apostrophes in each word, indicating that it is a gematria [Jewish numerology]. The equivalent number is 506, which is a reference to the Hebrew year. The practice of using a phrase as an innuendo to a date is common in rabbinic literature.
2. A fascinating dating schema was used here. The month of Av was not mentioned directly, but rather through its nickname Menachem (the comfort, given that the month marks the destruction of the two Temples, and includes Tisha B'Av). The year is provided with the gematria of *Mevaser* (the bearer of good news, referring to the Messiah). Thus the phrase *Menachem Mevaser* means: may the comforter bear good news – i.e. expressing a hope for the coming of the Messiah.
3. Israel here refers to the Jewish people, and not the land.
4. This long, run–on sentence is replete with obscure, kabbalistic terminology. I translated it as literally as I could, although I glossed over some of the more obscure innuendoes that did not lend themselves to easy translation. It can be summed up as: there are great sages in Slutsk.
5. This long sentence fragment seems to imply that individuals may belong to the community of Slutsk and use its cemetery, even if their location is beyond six parasangs.
6. The last part of this sentence is unclear. I translated it literally. The entire style of this piece is highly repetitive and wordy.
7. The concept of "interchanging" seems to imply that neither community should overrule or overlord the other community, and only the rabbis of each community have the rights to negotiate on behalf of the community.
8. The acronym of this gravestone is Yona the son of Avraham.
9. The acronym on this gravestone is Shmuel the son of Tzvi S A. The last two letters may be a short form of his surname Simchavich.
10. The gematria of this phrase is 660. The acronym of the gravestone is Raphael Yosef the son of Yitzchak.
11. There is a footnote in the text with an alternate version: He loved the early ones, and heeded and rectified good customs.
12. There is a footnote I the text with an alternate version: The holy one of G–d, prepare to meet your G–d.

[Page 23]

As Reflected in Periodicals

Translated by Jerrold Landau

Economics

The sale of lottery tickets under the permit of the government. The lottery was in the hands of the agents of the regions of Mohilev and Minsk: Yehoshua the son of Menachem Mendel Ratner of Mohilev and Yehuda Leib the son of Aharon Pacjak from Slutsk.

The expensive lottery was 140 rubles. Simple lotteries: full 130 rubles, half 70 rubles, quarter 36 rubles, tenth 15 rubles, one twentieth 8 rubles, and a hundredth 1.60 rubles.

(*Hakarmel*, issue 38, 4 Nissan 5622, 1862

The situation of the liquor merchants is bitter. Of the approximately sixty tavern owners in our city, a permit was only given to the five who had rights over their houses that they had purchased prior to last May 3 (the day that the decrees were issued). As of now, eight people are missing out of the twenty whose lot it was to go to the army. The responsibility lies with our directors who did not collect donations to protect those who were to go into the army, as is done in other cities. A Jew who goes to work in the army in place of his younger brother receives a stipend of five rubles from the chairman of the committee of those who take people from the army, and they praise him to his face.

(*Hameilitz*, issue 34, 1881)

Yeshaya Chorgin

Simcha Zak announces from Slutsk that the high tax officials came there and placed an army guard over the shops until they would come to inspect their merchandise. Even if they did not find foreign merchandise, they took merchandise from Moscow and Łódź if they did not find the lead seals, and imposed a large fine.

Only when they came to a Christian store did they believe the words of the owner that they did not have foreign merchandise.

(*Hameilitz*, issue 22, 1883)

The great benefit for [the people of] Israel from the factories can now be seen in our city, for in the new year, a tobacco factory (Macharka) has been founded in our city. Many of those who had been unemployed now work in the factory and receive their salary. Had the wealthy people of our nation not founded factories for work and manufacturing, many of our people would earn their livelihood in degradingng ways and live from the work of their hands.

(*Hameilitz*, issue 22, 1893). M. A.H.

Signs of revival and vitality could be seen in our city with the appearance of engineers who came to repair the railway tracks in the area 70 verst from the Gorody station. The merchants who to this point went about with lowered heads from lack of work are anticipating changes for the benefit of Slutsk, which is situated in a very fruitful area in the Minsk region. Most of its residents are involved in the marketing of grain and fruits, and the railway will ease transportation and commerce. Through the initiative of Sh. Migdal, L. Kontorovitch, and Ch. Bronstein, an assistance fund for the benefit of the impoverished Jewish high school students has been set up, to furnish them with food, school supplies, clothing, and tuition.

Upper grade students in the gymnasia collect donations and pledges every Sunday.

(*Waschod*, issue 9, 1883) B. Goldberg

Once again this year, the wealthy philanthropist Mr. Yehoshua Ceitlin of Moscow sent one hundred rubles before Passover for Passover flour[1]. For this, those involved in the preparation of Passover needs for the poor in the city of Slutsk will bless him.

(*Hameilitz*, issue 34, 1884)

This year as well, the call to army service in our city ended in a positive manner. Of the two-hundred youths who were selected by lottery, only a few were missing, who did not show up on the designated day for various reasons. Therefore, it is no surprise that even from among those who lacked privilege, about ten went free to their homes. Approximately fifty people went to the army. This number also included youths from wealthy families. Everyone was given twenty rubles. All the ministers were filled with feelings of joy and love when they saw this large crowd. They expressed these feelings to us with their mouths, and also treated us kindly. Our hope is that the mouths of our accusers and detractors, who say that we do not fulfil the law of citizens to their homeland, will from now on be shut. However, we have now heard the news that a few of those who went to the army from our city, as well as from other towns of our region, have escaped for their lives after they took an oath of allegiance to their king and homeland. – – –

Many from our city travel to America. Even next week, approximately ten families are preparing to leave our city. Most of those are tradespeople, and as is known, they do well there.

(*Hayom*, issue 268, 1887) Binyamin Epstein

Immigration

Immigration to America has increased greatly during the latter period. After the Sabbath of the Torah portion of *Vayigash*, nine families left Slutsk to forge their way to America. Another ten went on Tuesday of the Torah portion of *Vayechi*. Another fifteen families are ready to cross the ocean. This is despite the news that two ships bringing refugees to America have sunk in the ocean, and that the new country, which to this point has served as a refuge for any person in straits and difficulties, is now only pleasantly welcoming those who are coming with significant sums of money. Nevertheless, those who are leaving do not pay attention to this, for the name "America" is magical and everyone is attracted to it.

(*Hameilitz*, issue 9, January 12, 1888) Binyamin Abramovitch

Zionism

In *Hayom*, the pen of a writer from Jerusalem has written words of judgment against the rabbi who oversees the charitable fund for Israel [*Chaluka*], and against Chovevei Zion, for in recent times, the sending of money from our city to the Holy City has stopped for some strange reason. Has a reason been found from this in the name of "they are saying that it is said"? "For the hands of the rabbi who is the *gabbai* [trustee] is guilty in this matter, for chaos reigns, and they should assist Chovevei Tzion on behalf of the poor of the Kolel."[2] Now, regarding matters affecting the rabbi *gabbai*, he should come himself to respond to them and demonstrate that his hands were clean. However, regarding matters related to Chovevei Tzion, I am issuing a public protest, and

[Page 24]

with clear words I say that those who "are saying that it is said" are lying. I, who am aware of all the deeds of Chovevei Tzion from the time the organization was founded up to now, can testify that through this entire time, the rabbi *gabbai* did not give the organization fund one cent of his own or from the *Chaluka* fund. His hands were faithful to thwart the steps of the organization at all times, and to disparage it, to the point that he barely let this idea to even take a footstep into the *Beis Midrash* in which he worshipped. – – – The hands of Chovevei Tzion were not sullied by the blood of their brothers, the residents of the Holy City. They only toiled to build the ruins, and Heaven forbid would they destroy the holy building that was founded by the great ones of our people, and to which the lives of hundreds of souls depended upon.

(*Hayom* issue 14, 1887) Asher Ebin

Some time ago, the Zionists of our city celebrated the *Beit Mishteh Hachamim* [Party Houe of Warmth] with great pomp and ceremony. The chairman explained the purpose of the founding of *Beit Mishteh Hachamim*. The Zionists donated great sums to this endeavor.

Some time ago, the *Talmidei Tzion* organization performed the Vision of Bar Kochba with great splendor.

(*Hatzofeh*, issue 11, 1902) Mordechai Lipa Goren

Last week, Rabbi Yitzchak Reines appeared in our city. In his sermons, he aroused the gathering to put their efforts toward Zion. Our organization was founded with his assistance, and has fifty members.

The *Talmidei Zion* [Students of Zion] organization was recently founded here. Its members speak Hebrew.

(*Hatzofeh*, issue 27, 1903) M. L. Goren

The rabbi and *Gaon* Rabbi Yitzchak Yaakov Reines stayed in Slutsk and delivered his speech. The *Beis Midrash* was full to the brim with people from all the factions who came to hear about the idea of a national fund.

(*Hatzofeh*, issue 22, 1903)

The Zionist movement in our city is successful, and had already succeeded in gaining members from all factions. The main organization is *Kedma*, which excels in its activities. *Beit Mishteh Chamim* was founded by it. Many people gather there daily. There are about fifteen Hebrew and Russian newspapers there. A book bindery was also founded by it, which contains approximately 2,000 exemplars, and is conducted with proper protocols. The second organization is Mizrachi. Its activities are still limited, because it was only founded half a year ago. We have another organization, Poalei Zion, whose members are workers and tradespeople. It is also conducted in a good fashion.

(*Hatzefira*, issue 139, 1903) Y. Ch. G.

The Zionists of our city founded a matzo bakery for the poor. Many young women, even from wealthy families, work in baking matzos. At first, we thought that nobody would object to such an enterprise, but we have now discovered that even such an enterprise has opponents.

(*Hatzofeh*, issue 65, 1903) A. M. Chaikin

Already from the early days of the revolution, the few young Zionists hastened to meet and decided to conduct strong publicity among the strata of the people.

A Zionist organization quickly began to be formed in our city. With the help of excellent orators sent here from the district, comrades Abramovitz and Greenblatt, a large Zionist organization of 250 members was formed from amongst the active male and female youths.

A Zionist club, a library, and a reading hall were founded. Large assemblies and meetings were arranged on occasion. Various committees were chosen for all the Zionist activities. Approximately 1,100 *shekels*[3] were sold, and five delegates were sent from here to the Zionist convention in Petrograd.

A flower day for the benefit of the Jewish National Fund [Keren Kayemet] was arranged on Lag B'Omer. Approximately 700 rubles were earned for the treasury that day.

An organization of Zionist householders, called *Kadima*, was also founded. More than sixty members participate in it. The Zionists demonstrated life and movement during the elections for the city duma [government]. Thirty-one members were candidates for the elections of June 18th. The Bund joined with the S.D., the S.R., the Russians, and Kyva, and with the assistances of the local *garnizon* [garrison] were poised to elect a decisive majority for the duma, but they failed. The bloc only received nine mandates from all the candidates. The Zionists, along with lists submitted by the other Jewish organizations, elected thirteen candidates. Th eight remaining spots fell to the hands of the local Russians and Poles. Of the thirteen Jews elected, aside from the Bundists, seven were Zionists and the rest were non-factional Jews. Apparently, the Zionists won a decisive victory in the election. This made the Bund angry. From that time, the Bundists always tried to interfere with the Zionists and to denigrate them in the eyes of the soldiers. They called them counterrevolutionaries" and "supporters of the Black Hundreds"[4].

On 20 Tammuz, a memorial was arranged for Dr. Herzl. The large *Beis Midrash* was filled to the brim. Several speakers from *Kadima* and Achdut described the holy duty for us to continue his great testament. – – –

A Flower Day was arranged that day for the benefit of the Herzl Forest. Four hundred rubles were collected. On 25 Tammuz, the young Zionists arranged a celebration. They performed Sholom Aleichem's *Tzezeit un Tzeshpreit* [Scattered Far and Wide], showed pictures from the Land of Israel, and sang and declaimed songs of Zion. The celebration went very well. Approximately 800 rubles were earned for the organization after expenses.

It has been now about two months since the Agudas Yisroel organization was founded here. Among the other sections, there is a section related to work in the Land of Israel, but there is no living spirit in the Aguda. – – –

The Chovevei Sfat Ever society, which was founded before Passover, has opened evening classes at five levels. More than 150 girls attend the classes. Four male teachers and one female teacher are teaching, and are successful in their work.

On June 28, a splendid manifesto was arranged for the benefit of the free loan. Many Jews and Russians signed for the loan.

A representative of the Petrograd *Briut* [Hygiene] organization came to open a chapter in our city, under the leadership of the Zionist Gutzeit. Representatives of all the societies and organizations gathered together and the question was raised as to whether

[Page 25]

the protection of the health of the Jews, and the founding of hospitals, old age homes, etc. should be given over to the Jewish community? The Bundist declared that the role of the Jewish community organization was only to protect our culture, and that we are no different than the rest of the residents with respect to other questions. When they voted, and their declaration was not accepted, they left the hall as an act of demonstration. A committee was chosen from amongst the Zionists, whose task it was to immediately begin the work of founding the chapter of the organization in Slutsk.

(*Ha'am*, issue 2, 10 Av, 5777, 1917) Yachin

To my friends, many greetings:

Please G-d, I will be travelling from here today in peace (but not with my money, for there is no money for this master!) to my home and native city of Slutsk. Please G-d I will stay there for two months. Therefore, my friends, if you wish to send me letters or responses to my letters, send them to my house.

May G-d renew for you, for us, and for all those created in His image a good, blessed year, in accordance with your desires and the desires of those who love you and your friends. Here from Kiev, Monday, 18 Elul 5631 (1871)

Tzvi Hirsch Dinov, Magid, native of Slutsk

(*Hameilitz*, issue 34, August 31, 1871)

New York, 12. The Renowned Zionist preacher Rabbi Tzvi Hirsch Masliansky died at age 87.[5]

SP'A

With the death of Rabbi Tzvi Hirsch Masliansky, a large branch of the annals of Chibat Tzion and Zionism departed the stage of life. He was one of the great Zionist orators, a wonderful character of an educator of the nation to the love of Zion in a manner blender with old-style oratorial charm and signs of the new publicity. In his wonderful, enthusiastic lectures, he preached love of Zion and Zionism to the masses of people in Jewish communities on both sides of the ocean, as he moved and enthused the hearts of tens of thousands of listeners. It is appropriate to have a chapter on orators in the annals of Zionism – and he was one of them.

He was a native of Slutsk. Already in his youth, he demonstrated the traits of an excellent memory and breadth of knowledge, but his greatest surprise was in his oratorial skill. AT the age of ten, he would wrap himself in a sheet and preach to his young friends regarding the destruction of the Temple. The power of his imagery would move their young hearts to weeping. The many scenes during his youth and young adulthood were just like this miniature scene during his childhood – in front of large gatherings, in synagogues and halls. He was educated at the Yeshiva of Mir, and he went to Karlin. His first job was as a teacher, but with the Storms in the Negev (5641 – 1881)[6] he was caught up in the surge of awakening of Chibat Tzion, and preaching became the trademark of his life and his occupation. At first, he lived in Ekaterinoslav where he conquered the hearts of the community with his sermons on Sabbaths and festivals. He moved to Odessa in 5651 [1891]. The greatness of the impression of his preaching can be seen from the fact that Y. L. Pinsker, M. L. Lilenblum, and Ahad Ha'am aroused him to believe in the great power hidden within him, the power of speech that encourages and proves. He knew how to utilize all type of Agada [rabbinic lore] and parables, and all modes of sharpness and rhetoric in order to move the hearts. His preaching route throughout the Pale of Settlement in Russia and outside of it was like a circle of great populist enthusiasm. He knew how to win over the heart of the *Maskil* who tended toward assimilation and to fan the coal of nationalism so it would reignite. He knew how to win over the heart of the Orthodox, strict in tradition, and to cause their hidden strands to vibrate. Police persecution forced him to leave the bounds of Russia and move throughout the communities of Europe. The impression he left in the ghettoes of the East was the same as in the ghettos of the west. In the growing Jewish settlement of the United States, he found an arena for his activities – as the most famous nationalist preacher, as an active communal worker. He was served as the vice president of the Zionist organization, as a journalist (He published *Di Yiddishe Velt* with his son-in-law P. Turberg), a Hebrew writer – he was still among the writers of *Haboker Or* of A. B. Gutlober – and a Yiddish one. Some of this fine oratory skills carried over to writing. He published several books, the most precious of which is the chapters of his memoirs.

(*Davar*, issue 5330, 7 Shvat 5703, Jan. 13, 1943).

Education

Like me and like you , honored readers! – – – I cannot restrain my grief and control myself from proving before the community and congregation, before the sons of Yeshurun[7], to whom the peace of your brethren is also their peace – perhaps you will come hasten to bandage the pressure on our heart – and you will return and heal yourselves.

My hometown of Slutsk in Lithuania[8], formerly a major Jewish city, fine in its greatness, with great searchers of the heart living there, wise people, writers, and philanthropists who have also succeeded in splendid charitable deeds in peace and truth. – – – How is it that all hearts do not melt, for to our dismay a new generation has arisen, a generation wise in its own eyes – – – That which our fathers have nurtured and grown has been destroyed, ruined, and removed by the hand of – – – The hospital of which we took pride is continually becoming impoverished, there is no supporter or benefactor, there is nobody who is responsible for gathering in the poor who have become ill – The Talmud Torah about which we have said that from it our Torah will spread, behold mischievous children have gone forth from it. There is no sick person from all the masses of Israel, whose teachers lead them to the waters of knowledge and wisdom, to pay attention that they do not go about naked and barefoot, and wander around outside all day. They wander about the city without any guide or advisor. The Gemillut Chasadim organization [for charitable loans], the Malbish Arumim organization [providing clothing for the needy], and the Hachnasat Orchim organization [providing lodging for wayfarers], these organizations of support and protection have become impoverished – – There is no helper or supporter, no pillar or support – – – They have become impoverished, the sources of money have dried up – – – They lie down naked without clothing. They ask for bread and there is not even a morsel. For those who have sufficient energy to work at any trade, nobody approaches them. The Yeshiva building, which was established from days of yore, its honor has gone down to the ground – – – A bit here and a bit there. Young children and youths, for their path to the route of life is covered over for them from all sides. Those who figured out how to get into the Yeshiva are forced to go from door to door, to bow down to a coin of money.

Woe, for these our souls are grieved! For such an important city among the people of Israel such as the adorned Slutsk can fall so much and fail in charity on the streets. Mercy has declined precipitously, and Torah and faith have been laid on the ground. Shall we not be ashamed, shall we not be embarrassed, dear readers? – – – Let us repent and return from our ways – – – We should be a father to the orphan and savior to the widow, the oppressed, and those bent over. We should extend our hearts to the ill of our nation, to save their souls from descent to the pints. Sh'sh ShM'ch.[9]

(*Ivri Anochi*, issue 49, Brody, 13 Elul 5632, 1872)

[Page 26]

In the district of Slutsk – 70 *cheders* and 894 students. In the district of Pinsk – 85 *cheders* and 1,925 students. In the district of Novogrodok – 44 *cheders* and 619 students. These numbers are not all exact.

(According to information on the leadership of the general schools in the region of Minsk)

I have already announced in *Hameilitz* that the winds of the times influence our brethren here to teach their sons language and books, to turn them into effective people. That is not the lot of the girls in our city. Nobody is concerned with educating them, for there is no girls' school among the people, and their parents cannot afford to pay three or four rubles monthly to the private girls' school, as do the wealthy of the city. For this reason, no attention is paid to the Jewish girls who are being raised without the knowledge and education that leads to productivity. The many teachers in our city are not acting effectively, and who is not guilty? Is it not the leaders and educated people of our city, who pay no attention to concern themselves with the upcoming generation. They waste their energy and time in dispute and discord. How strong is the breach and separation of hearts regarding the cantors Z.M. and Tz.L. It has been three years that he has served in the holy post in first place, and his listeners are satisfied with his pleasant melodies in accordance with musical theory. However, the people of the older generation tried to denigrate him for singing with foreign writing and musical notes that are strange to them on top of the *Siddur*. They do not understand it. One day, when their hearts were merry at the Chevra Kadisha celebration[10], they chose Tz.L. who was the scion of wealthy people, his throat groans and wails, and musical principles are lost on him. They rejected Z.M. A dispute such as this in a Jewish community is sufficient to weaken the power of all those who wish to institute needed improvements in the community.

(*Hameilitz*, issue 21, 1881) Shalom Epstein

How soured are our hearts to witness the situation of the Talmud Torah in our city, for it is bad: The youths who study there are abandoned and unsupervised, without a teacher or principal. They go from house to house asking passers-by for donations. My masters! For whom have you abandoned the poor of the flock of our community? The two *melamdim*, impoverished personalities. – – – No my brothers! Your silence during these bad days is not good!... – – – Prepare the Talmud Torah with a trade school. Appoint faithful teachers and supervisors. Pay attention to its protocols and customs. Then the blessing of those lost will come upon you.

N. N.

There is also a Machzikei Yetomim [Upholders of Orphans] home in our city. (more accurately, damagers of orphans[11]. The older ones go wild on the streets of the city. They do not learn Torah and proper behavior, and they do not even know how to read Hebrew.

(*Hameilitz*, 1881)

It is pleasant duty to give praise to the students of the seventh and eighth cohort of our brethren here, and especially to the high school students Mr. L. Eliashberg and Mr. L. Gutzeit, for they aroused their friends to found a school to teach youths who are under their hands, and to hire a teacher for them to prepare them for the gymnasia [high school]. The volunteer students have taken it upon themselves to teach for three hours a day, each one three high school students. On Sundays, when they do not attend the gymnasia, they teach for five hours. Aside from this, they have given donations from their own pockets, each in accordance with their means, to pay for the room that they have rented for this. Approximately ten lads come to hear their lessons.

Yeshayahu Chorgin

Mr. Yeshaya Chorgin of Slutsk states that several intelligent girls and enlightened youths from the upper grades of the gymnasia school have taken note of the fate of the poor children who are going around without anything to do, without any work, and without good education. They founded an organization to give over various jobs to the poor children, to teach them trades and professions that can sustain them. The students of the gymnasia teach them the following subjects at set times: the Russian language, arithmetic, and writing craft. To this point, the group has succeeded in teaching trades to ten boys and three girls, and that there is hope that, in time, the group will succeed in growing its activity and glory.

(*Hameilitz*, issue 44, 1884)

The motto "seeing is not like hearing" is apparently to the point and true. The terrible situation of students of the Talmud Torah in our city has been mentioned in the newspapers more than once. If some of the members of the intelligentsia were to go to the Talmud Torah, they would realize the great need to change and improve the deficient methodologies of the institution.

More than forty naked[12] and barefoot youths are crowded into a single room. The classes are disorganized and the knowledge of the students is deficient. The teacher is a schlemiel, lacking pedagogic understanding and training. An organization called Temicha LaYatom [Support for the Orphan], the purpose of which is to provide material assistance to poor youths, has been founded.

A raffle was organized for the benefit of the Talmud Torah, which brought in seventy-five rubles. That money sent three youths there to study a profession. The rest of the money was used to provide clothing and shoes for the rest of the youths. The Orthodox people of the city are not interested in changes and improvements in the Talmud Torah, or in collaborating with the new organization.

(*Waschod*, issue 31, 1884)

Questions were received from Slutsk to the committee of the organization of dissemination of Haskala in Russia, regarding how to act, for they wish to have a night school in which adult workers and apprentices can study during the evenings.

(*Der Yud*, Vienna – Krakow, issue 16, 1889)

Torah Students

Blessed be G-d, Memel, Friday of the Torah portion "And your brothers the entire House of Israel shall weep over the fire"[13] 5620 [1860].

To my dismay, and the dismay of all scholars, I inform your honors that I have received a letter from my father-in-law, the Rabbi and *Gaon* M. Yosef Peimer, the head of the rabbinical court of Slutsk in Russia, that his wise, wholesome son, renowned to the public, my brother-in-law, honor to his name Rabbi Yisrael [Behmer][14] has taken ill on Thursday, 6 Nisan. He passed away on Wednesday, 12 Nisan. May his soul be bound in the bonds of eternal life, may his soul rejoice in G-d, and may G-d comfort us among the rest of the mourners of Zion and Jerusalem.

From he who honors and appreciated him.

Yeshaya Wohlgemuth, rabbi in Memel

[Page 27]

Our soul also mourns over this bad news. Our souls weep privately over the death of this friend of ours who was cut off in his prime, and is no more! With sorrowful hearts, we inform this to all those who love him and all those who know his name from his works that he has published! Woe over he who has gone and woe over the loss! The great things and the things of high splendor have been covered over. Here too in *Hamagid*, in which the late scholar worked for about nine moths with the good grace of G-d upon him, we shall hereby erect a monument of eternal memory! May he rest in peace and may his memory be a blessing!

(*Hamagid*, issue 16, April 25, 1860) The editor

Thursday 23 Adar I, 5630

During these days, the great, sharp, expert, and wise rabbi, a case full of books, Rabbi Pesach Aharon, may the memory of the holy be blessed, has passed away. The deceased was one of the excellent remnants [of past generations], filled with Talmud and rabbinic *halachic* literature, *Sifra, Sifrei, Midrash, Mechilta*[15], and all the early and late responsa literature. He delved into Torah day and night. He pursued justice, and his motto was to be useful and to do good. He founded the "*Maskil* el Dal" [Educating the Poor] society for the benefit of the poor, widows, and orphans. He gathered approximately forty abandoned lads from among the poor, hired teachers for them, and ensured that they would not be lacking in bread or any of their needs. He only lived for 43 years. Masses followed behind his bier. He was eulogized in the synagogue courtyard. Rabbi Yekutiel Schwartz eulogized him in the cemetery.

(*Hamagid*, issue 11, 1870). Yitzchak Yaakov ben Pesach

There are very few people in our day, remnants from the old generation, who are accepting of the members of the current generation who follow the new paths, and more so that they understand, and agree, that their ways are proper and that there is some improvement over past generations. Therefore, these few people are very precious in our eyes. They are few in number. – – – We have lost such an excellent person this past winter, the great rabbi, luminary and *Tzadik*, Rabbi Naftali Tzvi Cheifetz, the author of the book *Gan-Tzvi* on the five books of the Torah (the title of his book hints to his name, for it is the *gematria* [numerology] of Naftali Tzvi the son of Rabbi Yisrael). He was 75 years old at his death. He occupied himself in Talmud and rabbinic decisors day and night, and he delved deeply into books of research and exegesis all his days. He was a sublime, erudite scholar. He understood the ways of the world and the pathways of business. He would make peace between man and his fellow with soft words and a pleasant countenance. He was the rabbi of the excellent orator Rabbi Dinov, whom he loved boundlessly.

A public courthouse was opened in our city in the month of May.

(*Hamagid*, issue 34, 1872) M. Y. Hirschbein

For he is not one of those who sit behind the oven. So that he not be suspected by his readers as someone who sits behind the oven, he writes that he was forced to announce that he is a student in the government school of surveying, may its splendor rise.

In his article, he presents me as a target for shooting his arrows (not mighty, and not sharp, and unharnessed coals) of his nonsense and lies. – – – In his article, he also flatters with lies the local rabbi who currently lives amongst us. Every time he mentions him in is article, he describes him as "The great rabbi and *Gaon*," and he dishonors the honor of the deceased local rabbi (even though our sages of blessed memory have said that *Tzadik*im are greater in their deaths than in their lives). Every time he mentions him in the article, he refers to him as "The late Rabbi Beimer of blessed memory." – – –

He denigrates the honor of the true rabbi and *Gaon* who was unique in his generation, the Rabbi of the Entire Exile[16] the Admor Rabbi Yosef Beimer, who was known in a praiseworthy fashion throughout the world as Rabbi Yosef Slutsker. – – – The writer of the article mentions that my wife hates him, the dark and unilluminated family members hate him because the rabbi hates him because he has become a *Maskil* and a student in the school of surveying. He wrote that article because he wishes to appease his wife and family members, and the local rabbi who is at the head of them. O would it be that they would be appeased by this article, and then I would say, "rejoice my children, rejoice." – – – Indeed I have sacrificed my soul as a sacrifice for the love of truth and peace. – – – If I were to have asked the writer to write about the rabbi, I would have confessed and said that this is so. But, by faith! That is a lie, I never requested this of him for I do not think the matter of the local rabbi to speak important things on his behalf. The writer praised Y. A. the local rabbi because he loves his fellow. By faith, this is a complete lie, and this should be understood. And that Y.G. wrote that the rabbi created the "Maskil El Dal" society, this is an absolute lie, for the late Rabbi Pesach Horn of blessed memory created it, and the rabbi annulled it with his spirit. He also wrote that he distributed more than half of his salary to the poor – a liar! How can he be so brazen as to state such? And you the rabbi, how can you be silent when you hear false praises about yourself? That which Y. G. wrote, that those who are wholesome in the faith of Israel hate me because I denigrate the honor of the rabbi, that is indeed true. – – – That which he wrote that the late Rabbi Beimer of blessed memory did not allow me to cross the threshold of his home, accept it if I state that the true rabbi and *Gaon*, may his saintly memory be a blessing, loved me very much, and I was one of his prime admirers in this, my city.

After all my words, I state that I my heart would rejoice and be happy if the writer would make peace with his wife.

(*Haivri*, issue 18, 1873) Tzvi Hirsch Dinov, Maggid, native of Slutsk

Friday, 18 Sivan 5633 [1873]

To the honor of the rabbi, the publisher of *Ivri Anochi* [I am a Hebrew], may G-d protect him:

I imagine that you will quickly publish my article, for indeed you are a Hebrew [*Ivri*], you fear the G-d of Heaven, and it is fitting that my article should be in the very place where you have disparaged my honor in vain,

When I returned in peace from Peterburg this past Shavuot, they gave me issue twenty-nine of *Ivri Anochi*. I read the article from Horodno entitled "Public Rebuke." The writer announced at the end of his article that he was trying to scare me.

(*Haivri*, issue 16, 2 Tammuz 5633, 1873)

The wonderful tycoons, G-d-fearing and pure Reb Yona Isserlin and his son the rabbi and *Gaon* Rabbi Shachna of Slutsk are exemplary. They concern themselves for the welfare of all the members of the community in the same manner that they concern themselves with the welfare of their own households. Every person in straits who has built a house or married off a son or a daughter knows that he can receive a specific sum of partial support from these tycoons. It will be given with joy so that nobody will feel that he is receiving a free gift, rather that it is something he earned. Gifts for a lecture

[Page 28]

are sent to any resident of the city, from rich to poor, each in accordance with their value. All residents of the city, from young to old, came to honor them with the appropriate honor, and they distributed portions and honors to each person as appropriate. Their entire satisfaction and honor comes from doing good and benevolent deeds to the poor and oppressed. They befriend them, and are only pretentious regarding their honor. They have a wine cellar for the sick and poor, consisting of choice types that cannot frequently be found in commercial establishments. They distribute portions of flour and meat to all the poor on Sabbaths and festivals, to anyone who stuck out their hand and requested. They also give gifts to the poor discreetly, so that nobody should recognize it and be embarrassed.

(From *Hakerem*, 3612, 1882)

The great rabbi, illustrious in Talmud, is the true *Gaon* and *Tzadik*, who is a ruler in the pure fear of G-d, honor his holy name in splendor, is Rabbi Yosef, may he live, the rabbi of the holy community of Slutsk, may G-d shield it. Let light and brightness not cease from shining from his dwelling place as he goes to Raseiniai (a city in the Kovno Gubernia), but it should continue to shine with sevenfold illumination (as our sages of blessed memory have said: To the extent that scholars age, their knowledge continually increases) in the honorable city of Slutsk, which is the large city (also large in opinions) from a long time back. For the great ones of the world have always settled there to teach doctrine, to disseminate Torah and holy knowledge. The holy community and its leaders know how to appreciate the value that G-d has given to it by causing the aforementioned man of portents to dwell therein.

(*Hamagid*, issue 34, year 1)

"My heart rejoices greatly when I see at this time, when the horn of Torah is cast low and those who grasp Torah are considered as senile, approximately two hundred youths have gathered together, who are dedicated solely to Torah and religion. From you, the hope spreads forth, and you will be able to illuminate the coming generation. You should only be strong and become men."

(The blessing with which the *Gaon* Rabbi Yitzchak Yaakov Reines, may the memory of the holy be blessed, gave as he concluded the class that he gave in the Eitz Chaim Yeshiva of Slutsk on Thursday, 11 Shvat, 5663 [1903].)

(*Hameilitz*, issue 22, 5663, 1903)

Illnesses and Epidemics

The frightful illness that caused many to fall sick in many cities this summer also did not skip over our city.

This past 28 Av, we found out that several people died suddenly. The illness spread quickly, tearing away many children from the bosoms of their mothers, and also not sparing adults. Then those of precious spirit were aroused to stop the plague. They called meetings and founded a committee with all types of medicines and remedies. – – – They paid the salary for two Herew physicians to be available at all times to aid any person. They also paid Dr. Mashevski to go around and visit the sick (from among the poor). Medicine from the pharmacy was given to them by his order. Along with monetary support, he warned them to refrain from eating foods that are difficult [to digest], and not to prepare the customary hot dishes for the Sabbath. Signs were posted on Tisha B'Av that women, and young girls and boys below the age of eighteen are forbidden to fast. Men who feel that the fast will damage their health are allowed to eat and drink. On Tzom Gedalia, they announced that people should not fast. On the morning of the eve of Yom Kippur, they announced three things: a) women should go home on Kol Nidre night after the *Shmone Esrei* prayer; b) the wearing of shoes is permitted for anyone who leaves the synagogue; c) it is permitted to place bottles of water in ovens that have been lit from the day [i.e. before the start of Yom Kippur] as on every Sabbath eve. – – – Hot food was prepared in the committee building in case of a deathly panic. – – – People came to stand watch at the committee building all night. Those who were moved to work in this great matter should be praised.

The honorable leader who is occupied with communal needs, Reb Tzvi Hirsch David Travin, the honorable tycoon Reb Tzvi Hirsh Getzow, Reb Binyamin Wolfson, Reb Moshe Yechiel Eberil, Reb Yehuda Landau and his honorable brother the honorable Reb Betzalel Landau, Reb Chaim Mintz, Reb Nachman Oko, Reb Meir Reiser – – – collected *sheimos*[17]. They placed all the torn pages in earthenware pots, loaded them on four wagons, spread black garments over them, and transported them through the streets and the marketplace to the cemetery. They collected donations with the call "charity saves from death." – – – The name of Israel has become an accursed through such boorish deeds – – –[18]

There was a consultation in the large *Beis Midrash* regarding the many orphans who remained after the cholera plague. All the leaders of the city gathered together, headed by the *Gaon* Rabbi Menachem Mendel. – – – However, this time, they did not make any enactments. Rather they called for donations from al the residents of the city, each according to their means, to support the orphans and feed them until after the month of the High Holy Days. Then, a second meeting will be called to see what can be done with them.

The regional minister came to visit our city on the Sunday following Yom Kippur. He remained in the city for about three days. He took interest and asked about how many people died in the plague.

Yitzchak Yaakov Hirschbein

(*Hameilitz*, issue 15, 5633, 1872)

It has been about a month since the wealthy people of our city, headed by Mr. Sh. Migdal and Mr. B. Wolfson, girded themselves and sent a letter of request to the regional minister, who gave them permission to take a sum of 3,000 rubles from the meat tax fund in order to renovate the exterior of the old hospital, which had no form and no splendor, and was also too small to house all the sick people who come to request cures for their illnesses. They approached the building effort in a high fashion, to build a new hospital with spacious, clean rooms, and a grove of trees outside for shade. They would also renovate the old building so it could serve as a hostel for elderly, poor people, so they can spend their latter days and not suffer from the afflictions of hunger and cold during their old age.

The words of the heretic in issue 15 of *Hameilitz* are not believed when he continued to praise the efforts of our wealthy people, and their attempts to obtain 3,000 rubles from the meat tax to renovate the hospital. Had they indeed paid attention to the hospital, they would have made efforts to fill the more urgent needs – food, drink a place to sleep, etc. – rather than new walls instead of the old ones, which were still strong.

I have heard complaints that a liter or meet will be divided among ten sick people. Were it not for the help of the merciful women, who gather food for the sick, they would have perished from hunger. They would have also concerned themselves with mattresses filled with straw and hay. There is no expert physician. Therefore, only few come to request relief in the hospital.

[Page 29]

The words of the publisher of *Hameilitz* relating to the leaving over of the dead[19] have made a great impression in our city, for when a young man died a sudden death a few weeks ago, the rabbi did not allow him to be buried until three days had passed.

(*Hameilitz*, issue 15, 1881) Shalom HaLevi Epstein

A few years ago, a "hospital" was built here from the communal funds. It was surrounded by a lovely garden, which grew trees that spread an aroma around. At first, the conduct of that institution was proper and orderly under the direction of the faithful, upright Mr. Binyamin Wolfson. His entire field of interest was directed toward that institution. With the help of the philanthropists of the community, he provided the sick with all their needs. However, from the day that the Satan began to dance in its midst, and discord grew in the city, the institution began a downward spiral. The sick people were lying down with nobody to respond to their needs. Their clothing was torn down to the skin. Had the wealthy Mr. Dov Ber Lifschitz not provided help, the building would have already been smashed to pieces and destroyed to its foundation. That philanthropist donated three hundred rubles from his own pocket to repair the building . His hand is still outstretched, a single philanthropist cannot himself sustain the entire institution and fill all of its needs. If the other wealthy people of the city do not rise up to empathise with the pain of their brethren who are sick and poor, there is no hope that the institution will be able to exist for a long time. Therefore, I have decided to arouse the hearts of all the communal heads and important people of the city to place their eyes and hearts upon this institution, which alone serves as a refuge for our brethren during bad periods, and to distance themselves from disputes and discord.

(*Hameilitz* issue 45, 1886) Aryeh Leib Rubinstein, deputy government appointed rabbi

During such times when the wellsprings of livelihood have been closed and the ways of business are mournful, and people eat the flesh of their arms, the people of Slutsk are not satisfied with one cantor who has served in his position for a long period. They added a new cantor who made the rounds to cities and towns, and also came to our city during his travels. The cantor arrived, caused confusion in the entire city, and fomented great, deep hatred between fathers and sons, man and his friend, man and his wife. Now, there is only discord and dispute. Curses and castigation are heard in the outskirts of the city of Slutsk, and the houses of prayer have been turned into houses of revelry. Not one prayer services completes without the arrival of the city minister with officials who are close with him to quiet the commotion and noise rising from there. – – – The abandon and disturbance in the local hospital is great. Tens of lads with no purpose wander through the outskirts of the city, with no place of refuge or study. I cannot hold back my words, and I call out: Stop the discord. Leave the cantors, and concern yourselves with your sick and poor people! Direct your hearts to effective, honorable matters.

(*Hayom*, issue 416, 5 Tammuz 5646 [1886]) Ish Pinsk

Fires

On the bitter day of Tisha B'Av, the harsh, directed hand reached out to smite us with all sorts of beatings in ancient days and during various times. For the day has almost passed, the source of our eyelids have almost been sealed in the memory of the burning of our Holy Temple – – – And behold, a voice called out to struggle with fire. Our ears rang from the noise of the drums, the sound of the bells, and the screaming outside: Come and save yourselves, for fire has been cast upon our dwellings. The Jews, weary from their fast and their agony on this day of mourning, rose from their beds without energy to go to the place of the fire. But woe! The fire had taken hold of the four corners of the shops, and a pillar of fire and cloud of smoke were ascending skyward. The fire consumed two rows of shops, approximately eighty in number. Fifty houses also went up in flames. The fire consumed from the first hour until the third hour. – – – The great, vast damage cost up to 150,000 rubles. – – – One Jewish soul also went up in flames, a seven-year-old boy. – – – The name of the Cossack fire chief Artemi Andreievich Astachov should be remembered positively, for he gathered his army to fight against the terrible fire.

MTz'K Ish Vilna

(*Hakarmel*, issue 5, 19 Av 5622, 1862)

On Tammuz 2 – – – Last Tuesday, the fire went forth (the reason is unknown) and consumed approximately a thousand houses in our city. The flame went forth at 3:00 p.m. and the city was destroyed within three hours. The Great Synagogue, built like a citadel, the large *Beis Midrash*, the *Kloiz*, the *Beis Midrash* of the late wealthy *Tzadik* Reb Yona of blessed memory, the *Beis Midrash* Racha'g of the wealthy rabbi Sh. Simchovich, the house of the rabbi, the hospital, and eight other houses of worship were also destroyed. Several people were burnt by the fire, may G-d save us. Several Torah scrolls and books of the prophets, and books on the oral Torah of great value were also burnt. Most of the victims of the fire had their property wiped out, and they have no bread to eat or clothing to cover their nakedness. Prominent householders, strong leaders with their wives and children all fed to the field, where they spent the night, sated with wandering, in weeping and wailing. The voice of the children of the holy flock ascended Heavenward, may G-d have mercy. – I was among them as well. Several sick people and women who had just given birth with their babies were carried out to the field on their beds. – – – Few in number had their houses insured by the insurance company. – – –

On the second night, there was nobody in the fields, for the merciful ones the children of the merciful took the unfortunate people into their houses. Nobody said that they had no room.

Many gave of their meals to the guests who they had taken into their house. The honorable people of the city distributed bread, pulse, and potatoes. Food was brought in daily from our Jewish brethren as well as the Christians villagers from the nearby towns. Kasinov, the governor from Minsk, promised to stand to the right of the unfortunate ones. The mighty, merciful Czar sent his donation of 5,000 rubles for bread for the poor of our city. Potoposh[20], the governor of Vilna, sent 1,000 rubles. Now my honorable sirs, my brothers, friends, and masters, honorable wealthy people in the city, as you dwell in your closed off houses, just as you sheltered your brethren to this point, shelter your brethren today as well. – – – You as well, the exceptional wealthy people of the world, Simchovich and Isserlin, do not abandon your unfortunate brethren. As well, the praiseworthy brothers of the Simchovich family of Mohilov and the wealthy citizens of Dynaburg[21], do not forget the natives of this praiseworthy city. You too, shelter and have mercy on this praiseworthy city, full of Torah and fear [of G-d], grace, mercy, and charity.

(*Hamagid*, issue 27, 1868) Tzvi Hirsch Dinov

They brought bread from all the nearby villages. Christians brought their contributions.

The Osei Tzedaka [Doers of Charity] organization of Memel sent through the rabbi and *Gaon* Isserlin

[Page 30]

seventy-five rubles, from Bobruisk 85 rubles, from Lechevich 100 rubles, from Uzda 25 rubles, from Niesvizh 70 pod of bread, from Kletzk 45 pod of bread, from Starobin 40 pod of bread and 200 rolls of wheat flour. The wealthy man Matzkevich from Hresk sent as donation 1 ½ chechve[22] of fine flour, 1 ½ chechve of groats, 40 pod of bread, and 600 challahs baked from wheat flour. The wealthy Reb Yosef Pulman from the village of Hresk donated 2 ½ chechve of flour. Twenty pod of bread were donated from Ureche, 20 pod of bread from Vizhne, and fifteen pod of bread form Hrozova.

(*Hamagid*, issue 37, 1868)

Wednesday, 10 Av

– – – A committee of Christians and Jews was chosen to distribute financial assistance to the unfortunate people, so that they do not perish from hunger. – – – A representative came from the honor of our glorious king, and brought 5,000 rubles. The distribution was concluded on Wednesday, 11 Tammuz. The Ispravnik [district official] Labonzov and the judge Lisovich, and the honorable people from amongst our brethren: Tzvi David Travon, Reb Moshe Moshelov, Reb Shmuel Migdael, Reb Tzvi Hillel Bezborodkin, Reb David Kosovski, Reb Matityahu Grajovski all distributed [aid] in a pleasant and understanding manner.

There were approximately ten Christians from amongst those who were burnt. – – – By Friday, a sum of 3,260 rubles had been distributed. A mass meeting in honor of the high-level guests was arranged in the *Beis Midrash* on Vilna Street, as they were planning to leave the city.

The government rabbi M. Lipman opened with strong words, and words of Torah. – – – Following him, the great musician Betzalel Landau, faithful to the house of the rabbi and *Gaon* Rabbi Isser Isserlin, along with his choir of singers, sang *Hanoten Teshua*[23], and *Kel Melech Netzor*[24]. – – – The lord Kovelin also spoke and promised to intercede before his glorious kingship for immediate assistance. The city notables presented him with a letter of thanks with their signature.

(*Hamagid*, issue 37, 1868)

As is known, a large, terrible fire broke out in our city four years ago and consumed half of the city. Many houses of worship and dwelling places of Jacob went up in flames at that time. Throughout these four years, the ruins have already been rebuilt, and all the houses of worship have risen from their ruins. The Great, splendid synagogue was built in a lofty manner, and is known in a praiseworthy fashion throughout our entire area. The fire had afflicted it and caused ruin inside. Only the stone walls remained, casting a pall. To this point, more than 3,000 rubles have been spent on its restoration after the fire. However, darkness still covers its walls, for the plaster fell off of them during the fire, and the stones are also covered in soot.

This summer, G-d moved the heart of a certain person (who is anonymous), from among the notables of our community, to give 150 rubles to began to plaster the walls from the inside. Several others were aroused to donate approximately 300 rubles, so that the work could be completed. To add glory and splendor, they made a fence around the holy ark, not the work of an artisan: two square pillars on each side, with a sort of dome on top in a decorative fashion. When all this work was finished, they made efforts to arrange a dedication celebration with musicians and instruments. May G-d reward the upright individuals who made efforts in the renovation of the building.

(*Hameilitz*, 1872, 5633[25]) Yitzchak Yaakov Horabein

In response to the appeal for help in *Hameilitz* issue 32 for those afflicted by the fire in our city, Dr. Rilf of Memel and the lofty wealthy man, renown in most of our Diaspora, Mr. Yehoshua Ceitlin of Moscow, were aroused. The former sent us 200 rubles, and the latter 60 rubles, over and above the 18 rubles sent to one of those afflicted by the fire. Even though twenty years have elapsed since Mr. Ceitlin moved out of our city, he does not forget it, and he is available for it without being asked. Aside from this, he has set for himself a firm rule to send a donation for distribution to the poor of our city before all the festivals. Last Passover, he sent 40 rubles to the Maos Chittin fund, and 50 rubles for the poor of our city. It is our hope that he will not avert his eyes from the poor of our city in days to come.

We the undersigned offer our gratitude and blessings in the name of our entire community to these chief benefactors of ours. May it be the will of our Father In Heaven to raise their profiles in honor, and grant them from His bountiful blessings. May the blessings of those who depend on them come along with the blessings of the members of the committee:

Elazar the son of Rabbi Michael of blessed memory Rabinovich

Chaim Yavorav, Tzvi Hirsch Ofos

(*Hameilitz*, issue 48, 1881)

The hand of G-d came upon our unfortunate city. On Sunday night, 4 Av, fire broke out in one of the houses, and within moments, approximately forty houses were burnt. Among them was one *Beis Midrash* built as a fortress, and twenty-five shops. Due to the fear of the night, our brethren were unable to save all of their toil, and their merchandise also went up in flames. They were only able to save themselves. On Monday, one child was found burnt, with his bones dried up. The screams of the unfortunate people were very great, for the fire spread throughout almost the entire area of Jewish settlement. Their many needs cannot be filled by donations of people from our city. Therefore, our eyes are turned toward the philanthropists of the nation, the pillars of charity, who join in the difficulties of our people, that they shall have mercy and pity, to hep us with their donations. Even the good benefactor, Rabbi Dr. Rilf, shall please help us with the righteousness of his heart.

All donations should please be sent to the address of the local rabbi and *Gaon*, Rabbi Meir Peimer.

(*Hameilitz*, issue 32, 1881) The writer: M. Polyak

The writer in Hamelitz 32 made us into a laughingstock through his request for assistance for those in our city afflicted by the fire, for they never thought of this, and it would be disgraceful for most of them to ask for help. They succeeded in salvaging everything that was in their houses, and for the poor (few in number) who need to call for help, the donations from the philanthropists of our city will be sufficient.

Yehoshua Grynberg

We will repeat once again that, from this time, we will not publish such announcements unless they come with the signature of the rabbi or heads of the community.

(*Hameilitz*, issue 35, 1881)

On the second day of Rosh Chodesh Iyar, a fire broke out in the city at noontime. Within two hours, sixty shops and twenty-two large houses, built like fortresses, became heaps of ash. The damage reached 200,000 rubles

(*Hameilitz*, issue 44, 5647, 1887)

[Page 31]

Mr. Moshe Mordechai Portman announces from Slutsk that the wrath of G-d fell upon all the residents of the city in the wake of the fires that have been ignited there for about the past two months by a group of traitors and wicked people. Guards and police make the rounds throughout the day and night, and even the householders do not let themselves fall asleep at night. The rabbi and the city notables have also met together to deliberate about how to stop this evil. They decided to issue a strong "ban," the likes of which have not been heard in the city for many years. They did so. The shamash proclaimed the ban in a loud voice. It is written in Kol Bo. All those who heard this were afraid and vexed from this.

(*Hameilitz*, issue 148, 5648, 1887)

The Czar's Birthday Celebrations

We have heard about the celebrations of His Majesty the Czar. There too, they people gathered for prayer in the synagogue. Ministers and army officials, headed by the Cossack army chief Master Astachov, and the city officer also came to hear how the Children of Israel were praying for the welfare of their king. The synagogue was enveloped with holy splendor. The renowned cantor Reb Nissan of Shklov recited the prayer *Hanoten Teshua Lamelachim* [23] and sang the song *Elyon Melech Shamor*. Following the services, the heads of the community presented the chief Cossack official with a letter of allegiance in the name of the Czar. When the letter was presented, the entire gathering shouted out the accolades of the Czar. That day, they also made a feast for all the military personnel, numbering about 1,100, who were camped in the city to protect it. The military officers greeted the people and acknowledged their allegiance and kindness.

(From the writings of Dr. E. L. Steinberg)

(*Hakarmel*, issue 5, Tishrei 5624, 1864)

On February 19, the city notable went to General Nikolai Alexandrovich, and the brigade chief Varanovsky to greet them with the joy of that day. They requested that they, with all the officials standing alongside them, come to the Great Synagogue in the evening to hear the song and prayer that the Children of Israel will recite for the welfare of the Czar and his royal family. The officer should greet them in joy, and say good, comforting words to them, for the heart of the Czar is positively inclined to the Jews. – – –

The day passed, and all the residents of the city lit their candles and illuminated the night. The light from the Great Synagogue shone afar, and masses streamed to the building. Two leaders of the community, the great, wise Rabbi Shmuel Simchovich, and his brother-in-law, the wise, philanthropist Rabbi Yehoshua Isser Isserlin, stood at the door to greet the minister, along with his entourage and officials. All the chiefs of the city officials, judges, leaders, high school officials and teachers came along with them. They sat in honorary seats around the table that was placed for them between the *bima* and the Holy Ark, near the great, elderly, rabbi and *Gaon*, Rabbi Yosef Behmer. A band of musicians playing their instruments greeted them as they entered. After that, the cantor recited the *Hanoten Teshua* prayer. At the end of the prayers and the song, the general drank a toast for the welfare of the Czar. – – –

Menachem Tzvi Kolkes

(*Hakarmel*, issue 27, 10 Adar II, 5621, 1861)

The Jewish community of Slutsk celebrated its joyous festival on April 17. Everyone gathered in the Great Synagogue, wearing festive clothes. Even all the military and city leaders gathered there. The cantor and his choir of singers recited the prayer for the government, accompanied by musicians. Twelve school students sang the popular song *Kel Melech Netzor* in Russian. A cup of salvation was raised for the life of our noble master.

(*Hakarmel*, issue 5, 10 Sivan, 5626, 1866)

Menachem Kolkes

The teacher and *Maskil* Reb Menachem Tzvi Kolkes announces that when the news came of the salvation of Czar Alexander II on the Sabbath of the eve of Shavuot in the afternoon, the wealthy, wise rabbi, Rabbi Shmuel Simchovich, may his light shine, arose along with the rabbi of the *Maskil* community Lipman and commanded that this great salvation be announced to all the people of the city. Masses streamed to the Great Synagogue at *Mincha* time. Chief of the army and ministers came to the prayer. Reb Betzalel Landau, the cantor of the synagogue of the wealthy philanthropist Reb Isser Isserlin, and his choir, sang *Kel Melech Netzor* in Russian. The next day, the first day of Shavuot, the heads of the community distributed loaves of bread and liquor to all the soldiers in the courtyard of the Russian house of worship.

(*Hakarmel*, issue 44, 9 Tammuz, 5627, 1867)

Miscellaneous

Chaya, the daughter of Reb Yitzchak of Slutsk, is seeking her husband after he had already been gone for nine years. His name is Mordechai the son of Reb Pinchas of Kletzk. He had lived for many years in Slutsk. His is of average height, dark haired, with a full beard, and heavy. His left thumb is missing two sections, with only the bottom section, closest to the hand, remaining. He is hard of speech, and his eyes are soft. Let our Jewish brethren pay attention, for perhaps he can be captured and returned to his abandoned wife.

(*Hakarmel*, issue 31, 28 Shvat 5621, 1861)

A terrible accident took place in the district of Slutsk on 27 January 1861. A wild wolf emerged from its den and started to inflict damage. It forged a path for its wrath through Kapolya. At a distance of two verst from there, it killed a Jewish man who was passing by, Reb Yosef Eliyahu of Kapolya. From there, the wolf went to the yard of the guard of the forest of Count Wittgenstein. It hit and injured a person. The guards shot at it, but missed their mark. The wolf broke through to the village of Evanelevich, owned by the Lord Reitman, where it tore apart and trampled thirty-five male farmers, and 203 women. The wolf later attacked a brave person. When the wolf opened its mouth to tear him apart, the man placed his left hand into the throat of the wolf, and pushed it against the wall, while strangling it with his right hand. The man shouted out for help. – – – A soldier came to the rescue. He hit the wolf with an axe and chopped it into pieces. Sixty people were killed by the wolf, including one Jew.

From the report of the police chief Zdroviechki on January 29, 1861.

Menachem Tzvi the son of Reb Shmuel Kolkes of Vilna

(*Hakarmel*, issue 34, 19 Adar 5621, 1861)

[Page 32]

I have seen in the first issue of *Hakarmel* of this year that the rabbi and *Gaon* Rabbi Yosef, may he live, the head of the rabbinical court of our city, has been chosen by the community of Minsk to be the head of the rabbinical court. Therefore, I inform the community that this rabbi and *Gaon* has lived in our city for 34 years, and we know how to appreciate this high honor. We too were honored through his honor. He responded immediately to the letter of appointment sent by the community of Minsk. I inform the public so that we an remove the disgrace that we did not know how to appreciate the preciousness of the rabbi and *Gaon*, may he live.

Reuven the son of Avraham Maharshak

(*Hakarmel*, issue 8, Elul 5622, 1862)

My heart rejoices to announce that the wise, wealthy, philanthropic sage, who rejoices to do righteousness and all times, Rabbi Yehoshua Isserlin, may his light shine, has been raised to the ranks of an honorable citizen in his generation. This honor is fitting for him and his family. Our brethren the children of Israel, raise your hearts in joy to hear that from time to time, the good government continues to grant honor and strength to our honorable brethren in all places that they live.

Menachem Tzvi Kolkes

(*Hakarmel*, issue 27, II Adar, 5624, 1864)

On Friday night, thieves and murderers attacked the hotel in the center of the city and murdered the hotel owner, Yaakov Moshe, his wife, their daughter, and also a guest who was staying with them for the Sabbath. After they pillaged those four people, they set the building on fire. Within an hour, it turned into a ruin. Of the burnt bodies, only the head of the hotel owner was found.

(*Hameilitz*, issue 19 1878)

з Слуцк. Вид с моста близ гимназии
Sluck. Widok z mosta koło gimnazjum

City scenery near the Gymnasia

The government rabbi in our city and region from 1860 to now, Rabbi Shlomo Zalman Shapira, was honored with a gold medal that he could place on his neck with the Stanislav ribbon for his faithful work and for his lessons in faith that he teaches to Jewish children in the local Gymnasia.

(*Hameilitz*, issue 35, 1883) Eliyahu Rubinstein, deputy government rabbi of Slutsk

Yehoshua Karlin announces from Slutsk that the society formed there in memory of Moshe T'L continues to strengthen. The local rabbi and *Gaon* has also signed up to it, leading many of the mighty ones of the city to do so as well. The number of members is currently more than 400 (may they grow). They all gather together once a month to deliberate together and to strengthen each other in the holy work.

(*Hameilitz*, issue 7, 1885, 5645)

Workers have excavated near the house of B. Z. and found a chest with silver coins (some say gold) that were buried there four hundred years ago.

(*Hameilitz* 5647, 1887)

On the first day of Passover, an elderly Jew died at the age of 110. His 93-year-old wife died on the second day. They were healthy and strong. Every day before the festival, the old man helped his son in his store. Only when he was returning from the synagogue on the first day of Passover, he tripped on a stone and was seriously injured. He died in the morning. His wife fainted from excessive weeping, and became ill. She died as well on the second day of the festival.

(*Hayehudi*, London, issue 15, 5670, 1909)

Translator's footnotes:

1. i.e. *KImcha Depischa* or *Maos Chittin* – provision of food for Passover for the poor. The term is based on the requirement of eating matzos on Passover. The poor would be provided with the flour for the baking of matzos. In time, the term took on the meaning of providing the poor with Passover needs in general.
2. The charity was called *Chaluka*, and went to support those studying in the various Kolels of Jerusalem in the era prior to formal Zionism. See https://en.wikipedia.org/wiki/Halukka
3. Tokens of membership in the Zionist movement.
4. See https://en.wikipedia.org/wiki/Black_Hundreds
5. See https://en.wikipedia.org/wiki/Zvi_Hirsch_Masliansky
6. A term for the pogroms of 1881-1882.
7. A poetic form for the people of Israel (see Deuteronomy 32:15, 33:26).
8. The term Lita is used here in the broad sense of the term
9. Seemingly the initials of pseudonym of the author.
10. A Chevra Kadisha customarily holds an annual feast for its members.
11. There is a one letter difference in the Hebrew.
12. Although the word used is naked, it means poorly clothed.
13. There is a literary mode of naming Torah portions by a prominent verse in the portion. This verse refers to the Torah portion of Shemini.
14. According to the profile on Geni, the surnames Peimer and Behmer are interchangeable in that family.
15. *Sifra, Sifrei, Mechilta* are all early rabbinical *Midrashim* on the *Chumash*.
16. A flowery term (here as an acronym) for a great rabbi.
17. A term used for torn and unusable pages of holy books (or entire holy books), which require burial. They are called *sheimos* [names], as they are rendered holy since they contain the Name of G-d.
18. This sentence seems very out of place here.
19. i.e. delaying the burial.
20. This would be Aleksandr Potapov. See https://en.wikipedia.org/wiki/Aleksandr_Potapov_(statesman)

21. Dvinsk or Daugavpils.
22. A Russian unit of volume, close to 6,000 bushels.
23. The opening words of the Prayer for the Government,
24. G-d, King, please guard. – Evidently the opening words for a prayer for the Czar.
25. There is an error here, probably in the Hebrew date, which says 5532 (one hundred years off).

[Page 33]

Rabbis

Translated by Jerrold Landau

Rabbi Yechiel of blessed memory the son of the *Gaon* The Rasha'l

The *Gaon* Rabbi Yechiel the son of Rabbi Avraham Luria, the head of the rabbinical court of Slutsk. The responsa of the Mahara'm Padua, section 83, was sent to him.

He was the father of the *Gaon* Rabbi Shlomo Luria, who was known as the Maharsha'l.

He died on 12 Kislev 5334 (1574). (See: "About the Lurias" by Avraham Epstein.)

Rabbi Moshe the son of Reb Pesach the son of Reb Tanchum Krakow

He was the head of the rabbinical court and head of the Yeshiva in the Brisk Kloiz and in the holy community of Slutsk. In the year 5424 (1664) he wrote an approbation of the book *Amudeha Shiva* by Rabbi Betzalel Darshan of Slutsk. He signed his name as Moshe Kahana the son of Rabbi Pesach Katz, may the memory of the holy be blessed.

Rabbi Nachum of blessed memory Katzenelenboigen

The *Gaon* Rabbi Nachum Ke'b (Katzenelenboigen) the son of the *Gaon* Rabbi Meir Ke'b was a fourth generation descendent of the Mahara'm of Padua, the head of the rabbinical court of the holy community of Slutsk in the year 5419 (1659). He died there before the year 5447 (1687). There is a eulogy for him in the book *Zecher Hachayim*.

Rabbi Naftali Hertz of blessed memory Ginzberg

Rabbi Naftali Hertz of blessed memory Ginzberg was accepted as the head of the rabbinical court of the holy community of Slutsk. In the year 5430 [1670] he signed in the council of Selits and the council of Chomsk as "Chobe'k Slutsk." In 5439 (1679) he wrote an approbation for the books *Keneh Chochma* and *Divrei Chachamim* by Rabbi Yehuda Leib of Pinsk. He was husband of the sister of Rabbi Nachum Katzenelenboigen. (See "City of Vilna" page 151).

He died at an old age on 22 Tammuz 5447 (1687), and was buried near the *Gaon* Rabbi Nachum Katzenelenboigen. During the third decade of the fifth century, he was among the leaders of the Jewish community of Poland and Lithuania. The *Gaon* Rabbi Naftali Hertz Ginzberg occupied the rabbinical seat as the head of the rabbinical court of Pinsk and Slutsk.

The story taken from the book of Torah novellae by Rabbi Zekil of Worms is apparently relevant to Rabbi Naftali Hertz Ginzberg the son of Rabbi Yitzchak Izak, the rabbi of Slutsk. Regarding that, Rabbi Yissachar Ber Sokolski published in the *Hachoker* publication, year 1, pp. 154-5 that his name really was Rabbi Naftali Hirsch. These are the words of the story: The rabbi and *Gaon* Rabbi Hirsch Ginzberg, who was the rabbi and teacher of righteousness in the holy community of Slutsk, where he is buried, was more than eighty years old.

– – The Rebbetzin conducted herself with a high hand and with great honor until her old age. When he became elderly, the heads of his city urged him to permit them to take on another rabbi and teacher of righteousness in the city, for he was not able to function properly in the rabbinate due to his old age. His income and honor would not be affected one iota. The other one would be the rabbinical judge and teacher of righteousness, as a student sitting before his rabbi. He responded: "I do not permit you to do this. If you appoint a teacher of righteousness, you will be going against my will." Since the city of Slutsk was under the Duke of Brandenberg, and the *Gaon*, the author of *Nachalat Binyamin* was the rabbi in Landsburg in the province of Brandenberg, they appointed the rabbi, the author of *Nachalat Binyamin*, as the rabbi of Slutsk. When the author of *Nachalat Binyamin* arrived in Slutsk and went to the home of the aforementioned Rabbi Naftali Hertz[1] and urged him to permit him to settle in Slutsk, the author of *Nachalat Binyamin* told him as follows: "If I want to settle here I can conduct the rabbinate with full honor and a high hand, even against your will, for my hand is strong, and I am beloved by the Duke of Brandenberg. I will not do all this against your will, and I will grant you all the honor. The income of the rabbinical position should be yours only (for the author of *Nachalat Binyamin* was wealthy). I will only serve as the head of the Yeshiva, but it should not be against your will." The rabbi and *Gaon* responded to him: "I do not give you permission. If you desire, you can do this, but it will be against my will, author of *Nachalat Binyamin*." When he realized that he had urged him and spoke many things, but he nevertheless did not give him permission, he accepted the rabbinate without the permission of the rabbi and Gaon. A month had not passed before the author of *Nachalat Binyamin* became ill and passed away. The rabbi and *Gaon* survived him.

Rabbi Betzalel the son of Rabbi Shlomo

The *Amudeha Shiva* book, great, wonderful explanation on the Torah, Prophets, and Writings – – – compiled by the great rabbi and *Gaon* Rabbi Betzalel may the memory of the righteous be blessed from Slutsk in Lithuania, was published for the first time in 5434 (1674) in the city of Prague, with the approbation of the *Gaonim* of the land, including our great rabbi, the Turei Zahav. I brought it to print, me, the young Tzvi Hirsch Kopil-Bachner of Kalish – in Lemberg, published by Uri Zeev Wolf Salat, may he live, 1887.

From the introduction of the author – – – I had already had the idea of publishing (a golden book). I succeeded when I came to my land and birthplace in the country of Lithuania, and I found favor in the eyes of the chiefs, the heads and leaders of the country. They gave me a large gift to publish the book. I also found favor in the eyes of the captains, the heads of the country of Poland, exemplary people, members of my community, the holy community of Slutsk. – – –

He died on 12 Nissan, 5482 (1722).

(Note: Nine rabbis of the great ones of that generations are listed in the cover page of the book.)

Rabbi Binyamin Wolf (author of *Nachalat Binyamin*)

Rabbi Binyamin Wolf (author of *Nachalat Binyamin*) was accepted as the head of the rabbinical court of Slutsk in the year 1687. He was called by the members of his generation: Rabbi Wolf the son of Rabbi Lipman.

[Page 34]

His book *Nachalat Binyamin* was published in the year 5442 [1682]. He did not live long in Slutsk, for he passed away.

He died on 28 Cheshvan 5447 [1686].

Rabbi Yitzchak Meir of blessed memory Teomim

Rabbi Yitzchak Meir of blessed memory Teomim was one of the deportees of Vienna. "The young orator Yitzchak Meir the son of the renowned *Gaon* Rabbi Yona of blessed memory Teomim, who lives in the holy community of Slutsk. He was the fifth signatory in Pinkas Heilprin of the council of Chomsk in 5451 (1691). The rabbi and *Gaon* Rabbi Yitzchak Meir the son of Rabbi Yona Teomim Frenkel, head of the rabbinical court of Slutsk, published *Ein Yaakov* with all the commentaries, entitles *Kutonet Or*. (*Chevel Hakesef*) on the book *Shabta Deraglia*, Rabbi Tzvi Hirsch the son of Rabbi Yerachmiel Chotsh (Fiurda, 5453 – 1693), he signed there: "Living in the holy community of Slutsk."

Rabbi Shlomo of Zelkova the son of the *Gaon* Rabbi Elchanan

Rabbi Shlomo of Zelkova the son of the *Gaon* Rabbi Elchanan, Rabbi Shlomo Charif, was accepted as the head of the rabbinical court of Slutsk in the year 5452 (1692). On Wednesday 25 Tammuz 5466 [1706] he gave an approbation for the books: *Netiv Hayashar*, *Rosh Yosef*, *Naftali Sva Ratzon*, and others.

Rabbi Moshe of blessed memory of Radom

"The community of Minsk must pay Rabbi Moshe of Slutsk 820 zloty." …

(The council of Selits, 5460 (1700), Pinkas Heilprin)

Rabbi Aryeh Leib of blessed memory the son of the *Gaon* Rabbi Yudel of Kovela – Epstein

Rabbi Aryeh Leib the son of he *Gaon* Rabbi Yudel of Kovela – Epstein. (Died on 12 Nissan 5482 -1722).

Rabbi Aryeh Leib the son of the *Gaon* Rabbi Yudel (Gvurat HaAri) was called Reb Leib dem Rebbe's in Slutsk.

"Signed by Ari Leib who lives in the holy community of Slutsk."

He was the fourth signer in the council of the Admor T'p (Pinkas Heilprin). "Our rabbi and teacher Rabbi Aryeh Leib the great, renowned *Gaon* in his generation, head of the rabbinical court of Slutsk." (Anshei Shem)

The Council of Mir 5457 [1697]

"And signed by Ari who is nicknamed Leib the son of the famous rabbi Rabbi Yehuda Yudel, may the memory of the holy be blessed." (Pinkas Heilprin). There, he is also the seventh: "And signed by Ari who is nicknamed Leib of Slutsk."

Rabbi Yehuda the son of Rabbi Asher Enzil

"Rabbi Yehuda Leib the son of Rabbi Asher Enzil, head of the rabbinical court and Yeshiva head in the Ostraha Kloiz. Later accepted as the head of the rabbinical court of the holy community of Slutsk and the holy community of Pinsk.

(*Daat Kedoshim*)

He gave an approbation for the book *Zera Yisrael*, and he signed Yehuda Leib the son of the late rabbi and *Gaon* Rabbi Asher Enzil of blessed memory, "Who lives here in the holy community of Ostraha, in the local Kloiz. 13 Av 5482 (1722), and now head of the rabbinical court of the holy community of Slutsk."

(*Daat Kedoshim*)

He served in the rabbinate following Chaim Cohen Rappaport (*Luchot Zikaron, Rabbis of Slutsk*, page 34).

Rabbi Aryeh Leib the son of Rabbi Natan Nota

Rabbi Aryeh Leib the son of Rabbi Natan Nota died in Grodno on 29 Nissan, 5489 (1729).

He gave an approbation on the book *Zera Birech* on Tractate *Brachot*, and signed, "The Kattan[2] Aryeh Leib, who lives here in Slutsk."

Rabbi Avraham Katzenelboigen

("Signed, Avraham the son of the *Gaon* Rabbi David of the Katzenelboigen family" a resident of the holy community of Slutsk).

He was the first signer of the council of Mir, 5512 (1752).

(Pinkas Heilprin)

"And signed by Avraham Katzin Nellen Boign who lives in the holy community of Slutsk."

He gave an approbation for the book *Kochvei Yaakov* and the book *Beit Avraham*, the booklet *M'T Kasher*, and was included in *Aliyat Eliyahu*.

When he was at first the head of the rabbinical court of Slutsk, he signed at the head of the *Gaonim* of his generation in the book *Luchot Habrit* in the year 5512 [1752].

Mr. Binyamin Trachtenberg of Jerusalem has his family tree. Rabbi Yom Tov Lipman Heller in the council of Mir signed the agreement on the ban against Rabbi Y . Eibeschutz in the year 5512 [1752]. In the year 5487 [1727] he was in the home of his father-in-law in Vilna. The aforementioned Rabbi Avraham saw the Gr'a when he was seven years old, and he took him and brought him to his father in Keidiani (*Aliyat Eliyahu*).

Rabbi Yissachar Ber of blessed memory

Rabbi Yissachar Ber of blessed memory.

"Signed Yissachar who is known as Ber, who lives here in the holy community of Slutsk."

He gave an approbation for the book *Shirat Moshe* by Rabbi Moshe Meizel of Vilna (Shklov, 5548 [1788]).

(Council of 5521, Slutsk 1761)

Rabbi Chaim HaKohen of blessed memory Rappaport

In the year 5482 [1722], he was accepted as the head of the rabbinical court and Yeshiva head in the holy community of Slutsk, which at that time was a city full of sages and scribes. His book *Zecher Hachayim* incudes explanations and eulogies.

"The *Gaonim* of his generations bent their knees before him, made a fence, and filled the breach in all his matters. Everyone knows how he persecuted the accursed group of those who contradicted the Oral Torah. Sh.T. [Shabtai Tzvi], and M. Sh., Sh.R.'Y. [May the names of the evil ones rot]."

(From the introduction of the grandson of the author, the compiler and publisher of Responsa Rabbi Chaim HaKohen).

The approbation to the book *Seder Hadorot*, 5529 [1769] – – –

"Today is Sunday 3 Tammuz, 5490 [1740], when he was the head of the rabbinical court and Yeshiva of the holy community of Slutsk. Chaim the son of the *Gaon* Rabbi Simcha Katz, may the memory of the holy be blessed, the rabbi Rappaport, who lives her in the holy community of Slutsk, may G-d protect it."

He died on 17 Tammuz 5531 – 1711.

[Page 35]

Rabbi Chaim Zeldes of blessed memory

Details are not known.

Rabbi Yosef of Hlusk

Rabbi Yosef the son of Rabbi Menachem Mendel of Hlusk, head of the rabbinical court of the holy community of Slutsk. In the year 5531 (1772) he gave an approbation to the book *Tiferet Yisrael* by the *Gaon* Rabbi Yisrael Yaffa of Shklov, and signed "Yosef the son of the *Gaon* Rabbi Menachem Mendel, head of the rabbinical court of Slutsk and Hlusk."

(*Daat Kedoshim*)

Rabbi Yudel the son of Rabbi Avraham HaLevi Horowitz

In the year 5504 [1744], he signed on the *Chumashim* of the Rasha'd with a *Tikkun Sofrim*[3] and his commentaries: Rabbi Yehuda Yudel of Slutsk, gives and approbation on the book *Kutonet Pasim*, also called *Chaluka Derabanan*, on the Passover Haggadah of Rabbi Yosef the son of Rabbi Moshe Darshan. He also wrote two books titled *Kol Yehuda* on the entire *Shulchan Aruch* and *Orach Chayim*. The books were given over to be published, but for various reasons, he did not succeed in publishing them during his lifetime. They were also not published after his death.

"Signed, Yehuda Yudel the son of the Kattan Rabbi Avraham HaLevi Horowitz, may he be remembered for life in the World to Come, of Slutsk."

(Council of 5512 [1742], Mir, Tenth signature).

He died on 7 Shevat, 5534 (1774).

Rabbi Shlomo Zalman Lifschitz of blessed memory

Rabbi Shlomo Zalman Lifschitz, the head of the rabbinical court of Slutsk, the son of the great rabbi and *Gaon* in his generation, Rabbi Menachem Manush Lifschitz of blessed memory.

In the year 5528 [1768] the even town notables decided to become enemies of the *Gaon*, and they forced him to forgo some details of the rights that were granted to him in the rabbinical contract. They imposed new conditions on him, and the head of the rabbinical court swore to fulfil all their words. Then, he presented his case before the chiefs and leaders of the holy community of Horodno, stating that he was forced into everything that happened, and requesting that the community present their petitions to the rabbinical court and the chiefs of the holy community of Horodno. After the majority were rejected by the community, they went together to a judgment. The rabbinical court of the holy community of Horodno issued a verdict on 3 Tevet 5531 [1771] stating that the rights of the *Gaon* have been restored. – – – The opponents of the *Gaon* appealed the verdict for various reasons, and increased the dispute with him for several years, until they made a compromise in the year 5537 [1777]. The compromise was only for show, for the anger did not abate in the hearts of his opponents. Based on the rabbinical rights (from council of Chomsk in the year 5480 [1720]), he brought his situation before the main community that chose him. The coals of hatred smouldered until the year 5541 [1781] when he left for Lachva. After a series of complaints, the community summoned the head of the rabbinical court to the communal hall to stand trial. They decided to remove him from his rabbinical position on 26 Shevat 5545 (1785). Then, the head of the rabbinical court approached the duke and expressed his wish that his words be presented before the judges of Slutsk and the leaders of the community. – – – In any case, his opponents made attempts to change the first thoughts of the duke, and he sent a commission to Vilna asking that they become the masters of the situation.

(*Kirya Neemana*, Vilna, 5620 [1860], page 272)

His sister was the wife of the rabbi, *Gaon*, and Tzadik, known in glory in the council of the upright, our rabbi Yona Isserlin, who was called Reb Yona Slutsker, may his merit protect us.

(Book of the Annals of People of Renown, volume I, pp. 35-36, section 59)

Rabbi Yitzchak Yosef Teomim of blessed memory

Rabbi Yitzchak Yosef Teomim of blessed memory died in Breslau on 16 Cheshvan 5554 (1793)[4]. He was the brother of Rabbi Yitzchak Meir Frenkel. They were the sons of Reb Yona Teomim. He sat on the rabbinical seat of Slutsk until the year 5505 [1745]. In the year 5527 [1767] he gave an approbation for the book *HeAruch*.

Rabbi Shlomo Zalman Menachem Manish

The rabbi and *Gaon*, Rabbi Shlomo Zalman the son of the leader Mr. Menachem Manish died on the Sabbath of the second day of Rosh Chodesh Adar. See the book *Shem Gedolim Hechadash*, section 7, point 29. Rabbi Shlomo Zalman, the *Gaon* of renown in his generation, the head of the rabbinical court and Yeshiva head of the holy community of Slutsk, etc. was buried in the year 5532 [1772]. He made a mistake in this, as it should have said second day of Rosh Chodesh Adar of the year 5558 [1798]. See the book *Dor Vedor Dorshav*, section 7, point 106, where he too made an error in this regard.

(Copied from Ledgers of the Cemeteries of the City of Slutsk by the rabbi of Slutsk, Rabbi Yosef Peimer the Second.)

Rabbi Simcha Bunim of blessed memory

Rabbi Simcha Bunim Z.z. (Died in the year 5584 1824). The *Gaon* Simcha Bunim the son of Rabbi Kalonymus of Druya.

(*Sefer Hayichus*, A. Rivlin)

The *Gaon* Rabbi Yosef Peimer of blessed memory

(Copied from the article by Shmuel David Maharshak, the Shochet of Slutsk in *Hamodia*, 5624 [1864] with omissions.)

The *Gaon* Rabbi Yosef Peimer was accepted as rabbi in the community of Slutsk in the year 5589 (1829). He guided us in Torah and fear of G-d for 35 years. As is told in the book *Sheerit Yosef* – there is a bitter eulogy on the aforementioned *Gaon* delivered by Rabbi Yosef Gibianski (published in Vilna 5624 [1864]), the year that the aforementioned *Gaon* died, may his merit protect us. The following is engraved upon his tombstone.

Here is buried
Rabbi Yosef the son of Reb Meir
From the city of Shkod in the State of Zamet
He was the rabbi of our community for thirty-five years
And he died on Friday, the eve of the holy Sabbath, first day of Rosh Chodesh Iyar, the year blessing
Of mourners, the year 5624 (1864) in the holy community of Slutsk. May his soul be bound in the bonds of
eternal life[5]

When a new gravestone was erected over his grave in the year 5559 [1799], his son, the *Gaon* Rabbi Meir, may the memory of the holy be blessed, the head of the local rabbinical court, inscribed the following: "This is the text that the deceased of blessed memory commanded, and we must not add praises, for his praise comes from the mark he left on the world." It is worthwhile to publicize the ancestry of the *Gaon*, for the annals of the *Gaonim* and *Tzadikim*, their education, and their holy ways impart good lessons to us. – –

[Page 36]

Rabbi Yossele Peimer (the first)

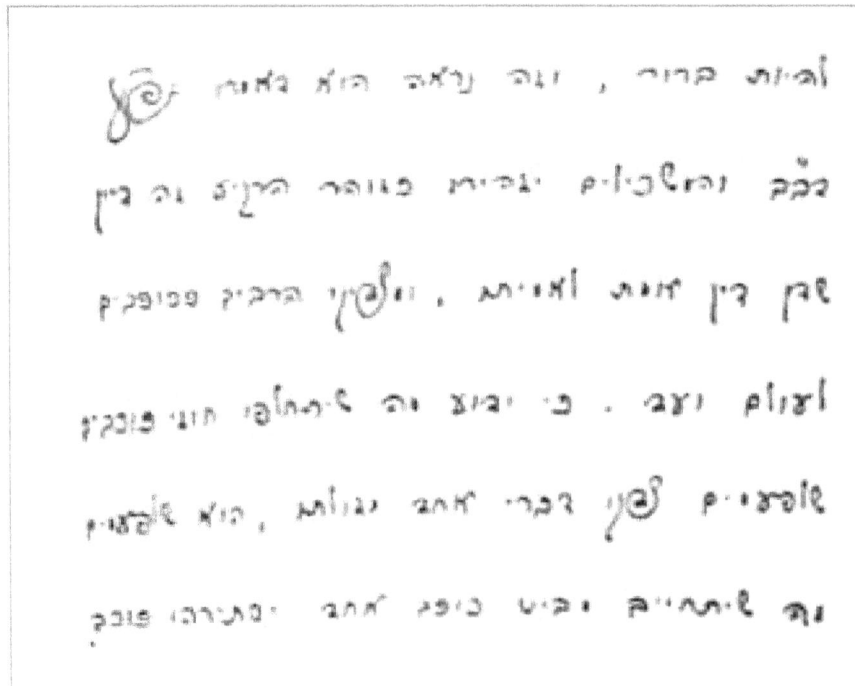

The handwriting of Rabbi Yossele

Translator's note: The following is a rough translation, as parts are difficult to make out, and the language is obscure:

To be clear, and this appears in that [??] have said, and the educated ones will sine as the splendor of the firmament refers to a judge who judges truthfully. And before the necklace like the stars for ever and ever. For it is known that the statues of the stars change, for sometimes the words of one come before the other, that is, sometimes what one star seems as obligatory is contradicted by a star.[6]

The history of the *Gaon* of blessed memory, his way of life and customs, were written by his grandson the rabbi and *Gaon* Rabbi Yosef Peimer, may he live long, but are not yet prepared and edited for publication. Therefore, I find it necessary to publicize several things from which we can derive an accurate portrayal and concept of the traits of the *Gaon* Rabbi Yosef the Tzadik, who poured water over the hands[7] of the *Gaon* Rabbi Chaim of Volozhin.

"He was 32 years old when he was appointed rabbi in our city of Slutsk. His praiseworthiness, breath of heart in Talmud and rabbinic decisors, and depth of understanding made wings [i.e. spread] through the country.

When he was accepted as rabbi in the year 5589 [1829], he already was able to demonstrate his breadth of Torah knowledge. – – He was wise and understanding in the ways of the world. He had wit upon his mouth. His sharp words and adages spread through the city. The extent of his alertness and dedication to the benefit of the public can be seen from the testament he issued a day before his death, which he wrote as follows: "I request from honorable leaders of Vilna, and the honorable leaders of Minsk, my they live, that they conclude the peace that they had begun. May G-d grant them life, blessing, and peace. (This is one section of his will, and I am sending it to you).

He left behind many manuscripts of responsa that he responded to several *Gaonim* of his time, especially [regarding] the dispute in the name of Heaven[8] that was conducted by the *Gaon* Rabbi David of blessed memory, the author of *Galia Masechta*. In his writings there is an explanation of the four sections of the *Shulchan Aruch*[Code of Jewish Law] as well as a commentary on the Torah – all of which are mentioned in the book *Sheerit Yosef* by Rabbi Yosef Gibianski.

His livelihood came in a meager fashion, but he never complained about all this. When Rabbi David Tevil of Minsk died, a rabbinical contract was sent to him, and he agreed to it. When the people of Slutsk urged him to not leave them, he acceded to their request on the condition that they return his contract to Minsk, and that they do not increase his salary.

The rain that penetrated his home ruined and dampened a large portion of his books, but he did not complain. He did not show fear before anyone. He was careful with the honor of scholars, and when he saw a denigration of their honor, he would not act in a sycophantic manner even to a great person of Israel.

When the *Gaon* Rabbi Yitzchak of Volozhin, may the memory of the holy be blessed, died on Friday 26 Iyar 5609 [1849], and the news of is passing reached Minsk, and the *Gaon* Rabbi David Tevil of blessed memory found out about it, he said that said that he lived like a Rebbe of Hassidim, and died as a Rebbe of Hassidim. The *Gaon* Rabbi David Tevil of blessed memory died in the year 5620 [1860], and the news reached Slutsk. They asked my grandfather the *Gaon* Rabbi Yosef, may the memory of the holy be blessed, of Slutsk to eulogize the eminent deceased. He responded that the there is time. When thirty days passed without a eulogy, Rabbi Tzvi Hirsch Chefetz of blessed memory came to him and told my grandfather that the community is complaining about the denigration of the honor of such a great deceased scholar. He responded that which he responded.

On the memorial day for the *Gaon* Rabbi David Tevil on Shemini Atzeret, they asked my grandfather the Gaon: "Why did you not eulogize the *Gaon* Rabbi David Tevil of blessed memory?" My grandfather said, "When the news of the death of the *Gaon* Rabbi Yitzchak of Volozhin, that city reached Rabbi David Tevil, since he lived as a Hassidic Rebbe and died as a Hassidic Rebbe, he was not allowed to say such things, for he had to rend his garments as I did and put ashes on his head, for a great leader of Israel had died. For this reason, I did not eulogize the *Gaon* Rabbi David Tevil of blessed memory, so this should be an atonement of sin." (I heard this from my friend the honorable elderly man Mr. David Kosovsky, may his light shine.)

The Will of Rabbi Yosef Peimer of blessed memory

We, the witnesses who signed below, went to visit the honorable rabbi and *Gaon*, may he live, and found him lying on his sick bed, may G-d protect us. His mind was sharp and clear like a healthy man walking in the marketplace and talking coherently. The rabbi and *Gaon*, the aforementioned Rabbi Yosef, arranged before us his entire estate that will remain behind him after a hundred years, in accordance with the commands and gifts of a seriously ill person[9] in accordance with *Yoreh Deah*.

[Page 37]

His words were as follows: The 550 rubles that I have designated for the publications of my book, which I have in my possession, R.D. Beer Lifschitz, Bh'k, A.Y. RM.Sh.[10] shall be given to my wife, may she live, for her *Ketubah*, without any issue or lack. I request of her that she forego the rest, and she will certainly overlook, and she has no other money.

To my son Rabbi M., I owe three hundred rubles. In lieu, he will get all my books. He should accept some rabbinical position, for it is appropriate to him, and I am sure he will accept upon himself the yoke of Torah.

My son Rabbi Z. will get one hundred rubles, and the debt payment as is explained below.

My grandson Rabbi M. of Kapolya will get one hundred rubles as a gift from a seriously ill person. This is a gift to Rabbi M. my aforementioned grandson. There are one hundred rubles that are owing to the known Anana'ch and to the well-known Rabbi Tz. Chefetz to use according to my will. Now, the authority is given to my son Rabbi M., may he live, and Rabbi Tz. Chefetz to use as they see fit. Twenty-five rubles are owing to Reb Moshe Gershon, and it shall be discharged, as is explained below.

There is close to one hundred rubles owing from the community for the needs or the building. Fifty rubles owing to my daughter Mrs. Rivka, may she live, and it shall be discharged, and fifty owing to my daughter Mrs. Feigel may she live, and it shall be discharged.

All the household utensils go to the Rebbetzin, may she live.

There are fifty rubles owing, as is known, to Reb Tz. Ch., and it shall be discharged as is explained below. There are one hundred owing to the Ana'ch and one hundred to my son the aforementioned Rabbi Z, and fifty for the aforementioned Rabbi Tz. The rest that is owing to my aforementioned daughters shall be overlooked by them.

My study lectern shall not be touched by anyone other than my son Rabbi M., may he live, and Rabbi Tz. Chefetz, may he live.

The expenditures regarding my illness, I do not know from who or to whom.

The printing of my books will be in accordance with the will of G-d, and the will of my household members, may they live.

Regarding my unmarried granddaughter, the daughter of Rabbi Abba, the members of my household shall consult among themselves.

I request that the spiritual leaders of Vilna and the spiritual leaders of Minsk conclude the peace that they have begun, and may G-d give them live, blessing, and peace.

All the aforementioned was commanded by the rabbi and *Gaon*, Rabbi Yosef, the rabbi of the local community of Slutsk, as a command and a gift from a seriously ill person, with the strength of documents of testaments made on the selfsame day by the enactment of our sages. He commanded that it be written in a book. We have done thus, and have written it before the eyes of the aforementioned Gaon. As proof, we have signed on Thursday, the eve of Rosh Chodesh Iyar, in the year of *Bebirkat* [see footnote 5].

Signed by Naftali Tzvi Chefetz. Signed by Yosef Zundel son of Rabbi Dovber of blessed memory.

In a letter from Jerusalem to Rabbi Meir the son of Rabbi Yosef Peimer dated Friday 2 Av 5632 [1872], they describe the death of his mother, about which he had already been informed by a telegram dated Monday 14 Tammuz. They tell of the rebbetzin's final wish, they give an accounting of her property, and ask where to send it, since there was a second heir, a grandson, and my grandfather Rabbi Mordechai Leib Yaffa who requests that they send the designated [amount] to the rabbinical court in Slutsk, where it will be divided. It is interesting that the rebbetzin asked that the pillows and bedding be sent to her granddaughter in Slutsk. When they informed her that the expenses would be more than the value, she agreed that they be sold, and the money should be sent.

Rabbi Yosef Dov HaLevi of blessed memory Soloveitchik

Rabbi Yosha Ber Soloveitchik

Rabbi Yosef Dov Ber Soloveitchik was a unique *Gaon* in his generation and a unique, wonderful *Tzadik*. He was born in Neszvizh (Minsk District) in 5580 (1820). During his youth, he was brought by his father, the *Gaon* Rabbi Yitzchak Zeev (grandson of the *Gaon* Rabbi Moshe Soloveitchik, the head of the rabbinical court of Kovno) to Volozhin. The great ones called him the second Shaagas Aryeh. In 5625 (1865) he was accepted as the rabbi of Slutsk. He left the rabbinical seat of Slutsk in the year 5635 [1875] and went to Warsaw. In the year 5638 [1878] he was accepted as the rabbi of Brest Litovsk. This *Gaon* was also an excellent scholar and most of his discussions were transmitted from mouth to mouth since they excelled in their sharpness and depth. In the year 5649 [1889] he was chosen to go to a rabbinical convention in Peterburg. His works include: a) Responsa *Beis Halevi* (Vilna 5625 [1865]); b) volume II of the aforementioned, responsa, halachic analysis, and exegesis (Warsaw, 5634 [1874]); c) Volume III of the aforementioned, exegesis on the Torah and legends of the sages (ibid. 5644 [1884]); d) Volume IV of the aforementioned, halachic analysis of the Order of *Nezikin*[11] (ibid 5651 [1891]). Many responsa and analysis sections from the book remain in manuscript.

He died on 4 Iyar 5652 [1892] in Brisk.

From the introduction to his book *Beis Halevi*:

"Since I was not graced with the language of scholars to know and to arouse the hearts of the listeners, I request that the preachers, those who give discourses to the nation of G-d, whom G-d has blessed with skills in the spoken language, reproof, and fear of G-d, please pay attention to this small book. Perhaps you will find in it some useful things for your work, the labor of G-d. I am not particular if you do not even mention it in my name. Your words of reproof shall be made more pleasant, and blessings of good shall come upon you. I, the young one, also bless you."

Rabbi Meir Peimer

(From the mouth of his son Rabbi Yosef Peimer of blessed memory)

On the morning of Monday, 20 Iyar, 5671 [1911], my father the rabbi, *Gaon* and *Tzadik* Rabbi Meir Peimer, may the memory of the holy be blessed, passed away and was summoned to the Heavenly court. He was the son of the *Gaon* and *Tzadik* Rabbi Yosef Peimer, may the memory of the holy be blessed, who served as the rabbi of Slutsk for 35 years. My father, may the memory of the holy be blessed, was educated in his father's house on the bosom of Torah and fear of Heaven. During his early years, it was noticed that he was created for greatness. He made his nights like days, and the sounds of learning never ceased from his mouth. He did not wish to accept a rabbinical position. However, when his father

[Page 38]

commanded him emphatically, he accepted a rabbinical contract from the community of Berezhany in the year 5629 [1869], and was a faithful shepherd to his community.

He left the rabbinate in the year 5636 [1876] and moved to Slutsk as a householder. In the year 5638 [1878] he was accepted as rabbi in the city. In the year 5648 [1888] he left the rabbinate again and traveled to Minsk to live as a householder. In the summer of 5650 [1890] he again took on the rabbinate of Lechovitz. He instituted several effective things in the town, such as: *Korban Eitzim*[12], the distribution of firewood to those in need; as well as *Lechem Evyonim* [bread for the poor]. He occupied the rabbinical seat of Karelitz until the year 5655 [1895]. That year he was accepted as rabbi in Lechovitz, where he remained for a few months, and returned to Slutsk as a householder.

He paid special attention to the Talmud Torah, and concerned himself with the spiritual and physical needs of the students. He became seriously ill on Passover 5671 [1911], and travelled to consult physicians in Minsk. He understood from them that his illness was dire. His desire was to be buried in the burial place of his ancestors in Slutsk. The power of his memory was strong until his final moments. He was approximately 71 years old at the time of his death. He is buried next to the great, famous crown of Torah Rabbi Yosef Zundel, may the memory of the holy be blessed, who was the teacher of righteousness in Slutsk for approximately sixty years –.

From the Will of Rabbi Meir Peimer

Now I will give the details of what I have in my hands. I have a Torah Scroll with everything that belongs to it[13]. It is located in the synagogue on Zareca Street in Slutsk. I also have 34 volumes of Torah topics. Some of them are with me here, and the larger portion of them are with my younger son Rabbi Yosef, may his light shine, in Slutsk. The aforementioned books are in manuscript, and have not yet been published. The manuscripts of my honorable father, the rabbi, may the memory of the holy be blessed, are with me. I have four volumes. Two volumes are half of Boigen[14]. They are responsa on the four sections of the *Shulchan Aruch* [Code of Jewish Law], one section is two quarters, and it is bound. It is on the *Orach Chaim* and *Yoreh Deah* sections of the *Shulchan Aruch*. Two unbound booklets belong to them. One section is on exegesis, also in two quarters, and is bound. There is also a manuscript from my honorable grandfather, the rabbi and *Gaon*, may the memory of the holy be blessed. They are in the hands of my son, the aforementioned rabbi, may his light shine. I estimate the value of all my aforementioned books at five hundred rubles. This also includes the rights that I have in the manuscripts of my honorable master and father, the rabbi, may the memory of the holy be blessed, as well as my papers on Torah novellae, with which G- graced me, and are in my hands. These are also included in my aforementioned estimate. It is my will that all those aforementioned books, manuscripts found therein, and the rights that I have in the manuscripts of my grandfather the rabbi, may the memory of the holy be blessed, as well as my papers on Torah novellae, remain in the hands of my younger son the aforementioned Rabbi Yosef, may his light shine. This is to be in the manner that half of the above valuation, that is the sum of 250 rubles, be given to my dear son Rabbi Moshe, may his light shine. The discharge payment shall be in cash. He shall be given the aforementioned sum after his gives a quittance, as is the custom, stating that he has no complaint regarding my will, neither on real estate nor on chattels. He should sign on the necessary documents. I trust that he will act in accordance with my will without any omission. In this merit, G-d should grant him success in anything that he wishes to do for the good. The aforementioned Torah scroll shall remain in the aforementioned synagogue. However, I have not decided on the synagogue, and I give rights to it for the future to my two aforementioned sons, that is my dear son Rabbi Moshe, and my son Rabbi Yosef, may his light shine, to do with as is appropriate for the times, etc.

Similarly, I have a house in Slutsk, on Zareca Street. It is registered in the name of both of us, me and my wife, may she live. I also bequeath all my rights in that house to my wife, may she live, and to my aforementioned daughter.

The Ridba'z Rabbi Yaakov David Wilovsky

The Ridba'z

He was the author of a commentary on the Jerusalem Talmud, and was also known as the Rabbi from Slutsk. He was the son of Reb Zeev Wilovsky. He was born on 30 Shevat 5605 (1845) and died in Safed on the first day of Rosh Hashanah 5674 [1813]. He was accepted as the rabbi and head of the rabbinical court of Izabelin (1868) and later in Bobruisk (1876). Vilna (1881), På‚ock (1883), Wilkomir (1887), and Slutsk, where he served as a rabbi for ten years until 1900 and founded a Yeshiva there. The power of his memory was very wonderful, and he knew several Talmudic tractates by heart. He was an expert in the Babylonian and Jerusalem Talmuds, as well as most of the rabbinic decisors. His diligence was very great. On long winter nights, the snow was effective in removing from his eyes the slumber that overtook him at times, but it caused redness around his eyes. He dedicated most of his days to the Jerusalem Talmud, which most of the rabbis were not accustomed to. His strong love for the Land of Israel was apparently effective in leading him to work constantly on the Talmud of the people of the west[15]. The publication of the Jerusalem Talmud cost 22,000 rubles. He took it upon himself to pay 40% of the publishing fees. He was forced to travel abroad to sell

[Page 39]

the sets of Talmud that he had in his portion. He came to America in 1900 and succeeded in collecting enough money to pay the publisher. Therefore, he dedicated the Order of *Nezikin* to his supporters in America (see the introduction opposite the title page of that Order). In 1903, he came to America once again, and was appointed as chief rabbi of Chicago and the country. Several communities banded together and promised him 10,000 dollars for four years. However, due to the opposition of some local rabbis, as well as the fact that the Ridba'z realized that he would not be able to introduce enactments, he left his position and did not want to accept his salary. After he travelled and preached in the large cities of the United States, he left America in 1905 and decided to settle in the Land of Israel. When he arrived in the Land, he decided to live in Safed, where he founded the Torat Eretz Yisrael Yeshiva. His son-in-law Rabbi Yosef Kamenetz assisted him. His books were as follows: His largest and most famous composition was the publication of the Jerusalem Talmud with his two commentaries called *Chidushei HaRidba'z* in which he details the difficult Talmudic passages, and *Tosafot Ridba'z* in with its sharpness and breadth. They were published along with previous form and commentaries (Piotrków, 5659 5660 [1899 1900]). He also authored the book *Migdal David*, which consists of novellae and didactics on the Babylonian and Jerusalem Talmuds (Vilna 5634 [1874]); Chana David – novellae on Tractate Challah of the Jerusalem Talmud (ibid. 5636 [1876]); *Teshuvat Ridba'z* (5641 [1881]); *Nimukei Ridba'z*, a commentary on the Torah, Volume I, *Bereishit* and *Shemot* (Chicago, 5664 [1904]), *Responsa Beit Ridba'z* (Jerusalem 5668 [1908]); an edition of *Peat Hashulchan*[16] with *Beit Yisrael* of the Ridba'z in which all the commandments pertaining to the Land of Israel, especially the law of the Sabbatical year, are explained (ibid. 5672 [1912]). The Ridba'z was also an excellent preacher, and his words left a powerful impression. His introduction to his books include honorable notes on the history of the times, especially on the annals of the communities in America (see his introduction to *Nimukei HaRidba'z* and to the Responsa of the Ridba'z Volume II) .

The name Ridba'z which he used for his books is the acronym of Rinat Yaakov David Ben Zeev, based on the verse Sing to Jacob with joy (Jeremiah 31[:6])[17]. When he came to America for the second time, he gave himself the name Ridba'z instead of Wilovsky, which had been his family name in Russia. The rabbi Ridba'z was one of the greatest rabbis of his generation.

(from the *Otzar Yisrael* Encyclopedia of Eisenstein)

Rabbi Yakov David Wilovsky (Ridba'z) – Rafael which was added (during his illness) Yaakov David ben Zeev.

From the year 5664 [1904] in Safed in the Yeshiva Torat Eretz Yisrael and the general Talmud Torah that was founded by him on 25 Iyar 5629 [1869]. He left a testament for his sons, also in the name of their mother Mrs. Miriam Bluma, with nine sections, most about life conduct. Responsa of Ridba'z for the commandments related to the Land, Jerusalem 5668 [1909] are at the end of the book.

(DovBer Wachstein, testamentary introduction, Kiryat Sefer, eleventh year, page 326)

The Ridba'z: known as the *Gaon* the Ridba'z from Slutsk. His books that were published: *Migdal David*, novellae on the Babylonian and Jerusalem Talmuds, Chana David, Responsa, a large commentary on the Jerusalem [Talmud]. (*Album Ivri*, A gift to the callers of the nation, New York, 5665 [1905], page 8).

Rabbi Isser Zalman Meltzer the son of Rabbi Peretz

He was a great *Gaon* and *Tzadik* of renown. He was born to a well-pedigreed family in Mir in 5630 (1870). He studied with the *Gaon*, the head of the rabbinical court in his city, Rabbi YomTov Lipman. He came to Volozhin and studied under the *Gaonim* the Netzi'v and Rabbi Chaim HaLevi. He became known as Zuna Mirrer as a symbol of extra love. He was accepted as a Yeshiva head in Slobodka.

Rabbi Isser Zalman Meltzer

In the year 5657 [1897], when the *Gaon* the Ridba'z founded the Mussar Yeshiva in Slutsk, he was invited to serve as the Yeshiva head. Six years later, when the Ridba'z left Slutsk, he was appointed as the rabbi and head of the rabbinical court in his place. He served in the rabbinate and as the Yeshiva head in Slutsk until the Soviet revolution. Then he had to escape, so he made *aliya* to the Land. He was accepted as a Yeshiva head in the large Eitz Chaim Yeshiva. Along with the *Gaon* Tomashov, he published the *Yagdil Torah* Torah anthology for three years. He authored many books the most famous of which is *Even HaEzer* on the Rambam, for which he won the Rav Kook prize in the year 5705 [1945]. He was one of the main editors of the full Jerusalem Talmud, Otzar Haposkim edition, affiliated with the union of rabbis who were Russian refugees. He served as chairman of the executive committee of the Vaad Hayeshivot.

He died in Jerusalem on 10 Kislev, 5714 (1953)[18].

Rabbi Yosef (Reb Yossele) Peimer (the Second)

He was the rabbi in Slutsk, and lived on Zareca Street. He was the son of Rabbi Meir Peimer (who was in dispute with the Ridba'z). He was of average stature, with a black beard, soft as silk, prominent *peyos*, and black eyes that exuded purity and generosity. He was modest and quiet in his comportment, wondrous in his breadth of knowledge. He was the grandson of the *Gaonim* Rabi Aryeh Leib of Kovno and Rabbi Yosef, may the memory of the holy be blessed, of Slutsk. He loved

[Page 40]

Rabbi Yossele Peimer, son of Rabbi Meirke

to peruse and delve deeply into Biblical commentaries. He loved the Hebrew language. He would rarely preach about the issues of the times. He would spice his words with statements of our sages of blessed memory. He lived in Baranovich and Warsaw during the First World War. In the year 5685 [1925] he came to America and became the rabbi of the Beit-El Synagogue in Boro Park, Brooklyn. His fellow native, the philanthropist Kulak and the philanthropist Reb Avraham Myers strengthened and supported him. He died on the Rosh Chodesh Kislev 5699 (1938)[19] at the age of sixty. (Some of his works are included in *HaBeer*, published by the *Gaon*Friedling, may he live long.) A fire broke out in the city of Slutsk on the eve of Rosh Chodesh Av of the year 5680 [1920]. His house went up in flames, and all the books of his grandfather, the *Gaon* Rabbi Yosef, of his father Rabbi Meir, and the manuscripts of his forbears the *Gaonim* were burnt. The manuscript of his Torah novellae and his book *Toldot Yosef* also went up in flames.

Rabbi Yechezkel Abramski

He was a rabbi in Smolovich. In the year 5684 1924 he served as the rabbi and head of the rabbinical court of Slutsk. He edited and published two booklets of *Yagdil Torah*, published in Slutsk during the time of Soviet rule. After that, he served as the rabbi of the Machzikei Hadas community of London. His book Chazon Yechezkel on the Order of Moed (*Shabbat, Eiruvin, Pesachim*) includes variances in redactions, explanation, novellae, and sources.

"With the publication of Order Zeraim, the publisher announced that the upcoming volumes would appear, G-d willing, in order. The long break came for reasons of the adventures that overtook me. Only with the mercy of G-d did I leave the darkness of prison for light, from slavery and backbreaking labor to redemption. Praised by the name of God who – – – And also who inspired my heart to save my manuscripts from utter destruction when I gave them – – – to the faithful hands of – – – Mr. Michel Rabinovich – – – who merited to make *aliya* to our Holy Land, and brought my manuscripts with him. They are guarded by him in good order, and not one page of them is missing."

Rabbi Yitzchak Hochmark

Rabbi Yitzchak Hochmark was an eclectic personality, since he was connected to the outside world as an emissary for Yeshivot and public institutions. He visited the United States and South America more than once. Rabbi Yitzchak Hochmark was the final rabbi of Slutsk.

List of Synagogues of the City in Alphabetical order

1. Ostrova
2. Isserkes
3. Baalei Batim
4. Beis Midrash Hagadol
5. Wygoda
6. Zarecer
7. Zovchei Tzedek
8. Tailor's
9. The old Hapashker, burnt
10. the new Hapashker
11. Yeshiva
12. Mishnayos
13. Smiths
14. Kalte Shul [Cold Synagogue]
15. Kloiz
16. Karnim
17. Kirznershe (hatmakers)
18. Kapolya Street

Translator's footnotes:

1. There is an apparent error in the text here, as it says Hirsch instead of Hertz.
2. *Kattan* means 'small', and when used by a rabbinical personality as part of his name, it is a sign of humility.
3. Emendations of Biblical texts made by early rabbis.
4. Text says 1794, but the month of Cheshvan of 5554 would be in 1793.
5. In the original, this is arranged in a triangle. In terms of the year "blessing of mourners," this is based on the numerology (*gematria*) of the year, a common literary device in poetic, rabbinic Hebrew.
6. I believe he is using the term 'star' here as a euphemism for a scholar.
7. I.e. he served and aided.
8. I.e. a dispute to clarify matters of Torah, with no ulterior motives. See *Pirkei Avot* 5:17.
9. According to Jewish law, a seriously ill person [*shechiv mera*] is entitled to issue a will orally.
10. I am not sure what all these abbreviations and mnemonics mean. In the following paragraphs, I skip some of the abbreviations without changing the meaning.
11. Dealing with civil law, torts, etc.

12. Literally: The wood sacrifice, referring to the donations of wood to the Temple to maintain the fire on the alter for sacrifices. See Mishnah *Taanit* 4:4-5.
13. Referring to the Torah mantle and other decorations.
14. I am not sure about what this means, but it may be referring to rabbi Katzenelboigen, mentioned earlier.
15. Israel being west of Babylonia. The Babylonian Talmud was compiled later than the Jerusalem Talmud, and is far more frequently studied.
16. Originally written by Rabbi Yaakov of Shklov, 1836.
17. *Rinat* means "*The song of.*" In the verse, the form is *Ronu* "*Sing to.*"
18. The original text states 1954, but Kislev 10 would be in 1953.
19. Here too, the original text says 1939, but Rosh Chodesh Kislev would be in 1938.

[Page 41]

Professions and Vocations

by Nachum Chinitz

Translated by Jerrold Landau

The area around Slutsk was noted for its pleasant forests, vegetable gardens, and splendid fruit orchards. The fertile ground yielded ample produce. The word *Slucizna* testified to the good soil and its yield. It is no wonder that many Jews were involved in forestry, grain, flaxseed, pig hair, and skins, either directly or as middlemen. A variety of vegetable gardens were in the suburbs of the city, and Jews tended to them with diligent hands. The cucumbers of Wigoda Street were well known in the entire region. Wigoda Street was noted for its vegetable gardens. "Slutsk cucumbers" were considered to be something. Jews leased plots of land from the *poretz*[landowner] Salwyta and tilled the vegetable gardens.

On Wigoda Street there were taverns; the storehouses of the Wigodski brothers, who were grain wholesalers; and the grain storehouses of Mote Eila. The pears of Slutsk were tasty and pleasant. They were kept throughout the winter until they rotted. There were none better for eating. Slutsk was blessed with a wide variety of apples and other fruit. Entire families leased fruit plantations, and devoted their entire energies to them. There, they slept and lived for months, and earned their livelihood from this. The pears of Slutsk, *Bere Wasofpozanks,* were marketed throughout Russia. Bread with a pear was literally the food of kings, and served as a satisfying and nutritious meal for both young and old.

Sluck Klermasz

On occasion, an entire family would move to the garden to live until the end of the harvest season. In the bosom of nature, in the clear, healthy air, the Jew guarded his property so that it should not be damaged by strangers. At the same time, things worked out that the garden would sustain him throughout all the days of the year.

The large market that straddled both sides of the street was well known. Rows and rows of stalls and booths filled the area, so that there was no space. On Sundays or the days of the various fairs, the farmers of the region gathered there, spread themselves out, and took over every place. It was possible only with difficulty to squeeze between the wagons, whose shafts were very high. It is impossible to describe the noise and the tumult. The farmers came with their produce and wares, and the Jews were noisy and quivering. A handshake or a pat on the back was testimony to a deal being sealed. On occasion, curses and arguments were heard, a sign of reneging. The farmers covered the market with fowl, eggs, strands of flax, pig hair, and flaxseed. They brought to market flasks of butter, a variety of

[Page 42]

cheeses, and also cows, calves, pigs and horses.

The Jews had great ability at business. After negotiation and haggling, the deal would be signed at a propitious time, and then they conducted the *magaritz*: they removed small or large liquor bottles from their pockets, and after an appropriate shot accompanied by a piece of pastry, both sides went out satisfied.

The farmers then would go to the stores to purchase their needs with the money that they earned. Butter and cheese of all varieties from the entire region was collected together by the merchants and sent to the large cities. Many Jews went around to the villages to purchase agricultural products. They paid cash, but for the most part they paid with varieties of haberdashery. Various businesses were attracted to Shasina Street on both sides of the market. Some of the buildings were of wood and others were of stone. Some were meager, small stores, and others were larger with show windows displaying shoes and clothing.

In the midst of the well-known stores that included those of Gachuv, Mendel Kantrovitch, Orah Zhidna, and Derchin, there were also stores for textiles, work implements, iron and skins. There were well-known stores for the sale of salted fish, kerosene, naphtha, glass implements, earthenware, and household implements.

People would remove their hats as they entered the pharmacies of Tsipchin and Franchikovski on the Street of the Road [1] . The healing potions gave off an intoxicating and irritating odor, and a semblance of a feeling of awe was felt as one entered; as if there awaited the fate of the sick person, whether to life or, Heaven forbid, to death. Aside from the pharmacies, there were the medicine and spice stores of Bronstein, Vitkin, Shaykovitch and Karmin.

Feigel Sperling, the cake maker
("the sweet")

Reb Zeev Greisvach, a dedicated Zionist, who made aliya to the Land in 1932. He died in Tel Aviv at the age of 80.

The stores of Zeev Greisvach and Malka Eila were also well known. They specialized in the sale of fruit from outside the country that were not common in Slutsk, and the prices were outrageous. There, they sold grapes, watermelon for the blessing of *shehecheyanu* on the night of Rosh Hashanah [2] , aromatic oranges – even though their skin was yellowing, and a lemon that had shrunk with age. These fruits were purchased by well to do Jews and were used in particular for the ill.

The vast majority of the businesses were in the hands of the Jews, with the exception of a large store in the house of Efrat that sold valuable textiles. It belonged to a Christian by the name of Muchov. That store was nicknamed "Tania".

There were two watermills in the city that became obsolete with the establishment of the steam mills of Feiberg, Gutzeit, and Neikrug-Mishlov. These mills were located in three story buildings. A sawmill for planks was next to the flourmill of Gutzeit. Jewish middlemen and flour merchants earned their livelihood due to these enterprises.

There were people in Slutsk who earned their livelihoods by issuing loans for interest. Among these were some who served only as middlemen and to whom people related to with an unusual level of trust. These would lend money to the *poretzes*, who were the owners of large properties. The names of Bere Efrat, Leiba Baslovski and Reb Yosef Chernichov were considered pleasant in this area, for they would not wrong their customers, nor leave their money on the horns of a deer [3]. Aside from them, there were numerous middlemen and agents, who lived off the air and earned their livelihood in a meager fashion and with difficulty from various opportunities. They wore shabby clothing and were gratingly poor.

One of them, Zushe *Der Mekler* [broker], was very poor and had a large family. He was upright and straightforward. Later, he moved to the United States to join his children, who sustained him in an honorable fashion. Apparently, they spoiled him. Yet for with all this, he longed for his meager life in Slutsk, which had occupied him and kept him busy.

Slutsk was known for its famous conditoriums [4]. One of them was owned by Solomiak and was on Soan Street [5]. It was known for its cakes and baked delicacies that beckon and hinted: come in and taste of the taste of the Garden of Eden, and of the tasty treats that come to whet the appetite and attract the eye.

The studying youth loved to sit and spend time in the tavern hall of the Turkish Conditorium on Zaretze Street. Although it was of the second tier, it had fine and tasty baked goods.

[Page 43]

Most of its clientele came from the masses and the youth. This place was first and foremost a store, with a bakery in its back. It was owned by the two Turks and their families who settled in Slutsk. One of them used to go out on the streets in his Turkish garb, with a decorated basket on his head, full of treats. He would shout out " *maraz* merchandise", and women, children, and wayfarers would immediately surround him until he had sold all of his wares.

The Slutsk merchant Moshe Aharon with his
wife and grandchild. These are the parents
of Aryeh Shapira

Reb Yudel Sperling, the husband
of Feigel (the cake maker) [6]

The woman "Feigel the cake maker" was known in Slutsk. Her home made products – fried pieces of dough and honey, a tasty pastry – were cut into pieces with a small saw, and were literally grabbed up from her hands. These "Slutsk cakes" were something special, and nobody could duplicate her products. She literally ran a small factory in her house, and her hands were always busy, for she received hundreds of orders, even from the depths of Russia.

Slutsk also excelled in the working of *Garibalnies* skins. Tanners provided leather to the local shoemakers, and also for sale outside the city. Skins were also produced for the needs of holy objects [7] on Podbalania Street, Shul Gasse, and Shkolania Street.

There were many artisans and craftsmen of various types. Scribes (Sofrei Stam [7]) wrote Torah scrolls, *Megillas*, *Mezuzas* and *Tefillin*. These products were exported particularly to America and the breadths of Russia. The well-known scribes included Reb Hillel Nuzik the scribe, a scholarly Jew who conducted a study group in the Kranim synagogue; the son-in-law of Reb Shmuel the *shamash* [sexton] of the *kloiz*, Ben Zion Shpilkin; the son-in-law of Reb Refael Yosef, Chaim Leib the scribe, who also organized the eating rotation for the Yeshiva students [8].

Combs and *shofars* were also produced from the horns of animals, and entire families were employed in these endeavors. The combs of Slutsk were famous for their quality. Many people earned their livelihood from this manufacturing. The "Kranim" synagogue was established with their effort and support [9].

One of them, "Zelig the comb maker," excelled in his generosity for the benefit of the poor. During his free time, he went around with a sack in his hand to collect bread and challas for the poor and needy. Even the father of the head of the Yeshiva Reb Berl Grebenchik occupied himself with combs, and indeed his name testifies to this – Grebenchik – a maker of combs.

The hat makers produced hats and caps in various sizes, both for the summer and winter seasons. The members of their families worked on this endeavor in their homes, and their stores were in the marketplace, on the Street of the Road and on Zaretze Street. They even had their own synagogue, known as Kirznershe Shul [10]. For the most part, they supported themselves by the sale of hats to the farmers of the area, who loved to outfit themselves by wearing these various glittering hats on their heads.

The water drawers walked along the street with a pole and two buckets, *Bagrashan* buckets [11]. At times they lowered the price in accordance with the competition. Other water drawers provided higher quality water from a pitcher on top of a wagon, hitched to a horse. They were considered to be well-placed people. Each had his own territory. People would eagerly await their drinking water. They had a different fee, depending upon whether the water was provided in a corner or at the home itself. The water drawer would wait a bit, he would remove the stopper from the pitcher, and the water would flow out into the buckets. The children loved to watch with curiosity the streaming of the water and the filling of the buckets.

The latrine cleaners came around at night, and did their work for a set fee. They entered into every courtyard and house with special wagons with special buckets atop the wagons. As soon as these wagons came into view, the windows would shut and people would begin to plug their noses, for the odor wafted from afar. The owners of these wagons would say: "See how well-placed and honorable are the people of the holy community of Slutsk!" The latter did not desist from the sarcasm [12], and they called the cleaners: "The leaders of the holy community of Slutsk"...

An entire street bustled with the banging of paddles and wheels, the clanging of wagons, and the pulsating of fasteners. Weary, sweaty men operated wheels,

[Page 44]

and thrust together parts of wheels. These were the workers who produced their wares for the needs of the city and the environs. The name of the street testified to them and their activities – Kalesnichkia Ulicha – the street of the wagoneers. They would say " *Vehaofanim Yeshoreru* " – this is the song of the workers [13], who earn their livelihood from the toil of their hands. They worked on a narrow and poor street, with small houses – poor wooden houses that were covered with moss. On both sides of the street could be found a mixed variety of wheels and wagon parts that were awaiting repair in the world of the wheel of fortune.

The smiths had their own street – Shmidshe Gas. It was a narrow side street with small, forlorn houses, as well as a few new houses. On both sides, the welding machines were fired, as the anvils, hammers, and sledgehammers rose and fell. There would be sparks of fire, pieces of white hot metal, and by their side were the smiths, second generation smiths, with narrow, thin, and poor faces. Some would be strong of heart, with thick heads of hair, and the fire of rebellion inside them. They would place shoes on stubborn horses, who did not want to have iron shoes. There would be scraps of junk and pieces of metal wherever your eye would alight. Women and children would conduct business, and wait for their various vessels to be fixed. These smiths also had their own small, clean synagogue in the middle of that street, known as the Shmidshe Shul. It was their own, and they would define its characteristics and way of conduct. Reb Zalman Zitzin was a Rosh Yeshiva (Yeshiva Head) who opened up a small yeshiva in that synagogue. The ears of the studiers would also hear "the sound of implements of horsemen, and the riding of horses". The "voice is the voice of Jacob and the hands are also the hands of Jacob" would be intermixed [14].

Itze Katznelson the carpenter, the father of
Baruch Katznelson

There were butchers and cattle merchants who earned their livelihood by selling meat to others. There were butcher stalls next to the *Kalte Shul shtibel*. The synagogue of the butchers *Zovchei Tzedek* [15], known as the *Katzavishe Shul*, was not far from these butcher stands. This fulfilled the statement, "And all sons of flesh shall call in your name" [16]. It was said regarding them: "They slaughter the *Tzadik*," and therefore they have no righteousness, so why do you complain about them? The cattle merchants sold their wares throughout the depths of Russia.

The shoemakers and carpenters earned their livelihoods with difficulty. Many immigrated to the United States and other places. The great poverty that prevailed in the city did not allow for the residents to purchase many shoes or other items. Boots were sold in great numbers on account of the mud and grime in the city.

Two wheeled wagons, known as the Slutsk Rickshaws, were prevalent in the city. A thick rope was bound to the wagon, to which the drawer was hitched. For a few coins, objects and merchandise would be ported from place to place. These were personages such as "Tovia the Porter" of Y. L. Peretz, who was always waiting "from whence his help should come," and "whose corners of his garments were hitched with a rope around his waist." He was ready and prepared to port carry anything on his shoulders – if only someone should stop by.

The steady wagon drivers had a different honorable task – to carry on their long wagons (*drages*) all types of merchandise from Bobruisk or Starye Dorogi, and later from Urechye to Slutsk. They unloaded all of the merchandise from the train, and also loaded merchandise from Slutsk onto the train. Wagon drivers from nearby villages worked along their set lines: Kopyl, Starobin, Grozovo, and Glusk. These men of labor had set days when they would go along their journey, and days when they would not. They were known as the Slutsker wagon drivers, Glusker, Urechyer, Starobiner, Lyubaner, etc.

During the summer, these wagon drivers would drive wagons, and in the winter they would drive sleighs. Some were only involved in the transport of merchandise, and many others brought passengers from the nearby towns and the train. With the laying of the railway line into the city, their livelihood dwindled, and they were forced to add routes to various towns. A portion of them got used to the conditions, and began to transport merchandise from the train station, and others sold their wagons and purchased carriages to transport passengers to various destinations. Many claimed that, just as they had adapted at first to the *diligens* [stage coaches] that transported passengers from Bobruisk and Leshchevtsy to Slutsk, and later from Starye Dorogi to Slutsk, they would also get used to the train.

The double decker automobile also plied its route on the road from Starye Dorogi to Slutsk, despite the comfort of the train.

There were many fires in Slutsk, which on occasion wreaked havoc in the city and destroyed the livelihood of many, to the point where all that was left was a loaf of bread. For the most part, the fault lay with the homeowners, the artisans, the contractors, and the owners of lumber storehouses, who would anonymously start fires so that they would be able to sell their merchandise, which would be sitting like a stone with no turnover. The guilt became so great that a ban of excommunication was issued by order of the rabbinate. I was present at such a declaration of excommunication in the *kloiz*, where black candles were lit, a coffin covered in black was brought in, and Reb Shachna the *Shammas* read the ban of excommunication at the behest of the rabbis. The faith that the guilty would be punished found support, at times, with attacks upon people whose fate came upon them by chance. It was seen as the finger of G-d when Yankel Minnes, the owner of a storehouse of wooden building materials and who was suspected of arson, severed an artery in his hand with the knife as he was cutting the Sabbath challas, and subsequently bled to death.

Most of the structures in the city were made of wood, and when a fire broke out, it spread quickly from house to house and destroyed complete blocks. The firefighters did not always have the appropriate means to put out the fire, due to the lack of modern fire fighting equipment. With the building of entire blocks of stone structures, the danger abated, but, nevertheless, fires broke out from time to time.

Four Jewish doctors were involved in tending to the sick.

[Page 45]

The most well known of these included Dr. Shildkraut and Dr. Feinberg. The important ones published a monthly called *Grayev*. There were also Christian doctors in the city, who functioned as private doctors and also at the government hospital. These include Vatsur and Yanishevitch. Dr. Shildkraut and other important doctors worked at the poorhouse.

Transportation from Slutsk to Starye Dorogi [17]

The most well known of the slaughterers of Slutsk were Necha the *Shochet*, Areh the *Shochet*, and Alter Maharshek. Necha the slaughterer, with a white beard, a tall stature, and pleasant mannerism had a name among the *shochtim*. He used to say: "Most of the boys of Slutsk passed under my hand, as I brought them into the covenant of Abraham our father. [18]" Areh the *shochet* was a faithful Jew, an expert *shochet*, pleasing to his fellow man. His son Nathan also served as a *shochet*. Alter Maharshek was a Zionist with all his soul and money. His house was a gathering place for the wise and for the Zionists. He was a faithful Hebrew speaker, who loved the Hebrew language. He published articles from time to time in the Hebrew newspapers, and authored books.

Guards, whose job was to chase away thieves, circulated in the streets of the city during the night. They were armed with *Kalakatekes blez* – wooden noisemakers similar to the type that children would use during the reading of the scroll of Esther to blot out the name of Haman [19]. These guards would go from street to street, making noise with their noisemakers in order to assure the property owners that there is an eye that sees and an ear that hears. The residents of Slutsk were disappointed with their policemen, who stood on guard in their booths. The guards took pride in their implements and in their song--"Do not fear, my servant Jacob [20]."

The inns and hotels excelled in their cleanliness and in their special meals. There was a special place set aside for the wagons and carriages of the guests.

The guests included tenants and "portly people" who were involved in business, and who came to visit the city with their wives and children. The Migdal Hotel and Europe Hotel were considered to be first class hotels. Their guests included government officials and squires (*poretzes*), as well as other individuals of high rank.

Second class inns included *Bokshitzki, Kreines, Yabrob*, and others. They had separate rooms for merchants, agents, and other guests from the middle class.

Lower class inns served for the most part the average people and townsfolk who would come to the city to shop or to attend to their affairs. These inns included Neiman, Tatelech, Lewik, Chaim Itzkes, Der Teitzel, and Nakritz. The wagon drivers set up their headquarters at these inns, which served as a gathering place, a meeting place, and waiting area for guests from the region.

The well-known sellers of drinks were Chaim Itzkes, and Ratner who owned a government concession. They sold wine in measured amounts for *Kiddush* and *Havdalah* [21]. On Fridays, there was a long lineup of purchasers. The wine was poured out into bottles of various sizes, some smaller and some larger. Not far from there was the tavern of Yoshe Pozniak, who sold wine. People would sit around his tables and enjoy an abundant meal, along with a bottle of wine or a can of bear.

Meir Rips sold wine on Kapola Street. Finkelstein had a brewery on Vilna Street.

There were two bands that would play at weddings. One, headed by Eizel the *Klezmer* [22], was well versed in music and well organized. Its members knew how to gladden the hearts of the audience. They would move the audience to tears when they played sad tunes. The head of the second *Klezmer* band was Shimon Leib. He was still quite young, but he gathered around himself Jews who had a good sense for music, who thrived under his direction. The *poretzes* would from time to time throw parties and celebrations on their estates, and they would invite these two groups to gladden the hearts of the *poretzes*, their families, their guests, and their many servants. The Orthodox Jews pretended not to notice that the members of the bands went bareheaded, and some of them even clean-shaven. One Orthodox musician, Chaim David the *Badchan* [23], was well known. A book of Psalms stuck out of his pocket, and he would read from it at every available moment. He was good looking, with a pale face,

[Page 46]

a full-grown beard, and sparkly, black eyes. On the eve of the Sabbath, he would concern himself with insuring that the Yeshiva students had a place to eat. If he could not find a host, he would invite them to his house where he would feed them in a generous manner.

From among the chimneysweeps, one character stood out. He was a tall Jew, thin, with a face covered with soot. He would stand on the roof and clean out the chimney with a long brush, as the soot came out through the kitchen stove.

Kaniuch would occupy themselves with horse corpses. They would take rejected colts [24] to a place outside the city, kill them, strip their skin and sell it to a tanner.

Plikers – pluckers – were poor women who earned their livelihood by plucking feathers at the slaughterhouse in exchange for a few coins.

Men and women stood next to the *cheders* with pots in their hands. These pots would be enclosed in baskets and covered in rags. Inside were various types of cooked legumes. There were three measures in the pot, the largest was two Kopeks, the middle was one Kopek, and the smallest was ½ Kopek, known as Groshn. The children would hover over the baskets, and obtain food to sustain themselves.

Men and women busied themselves with fattening geese and ganders in order to sell *gribenes* (hunks of hardened fat). The fattening began at the beginning of the fall, and continued until Chanukah. As a result of standing in one place and being stuffed, the geese became fat. Then they were slaughtered. Their thick skin was fried with onions, and the fat was separated. The rest was the tasty *gribenes*. This was a very tasty food, and even the poor people would purchase it. They would purchase the fried onions and also a very small amount of the hunks of fat, either a quarter or an eight of a liter of *griben*.

At Chanukah time, there would be a woman sitting over a pot of burning coals in the market. She would be covered with layers of clothing, and she would weigh out a bit of *griben* for a few small coins. The women would spread this on bread for young children.

The *Shamash* of the *Beis Din* [rabbinical court of law] had the task of summoning litigants to judgement in front of the judges, and of proclaiming communal affairs in the synagogues on Sabbaths and festivals in the name of the rabbis.

It is worthwhile to mention one other lowly form of work – licking of eyes. Rabbi Goldberg of blessed memory of New Orleans related that once during his youth, he was chopping wood. Grains of soil injured his eyes, and his world became darkened. They brought him to the eye licker (*oygen lekere*), and she put the tip of her tongue onto his eyes, removed the granules of soil with a quick lick, and his eyes were healed. Her face was thin and wrinkled, and her house was poor. She was very poor. People wanted to pay her for her efforts, but she refused to receive any money for the *mitzvah* [25]. Since the High Holy Days were approaching, she requested that Reb Kadish the *melamed* [teacher of young children] pray that she be blessed with a good inscription and sealing [26].

Yochnin on the Street of the Road was considered to be a first class photographer. His photographs received awards at various competitions. Residents of Slutsk and its environs streamed to his studio by the thousands in order to be photographed. Rakuva also had a studio, as did Grozobski. These three photographers also employed several employees. There were private *cheders* in Slutsk that employed hundreds of *melamdim* and tutors. There were 18 *Beis Midrashes* served by various clergy: cantors, chief *shamashes*, collectors, emissaries, *shochtim*, *dayanim* [rabbinical judges], two rabbis, and Yeshiva heads.

Reb Zecharia Finkelstein
(Zecharia *der Falashnik*)

The residents of Slutsk earned their livelihood from the gentiles and from their environments, and they also fulfilled in themselves the adage: "Go forth and earn your livelihood one from another."

The peddlers, referred to as "*Koder*" [rags], were also known. They would purchase scraps, bones, and rags, and collect various objects and old items in the city and in the neighboring villages.

* * *

The famous interior decorations of the synagogue of Mohilev on the Dnieper were drawn in 1740 by Chaim the son of Reb Yitzchak Eizik Segal of holy blessed memory of Slutsk, who engaged in this holy work. It is related that this Segal produced the interior designs for two other synagogues, in Kapust and Dolhinov.

(*Rimon*, volume 3, 5683 –1923, Berlin)

* * *

The stories of the *Magid Moshe Yedaber* [27] and of Reb Aryeh Leib Neimark (the *Dayan* of Slutsk) called "*Even Yaakov*", with the acronym of Aryeh the son of Nissan, were published in the printing press of M. Tomashov, in the *Yagdil Torah* anthology.

The book of Reb Meir Soloveitchik (the name of the book is not known) was also published in that publishing house, as was a commentary on the Torah by Reb Zeev (Velvel Prizivitzer) Katznelson – a well-known *melamed* in Slutsk.

Various publications, the majority in Russian and the minority in Hebrew, were published in the printing presses of M. Yavrov and Friedlind.

Translator's footnotes:

1. In Hebrew, *Rechov Hakvish*, i.e. Road Street – admittedly a strange name for a street.
2. The '*shehechayanu*' (He Who has kept us in life) blessing is a blessing of thanksgiving for survival that is recited on various festivals throughout the Jewish calendar, as well as on private moment of joy, such as wearing a new suit for the first time, and eating a fruit that one has not partaken of yet during the current season. On the second night of Rosh Hashanah, there is a question if this blessing should be recited (the details of the halachic debate being beyond this footnote), so a new fruit is generally eaten to resolve the doubt, and enable the blessing to be able to be recited with no question. Interestingly enough, the blessing is only recited on tree fruits, and would not be recited on a watermelon.
3. I am not familiar with this expression, but I expect it means that he did not invest money in places where the money was sure to disappear quickly.
4. I am not familiar with this term, but I expect it refers to bakeries of fancy pastries.
5. This literally means "Noisy Street", and may be a euphemism for one of the busy streets of the town.
6. The Yiddish word *Foldn* translates in my Weinreich dictionary as "fruit layer cake," but from the context, it is not limited to that.
7. Torah scrolls, *tefillin* (phylacteries), *mezuzas*, and *megillas* (the biblical scroll of the book of Esther, and other such scrolls) are written on parchment scrolls. Scribes who write these parchment scrolls are called "*sofrei stam*", with *stam* being an acronym for *Sifrei Torah* (s), *Tefillin* (t), and *Mezuzos* (m)
8. The eating rotation refers to the custom at that time for non-local Yeshiva students to take their meals at various homes on a pre-set rotation basis.
9. *Kranim* means "horns" in Hebrew.
10. *Kerzner* being Yiddish for hatmaker.
11. I am not sure of the meaning of this.
12. Literally, did not hide their hands from the plate.
13. This is a take off from a portion of the morning liturgy, referring to the singing of the celestial angels. An *Ofan* (plural *Ofanim*) is a type of angel. The word *Ofan* is also a wheel, hence the pun.

14. These are two biblical verses. The second is actually a take-off of the verse "The voice is the voice of Jacob and the hands are the hands of Esau," which Isaac said as he was being tricked by Jacob into receiving the blessing.

15. Literally "Slaughterers of Righteousness". In the Yiddish name, Katzavishe, means "relating to butchers" – *katzav* is the Hebrew word for butcher.

16. Sons of flesh in this excerpt from the aleynu prayer refers to all humanity. The take-off here has it referring to workers of flesh.

17. The caption in Russian Cyrillic and Polish on the postcard itself says Sluck. *Tor automobilowy* (the Polish text). The photo is of the double decker wagons referred to a few paragraphs earlier.

18. Evidently he was a circumcisor (*mohel*) as well as a *shochet*.

19. During the reading of the scroll of Esther (the *Megilla*) at the synagogue on Purim, noise is made whenever the name of the villain Haman is mentioned.

20. A refrain from a hymn sung after the conclusion of the Sabbath, assuring the Jewish people (the sons of Jacob) that they should not fear as they are under protection.

21. *Kiddush* is a prayer at the beginning of the Sabbath and festival meals, recited over a cup of wine. *Havdalah* is a ceremony marking the conclusion of a Sabbath or festival, also recited over a cup of wine.

22. The word *Klezmer*, that has now made it into English, comes from the Hebrew words "*Klei Zemer*", literally meaning musical instruments. In this sentence, as in the English, it has taken on the connotation of "player of musical instruments".

23. Literally "jester" – someone who put on skits and other forms of entertainment at a wedding.

24. Either referring to untamable colts, or colts that were rejected by their mothers.

25. Generally *mitzvah* refers to a commandment, but here it refers to a good deed.

26. Tradition has it that on Rosh Hashanah, the fate of a person is inscribed for the coming year, and on Yom Kippur, it is sealed.

27. A *Maggid* is a roving storyteller. *Moshe Yedaber* means "Moses Spoke".

[Page 47]

Movements and Factions

In the Era of *Chovevei Zion*

(From the 1890s until the 7th Zionist Congress)

by Sh. Menachem

Translated by Jerrold Landau

Slutsk was far from the centers of *Haskalah*. Hebrew newspapers were hard to find there. In a city with a population of 15,000 Jews, which was the vast majority of the general population, only a few people received copies of *Hamelitz* and *Hatzefirah*. Pretty much the only *Chovevei Zion* activist in town was Reb Pesach Karon (the teacher Pesach Ezras). He would place charity plates for the settlement of the Land of Israel, sponsored by the Odessa committee, in the synagogues on the eve of Yom Kippur. A special article, the fruit of the pen of the native of our city, the writer Y. D. Berkovitz, is dedicated to this dear Jew.

The Feinberg family was also numbered among the supporters of *Chovevei Zion* [literally: Lovers of Zion] in Slutsk. One of the children of that family was sent to study in *Mikve Yisrael*. Characteristic of the scoffers of Slutsk, when he returned from the Land of Israel to Slutsk, his acquaintances gave him the nickname of "Moshe Terk" [1]. His photograph appears in our book among the members of the committee of the *Bonei Zion* [literally: Builders of Zion] group.

The echoes of the First Congress [2] reached Slutsk, and a Zionist group was set up in the city by the name of *Bonei Zion*, which was headed by the physician Dr. Melzer, who at the time was living in Slutsk. The members who appear in the photo that was taken in the year 5662 (1902) joined him. These were the Zionist activists of Slutsk, whose sole motive was the distribution of shekels [3], and the selling of the stamps of the Jewish National Fund and shares of the Colonial Bank. They would meet in the *shtibel* of the synagogue (The Oposhker Shul).

The Zionists in general were an isolated stream in a traditional city that strongly opposed any Zionist activity. On the other hand, members of the intelligentsia were also opposed. These included those who read Russian literature and newspapers, such as the teachers of the public school (Yereskoye Uchleyushchle) [4]. From among these, the teacher Yellin should be remembered positively, for he secretly maintained a close connection to Zionist circles.

The active committee of the *Bonei Zion* group in Slutsk in 5662 (1902)

Sitting, from right to left: 1) Zevin, 2... 3) Eizik Ratner, 4) Dr. Meltzer, 5) Shmaryahu Beilin, 6) the lawyer Ratner, 7) Sheikovitz, 8)...
Standing: 1) Avraham the son of Kadish-Dov (Ber) Epstein, the teacher and scribe, 2) Leib Ladovski, 3) Dr. Zonin, 4) Moshe Vatner, 5)... 6) Hillel Dobrow, 7) Avraham the son of Moshe Yechiel Epstein, 8) Freiberg

Those who were afflicted by the plague of assimilation included the rabbis of the Shapira Veshman stream, and also the well-known Dr. Schildkraut. At that time, the first sparks of the S. D. and Bund began to appear and spread. This will be described in detail in the article by Moshe Tulman.

In the year 5660 (1900), the Zionist winds blew across the young intelligentsia who were enthralled by modern Hebrew literature. This group was headed by Hillel Dobrow, who in his time was a student at the *Beis Midrash*, and later acquired general secular knowledge and the knowledge of the Hebrew language in particular. The committee of *Bonei Zion* took no interest at all in the issues of Hebrew culture, the spreading of the Hebrew language, and questions of modern, nationalistic education. The young people founded the *Kadima* [literally: forward] group, which was headed by Hillel Dobrow.

Another young lad, an excellent orator who was blessed with many other talents as well, became very active in this group. This was none other than Aharon Singelovski, who later on became known as a national activist with a worldwide scope, the chairman of the world ORT organization. In Slutsk, he would appear at publicity gatherings for Zionism, and he was also active in the Hebrew speaking circles.

The group of young people headed by Hillel Dobrow revolted against the *Bonei Zion* committee. From among these, the following stood out: Avraham Epstein (Abba Aricha) [5], Meir Wachsman, Y.D. Berkovitz, Avraham Epstein the second, Yehuda Leib Dadovski, Avraham Mirsky, the carpenter Yosef Mechanik, and others. Through the efforts of Hillel Dobrow and with the participation of the young Y.D. Berkovitz and their friends, the Zionist hall *Chanaya* [4] (house of wheat) was established. This building contained a reading room for Hebrew, Yiddish and Russian newspapers. Next to it was the first public library in Slutsk. At the time of the founding of the Zionist library, there was not one book in Hebrew, Yiddish or Russian available for borrowing. These institutions were established and developed thanks to the activities of the members of *Kadima*. The lawyer M. Karpman joined it, and devoted himself with dedication to all Zionist and cultural activities.

No representative of the Bonei Zion group was chosen as a representative to the all-Russian convention that took place in Minsk in the year 5662 (1902). Instead, the lawyer Karpman was chosen, who represented the entire Zionist movement of Slutsk. From among the important activities of the *Kadima* group, we should especially point out the *Dovrei Ivrit* [Hebrew Speakers] group, whose members gathered weekly in order to converse and lecture in the Hebrew language on current events and on literary and educational issues. Not only members of *Kadima* joined this group, but also members of other circles in the city, people who loved Hebrew

[Page 48]

and its literature, including many young people. From among the young women, we should point out those who appear in the photograph of the supporters of Hebrew students: Stusia Eila, Chania Ratner, Batya Schorr, and Ita Blumstein.

Courses were also set up there – evening courses to teach Hebrew and general knowledge to the students of the elementary Yeshivas. Hillel Dobrow interceded with the Yeshiva heads, who recalled his youth in a positive fashion (as a former genius) and permitted the students to attend these lessons. At first, the Hebrew teachers taught without receiving any compensation. As the enterprise grew larger, and it became necessary to rent premises and to invite teachers, a committee was founded that concerned itself with the support of this institution by donations from friends, arranging parties, and other such means. From among the Russian teachers, we remember positively Yosef Goldberg who died in Tel Aviv, and Moshe Katznelson who perished in the Holocaust.

After the pogrom of Kishinev [6] independent defense was organized through the efforts of the young Zionists. People joined from all segments of the Jewish community, including the *Bund* circles. When the first Zionist activists, Dobrow, Avraham Epstein, Y.D. Berkovitz, Yehuda Leib Sadovski and others left Slutsk, their friends in the movement took their place. During those years, a *Poale Zion* group was organized. It was founded by Yitzchak Berger of Minsk (Minsker Tolk). There was also an extremist stream among the general Zionists in Slutsk, known as *Hatechiya*. Both sides of Shusanya Street were occupied on Sabbath and festival evenings by members of the proletariat factions: Poale Zion on one side and *Bund* on the other side. They would often participate in joint meetings, which dealt with nationalistic and socialist issues. On occasion, these meetings ended with quarrels and blows.

When the left wing Zionist movements, such as S. S. and *Poale Zion*, grew, strikes of the workers in the small workshops of the city and of the officials of the shops were organized. They competed with *Bund*. In 1905, prior to the seventh Congress, there was a heavy battle within the Zionist organization, between the general Zionists on one side and *Hatechiya* and *Poale Zion* on the other side. Secret information reached Slutsk that on May 5th of that year, the regional committee would meet secretly in Minsk, headed by the regional delegate, the well-known Shimshon Rosenbaum.

The battle regarding the elections in Slutsk was fierce. The candidates were: the lawyer Karpman from the general Zionists and Sh. Nachmanovitch from the left wing factions. The left wing was victorious. Issues were raised regarding nationalism and socialism, territorialism and Zionism, and Zionism in the national realm. Ber Borochov [7] of blessed memory also participated in this convention. Sh. Nachmanovitch returned from the convention, and a large crowd from all the Zionist factions came to hear his accounting. The lawyer Karpman was among them.

When organizational questions arose in the Congress, and the Zionists divided into yea sayers and nay sayers, a territorialist faction arose in Slutsk as well and attracted many of the general Zionist circles to itself. Testimony to this is provided in the writings of the writer Y.D. Berkovitz, who was 17 years old at the time and living in Lodz. (See the exchange of letters regarding Zionism and the "Hebrew Speakers".)

Hillel Dobrow and Singelovski

After the Russian revolution of 1905-1906 was crushed, the government banned the Zionist movement. The young activists spread in all directions. The social groups went underground, including the Zionist movement. The Zionist hall (*Tzania*) was closed. The library that was founded by the Zionists continued in existence, and brought rays of light into the communal apathy that prevailed in the city. A large portion of the youth strove for the life of this world, spent time in the various conditoriums, and were attracted to an empty life that lacked real content. Even the Russian literature of that era, symbolized by Asher Sanin the hero of the writer Archivshev, tended to that direction. A frivolous group, known as *Trumpatel*, was known in Slutsk.

The *Cheder Hametukan* [8] continued to exist and flourish under the direction of Chazanovitch and his friends. There were also numerous Hebrew newspapers that were distributed by the booksellers Reiser, Robnitch and others. The Zionist embers crackled in secrecy until they found their place in the *Tzeirei Zion* movement. With the silencing of the secular nationalistic movement in that era due to government edicts and ideological decline, the institutions of Torah and the Yeshivas rose in stature, and continued their activities with greater strength.

[Page 49]

Letters
(From his legacy)

by Hillel Dorbow

Translated by Jerrold Landau

Letter A

28th of Shvat, the year 1834 of our exile[9], Yekatrinoslav.

To the members of the "Hebrew Speakers" circle of Slutsk. Shalom!

Dear Friends!

In response to your letter, we express our feelings of joy to you, for the proclamation that we published in the newspapers was not a proclamation in the desert, but indeed, it met attentive ears. The letters that we receive from the various organizations in all cities bring joy to our hearts, for the idea of the revival of our national language as a spoken language has found adherents throughout the entire Diaspora, in all remote cities and "dark corners." The nationalistic and educational value of this movement is very honorable, and its influence in spreading our language and literature is so great and strong, as can be shown by the frequent letters that we receive from the various organizations. Pretty much every group, aside from the great effort directed toward the main goal – spreading the language, surrounds itself with many other activities and actions that have a direct or indirect relationship to our language. The arranging of Hebrew festivals and literary celebrations, the founding of groups for the study of the language, the regular readings, the speaking and conducting of debates – all of these are honorable deeds, of which it is difficult to estimate from the outset the extent of their influence in the development of our language and literature. If we indeed succeed through "*Kol Koreh*" ["The Voice of the Proclamation"] to give a small push in that direction, if indeed we succeed "in instilling a bit of light and hope" to the life of the organizations – this is a great thing for us! We can view ourselves as fortunate for we fulfilled our objective.

With respect to your organization "*Dovrei Ivrit*" ["Hebrew Speakers"] in Slutsk, we see that you have done a great deal for the benefit of our idea, by means of your rich and variegated activities. Things such of this are indeed invaluable, and the more one engages in this, the more praiseworthy it is. Nevertheless, everything depends on the time and the place, and in accordance with your capabilities and the conditions of your small city, you have done great things and we hereby say to you: well done!

We willingly give answers to all of your questions. The status of our organization in general is not too bad. There are cases where members drop out; however on the other hand new members come to almost every meeting. The number of regular members is not less than thirty, plus or minus a small amount. There are always a significant number of guests, sometimes up to twenty people. The content of our meetings is as follows: a) an investigation into current events that affect the larger or smaller communities in Israel, from the newspapers; b) some interesting, nice item of literature or publicity; c) a lecture from one of the members on a current topic. Relating to this content, our meetings are divided into three parts. In the first part, after the reading of the minutes of the last meeting, we discuss the news, or one of the members speaks on the weekly chronicles. A recess follows. The recess is of great benefit to those of our members who are not willing or able to speak publicly, for during the recess, private conversations occur that do not require special skill. After the recess, one of the members reads some story, article, or other such item. The debates take place during the third portion[10]. If the truth be told, our group excels greatly in this area. The members deal with each question seriously and sincerely. With the readings, we touch upon various questions, of a personal, nationalistic, traditional, or esthetic nature. Each question is debated in depth, until the issue is well clarified. The debates are conducted in the finest possible manner – nobody interrupts his fellow, in accordance "with the custom of Jewish people". Our meetings obviously leave a pleasant impression.

We will now move from the external qualities of our group to the internal, fundamental qualities. In order for us to present to you some idea of the essence of our group and its fundamental aspirations, we will transcribe a few minutes from the ledgers of our group:

1. The purpose of the *"Safa Chaya"* ["Living Language"] group is to broaden the knowledge of our language as a living, spoken language, and to expand the knowledge of our literature… (Chapter a, paragraph b).

2. The means… the organization attempts to find teachers for those who express an interest in learning our language… The organization maintains relations with all of the other organizations of Hebrew speakers. (Chapter b, d, e).

3. Any male or female above the age of 18 who agrees with the charter of the organization is eligible to be a member of the group…
    New members are accepted upon the recommendation of two members after they attend a meeting no less than two times. (Chapter c, paragraph b).

4. …Every man or woman has the right to attend meetings and to take part in the debates. (Chapter f, paragraph a).

5. The organization chooses a director, secretary and treasurer for a term of a half a year (Chapter e, paragraph a).

Letter B

Slutsk, Minsk region (Russia)
23rd of Av, the year 1835 of our exile

To the general meeting of Hebrew Speakers in Basle – Shalom!

Members of the *"Dovrei Ivrit"* ["Hebrew Speakers"] organization realize the great value of the founding of a central organization that will unite all of the organizations that are busy with the revival of the Hebrew language as a spoken and written language; but to our great anguish, we cannot send a delegate to the meeting in Basle. Therefore, we hereby desire:

1. That the meeting registers our organization among the groups that are joining the central organization.

2. To give a small idea of our group and its work.

[Page 50]

Avraham Mirsky

3. To express our opinion on various issues relating to the revival of the language. Our group has existed for two years already. Its purpose is to disseminate among the members of our city the speaking of Hebrew, and the Hebrew language as a living and spoken language. The number of members is now 30 (26 men and 4 women).

Activities of the Organization

1. Meetings take place one a week. The meetings deal with: 1) Current events that deal with general or specifics of life in Israel. 2) Lectures by members on issues of Zionism, literature, and publicity. 3) Lectures on specific period of the history of our people.

2. The setting up of groups for the study of the language. More than 40 poor boys and girls study the Hebrew language in groups that were founded by our organization.

3. The planning of Hebrew literary celebration.

The Influence of the Organization

1. Members of the organization influence the students of the elementary Yeshivas to speak Hebrew among themselves.

2. Hebrew conversation can always be heard in the Zionist institutions, such as the library and the coffeehouse.

3. Members present speeches in Hebrew at all of the Zionist celebrations and festivals.

4. The literary celebrations that were arranged by the organization have had a great influence in the speaking of Hebrew, and ignited the hearts of hundreds of people.

Possibility of the Renaissance of the Language

The experience that we obtained in "our dark corner" over two years permits us to hope that the renaissance of the language is within the realm of possibility. The gathering should pay attention to the following, which are among the most urgent and effective means: a) to obligate the members to speak Hebrew during all of their activities in life. b) To attract women and girls to the groups, or to establish special groups for them, so that the mothers will rear the next generation in Hebrew.

In conclusion, we give our blessings to the first general convention of Hebrew speakers, that it should succeed in its activities to actualize the founding of a central organization for its fruitful deeds and activities.

With blessings of Zion.

Letter C

A portion of the letter of E. Epstein to Dobrow, from Yekatrinoslav, March 13, the summer of 5664 (1904).

My brother Dobrow!

Mr. Zirkel, who will bring you the letter, is a native of Slutsk, and lived here in Yekatrinoslav for two years. During this time, he participated in local Zionist activity, and became an active member of the local branch of *Poale Zion*. I do not know whether or not there is such an organization in our town, thanks to your trait of putting your hand to your mouth and being quiet. However, A. Mirsky, in his last letter from Slutsk, hinted to me that there is an organization of that sort in Slutsk; if you take part in it, you can sign up Mr. Zirkel to it, and he will assist you in no small measure, for he has experience in this matter. However things turn out, try to draw him near to you and to the local Zionists.

In conclusion, we give our blessings to the first general convention of Hebrew speakers, that it should succeed in its activities to actualize the founding of a central organization for its fruitful deeds and activities.[11]

With blessings of Zion.

Letter D

My brother and friend!

I received your letter today, after I had already sealed my letter to you and was ready to send it to the post office. You yourselves can imagine how happy I was to receive it. I read it over and over, and each successive time I had more and more pleasure.

Berkovitz stole my heart with his soft, warm words, and turned my anger to love. There is enchantment on your lips, Berkovitz, and I always read your words with great pleasure.

I am very happy with all the news that you informed me of. I see that there is life, movement, work, and action in our "camp". I am particularly happy that your small organization was founded under the supervision of Yellin. Apparently from your letter, "*Dovrei Ivrit*" is growing and sprouting. I have also become a member of the "*Safa Chaya*" ["Living Language"] organization, and I am now one of the most faithful and significant members. A great future is awaiting me here, for the chairman registered my name in the list of candidates for the position of secretary. (Incidentally: why do you not come in contact with the "*Safa Chaya*" organization here, as I have already written you a few times!) Next week, at the meeting of "*Safa Chaya*", I will relate before all the members all of the news and activities and discreet deeds that have taken place in our city Slutsk

[Page 51]

concerning the "*Hakol Kaasher Lakol*" ["Everything For Everyone"] festivities and warm celebration. The teacher Belkind from the Land of Israel, one of the first *Chalutzim* [Zionist pioneers] now lives in Yekatrinoslav. On Wednesday, he lectured at our "*Safa Chaya*" group on the topic of an agricultural school – that is to say, not for agronomists, but rather for simple Hebrew farmers – that he intends to found in the Land of Israel. Of course, he spoke in Hebrew. Our language lives on his lips in the full sense of the word, but he uses the Sephardic pronunciation. According to him, this is the pronunciation that is prevalent in all of the *Moshavim* [settlements] in the land of Israel. Nevertheless, it is very easy to understand.

* * *

Photocopy of the Hatzair newspaper. The title and header information is

"Hatzair, a newspaper of Hebrew literature and life issues, published by the '*Dovrei Ivrit*' organization, edited by A. Aran. [note, the word Epstein is superimposed in script.

9th of Tishrei

Price: 2 rubles annually; 1 ruble every six months; 50 kopecks for a quarter of a year; 4 kopecks per issue. Published in Slutsk once a week. Number 1, First year.

5663 (1902)

The proceeds of this newspaper are dedicated to the national Zionist library of Slutsk."

A table of contents and the first article follow. They are in Hebrew script as opposed to printed Hebrew, and the photocopy is not completely clear. It is not translated here.

The caption below the photocopy is as follows:

"The chief editor (the author of the first articles) was Avraham Epstein (who was about 25 years old).

The editor, director, advertising chief, and copyist was Y.D. Berkovitz (16 years old, close to his 17th year).

Meir Wachsman, the author of the article for Rosh Hashanah[12], was 19 years old. His article was edited (primarily shortened, due to its excessive length) by 'chief editor.'

Only one copy was produced of this first issue. It was available for reading by the patrons of the 'Zionist Library' in Slutsk (which itself was founded by the group that dealt with the newspaper).

Two more issues appeared. Dozens of copies of them were printed, but all were condemned to be burned out of fear of the Slutsk police[13], who threatened with a "search" the mistress of the home in which the printing of this newspaper took place during the nights. (The teacher Hillel Dobrow lived in that house, and his apartment turned into "the printing house" for the newspaper.)"

* * *

Regarding the reading house, I find it correct to advise you to sign off for other newspapers and journals. Many people will jump upon these newspapers, and I am certain that the income that they will bring in will exceed the expenditure. In general, I find that there is no life in our library, and it stands upon the point of darkness. Dobrow has a certain natural inclination to purchase old books, rags Heaven forbid. Do we really have a "Hebrew library" in the full sense of the term? I am very doubtful. It is necessary to use whatever means are available to purchase the missing books, and to collect them together so that we will have a full collection. It is necessary to place a ledger in the library, so that people can list the books

[Page 52]

that they wish the library to obtain. It is necessary to subscribe to some sort of Russian periodical such as "*Znania*", and then we will receive some respite.

I will immediately send you a letter and an article when I receive "*Hatzair*".

Mirsky has not come to me for about one week. I cannot wait until he comes and writes as well – I am waiting for a letter.

Peace be with you. We will see each other again.

Your brother Avraham

Letter E

A letter of Y. D. Berkovitz to the "*Dovrei Ivrit*" organization of Slutsk.

Lodz, 10 Elul, the year 1835 of our exile (1904).

My brothers Hillel, Leib and Avraham![14]

I am not writing this letter in your honor or in honor of your deeds, for you are not worthy of this at all. When "the screen was lifted." I was dumbfounded and astonished to find out what was revealed before my eyes from those things that took place "behind the screen," and "inside the walls." However, I stood and stood, my feet swelled from all the standing – and I was not able to see anything, therefore I decided not to rely on false promises, and that I must completely abandon any thoughts of "brotherhood" from hypocritical brothers. I am not writing you this letter to reawaken forgotten brotherhood, and to reestablish it in its original form, but rather since we are ideological brothers, and the innovations that were made in that common ideology have inspired me to write what I am about to write. These innovations had so great an effect on me that I cannot restrain myself from speaking about them to anyone. Here in Lodz, I was not able to find such ideological brethren, whose outlook and ideas regarding the national movement are as clear to me as yours. With my Zionist acquaintances here, I can only skirt around the issue but not touch it; and this causes me much suffering, plagues me with doubts and drains the vigor from my brain. Yes, my brothers! The Sixth Zionist Congress caused me to write you this letter. –

Palestine and East Africa[15]. – This news, that came to me recently, did not have the impact upon me that it should have had upon every Zionist Jew. It was so sudden and poorly defined, that I did not know how to relate to it. It seems to me in retrospect that this suggestion was not important at all, and that it was said solely for the purpose of uttering words. However now, when this idea is being further defined, it sticks in my mind from day to day, – and I feel some shame, some injury to the honor of our nationalistic feelings. What is this that G-d has done to us? – Should the epitome of our ideal, the sum of our national aspirations should be some country in East Africa, to which at this point we do not even know, and we have never set foot upon it – for there is no connection between us and it? Do you hear? – No connection! Not a connection of having lived there for hundreds of years, and not a connection of a long hopes and expectation in the hearts that beat and the eyes that wasted away for 2,000 years. Not a connection of longing and early memories, not a soul and not a spirit… Should we exchange our land, the Land of Israel, for a land that we do not know and that our fathers have not known until this day? – It has no past and no future, but rather only a present; there, there is no permanent dwelling, no safe sanctuary for the generations for a washed out and anguished nation, but rather only a temporary inn, a "night camp." My brothers! How much bitterness and mockery is awaiting in these matters! Did we dedicate our souls up to this time for such an inn, is this what we were waiting for from the day that we went out into exile, is this our hope that "has up to now not been lost?"[16]

I understand, my brothers, very well the psychology of the Russian delegates, whose Jewish nationalism takes precedence over "their Jewish state." When I read in the papers that many of them wept when the suggestion was accepted, my heart also wept inside of me. Instead of singing "it has up to now not been lost," I wanted to lament: "surely the people are grass"[17]. "grass" is the nation, who no longer have the power to endure and wait more than seven years. "Grass" is the people whose patience is wearing thin, whose powers are weakening, and whose despair is growing. When "night" arrives, it feels itself as tired, and has no energy to continue onward. It falls down in the midst of the journey to take a rest in any place, without looking around to see if this "rest" is a complete rest, an eternal rest, for the pained and afflicted soul.

Indeed, "grass" is the people…

Nevertheless, from the midst of the cloud of bitterness and agony, from the shame and heartache, the voice of our people rises up:

We will not go to Africa!…

The bent nation has awakened, they have shaken off and straightened up, and knows its protest… we no longer believe in the mercies of G-d, as our fathers believed. Many of our holy fathers, who up to this point have been the mainstay of Judaism, were turned into profane things in our mindset, however the ring that still surrounds them all remains with us, and is the source of our Jewish soul – and you come and wish to take this too from us? – We will not give…

I do not know if all of the people accepted the African recommendation with joy, but I know clearly that the opposing spirit that pervaded among the Russian delegates was a joyous and heartwarming sign for all of our good Zionists in the lands of the east. Our task after the Sixth Congress must be enriched, deepened and broadened into different facets. Our work among ourselves must strengthen, and through it our nationalist work must be in the direction of the opposing spirit. That is my view now, at the time of the storms of the spirits and the battles of wits, that is to say: now, at the time that everything is still theoretical. What will be later – I do not know. I feel now, that beneath the multitude of thoughts that are storming inside of me, beneath the waiting in fear and trembling for the realization of the Sixth Congress – beneath all of this I feel myself abandoned and cheated… What is your opinion, my brothers, with regard to this? I wanted very much that you should all write me about this. I request that you write me how Slutsk received this news, and what is the situation in general with regard to this. Was a delegate sent from our organization, and did "*Dovrei Ivrit*" and "*Ivriya*" answer the proclamation? – Did not the coffeehouse and the library encounter obstacles after the circular appeared from the minister of the interior? – In general, demonstrate to me for the first time since I left you that you still are alive and toiling.

[Page 53]

Here in Lodz I am no longer part of the Zionist organization, but I rather stand near to it. The reason for this is that I lived outside of the city during the summer, and I was not able to take any part in Zionist activities. I do not know what will be in the upcoming winter. At the present, I am attempting along with a few other Zionists, to found here an organization for speaking of Hebrew and for Hebrew literature. We will know in time if our dream becomes reality. Not all of the Zionists gave their hands to this cause, for if they did we would have been able to found a Hebrew club, in accordance with Epstein's advice. I do not know anymore whether I am a "resident of Lodz." It could be that one clear morning I will lift up my wings – and fly… Please write to me what Epstein from Yekatrinoslav has written you, for I have not received a letter from him in a long time. –

I am making haste to end this letter with a request that "you gird your loins" and answer this letter immediately. If you are stubborn this time and do not answer me – then woe, woe to you!…

With blessings of Zion,

Your brother Yitzchak Dov

Please send regards to Meir Wachsman. This letter is also intended for him. Please request that he write me –

A group of *Chalutzim* in Warsaw at the beginning of 1921, on their way to the Land of Israel

1) Berl Sinigovski, 2) Chana Soloveitchik-Cohen, 3) Shalom Shpilkin, 4)..., 5) Eliahu Altman, 6) Dov Tiroshkin, 7) Shachnovits, 8, 9) ... 10) Bela Katznelson-Kikaon, 11) Musia Harkavi-Katznelson, 12) Binyamin Katznelson, 13) Klibanski, 14) Chaim Berlas, 15) Yitzchak Levinstein, 16) Ruth Mirsky-Goldin, 17) Pesach Litvak, 18) M. Hershberg, 19) ... 20) Tzipora Lachover Berlas, 21) Yosef Dinstman, 22) Miriam Dankigenbaum, 23) Tzvi Grinfeld, 24) Sadeh, 25) Rubinchik, 26) Mrs. Rosenzweig, 27) Shifman, 28) Aryeh Ben Moshe Shapira, 29) Chana Fieirstein-Handel, 30) Dina Kaplan-Kopilov, 31) Sarah Tadik, 32) Chaya Kordon, 33) Katz Litvak, 34) Yaakov Zolibanski, 35) Dina Stambulchik, 36) Yamima Katznelson, 37) Bar-Natan... Sara Zazik. 38) Sarah Smiatichki-Winson, 39) Zahava (Golda) Berger-Stern, 40) Esther Halpern Schneerson, 41) Goz, 42) Fania Stambolchik, 43) Yoel Berg, 44) ... 45) Guberman, 46) Moshe Fogel.[18]

Translator's Footnotes:

1. Probably because Palestine was under Turkish rule at the time.
2. The First Zionist Congress, held in Basle, Switzerland in 1897, under the directorship of Theodore Herzl.
3. A shekel is a name of an ancient Jewish coin, and is also the name of the currency of the State of Israel. Here it refers to the dues of the Zionist movement.
4. Transliterated from Cyrillic.
5. Abba Aricha is a Talmudic nickname for a sage who was very tall. *Aricha* means tall in Aramaic, as does *Aroch* in Hebrew.
6. The pogrom in Kishinev took place in 1904.
7. A leader of extreme left wing Zionism.
8. A term for a modern style *cheder*.
9. This is a poetic way of recording the years. The exile took place in the year 70 of the Common Era, so the year of this letter would correspond to 1904.
10. There is a footnote in the Hebrew text at this point, stating that the debates and discussion take place according to the musical protocol. (I am not sure what this means, with a one letter change in the Hebrew, it would mean 'the customary manner', so I suspect that there might be a typographical error here.)

11. This paragraph, and the following one sentence paragraph, are equivalent with the end of the previous letter. I suspect that they were repeated here in error.
12. The date of this issue, 9th of Tishrei, is the eve of Yom Kippur, one week after Rosh Hashanah.
13. The word here is "Ganders". I am not sure what it means, but it may be short for Gendarmes.
14. There is a footnote here in the text: "Hillel Dobrow, Leib Sadovski, and the young Avraham Epstein, the son of Yechiel who was the brother of the "elder" Avraham Epstein.
15. This is evidently referring to the idea that took hold in the early years of the Zionist movement that a Jewish state should be founded in Uganda.
16. A quote from the *Hatikva* anthem – the Zionist anthem and now the national anthem of the State of Israel.
17. A quote from the book of Isaiah.
18. The gap between 31 and 38 was in the list of names.

[Page 54]

Bygone Days

by Dr. Meyer Waxman

Translated by Sara Mages

It is difficult for a man who left his hometown fifty-five years ago, which constitute a period of changes in the circle of life of humanity, the life of our nation and this person's private life - to uproot himself from the present, go back and review the days of his youth in a quiet city like Slutsk that nestles in a far corner in White Russia. However, there are moments when, unintentionally and without thinking, images of this life rise from the depths of my soul and memory and evoke longings for days gone by and a world that has passed and will never return. I want to list some of these images as a tombstone for the city and its life during the last eight years that I spent there, years that rode on two centuries, the end of the 19th century and the beginning of the 20th century.

Slutsk, although the number of Jews, who lived there, did not excel in quantity, its community occupied an important place in the life of the Jews in Poland and Russia. Already at the beginning of the 18th century it was added as a fifth member of "*Va'ad Medinot Lita*" [Lithuanian Council], which oversaw the social and cultural life of the country's Jews. The importance of this community came from the dedication of its members to the study of the Torah and its sages who have earned a reputation in the Jewish world. The community administrators have always endeavored to elect great scholars as community rabbis. From among those who served in this position during the first seventy years of the 19th century were: HaRav R' Yosef Peimer ["Yossele Slutsker"] a student of R' Chaim of Vałožyn, and R' Yosef Ber Soloveitchik, the son of R' Chaim's grandson who participated for some time in the management of the Great Yeshiva.

Slutsk was known for its opposition to the Hassidut. I still remember the saying that was spoken by many in those days - if a small Hasidic synagogue would be founded in Slutsk, even just for a *minyan* of men, then, the Messiah will come. I do not know if this saying came from those who were drawn to the Hassidut, who intended to say that such a *minyan* would hasten the coming of the Messiah, or vice versa, from the opponents, that this miracle can only happen in the days of the Messiah, but whatever it may be, it indicates that the Hassidut did not occupy a place in the life of the community. And because of this lack of fanaticism, the Haskalah Movement penetrated it at the beginning of its spreading. Even Yisrael, the son of HaRav Peimer, was captured by it. He moved to Germany, changed his name to Behmer, and earned a reputation among the scholars of Jewish wisdom by writing several important books in Hebrew. He returned to Slutsk and died there in 1860.

Therefore, these two faces stood out in the life of the community during my youth. In the 1890s, there were many small yeshivot where most of the homeowners' sons were educated. A large number of them gained a deep and wide knowledge of the Talmud and many entered the famous yeshivot: Vałožyn, Mir and Slabodka.

Some of them also served as rabbis and held important positions in Jewish cities. A small number even reached the virtue of great Torah scholars like: HaRav R' Baruch Ber Leibowitz, who became famous in the 1920s as head of Slabodka Yeshiva and later founded a large yeshiva in the city of Kamenitz D'Lita. Some of Slutsk's scholars served as rabbis in important cities in the United States.

I remember, when I was a little boy it was announced in the "*Shulhoif*" (a square that was entirely surrounded by synagogues), that after the 15th of Av, when the nights begin to lengthen, the sound of the Torah will be heard in the synagogues. On these nights my friends and I visited the synagogues, the Great Beit Midrash, the Kloyz and also the Tailors' Synagogue, to enjoy the great light that came out from them and the melodies the yeshiva students sang during their studies.

The rabbi of Slutsk in those days, R' Yaakov Dovid [Wilovsky - known by the acronym Ridvaz], author of "The Ridbaz Commentary on the Jerusalem Talmud," was not satisfied with the local yeshivot and made efforts, and also succeeded, in moving part of Slabodka Yeshiva to Slutsk with its Rosh Yeshiva [dean], HaRav R' Isser Zalman Meltzer. In this way, one of the largest and famous yeshivot in Russia existed in this city.

However, on the other hand, there has also been an increase in the pursuit of continuing education in secular studies to acquire a scientific profession such as medicine, or just a university education.

Since the entrance to the gymnasium for Jews in this city was limited to a small percentage, and only the children of the rich were able to squeeze in there, what did the children of middle-class, or the children of the poor, do? They used the privilege given to them to prepare privately and take the final exams in the gymnasium.And so grew the number of yeshiva graduates, who reached the age of maturity, and devoted their time to these studies. They were also joined by the girls who hoped to enter university and study to become a pharmacist, a dentist, or a certified midwife. Not many days passed and groups of such students, boys and girls, formed the intelligentsia of Jewish youth. Their number increased by the arrival of young men and women from the surrounding towns. They even flocked from the villages to the district city to attend a continuing education program.

This strong desire to expand their knowledge in secular studies did not take the place of the spirit of Hebrew and national education which found its place in Slutsk in these years. Many young people acquired the love for the Hebrew language and its literature in their childhood. This desire intensified by the Zionist movement whose echo also reached this city. In Slutsk, there were no municipal libraries and certainly no public Hebrew libraries, but there were two men, one a book seller and the other a teacher, who had a room or a school. They purchased Hebrew libraries for themselves and provided books to read for a few kopeks, but the demand was larger than the supply.

There were also young people who dreamed of becoming writers in the future, or to study Jewish wisdom in universities abroad. Among those dreamers were two sons of wealthy families. One of them was Schmowitz's son, who was close to the Galician-educated circles and was married to a privileged family in Slutsk that Mendele [Mocher Sforim] already mentioned in his memoirs.

[Page 55]

A group of members in 1900

From the right: Yehudit Ratner, Hilel Dubrov, Yosef Lisbron, Moshe Chipchin, Stisia Ayala

He became known outside Slutsk as a wise man and a public activist, and was also invited by the government to meetings on which Jewish matters were discussed. The second was the son of a moneylender who received a comprehensive Hebrew education. Both realized their dream. The first is the late Dr. Yakov Naftali Simchoni, the historian and Jewish literature researcher, and the second Dr. Peitel Lipschutz who moved to Germany, specialized in economics theory and published several articles on this topic in "*Haschiloah*."

The influence of the Zionist movement on the spiritual life in my hometown, Slutsk, takes an important place in my memories. As far as I know, there were also a number of people in the city who were members of "*Hovevi Zion*" from the beginning of the movement. One of them, Zev Gluskin, was a member of the Odessa Committee and his name is mentioned a number of times in the committee's reports. Indeed, these were individuals who did not join the association, but the appearance of the Zionist movement, and its impression on the Jewish world, also aroused the people of Slutsk.

I do not remember exactly, but it seems to me that already in 1899 a Zionist association, whose number has risen to a hundred, and maybe even more, was founded. Among the members were many of the intelligentsia strata and also professionals. The chairman was a private lawyer, the official language, or the language of discussion, was Russian. Obviously, they were able to debate in Yiddish, but also the Hebrew language was not forgotten. Two secretaries were nominated, for Russian and Hebrew, a post the writer of these columns had won. This association raised the spiritual life in the city and increased the interest in Zionism and Hebrew culture.

Not many days passed and the Zionist association, with the help of people interested in Jewish social life, established a center for Zionist and cultural activities in Khapashker Street. Officially it was called the Tea House - *Teshema* in Russian. This house became a place for Zionist meetings and home for various companies interested in developing Jewish cultural life. It also had a library in the three languages of the city's residents.

A few weeks went by and the house was bustling with people. Some came to read Jewish newspapers in different languages or books in Hebrew, and some just visited for a friendly conversation over a cup of tea. Young men and women gathered for meetings, debates and lectures, and a short time later the sound of the Hebrew language echoed in the air. A Hebrew-speaking association was founded in the city, and it was not only concerned with speaking, distributing and learning the language. From time to time Hebrew banquets were held and those, who dreamed of a literary future, read from their works.

It didn't take long and their dreams began to come true. Some left Slutsk to try their luck at literary centers such as Warsaw, Lodz and others. Soon, a rumor spread that Y. D. Berkowitz had won the first prize of the newspaper "*HaTzofe*" for his story "*Mashke'le Hazir*," and Avraham Epstein's articles were published in the press. Some of their friends were proud of them, others were jealous of them, but directly or indirectly, it led to the glorification of the national and the Hebrew spirit in the city. The number of members of the Zionist and Hebrew associations grew, and the interest in the Hebrew language and its literature increased.

Even though the Zionist association official language was Russian, this association always emphasized the value of the Hebrew language. In 1902, when the Russian Zionists gathered for the national conference in Minsk, the writer of these columns was asked to send a greeting letter in Hebrew to the conference and frame it in the shape of a Star of David using the stamps of *Kern HaKayemet* that were seen in the world only a few months before.

[Page 56]

It is worth noting to the generations the harsh conditions in which the Zionist activity was carried out in the first years of the present century.As is well known, at that time there were many illegal movements in Russia and in Slutsk. It was impossible to hold a public meeting in a hall because the government suspected its purpose, but the meetings were necessary.Therefore, the meetings were held in Beit HaMidrash around tables on which Gemara, Mishnayot and open Chumash books were placed. And if, God forbid, a policeman or an official glanced at the gathering, it was clear that it was not a meeting but a study group in sacred books. Often, the lecturers and many of the listeners, who sat bareheaded, had to cover their heads against their wishes.

I will conclude in one case that illuminates the difficulty of the situation in a special way. In the summer of 1904, when the terrible news of Herzl's death came and shocked the hearts of all members, the question arose on how to hold a memorial service for the leader's death. It was difficult to find a place and the date was postponed day by day. And suddenly, a large number of young men and women woke up, chose a weekday, and in the middle of the day flocked to the cemetery. And there, on the fence posts, the speakers delivered their eulogies with the assurance that no secret policeman would suspect such an assembly. The eulogies were given by the writer of these columns and a young man who came from the village to study and prepare for the final exams at the gymnasium. His name is Aharon Singalowsky, who later became famous as the founder of the international "ORT" company and was its director for decades.

In this manner Slutsk contributed, in the ten years that ended the 19th century and opened the 20th century, to Hebrew literature, Zionism and social life, when it helped a number of young dreamers to realize their dreams and enrich the life of their nation.

At the conclusion of the article on the memories of my hometown, I want to fulfill the words of our sages who said: "While the wine belongs to its owner, the gratitude is given to the one who pours it." [Rava Kamma 92b]. If there is a taste of wine in my words, you must know that the one who poured it is my relative, HaRav R' Nisan Waxman, a native of Starobin and student of Torah institutes in Slutsk, Mir and Slabodka. He, who stood by me for several months and encouraged me to pay my debt to the city that instilled in me the love for the Torah and Jewish culture. If it was not for him, who knows if I was able to cut myself from my world and concentrate on days gone by. *Chaza*l ["Our Sages, may their memory be blessed"] were right when they said: "Good deeds to be fulfilled by the worthy." The worthy is my relative, who served as rabbi of the community of Lakewood in the United States for many years, and enriched from his spirit the thousands of guests who visited this city, which is known as the resort city, over the years. He also made important contributions to religious literature, when he edited and published important books with introductions and comments, and taught Torah in broad circles in Brooklyn with dignity and splendor.

The association "Supporters of Hebrew Learners" in Slutsk, 1904

1) Y. D. Berkovitsh, 2) Avraham son of Moshe Yehiel Epshteyn, 3) Mrs. Blumshteyn, 4) Avraham son of Kadish-Dov-Ber Epshteyn,
5) Hillel Dubrov, 6) Dr. Binyamin Ostrovsky, 7) Batya Shor, 8) Dov Cohen,
9) Moshe Katzenelson (later a doctor and a Zionist activist in Bialystok, perished in Auschwitz), 10) Stisia Ayala- Goldberg,
11) Shimshon Nachmanovitsh (Nachmani), 12) Henya Ratner, 13) Yehudah Leib Finkel

[Page 57]

Self Defence in Slutsk

by S. Menachem

Translated by Sara Mages

During the period of pogroms in Ukraine, in 1905-6, there were no pogroms in Slutsk but the Jewish community, with all its parties, was ready for a day of trouble and distress and to defend itself.

The defense was organized from all walks of life, starting from the ordinary people, the General Zionist, Zionist Left and the "Bund." A committee, which was composed of all streams, was elected, starting with Yisrael Brahon who was close to the authority, from the heads of the fire department to the "Bund."

The writer of these lines was one of the committee members who visited, in pairs, the homes of the wealthy to solicit donations for the needs of the defence according to the committee's assessment. Many responded and donated generously and without opposition, while some objected and threatened to report us, and, of course, they avoided it because the fundraisers warned them not to do so.

My fundraising partner was a member of the "Bund" and when we arrived to M.G., one of the richest men in the city, he threatened that he would remember my hat and my glasses (for he didn't know me and didn't know my name). It is possible that it caused results in the future.

Another amusing story about a wealthy Jew named Y. M. that we found sitting on a stool in a house that was empty of furniture. We thought he was in mourning and prepared to leave, but he stopped us and asked: what do you want? We explained to him that we had come to receive a donation from him for the self defense and he replied: I'll give you ten times of what you demand of me, provided you will save me from my hooligans.

We were very curious to know who they were. It turned out that while he was away from his house for his business, his sons moved from their apartment in the old house on Tritshan Street to his house, which was purchased from one of the Polish landowners, on Broad Street (*Breiter Gass*).

On the right: Rachel Efrat

With the money collected we purchased firearms: a few dozen pistols and a large quantity of bullets which were hidden under the stove in my apartment on Zaretzer Street. When it seemed to me that undercover policeman was sniffing in the area, it was decided to move the weapons to a safer place.

Rivka Efrat

The act was done by female members who transferred the weapons to Bere Efrat's home. He was a wealthy widower who loaned money with interest to merchants, shopkeepers and just Jews, with the help of speculators who always came and left his house. The man was wise, involved with people and loved to talk about daily affairs. He was cynical in his conversation and also in his habit. He only walked in his underwear at home and sometimes appeared the same way outside to oversee his vast property that included a large number of stores in the middle of the market. During the emergency years of the revolution the lenders, and the borrowers alike, were impoverished, meaning, they were left without their pants...

I, and my dear friend Eliyahu Charnyi, were frequent visitors to his home. I taught Hebrew to his daughters and Charnyi, the wise and witty, was a friend of the family. That strict old man loved to talk to us. His daughters have long since reached adulthood and the amount of their clothing grew from year to year. The weapons, and the seal of self defense, were buried in the large cupboards, in bedding and stacks of embroidery and lace. Thanks to our friends, Rebecca and Rachel Efrat, no one could think, and no police officer could guess, where the weapons were hidden.

In 1921, during the hunger years in Russia, Rachel Efrat died of starvation in Petrograd. Rivka Efrat, who immigrated to Israel, told me that after I left Slutsk, Eliyahu Charnyi moved the weapons to another hiding place with the help of a number of female members.

[Page 58]

Three Encounters
(In the presence of "*Poalei Zion*" and the "Bund")

by Dr. Aaron Domnitz

Translated by Sara Mages

It was at the beginning of the winter, when I was a student at Yeshivat R' Nehemiah. Beit HaMidrash of R' Issar (R' Issarkes Shul), where the yeshiva was housed, was located near Synagogues Square (*Der Shul Hoiyf*). Houses of worship, and various Batei Midrash, concentrated there. It was the public center of Jewish Slutsk. The sound of Torah emerged from all the synagogues. In every house of worship were young men who "studied alone" ("*Gelernt far zich*") and prepared for ordination. Boys, age eleven and above, flocked to the permanent yeshivot, most from the small towns near Slutsk. Among them were also from Babruysk, Mazyr and others. All of them ate by "days," meaning: a regular day every week on the table of a particular homeowner. Sometimes, a homeowner also housed yeshiva students in his apartment, but for the most part they slept on hard benches in Beit HaMidrash.

Once, a rumor spread that there was a thief among the yeshiva students. It was discovered that a pillow and a blanket had been stolen from one of the boys. Also, a food package disappeared to one and to the other - a shirt for the Sabbath. The boys didn't know what to do and the concern encircled all Batei HaMidrash. In their grief, everyone began to suspect his neighbor and followed him. One evening, after "*Ma'arive*" prayer, a boy burst into R' Isarka's Beit Midrash and announced that the thief had been caught near the Butchers' Synagogue. Many burst out, I was slightly delayed. I remembered the stories that when the farmers in the village caught a thief, they beat him to death. I couldn't restrain myself. I went out. The boys ran and I among them. A horrific sight was revealed to me - a youth was lying on the ground, the boys were beating him and he screamed and shouted for help: Take pity of me! I raised my voice. "Enough! Leave him alone! To my surprise, they listened to me and released him. When the thief got to his feet, he straightened up, looked around, stared at his rescuer as his face expressed rage and hatred, and left.

He was from my hometown, a friend of mine from my youth in Romanova, the blacksmith's son. We studied Hebrew and the beginning of the Chumash in the same *heder*. He was seven at the time and didn't know his verse at the end of the week, and I was five and a half years old and was well versed in it. At the teacher's command I had to slap his cheek, as was the custom of those days, and he took revenge on me after that. When we left the *heder* I complained to my mother, with abundance of tears, that blacksmith's son is beating me.

Years later we met again in Slutsk, and what a big change that was: I am a student of R' Nehemiah in the upper class, and he steals the food and the meager bedding of the yeshiva boys.

Seven years have passed, and what are they in the life of the individual? Seemingly, there are also many changes from the age of twelve to nineteen, and even more so, during the years of the first revolution in Russia that its echoes reached the remote cities of White Russia.

In Slutsk, and its neighboring towns, the youth awoke to action. I went through adolescence in Minsk where I lived for five years. I was involved in the youth movement circles that sprang up in the Jewish street: Zionism, Socialism and Socialist Zionism. I joined "*Poalei Zion*" and also knew the Bund'aim [members of the "Bund"]. Among them I had many acquaintances, my schoolmates from the yeshivot. We spent days and nights debating: "which is better, Zionism or Socialism? Sometimes, the personal interaction between the opponents increased. There have been many instances where individuals have gone from party to party without a conscience. There was, indeed, a feeling of confusion in the hearts, rushing around between idea and emotion, a deliberation in the soul that was caught between two authorities. But, the mutual hatred, which was discovered later and turned former friends into enemies, was still missing.

When I came to Slutsk in 1905, I found in it almost everything that was in the big city, but on a small scale - youth movements of all the rebellious parties, with their flags and slogans, but something was missing in them. Instead of holiness, idealism and youthful purity, I found here Insolence, bullying and ugly party quarrel. Instead of idea, the fist and the violence dominated. *"Poalei Zion"* got off the stage, split, disintegrated and was eliminated. The Zionist Socialist Party in Russia (S.S.), and its platform, inherited their place: just territory, but not Eretz Yisrael and socialism in the entire world. The territory is needed for the realization of socialism, the Jews will become proletarians and in this way the socialist redemption would come.

And the Bund'aim? They ruled the street, waved flags, demonstrated slogans and showed their strong arm. The "Bund*"* became a mass movement. Already then I have discovered in them the buds of contempt for the "intelligent," the dreamers and the theorists. I no longer recognized my Slutsk the quiet and humble, lawlessness took over its streets.

In those days a rumor spread in Slutsk that the villagers in the area were planning to come to the city and conduct a pogrom. It was told, that unknown people were wandering in the villages and inciting the crowds to gather on market day, to attack and rob. Self defence was organized. There were two separate organizations, the "Bund" and the Zionist Socialist Party. Out of my opposition to the Zionist Socialist Party, I signed up for the "Bund" defense organization. The center gave an order to all registrants to come at midnight to a secret meeting at the Great Beit Midrash. I felt as if I was desecrating a holy place. Indeed, I already abandoned Batei Midrash as a place of study, but to come in secret in the middle of the night to the Great Beit Midrash, which I knew in its greatness, and attend a socialist meeting, was to my dismay.

I came. The building was full. Speaker after a speaker climbed on the stage, spoke against the Czar, the police, the rich, and defamed Zionism, the "backward country" and the dead language. It was a typical "Bund" meeting. The defence matter was not mentioned at all. A knock on the door was heard. Those standing on guard opened it slightly, observed, exchanged words between them and let the man in. It was the head *shamash*: who knew nothing about the meeting. The *shamash* [beadle] stood at the door, alarmed and amazed and asking: What is going on here? - "Be silent, don't interrupt." - "I do not obey your commend. I am in charge of this place and not you" - the *shamash* scolded and his lips trembled - "I'll call the police!" As he turned to leave, those standing on guards held him back, threatened with a gun in front of his face, sat him on a chair and warned him that if he kept silent nothing bad would happen to him. The *shamash* understood and obeyed. He murmured softly:

[Page 59]

"Who would have thought? ... I know many of them. They are the sons of important homeowners. Are they also among them? Indeed, a new and insolent generation has risen."

A surprising incident occurred during the meeting. One of the speakers got on the stage bareheaded. The *shamash* jumped out of his seat, as if he had been beaten by a snake, and shouted: it's not possible by any means, you can shoot me, I will not allow to turn Beit HaMidrash into a cloister!! A commotion broke out. There was a danger that the noise would be heard outside. Two of the leader's bodyguards leapt off the stage with clubs in their hands to silence him. One intended to strike a blow on the *shamash*'s head. In the blink of an eye I held his hand to prevent it. Meanwhile, the chairman ordered in a commanding voice: don't strike! Quiet! The violent man lowered his arm, looked at the chairman and also at me, we knew each other: the blacksmith's son from Romanova, "my friend" from the Chumash *heder*... Now he is a member of the "Bund" and his weapon - a strong club to defend the revolution with it.

In anger these words came out of his mouth: "You are also here? You rotten intelligent! Come. Let us confront each other." I haven't seen him since.

These are my three encounters with him. That same winter I left Slutsk and Russia. I immigrated to America. Occasionally thoughts rise to my heart. Maybe a fourth meeting would have taken place during the October Revolution. He - armed and marching as the ruler of the *Tsheke* [prison], and I - a prisoner of Zion in the cellar, in the depths of that same building, waiting for further investigations and tortures by the rulers of the holy proletarian revolution.

Chills attack me from the fourth imaginary meeting that did not take place.

[Page 59]

"*Tzeirei Zion*"

by Noah

Translated by Sara Mages

The General Zionist Association, which was headed by the affluent Zionist, Leibush Gutzeit, existed, and continued its activities, until 1913. The Zionist activity was expressed in the sale of the Jewish National Fund stamps, shares of the Colonial Bank, the placing of bowls on Yom Kippur eve in the synagogues to raise funds for Eretz Yisrael on behalf of "*Hovevei Zion,*" conducting balls and lectures with Zionist and national content.

Since Gutzeit was known to the police as a man of great personality, it did not pay attention to the nature of the Zionist work and sometimes also turned a blind eye.

From among the well known Zionists in the city were: the slaughterer R' Alter Marschak, a learned Jew, intelligent and a lover of the Hebrew language in all his soul, the teachers Hazanovitsh, Shveydl, Gutzeit, and also the drug store owners Karmin and Shaykevitsh, Chipchin, the elderly Faynberg the owner of the flour mill and others.

However, at the beginning of 1913

"*Tzeirei Zion*" in Slutsk, 1914

1) Moshe Brahon, 2) Dvora Epshteyn, 3) Musia Harcavi, 4)... 5) Masha Epshteyn, 6) Shmaryaho Brahon, 7) Shkolnik, 8)... 9) Nachum Chinitz, 10) Moma Lashovsky,

11) Trasova, 12) Z. Radunsky

a group of "*Tzeirei Zion*" began to organize. They set and marked for themselves an independent and responsible work: to get closer to the high school students, put them under the wings of Zionism, and create small classes for Zionism, Hebrew and lectures. In order not to get the attention of the police there were five to eight young people in each class. They read, discussed and argued. In addition, certain activities also took place in various places in the city.

The center of activity was in Shpilkin's house on Podblenya Street. This house was completely imbued with a Hebrew and Zionist spirit, and a great person lived there - R' Ben-Zion Shpilkin, son-in-law of the well known *tzadik,* R' Rafael Yosel. He was a scriber, a modest man who served as a *shamash* in the tailors' Beit Midrash. His wife was righteous, modest and kindhearted.

His son, Avraham Yitzchak Shpilkin (A.Y.S) was a scriber like his father. He read a lot and was a humble man. He undertook the Zionist activity and his apartment served as a center for fertile work. Papers and circulars were destroyed immediately after they were received. One evening the house was surrounded and the police conducted a thorough search. After a vigorous investigation all those gathered were released for lack of evidence.

The police eye watched and followed. Once, an emissary of *"Tzeirei Zion"* came from Vilna and, in order to talk with most of the young member, it was decided to gather behind the city in the *"Syolka."* There, on the lawn, lay about sixty young men and women and in the center, the emissary, an educated young man and an enthusiastic Zionist. His words were brief and a plan of action was proposed. In the meantime, one of the members noticed a policeman approaching. All the pieces of paper were carefully destroyed and hidden and, therefore, the gatherers were not surprised when the police company appeared. They were surrounded and asked, why did you come to this place? It was explained to them that the day was a holiday and a trip was arranged for this occasion.

Indeed, the answer was unsatisfactory, but since nothing illegal was found - the gatherers were released and only two had to appear at the police station for a certain period of time.

On 20 Tamuz we, about 15 people, gathered at the home of the member Berkovitch. A female member recited the poem "Stile Alive." A few members spoke briefly and read from Herzl's writings.

Active at that time were: the sons of the well known dentist, Dr. Epshteyn, his daughter Dunia (a doctor) and his son Sasha a student from Petersburg, Schmeril

[Page 60]

Noah Goldberg, Tzvi Razarn, Tarasova, Chaya Rachel, H.M. Apelsin, Shpilkin and Chinitz.

In this manner the work continued in the underground until 1916. Speakers, who gave public lectures in Russian on well-known topics, were brought in. Dr. D. Pasmanik, the student Natan Greenblat from Minsk, Dr. Alexander Goldstein and Bistritzky (Agmon).

A group of *"Tzeirei Zion"* in Slutsk

The days were difficult in the city and, since it was near the front, it was flooded with refugees. Many Jews were accused of espionage, a matter that caused a greater impact and prepared the hearts for a Zionist and national spirit.

Many of the Jewish soldiers at the front were eager for a Hebrew word and a lecture. Even though the subjects were literary - there was in them kind of a power of speech and longing for something hidden and out of sight. This discontent was expressed, in all its validity, at the outbreak of the revolution against the Tsarist rule.

"*Tzeirei Zion*" participated in first procession. They gathered around the anonymous soldier (\member of "*Tzeirei Zion*"), who proudly carried and waved a blue and white flag on which was written, in Hebrew and Russian, "Land and Freedom."

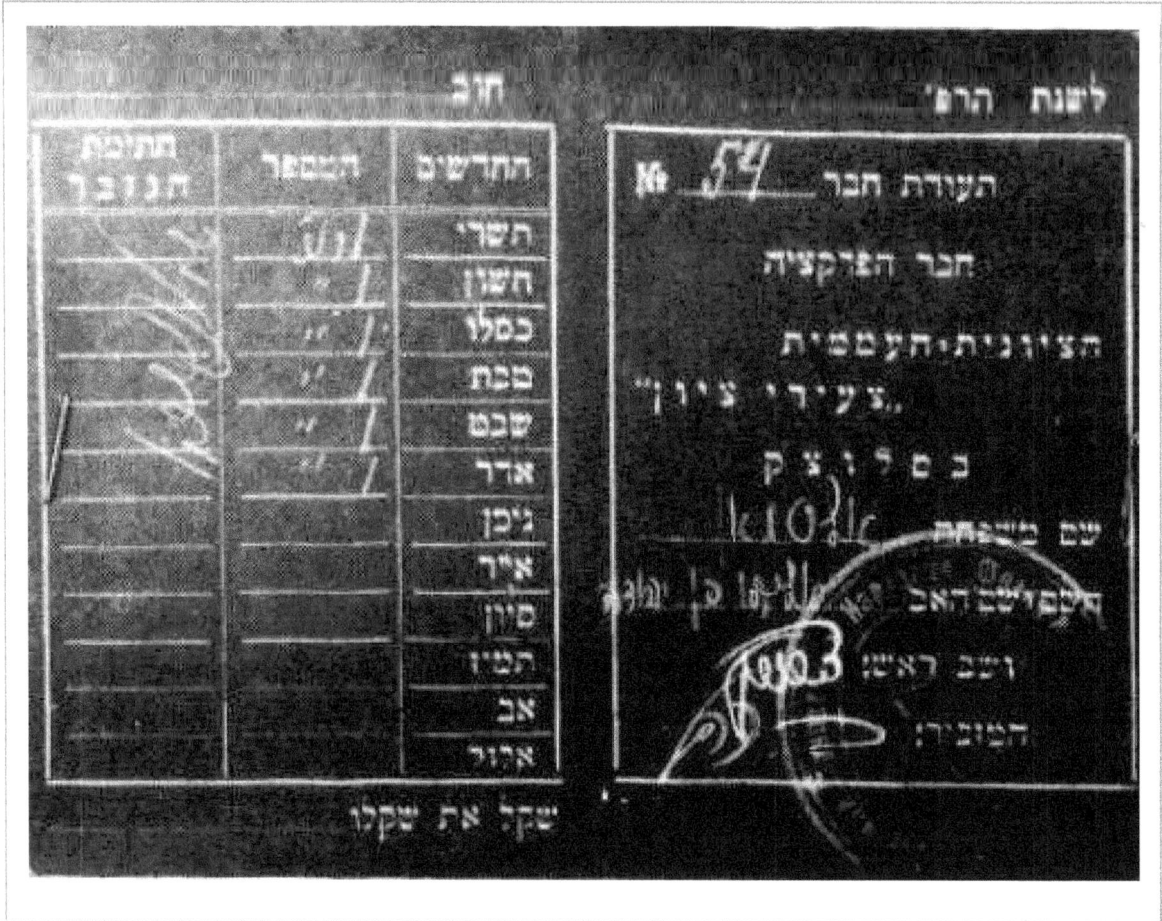

Membership card for *"Tzeirei Zion"*

"Tzeirei Zion" meetings were held during the German occupation, but it was necessary to give advance notice of their content and trend. Among the German soldiers were also Zionist Jews who wanted to vent their longing to Zion. Sometimes it was necessary to be careful and make sure that the soldier was not a spy.

The active members at that time were: Landa, Shpilkin, Chipchin, the Harkavi brothers, the son of Gutzeit Yasha, Gabai who was a passionate Zionist, Musya Harkavi, Avraham Tshernikhov, A.Y. Nozick and Altman.

With the Polish occupation in 1919, the Poles restricted the freedom of action of the Zionist activists.

Despite everything, "Tarbut" school was opened and various meetings were held in the school hall. Various activities were conducted under special permits. In 1920, groups of young people still managed to leave Slutsk and immigrate to Israel.

With the signing of the Peace of Riga, the Poles had to leave Slutsk and upon their withdrawal dozens of *"Tzeirei Zion"* members were able to move to Poland. Some immigrated to Israel and some to the United States.

"Tzeirei Zion" in Slutsk , 1917

First row (on the floor, right to left): 1) Shalom Shpilkin, 2) Eliyahu Altman, 3) Dov Sheptel, 4) Ashka Lev.
Second row (seating): 1) Arnbaum, 2) Avraham Tshernikhov, 3) Avraham Yitzchak Shpilkin, 4) Mordechai Melinski 5) Moshe Harkavi, 6) Motya Pehmer-Melamed.
Third row (standing): 1) Lipa Yom-Tov Gabai, 2) Ester Rachel Tarasov, 3) Musya Harkavi-Katznelson, 4)... 5) Chaim Moshe Apelson, 6) Yisrael Noah Goldberg, 7) David Neimark, 8) Shmaryaho Brahon, 9) Fanya Krepkh

[Page 61]

Movements and Parties

by Zvi HaGivati

Translated by Mira Eckhaus

The Zionist Youth in the Underground

Slutsk - a provincial city in White Russia. Known all over Russia for its fine fruits, which earned its reputation; Immersed in the summer in greenery, in the autumn and the spring - in mud and in the winter - in snow. City - mostly Jewish, famous in the "Reformed" Cheder, in its Rabbis and in the great Yeshiva, that many from the near and far surroundings come to learn in it. A city with a juicy and vibrant Jewish community.

With the February revolution and with the beginning of the October revolution, the Zionist parties began to develop in it: "Tze'irei Zion" (Zion Youth), General Zionists, Mizrahi, Poalei Zion. The Bond party was fighting Zionism, but the Zionist spirit in the city was strong and conquered hearts, and had an impact not only among the adults, but among the youth and children as well

These days were very good days for the Zionist movement, which flourished and prospered. The restrictions and decrees against the Jews have been abolished, the percentage norm in schools has been abolished, the "living area" has been abolished. The Jews were equal in their rights with all the residents of Russia. The removal of all the restrictions and decrees and the freedom, made everyone enthusiastic. Bold dreams, it seems, are on the verge of coming true. Zionist Conferences, the gathering of the Jewish Communities in White Russia in Minsk. Soul-stirring news came from afar: the Balfour Declaration, the Jewish High Commissioner in Israel, every Jewish soul elevated.

However, the days of glory did not last long. The sky darkened over Russia in general and the Jews in particular. The civil war broke out. The Jews were caught in the middle and suffered a lot.

With the victory of the Bolsheviks, the ax was waved on Zionism. It was clear that the roots of the Hebrew spirit would be eliminated and destroyed. Therefore, the Zionist movement in 1920, when White Russia was under the rule of the Poles, was very active and feverish action was carried out. Many members of "Tze'irei Zion" (Zion Youth), among them a group of university students, left Slutsk and traveled to Warsaw, in order to immigrate to Israel, because they knew that when the Poles withdrew from the city and the Bolsheviks return, the borders would be closed and they would not be allowed to leave Russia.

And indeed, with the return of the Bolsheviks to White Russia, the major Zionist parties ceased their operation and the initiative passed to the youth, who were educated on the principles of the Zionism and the Hebrew language.

This youth did great things and sacrificed his life for the fight with the almighty government.

* * *

Slutsk excelled in its Zionist and Hebrew work. It had 2 "Reformed Cheders", where the teaching method was learning Hebrew in Hebrew and which were conducted by the best Hebrew teachers. In addition to the "Reformed Cheder" there were also teachers for private lessons in Hebrew. The teachers were kind and loved by the students. In the summer, at every opportunity, on Lag Ba'Omer, on Shavuot, the students would go out with their teachers outside the city, to the countryside, a place of meadows and forests. There everything was allowed. The young teachers, full of excitement, competed in running with the students, had fun with them, played various games. And suddenly, everything went silent, the noise and commotion died down. The teacher told them about the Land of Israel, about the heroes of the Jews, about different periods in the history of the Jewish people. The teacher cultivated love for the people, for the spiritual assets, for the ancient language. And the children's eyes, which just sparkled in mischief, now shined in a completely different light. They were fascinated, their hearts were receptive and they listen attentively to the teacher.

Indeed, the seed was sown, tamed and planted deep, deep in the soul of this group of children. Later, as the children matured, the seed sprouted, were fruitful and prospered. This group organized the Children's Organization, "Pirchei Zion" (Flowers of Zion). This children's organization organizes many children and they engaged in various activities: founding a library, writing essays, reading books and discussing their content, making connections with the adults of "Tze'irei Zion" (Zion Youth), helping in the election process, inviting lecturers on various topics, develop action for the KKL (Jewish National Fund), participate in collecting funds on film day, organize plays.

In particular, one play is remembered, which was presented in the municipal theater, called "Musar Na'ar Ra" (Bad boy morals), which was composed by the Hebrew teacher, who was also the director of the "Reformed Cheder", M. Hazanowitz. The play was very successful. It brought together a large audience from all classes and strata, who came to watch it. There was thunderous applause for the young actors and it had a great echo in the city.

The "Pirchei Zion" (Flowers of Zion) Association extended and had branches. Many children joined the association. It is true that many of them, when they grew up, got rid from all their childhood activities and turned their backs on them, and turned to foreign ways, but this group of children, whose members were connected to each other from a very young age, who studied together in the "Reformed Cheder", founded together the "Pirchei Zion" (Flowers of Zion) Association, entered together to the Russian schools - the gymnasium and the trade school - accepted Zionism in an instinctive manner and imbibed of its origins. No frenetic wind had the power to shake it and divert it from its path. It remained loyal to Zionism all the time despite all the strong temptations, even when the misleading and deceptive light of communism shone in its eyes, even when it promised a comfortable path, safe and complacent life, the life of an apprentice, the life of a student, a life that is much more worthwhile.

* * *

In 1920, after the expulsion of the Poles from White Russia and the complete victory of the Bolsheviks over the White armies, the situation in Russia became quieter and more stable. The civil war was over, the agitated spirits have calmed down, the hearts have calmed down. They began to build what was destroyed, to repair what was ruined during the world war and the civil war.

But, if Russian Jewry was sentenced to a physical extinction during the civil war, then now, a spiritual extinction was decreed for it, not from the outside, but from the inside. The Jewish Yevsektsiya was established by the Communist Party and decreed extinction of the life of the people as a nation, of any manifestation of national awakening, of any desire for a new life in the homeland that is being built. However, the Jewish youth did not remain indifferent to the life of their people and their destiny and there was a fight between the all-powerful rule and the youth.

At the beginning of Soviet rule, the Zionist movement was in a semi-legal state and was not touched. They would get permission to open clubs

[Page 62]

for various sporting actions, in which disguised Zionist work was carried out. We no longer knew malicious acts and persecution, until the Yevsektsiya began with a momentum war, with means of repression, with imprisonments and deportations.

The years 1920-1924, when military communism ended and the NAP began, were boom years for the Zionist youth movements all over Russia. Until 1924, they did not know about any deportation from it. It was only from this year onwards that they began to deport the Zionists, first to Israel and later - to Solovki, Siberia, the Urals, Kazakhstan, etc.

The Zionist movement was included among the regime's enemies, which needed to be rooted out. The Yevsektsiya raised its head and called for a holy war with Zionism, declared it as a reactionary, chauvinist, bourgeois movement, who helps and serves British imperialism and who must be fought to the bitter end.

Thus, all the Zionist organizations were disbanded and the underground period of the youth began.

The small group of the youth mentioned above, whose members were now studying in the upper classes of the Russian secondary school, brought about a complete revolution among the youth. The major parties: the General Zionists and "Tze'irei Zion" (Zion Youth), with the announcement of their ban, ceased to operate. Their members supported their families and could not risk their livelihood. However, this youth group could not sit idly by, it began to operate under underground conditions and persisted in it. They abandoned their parents' discipline, some of whom wanted their sons to go with the flow, adapt to the new life and enter the university; It aroused the embers of Zionism that was blurring; It rose up and stood at the head of the protests against the Yevsektsiya, against the Komsomol and against the communist rule.

* * *

In December 1922, an apolitical Zionist youth organization was organized under the name of "Kadima", which included studying youth and working youth, operating illegally and placing itself at the head of the Zionist campaign.

Several of the founders of "Kadima"

Sitting from right to left: 1) P. Efron, 2) Y. Ratner, 3) Zvi Hazanowitz (HaGivati)
Standing: 1) Zusha Peker, 2) Shabtai Baskin (Beit Zvi), 3) Shlomo Neikrog (Noi)

The small initiative group worked wonders and completely changed the way of life of the youth in the city and gave them a different motivation and other concepts.

It attracted to it wide circles of students and working youth. The operation was branching out and expanding. Many boys and girls joined the movement. We have taken over the archive of the "Tze'irei Zion" (Zion Youth) and from there we published all kinds of pamphlets about the Land of Israel, Zionism, various photos and postcards of the Land of Israel and of personalities in the world Zionist movement. We read the books, studied problems and also taught others, who joined the movement at a later stage. We held balls, parties, lectures, readings, raffles and different games as is customary with youth, in various members' apartments.

A group of members from the youth studying in "Tze'irei Zion" (Zion Youth), Slutsk, the year of 1918

From right to left: Shapira Aryeh, Shpilkin Shalom, Apelsin Moshe (died in Russia), Nozik Avraham (died in Tel Yosef), Winograd Aryeh, (died in Tel Aviv)

The operation was mainly concentrated in the house of Reb Alter Maharashak, which was a little far from the city center. He was a veteran Zionist, whose sons and daughters all received a Zionist education and knew Hebrew. He would greet us with a pleasant hospitality. Despite the danger, he did not object to holding gatherings and parties in his house and this house, which was full of love and warmth, was like a magnet for us and from it thin threads stretched to the hearts of the members.

We established a children's organization for children at the age of 13-14 called "Yok" – Yogand Kadima, which also brought together many children. Among them were talented children, who had a promising future. There was a lot of activity. They were very dedicated to their organization and were a loyal help for "Kadima", as the organization considered itself as one that follows the Kadima path in the future and as its heirs.

We had help, that was given by several of the older members. Azriel Nakritz was one of the founders of "Kadima" and its living spirit in the first period. One member, who studied at the university and came to Slutsk on his days off, also participated in the training. Later, another member, also a student, a member of SZ, who was loyal to its principles, explained to us about the Socialist Zionism.

We held a literary trial at Maharshak's house about Aman – the Yevsektsiya - for which we had been preparing for a long time and which was held in all the court's formalities with a prosecutor, a defense attorney, the head of the court, witnesses, etc. The trial was very successful, and it was of interest to the members. In it, it was as if we agreed and consolidated our Zionist identity.

[Page 63]

I still remember one evening, when several members of the "HaChalutz" from Bobruisk passed through Slutsk, on their way, illegally, to the Polish border, in order to immigrate to Israel. Many members gathered at Maharashak's house, where we held a party for them, sang songs, talked about the Land of Israel, our heart's desire, and we spent a long time together. We looked at them with envy: In a little while they will be in Israel. And what awaits us?

We were thirsty for any information about Israel and Jewish life, beyond the Russian region. Every piece of news, which came randomly from there, would make us happy. We sang songs from the Land of Israel: there are foxes there, there in the land of the lust of fathers, there in the land of the deer, the return of the Lord, and we also learned the Hora dancing, according to the melody: Gilu HaGlilim. We would go to the parents of the members, who traveled to Israel during the time of the Poles rule, and we drew encouragement from their letters.

The activity, as mentioned, was many and extensive: the youth organization, assemblies and conversations about Zionism, socialism, communism, about the bridge between nationalism and socialism, many debates in high school and outside with the Komsomol, the Yevsektsiya, the secret publication of a newspaper about Shapirograf, the organization of Zionist groups in various institutions. A struggle began for the souls of the Jewish youth and against communist assimilation.

This activity of ours began to anger the Yevsektsiya and the Komsomol. They realized that we would soon take over all the Jewish youth and decided to uproot the "bad one" from its root.

* * *

In August 1922, a thorough search was conducted in Shabtai Baskin's house. They searched, but did not find forbidden things. This time they had to be satisfied with a search only.

A short time later, the G.P.O. placed a siege on the houses of previously active Zionists. Former "Tze'irei Zion" (Zion Youth) activists and 4 members of the youth organization "Kadima" were banned. Unintentionally, the last three did not sleep in their houses. And this was the affair of their imprisonment.

We would carry out our activities in different places: in the parents' houses, in the rooms of relatives and friends, in the summer - in the fields and in the meadow. Reb Alter Maharshak then leased a large garden of fruit trees. We would often gather in this garden, talk and dream about the Land of Israel that we longed for. Sometimes we would also sleep in it, build a fire and sit around it, roasting potatoes and apples. That night, when the G.P.O. surrounded the Zionist houses and searches and arrests were conducted, a group of members stayed in this garden. And so, when the dawn began to break, they came running from the house of Maharashk and talked about the searches that were carried out in the city. They were also held at Maharshak, Nakritz, Baskin and at my parents' house. Since we were absent from the house, the G.P.O. soldiers remained at our houses to wait for us, and to arrest our parents if we don't return home.

We arranged a short consultation, deciding between us how to talk and what to answer in the interrogation. I came home and found a complete chaos in it. They searched every corner, to find incriminating material against me, but could not find anything in their search. The soldier looked at me strangely, he measured me from my feet to my head and blurted out: "Are you the criminal?" He thought he would see an older man and here stands a 15-year-old boy instead. I'm being led to the G.P.O. The soldier walked after me, with the machine gun aimed at me. I met acquaintances and neighbors on the street. They looked in wonder, mixed with pity and shook their heads.

17 of us were in prison. From "Kadima" - myself, Baskin, Maharshak and Nakritz. The rest were former members of "Tze'irei Zion" (Zion Youth). Anyway, there was a reason for the imprisonment of myself and the other members of "Kadima" - after all, we were activists and acted against the government, but what did they want from the older Zionists? They long ago withdrew from any action and had no organizational connection with any Zionist organizations. Indeed, apparently, they remembered their past.

Our first imprisonment was easy. They had no facts to prove our guilt. We were in prison for 3 weeks and were released.

However, the war against us was already in full force and was being conducted in a raging fury. We started to be more careful. We didn't walk the street with forbidden papers in our pockets, we learned how to avoid the eyes of spies, we acted with a serious conspiracy. Our organization became a mass, grew and expanded and finally, even, provocateurs were also discovered in it.

* * *

Our operation went beyond the borders of the city of Slutsk and began to spread in the nearby towns. Boys and girls from the same towns studied in the high school. Many of them joined our organization and when they came, on their days off from school back to their homes, they organized branches of "Kadima" in their towns. This is how the organization expanded and we were already in control of many towns: Grozovo, Kapoli, Wizna, Timkovitz, Ljuban, Pohust and Strubin.

The branches in the towns conducted their operations under our direct guidance. We sent, from time to time, members to lecture them, deliver news and give the necessary instructions. In Slutsk, a district committee of Kadima was organized, which managed all the activity in the district, often convened conferences and councils, that were composed of representatives of the branches, in which each branch gave a report about the activity of the branch and its probability of success.

The ties with the branch in Grozovo were the closest. The distance from this town to Slutsk was not large. We would go out, every once in a while, on foot, to Grozovo for meetings and talks of the branch. Sometimes all the members of the branch would go out to the fields and forests halfway to Slutsk and we would meet them there. They would arrange shifts, so that we wouldn't be caught and we would give lectures, giving the main information about the Zionist activity, about what was happening throughout Russia and a tiny bit, from what we would raise, about what was happening in Israel.

One of the most typical and visible actions was in Grozovo. The Yevsektsiya held a public trial against "the Zionist" with the composition of a jury, prosecutor and defense attorney. Members of the audience were allowed to appear as witnesses on behalf of the prosecution or the defense. We decided to use this opportunity and appear openly at the trial in defense of Zionism.

We sent Baskin and Shimon Maharashak to participate in the trial. However, the trial was postponed until the next day. They took advantage of this delay and walked to Capuli in the bitter cold, which prevailed that day, to visit there at the branch and provide information about the situation.

The next day, when the trial began, they both appeared: Baskin on behalf of the defense and Maharashak on behalf of the prosecution. As the first witness appeared

[Page 64]

Maharashak. The judges were hoping to hear real prosecution words about "the Zionist", however, they were embarrassed when they heard his fiery words when he accused the Zionist who is not a real Zionist, is not Zionist enough, and is a caricature of a Zionist. Baskin did not have time to reach his speech. The G.P.O. arrived and they were both banned. They were banned for a few weeks and then released.

Another typical visit that I remember, was when me and Baruch Lifshitz went to the town of Vizna at night. It was a harsh winter day. The cold was great. We traveled in a convoy of three sledges. Two Russian girls from a village near Vizna were riding in one sledge and we introduced ourselves as members of the Komsomol.

When we arrived to Vizna, we gathered with the members of the branch in the room of one of them. We started lecturing and finding out the topical questions. A short time later, members, who were on guard, suddenly announced that the members of the Komsomol heard about our arrival and they were following our tracks. A great danger was involved with it, because Vizna was near the border and a special license was needed to be in it.

We sneaked out of the house. They led us along winding paths, behind fences, arranged a sledge for us, and we barely made it to Slutsk.

* * *

Our Zionist activity expanded day by day. New members joined. The financial expenses also increased. Therefore, we collected membership tax. We held various raffles. We received from the members not only money, but also wheat, which was equivalent to money at the time. Collecting money only from our members was not sufficient, so we also turned to older Zionists, who were not active for a very long period but who followed our bold actions with whimsy and admiration, and collect various donations from them as well.

We had contacts with the central bureau in Minsk and we used to travel to central conferences of "Kadima". New branches appeared not only in the vicinity of Slutsk. They were also along the railroad Slutsk - Minsk: Oratsia, Sitria Dorugi, Osipovici, Holoy, Lefitz, Svislots. The action was in full scope.

We were active in the high school in its two upper classes that were called courses for general education. We developed a branched Zionist operation. Many students were attracted to our ranks. It was the glory of "Kadima", whose members were active, energetic and ready to act.

In the student assemblies, the Komsomol usually behaved as the ruler. It was enough for the Komsomol representative to announce: On behalf of the Komsomol, I offer this and that, and no one would dare to open his mouth, as it was customary at all meetings in greater Russia. And here, suddenly, students dared and announced that on behalf of a group of members who are not related to any party, they offer a counter proposal and sometimes their proposal gained a large number of votes. There were also students, who were afraid to publicly vote in favor of the proposal, which the Komsomol did not propose. But secretly they would encourage us. It is worth noting the fact that in the elections to the Otzkom (the students' committee) the members of the Komsomol were afraid that they would be defeated and their representative, Sinitzky (whom I will talk about further below) negotiated with us and suggested that Fayvel Efron should also join the Otskom.

This is how the Komsomol members realized that our action was interrupting them and their influence on the students was diminishing and they decided to take vigorous measures against us.

Then came the great purge and all our active members were expelled from the school as an undesirable element under the excuse that they were, so to speak, of bourgeois origin. Indeed, some students, who proved their proletarian origin, were accepted back, but many were expelled altogether and had to continue their studies in other cities.

* * *

After the first imprisonment in 1922, a series of imprisonments began from time to time. In November of that year Baskin was arrested and taken to Minsk. He was accompanied by a soldier from the army of the G.P.O. Our members Ratner and Skaklasky traveled with him on the same train. They befriended the soldier, and he fulfilled all their requests. In Osipovici, during the long waiting time, everyone went down with the soldier to the house of one of our members and the soldier even gave his rifle to one of the members.

This imprisonment did not last long and after an interrogation with one of the members in Minsk, Baskin was released.

Our action at that time reached its peak. The center of "Kadima" was in Minsk and was called C. B. (Central Bureau). Once in a while we would meet with the members in Minsk, at the councils and conferences of "Kadima". However, the operation that was conducted by the Central Bureau did not satisfy us, the members from Slutsk. We were full of energy and a strong desire to act. We had a lot of organizational power. We organized many branches in the towns. We acquired a lot of experience. The operation of the Central Bureau was too weak in our opinion. We demanded to transfer the center to Slutsk, as well as the publication of the central newspaper on behalf of "Kadima".

In this regard, members of the Central Bureau visited Slutsk several times to clear the atmosphere between us. At the end, the central journal of "Kadima" was transferred to Slutsk and we edited and printed it. 7 members were elected to the Central Bureau: 3 from Minsk, 3 from Slutsk and 1 from the nearby branches, I think from Osipovici.

* * *

And here is a sensation in Slutsk. On March 12, 1923, 5 members were arrested by the G.P.O.: Nakritz, Lifshitz, Skaklasky, Hazanovitz and Karina Maharashak, while they were printing the newspaper of the movement "Kadima". This was, of course, a "big deal" for the G.P.O. and the Yevsektsiya, and they lunged on us, as if they had found a big treasure. We were arrested, interrogated, and sent to Minsk. The trial day in Minsk had already been set, but Nakritz who then was serving in the Red Army could not be released and come. Finally, it was decided to hold the trial in Slutsk, and not just a trial, but a process. We have pledged not to leave Slutsk until the trial and in the meantime, we were released.

Of course, during our imprisonment the action continued, and we, when we were temporary released, returned immediately back to work. Before the trial, we decided to call a large gathering of members and say goodbye to them, because we feared that the punishment that is expecting us is severe. The meeting was held at the edge of the city, at the house of a relative of our friend. The room was too narrow to contain all the members, who sat crowded and listened to the farewell words.

[Page 65]

Suddenly beeps and whistles were heard outside. We didn't have time to come to our senses when the two G.P.O. soldiers broke into the apartment. We were amazed. Admittedly, among the present were members that the G.P.O. knew them as active Zionists, but most of the members were not known as Zionists. They were not suspects and their revelations threatened them with serious consequences. The people of the G.P.O. began to register the members and suddenly one of the members was heard calling to the soldier: please do not address me in the present tense, and in Yiddish: Comrade do not be afraid, give false addresses and names. They won't arrest all of us, we are too many and they are only two".

The compressed atmosphere dissipated. The tension was over. The young members cheered up. As a reply to the questions of the soldiers, names from the Haftarah were given: Feinfinkelkroit, Wolkenkratzer, Lamaffernstein, etc. Here and there a laughter was heard as a response to the names invented.

The soldiers wrote down the names and addresses that they had given them, and when they realized that they would not be able to take over all those gathered, they released them. Us, the ones who were awaiting the trial, they knew personally and there was no point in imprisoning us, when, in a few days, we will stand trial,

All the Yevsektsiya forces were recruited for our process. One of the judges was Avraham Yaakov the cheese maker, who was known for his virulence that permeated everything that was related to Zionism. The prosecutor was Shelchovitz, the secretary of the professional associations and on the bench of the accused were sitting boys and a girl aged 16-19. Indeed, all this honor was given to them.

And I was sitting on the bench of the defendants and looking at the crowd of people that was filling the great hall. My gaze reviewed the audience and tried to find sympathy for us. Our groups of members were scattered in several places. Their faces reflected anxiety for our fate, in the faces of some of them I read admiration for us, love and sympathy. But the majority of the public was cold, indifferent, expressing their agreement to the accusations by clapping their hands – was it out of true agreement, or out of indifference, servitude and stagnation, out of the habit of obeying whatever the government says?

And the prosecutor thundered in his speech and poured out all his anger and wrath on us, and not on us only, but on Zionism as a whole. And he accused the twelve sections of the counter-revolution; And the twelfth section was the most terrible crime: reviving a dead language, that was destined to extinction, like the Latin language, a language that is religious, mystical and counter-revolutionary.

And I listened to the words of the prosecutor and thought: "how can people say so many stupid words? Did the hatred, stupidity and the hardness of the heart grow so much? Will these people be able to overcome us and defeat us? No way! If we will be punished - others will come in our place and the war will continue and the chain will not be broken".

A verdict was issued: three were released due to their young age and they were - Lifshitz, Skaklasky and Hazanovitz; Karina Maharashak was sentenced to a year of probation; Nakritz was sentenced to a year in prison.

Sometime after the trial, ideological debates began in "Kadima". In Russia, there were three apolitical youth organizations: the "Hachaver" - in Great Russia, the "Histadrut" - in Ukraine and "Kadima" - in White Russia. A proposal was offered to unite all these three organizations into one apolitical organization in the name I.W.O.S.M. On the other hand, the question of the politicization of the youth organizations and their party affiliation was presented.

We debated this question a lot. At the beginning, we had a tendency to unite with I.W.O.S.M. and Fayvel Efron came to Moscow to carry out this unification, where he met with the late Misha Efrat, one of the active members, who was one of the founders of "Kadima" in Slutsk, who made all the efforts regarding the unification of Kadima union with one youth organization, which had split from the "Hachaver", and was named A.S.Y.P. (Yidishar Socialistishar Yogand Perain) and sent special letters to various members in Slutsk.

Efron met with the members of the center of A.S.Y.P. and the unification with I.W.O.S.M. was postponed for now. It should be noted that in a political sense the members of Slutsk were very close to the organization A.S.Y.P. and the unification with it captivated many members.

The unrest all over "Kadima" in White Russia was great. The question that was raised was whether the apoliticality of the youth should be maintained and the organization should be unified with the I.W.O.S.M. and by this to establish a large and extensive Zionist youth organization, whose power will be great, or to define the movement as political and accept the principles of A.S.Y.P.

In this regard there were disputes, there were differences of opinion and finally a conference was called in Minsk and there was a division. Some members joined the I.W.O.S.M. and most of the members joined.

A.S.Y.P. A branch of A.S.Y.P. was founded in Minsk and it began to develop a wide operation in the close area. "Kadima" in Slutsk and all the branches in the towns in its entire district, joined A.S.Y.P.

In March 1924, mass imprisonments began among Zionists throughout Russia and even in Slutsk. The people of the G.P.O. went from house to house in the city and banned active members as well as ordinary members. One day before all the prisons, I was banned and my prisons were in somewhat unusual conditions. I went to the train station, at the edge of the city, to deliver a letter to the center of A.S.Y.P., to the father of one of our members, who went to Moscow. The cash register was in a small, narrow box. I went in there and handed over the letter. And here I see two soldiers from the G.P.O stand by the door. I understood what it meant for me. My mind was working hard on how to get out of this trouble. Suddenly I saw that one of the soldiers made a movement and moved a little to the side of the door. I immediately exercised the opportunity. I leapt through the opening and like an arrow from a bow I ran in the direction of the city.

The soldiers chased after me shouting: "Stand up, we'll shoot you". But I trusted that they wouldn't shoot in the crowd that was at the station. The railroad was already behind me. The soldiers were at a large distance from me. I ran forward and I thought I've already been saved, and here in front of me I saw a friend from school, with whom I studied for many years in the same department, Haim Sinitzky, the representative of the Komsomol in the high school. He stretched out a leg. I failed and fell to the ground. He attacked me and I wrestled with him. In the meantime, the soldiers arrived and caught me.

I was put in a barrack at the train station. My first thought was how to get rid of the illegal substance, which I carried with me. Luckily, they left me alone in the room for a moment and I immediately used it and stuffed all the papers into the cracks in the walls of the barrack.

They brought me to the prison and put me in a cell. I was already used to

[Page 66]

prisons and I was not so depressed. And here the next day I heard familiar voices in the prison yard. I looked through the window and saw that almost half of the members from the branch were in prison. Indeed, that night the people of the G.P.O. went for hunting, they went, according to well-known addresses and banned many members.

All the members were kept together in one room, while I was kept separately. Of course, I found tricks on how to communicate with them and pass them notes. I was already a "veteran" and used to prisons and knew all the tricks. For a week we were all in the prison in Slutsk and after that we were sent to Minsk to the G.P.O. Only when we left the prison, at the train station, I was joined to the rest of the members and since then we have not been separated. On the way, at the various train stations, members from different branches joined us and our number increased. That's how we arrived in Minsk and were brought to the G.P.O.

The building of the G.P.O was a huge building and all the prisoners, including me, were locked in the big basement. The cell I was sitting in was for 15 people. The window was at the top, near the ceiling, and was made of iron grating. I used to lie curled in the corner, on the hard plank, among the other members of the cell, pondering: what is happening now outside the prison? What are the other members doing? How is the work going on in the organization? And you wait impatiently for them to call you for interrogation - maybe you will know a little about their fate.

And the interrogation is also conducted in a unique way: they are not satisfied with daytime interrogation, but also interrogate at night. In the middle of your heavy sleep, you feel a hand that shakes you and you hear a rude voice: "to interrogation"! And you jump up from your bed confused: where, for which interrogation, for what, which room is it here, which soldier? But the bitter reality slaps you in the face. In silence you get dressed, wrap yourself in a coat and leave the cell with the soldier.

Night. Darkness. A cold attack you. Quiet is everywhere. And you leave the basement to the inner courtyard. The building of the G.P.O. towering before you in all its height. And you start going up with the soldier to the first, second, third floor, you go forward, and the soldier with the rifle is behind you. And he commands you: "to the right, to the left, forward, to the side". And you open a door and close a door. Electric lamps are lit on the stairs and the rooms in a dark light, darkness, you meet no one. And you go and go, from room to room, from floor to floor, and there is no end to this walk. A shivering attack you, you are cold. And you imagine what kind of meeting you will have with the interrogator, and you feel bad and bitter. And you are attacked by the desire to get out of the prison at any cost and be free... You barely control your nerves, get over yourself, wrap yourself in the coat and keep walking on (this whole walk in the middle of the night, on a long and complicated road is just a ploy of the G.P.O. to scare the prisoner). But here we come to a door on the fifth floor. The soldier puts his rifle in the corner, lights a cigarette and orders you to knock on the door. With all the courage left in you, you knock on the door.

An answer is heard: "Come in". You open the door and enter. A large and spacious room. In one corner stands a small table, next to it are two chairs. Above the table descends an electric lamp with a green marble. The room is half dark. I go to the table.

The interrogator sits there, as if he doesn't notice me at all. I sit in front of him and remain silent. He is also silent. Suddenly he raises his head, as if he just noticed my presence and greets me with a sneer. The interrogation begins. The questions are common, and so are the answers. He tries to complicate me, asking me a lot of relevant and irrelevant questions; Wants me to tell him the names of members; Wants to put me in an iron circle, from which I cannot get out; Weaving thin, invisible spider webs around me and I answer him, carefully, tearing his webs, severing the tuber; All my senses are alert, tensed. We play the cat and mouse game. If there is a question that I have difficulty answering, I say: "I don't know". And when my answer does not satisfy him, I add: "It may be look as if my words appear to be incorrect; but this is so, this is a fact".

At first, the interrogator behaves politely, coaxing me, seducing me, promising to release me, complimenting me, as if he spared me, that I am so young and have to sit in prison, and how I, who am of proletarian origin, can be a counter-revolutionary; He suggests that I move to the Komsomol, go to work for the G.P.O. When he sees that the temptations are not useful, he begins to get angry, takes out papers from the drawer in the middle of the interrogation, as if these papers contained all my fate; Suddenly runs to the other side of the room, rings the phone and comes back to me with a triumphant expression on his face. Finally, he takes out a gun and places it on the table. He gets more and more excited, his face turns red, his voice is irritating. He starts threatening to put me in prison forever, to send me to Siberia, to Solovki, to kill me like a dog. Finally, he is unable to stop himself, and all red with anger, he begins to curse in crude Russian slurs. When I ask him to be more polite and be careful with his language, he attacks me with clenched fists, starts shaking me with the chair, grabs the gun, puts it in front of my temple and shouts: I'll shoot you soon, son of a bitch!" A shout erupted from my throat: Put down your hands, barbarian, Huni!" The interrogator looked at me with intense hatred, breathed heavily and ordered me to leave the room.

I was all shocked and left. The soldier who was waiting for me in the corridor looked at me curiously and led me back, but not to the previous cell. As a punishment the interrogator sent me to the terrible cell of the G.P.O., to the single cell No. 6, which was considered by all the prisoners as a monster...

And so, days and nights went on, turning into weeks and months, everything was sickening. Every day prisoners were taken out and new ones were put in their place, and only we were not touched. Every once in a while, they called us for an interrogation, repeating the same questions; Tempting and threatening again - and you returned to the prison, heartbroken, your nerves were on the edge, tensed; A light touch and they will explode. You go to the window and look impatiently at the sky. Oh, the sky, the sun, the freedom!... How you long to see them again! Is it true that there are people who walk freely, who can do whatever they want, that no damn soldier follow them everywhere; People who breathe the smell of the fields, the fresh air?.. And the nights and days pass. And all the days have one form and one tone... We have been sitting in prisons for about six months, and the end is not seen in the horizon. And it was annoying, just to sit there, without a trial. And a desire arose in us

[Page 67]

to do some bold thing, to take drastic measures, in order to force the interrogator to put an end to our unknown situation. Let them send us wherever they want, provided that they do not continue to torture us with this state of ignorance.

Seeing that the imprisonment continues and has no end, we went on a hunger strike, which lasted 4 days, demanding to have our interrogation intensified.

The strike was successful and the interrogation was over.

We were informed of the verdict:

Deportation for three years to the Urals, or deportation to Israel. We stood amazed and confused. Deportation to Israel or to the Urals? To the Land of Israel! Even in our wildest dreams we could not dream that we could be so soon in the Land of Israel. Because it was impossible to leave Russia, and they had not yet deported people to the Land of Israel. These were the first deportations to the Land of Israel. And the interrogator presents us with a dilemma: the Land of Israel or Ural! Well, this was the end of working underground, of the prisons, of running from the G.P.O... we go to Eretz Israel!

I was deported from Russia. And as I stood on the deck of the sailing ship and looked at the shores that were getting farther and farther away from me, my heart contracted: you, the great and wide Russia. You expelled me as a despicable child, why, then, was I imposed to suckle, to be feed on your culture, that is foreign to me at its core, for so many years?

Members of Kadima and A.S.Y.P., the first to be deported to Israel from Slutsk

From right to left: Israel Ratner, Zvi Hazanovich (HaGivati), Nakritz Azriel (Shalev), Lifshitz Baruch, Shimon Maharshak

Why this tragic duality in my fate. The fate of a young Jew, to absorb and digest foreign culture and education? Why did I have to draw from a foreign country, from springs not mine, why?

The Trial of the Zionist Youth

by Azriel Nekritz

Translated by Sara Mages

At the beginning of 1922, a Zionist youth organization called "*Kadima*," that I was among its organizers and instructors, was established in Slutsk. This organization developed and expanded. One of its activities was the publication of the central newspaper of the entire movement, also called "*Kadima*."

On 12 March 1923, one of the newspaper's issues was printed in my house. Suddenly, in the middle of the printing, the men of the GPU[1] burst into my house (later we learned that one of the neighbors informed us), arrested the printers - four male members and one female member - and confiscated all the material.

Members of "*Kadima*" in Slutsk who were tried in November 1923

1) Azriel Nekritz (Shelef), 2) Baruch Lifshits, 3) Yehudah Skakolsky, 4) Krayna Maharshak-Baskin (Beit-Tzvi), 5) Tzvi Hazanovitsh (Hagivati)

The GPU arrested us and four days later transferred us to Minsk. Along the way, we agreed that during the interrogation the members, who were young in age, would lay all the blame in regards to the newspaper on me, and I will answer all the questions that directly concern me. And indeed, so it was during our interrogation and we all stood the test.

At the end of the investigation we were told that we would have to stand trial, we will be released until the trial out of a commitment on our part not to leave Slutsk without a permit from the GPU. I had to report to the army to which I was drafted prior to imprisonment.

Our indictment contained two clauses: clause 72 of the criminal code which dealt with the ownership, preparation and distribution of illegal literature, and clause 83 which dealt with incitement and the seeding of international animosity. After a while they added to me, the adult among the prisoners, another clause - disrespect for the Yevsektsiya[2] as an integral part of the Communist Party. Our trial was set for 24.9.1923 in Minsk.

On the day designated for the trial in Minsk, the four members appeared without me because I did not get a release from army to appear in the trial.

The chairman of the court opened the trial and announced, that since the main defendant was absent the court decided to postpone the trial until a special announcement.

The Yevsektsiya in Slutsk was not interested that the trial would take place in Minsk, because it wanted to turn it into an "exemplary trial," to prove to the masses of Jews the revolutionary nature of the Zionist movement. Therefore, it used the opportunity of the postponement of the trial

[Page 68]

and started to take care of the transfer of the trial from Minsk to Slutsk, a place were the defendants were known. The Yevsektsiya succeeded and the trial was set, for the second time, to 27.11,1923, and this time in Slutsk.

From the correspondence with the members, which did not stop all the time, I learned that our file in the hands of the investigator was getting fatter day by day. It was clear that there was a need for an early meeting of the members with me to clarify our position and coordinate our appearance at the trial.

I tried to get permission from the military authorities for an early travel. I explained to the commander that I have a political trial. I am being accused of counter-revolution, I want to prove my innocence at the trial and for that I want to be given the opportunity to arrive early in Slutsk to contact a lawyer. During our conversation a political debate developed over the Zionist issue, and even though the commander - a member of the Communist Party - was not a Jew, the question seemed reasonable. My stand in this debate was well-liked by this gentile and he helped me to get the permit. I managed to get to Slutsk a few days before the start of the trial for a joint meeting of the five "defendants." I first went to the court house to review our file. I was referred to the judge himself, a local man, who was the only judge in the trial, and without his approval I could not get the file for a review. He graciously received me and said that he was happy to have the opportunity to talk to me as the central personality in the trial. We talked for a long time. The judge tried to influence me "to express my remorse" for my wrong way, and promised and declare, that from now on I will be loyal to the social revolution, etc., etc. For his part, he promised that he would do everything for the cancellation of the trial, or, that only a symbolic judgment would be given. I explained to him, during a convincing and serious conversation, that our path is not wrong and that we have nothing to regret. We are interested in a profound and serious public inquiry and we are sure that we will prove the righteousness of our war and actions. From our conversation it became clear to the judge that we would defend our way, vigorously and warmly, and that the trial could become a public political debate.

The next day we learned that the judge had approached Minsk and demanded to send a special session of the Supreme Court because he was unwilling to assume responsibility for the administration of this trial. His demand was fulfilled and a special session was sent in the composition of three judges with a chairman. I contacted a well-known Russian lawyer (Petkavitch), a former member of SRs [Socialist Revolutionary Party]. After I lectured the matter to him and answered his questions (which, by the way, proved to me that he understood the matter nicely, as if he were a Jew), he enthusiastically accepted the defense and refused to accept a payment for his work. "I do not get paid by politicians" - he declared. The layer had to read the file and I had to get an agreement from the presiding judge that the trial would be conducted in the Russian language. The next day, when I came to the court, I learned that a special assembly was already sent from Minsk. The new judge accepted me with a noticeable and deliberate coolness and refused to conduct the trial in the Russian language. My explanation that our lawyer is Russian and doesn't know Yiddish did not help. A few hours later, when I met with the lawyer Petkavitch, I told him about my conversation with the judge and the results of my request to conduct the trial in the Russian language he announced that he is forced to step away from our defense. From his remarks I understood that he was hinted about his political past and was advised not to stick his nose in a matter bordering on "counter-revolution."

After consideration we came to the conclusion that we also wanted the trial to be conducted in Yiddish since most of the Jewish residents of Slutsk did not master the Russian language. And we, after all, needed a Jewish audience because we were interested in convincing the Jews of the righteousness of our ideas.

In a joint consultation with the members, in light of the situation that has arisen, we have decided to not to accept the official defense provided by the college of lawyers and take on the defense. We also decided not to publicize the matter ahead of time and announce it as a fact at the trial. The college of lawyers informed us that it has appointed the attorney Repp, as was customary by rotation.

The trial was set for Wednesday, 27.11.1923, at the Slutsk municipal theater, which was the largest hall in the city and contained more than a thousand people sitting and standing. The Yevsektsiya's choice of this hall, and setting the time for seven in the evening when everyone was free from work, proved the Yevsektsiya's intention to turn the trial into an event in the city.

And indeed, it was a powerful and wonderful Zionist demonstration that I do not remember anywhere else in Russia since the Zionist movement was declared counter-revolutionary by the government. Even though the entrance to the hall was by special tickets distributed to the members of the Communist Party, the Komsomol, the members of the professional associations, etc., many Jews, and members of the youth movement, also entered in various ways despite the efforts to prevent them from entering the hall.

The hall was full to capacity. The ushers couldn't control the large crowds that gathered at the entrance and sat on the windowsills. Outside the hall hundreds of people stood around the building and besieged it. The trial opened at seven in the evening as the three judges, the prosecutor and the appointed defense attorney - the lawyer Repp, sat on the stage, and on the side, on the defendants' bench, sat our five members. After the usual formal questions (names, age, profession, etc.), I announced, on behalf of all the accused members, that we are removing ourselves from the protection given to us by the law and take on the defense. The effect was full. The defense attorney - the lawyer Rapp, was confused and was forced to apologize. He left his seat next to the judges table and move to the audience benches.

The prosecutor's speech was in the well-known style: he started to talk about the social origins of the defendants, who were the children of traders, speculators and clerics (Krayna's father was a slaughterer), but, also here he had to be somewhat reluctant because I was a soldier in the Red Army and sat on the defendants' bench in military uniform. Before I joined the army I belonged to the working class, I worked (as a pharmacist) in pharmacies and was a member of the Professional Association of Medical Workers. After that came the political affair - the counter-revolutionary activity of Zionism in Russia. The agreement between Jabotinsky-Petlura,

[Page 69]

that came to prove the connection between Zionism and imperialism. Together with that, the prosecutor announced that he was removing the third clause in the indictment - disrespect for the Yevsektsiya as part of the Communist Party, a matter that was very unpleasant for the members of Yevsektsiya in Slutsk. He ended his speech demanding that the defendants, especially the main defendant, Azriel Nekritz, who guided the other defendants and had a devastating and criminal effect on them, will receive the maximum penalty.

After the prosecutor's speech, the judges turned to questions, more precisely, the presiding judge to the defendants. Among other questions I was asked about my attitude to the Red Army and whether I was serving out of choice or against my will. I replied that as a citizen of the Soviet Union I consider it my duty and fulfill my civil duty willingly and faithfully. With that I shut his mouth and disappointed him, and he lost the urge to ask me more questions. He only "commented" to me that the Red Army would not tolerate counter-revolutionary elements like me.

After the questions the members' speeches began, but, as we agreed earlier, the members spoke briefly and each touched one particular point. I gave the main defense speech and spoke last.

The trial lasted two consecutive nights, from seven in the evening to dawn on the 27th and 28th of November 1923, and during all hours of inquiry on both nights. The huge crowd didn't move from the place and remained tense and listening. My speech began on the second night of the trial, at about midnight, and lasted over three hours. I prepared for this speech while I was still in the army. I read, with great care, everything that was written about the national question by the leaders of the communist movement: Lenin, Stalin, Bukharin, etc., and copied many quotations from their words in a special notebook. Close to that time, the fourth All-Russian Conference of the Comintern [Communist International] was held, and I also drew a lot of material from it for my upcoming speech.

I lay before the judges, and the huge audience in the hall, the history of Zionism, the aspiration of the Jewish people for the homeland. I proved with many quotes from the words of the communist leaders, which I read from my notebook, that the national aspiration, the nation's longing for the homeland, is not counter-revolutionary, nationalism does not contradict socialism, if there is no territorial basis under its feet, and if it is without a homeland. I contradicted the prosecutor's accusing points. I proved that the Zionist youth movement is not chauvinistic and reactionary, and no less socialist than the Komsomol. I destroyed the blame that there was a connection between the Zionist movement and the Jabotinsky-Petlura agreement.

It was a typical public Zionist speech, which made a great impression on the audience who listened to every word with great tension, and angered the judges and the members of Yevsektsiya. The presiding judge stopped me from time to time and demanded that I should talk on the topic, but I informed that I answer, one by one, to the prosecutor's points of charges, and therefore I'm talking about the topic and the court does not have the right to deny, or restrict, the defendant's last speech. I continued to speak through the frequent interruptions of the presiding judge until I reached the point of proof based on the words of the communist leaders, that if to blame an idea and national ambition with counter-revolution, therefore, the Comintern is also counter-revolutionary. With that, I exaggerated and the chairman stopped me and announced that since I was not talking about the topic, in spite of his many warnings, he is not allowing me to continue and finish my words. I protested against it and demanded that my protest be entered to the protocol. The presiding judge stopped the court's meeting and entered the consultation room together with the other judges.

The consultation lasted approximately three hours, and in the early hours of the morning a verdict was issued: I was sentenced to one year in prison, expelled from the ranks of the Red Army and denied the right to vote. The member (Krayna Maharshak) was sentenced to one month imprisonment, but since she was already jailed for four weeks before the trial, she only had to stay in jail for two days. The other three members were released due to their young age.

I should point out that the maximum penalty of clauses 72 and 83 of the criminal code is: one year imprisonment under clause 72, two years under clause 83, together, three years in prison. And indeed, during the consultation of the judges with the prosecutor, as told to us by one of our members who secretly listened to their discussions, the latter strongly demanded this maximum penalty for me, but the judges told him that after the defense speech, clause 83 (incitement and the sowing of international hostility) should not be taken seriously and it is necessary to turn a blind eye to it without informing its cancellation. In this manner, a verdict was issued for only one year in prison and with that the Yevsektsiya suffered defeat. But, that was not enough. Its main defeat was that instead of proving to the general Jewish public, by turning this criminal trial into an exemplary political process, that the Zionist movement is counter-revolutionary and the Zionist youth movement is chauvinistic and reactionary, the Jewish public came to know the opposite, and expressed open sympathy for Zionism and our movement. Shortly after the trial, as I sat in prison, I learned that new members, from the working and studying youth, had entered the ranks of the youth organization "*Kadima*" in Slutsk and other locations in White Russia. It was a reward for our proud standing in this trial.

[Page 70]

The Yevsektsiya in Slutsk felt well the defeat brought by the trial. A closed meeting of the Yevsektsiya was held immediately afterwards and it was decided to turn to the party center and demand that it would no longer arrange public trials against the Zionists because the results of these trials were to their detriment (one of our members managed to copy several sections from the minutes of the Yevsektsiya's meeting). And indeed, it was the second public trial (after the Kiev trial) and the last of the Zionists in Soviet Russia.

Translator's footnotes:

1. GPU - the State Political Directorate (also translated as the State Political Administration) (GPU) was the intelligence service and secret police of the Russian Soviet Federative Socialist Republic (RSFSR).

2. Yevsektsiya - the Jewish section of the Soviet Communist Party and its stated mission was the destruction of traditional Jewish life, the Zionist movement and Hebrew culture. Retu

Everything That Has happened

by Fayvel Efron

Translated by Mira Eckhaus

In memory of my late mother Itke - the pure and noble soul.
In memory of my late father Yosef Dov Ber - the sharp and daring.
In memory of the destroyed house.

Widowhood and bereavement. The exterminator exterminated everything.

The sentence was decided a long time ago. The shadow of the total destruction was everywhere. But the end was horrible. And the destruction was in its diabolical and terrible shape - who could have imagined and think what will happen?

Slutsk - my hometown. Why it was so special to me? - Because it was mine, it was my home, my childhood, my youth, the beginning, the dreams, ambitions, hopes and faith. Faith in man and humanity.

I lived in it only for a few years. But my longing and cuddling are numerous. My love and gratitude are strong. And at the same time, I remember the driving force, the aspiration, the desire and necessity to leave, run away, depart from Slutsk. Many left Slutsk, mostly teenagers. And I wish those who remained would have left as well.

The Jewish Slutsk - seriousness, severity, strictness, fanaticism and honesty together with innocent faith, longing and yearning. Quietly restrained grief and trembling sadness spread over everything. The whole landscape seemed sad and serious.

A few years, a shocking crisis. From way of life of innocent faith, conservative piety and zealous observance of the religious commandments - to a heresy that takes over and fights and breaks everything that is accepted and sacred, even to the point of marriage without a Rabbi, mixed marriages and uncircumcised children. Who can count how many fathers were in sorrow and how many mothers' hearts were broken? Who can mourn the shock and anxiety from this generation?

And with the background of a few general events in this short period of time - here are some fragments of memories and impressions of a boy and a teenager in Slutsk as he saw them, felt them and lived them.

Baylis' trial. World War. Refugees. The first revolution. The second revolution. Exchange of regimes and authorities. Crisis and destruction of Jewish life. Zionist underground. Imprisonment and leaving home. A distress came down to the calm life and the childish peaceful. The distress by the Baylis' trial. And fear of the future. The boy's heart also felt that something crucial was about to happen. In the evenings, neighbors would gather and excitedly read newspapers.

On Simchat Torah, restraints were loosened among the crowd of the young people, and they used to outburst into the courtyard of the synagogue and out into the streets of the city, with fireworks and sipping a drink. On this Simchat Torah holiday, before the verdict in the Baylis trial, all joy was nullified. (As fate would have it, and since then the celebration of Simchat Torah has not resumed publicly and cheerfully in Slutsk) ... An enormous fear and depression. With a great sadness, the prayer was quietly and we approached the encirclements of Simchat Torah. A stranger suddenly appeared, a guest from the Hassidim, who was an unusual sight in Slutsk, which opposed the Hassidism. The guest approached the holy ark and began to dance, something we were not used to see, an adult dancing... - And I remember the silent typical movement, the slow and restrained speech without raising a voice, all the anxiety and sadness were expressed in the words: "Fe, Reb Id - Maacht Zich Nit Naresh" ... Yazt... (Fe, Jewish Reb, don't lose your mind now...) which were said by the Shamash Reb Yaakov (Reb Yankev, as it was pronounced in Yiddish), a kind and respected Jew, pleasant.

How can I forget the joy of liberation from anguish. Constricted and restrained joy, so as not to upset the gentiles... lest... it was not over yet? Baylis was indeed released but the Jewish people were not cleared of guilt. And severe insult and bitterness accompanied the joy. Who knows what will happen.

And indeed, the evil forces did not rest in Russia. They did not disappear when the verdict was given and they did not silent, but continued and increased their propaganda and incitement against the Jews.

Also, in Slutsk they decided to take advantage of a young gentile man named Gabrila, who many years ago was murdered by Christians, and years later a part of his body was found intact. In the spring of 1914, they recollected him and declared him a saint. And to denote this event, they decided on a large conference and a magnificent religious parade in Slutsk. The incitement against the Jews of Slutsk and the surrounding area increased. They spread the rumor that the Jews were the ones who killed Gabrila. The fear grew. There was a real danger of a pogrom. The rich Jews fled and left the city.

The conference took place, the magnificent parade passed, a large crowd gathered and came to Slutsk. But the enthusiasm was not great as the planners had planned. And there was no pogrom. And they said then, that it was mainly due to a generous gift that was given to the governor. And in any case, a reinforcement of police officers was brought, as they said that the youth of Slutsk also prepared and organized for self-defense.

And then, a natural phenomenon occurred. A total solar eclipse, which left a great impression on the children as well as the adults.

A sign of evil, new troubles, a sign of war, mumbled and prophesied women and men alike.

And indeed... - a very short time later, in August 1914, the war broke out. It was on 9 Av. The First World War with all its horrors. The world as we know it had changed. Slutsk, who had never excelled in publicly expression of joy - became completely silent. No

[Page 71]

weddings or any other celebration were held. Melancholic was everywhere. The Jews felt themselves outcasts and strangers to the country in general and to the war in particular. They resorted to all kinds of means of evasion. They even reached to the point of mutilating each other with minor as well as severe and serious disabilities. Professionals were specialized for this purpose. The bribery business flourished. And there were also those who disappeared completely from the area and went underground.

In the rotten regime of Russia at that time, after small victories at the beginning, the great and shameful retreat began. And of course, the Jews were also to blame for this discriminating retreat. The Jews were accused of extradition, sabotage and espionage. Nikolay Nikolayevich, who was from the royal family and the commander-in-chief at the time, ordered a global and immediate deportation of all the Jews in the area of the battles. All Polish Jews were deported. The "Bezantsim" Affair began, the refugees.

The late Elisheva Eshkol (Elka Kaplan)

From the nearby town of Snyavka, she stayed in
Slutsk as a refugee in 1917-18 and was active in
"Tze'irei Zion" (Zion youth).

In the fall of 1915, many refugees arrived in Slutsk. They were received with great care and hospitality. They were fed and treated with brotherly love. Most of them were housed in synagogues and private homes. Women and young women collected clothes and food needs, cooked He cooked, brewed and fed them.

But these Jews were strange to us. Hasidic Polish Jews, with long, curled and embossed sidelocks. The people of Slutsk would humble them, without exaggeration and external bragging.

And their special clothing. The small hats, the socks over the pants, the various capote with "belts" worn on them - until then, Slutsk had never seen such Jews. Also, their Yiddish speech was different and strange, foreign and odd, unclear and unpleasant to the Lithuanian Jew in Slutsk. The children would call them with a special melody "Itshe-meye"... (r). - They would also add "Heing afen tye"=8; (r). And for a complete relief, they would harshly add – "Poilishe dribkes"...- Indeed, contradictory groups. And there was mutual reluctance and a partition between the residents and the refugees. (Different partitions were also within the residents among themselves. Between different classes, professions and degrees - special Beit Midrash houses. And the main partition was according to genealogy, ancestry).

And the refugees also established special Minyans for themselves. Minyans of Hassidim. But over time, the differences and contrasts were blurred. The refugees recovered and acclimatized and the residents helped them. And there were among the refugees both rich and beggars, and also professional beggars. And over time, the integration increased. Partnerships were established and they even reached to "mixed marriage". Indeed, integration of exiles.

The Russian retreat stopped not far from Slutsk, near the town of Liakhovitz. And from there, they did not expel the Jews, and most of the Jews did not leave the town. The town was bombarded continuously, there were many victims there. Only a few came from there to Slutsk, broken and ragged.

And at the same time, in the atmosphere of war and a close front, a new doctor appeared in Slutsk. A young Jewish man, quick, smart and cheerful. He only spoke Russian and was dandy. No one knew where he came from. And he immediately stood out. He joined and became a member in the circles of the Naichelstavo", beginning with the Ispravnik" and ending with "Vainski Nechelknik" (from the police inspector to the military commander). He was appointed as a military doctor and was promoted to sit in the "Prisotstva", the committee for examining and accepting recruits for the army. And here he found an open door for accepting bribes. And he took advantage of it with a broad hand and brutally. And the Jews of the city hated him, especially the Slutsk women, who would accompany him on his carriage ride with bitter curses. He established a high and luxurious standard of living for himself. He lived in the spacious house of one of the richest people in Slutsk, who left the city when the front approached it. He married a beautiful woman. Four Christian servants and maids served them in their house. And almost every evening, and night after night, debauchery balls were held in his house, and all the members in the "Naichelstavo" were its guests.

From time to time, one would see in his apartment a Jew with a distinguished face and a well-kept beard, staying in his house for a few days. In the summer, this Jew would be seen sitting in the porch and studying Gemara. "It's his uncle" - the servants would tell. And it was an enigma to the neighbors. And one evening - it was at Sukkot (5677) his regular guests came to him unexpectedly, without invitation and without prior notice and arrested him.

It turned out that he used a name that was not his, and he was not a doctor at all, but a third-year medical student.

The government officials were afraid about their fate so they held a party in his cell and poisoned him.

The Slutsk Jews were amazed. They shook their heads, even those who once cursed him, out of pity, participation in grief and powerlessness over the corrupt, hostile and Jew-hating government. And when the revolution broke out a few months later, the Jews would still be reminiscing him and saying among themselves: "If only he had lived a few more months, he would have risen to greatness"... There was something about him that charmed the people of the city. Like a stray star, he appeared and surprised, deviated from the straight path, misled the people and fell into the oblivion.

The revolution broke out, the February Revolution. At first, the people whispered with hesitation and while looking to the sides. It was said, word of mouth,

[Page 72]

that something was happening in the capital. The emperor resigned... in favor of his sick son Alexei... in favor of his brother Michael... Michael Caesar... Michael did not agree... Michael resigned... Republic... Provisional Government... –

I remember the first Shabbat and the fierce debate at the synagogue. "The one who gives salvation" to whom? Opinions were divided and the spirits were agitated. There were distinctly conservative monarchists - who sided in favor of King Nikolay. And progressive monarchists who were in favor of Michael. And there were also republicans who were in favor of the provisional government. And on that Shabbat, there was no "the one who gives" and there was no "salvation" in the synagogue. It was as if something was missing. It was as if they were after a surgery in which a vital organ was amputated.

The emperor was dethroned. Russia was a republic. There was a provisional government. It was a dream. Spring. General joy. Joyful face. The heart sings and aspires to wonderful things. An outburst of feelings of mutual brotherhood and a desire to operate. Aspiration for heroism and self-sacrifice. A great experience. And the deserters (the skivers) came out of their holes, - now we know what we should fight for - they said.

And the demonstration of gratitude in the market square was general. Christians and Jews. The intelligentsia and the common people. The clergy too. - The entire population. - The revolution of the entire people, a revolution - without bloodshed.

Even then, there were indeed skeptics who remembered the year 1905. With a heavy sigh they would express their fear and hesitation, who knows what will happen and let's hope that everything will not end like in 1905.

All parties came out of darkness and organized. Groups, associations and organizations were created and organized every now and then. Also, the Zionist movement in all its wings and nuances. A Zionist youth movement, and even a children's association - "Pirchei Zion" (Flowers of Zion).

And as if there is no longer a war. Only freedom, endless freedom. And they enjoyed this freedom as much as they could. The youth wanted to share this celebration even with the dead and would spend and walk at night in the cemetery. Even the fear of death and the dead disappeared. The spirit of freedom and a light mischievous spirit took hold of everything. It also touched the members of the yeshiva and the sons of the Rabbis even started learning Russian and playing in the lord's gardens (albeit secretly) with the daughters of the lords and the intelligentsia - crackat. The election cauldron and the election war have begun. Assemblies and speeches. Those who were held in the katorgas also came to speak and preach. And these were admired heroes by the entire residents of Slutsk. The director of the commercial school, Dmitry Ivanowitz Ivanov, a liberal Christian, also came to give a speech on Shabbat, in the Great Synagogue (the cold). He was unlike the director of the Sokolov Gymnasium, who was a reactionary. The election war was conducted furiously, with everyone believing in their own way with complete faith. Everything was reorganized. A city management was elected in general elections. There was a militia instead of police and the head of the militia was a Jew, and Daniel'ke was a militiaman. And on the evenings of his guarding - in the policeman's pavilion, girls and boys and children gathered around him - and there was joy everywhere. Politerke the policeman, the monster and the fear of the Jews, was fired. Chastened, he greeted loudly every Jew he saw from a distance. How he fell from his grace and lost whole his threatening power. – Finally, he was recruited and sent to the front.

The dreams were beautiful. The hopes were big. But the spring was short. The reality became difficult and gloomy day by day, the new soldiers were not useful either, the former skivers, and at the front - defeat after defeat. There was a great anarchy in the entire country, one government was replaced by another, everyone longed for the Constituent Assembly.

The October Revolution came. The power was taken by the Bolsheviks. Their slogans were: give the land for the farmers immediately, and end the war – let the soldiers return to their homes - had an effect and charm. They especially captured the hearts of the tired soldiers. The Bolsheviks were neither harmed nor disturbed by the talk of the Slutsk Jews about them: they are disturbed, unscrupulous, anarchists, just thieves, and as they shouted all over Russia – they were German spies... - they seized power, - but the anarchy prevailed. In the meantime, there was a pause in Slutsk: according to the Brest-Litovsk agreement, the Germans also entered

Slutsk, and if at first they left a hard impression when they entered the city, when they took hostages from among the city's dignitaries, over time their attitude was revealed to be kind and fair. And it was long ago when the Jews had such good days, days of well-being, peace and quiet. And perhaps this was the case with the Slutsk Jewish refugees during World War II, who did not believe in the wickedness and cruelty of the Germans. Perhaps this was one of the reasons that the Jews did not leave and did not run away from Slutsk.

At the time of the revolution in Germany, the Germans also left Slutsk.

A period of great suffering and many upheavals followed. A severe and brutal civil war was going on in Russia. There was a continuous change in the governments and the suffering increased. There was a shortage of everything. And a real hunger. The Jews were always to blame. Anti-Semitism increased and visible banditry appeared. A despicable wave of riots swept over the whole of Russia. "Hit the Jews, save Russia" - this was the slogan of all those who were fighting the Bolsheviks. The Jews, against their will, became accomplices to the Bolsheviks. The Bolsheviks appeared as their saviors. And unfortunately - it was not always possible to trust the Bolshevik saviors either. I remember the funeral procession of murdered saints, which passed in a demonstration in front of the offices of Cheka in Slutsk demanding protection and an effective war against the banditry (at the time, such a thing was still possible). The person who headed the Cheka at the time met with a delegation on behalf of the protesting funeral participants and promised them things. After a while it became known that he himself was later shot on charges of association with the gangs.

The banditry did not affect the city of Slutsk itself, but it spread in the surroundings, in the towns, in the villages and on the roads, and cast its heavy shadow on the city as well, shocking and poisoning life. The change of government in Slutsk was relatively amicable. Bolsheviks and Poles and once again Bolsheviks and again Poles and finally Bolsheviks. The days of distress and oppression have come. Every rule and its decrees. Every period and its troubles.

The first withdrawal of the Poles should be noted in a special disgrace. The retreat lasted for days and weeks. The abuse then reached its peak before it reached to Slutsk. They robbed, looted, beat and flogged. Riots broke out - it was literally a pogrom. They destroyed and burned houses and even raped women. There were also victims. The Jews shut themselves in their houses and basically, life stopped.

The actions and conduct of the late Dr. Schildkroit, the leader of the Jewish community at that time, who did not sit idly by, were well known. Perhaps the activities of my late father were less known. Many knew that he would go around and help those in need with food and comfort them with a word of encouragement.

[Page 73]

More than once he was beaten on his way. Once he encountered a group of high-ranking officers. He approached them and rebuked them about the barbaric acts, in the name of the nobility of the Polish people and their culture, in the name of Adam Mitskevich, in the name of the Polish people's war for their freedom, among whose fighters were also Jewish heroes - he demanded that they stop the rampage. The group of officers listened to his words and promised him faithfully to end the riots. And indeed, after this conversation, a few days of relative silence came.

And as to the Polish nobility - during the second retreat of the Bolsheviks from Slutsk, the Polish doctor Silitsky and his son were captured, while crossing the railroad tracks in the direction to the front. There was no doubt that they were engaged in espionage. And yet they were not executed. One of the Parfontov family, one of the sons of the converted Hannah Bilka, who was a communist and close to the government, intervened in their favor and saved them.

Hannah Bilka and her sons, this is a story for a separate chapter. It was said that in her youth, she was beautiful and because of the love of the priest's son Parfontov, she converted and married him. But the great love expired and her life was very difficult and she was even beaten by her husband. She had beautiful sons, who resembled more to the Jews. They were talented for every handicraft, work of art and especially for painting, singing and playing. But they were lonely and isolated. They could not associate with deep friendships either with the gentiles or with the Jews. Both sides have rejected them. They called them "Palzshidki" – half - Jews. Nevertheless, they were closer to the Jews. I studied in the same class with two of her sons. I was in their house a few times. It gave the impression of a sad and untidy house. Hannah Bilka was no longer young, but the impressions of her beauty were still visible in her face. And her eyes were sad, the eyes of "a Yiddish Maame"...

And when the Poles re-entered Slutsk, Parfontov, the communist son, was caught and imprisoned. Hannah Bilka ran to Dr. Silitsky, who was saved thanks to this son, and asked for his assistance. The Silitsky family members locked themselves in their house and did not open the door for her. Hannah knocked, cried, shouted - and to no avail - the son was executed.

It was an evidence and expression of the Polish nobility.

In the end, the Bolsheviks remained in Slutsk. Their rule was solid and well established. And at the same time, the situation of the city's Jews worsened. And this time not out of malice and evil, nor out of anti-Semitism – it was purely the essence and purpose of the regime. At the head of the government were both Jews as well as residents of the city, but it didn't ease the situation of the population. On the contrary - the Jews were more strict, pious and zealous in their new Torah. Synagogues were closed and all the cheders were destroyed. The teaching of the Hebrew language was prohibited. Teachers (melamedim) and Rabbis were put on trial. There was a crisis in the spiritual life. The cheap and crude heresy came to rule. The spirit of freedom disappeared. The organizations, associations and parties were eliminated. An underground Zionist youth movement was established and developed.

The economic situation was also very bad. And this should be known, in Slutsk, the war against the bourgeoisie - meant a war against the craftsmen, who themselves were paupers, and against the shopkeepers, whom mostly lost their property. And they were the majority of the Jewish community. The status of the Jews was destroyed, all their livelihoods were eliminated, new and different types of livelihoods were created - that even Shalom Aleichem neither knew nor thought about them. And first and foremost - the trade in valuta. There were all kinds of valuta and money. There was a difference between new and old money, between wrinkled and smooth, dollars, Polish money, Soviet money and even tsarist money, of the king. There were notes with holes (pin holes) and without holes, Kanak money, and the value of all the various notes was different. They would replace valuta with valuta, create holes and plug holes with all kinds of soap (a whole industry was developed around it), and iron the money bills, buy, sell, and make money from it and make a living.

Individuals also started to engage in smuggling. The border was close. The trade of the mashochniks (sack owners), who were merchants that all of their goods were contained in a sack, developed and became widespread. This trade developed because of the great shortage and the huge differences in prices, which were created between the village and the city and between the cities themselves. This trade spread despite the severe prohibition by the government and the great danger that was involved in it. More often than not, these mashochniks were left without goods and imprisoned as well. The population was then divided into three types: those who had been sat (in prison), those who were currently sitting, and those who will sit in the future. This Jewish joke did not stop. The "Agot wort" and "Agot wertel" - were always acceptable and desirable in Slutsk.

There was a shortage of everything. Even in essentials needs, food needs and also in clothing. They came up with various inventions and all sorts of tricks in order to overcome this shortage. They tried to fill their stomach and cover their body. Various substitutes were invented instead such as bread made from flour mixed with bran, crude oil, crushed and dried beetroot tea, saccharin, black salt, etc.

Girls sew clothes from sacks and old weavings and all kinds of diverse scraps until eye-catching combinations in abundance colors were obtained.

A complete home industry was established of shoes made of old cloth and their soles made from ropes. Shoes were also made from cork wood. There were also girls who were able to sew and prepare fancy shoes and elegant clogs.

But this was not what the Jewish youth dreamed of, nor what did they strive for. The high schools did not accept the young Jews due to their non-proletarian genealogy. They were not welcome anywhere, they were without any shred of hope, with no way out. And this situation increased the quest of the youth to the Zionist movement, the underground movement - the only solution, the only way - the way to Zion.

And at the same time, like a miracle, the new theory of the Communism grew stronger and stronger and took over the minds and conquered the hearts. And over time, even more and more. At first, it swept the youth and then also the older population, either out of recognition or out of careerism.

A typical tragic case was with a Jew, who was approached by a woman that wanted to console him in his mourning for the death of his young son. The mourner sighed and said: death is better after all, than if the son had been a communist. And the woman had a communist son. No man is judged when he is in sorrow. The reluctance and hatred for the communists was indeed great at the beginning. But only two, three years later, when the same Jew spoke with the son

[Page 74]

of that woman (not the communist) about his Zionist son who was exiled and in prison, he consoled himself and boasted with satisfaction, that his younger son is no longer following dangerous paths. He, thank God, is a Komsomol and is a member of the Communist Youth Organization.

The communist ideology and terminology penetrated the ranks of the Zionist underground as well. Both the foundation and the formulation were Marxist. And in the evenings, young men and women sat in the underground and argued, and made excuses for themselves why they did not follow the crowd, on the wide and wonderful road of the global socialism, but rather followed a side path, a crooked path of war for socialism within a small nation - doubtless a nation, a proletariat that is not a proletariat, that was not yet born, on an unknown path of immigration and concentration in a very problematic and remote country (with malaria). In addition to all this - being underground in the land of socialism being realized... they justified themselves. And out of self-righteousness they accused the Bolshevism of deviation. And there was a debate about what was the deviation. There were those who claimed that the deviation was only in the question of the Jews. And there were those who said that the deviation in the question of the Jews was a result of the general deviation. And here they found help, reinforcement and encouragement for the Zionist idea and the underground Zionist movement from an unexpected source, a Bolshevist government source... In 1924, a booklet by a man named Bergin appeared in Russian and contained an analysis of the situation of the Jews in Russia at that time, a truly Zionist analysis in the full sense of the word. And the proposed solution was a settlement of the Jews. Where? - by their places of residence, and by implication to the Crimea.

A public committee, "Gezard", was established, a government committee, "Kammerd", with the enthusiastic support of several important figures in the central government led by Smidovich, the deputy of the Soviet President Kalinin. A movement arose, gatherings were held. Also, in Slutsk, Minsk and all of White Russia. As a result of this movement, a small number of Jews also moved to agriculture. Both in White Russia and around Slutsk, the Jews were indeed willing and wanted to move to agriculture, but there was no available land. Not even in Crimea.

Itke Efron, wife of Rabbi Yosef Dov Ber Efron

Rabbi Yosef Dov Ber Efron

Together with the establishment of committees and a movement for Jewish settlement within Russia, the authorities increased the persecution of Zionism. The authorities realized that Zionism had become stronger and stronger because of this movement. And they decided once and for all to completely eliminate the Zionist underground. They did not succeed in eliminating the settlement, even after reaching Birubidzin. However, they succeeded in eliminating the Zionist underground. But Zionism was not eliminated, the Jewish spark was not extinguished in Russia to this day. With the extermination campaign and the elimination of the underground, it was also my turn (in January 1925) to be imprisoned together with a group of members and to be sent to a foreign country. Until then, I managed to avoid imprisonment. And it was my first and last imprisonment. And the dangerous political criminal, 18 years old, was imprisoned in the prison cell of gthe GPO in Minsk with many criminals, smugglers, bandits, spies, vagrants and the unspecified. Despite the concerns, cordial and beautiful mutual relations were formed among us.

After the interrogation ended, the entire material was sent to Moscow. And about two months later, the stereotyped decision of the collegium of the G.P.O., which discussed human rights without seeing or hearing the accused, was given – exile for three years to various remote places in Asian and Northern Russia. The great and wide Russia.

It was said, that instead of being exiled to remote places, we will immigrate to Israel, as was customary at the time for those convicted of Zionist crimes. Upon receiving the verdict, we were given a two-week leave to prepare for the trip. Liberal times! And it was clear that within two weeks all the formalities for traveling to Israel would be sorted out. But a week later we were banned again. What happened - we do not know to this day. Conceivably because of betrayal, provocation by one of the members. We wanted to bring her to Israel as the wife of one of the "deported" members. She agreed to this - both by force of discipline and by force of her true desire, so to speak, to immigrate to Israel.

[Page 75]

But... - Apparently our plan was delivered by her to the G.P.O. and the G.P.O. decided to send us to the remote exile places and not to Israel. The "bride" was still needed by the G.P.O. She has not yet finished her role. And indeed, she worked a lot for the G.P.O. For a long time, I tottered along the way and passed through multiple prisons until I arrived at the designated exile place in the northern rear.

And then my father began more seriously to take care of my release and the exchange of my exile with immigration to Israel. I didn't like it. I felt a violation of my honor, the honor of a political warrior. My father also came to the exile place and visited his son, his youngest son. And then, he was no longer young and he was very weak. My father was great in the Torah, a member of a family of Rabbis for generations, the sister's son of the late Rabbi Yosef Dov Ber Soloveitchik. During his visit to me in the exile village, he recited to me by heart entire chapters from the Bible and songs of Zion - beginning with Yehuda Halevi, through Dulitzki and ending with Bialik. He also read some of his poems in Hebrew and Yiddish, which he wrote and did not publish. He had a wonderful memory. A complete and detailed map of cities, Jewish settlements, was in his head. He was knowledgeable like no other in the biographies of many families in the three aspects of their attribution, origin and branching. Thanks to his great energy, his firm strength and great ability, he reached the leaders of government in Moscow: Katanyan, the prosecutor at the time, Kalinin, the president of the Soviets and Smidovich, his deputy. Dad indeed spoke Russian, but his Russian was not excellent. He was very knowledgeable in Russian literature.

He was received nicely by the Russians and he held interesting conversations with them. Kalinin was especially enthusiastic by his well-groomed beard, which was very long. How, how do you grow such a beard, - he repeated and asked several times. (Kalinin himself had a sparse goatee beard). But the matter that father acted for, was not settled so easily. It also took a lot of time. Lots of rushes and postponements. Everything was in the hands of G.P.O. But finally, the exchange-release decision was received.

And indeed, I was the first of all the people deported to the remote exile place, (the region of the Zirians or the Komi region as they called the place) - to leave to Israel. This opened the opportunity for the other deported as well. On the way to Israel, I was not allowed to visit Slutsk. And I won't see it anymore -the Jewish Slutsk no longer exists...

A group of pioneers on their way to the Land of Israel

First row, from right to left: Altman, unknown name, Shomroni, Podlipsky, Shalom, Shifman, Podlipsky, Birg Yoel, Peskin Mandelwitz
Second row, from right to left: Mizel, B. Katznelson, his wife Mosia Harkavi and their daughter, Shapira Pesia, Shapira Aryeh, H. Kaminer, Epstein
Third row, from right to left: Ostrovsky, S. Shpilkin, Yoel Birg, Hannah Mizel, Aharon Rolnik, Bashevkin

[Page 76]

Institutions

Educational Institutions

by N. Chinitz

Translated by Yocheved Klausner

Slutsk excelled in its scholars, as a place of Torah study, its *hadarim* (plural of *heder* = a school where little children learned Torah), where they taught the Pentateuch [*Humash*] with RASHI commentary, the Bible and Talmud. Even the very poor made every effort that Torah would not be forgotten in Slutsk. Some of the *melamdim*(teachers) were well dressed and "learned in the ways of the world" and their teaching rooms were clean and nice, but these were few. We should mention "R'Welvel Prizivitzer", a handsome Jew, who treated his pupils softly, taught them the Bible (*TANACH*) and the first pages of the Talmud.

The *heder* of R'Shmuel-Yosef Regelson was modern for its time. R'Pesach Karon, a short Jew, with a warm and sensitive heart, was attracted to Eretz Israel. He had a large library and would lend books for a small fee. This Zionist man and his library were famous. His body was bent, and through his glasses one could see two dreaming and smiling eyes. His library and his room filled his heart with love.

The Rav R'Berl Griboshthcik, Head of the Yeshiva in the "Karnayim" synagogue.

R' Zalman Zitin, head of the Yeshiva in the Ironsmiths'
synagogue, member of the religious Court in Slutsk.

Rav Goldberg is telling:

"I was in the *heder* of R'Pesach Ezra's, one of the best *melamdim* in town. The rabbi was a short man, his head sunken between his shoulders, his face, with a white beard, radiating nobility, his forehead wrinkled like an old yellow parchment, his eyes shining with love and his lips smiling.

The rabbi made me sit on a bench near a long table, where several children already sat, their books open. He opened a prayer book and showed me the large letters, saying: "This is 'alef' – alef, child, and so on." As I was repeating the words, some copper coins fell on the table from above. "See, child" – he said – "the angels are sending you a present from Heaven."

In R'Pesach Ezra's *heder* I learned *siddur* (prayer book) and the Hebrew language. R'Pesach Ezra's had a library of children's story books and every Shabat eve he would lend his pupils little books that would capture the hearts of the children by their beautiful legends and charming stories.

In the rabbi's courtyard several fruit trees grew – how good and pleasant it was to play in their shade! His wife would gather apples or pears that had fallen from the trees and give them to the children playing around, who would find in them the "taste of paradise."

The little Yeshivas were well known: R'Nehemia's, in

[Page 77]

The Talmud Torah in Slutsk. Its pupils, *melamdim* and teachers.
In the 4th row, the second from right, is "Kadish the *melamed*."

R'Iserke's synagogue, the lower and the higher class. Who didn't know R'Nehemia, with his sharp mind!

The spacious courtyard of the synagogues – "the Big Bet Hamidrash, the Cold Bet Hamidrash, the Taylors' Bet Hamidrash, the Kloiz and the synagogue Karnayim" – served as a formal meeting-place for the students of the "Little Yeshivot". R'Yashe Tritzaner, a great scholar and a quiet person, was loved by his students. In the women's section of the Karnayim synagogue R'Beril Gribentchik was teaching. He "had" two tables, a long one and a smaller one. He was a tall Jew, skinny and with large protruding bones, yellowish hair, long sidelocks and a small beard. He was honest and straight, with an appearance of a monk or hermit. His father was making combs, and he himself was an ordained rabbi from the Volozhin Yeshiva, a friend of the writer Michah Yosef Berditchevski. He was complaining about the writer, sighing and coughing: "Such a great scholar, and lost his right path"....

In the Taylors' synagogue, the great Yeshiva *Etz Hachayim* ["The Tree of Life"] was situated, relocated from the synagogue on Ostrova Street. Here the *Gaon* (genius) R'Isser Zalman Meltzer would give his lesson. The yeshiva employed two supervisors [*mashgichim*], R'Pesach and R'Sheftil Kremer, and later it relocated to the special building at the end of Shkolania Street. The supervisor was the Rav R'Asher Sandomirski, who served until the Yeshiva was closed by the Soviets. Rabbis, teachers, authors have graduated from the Slutsk Yeshiva: I.D. Berkwitz, Rav Prof. S. Asaf z"l, Dr. Nathan Klotz, the poet Lisitzki, Prof. Meir Wachsman, Rav

Rubinstein from Vilna, Chief Rabbi Katz of Petach Tikva, the son-in-law of R'Isser Zalman, the scholar Kotler and others. Another small Yeshiva was situated in the Blacksmiths' synagogue, and Rabbi Pesach Mamosh was teaching there. It is worthwhile to see what the poet A. A. Lissitzki said about him. Later, Rav R'Zalman, a merchant in coals, was teacher there, a short Jew, full of Torah. Most of his trading was done by his wife, a true "woman of valor" – sometimes he would help her. At the synagogue on Vilna Street the head of the Yeshiva was R'Yitzhak Leib Rabinowitz

The "Modern Heder" had a special place in the community. It brought a ray of light by the method of "Only Hebrew" [lit. Hebrew in Hebrew]. We remember with a blessing its first founders-teachers: Kagan, M. Hazanowitz, the well-known writer Avraham Epstein (Aba Aricha), Yarkoni, Berger, Gutzeit, Sweidel z"l and, may he be inscribed for a long life, the teacher S. Nachmani (Nachmanowitz), who is now in Eretz Israel and was one of the first founders of the "Modern Heder".

In 1914, a second Modern *Heder* was established in Slutsk by the teacher Yitzhak Katzenelson (Hazanowitz' brother-in-law) and Reuvke Altman,

[Page 78]

АТТЕСТАТЪ

Содержательница Пансіона.

a great scholar, very knowledgeable in Hebrew Literature. Nahum Chinitz and Israel Aharon Sviranovski were also teachers in this Heder.

In Slutsk was known the "Old Talmud Torah," where there was more shade than light, yet it educated an entire generation of poor people and laborers, who later headed several movements and institutions. Two of them I remember: Kadish the melamed with his thin beard, an honest and righteous man, who continued his holy work to the end of his days. He taught Talmud calmly and tried to make his pupils understand difficult passages. I shall mention also the director of the general studies Mishkovski, a Bund man, who opposed Hebrew and all that was connected with it. He was an honest man, was married to Klara Mironovna, a Zionist woman, who gave fiery speeches.

Another Jewish-Russian institution was the Jewish school "Evreiskvya Utchilishtza," but this was a "Jewish School" only by name, since the instruction language was Russian, except very little "religion" and "Hebrew" and a few prayers. During vacation days and formal holidays, as the king's birthday and the like, the principal Levinsohn would appear in the synagogue with the School Choir and the officially appointed rabbi, Levinsohn would speak and the ceremony would end with the performance of the choir.

During WWI, as the flow of refugees grew, in 1914-1915 the Talmud Torah became full of children of refugees and a new branch of the local Talmud Torah was opened. The Rav R'Yosef Feimer introduced Hebrew and Bible [Tanach] as mandatory subjects of study. A girls' school, of four grades, also opened. The principal was Chaim Kagan, the language of instruction was Russian, but they taught the Yiddish and Hebrew languages as well. They also began to teach the girls Hebrew and Yiddish songs. Most of the teachers were members of the BUND and the Bundist spirit was beginning to rule, little by little.

The "Tarbut" School that opened at that time in Slutsk was soon closed by the Soviet regime, then was opened again during the Polish rule. Among its teachers were: Azriel Nakritz, Shemaryahu Barhon, N. Chinitz, Lipshitz and others. In the evenings they had "evening courses" in general education, Hebrew and various other subjects.

Slutsk had a wonderful Library, with books mostly in Hebrew, Russian, Yiddish and some other languages. Annexed to the library were a reading room and a club. The library played a major role in the cultural development of the youth and the laborers. For the Yeshiva students, as well, the library was an important source of development; they drank with great thirst whatever they read.

[Page 79]

Among the Russian important institutions stood out the classical Russian High-School, of 8 grades. The graduates of this school were known for their extensive general knowledge. The school was known through Russia, and many students were "externs" (studying elsewhere) and came only to pass the exams and receive the matriculation diploma. Those who passed the exams were happy – many failed. Sometimes an anti-Semitic teacher would ask a non-relevant question, only to be able to give the grade "failed." The historian and writer Saul Ginsburg wrote in his book "Historic Writings" about the school:

"In the Slutsk region lived many Polish Calvinist estate owners, people of culture, who were free of the Catholic fanaticism and treated the Jews with tolerance. The contact with them influenced the Jews culturally and enlarged their spiritual outlook. Moreover: among the enlightened estate owners were often people who openly assisted Jewish young people who aspired to a good education, while the environment was in total opposition. In Slutsk there was a large Polish Calvinist community. Two of them, noblemen of the House of Domanski had business relations with Kaplan Yakov of Minsk, and they suggested helping him enroll his son in the Slutsk High School. Indeed, in 1840 Meir Kaplan was accepted as a student in the school, in the 4th grade. Most of the teachers were Calvinists. It is worth mentioning, that one of them, Vanovski (the Vanovski who was later the Russian Minister of War was from the same family) studied Hebrew with Meir. The high school was impressive: a large two-story building, long and wide, with a large entrance, on the "Boulevard Street".

The Boulevard was always full of students, wearing coats with shining buttons. The teachers were well dressed, walking around proudly as if saying: Here we are the rulers, and everything is in our hands – good or bad.

A high-school for girls, of seven grades, was also opened. There was also an elementary private school, of six grades, headed by Rav Ashman and a commerce school of 8 grades, situated in a large and beautiful building, on the road to the train station. The building was well planned and had laboratories, reading rooms and meeting halls. It was headed by Ivanov, a liberal and respected man. The commercial school had a norm of admission – for every 10 Cristian students one Jew was admitted, and the other school admitted 2 Jews to 10 Christians. The Jews covered the cost of managing the school; otherwise it would have ceased to function. The town maintained also a 2 grades school by the name of Smena, for girls of poor families, where they taught Russian and arithmetic and very few other subjects.

A Center of Torah

by Rabbi Nissan Waxman

Translated by Jerrold Landau

Edited by Jane S. Gabin

The Jewish community of Slutsk was one of the most important in the countries of Lithuania and Russia for hundreds of years. At the beginning of the fifth century C.E. there were already the origins of a community where. Large houses of worship and *Beis Midrashes* were founded and set up. The people of the city were known as benefactors of charity and benevolence to anyone who came to their midst, and "first for any holy matter in the world"[1]. There was also a large Yeshiva there, under the leadership of the Gaon Rabbi Yaakov, the son of Rabbi Uri Feivish of Tomaszów. The good name of Slutsk went before it and attracted the hearts of rabbis from the entire Jewish Diaspora.

The times were days of storms and horrors in the world. Powerful forces burst forth from near and far, as usual beating down on the skulls of the Jews first. The disturbances and tribulations in Ukraine and Poland drew near to the borders of Lithuania and White Russia, and the ire of the inimical Bogdan Chmielnicki, may his name be blotted out, reached the gates of Slutsk[2].

On the other hand, the Thirty Year War (5378-5408, 1618-1648) in the lands of Germany and Bohemia heavily affected our brethren who lived there, and forced them to escape and seek refuge from the rotating flaming sword[i] that was set against them. Many honorable families were cordially welcomed to Slutsk, and there found comfort for their souls[3].

The Gaon Rabbi Meir Katz-Ashkenazi, the father of the wonderful Gaon Rabbi Shabtai, the author of the Sha'ch[ii], one of the great ones of Frankfurt, and later the rabbi of Brisk, sent his young son Rabbi Yona (Menachem) Nachum to study Torah in the Yeshiva of the aforementioned Rabbi Yaakov in Slutsk[4].

The residents of Slutsk escaped from their city and communal life was interrupted only for a few years in the midst of the tribulations of *Ta't ve Ta'ch*[iii]. However, after the fury passed and the land quieted, the community of Slutsk returned to its original strength and honor. In the year 5458 [1698], the famous emissary from Chevron, the Sephardic rabbi, Rabbi Avraham the son of Rabbi Levi Kunki, passed through most of the countries of Europe. When he reached the lands of Lithuania and Reisen [White Russia], he found there "four goblets with almond blossoms[iv] standing for the four languages of redemption, that is: Brisk, Pinsk, Horodna, and Vilna. After that he adds and details: "And there is yet another holy community,

[Page 80]

Slutsk, filled with the satisfaction of Torah and greatness together!" – this is from the preface to his book *Avak Sofrim*, Amsterdam 5464 [1704].

The wonderful description of Rabbi Natan Nota Hanover and the end of his book *Yaven Metzula*, regarding the leadership of the communities in the country of Poland, is fully applicable to the splendid community of

Slutsk. The tradition was maintained in Slutsk in a restricted manner during most times, that their rabbis of Slutsk, who were always from among the great ones of the generation, served in the dual role of "Head of the Rabbinical Court" standing at the helm of the rabbinate, as well as Head of the Yeshiva. Even during the first decades of the sixth century C.E., before the founding of the Yeshiva of Volozhin in the year 5564 [1804], at a time when Lithuanian Jewry was lacking in great Yeshivot, there were important groups of Torah scholars in Slutsk. They studied Torah constantly in the local *Beis Midrashes* – over and above the people of the city who filled the *Beis Midrash* and studied Torah alone or with the congregation. In general, the Jews of Slutsk were able to state with pride: "From the times of our forefathers, Yeshiva never ceased among them."[5]

Rabbi Nissan Waxman

. They would relate the following in Slutsk: When the rabbinical seat of the city became vacant around the year 5590 [1830], the leaders of the community of Slutsk approached the Gaon Rabbi Chaim of Volozhin to send them an excellent student suitable to serve as their rabbi. He recommended one of the best of his students, Rabbi Yaakov Meir Yalovker. When they came to inform him of the opinion of his rabbi, he responded that he had no intention of serving in the rabbinate. His mother was present a that event, and ordered him to accept.

Note: in the book *Kol Yehuda* by Rabbi Yehuda Leib the son of Rabbi Eliezer, the head of the rabbinical court of Zeleny (Jozepol, 5587 [1827]), we find a eulogy of him, referring to him as: the Lamp of Israel, a father in wisdom but young in years, who enlightened the eyes of his generation with the light of his Torah, and gathered to himself every orphan and every widow. He established tens and hundreds of students. (Brought in a note in his article on the Yeshiva of Volozhin, page 27), from Rabbi Dr. Shmuel Kalman Mirsky in his book "Torah Institutions in Europe" (New York, 5716 [1956]). It appears from this, that he served as the head of the Yeshiva in Jalowka.

Rabbi Yaakov Meir immediately told them: "I am prepared to forgo my opinion because of the honor of my mother, and to accept the yoke of your rabbinate. But give me one year so I can review the four sections of the Code of Jewish Law before I come to your camp."They accepted this. At the end of the year, he died.

Then the city notables approached Rabbi Chaim once again, and he sent them his dear student, the Gaon Rabbi Yosef the son of Meir of Bohemia (Poymer), who spent a long period of 36 years in Slutsk.

When the Gaon Rabbi Yosef came to Slutsk, he called the prominent elderly Reb Avraham, the *Shamash* of the Chevra Kadisha for 50 years, and "[where does this quotation end?]asked that he show him the graves of the Gaonim Rabbi Naftali Hertz Ginzburg and Rabbi Yitzchak Binyamin Wolf, the author of the book *Nachalat Binyamin*, who were buried in the city cemetery. Rabbi Avraham showed him one burial canopy, and only the grave of the Gaon Rabbi Nachum Katzenelboign-Wahl, the grandson of the prince Reb Shaul Wahl[v] between them. The Gaon Rabbi Yosef groaned: These righteous people did not make peace with each other to this time. He told the *Shamash* the following:

With the passage of time, when the Gaon Rabbi Naftali Hertz, the rabbi of Slutsk, was very elderly, he took on many householders who had difficulty discussing religious matters with him. There were large fairs in Slutsk, and many people would come for the market days. When some dispute arose among any of them, even between gentiles, they would go to the rabbi to have the case adjudicated by him. They would accept his decision without dispute. Therefore, even the gentiles complained that it was hard to come to the rabbi on account of his great old age. The city leaders decided to choose a younger rabbi to direct the Yeshiva, to preach the word of G-d, to teach, and to judge any matter that came before him.

When the book *Nachalat Binyamin* was published in the year 5402 [1642], and the author made a great impression upon the Torah world due to his great sharpness, the leaders of the city of Slutsk approached the author, Rabbi Yitzchak Binyamin Wolf, and offered him the rabbinical seat in their city. But he refused, saying that he would not turn his ear toward them without the permission of the elderly rabbi. They interceded with the elderly Gaon and received a letter of permission from him. Then, the author of *Nachalat Binyamin* acceded to them. When he arrived in Slutsk, he immediately went to the elderly rabbi and told him that he relied on his letter, and came to the city with his agreement. The Gaon Rabbi Naftali Hertz told him: If your honor would have pondered my letter, you would have seen that it had dots in order to minimize that which was written[5a]. The Gaon Rabbi Yitzchak Binyamin responded that he did not pay attention to the dots[vi].

In any case, he was accepted as the head of the rabbinical court and rabbi in Slutsk. It is unfortunate that these two luminaries both died in the year 5407 [1647]. They are buried on either side of the grave of the Gaon Rabbi Nachum Katznelboigen[6].

The legend continues that the Gaon Rabbi Naftali Hertz called upon the Gaon Rabbi Yitzchak Binyamin to a judgment before the Heavenly court. The Torah adjudication continued until Rabbi Yosele took over the rabbinical seat of Slutsk. Then, the Heavenly court decided that they should stand before the rabbi of Slutsk, the place of the deed, and he would declare the verdict. The legend continues that these two Gaonim came to Rabbi Yosele in a dream and he accepted to adjudicate between them. When the *Shamash* showed them their graves, he commanded [who? Rabbi Yosele to depart from there and to wait at the cemetery gate. But Rabbi Yosele tarried next to the

[Page 81]

canopy alone for several hours. When he returned to the *Shamash* at a late hour, his face was flaming, and he did not speak much. He only said, "Blessed be G-d, that the matter has ended properly, and now there will be peace between them."[7]

In time, a large tree grew between their graves, spreading its branches over both graves. (The tree existed over their canopies until the time of the final destruction.)

Even though the legend was not appropriate at all, for the skeptical spirit of the Jews of Slutsk, several notable things can be learned from it. An important Yeshiva was flourishing in Slutsk in the year 5442 [1682]. In any case, it is clear that the primary condition for the Slutsk rabbinate was that the rabbi should preach the words of G-d at the Yeshiva. The official Yeshiva head at that time was Rabbi Aharon HaLevi Feinstein (the father of Rabbi Eliyahu, the head of the rabbinical court of Pruzhany) until around 5603 [1843], when he went to serve in the rabbinate of Starobin. After him, the Gaon Rabbi Menahem Mendel Epstein, known as Reb Mendele, was appointed as head of the Yeshiva, and served in that position for many years.

When the Gaon Rabbi Yosef Dov Soloveitchik came from Volozhin to occupy the rabbinical seat of Slutsk in the year 5625 [1865], he was quite amazed with the learning methodology of Reb Mendele, to) the point that he gave over to him his dear son Chaim, aged twelve at the time, and asked that he study together with him. Reb Mendele conducted his work honorably, and the following year, the rabbi asked that he continue studying with his son and another lad named Yosef Rozen. The latter, even though he was several years younger than the rabbi's son, was already known as a wonderful genius, astounding everyone who knew him. Although the father of the lad, Reb Fishel, was a Chabad Hassid, he brought him from his home in Rogachov and gave him over to the oversight and supervision of the "cold *misnaged*," the rabbi of "Chilly Slutsk." This lad studied together with the rabbi's son for about one year. Rabbi Yosef Dov did not take his eyes off of them, and would test them from time to time. Chaim, the son of Rabbi Yosef Dov, remained in Rabbi Mendele's Yeshiva for several years, and we can surmise that Rabbi Chaim learned from Rabbi Mendele of Slutsk the foundations of his learning style, separating the principles and roots of the *halacha* into their primary factors. That was the methodology that caused wonders in the world of Torah and conquered most of its fortresses under its banner, the banner of Rabbi Chaim Soloveitchik of Volozhin and Brisk. Without doubt, Reb Mendele imparted his stamp upon his second student, albeit in a more restricted manner. That student later became known as one of the great ones of the generations, the Rogachover Gaon, the rabbi of the Hassidic community of Dvinsk [Daugavpils]. (He died in Vienna on 11 Adar, 5696 [1936].)

When the Gaon Rabbi Isser Zalman Meltzer came to Slutsk in the year 5657 [1897], bringing his Yeshiva with him, he thereby returned the crown of the splendid past of that Torah community to its former glory. His forced separation from there in the year 5683 [1923] marked the bitter end to a glorious period of the rabbinate in the Diaspora of White Russia. I was unable to repress those feelings when I was invited to give a greeting at the dedication of the Yeshiva of Slutsk in the city of Kletzk in the year 5690 [1930] at a gathering of several Gaonim of the region, headed by the Gaon Rabbi Isser Zalman, who came specially from the Land of Israel to participate in the dedication. As an alumnus of Slutsk, I felt myself as a mourner among the bridegrooms, and I expressed my thoughts in accordance with the dedication of the Second Temple: "And many of the Kohanim, Levites, heads of dynasties and elders who had seen the First Temple when it was standing were weeping" (Ezra 3:12).

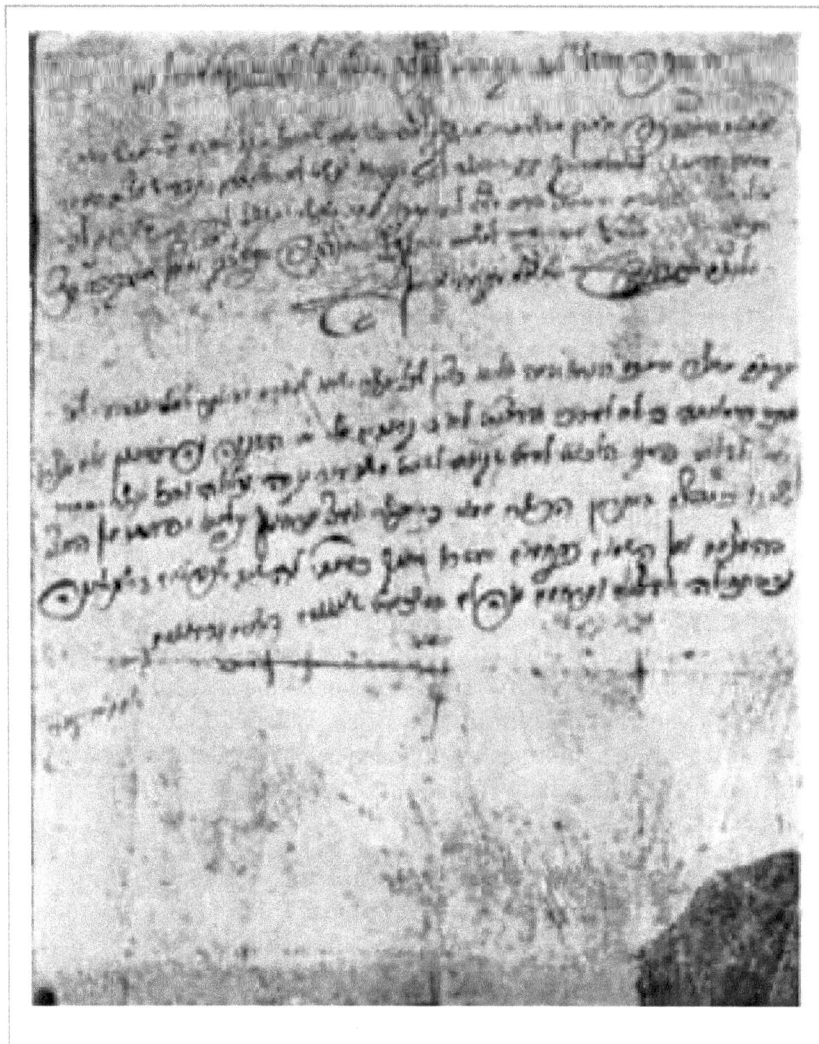

A letter of Rabbi Mendele to the community of Kozlovich,
stating that they should appoint Rabbi Aryeh Leib Charif of
Slutsk as their rabbi. In section II of the Responsa of Rabi Aryeh
Leib, he states that he refused to serve in the rabbinate.

Indeed, when the Gaon Rabbi Isser Zalman was in Slutsk, he succeeded in innovating something there and turning it to a bastion of the written Torah. He was the initiator and influencer of the publication of the *Yagdil Torah* Torah anthology, in which the Torah giants of the generation participated and considered as second in importance to *Hatevuna*, published a half century previously by the Gaon Rabbi Yisrael Salanter (Konigsberg, 5621 [1861]). The Gaon Rabbi Isser Zalman found a person equal to him in wisdom, fitting to his Torah, wisdom, and dedication to the goal – the Gaon Rabbi Moshe Binyamin Tomashoff, whom he appointed as editor and to whom he assigned the directorship of the anthology.

The *Yagdil Torah* Anthology and its Editor

Rabbi Moshe Binyamin Tomashoff was born on 7 Adar 5638 [1878] to his father Rabbi Alexander Yehoshua and his mother Basha. His father earned his livelihood honorably from the Russian bookstore in

Slutsk. When Moshe Binyamin reached the age of Bar Mitzvah, he began to study in the Yeshiva of Rabbi Nechemia, which was in the *Beis Midrash* of Reb Isserke at that time. He studied there for about three years, and his name became known in the scholarly circles of Slutsk for his breadth and diligence.

During those days, the name of the Gaon Rabbi Boruch Ber Leibowitz began to rise. He was also a native of Slutsk, or, more accurately, of Podlivtsi outside of Slutsk. Rabbi Boruch Ber married the daughter of Rabbi Avraham Yitzchak HaLevi Zimmerman, the rabbi of Slutsk. His father-in-law Rabbi

[Page 82]

Zimmerman was appointed as the rabbi of Kremenchug, and then Rabbi Boruch Ber took his place in Slutsk.

In the year 5654 [1893], immediately after Sukkot, Rabbi Baruch Ber went to the Tomashoff residence in Slutsk to convince the father to send his son Moshe Binyamin to his Yeshiva in Hlusk, and promised to supervise him. Rabbi Boruch Ber fulfilled his promise, and he himself studied together with him each night until 2:00 or 3:00 a.m. During the winter nights, they succeeded in going over only four chapters in the *Choshen Mishpat* section of the Code of Jewish Law (sections 39, 40,41, and 46). Only a person who knows the manner of Rabbi Baruch Ber's great depth and toil can believe such a thing.

After that, Rabbi Moshe Binyamin split his years of study between the Yeshivas of Slobodka and Slutsk until the time of his marriage in 5663 [1903] to the daughter of the Gaon Rabbi Tzvi Yaakov Oppenheim, the rabbi of Kelm in Lithuania.

After several years of study in the home of his father-in-law, he returned to his native city of Slutsk and was close to the Gaon Rabbi Isser Zalman, who already knew him from Slobodka. In time, the Slutsk Yeshiva grew as did its expenses, and there was no source of money, for in accordance with the law in Russia at the time, it was forbidden to send out emissaries to collect money for the benefit of the Yeshiva. The Gaon Rabbi Isser Zalman, who by nature was a visionary and a dreamer, did not rest, as he searched for ways of easing the difficult situation. On Purim of 5668 [1908], when he was in a jovial mood, and several of the illustrious students of the Yeshiva were feasting in his house, he turned to Rabbi Meir Binyamin Tomashoff and expressed his intention to found a weekly anthology for Torah and wisdom. This would have several purposes, first, as a collection for its own purpose, and second, as an opportunity for the emissaries of the Yeshiva to collect money under the pretext "for the anthology." Therefore, he advised Rabbi Tomashoff to approach the regional minister in Minsk with a request for a permit to publish a Torah anthology in Slutsk in his[whose?] father's printing press.

These words resonated with Rabbi Tomashoff as timely, since he was already looking for a source of livelihood, and he regarded this as something fitting to his personality. However, at first, he accepted the suggestion of the rabbi as a Purim joke that came to the imagination of the genius at a jovial moment, for why would the governor in Minsk give such a permit at a time when the government was refusing to accede to the requests of people more famous than he, and of known institutions more influential than the Yeshiva of Slutsk? In any case, he sent a request to the regional minister after some time, and turned his attention away from this matter. To his great surprise, Rabbi Tomashoff received the permit after a few months, and dedicated himself to the preparations for publishing. He designed an announcement, which he sent to all the rabbis and Torah greats, urging them to take part in the anthology, which would be a "unique organ" in the field of Torah and rabbinics.

Most of the Gaonim of the generation gave him their blessings and promised to participate. Only a few did not understand the entire matter, and suspected that this might be a matter from which the "odor of *haskalah*" would emanate. The famous rabbi and preacher Rabbi Elyakim Getzel Leviatan, the preacher of righteousness in Brisk, asked innocently, "What is an organ? You do not have another word for this. Also, what is 'unique,' for is there not only One who is unique?"

When the matter came to be carried out, Rabbi Tomashoff realized that he had to start everything from the beginning, that is: to acquire publishing machines and typography letters with all their accessories. He did the calculations and found that everything necessary would cost about 1,000 to 1,200 rubles. The Gaon Rabbi Isser Zalman gave him 100 rubles, and Rabbi Tomashoff took the rest from his dowry money. Even his parents helped him in purchasing the machines. Rabbi Tomashoff himself arranged the lettering, conducted the entire publishing task, corrected and edited the articles, and wrote his own Torah articles as well as notes on almost every article by the rest of the participants. He only had assistants for known tasks. Among them was Rabbi Moshe Aharon Poleyeff of Timkovichi, who studied at that time in Slutsk (currently he is one of the heads of the Rabbi Isaac Elchanan Yeshiva of New York). He would transcribe most of the manuscripts of the participants into clear print, for a salary of three rubles per month. The headings for the issues were written by the young girl Chana Perl, the daughter of Rabbi Isser Zalman, on a voluntary basis. She later became the wife of Rabbi Aharon Pines-Kotler.

To the joy of many, the first issue of the *Yagdil Torah* anthology was published on Tuesday of the Torah Portion of *Miketz*, 28 Kislev 5669 [1908], "through the efforts of the editors and publishers: Isser Zalman Meltzer, the head of the rabbinical court and head of the Yeshiva of this place, and Moshe Binyamin Tomashoff."

The cover page had a detailed table of subscription prices in the local currency: in Russia, 2 rubles and 50 kopecks, 1.50 for a half a year, 30 kopecks for a month. Abroad: for a year with monthly mailings – 2.50, weekly mailings, 4 rubles. For an individual edition, 5 kopecks. The price of advertisements: 25 kopecks for each small line. Indeed, no secular advertisements were even published in it. The cover page indicated that it was published in Slutsk, and its purpose was "novel Torah ideas, halachic didactics, questions and responsa in decisions of Jewish law, exegesis, *mussar* [moral lessons], and articles on issues of religion, Torah, and fear of G-d." Under the title heading, the title and place of publication were printed in Russian. On page 2 of the issue, the Gaon Rabbi Isser Zalman wrote "A few words of introduction," explaining the purpose of the anthology, and the reason for his participation in its publication. Among other things, he writes: "We will now illustrate a bit at a bad, bitter time, when the cold is very great, the house is full of holes and cracks, and the children stand shivering with cold, their clothing is thin and soft, their faces are white as lime, if we do not make an effort to obtain a bit of wood and kindling to make some sort of fire, some flame to bring a bit of warmth into the house, they will perish from cold and freezing." After that he continued: "I know the weight of the task, and the difficulty in establishing the anthology, but I did not take upon myself all this work until my friend the Gaon Rabbi Meir Binyamin Tomashoff, may he live, told me he would take upon himself this task, and that his great powers are quite fitting to work on this – – and I see before me the conditions of the physical and spiritual situation of my honorable friend the Gaon Rabbi Meir Binyamin, may he live, that the periodical will be able to maintain itself for a long time with the help of G-d. Therefore, I have agreed to take this sublime periodical upon myself as well" – – –

The booklet was sent to five hundred subscribers, including about two hundred rabbis, and most of the Torah greats, who were to pay the subscription fee later.

Rabbi Tomashoff indeed did not disappoint. He fulfilled his task completely, and brought the anthology to a very high, honorable level, even though it did not meet his expectations from a material perspective. As has been stated, he would write notes and react to the articles of the writers. He became known in the Torah world as a serious editor and a sharp critic, who did not hesitate to reject those items that did not seem fit to print, even

[Page 83]

if they came from famous people. On the other hand, he brought in many unknown researchers, and encouraged and publicised them.

Rabbi Shmuel Yosef Zevin, who was the rabbi in Kazimirov (Minsk region), wrote a two-part article on the *Yagdil Torah* anthology in *Hamodia*, published by Rabbi Akiva Rabinovitch in Poltava. After Rabbi Zevin complained about the Gaonim of the generation, that they were not following in the footsteps of their predecessors and were not placing the fruits of their spirits into a book; he praised the anthology, which would preserve the splendor of the Torah of our generation in general, and the Torah of the Gaonim of Lithuania in particular, which succeeded in developing and broadening during the latter period in a special manner of "logic, explanation, clarity of feeling, and strength of reasoning, delving into the depth of each and every issue." In his opinion, the anthology also fulfilled another task, important in and of itself, "to explain and delve into the questions that have arisen during the recent period on account of the new needs and realities." At the end of his words, he gives a warm caress to the face of the rabbi who was the editor: "The proficient rabbi and Gaon, which is Mr. Tomashoff (even though he did not use that title), who knows how to separate the wheat from the chaff with his proper notes and clear responses. His diligent hand is recognized in all Talmudic subjects of the anthology." (*Hamodia*, numbers 3-4, 12 Cheshvan 5672 [1912]).

Uncaptioned. The title page of *Yagdil Torah*, first year, issue 1. Tuesday of
the Torah portion of *Miketz*, 28 Kislev, 4th day of Chanukah 5669 [1909].

הערות מאת המערכת

לסוכנים יתן ראבאט כנהוג

Редакція „ЯГДИЛЪ ТОРА" Слуцкъ, Минской губ.

Redaction „IAGDIL THORA" Sluzk gouv. Minsk

Uncaptioned. The page opposite the title page (i.e., the copyright page). The text is as follows:

Notes from the Editors

a. We hereby ask forgiveness from the writers if is necessary to change and fixe their words. They should forgive us if it is at times difficult, given the plethora of articles, to give them a place in a timely fashion, and that we are forced to delay.

b.   Articles that are not published will not be returned to their owners.

c.   At the end of one year, every subscriber will be sent a table of contents.

d.   The subscriber must prepay their subscription fees.

e.   The fees for the anthology can also be sent through the Russian postal system, but the writer must accept responsibility.

f.   Place will be allotted in the anthology for announcements on issues of Judaism, such as copies of rabbinical meetings in cities that ask for such, notices of new books, announcements from Yeshivot, etc.

g.   Out of respect for the rabbis, may they live long, in every place, we ask, aside from supporting and strengthening the anthology themselves if they can afford it, they should also try to support it from the book funds of the *Beis Midrashes*, for at the end of the year, G-d willing, they will belong to the library.

Agents will be granted their customary rights.

The address for sending money and letters:
Redaction, IAGDIL THORA Sluzk gouw Minsk
Editors and publishers; Isser Zalman Meltzer head of the rabbinical court and yeshiva head of the local city. Moshe Binyamin Tomashoff.

The Gaon Rabbi Chaim Ozer Grodzinski of Vilna wrote a special letter to Rabbi Tomashoff, stating that in his opinion, the anthology stands at a level close to that of *Hatevuna*, which was published by the Gaon Rabbi Yisrael Salanter of blessed memory (Konigsberg 5621 [1861]).

When the Gaon Rabbi Boruch Ber came to America in the year 5699 [1939] and visited the home of Rabbi Tomashoff, he noticed the *Yagdil Torah* anthology, which stood bound in his bookshelf. He opened it and perused it with reverence and love. Then he turned to Rabbi Tomashoff and said, "Does your honor know why I am looking at it? It is because my rabbi, the Gaon Rabbi Chaim Soloveitchik, would also look into it, and appreciated it."

Indeed, as has been said, despite the acclaim that was brought to him in the world of Torah by the anthology, the material situation of the editor did not improve on its account. Rather, it apparently declined further, and he was forced to take a hiatus on occasion and issue a call to the subscribers to pay their subscription fee. Later he was forced against his will to request "help and side support of certain sums on an annual basis from various benefactors." When the appeals did not bring their desired results, the editor extended past his usual bounds with bitter words to explain the reason for the cessation of the anthology, that was caused only by his personal situation. In a main article called "A person does not know his time" Rabbi Tomashoff writes among other things: "Until this time I do not have a reliable source for my livelihood, other than from my parents, may they live, who are my supports at my right hand. However, now, they have taken from me, and almost stolen the narrow, meager flow, my publishing house, that we have succeeded in founding and creating through great toil and self-sacrifice. Now, my eyes are lifted toward the mercies of G-d, that He should prepare a source of livelihood for me. This is the reason that has prevented me from publishing *Yagdil Torah* in its right time."

[Page 84]

Rabbi Moshe Binyamin Tomashoff (the Mabi't)

(See issues 12 and 24, year 1, and issues 20 and 23, year 2.)

With all this, Rabbi Tomashoff rose above is situation and continued to publish the anthology until issue 8 of the third year, 5672 [1912]. Then his illness became more serious, and he had to travel to a doctor in Berlin. There, he decided to immigrate to America, to where his parents had immigrated in the interim.

Rabbi Tomashoff was greeted with joy in New York by the great rabbis who knew him from his youth in the Yeshivas of Slobodka and Slutsk, and especially on account of the anthology that he edited, bringing fame to his name in the world. However, he was not able to continue to publish the anthology in his new place.

Rabbi Tomashoff attempted to renew the anthology in New York in the year 5676 [1916], and he succeeded in publishing several issues, with the participation of the Torah greats of the United States. However, they were lacking the vibrant living spirit that was present in all the issues published in Slutsk.

At that time, Rabbi Meir Berlin, who had arrived in New York from Germany, where he edited *Ivri*, met him. He told him, "As a brother in craft, I advise you to not conduct your editing here as was your manner in Slutsk. There, the rabbis of Israel occupied themselves in Torah and created novel Torah ideas, which they wrote down and sent to you to publish. From your side, you conducted yourself as per the custom of the wise people of Israel from generation to generation: 'Even a father and his son, or a rabbi and his student, who are occupying themselves in Torah, and become enemies with each other'[lvii]. You have hit them on the thigh as you have illuminated their words. Afterward, certainly the end of that [Talmudic] statement was certainly fulfilled: 'they do not move from them until they become friends with each other.' However, in this country, where the numbers who occupy themselves with Torah for its own sake are diminishing, and those who devise new halachic ideas are becoming fewer, if some day someone comes by chance to publish something, and you use your editorial powers to contradict his words, you will destroy him completely, and he will hate you thoroughly!"

In the year 5685 [1925], Rabbi Tomashoff made efforts to once again revive the anthology. After the First World War, several Torah giants arrived in America, including some who had participated in *Yagdil Torah* in Slutsk. Therefore, Rabbi Tomashoff felt that the time was ripe for this. However, rather than publishing it in a private manner as he had done to this point, it was now edited and published collectively by all the participants. The name of the anthology was also changed to *Migdal Torah*. In his introduction, the editor explains the reasons he used the *segula*[viii] of changing the name: "for no longer do we have any surrounding and separating wall. Breaches were made in the wall, and the air of the secular world has penetrated. The borders have become blurred, and the spirits have become intermixed. The secular air has become a stormy stream that uproots our limbs in its path. The holiness of Torah is evaporating from all the minds and secular cultures are coming and filling the space in the minds. When there is no wall, we must at least build a fortress [Migdal] to protect the status of the scholars who are sharpening each other in *halacha*, with live questions on deep matters of Torah, through which the debates themselves arouse is us the disappearing life force and the concealed light hidden within us."

The booklet indeed made a great impression in the world of Torah, and many thought that the anthology will "return to its former strength." But the "Mabi't" (as he always signed his introductions and notes in all issues that he edited, with the acronym of Moshe Binyamin Tomashoff) saw with his sharp eyes that this was merely an imaginary rally before its death throes, and that it would certainly not exist for long. After all the adventures that he endured in editing the anthology from Slutsk to New York, he was able to realize that he did not have the ability to continue that work at the level that he was used to, and he absolved himself.

After Rabbi Tomashoff decided to no longer continue as editor, he collected his numerous articles and novel ideas on *halacha*, and succeeded in publishing them. These include: *Tikkun Gittin* on the laws of *Gittin* [divorce], and his significant, three volume book, *Avnei Shoham*, on all areas of Talmud and rabbinic decisors. His books were accepted with love and reverence in all Torah circles, and the majority of rabbis use them for practical *halacha*.

After Rabbi Tomashoff came to New York, the publication of the anthology stopped in Slutsk, as is known, until Rabbi Yechezkel Abramsky arrived during the 1920s to serve in the rabbinate. During those stormy years of fury, Rabbi Abramsky was inspired, together with Rabbi Shlomo Yosef Zevin, who was then the rabbi of Novozybkov, to renew the publication of *Yagdil Torah* in Slutsk, in order to blow a living breath among the other rabbis who remained in Soviet Russia. This period of self-sacrifice is indeed important, and it should be written about on its own. However, as far as our knowledge extends to the other side of that hidden [i.e. iron] curtain, it is possible to justly state that the *Yagdil Torah* anthology of Slutsk was perhaps the final one to utter a word of living Torah in that country, and also the first of its kind in the new country of America.

From among the participants in *Yagdil Torah* in Slutsk, under the editorship of M. B. Tomashoff, who are still alive, may the following rabbis and Gaonim live long (in alphabetical order): Eliyahu Yosef Henkin, Chaim BenZion Notelewitz, Yoel David Mozeszon, Yechezkel Abramsky, Yechiel Yaakov Weinberg, Nissan Telushkin, Tzvi Pesach Frank, Reuven Katz, Shlomo Blazer, and Shlomo Yosef Zevin.

Editor's note: The sad news that Rabbi Binyamin Moshe Tomashoff died in New York on 6 Tevet, 5720 [1960] has reached us. May his memory be a blessing!

Original footnotes:

1. *Daat Kedoshim*, page 228. Through the testimony of the author of *Kaneh Chochma*, Prd'a [Perhaps *Pirkei Derabi Eliezer*], 441.
2. *Yaven Metzula* by Rabbi Natan Nota Hanover, page 58.
3. *Daat Kesoshim*, ibid.
4. *Kiryah Neemana* by Rabbi Sh. Y. Fuen, page 92, Vilna 5675 [1905] (in the book *History of the Great Teachers* by Shevach Knobil, where Lutzk is written in error instead of Slutsk. Return
5. Tractate *Yoma*, 28b.
    a. (trans: there are two footnote 5 on this page, so I made the second one 5a) *Shir Hashirim Rabba* 87: "Every place where you find a large dot on what is written, capture the dot and leave what is written." (trans: i.e. take an innuendo from the word or letters that have a dot on top.)
6. *Daat Kedoshim* page 47.
7. From the mouth of the elderly Rabbi Natan Kaplan, who learned in Slutsk during the times of Rabbi Meir the son of Rabbi Yosef, and the Ridva'z, and heard several statements on these matters from him.

Translator's footnotes:

1. Based on Genesis 3:24.
2. See https://en.wikipedia.org/wiki/Shabbatai_HaKohen
3. A term used for the Chmielnicki uprising and the destruction of Jewish communities in its wake. The term itself is the Hebrew acronym for the years 5408-5409, i.e., 1648-1649.
4. Based on Exodus 32:20.
5. See https://yivoencyclopedia.org/article.aspx/Wahl_Shaul
6. The innuendo here seems to be that the letter from Rabbi Naftali Hertz may not have been written completely willingly.
7. Tractate Kiddushin 30b.
8. Roughly translates to "folk remedy" or "talisman."

[Page 85]

The Head of the Yeshiva

by Rav Yosef Eliahu Henkin

Translated by Yocheved Klausner

The great scholar R'Isser Zalman Melamed z"l – all days of his life were one long chain of learning, teaching and acitivity. The days of his study in Volozhin were the days of the hunger for "enlightenment"; many of the students were attracted, but not this student. He continued studying Torah and was a good friend of the Rav, teacher in the Yeshiva, R'Chaim Soloveitchik z"l. When Volozhin was closed, he went to Radin.

After he married the daughter of R'Feivel Frank z"l from Kovno, his wife took upon herself the duty of providing sustenance, so that he could continue studying. He and his brother-in-law R'Epstein z"l were appointed heads of the Slobodka Yeshiva, without a salary.

At the time, the Sloboda Yeshiva was supported by the well-known donor R'Ovadia Lachman. During the great controversy concerning the study of "Morals" at the Yeshivas, according to the method of R'Salanter, the Kovno and Slobodka Yeshiva Heads were part of the opposition.

After arguments and changes, R'Isser Zalman had to decide whether to return to Slobodka or to settle in Slutsk. He was also busy at the time with taking to print his work on the Jerusalem Talmud.

After many hesitations, he decided to go with his family to Slutsk. Yet, the arguments between the rabbis in Slutsk deterred him from stabilizing the situation of the Yeshiva; therefore he took upon himself to take care of the ordinary physical needs of the Yeshiva as well – and he did both things with great success.

His lessons were liked and appreciated more than the lessons of the other teachers in the Yeshivas, and his talks on the subject of Morals made a huge impression, and I remember some of the talks he gave between the afternoon and evening prayers [*between Mincha and Ma'ariv*], which filled our hearts with the fear of God, in particular during the month of Elul and the "Ten days of repentance," as he would often burst in tears. From 1897 to 1904 he served as teacher. He was also Head of the Religious Court in Slutsk, and was busy publishing his writings, as well.

After that, they appointed R'Isser Zalman Rabbi and Head of the Religious Court and the other rabbi remained only in the yeshiva in Zaretse Street and surroundings.

Since then, the Yeshiva developed more and more, until finally it built its own fine building, after having wandered from the synagogue on Zaretse, to Ostrover, to the Taylors, to the Kloiz, all in parallel to the well-known "exiles" of the Sanhedrin. Hundreds of students flowed to the Yeshiva of Slutsk and its name became famous. One of its branches became the Yeshiva of Shklow, as the scholar Fruskin z"l was sent there to serve as teacher. The Slutsk students opened a Yeshiva in Stołpce as well, with the help of the Head of the Religious Court there.

At the time the yeshiva was located in the Ostrova Bet Midrash, the "enlightenment" movement and secular studies spread among the students. The Yeshiva immediately prohibited secular studies and reading newspapers. Some of the students left and opened a new yeshiva. Rabbi Isser Zalman, firm and stubborn, fought against any deviation from the accepted ways of the yeshivas – only our holy Torah and its commentaries should be the guides of Judaism.

The Odessa Yeshiva was different from the others: its leaders introduced Torah and general Education together and it became known as a shelter for those who left Torah, and the name "Yeshiva" was kept only as a cover.

At that time, however, the Rav Reines z"l founded a yeshiva in Lydda, for the study of Torah and other studies, but his hopes that its level of Torah study would be high were not fulfilled and the students' bags were full of books by the new Hebrew writers and writers in other languages. The same was the fate of other yeshivas, founded next to older yeshivas, as that of Slutsk and some others. However, the *Etz-Chaim* Yeshiva, under the directorship of Rabbi Isser Zalman, grew, and hundreds of students from near and far came to study. During WWI, the worries of the Head of the Yeshiva were great: he had to watch and make sure that the students should not be mobilized and sent to battle and he was concerned with the city matters as well, as the chief rabbi: refugees from Poland and Lithuania filled the town and he had to take care of their needs. Epidemics erupted, and the rabbi fought like a hero to keep everything in order.

During the days of the Revolution and the victory of the Bolsheviks, he made every effort to keep the yeshiva and the Talmud Torah functioning and he was arrested and saved by the fact that he was liked and respected by the leftists for his deep devotion to the poor and the oppressed. Finally he was forced to escape to Kletsk, which belonged to Poland, and remained there several years; after his son-in-law the scholar Rabbi Kotler became the Head of the yeshiva, he made Aliya to the Holy Land.

In addition to his holy work at the Etz Chaim Yeshiva in Jerusalem,

[Page 86]

and printing his writings, he became the main authority in all religious matters and was a great help to his fellows. I shall not exaggerate if I say that thousands of letters asking for help for individuals and institutions were received from him in New York, most of them in his own handwriting. Only during the last year of his life somebody wrote the letters for him and he would sign them. Some of the letters reached our office after his death.

Here are described some of the ways of the scholar, who brought light to the children of Israel by his study, his deeds and his merits. He was the father of his students and the teachers who worked with him.

He supported me personally as well and helped me establish the yeshiva in Stołpce and sent me students from Slutsk.

May he rest in peace and may his eternal rest be of honor.

(From his book that appeared in New York 1951)

The Eitz Chaim Yeshiva

by Rabbi Tzvi Yehuda Meltzer

Translated by Jerrold Landau

Edited by Jane S. Gabin

This great wonder that is called the nation of Israel, in exile for two thousand years, is accompanied by unique phenomena that have no equal among any nation or language. Even its history, which developed in accordance with its own internal statutes, is almost wholly a concealed mystery in the eyes of the researchers of the world.

The personalities, which stem from this or that corner in a specific era of the history of the nation of Israel, did not have physical dominion, and had no power to actualize things. Nevertheless, their holy teachings were for all the members of our nation, and nobody would dare contradict their words.

Under such circumstances, a great person who makes history is not forced to serve in the rabbinate in a large city, in a splendid metropolis. It is possible that he is not even a rabbi at all, and is nevertheless a leader with high authority. Therefore, even small towns became famous for being the dwelling place of a prominent person. Torah and teaching would emanate from them to the Nation of Israel in each and every place.

Slutsk also belongs to towns of that type. It is a modest sized city in White Russia. Its name became synonymous for Torah and wisdom in the Jewish Diaspora. We have clear information about the beginning of the Jewish settlement in Slutsk one thousand years ago. I saw a family tree from Rabbi Aharon Kotler, may he live long, that details eighteen generations of rabbis, son following father. Sixteen of them are from Slutsk. Eleven generations ago, Slutsk also served as an administrative center, as one of the capitals of the Council of the Four Lands. Brisk, Litovsk, and Slutsk competed for that honor. This matter was decided in favor of Slutsk for the reason that the number of complete sets of Talmuds in Slutsk was greater than the number of individual tractates in the city.

Memories from My Childhood

Impressions of childhood are etched deep in the heart of the tender child, and are never erased. The adult recalls with awe his bright childhood days, connected to the home of Father and Mother with an abundance of affection and love that will never return, and will not be granted to an adult in his difficult struggles of life.

The image of Rabbi Shimon the Shamash is painted before me as if alive. His relationship to this position reached back to several generations of rabbis, all of whom served in faithfulness and respectful awe. He served the great Gaon, Rabbi Meir Feimer, the son of Rabbi Yossele Feimer, one of the primary students of Rabbi Chaim, the founder of the famous Yeshiva of Volozhin. After him, he also served the Ridba'z[1].

I also recall the stories of Rabbi Yosef Feimer, may the memory of the righteous be blessed. The glory of royalty was etched on his face. He was meticulous about manners. They said of him that he never changed the paved stones upon which he walked over the course of decades on the way from his house to the synagogue. His relationships with members of the community was one of mutual honor. The community revered him, and he honored the community.

Following him, Rabbi Yosef Dov Soloveitchik served in the rabbinate. He was the complete opposite of his predecessor: a stormy soul, vibrant, dynamic, impulsive, triggered and prepared for the battle for principles and ideas. He arrived in Slutsk during the chilling era of snatchings for the army – the Cantonists – under the order of the inimical Czar Nikolai I. he fought against the accepted custom of giving over the children of poor people to the army, and decreed that the children of the wealthy be given in their place, for their parents could always find the necessary means to redeem them. It once happened that a poor child was snatched. The Gaon Rabbi Yosef Dov risked his life, broke through the gate behind which the child was imprisoned, and saved him. When the lessee of the meat tax once approached him in the slaughterhouse to request a ban on outside meat, out of suspicion of obstacles, the Gaon Rabbi Yosef Dov ordered his wife to remove from the cowshed the cow that that lessee had previously given over for the needs of the family of the rabbi, and to return it to him. When she did not hasten to do so, he arose himself, untied the cow, turned to the lessee, and said: "I have already taken out your cow

[Page 87]

and now you can present your complaint to me"[2]. He did not show favoritism to any person, and there was constant friction between him and the wealthy people of the city.

His custom was to descend on the Sabbath from his place at the eastern wall, where the city *parnassim* [administrators] would be seated with their boxes of aromatic tobacco made of silver or gold, and to give the poor tailor, with his wooden box, the honor of a snuff of tobacco. It is clear that these steps were offensive to the stronghanded *parnassim*, and they made his life difficult to the point that he was forced to leave the city.

Rabbi Meir Feimer was appointed in his place. He had the image of his father, may the memory of the righteous be blessed, and peace between the citizens of the city and the rabbi was restored. However, the revolutionary kernel planted by the Gaon Rabbi Yosef Dov began to bear fruit. New ideas and different outlooks changed the status of the *parnassim*. This apparently caused Rabbi Meir to depart.

In accordance with his recommendation, the Ridba'z was invited to take his place. He was quickly exposed as a new edition of the Gaon Rabbi Yosef Dov, who went with the masses and did not subordinate himself to the statues of the strong-handed city *parnassim*. His stance moved a portion of the city leaders to invite Rabbi Meir Feimer to live among them, not as a rabbi, but rather as a resident of the city who would serve as their spiritual guide. He acceded to their urging. Relations between him and the Ridba'z were tense, and he once again left Slutsk, leaving behind his son to serve as rabbi for a portion of the residents of the city.

The Idea of Establishing a Yeshiva in Slutsk

During that period, the Ridba'z considered the idea of founding a branch of the Slobodka Yeshiva in Slutsk. For this purpose, he approached Rabbi Nota Hirsch Finkel "The Elder" may the memory of the righteous be blessed, and asked for his consent to that plan. His request was based on the fact that Slutsk was the gate to White Russia and the areas of central Russia that border it and have large Jewish populations. "The Elder" approved his recommendation, and sent a group of excellent students (they were called the *Yad Hachazaka*[3] because they numbered 14) to Slutsk to found the Yeshiva. My revered father of blessed memory – in whose beat[?] the pioneering spirit of disseminating Torah – was chosen as the head of the new Yeshiva. As he was young at that time, he was considered one of the excellent Yeshiva heads of his generation, and was revered by all his students. It should be noted that all those who moved to Slutsk with my father later became known as Torah greats of good repute, leaders of stature, and famous rabbis throughout the entire Jewish Diaspora.

The Development of the Yeshiva

When it was first founded, there were serious doubts about the possibility of maintaining this enterprise. The difficult pains of spiritual and physical absorption placed the issue of the existence of the Yeshiva into doubt. As it forged a new pedagogical path based on the *Mussar* [moral teachings] doctrine of Rabbi Yisrael Salanter, the Yeshiva encountered opposition in Slutsk and its environs, where the traditions of earlier Yeshivas with different pedagogical styles still pervaded. The struggle of the rabbinate between the Ridba'z and Rabbi Meir also left its mark. There was even an attempt by the followers of Rabbi Meir to establish a competing Yeshiva. Since the other Yeshiva was based on negative foundations, its founders lacked the enthusiasm and dedication required to direct and organize a holy task such as this. For these reasons, that Yeshiva was set up for quick failure, and it closed.

The situation of the Yeshiva was difficult because the Ridba'z, who had promised to bear the yoke of maintaining the Yeshiva, left Slutsk a short time after my father, may the memory of the righteous be blessed, arrived. The entire financial burden fell upon the shoulders of the Yeshiva head. The young Yeshiva head only took upon himself the dissemination of Torah, and was not prepared to bear the financial burden. The situation was difficult to the point that my father, may the memory of the righteous be blessed, lost his strength, and decided to return to Slobodka despite his great intentions. He said, "'And when the cloud was raised up, thy travelled… by G-d's word they camped and by G-d's word the traveled.'[4] It has disappeared, and we must travel and return to Slobodka."

However, providence wished otherwise. A certain wonderful Jew named Rabbi Kushi (Rabbi Yekutiel) Izak Golda's hear about the decision of my father, may the memory of the righteous be blessed, and said to him, "I have the tradition that the Yeshiva is like the ark of the covenant, which bears its bearers, and there is no place for worry." He gave himself over to the enterprise, found sources for the maintenance of the Yeshiva, and saved the enterprise from collapsing. My revered father, may the memory of the righteous be blessed, decided to remain. This Reb Kushi was merely a shopkeeper who devoted most of his time to Torah. The Gaon Rabbi Yosef Dov said about him, "Would it be that I would merit to pray on the Days of Awe as Rabbi Kushi prays throughout all the days of the year."

Such were the Jews of Slutsk, who worked and toiled faithfully. Their entire essence was given over to Torah and its preservation. For its sake, they knew no weariness or tiredness. Their work was without expectation of personal benefit or even the hint of honor. They were in the category of hidden righteous people. They themselves as well as the world at large did not know the magnitude of their righteousness.

The Yeshiva continued to develop, and the size of its student body grew. At the outset, it moved from place to place, from the synagogue on Zarece Street to the Ostrowa Synagogue at the edge of the city, and from there to the Tailors' Synagogue in the center of the city. Only after several years did it merit its own splendid building.

The Yeshiva and the City

Hundreds of Yeshiva students became an inseparable part of the landscape of the city, because the lads were not housed in dormitories, as is the custom in our times, but rather, rooms were rented for them from various householders in all sections of the city {Stancia}. They took their meals with them, or with various families in the city for a fee – and a small portion of them for free (Yamim)[5]. The distribution to various places to sleep and eat in all areas of the city ensured that their presence would be noticed in every corner. They filled the city with their bustle and appearance.

Lads gathered in the Yeshiva from all areas of wide Russia. They came from Moscow, Petersburg, and even the far-off Caucasus. Their influence is noticeable in the Caucasus to this day, for the Yeshiva educated its students for pioneering and for the dissemination of Torah. Its former students established Yeshivas even in the Caucasus. The elderly Gaon Rabbi Eliyahu Henkin, currently, the director of Ezras Torah in the United States, was among the first students of the Yeshiva of Slutsk, and he was also the first to reach the Caucasus and found a Yeshiva there.

After him, the Rabbi and Gaon Rabbi Asher Sandomirski, may he live long, made *aliya* to the Land of Israel. He lives with us in Tel Aviv. With a delegation of rabbis from America, he tells us about the religious life that developed among the Jews of Dagestan in the Caucasus. One can state with certainty that this matter was to a large degree the fruits of the diligence of the students of Slutsk, who knew how to establish an educated generation in a far-off land – a generation that could stand proudly and strongly against the obstacles of the times and the strong pressure from the area and the rulers of the country.

[Page 88]

The Yeshiva gave forth a significant number of rabbis who served in important communities. Many of them are currently found in the entire Jewish Diaspora, especially in the United States. In Slutsk itself, the students actively participated in the organizing of cultural life, and they played an active role in various communal endeavours. Many of them bore the flag of Chibat Tzion, and the connection to the Land of the Fathers, in the spirit of the Yeshiva head, whose influence upon his students was strong.

As is known, my revered father, may the memory of the righteous be blessed, was imbued with a deep, boundless love of Zion. In his time, he was a member of the secret Nes Tziona organization in the Yeshiva of Volozhin. He invested his entire dowry into purchasing land in the area of Hadera.

Even though Zionism was not preached in the Yeshiva in the usual sense of the term, the aspiration to a return to Zion was the lot of the majority of the students.

The Role of Slutsk in the Maintenance of the Yeshiva

Just as the tabernacle [*Mishkan*] in its time, so it was with Slutsk; every man and woman brought their contribution to the building of the Yeshiva, from the screen to the rafters. The day of the dedication of the building turned into a great festival for all the residents of the city. In addition, the residents of the city concerned themselves with the Yeshiva students, and demonstrated their connection and love in various ways. Indeed, other Yeshivas existed in Slutsk, but this was "the Yeshiva" and the pride of the residents.

Its Objective and the Reason for its Success

The success of the Yeshiva of Slutsk can be attributed to several factors. However, the reason for its flourishing and influence is based on the principal that it had a clear objective in the eyes of its founders. It forged new, daring ways in understanding the light of the Torah and its dissemination among all strata of the people: it came to the point where the methodology of Torah study endangered the essence of Torah life. Along with other Lithuanian Yeshivas, the Yeshiva of Slutsk took a revolutionary step in the long tradition of Yeshivas. It had the good, unwavering support of the halachic giants, who stressed the essence of halachic depth.

This approach arose with the new winds in Europe that began to burst through the wall of Jewish separatism. New problems demanded their solutions before they would break and overwhelm the ancient structure. The time came to broaden the horizon, to deepen the understanding of Torah, and to expose points of contact that would strengthen its influence in day-to-day life.

The first one to take a step to realize this plan was Rabbi Yisrael Salanter. Following him, other Yeshivas recognized the need to educate the students in public affairs, and toward the responsibility of Torah studiers to forge the spiritual image of the generation of tomorrow, to fortify it against negative influences that might shake the castle to its foundations. Static thinking without new methodologies is bound to fail. The new Yeshivas, the Yeshiva of Slutsk among them, saved the foundation by creating new vessels for the youth who were fighting the battle for the existence and uniqueness of the nation. Students of those Yeshivas placed themselves as a fortified wall against the attempts of assimilation, whether from the side of the Berlin school, or from the side of the various socialist movements, all of which led to the path of spiritual, religious and national destruction.

Words of Conclusion

We are dutybound to admit and to beat our breasts in confession that Yeshiva education did not succeeded in bringing a decisive negation of the exile. Perhaps this was expressed through the desire and necessity of fighting against the worrying phenomena in their own locations. Due to the need to fight against the danger of spiritual annihilation, they did not sense the collapsing of the ground of the Diaspora beneath the feet of the Jewish nation, and they did not enlist in the battle against indifference to the idea of the return to Zion. This tragic episode is deeper than the abyss, and we cannot define it or judge it. The ways of Providence are hidden from us. "As the Heavens are higher than the earth, thus are My ways loftier than your ways, and My thoughts loftier than your thoughts, for My ways are not your ways, and My thoughts are not your thoughts, says G-d"[6].

We do not understand why the awakening for the redemption that began with the Baal Shem Tov and the Gr'a [Vilna Gaon] did not take hold with their students, and their students' students. Indeed, the Yeshiva of Slutsk will remain as a memory until the victory of the spirit and will over the various obstacles. Its contribution to the golden chain of the Jewish nation will be thought of as a firm possession. All the creativity of the great Yeshivas, even in their destruction, has recognizable influence in all aspects of our lives from generation to generation.

The Yeshiva of Slutsk-Kletzk also merited to strike roots in the Land. As is known, the Yeshiva moved from Slutsk to Kletzk during the time of the Bolshevik rule in Russia. The Yeshiva continued in Kletzk for approximately twenty years as one of the great Yeshivas of Lithuania and Poland. It was headed by the Gaon Rabbi Aharon Kotler, may he live long. However, destruction also overtook it during the time of the terrible Holocaust. The Yeshiva head, Rabbi Aharon Kotler, succeeded in arriving in the United States, and he immediately established a splendid Yeshiva in Lakewood. My revered father, may the memory of the righteous be a blessing, actualized his aspirations during his youth: When the Yeshiva moved from Slutsk to Kletzk, he remained there for about two years, and then moved to the Holy Land to disseminate Torah in the old Eitz Chaim Yeshiva in Jerusalem. He raised up hundreds of students, some of whom disseminate Torah in the Holy Land. This period was among the brightest in the life of my revered father, may the memory of the righteous be blessed, who aspired to education students who would be teachers of the children of Israel.

The Yeshiva of Slutsk also merited a second incarnation. Immediately after the great Holocaust, a memorial to the Yeshiva of Slutsk-Kletzk was set up in Pardes Chana. From there, the Yeshiva moved to Rehovot, and it is known today as "Yeshivat Hadarom" founded upon the Yeshiva of Slutsk-Kletzk. That Yeshiva takes an honorable place among the new Yeshivas in the Land, and it is developing with great speed.

Translator's footnotes:

1. Rabbi Yaakov David Wilovsky. See https://en.wikipedia.org/wiki/Yaakov_Dovid_Wilovsky.
2. He did not want to be influenced by the favor that the lessee did to him.
3. *Yad Hachazaka* is the title of the 14-volume *Mishne Torah* of the Rambam. It literally means "Strong Hand." The word Yad יד has the numerical value of 14.
4. Based on Numbers 9:15-23
5. The terms *Stancia* and *Yamim* are the known terms for the concepts described. *Yamim* literally means "days"=8; and refers to the idea of Yeshiva lad eating meals at various householders on a rotation basis.
6. From Isaiah 55:9-8 [i.e. in reverse order] with slight paraphrasing.

[Page 89]

The Trial of the Yeshiva

by Rabbi Asher Sandomirski

Translated by Jerrold Landau

Rabbi Sender Nachmanowitz
(father of Sh. Nachmani)

The Eitz Chaim Yeshiva existed until 1920 in its building. Then the Bolsheviks expropriated the building as well as my place of residence. We returned to the *Beis Midrash* of the Tailors. We studied in an unofficial manner, and we did not know who the Yeshiva heads were, for they made efforts to be discreet. I would go with Reb Leizer Itshe to collect donations of money and bread for the Yeshiva students.

When I was arrested, they placed me in a special prison cell for interrogation. I was there for a month. They interrogated me: Who directs the Yeshiva, and how does it maintain itself? What was my connection to the Yeshiva? Later, they freed me, and placed me on trial, which was conducted in Yiddish.

The chief judge Kort came from Minsk. Rabbi Isser Zalman of blessed memory and I appeared in court. He was accused, as they found with him a note, regarding receiving money for the Yeshiva. The postal receipt was in the name of Rabbi Isser Zalman of blessed memory. Mass'[?]son was also arrested for posting announcements in the synagogue calling for a revolt against the decrees regarding the study of Torah. Since the *shamashim* [beadles] permitted the affixing of announcements, they were also summoned for judgment. Among them were Reb Natan Fiszkinhorn, the *shamash* of the Karnaim Synagogue, and Reb Sender Nachmanowitz, the *shamash* of the Mishnayos Synagogue (the father of Sh. Nachmani).

A large crowd gathered in the hall of Rabbi Chaim Yoshia Frydman. The members of the court were: Kort, M. Efron, and someone named Trachnilowicz, who resided in a room confiscated by the government in the home of Rabbi Isser Zalman.

Mass was the first to be interrogated. As a Yeshiva student, he would tap his foot and bang his fist on the table during his testimony, as he was wont to do while studying.

His orderly claims, along with movements, changed the trial proceedings to laughter and mockery. Following him, the *shamash* Reb Natan of the Karnaim Synagogue was interrogated. He became perplexed. He got mixed up and declared that he was a matchmaker and broker. He wanted to prove that he did not earn his livelihood from being a *shamash*, and that he had various sources of income that was insufficient for his livelihood.

They asked him: "Did you read the counterrevolutionary announcement that was posted in the *Beis Midrash*?"

"I read part of it, but not the majority, for I did not have time."

"What did you read, and what did you not read?

"I did not read it at all."

"You are a broker, you are a matchmaker, is it possible that someone with businesses such as yours does not know how to take care of his matters?"

"I did read."

"If you read it, why did you permit counterrevolutionary matters to be posted?"

He retracted, "I did not read," and slunk weakly onto the chair.

I pointed out: "He will die of a heart attack. A physician must be summoned."

The judge Kort asked me in anger, "You are a communal activist?"

I responded: "I am not an activist, but rather a human being, and I want to offer him help."

Dr. Meizel was summoned, and they let the *shamash* Reb Natan go.

They summoned me to testify. The first question they asked me was: "What government is better, the Czarist, or the rule of the people?" I responded: "I am not a politician, and we believe that the law of the government is the law, and we must pray for the wellbeing of the government."

They summoned Reb Sender, the *shamash* of the Mishnayos Synagogue. They asked him for an explanation from a known verse in Genesis, and they pronounced it with errors and omissions, and suddenly paused. Then Reb Sender said: "O, o, continue on." Laughter broke out in the hall. Since he was elderly, they did not continue on with him.

The trial continued on Friday night, and we stood up to worship – I, Rabbi Isser Zalman, and Reb Natan. We worshipped aloud to attract attention. The trial continued on the Sabbath, and on Sunday to Tuesday.

I was asked: "Earlier you stated that the present government is preferable in your eyes – for what reason?"

I responded: "I have never visited a theater, and now under your rule, I have merited not only to visit a theater, but to also become an actor."

Laughter was heard in the hall.

An account of the proceedings of the trial was sent to the Chik (The central committee) in Minsk. To our joy, all the accused were freed.

After about a half a year, a nighttime search was conducted in my home, and they found papers of letters from America, proving that I was involved in the maintenance of the Yeshiva. The second judge was a Jew named Minkin. During that trial, I was again interrogated. Rabbi Isser Zalman of blessed memory was already in Kletzk (Poland).

They asked me if I had been fired from the Yeshiva.

I said: "It is obvious that I have been fired, since the government is not content with it."

[Page 90]

Left to right: Rabbi Asher Sandomirski, the *Mashgiach* of the Eitz
Chaim Yeshiva; his father-in-law Reb Shachna the *Shamash*;
Rabbi Asher's wife and his family

Question: "So, who stands at its head?"

Answer: "I do not know. Perhaps Rabbi Isser Zalman found someone to take care of this, but he is in Poland."

Question: "How do you sustain yourself?

Answer: "Since there are people who do not see the hidden light in the Bolshevik regime, and they heard about my first trial and feel that the trial is like the Beilis libel, and therefore do not see it as a just, proper trial. Therefore, they support me."

Question: What did you do in Petersburg?"

Answer: "I do not have what to sustain myself with. I traveled to preach in public as a *Maggid*, as is Jewish custom."

Question: "And how is this? Do you not receive money from America?"

Answer: "This is insufficient for my livelihood."

Question: "What is the content of these sermons?"

Answer: "That they should pray, observe the Sabbath, lay tefillin, and be careful about the laws of kashruth."

Question: "Did you ever preach about the benefit of the government?"

To this, I asked: "Are there questions and deficiencies in the government for which there is a need for preaching to correct?"

One of the judges asked: "Did you ever preach that the citizens should pay their taxes on time?"

Answer: "These are already new sermons. By the time it would take for me to prepare a sermon on this matter, you would have already received more than the sermon, and I would not have anything to preach about." One judge asked: "What is your Torah?" I responded with a question: "Why is your Torah not our Torah?"

Question: "What is the essence of the Torah? Is it socialist or bourgeoisie?"

Answer: "Our holy Torah is neither bourgeoisie nor socialist. The Torah of G-d is complete. Were you to have absorbed a scintilla of the socialism included in our Torah, you would progress much further."

Question: "If the Torah is socialist, why does it state, 'for there never will cease being poor people in the land'[1]. Therefore, the Torah is bourgeoisie to us." I told them: "Why do you delve only into this verse? Indeed there is another verse: 'For there will not be a poor person among you'[2]. They claimed: "What is the explanation of the previous verse, which expresses a specifically bourgeoisie concept? With a Torah such as this you force feed young children!"

I said: "I was in Peterburg [?]during the time of famine. A day came when they brought bread to the city and distributed portions of bread to the residents. The black worker received a liter and a half, the employer a liter, the free professional (doctor, engineer) ¾ of a liter, and the former bourgeoisie a quarter of a liter. Thus, your government discriminates between the poor and the wealthy. In our city, a commissar travels in a car, whereas Wendrof, the son-in-law of Reb Shmuel the Shamash – a black worker – receives only 40 rubles a month and his family is perishing of hunger. Is there not discrimination in your regime as well?"

Question: "On what do you base this?"

Answer: "In the Torah, there is simple explanation and hidden explanation. Everyone knows the simple explanation whereas only certain special people know the hidden explanation. I can tell you the simple explanation – I am a simple person and I see it as my duty to note the value of the head of the rabbinical court, who is also an expert in the most secret of secrets."

Question: "In the Torah, it is written, 'you may extort a foreigner, but you may not extort your brother'[3]. That means, from a foreigner, from a hard-working farmer you can flail his skin and suck his blood, whereas to your Jewish brethren – you cannot charge interest."

Answer: "I do not find any support that the term 'foreigner' refers specifically to a farmer and worker. Our Torah goes hand in hand with your Torah. Regarding the payment of taxes, the bourgeoisie pays heavy taxes and if he is late with a debt, he must pay interest. A member of the professional union pays smaller taxes. A Communist pays barely anything. Why? Because you fulfil, "you may extort a foreigner, but you may not extort your brother.'"

They continued to ask me on the story of David and Bathsheba. They asked in which Yeshiva I studied during my youth.

On the day of the verdict, the Jews of the city closed their shops and went to the courthouse (in the Zalewski building). They sentenced me to a five-month prison term and exile for five years – with a choice of a far-off place or somewhere 100 verst[4] distant from Slutsk.

Translator's footnotes:

1. Deuteronomy 15:11
2. Deuteronomy 15:4
3. Deuteronomy 23:20
4. A verst is a Russian measure of length, about .66 of a mile (1.1 km).

[Page 91]

The Modern Cheder

by S. Nachmani

Translated by Mira Eckhaus

At the beginning of the year 5667, the first modern cheder was opened in Slutsk by the Hebrew teachers Mordechai Hazanovich, Shimshon Nachmani and Dov Cohen. This institution gained a reputation all over the area and the number of its students increased month by month. Until the establishment of the "Modern cheder", the education in Slutsk was poor and dark, by the melamedim (teachers), who tyrannized their students with a cane and a leash, without a trace of Hebrew and a national spirit in their teaching. There was an enormous opposition to the modern cheder from the melamedim and the ultra-Orthodox. This issue also came to Delturia before the authority.

It is worth noting that Avraham Epstein, Hillel Dubrov and Y. D. Berkowitz conceived the idea of the establishment of a modern cheder back in the years 5662-3 (refer to Berkowitz and Epstein's letters).

Epstein's trip to Ekaterinoslav for training in the teaching method of Hebrew in Hebrew and pedagogy in general ended in disappointment. He realized that the three of them are not ready for this: they lack professional and pedagogical training. The trio dispersed. In the meantime, Berkowitz became known as a master Hebrew writer. Dubrov wandered from school to school in the cities of Ukraine. Epstein was a teacher in schools in Warsaw. A few private Hebrew teachers remained in Slutsk. Due to the aspiring for a matriculation certificate, there was a great demand for Hebrew teachers. Dubrov's activity left traces, such as: the Zionist library and club Tsheina (founded with the great help of Y. D. Berkowitz), which was closed after Zionism was banned by the government.

The Hebrew teachers and admirers of Hebrew literature were S. Nahmanovitz and Dov Cohen. It was the period of crisis in general Zionism and the Hebrew teachers belonged to the left-wing parties and Po'alei Zion.

In approximately 5664, a new teacher, Mordechai Hazanovich, was discovered in Slutsk. Hazanovich, who came from Stari Durogi, where he was a home teacher with Mr. Leib Berger. Hazanovich found him a partner in Slutsk and settled down with her. He was known as a gifted teacher, with a pedagogical sense, even though he did not receive pedagogical training in any Ulpana (school). In the meantime, he was content with teaching private lessons and there were many who knocked on his doors inviting him to teach Hebrew to children and adults.

The rumor about the modern cheders reached Slutsk. The traditional cheder and the Talmud Torah for the children of the poor still stood firm, although there was one young teacher who installed benches in his cheder, but the teaching method remained as it was. Hazanovich, of course, joined the Hebrew Speakers' Association, which continued to have a miserable existence. He visited or taught in the modern cheder in Homel under the management of Israel Adler and once he was familiarized with the teaching methods according to the natural method, he came up with the idea of opening a cheder of this kind in Slutsk. Some of the parents supported him and the main helper was the head of the local Zionists, attorney Karpman, even though he did not intend to send his children to the modern cheder. His story should be told in the chapter regarding the Zionist movement in Slutsk.

Hazanovich energetically approached to realize his idea and influenced his friends Nahmanovitz and Cohen to join him. The principles were: a) a mixed school for boys and girls, b) the method of teaching is Hebrew in Hebrew. A spacious, four-room apartment was rented, with a closed yard next to it. Furniture was ordered from the carpenter Tuviah Makhanik and his son Yosef, who was a devoted Zionist. The furniture was the same as those of the local gymnasium: benches, cathedrals, blackboards, cabinets and more. Ads have been posted in the city and in the synagogues regarding the opening the modern cheder. The Zionists helped with propaganda that was successful and in the fall of 5667, the modern cheder was opened, which was filled with male and female students for grades 1, 2, and 3.

The three teachers obtained "melamedim" (teaching certificates) certificates, which decorated the walls of the rooms, and they started teaching using the method Hebrew in Hebrew, from the first day. It was like a wonder to see the little children speaking and singing in Hebrew in the house and on the street. The lack of experience was made up for by their efforts and their study of Hebrew and general pedagogical literature. Language studies were made according to the books of Ben-Ami, S. Ben-Zion and the Bible. The special teachers, Moshe Katznelson and Yosef Goldberg, were invited to teach the general studies, in order to teach Russian in the evenings. The material achievement was also surprising. The investments in furniture and appliances were covered little by little. In the first winter, in addition to the teachers, they hired also a Shamash (beadle), Reb Meir the shoemaker, who took care of cleaning the house, heating the stoves and served as a messenger. The propaganda against the modern cheder by the melamedim

The teachers of the modern cheder

From right to left: S. Nachmani, Mordechai Hazanovich, Dov Cohen, Noah Rubenitz

[Page 92]

and the ultra-Orthodox circles was fierce. Is it possible? Can boys and girls study together and walk bareheaded? But all this was to no avail.

In the summer of 5667, many students were added and it was necessary to invite another teacher. They wrote a letter to Avraham Epstein, who was then living in Warsaw, and he responded immediately, returned to Slutsk and joined the group of teachers. Epstein, who had already gained experience in the natural method and was by nature a gifted teacher and an educator with supreme grace, increased the attraction to the modern cheder and many flocked to it.

The coordinator of the work was Hazanovich, who was already a permanent resident of the city and a father of a family, and so it was natural that he handled all the technical matters of the modern cheder. The rest of the teachers, who were singles and did not live in the town, did not take root in the modern cheder. They strived to do great things, some of them went far away, and some strived to immigrate to Israel.

The accusations against the modern cheder increased day by day in the ultra-Orthodox circles mainly, the rabbis announced a boycott of it and there was a case of one old man, who was absent from the city for a while and upon his return he found that his grandson had been studying in the modern cheder. That old man tore a tear and behaved mournfully and announced that he would not rise from his mourning unless his grandson leaves the cheder of the heretics.

One morning, the modern cheder was surrounded by the police and a thorough search was made in the children's benches, in the chimneys of the stoves and also in the attic. The police searched for a self-defense weapon. Indeed, there was a basis for the police's concerns, because one of the teachers was a member of the self-defense committee. He used to aggressively collect sums of money from the wealthy residents of the city in order to purchase weapons, and they probably snitched on him. Of course, no weapon was found, because it was hidden in the safest places. The panic that arose in and around the cheder was stopped by attorney Karpman, who suddenly arrived in a carriage. After a conversation with the police inspector Nadziratl Gaborski, the search was stopped.

The single teachers did not last long in the cheder. The first to drop out was S. N. that for reasons beyond the institution's control, was forced to leave Slutsk in 5668 and his place was temporarily filled by the teacher Eliyahu Greenfeld (who is of course Eliyahu Yarkoni, one of the first veteran teachers at Petach Tikva). He didn't last long at school either, and likewise, Avraham Epstein and Dov Cohen, who left Slutsk and traveled far away. Other teachers came in their place. However, the modern cheder was established and existed until the October Revolution and in addition to Hazanovich, other teachers such as Ze'ev Gotzeit, Berger, Noah Rubenitz, Nachman Schweidel, N. Enchantedin, taught there.

The writer Y.D. Abramsky dedicated in one of his "The Bridge" booklets warm words to Gotzeit, and these are his words:

- - - "Gutzeit was one of the best persons, he was an old bachelor all his life, as if he was born an old bachelor, with one blind eye, a Hebrew teacher, accustomed and experienced. A master craftsman. He set the foundations of the Hebrew language in Slutsk. Berkowitz and Lisitzky had a vision and high aspirations. Gotzeit was the foundation and the root of Hebrew. Anyone who is from Slutsk and knows Hebrew - he is one of Gotzeit's students, he was the "unknown soldier" and the Hebrew language owes him a lot and it owes him a favor for his acts. He supported economically his old mother and his sick sister, and dedicated his life to the Hebrew. Many teachers

The modern cheder in Slutsk, its students and teachers

In the center: The teachers Eliyahu Yarkoni (Greenfeld), M. Hazanovich, Avraham Epstein, Dov Cohen

[Page 93]

I have seen in my life. I have never seen someone like him. He had a passion for grammar. All his essence was dedicated to the Hebrew grammar. The one good eye he had was a good eye for the Hebrew, a straight eye, observes to the "roots" and observes the ways of the "declension", so they will not deviate from the right path. It was said of him, of Gotzeit: Gotzeit saw with his one eye things that the big "reviewers" did not see with their two eyes. The "stress" was never "lax" in his hands, he knew the difference between the "Vav Hachibur" and "Vav Ha'ipuch" and how to use them, and he practiced the expression of gutturals and the laxities letters according to all their principles… Gotzeit had a student named Yaakov, who also had a passion for the Hebrew language, that used to say: If you want to know more about the letter "Ayin", from which I learn Hebrew well, go to Gotzeit : "Gotzeit is the "Ayin of Ya'akov", he is the source. When my time to leave Slutsk came, I took a book and wrote on it: "To the man that only the truth was spoken from his mouth".

The Letters of Avraham Epstein

Translated by Mira Eckhaus

Letter A

Ekaterinoslav, 26 Shevat, 11.2.1903

My brother Dubrov!

My brother, please send me the latest notebooks - the verb tables for Zeldas, I need them very much. - - - The letter of our association, "Hebrew speakers", made a pleasant impression on our association. I myself served as the secretary that evening and I was assigned to prepare a reply to your letter. But you already know my answer, I'm a little lazy and I don't have much free time. Nevertheless, don't be desperate, as I am slowly getting to my main goal. I am now teaching a company of various artists, and if I will succeed, I intend to take the test to get a teacher's certificate - this certificate is of necessity. I am not sure if I will be able to complete it until May. The time has come to do something regarding the foundation of a modern cheder in Slutsk. It is necessary to collect material, to group a collection of various objects and things - necessary material according to the English method. It is necessary to encourage the people, to act according to the public opinion, in general, and to prepare the ground for it. It is necessary to buy different toys made of wood and stone. In one word, to take from everything that can be taken, small as well as large, and do not underestimate it. The details are in the letter.

Your brother,
Avraham (Epstein)

Letter B

Ekaterinoslav, 6.6.1903

My brother Dubrov!

I wonder about two things. I am amazed at myself that I could hold back for such a long time and not write you anything, but I am even more amazed at you, how could you go over this thing in silence, as if all this did not concern you in any way and as if there had never been anything between us. I can't believe that you have already stopped being interested in me, in my situation, in my ambitions and my future plans. We all had one goal, you and me and Berkowitz, and this goal brought the three of us together and created a special atmosphere between us, some kind of relationship and inner connection that goes beyond the usual friendship.

Believe me, my brother, I myself did not divert my mind for a moment from this goal, and the idea of finally founding a "modern cheder" in Slutsk was the main thing that directed all my thoughts, deeds and actions. And if I myself have not written to you until now, I deserve to be reprimanded and I hereby say "I have sinned!" But you - how could you completely forgot me and did not remind me of my duty to my city and did not ask me what I was thinking of doing and did not write me anything about the state of affairs in Slutsk and how your preparatory work for the benefit of our idea is progressing? It is an enigma and it will remain an enigma! However, I do not wish to settle an account with you. I know for myself that just as I do not write because of my organic laziness, which has been rooted in me since I was born, so do you, you do not write because... because writing is extremely easy work and therefore it's hard for you. This thing is a parable to a woodcutter who happened to sign his name and couldn't, because his hand was trembling, and he was amazed at the same thing: even the cedar in the forest explodes with the force of his hand, but to hold a pen – that is beyond his strength.

You are a lively man with many activities who love to work, and write a few lines - this is beyond your strength and it makes you to sweat. First of all, how are you? Is everything good with your health, your spirit and your financial condition? How did the loneliness affect you after Berkowitz was taken from you? (Berkowitz contacted me after he escaped in the middle and left you alone, but from the words of his letter I saw and understood the great inner battle he had before he decided to leave his safe place and try the big world).

Are you still dealing with public needs, like you've been dealing with up until now? What is the state of the Zionist movement in our city? Did you have an election and who did you choose? (Surely the "honorable delegates" who were in the Minsk church were elected again this time). What is the state of the library "the child of our plays" and who is managing it now? What is your attitude towards the library and the association, after you resign? And the Association of Hebrew Speakers - does it still exist?…

I'll now move on to the question that concerns us the most, the "modern cheder", which we want to establish in our city. It is difficult, of course, to limit the time in which our idea can come true in reality. But I am certain that the actions for its realization will start – I do not have any doubts about that for a single moment. This thing is necessary, and it cannot be otherwise.

During the time that I spent in the modern cheder in Ekaterinoslav (this is surely already known to you) I learned to know all the details of the matter, both from the material and technical side as well as from the descriptive side. I realized that

[Page 94]

the establishment of such an institution and its maintenance require much more forces and much larger sums than you can imagine. Only a social initiative, only the participation of some public institution, of some association, or an entire society, will be able to put this thing on a proper and strong basis. The efforts of individuals will do nothing, because the "modern cheders" are in a special situation, which originates from the nature and essence of the cheders themselves.

One of the main conditions of the cheders of this kind is: an arranged division between the students based on their knowledge and their languages. In the old cheders there is no regime and order in this regard. In almost every cheder, the number of students is the number of classes. The melamedim themselves are conducted according to some gradually known method: Bible - Chumash, Talmud and Hebrew, everything in taught in a mess.

The reason for this vision is understandable: the melamed must, according to the nature of things, always accept new students, because the number of veteran students naturally decreases. Therefore, if in a certain period of time, he had 20 students with similar knowledge, then over time, this number of students will decrease and their place will be taken by new students, who do not have the knowledge of the veteran students. Meanwhile, he already has two classes. And this process is expanding from time to time. This is how the mess occurs, which finds a place in almost all the cheders, and which brings the melamed to a loss of his strength and the students to a loss of time, apart from the immoral effect on the students, which is a direct result of such an abnormal situation.

Letter C

Ekaterinoslav, Tuesday, 1 of Chol HaMoed 2.4.1903

My brothers and friends!

You brought me to a great trial in your letter. You didn't make a mistake when you said that my "corner" is dear to me. From the moment I came here I would miss it and all my actions and thoughts were aimed at the main goal of returning to my corner and fulfilling the idea for which I traveled to Ekaterinoslav. However, for that very idea I decided not to listen to the voice of your call. I am still not ready enough, I still lack the experience, so that I can head a respectable enterprise as the foundation of a "modern cheder". The pedagogical information and the plans, which I have already gained, are not enough. They are news I picked up by hearing and sight. However, I desire to actually work and acquire the practical information. And such a case, as it seems to me, will be available to me in a few days.

One of my acquaintances, who is also the chief supervisor of the modern cheders, both here and in Nikolaev, promised to find me a position in the cheder in Nikolaev. Although there is more than an eighth of a doubt in this matter, nevertheless I promised him to wait for his answer. And regarding the companies that you want to establish, I say to you: I stand behind you! If you manage to open a cheder for little children that begin their studies, that would be great, and I ask you to guard the little orphans - the children of Haya Zelda - whom we all owe respect to. I think that you can have them even among the girls – there is no harm in that. After all these things I am telling you that I will indeed intend - even if it will be only in a long time from now - to return to Slutsk. Much of it depends on the state of affairs. But my return should not stop you from doing everything you have set out to do.

Zuta intends to reply to your letter, perhaps he has already written to you. I have already reconciled with Zuta, I spent the first seder night in his company.

Your brother Avraham

Letter D

Ekaterinoslav March 20, 5 Nissan

My brothers Dubrov and Berkowitz!

Forgive me for my late reply. I had a few things to take care of, things that were not so important, but kept me so busy that I couldn't turn my heart to other things. And now my mind is free in such a way that I could handle the question that occupies us with the proper seriousness. You want to found companies for beginner girls and you are asking for my advice on how to arrange this and how to introduce the natural method. I have already written to Berkowitz regarding the pedagogical information and the basics of the method of study, that they are one of the things that cannot be acquired only by sight and hearing. All the theories and lessons in the world will not give or add anything to you, before you have acquired a decent experience in action. Continuing education in the profession of teaching is not given from person to person in written classes; It was obtained with a lot of hard and continuous work, in total addiction to this thing. Although you can acquire the basics of the natural method according to Epstein and Sheltzel, but the technique and the pedagogical tact will only come after a while.

I myself also applied to the advice of the teachers' council of the modern cheder and here they also replied to me the kind of things I said above and they also offered that I would use the material collected and recorded in the journal of the cheder. This material is very respectable because it is not a theory that is created after a thorough and deep thinking first, but rather the result of live work. I will try to copy this material little by little and send it to you, and it will be of great help to you.

And now I would like to make some general comments on the matter regarding the companies you want to establish.

It is necessary as much as possible to reduce the forces and not disperse them. It is necessary to set up a "cheder" in the full sense of the word. It is necessary for the apartment to be spacious and the furniture, the benches and the tables, to be of the best quality available. This thing is very important because during their studies, the students have to do various movements and actions from time to time and therefore everything should be aimed at those actions, so that the students do not feel any pressure and distress and it will not be harmful to the order and the regime.

The natural method is visible and therefore it is necessary to prepare a collection of various objects: pictures, names of toys, earthenware, straw, dirt, hay and other trivial things. The bottom line: it is necessary to get the students used to bringing all the objects they find into the cheder. And all these objects need to be marked with numbers and called names. Mainly this is necessary for the sake of the students, to make them like the studies. It is necessary for this purpose to plan multiple things which bring them into motion, and to occupy them

[Page 95]

all at once. The teacher must speak only a little, only in the necessary time, and bring the students to the inventions by asking questions, in such a way that they themselves find the answer to the question. He must also treat the students with affection and sometimes also have fun with them, and the main thing is to prepare himself before each and every lesson.

In order for you to know for yourself the progress of the studies and how far the students have progressed, make a journal and write down in it every time the new words and everything that deserves to be written down. I am sending you one page as an example.

A month later, after the students have learned to chat and understand what is being said to them, start teaching them to read and write. Reading and writing will be learned together, in parallel. We need to purchase a movable Alef Beit, large letters that are printed on pieces of parchment. Maybe one of the Torah scribes in our town could make one? You can teach the writing according to Yalin: Reading according to the little children - the student's book.

But first of all, you must visit the municipal school for a certain time and watch the ways of teaching. I think that Yalin will do his best for you and this will be easy for you. And here I almost have nothing more to say to you. If something comes up during the time that could benefit you more or less - I will let you know at the time.

Letter E

Slutsk, February 6, 1908

Hillel!

I have to leave my hometown - Slutsk. From working here in the "modern cheder" for a whole year, I was left with a pile of torn hoodies and a swarm of debts on my back. In short, I have no purpose to stay here. In case some position is found around your place, in a village, in a town - it is all the same for me! As long as your poor body is still debating in the world of chaos, it needs to be fed. It seems that this is how I am destined for my creativity, that I will be constantly tottered from place to place, without status and without a path. The result of my stay in Slutsk – only despair in the heart and a row of graves in the soul.

Try to get me a positive answer.

Avraham

A small episode: our Nahmanovitz was really exalted, he was a real hero: in the middle of winter "on a stormy night", he suddenly left without his parents' knowing about his leave and without a government license! And he did not have enough time to take his belongings as well. It is said that his suffering soul found rest in

Rogtsov. "He traveled from Slutsk and settled down in Rogtsov". Oh Slutsk, Slutsk - my heart belongs to you, to your cheders and to your heroes!

Hillel my friend!

The conditions you propose me are accepted (although the salary is somewhat insufficient). I am willing to accept this position upon the agreement of the council.

The first-class delivery is aimed at my belongings. If God's decree is that I should be among the Hebrew teachers, - then I only want to be a teacher for little children. The little children are my sphere, in which I feel like a fish in a stream. I don't know, maybe it's a coincidence, but in Slutsk I gained a lot of publicity as the teacher who was more liked by the students. I think I have some talent about it.

When are the two months of vacation? It was appropriate to set them in the months of Sivan, Tamuz.

I am waiting for an official answer from the "teachers' council".

[Page 96]

Memories

Memories

by Zeev Gluskin

Translated by Jerrold Landau

Why was it called Slutsk? Because it was situated on the Sluch River. When I grew up and began to study geography, I searched for the city of Slutsk and its river on all the maps that reached my hands, but to my dismay, I did not find them. The elders of the generation used to say that the river is an "artery" of the great sea… and therefore, they took pride in it. The pride of Slutsk was on the river. Two gristmills existed on the river and were powered by it. Our Jewish brethren and the gentiles bathed in the river during the summer, each in their separate place. In the winter, the gentile lads, especially the gymnasium students, skated on the ice. Even Jewish youth desired to skate, and also succeeded in playing pranks.

Most of the Slutsk natives had never seen the sea, and only from *Barchi Nafshi*[1] did they know that there is a large sea through which ships travel and sea monsters frolic. Perhaps the wealthy householders knew that there was a sea in Odessa, from which one can travel to the Land of Israel… During my time, the number of residents of Slutsk grew to 30,000, the majority being Jews.

The Jews of Slutsk were divided into various classes: tycoons, wealthy folk, prominent householders, middle class householders, regular householders, tradespeople, people with various livelihoods, people living from the "air" [i.e., Academics], and clergymen.

The number of tycoons and wealthy people in Slutsk was small, not even reaching the number of fingers on one hand. First among them was Reb Isser Isserlin, the scion of a most pedigreed family (from the Remah). He was considered to be a tycoon in the city, and everyone counted and enumerated his fortune, which was close to "80,000 rubles." His house was large and spacious, located in the center of the city close to the main road. Its windows were large, and its courtyard was spacious. There was a synagogue in his courtyard, built of stone. It was a beautiful building, called Isserke's Shul. Of course, members of the Isserlin family and other prominent people, "scholars," and the ten idle people[2] supported by the tycoon so that they would never be short a prayer quorum, worshipped there. The head of that institution was a great scholar, Reb Mendele. Every day, nights included, young men, children of the householder who were supported by their parents, a well as lads over the age of Bar Mitzvah, who had already concluded their studies with the *melamdim*, sat there and studied. Three or four lads would study together a page of Gemara with its commentaries in a group. There were also ordinary Jews who studied on their own. The great scholar Reb Mendele, who gave a class every day, would sit at the eastern wall every evening after the *Maariv* service, ready to answer anyone who had a difficult question. Anyone who turned to him was answered pleasantly, as he explained everything. Every lad felt it an honor to approach him, ask him something, and hear his answer. I too tasted one time the honor of asking him a question, as I enjoyed his countenance.

Zeev Gluskin and his wife

Boys who were of marriageable age would consider it a great merit to study in Isserke's Synagogue. The house and the synagogue were called "*Hechatzer*"[3]. Indeed, there it was sort of like a royal court. The tycoon Reb Isser Isserke's was a pious Jew who was not a scholar. He was tall in stature, with a full beard, exuding splendor. One could see in his face that he was a tycoon. He had no business dealings in the city itself. His business was in Königsberg, where he would earn "millions." He had one source of livelihood in Slutsk. He was a *mohel* [circumciser] and served as the city *mohel*. He had very frequent opportunities to perform circumcisions, and he never missed a single one, including on the Sabbath. He went to the rich and the poor, and he went for the *Shacharit* service to the synagogue where the host of the synagogue worshipped, and he himself sang *Vecharot imo habrit* with joy[4] all the way to the end. This was his "recompense" aside from the mitzvah itself. He exempted the worshippers from the *Tachanun* prayer and from the long *Vehu Rachum* on Mondays and Thursdays[5]. He would discreetly give coins to poor mothers who had given birth.

His wife Bryna Reizel was a goodhearted woman. She responded to every indigent with an open hand. A poor sick person requiring a bit of good soup or a bit of jam would come to the chatzer, and would always be received politely, with warm encouraging word – from the good royal court.

The tycoon Isserlin had two sons: one aged fifteen and the other aged twelve. Neither of them intermixed with the children of the city.

[Page 97]

They studied all their studies in their home. They had a special *melamed* to teach them Judaic studies, and special teachers to teach them reading, writing, and secular subjects.

When Isserlin and his entire family moved to the city of Königsberg, they took with them all the honor, all the valuable objects, and also one of the *melamedim*, who was half Orthodox and half *Maskil* [enlightened] so that the studies of his children would continue and the traditions of the home would not cease, as per the custom of Slutsk. The entire city was very pained when the family of the tycoon left the city. The splendid house, full of honor, remained empty and abandoned. To anyone passing by the house, it seemed that the walls were shedding tear.

The synagogue remained in its previous function and protocols. Between *Mincha* and *Maariv*, when the householders were engaged in regular conversation, the main topic was "who is fitting to come to live in this castle?" However, what logic could not do, the times did. The Holy One Blessed Be He arranged a fire in the city of Slutsk. That house burnt down along with all its environs. The synagogue miraculously survived, and the entire city saw this as the finger of G-d. In the merit of the ten idle people who lived in the house, it was not affected by the fire…

After several years, a new, fine, large, but ordinary house was built on the lot. It was built in the style of the houses of the lesser wealthy people of the city. All the residents of Slutsk recall the size and grandeur of the original house of Isserke. When the saw the new house afterward, they shook their heads in a sigh, "Was Isserke's house like this?"

Two prominent householders lived in that house afterwards. One of them was my brother-in-law.

I recall that the first time that I entered my sister's home, I trembled a bit: "Are my feet indeed standing in Isserke's house?"

The second in stature was Reb Shmuel Simchovich, the father of Dr. Y. N. Simchoni. He was also a member of the Isserlin family, a unique Jew. He considered himself to be a tycoon, and looked upon the Jews of Slutsk with condescension.

The following is what was written about him in the book "The Generation, Its Rabbis and Its Scribes" by BenZion Eisenstat.

"The rabbi, Reb Shmuel Simchovich of Slutsk was one of the *Gaonim* of Israel, and an excellent scholar. He was a man of great stature, the scion of good pedigree from generation to generation. He was educated in wealth, and studied Torah and wisdom with comfort. He learned German, Polish, French, English, and Russian. He was known as a Talmudic genius and a wise writer. He published articles in the 'Peterburg Herald' German newspaper. He was appointed as a rabbi in Vienna in the year 5625 [1865], and called to serve as a rabbi in Warsaw, but he did not want to serve as a rabbi. In the year 5654 [1894], he was called by the government to participate in the rabbinical conference in Peterburg.

Simchovich conducted himself in the fashion of wealth, with a high fashion. He would stringently investigate every person and keep a distance from the commonfolk. Therefore, the community related to him with respect and honor. To sum up Simchovich! He was a philosopher, a rabbi, and a *Maskil*. He would worship in Isserke's synagogue on the Sabbath."

He died in Slutsk on 3 Adar, 5656 [1896].

The third in stature was Binyamin Ebin. He was a wise man, and everyone knew that he was wealthy. He would lend to the *poritzes* [estate owners] and also to Jews for interest, based on the *Heter Iska* as our sages have ordained[6]. Every "child on the street" knew that he was a miser. He worshipped in the Chapashker Shul, the synagogue in which Rabbi Yoshe Ber [Soloveitchik] worshipped. This added to his honor.

The fourth was Gershon Ostrovski, who was nicknamed for his wife "Gere Kreine's." He was an ordinary Jew, with a grey complexion. His wealth was doubtful. He had a two-story house, in which there was a large store that sold groceries and fine beverages. The business was run by his wife Kreine. Her customers were the gentile intelligentsia, officials, and wealthy estate owners. She barely had any Jewish customers. Therefore, they suspected that Ostrovski was wealthy. There were several tens of important householders, well-pedigreed families, people who earned their livelihoods comfortably, who sustained their families neither opulently nor meagrely. Nobody investigated the wealth of any of them, but everyone knew who the powerful ones were. It was difficult to differentiate between an important, average, and ordinary householder. However, in a city as full of wise and intelligent people like Slutsk, the bounds between these three classes were clear to everyone.

Feigel Shteises,
mother of Zeev Gluskin

A cholera epidemic broke out in the city, and it was necessary to arrange salvation and aid for poor families. Money was needed. The heads of the community found a source for money: with the agreement of the rabbi and *Gaon*, a strong proclamation was made in the synagogues that every householder was obligated to make a one-time donation to the charitable fund, equivalent to their expenditures for one Sabbath. Since it was impossible to know and also difficult to ask everyone what their expenditures for the Sabbath were, they imposed round figure for each stratum. The wealthy had to pay 36 gold coins, important householders 18, average householders 9, and regular householders 5. The rest of the residents had to pay what they could.

My mother of blessed memory gave me 18 gold coins to give to the community. That is how I found out that our family was considered to be one of the important householders. Those who brought 9 gold coins were considered average, and those who only brought 5 gold coins designated themselves, of their own accord, as ordinary householders, This classification

[Page 98]

later served as the paradigm when the community imposed a value tax on all the residents.

The families of householders of all classes had various obligations: Whereas a wealthy person would be considered to fulfil his obligation if he came to worship at the synagogue on Sabbaths, Rosh Chodesh, festivals, and secular holidays; they were particular that a regular householder was required to worship in a congregation each and every day. A wealthy person was exempt from being a scholar, whereas scholarship was demanded from a regular householder. A wealthy person was even permitted to be an ignoramus [*am Haaretz*], but woe to a regular householder if the community began to investigate his scholarliness.

Those who had various sources of livelihood, shopkeepers and those who lived a life "in the air" – they all had a grey form.

Tradespeople – this was the class that was most appreciated – ordinary people who lived from the toil of their hands, living simple modest lives. It was touching to see most of the tradespeople hastening early in the morning, before dawn, to worship in the synagogues. They would appear once again in their own synagogue toward evening, as they sat with a chapter of Psalms or *Ein Yaakov*.

The clergymen included rabbis, rabbinical judges and their assistants, communal *shamashim*, and the beadles of the synagogues and *Chevra Kadisha*.

The rabbis during my time were: the true rabbi, rabbinical teacher, whom the city of Slutsk was proud of. The rabbis were the leaders and spiritual directors of the city. Everyone listened to them. One would see them on the street on occasion, but their full honor was in their homes on the rabbinical seat.

The government rabbi (*der Kozioger rov*) maintained the registry of births and deaths. He was a scholar and also honorable. He moved with his family to the Land of Israel toward the end of his life. The rabbi was a sort of government official. His family name was Shapira.

The registry book of births, deaths, marriage certificates and the like was located in the home of the government rabbi. He was required to know about every circumcision ceremony. They would come to him immediately to register the name of the child in his ledgers. When a girl was born, they would inform him of her name, and she too would be registered in the ledgers. The son of this government rabbi was a great Torah scholar. He delivered a class every day in the synagogue. He made *aliya* to the Land together with his father.

Rabbinical judges were always invited to their post by the rabbi of the city, and were called the *Beit Din Tzedek*. The *shamashim* of the *Beit Din* were invited by the rabbis and certified by the rabbi of the city. They were called *Shamashei Beit Din*. The synagogue beadles were elected by them. Most of the synagogue beadles in those days were elderly and scholarly. I remember with honor the beadle of my family's synagogue, who was called Herzl der Shamash. He was wise, with good character traits. The synagogue attendees honored him greatly. He made *aliya* to the Land of Israel in his old age. I recall very well when he came to our house to bid farewell to my father and the entire family. When he extended his hand to me, he said, "so, be healthy, and learn with diligence." I said to him, "Reb Herzl, take me too to the Land of Israel."

He placed his hand on my head and said, "When you are older, you too will travel to the Land of Israel. And when the Messiah comes, you will all go there."

To this day, I recall those words with holy awe. If I have merited to have the first half of his blessing fulfilled, I hope that the second half will also be fulfilled. The Messiah will come when the generation is fitting for it, in our Land.

There were sufficient synagogues and *Beis Midrashes* in Slutsk. I recall Der Kalte Shul [The cold synagogue], where people would worship in the winter wearing warm coats or furs. According to what the elders said, this synagogue had existed for more than 300 years. Some said that the dead came to pray there after midnight, and they returned to their graves at dawn. Therefore, people were afraid to pass by Der Kalte Shul late at night… There was a large rock next to this synagogue. It was told that a rabbi of the Hassidim had been flogged there. Some said it was the Baal Shem Tov himself – since all the people of Slutsk were *Misnagdim*.

In my times, there was someone in Slutsk named Itza der Chosid. On the day of Simchas Torah, we would go to his house to see him dancing on the table. I did not know about Hassidism, and I thought that the entire idea of Hassidism was to dance on the table on Simchas Torah. There were several other synagogues in the vicinity of Der Kalte Shul. All were in a semicircle, and this entire area was called the Shulhof. The wedding ceremonies of the city residents took place there.

Cultural matters in Slutsk were straightforward: "the study of Torah was the most important thing." There were *cheders*, the Talmud Torah, the Yeshiva, and people studied in the synagogues. In the Talmud Torah, they studied *Chumash* with *Rashi*, a bit of Bible, and Gemara with all the commentaries. Slutsk was a city full of children, and they studied in *cheder*. The older lads sat in the synagogues, *Beis Midrashes*, and the *Kloiz*. Thousands sat in them and studied. Some people of Slutsk also began to concern themselves with *Haskalah* [secular knowledge]. They learned the art of fine writing and a bit of Russian from private teachers called *shreibers*. Both boys and girls studied. Small groups of three or four students studied together in return for a small tuition fee. All the children of the prominent householders studied privately with a *shreiber*. They hired a gymnast [high school student] of the fifth or sixth grade to study the Russian language. This was very expensive.

In the latter period, there was a decree that all *cheder* students older than ten were required to study Russian, arithmetic, and geography.

There were not yet restrictions on Jews in the local gymnasium. As far as I recall, only people of the age of ten were accepted to the preparatory grade or to the first grade and above. The government was interested in attracting Jewish students to modern learning, but the Jews of Slutsk, and especially the majority of the householders, objected to the gymnasium. They regarded it as a first step to apostasy. A few who did not heed the opinion of the community did send their children to the gymnasium. When those gymnasium students came to the synagogue on the Sabbath or festival wearing their uniforms with their shiny buttons, and a sparkling insignia on their hats, they aroused great jealousy in the hearts of all the lads who did not merit such greatness.

I was born in that city on the 9th of Elul of the year 5619 [1859]. I was the fifth child, the first son after four daughters who preceded me. The joy of my parents was great, and I was always given great honor, as if I was an only son, even though two more sons were born after me.

After Passover, when I was 4½ years old, my father brought me to the *cheder*, enwrapped in a silk *tallis*. In the *cheder*, the "angels" tossed sweets from the ceiling, and the joy was great. For that Passover, my father of blessed memory

[Page 99]

came from Königsberg, where he was sojourning for his work. He brought me a little silk *tallis*, something that had not yet been seen in Slutsk. He also brought me books, a *Siddur*, and tiny *Chumashim*, printed in German with great beauty. Every time that he came from Königsberg to Slutsk, he brought me a gift of various books published abroad in beautiful form, in order to attract my heart to books and learning. If I am a boundless lover of books to this day, it is no doubt that this is the fruit of the seed that my father planted in my heart during my early childhood.

Reb Eliezer,
father of Zeev Gluskin

I was raised and educated with a comfortable of life, but without excesses or extravagances. My mother sent me to the *cheders* of the renowned *melamedim* in the city, whose tuition fess were high. My friends of the same age were from good families. Not more than six or even students studied together. The curriculum of the *cheders* was *kometz aleph* [i.e. reading the alphabet] until one page of Gemara a week.

The students of the youngest level *cheders* were brought to school every day by a special lad called a *bahelfer* [assistant teacher]. He also brought the children back home. The mothers would give food and sweets for the children to the *bahelfer* to give to them at certain times in the *cheder*. His job was to guard the child as he came and went: from a barking dog, from a wagon, so that a *shegetz* [derogatory term for a gentile] should not throw a stone at him, and in general to protect him from any injury.

He would receive his salary from the students, but the *melamed* was responsible to the parents regarding the *bahelfer* that he fulfill his task faithfully both in the *cheder* and on the route.

The students would go alone, without special protection, to the *melamdim* of *Chumash* and *Rashi*. They had to guard themselves from any mishap on the way. This developed the sense of self-protection in the child. However, the fear of the *shegetz* and the dog remained as a legacy throughout their lives.

During the winter nights, when the studies in the *cheders* lasted until 8:00 p.m., the students returned home in groups rather than alone, out of fear of the night.

This is the order of the "stops" of the children during our childhood: from the *melamed* of young children to the *melamed* of *Chumash*, from regular *Chumash* to *Chumash* with *Rashi*, to twenty-four [i.e. the *Tanach*] – to the beginning of Gemara in accordance with the Lekach Tov book, the heads of the easy chapter from "two are holding on to a cloak" [*Baba Metzia* 2a], and from there to a page of Gemara with *Rashi* every week, to Mishnah, and then to a page of Gemara with *Rashi* and *Tosafot*. From then on, it was Gemara classes without restrictions on number of pages per week. The important *melamdim* began to enter their students into the foyer of the *Maharsh'a*, and slowly showed them the pleasant palace of the *Mahara'm Shif*. The studies of the *Chayey Adam* and *Shulchan Aruch halachic* works, books of morality, etc. were like dessert after the meal, which did not enter into the calculation of the orders of the day. Of course, success in studies was dependent on the abilities of the students, and to a certain extent, of the *melamed*.

Secular studies, which were required of every Jew who was a member of society and would at times encounter a gentile nation, included: the art of penmanship in order to write a letter in fine form, and basic knowledge of the Russian language. Since my father of blessed family lived in Germany, I also studied German. My teachers for secular studies were from among the gymnasium students. I also learned the Hebrew language and grammar, and read the book of Mapu and others, so that I could enter the group of *Maskilim*. My mother of blessed memory found Hebrew teachers for this purpose.

I would write to my father in Königsberg every month about my studies and my daily work. I knew Hebrew appropriately. I was fluent in *Tanach*, and I knew *Ahavat Zion* by heart. My knowledge of Gemara was barely passable. On the other hand, I knew the Mishnaic tractates of *Brachot* and *Shabbat* almost by heart.

My father of blessed memory was very happy about my letters, and always encouraged me. Once he brought me a large Romm edition of the Talmud, bound in splendid volumes.

That is how my friends and I studied. We had a one-hour class in secular studies in Hebrew six times a week, and one hour of "gentile" studies five time a week. We were taught Russian, arithmetic, and geography from the gymnasium student. We also learned Russian penmanship from the Hebrew teacher.

I have pleasant memories from my childhood days, especially of my childhood home and my sisters. My mother was happy when I read to her my letters to my father, and especially the letters that he wrote to me. They treated me with some honor as the child of a wealthy family throughout our neighborhood and in the synagogue in which my family worshipped. I knew from my mother, peace be upon her, that her father, my grandfather of blessed memory, built the entire eastern wall of the synagogue with his own money. Of course, our place was next to that wall, the first place to the right of the Holy Ark. Herzl the Shamash often honored me with *maftir*.

At *Mincha* on the Sabbath, I would at times read the first section of the Torah portion of the following week[7]. I would also read the scrolls of Song of Songs, Ruth, and Kohelet from the bima with the traditional trop. The members of the synagogue related to me with friendship, as one of them. To them, I was a wholesome lad, of good fortune.

I entered the district school at age eleven. There I studied for two hours every afternoon, except for on the Sabbath. There, they taught Russian, arithmetic, and other subjects. We sat there bareheaded. I concluded

[Page 100]

school when I reached the age of Bar Mitzvah. All of the mark on my report card were Very Good.

On the day that I received my graduation diploma and celebrated my Bar Mitzvah, the celebration was with great splendor and pomp. My lecture was on the Talmudic discussion of "A left handed person." It lasted for about half an hour. All of our family members, my *melamdim*, neighbors from the synagogue, and some of my friends then participated in the feast fit for a king.

After my Bar Mitzvah, I continued to study Gemara on my own in Isserke's Synagogue. However, at the same time, I studied the Russian language and other studies with a fourth-year gymnasium student, to the extent that he himself knew. I secretly prepared for gymnasium. After my Bar Mitzvah, my teacher, a Jewish gymnasium student, brought me a book to study a bit of Slavic, which was necessary to enter the gymnasium, as well as a book of gentile prayers with several pictures of priests. There was a large picture of a cross after the title page. My mother of blessed memory saw this book by chance. When she opened it, she saw the cross, and became perplexed and afraid. She came to me screaming, "Woe to me, your teacher wants to bring you to apostasy, and certainly he is enticing you to enter the gymnasium."

She immediately fired the teacher, and begged me strongly to remove any thoughts of gymnasium from my head.

"It is enough that you graduated from school. I will hire a different gymnasium student from who you could learn, and you will know than all the lads of Slutsk."

I loved my mother very much. Her tears touched my heart, and I abandoned the idea of gymnasium. I sufficed myself with a different gymnasium student, specifically a gentile.

Our family name Gluskin comes from the town of Hlusk. My grandfather and my grandfather's grandfather were rabbis in Hlusk for several generations, and authored many books. We kept some of their books in our home, such as *Agudat Eizov*, and *Marot Hatzivot* by the Gaon Rabbi Zev of Bialystok.

My father of blessed memory was a native of Hlusk, the grandson of one of those rabbis. My name Zeev was the name of the author of *Agudat Eizov*. Being named after a grandfather was considered as s certain foreshadowing of Torah and good deeds for the newborn baby.

My mother of blessed memory was a native of Slutsk, from the Lifschitz family, which was considered to be of good pedigree. The fact that the scion of famous rabbis of Hlusk married a young woman from Slutsk was testimony to this. My maternal grandfather died in Konigsberg before I was born. He was a merchant and an agent.

My grandmother owned a large store in Slutsk. After her husband died, Grandmother became blind and moved in to live with her daughter, my mother of blessed memory. I recall Grandmother very well. She died when I was five years old. Her name Stisya well-known in her time. My mother was called Feigel Stishe's by all the people of Slutsk. That name is etched on the gravestone of my mother of blessed memory to this day My father was called Leizer Stishe's. Many people did not know the name Gluskin, but they knew the name Feigel Stishe's very well. I traveled with my father to Konigsberg in the year 5633 [1873] when I was fourteen years old.

Tzvi Hirsch Dayanov
(known as the Slutsker Maggid)

He was a preacher to the people. He was born in Slutsk, Minsk district, in 1832 and died in London on 21 Adar I 5637 (1877). His father Zeev Wolf was a metal craftsman. Dayanov was the first modern preacher in Yiddish, without melody or gestures, without parables or riddles, without threatening the people with Gehinnom [hell]. Using simple language and charm, he drew a living picture for his audience from the lives of the Jews, their current reality, their destiny, and what was required of them. He dwelt on the tragedy and harm that was liable to come from distancing oneself from work and labor, leading to a proliferation of loafers and indigents. He proved with incisive portents that Torah and secular knowledge are sisters. He requested that the parents send their children to government schools.

He did not display favoritism to anyone. He earned many enemies through his words. They closed the doors of the *Beis Midrash* to him, and did not allow him to ascend the *bima* to preach.

He complained about this in *Hamagid* and *Hameilitz*, and described the many persecutions. Only in Odessa did he succeed in preaching in the Great Synagogue on Yom Kippur of 5630 [1869], in the place of Rabbi Schwaber.

Kehillas Ein Yaakov Adas Ro'p of London accepted him to be their preacher and sermonizer in 1874 through the efforts of the poet Y. L Gordon. There too, his detractors hurt him and slandered him before the Chief Rabbi N. Adler, who opposed him until he was convinced of his honorableness and good works. He then came to terms with him. Dayanov founded a free Hebrew school in London for the benefit of the youth.

He served in his post in London for approximately three years. Various rabbis eulogized him when he died.

Dayanov wrote a sermon entitled *Kvod Melech* [Honor of the King] in honor of Czar Alexander II (Odessa 1869), which was translated into Russian (*Hamagid* h'h 62).

He left behind books in manuscript form.

Yona Isserlin

Our rabbi and teacher Rabbi Yona Isserlin of Slutsk, a great rabbi, and wealthy man, known for his fine traits and actions. He was the son-in-law of the great, famous Gaon of his generation, Rabbi Menachem Manish Lifschitz, may the memory of the righteous and holy be blessed. The aforementioned rabbi, Gaon and Tzadik was the father-in-law of the true Tzadik and rabbi of renown, the wealthy philanthropist known throughout the entire world, Rabbi Shachna Isserlin. Mohara'sh [Rabbi Shacna Isserlin] was the father-in-law of the great Gaon, known throughout the Land and in all places of Torah, the esteemed tycoon, Rabbi Shmuel Simchovich, and was also the brother and son-in-law of the famous rabbi, known in a praiseworthy fashion for his traits and character, Rabbi Isser Isserlin.

(*Anshei Shem*, page 89)

Translator's footnotes:

1. Psalm 104, recited on winter Sabbath afternoons and Rosh Chodesh, mentions the great sea.
2. By tradition, a sign of a significant city is when it is large enough to support ten "idle people" who do not work for a livelihood, but rather study Torah all day.
3. Literally "the courtyard" – a term often used for the court of a Hassidic Rebbe.
4. A part of the daily morning service that is sung aloud by the *mohel* when a circumcision is to take place that day.
5. The *Tachanun* prayer is recited on non-festive weekdays after the amida. On Monday and Thursday, a longer version, called *Vehu Rachum*, is recited. *Tachanun* is omitted when a circumcision is to take place that day.
6. It is forbidden to lend money to a Jew for interest. However, there is a rabbinical enactment, called a *Heter Iska* [permit for business purposes] that enables such loans to take place as a joint business venture. See https://www.yeshiva.co/midrash/13712
7. At *Mincha* on the Sabbath, as well as on the following Monday and Thursday, the Torah reading consists of the first section of the Torah portion of the following Sabbath.

[Page 101]

My Childhood Days

by Tzvi Hirsch Matlianski

Translated by Jerrold Landau

a. My Childhood Days

I was born in a Lithuanian city, in which one hundred percent of its residents were *Misnagdim*, that is Slutsk, a district city in the Minsk region, on the third day of the third month of Sivan, 5616 (1856).

Hassidic legend states that the Baal Shem Tov of blessed memory came to Slutsk "as he was going into exile," and its citizens did not receive him politely. Then he cursed the city that Hassidim should not be found therein forever. The curse was fulfilled, and, to this day, Slutsk remains one of the four cities known by the acronym of Karpa's: Kosava Ruzhany, Pruzhany and Slutsk, in which no Hassid has any heritage. These cities never heard *Hodu* recited before *Baruch Sheamar*[1].

My father, Rabbi Chaim of blessed memory, was one of the most scholarly people of Slutsk. He disseminated Torah all the days of his life, teaching Talmud and its commentaries to the children of the wealthy. His students took pride and glory in the name of their excellent teacher, his explanations and his style of teaching. "Rabbi Chaim Moshke's" understood and knew how to evaluate the talents of each student. He nicknamed them: Yosefke who had a great grasp, Yisraelke with the fine memory, and me, who also was among his students, was called someone of understanding. By nature, he was a good person, merciful, and gracious. All his students loved and revered him even after they left him.

My mother Rivka, peace be upon her, was beautiful and wise. She was known in the entire city for her natural wisdom and talents in mathematics. Therefore, she was nicknamed "Rivka the wise."

She was a native of Mir, the daughter of Rabbi Pinchas Papak of blessed memory, who served as a rabbinical judge in that city throughout his life. He was a scion of the Harkavi family of Novorodok. Six sons were born before I was born. All were excellent geniuses and handsome, but they died in their childhood. My parents were left with only one daughter. Since my mother was forty years old when I was born, I was the only son of my parents for four years until my only brother was born. I can easily understand the concern that my good parents had for me. When I was five years old, they dressed me in white, linen clothes, aside for the *Arba Kanfos* [ritual fringed undergarment] with woollen *tzitzis* – as a portent from early generations for a long life.

A holy image as if alive appears before my eyes to this day as I recall my beautiful, good mother reciting the blessing over the Sabbath candles. She would grasp my little hand and place me to her right, around the table set in honor of the Sabbath, covered with a snow-white tablecloth, atop which fluttered the pure candelabra with their candles. With her tender hands, she covered her sparkling eyes, exuding brightness opposite the light of the candles. She recited the petition with a gentle voice.

"Merciful and gracious G-d, perform the following mercy to me, as the candles light up in honor of the Sabbath with their holy light, so may shine the light of my son in studying Your holy Torah that You gave to your people Israel atop Mount Sinai. Grant him a long life, and may my husband and I not add to our mourning for our children who were cut off from the tree of life while still in their youth."

The sound of weeping could be heard in her latter words.

When she concluded the petition, she kissed my cheeks, which were moistened by her warm tears.

Then she placed my sister in her place. She was twelve years old. She too recited the blessing over her candles, which he lit in her small candelabra that stood behind my mother's large candelabra. In my childhood imagination, I always imaged that my sister's small candelabra were daughters to my mother's large one. She also read out the petition prior to lighting, but the formula was changed somewhat. Instead of "the eyes of my son" she said, "the eyes of my brother" and instead of "my husband and I" recited by my mother, she said, "me and my dear parents."

The preacher
Rabbi Tzvi Hirsch Matlianski
of blessed memory

After the blessing of the candles, my mother took me into her arms, dressed me with the small linen coat and woollen *Arba Kanfos*, and carried me to the court of the synagogue, to the ancient office next to the large *Beis Midrash*, where the holy *Tzadik* of the *Misnagdim*, Rabbi Rafael Yosef of blessed memory was sitting. My mother brought me to him every week to bless me. I recall his image to this day. He was a tall Jew, with a full-grown, black beard, a high, wrinkled forehead, and bright eyes. Every Sabbath evening, he placed his hands on my head, lifted his eyes, and blessed me. My mother carried me home in joy.

Rabbi Rafael Yosef, or, as he was called by everyone, Rabbi Rafael Yosel, was a sort of "sublime man," a man of portents, whose path of life and deeds will be told to the generation, and whose memory will remain with the men of great deeds of that generation, such as Rabbi Nachum the Shamash of Grodno, Rabbi Shimon Kaplan of Vilna, and Rabbi Motel Weinshenker of Shevel [Šiauliai]. They were not rabbis, did not "make use of the crown"[2], and did not inherit their greatness as a legacy from their fathers. They were from among the simple, pure masses, dedicated to the nation with all the strands of their souls. The nation recognized them and revered them from generation to generation.

[Page 102]

Rabbi Rafael Yosef of Slutsk was a simple tailor. He did not perform his work in the homes of the tycoons, but rather with the masses. He sustained the members of his family with the toil of his hands. He set times to study Torah every day. He taught a chapter of Mishnah to his audience after the *Shacharit* service, and he explained to them *Ein Yaakov* and *Menorat Hamaor* between *Mincha* and *Maariv*. His students from among the masses revered his name, and none of them knew what their teacher did at night. They did not know that within a few years he had learned the Babylonian and Jerusalem Talmuds, Sifrei, *Sifra*, *Tosefta*, *Mechilta*, and early and latter commentators. His talents were great, and the power of his memory was wonderful. He secretly become one of the giants of the generation. Nevertheless, he continued with his role and never missed his classes to the masses, who did not know his greatness and strength in Torah.

His great deeds and righteousness even surpassed his Torah and wisdom. He sustained tens of families with food and money for rent. He visited many sick people every day, he comforted mourners, and healed the broken hearted who expressed their anguish to him. He married off the daughters of poor people and brought them joy at their weddings.

From where did he obtain the means to do all this? He took and gave, gave and took throughout all the days of his life. Those from whom he took and those to whom he gave looked upon him with awe and honor, and revered him. He divided up the hours of the day and night. During one portion, he visited the strong men of the community and its wealthy people, and solicited their donations, which they gave with a good eye and an open hand. Many of them brought their donations to his house so that he would not have to waste his precious time visiting them. This was his work throughout several hours of the day, every day. In the darkness of night, so that his way would not be known, he visited the poor, lowly, widows and orphans. With the radiating light of his countenance, he distributed their portions to them, bringing light and salvations into their dreary dwellings.

He was great amongst the scholars in his Torah, and revered and sublime among the mases for his deeds…

b. Holding up the Torah Reading

Holding up the Torah reading was one of the most effective and easiest means to save the oppressed from their oppressors. If the event that cases of theft, extortion, cheating, or travesty took place in the city, the victim would come to the synagogue at the time of the *Shacharit* service on the Sabbath morning to hold up the Torah reading. He would stand at the Holy Ark and would not allow the Torah to be removed for reading until the rabbi, monthly *parnas* or communal heads heard the complaints, and demands for those who owed him, and promised to fulfill his request. Then he descended from the *bima* and the Torah reading began. During the time of the rule of the Czars of the Romanov family, military service was not the obligation of the private individual, but rather of the communities. The communal heads were tasked with the duty of providing a specific number of youths between the ages of 20 to 30 for the royal army. They were given permission by the government to take them by force if they would not go on their own accord. At the beginning of the winter every year, the snatchers went out under the auspices of the monthly administrator and communal heads to snatch those of the appropriate age, bind them with rope, and take them to the communal headquarters, where they sat in prison until the day came to present them before the army committee. They government physician would examine their health. Then they would be taken to the army camp where they would serve for 25 years.

There were times when the government issued a decree to snatch young children of the age of five or six. The snatchers fell upon them in the darkness of the night and took them from their mother's bosoms, despite the frightful shrieking and wailing. There was nobody to save them. The snatchers were wicked people, cruel murderers by nature, who knew no shame. They received their salaries from the leaders of the community. Their names remain as a curse and a malediction in our new literature.

This took place in my city of Slutsk.

It was Sabbath of the Torah portion of *Mishpatim*. The *Shacharit* service had concluded and the sound of the words *Vayehi Binsoa Ha'aron*[3] was heard from the cantor. The ark cover began to roll off the ark when suddenly the voice of a young woman and her three children were heard, one of whom was a one-year-old baby in her arms. They were screaming, crying, and wailing, impeding the Torah reading: "Thieves, murderers, oppressors snatched my husband this past night, bound him in ropes, and hauled him to the communal building, leaving me and my children to groan without anyone to sustain us. Jews, merciful ones the sons of merciful ones, have mercy upon me, and return my husband to me! …"

The rabbi, Rabbi Yosef Dov Soloveitchik, took off his tallis, approached the unfortunate woman, took the baby into his arms, and ordered the shamash to bring a glass of milk. The glass was brought, and the rabbi fed the child and comforted his mother, saying that her husband would be returned to her shortly. A fearsome trembling overtook the entire congregation of worshippers when they saw the *Gaon* giving a drink to the hungry child, the son of the poor tailor who had been snatched that night by the snatchers for army service.

The communal heads quieted and calmed the mother and here children. The rabbi approached the renowned tycoon, and noticed that he was holding the Tractate of Shabbat in his hands and perusing it, for he was a great scholar. The rabbi removed the Gemara from his hands and scolded him, "You are a deserting soldier." Everyone present was astonished at the words of the rabbi, for the tycoon B. had never served in the army and had never deserted the army. The rabbi turned to the astonished people and said, "I will explain my words to you. There are two types of soldiers in the royal army: infantry and cavalry. The children think that the cavalry soldiers are more fortunate, and are jealous of them because they ride on horses and do not walk on foot. However, in truth, the work of the riders is ten time more difficult than that of the foot soldiers. When the infantryman finishes his work, he eats his meal and returns to his rest. That is not the lot of the cavalryman. He must take care of his horse, clean it, give it to drink, feed it, and then take it to its stable. Only then can the cavalryman go to his bed, weary and tired. In the service of the Creator there are also two types of soldiers. There are foot soldiers, simple workers, poor, indigent, who have no responsibility other than for themselves and their household. However, there are also cavalrymen with their possessions that were granted to them. They are dutybound to protect their wealthy and to use it to help their fellow at an appropriate time. A poor woman with her three unfortunate children has come to us. She did not come to the foot soldiers, for they do not have the ability to help. The foot soldiers have the obligation to study Torah and fulfil the commandments. She came to the cavalrymen with their means, who do have the ability to help. Now I ask you a question: What is the judgment upon a cavalryman riding his horse, who escapes from the brigade and says, 'I want to work among the foot soldiers, and I do not want to be with the cavalry.' His sentence would be that of any soldier who deserts from army service: 'Stand on your guard and do not leave your place!'

"Now you understand that Rabbi B. E'N is a deserting soldier. He descended

[Page 103]

from his horse-property, and took a Gemara to peruse like a foot soldier. Therefore, I scolded him to return to his position and save the unfortunate woman."

The tycoon extended his hand to the rabbi and promised that the travesty would be rectified that very evening.

After the reading of the Torah, the rabbi ascended his podium, turned his face to the *parnas* [administrator] and his assistants, and called out with a fearful voice, "Today we read in the weekly portion 'If someone kidnaps and sells a person or he is found in their hand, he shall surely die' [Exodus 21:16] – did we not sin last night with this terrible sin? Let us hope that we can fix the travesty tonight."

There was a large meeting that night, and all the city notables gathered. One of those who sold themselves to army service, called *Achatniki* in Russian, was brought to them, and the tailor was set free and returned to his wife and children…

The term "deserting soldier" (*Antlofener soldat*) spread throughout the entire land, and was a wonder.

That year was the final one for snatching and snatchers. The government imposed the obligation upon individuals.

c. My Visit to Slutsk

I chose my native city of Slutsk on my first stop in Lithuania. I had not seen it for 22 years, from when my father of blessed memory sent me to Paritz to study with his student Rabbi Michel Wolfson, the rabbi of the city of Paritz.

I arrived in the city at dawn. I recognized i., I recognized the old houses, and the streets that spread out without order. My childhood days rose up in my memory, and I became a child again. The childhood fear of remaining alone on the street fell upon me. Longing for my mother overtook me, and I hurried along – that is to say, I ran to my mother's house. I found that the mother whom I had left in middle age, beautiful as the moon and pure as the sun, had now become a bent, old woman. She fell into my arms like a young girl, hugged and kissed me with her small, toothless mouth, and wept. I too wept: "O, G-d in heaven! How did my healthy, strong mother, beautiful and wholesome, turn into an old, weak, thin, woman devoid of energy!" However, her eyes lit up like an eternal light, and her voice was like the ringing of silver bells and telephones.

The sudden changes from Volhyn to Lithuania made an unpleasant impression upon me. I suddenly passed from the joyous life of the Hassidim to the sad, dark life of the *Misnagdim*, cold as ice. In place of the sated, fresh faces of the Volhyners, the thin, lean face of the Lithuanians appeared before me.

All the members of my family, my three uncles and their families, came to greet me. I was as happy as a child to meet them.

I visited the synagogues and *Beis Midrash es* in which I had studied and worshipped during my youth; however, where are my teachers? Where are the Yeshiva heads? Where are the rabbis and cantors of that generation? All of them, all of them, went along the way of all people, along with my father of blessed memory, to their peaceful rest in the Slutsk cemetery. I felt as if all had died on a single day. For, it was in a single day that I left them all alive, healthy, and whole, and today I have come when not one of them remains. My good teacher, Rabbi Tzvi Hirsch Poliak was also no more. My heart was ripped to pieces inside of me from so much agony and mourning…

I delivered a few speeches in Slutsk. The elders of the generation who still remembered the preacher Rabbi Tzvi Hirsch Dinov issued their verdict, saying: "From Tzvi Hirsch to Tzvi Hirsch nobody arose like Tzvi Hirsch"[4]. That means, from the days of Dinov until this day, they had not heard such speeches. The Russian police gave me no rest even in my native city, and they bothered me in my work. They forbade me from speaking in public. I was forced to part from my family, relatives, and acquaintances, and move on.

My parting from my dear, eighty-year-old mother was a heartrending scene. She fell upon my neck like a young girl. Her thin, weak body was trembling. She stared at me silently with teary eyes. Her gaze penetrated my heart. O! The pure gaze, the gaze of a merciful mother who sensed that these were the final glances, and that she would never see me again. To this day, those gazes did not depart from my memory. I too could not open my mouth.

I remembered that twenty-five years earlier, she carried me in her hands to seat me on the wagon when she sent me to study in the Mir Yeshiva. Now, she was carried in my arms like a pure dove. We embraced each other strongly and exchanged countless kisses, as we wept quietly. "Live in peace, my dear mother!" "Travel in peace, my son Hershel!"

That was our final conversation.

Translator's footnotes:

1. A change in the ordering of the *Pesukei Dezimra* section of the *Shacharit* service which exists amongst Hassidic, *Nusach Sephard*, and true Sepharic rites, as opposed to Ashkenazic rites, which recite *Baruch Sheamar* prior to *Hodu*.
2. A reference to *Pirkei Avot* 1:13.

3. "And it was when the ark traveled" [Numbers 10:35] recited as the Torah is being taken out of the Holy Ark prior to the Torah reading.
4. Based on a traditional statement regarding Moses Maimonides (Ramba'm): From Moses to Moses nobody arose like Moses.

Highlights of the Life of Y. N. Simchoni

Translated by Jerrold Landau

Yaakov Naftali Hertz Simchoni (Simchowitz) was born in Slutsk on 22 Tevet 5644 (January 20, 1884) to Reb Shmuel Simchowitz and his second wife Zissel, the daughter of Reb Yaakov Naftali Hertz Bernstein of LwÃ³w. The boy was named from his maternal grandfather, who was known in a praiseworthy fashion to the Jews of Galicia due to his ancestry, fear of Heaven, and generous character. He was a precious memory to his children.

Reb Shmuel, Simchoni's father, excelled with his talents and sublime intellect. He was expert in religious and secular studies, and was knowledgeable in Hebrew literature. Already during his youth, he left his parents' home in Minsk and went to Slutsk, where he was occupied for several years in the study of Torah in the home of his first father-in-law Reb Shachna Isserlin. He earned the reputation of a scholar with above average understanding. However, he never desired to work in communal affairs, and did not heed the advice of many to become a rabbi. He was content to live within the four ells of *halacha*, and to occupy himself with Torah for its own sake. He wrote an article for the Peterburg German newspaper, *Petersburger Herald*, for a period of time.

On one occasion, in 1894, he was invited to Peterburg by the government for the rabbinical convention.

[Page 104]

He had four sons from his first wife. They all excelled in their talents, but only one of them, Shachna, inherited his inclination for the sciences.

That son died in 1881 at the age of 22, after he completed the composition *"Der Positivismus in Miasmus"*[1].

Shachna Simchowitz was diligent, and he dedicated himself to the tents of Torah. His father mourned for him greatly. When a son was born to him a few years later from his second wife, he placed all his hopes and demands upon him. When Simchoni was born, his father was around the age of sixty. Given this great age difference, the father did not understand how to educate the son in accordance with his way, and he imposed upon him things that would even be difficult for older people. However, the talents of the child were beyond the usual. He had already learned from his mother to read Hebrew and German at the age of 13 1/2. He earned the name of a genius [*iluy*] at the *cheder*, but his father never praised him. Similarly, he distanced the lad and mocked the imaginary stories that he enjoyed. The father's stringency left deep marks upon the soul of the lad. He was a loner during his childhood and did not have many friends. There was only one matter in which the lad did not listen to his strict father. After he found the Hebrew book shop in the city, he never ceased going there morning and evening. The mania for reading, which was his hallmark until his final day, already affected him during his early childhood years. This was accompanied by the urge to write. He wrote his first work at around the age of eight, called "The Thousand Year War of the Birds." In that book, he described the times of the battles between different species of birds, accompanied by pictures and maps. The lad worked for a year and a half on that work. He was fortunate in that his father was occupied at the rabbinical conference of Peterburg during that time, so there was nobody to impede the lad from acting as a child. When the father returned from his journey, the "author" continued with his literary work secretly for some time, until his hidden items were discovered one day, and all the notebooks were burned.

When Simchoni was about ten years old, he accompanied his father on a trip to Western Europe. That trip brought the two of them closer to each other. That time, they had many discussions about scientific matters, and the lad as influenced greatly by the investigative spirit of the older man. Simchoni lost his father at the age of thirteen. At the direction of his mother, he began to study gymnasium studies according to their curriculum, and took the annual exam at the city gymnasium of Slutsk. In time, he learned to write Hebrew poems. However, the influence of his late father was etched in his memory, and he regarded this as mere frivolity.

In, the year 1898, he went with his mother to live in Minsk. There, he found a broad arena for his development. That which he lacked in Slutsk he completed there, in the city with many books. He especially read a great deal of history. He learned Latin and Greek, and began to study Arabic. He dedicated three hours a day to the study of Talmud from an expert. In those days, he also began to work on scientific endeavors. His first work was a family tree of his ancestors, especially from his mother's side, who was related to the author of *Pnei Yehoshua*. From time to time, he would travel from Minsk to Galicia, where his mother was born, or to Germany.

In 1903, he was ready to take his matriculation exam but when he arrived in Slutsk to be examined in the gymnasium, the exam was set for the Sabbath. Even though he was not meticulous about fulfilling the commandments, he refused to take the exam so that he would not violate the Sabbath publicly. Therefore, his journey abroad for university was delayed. In the meantime, the first revolution came (1905), which turned the world of the Jewish youth into a ferment. However, Simchoni was not swept up in the stream. He read the newspapers of the various parties, but the matters did not touch his heart. During the revolution, he was engaged in deep research on "The Rabbis of the City of Horodna."

He left for Peterburg in 1906. He turned into a different person in that fruitful city. There, he became friends with the studying youth. He participated in various organizations and became involved with people. After he received his matriculation certificate, he went to the university of Leipzig. His mother supported him throughout his entire journey, so he was able to engage in his studies in comfort. He spent the summer months in Switzerland. There he became friendly with the poet Yaakov Cohen, who planned to publish a large anthology at that time called "The New Hebrew." Simchoni's first article, "Rabbi Yehuda Halevi as a National Poet Who Made an Impression," was published in that anthology in the year 5672 [1912].

Already before that, he published an article on the *Pnei Yehoshua* in German: *Monatshrift für Geshichte und Wissenschaft des Judentums* 1913.

That year, he published an article on the Prophet Ezekiel in *Heatid* of Sh. Y. Horowitz (volume II).

In 1914, Simchoni earned his doctorate for his work "Research on lectures of Arabic Writers Regarding the Khazars." From that year and onward, before and during the war, he lived in Berlin for a few years and was the living spirit of "House of the Committee for Hebrew," which he turned into an important, well-known stage. After Poland was conquered by the German army and *Hatzefira* was reconstituted (1916), Simchoni participated in it with two large research works, on Rabbi Yehuda Hachasid and Shadal [Shmuel David Luzatto]. In 1917, he was invited to be a teacher of Hebrew subjects and the Dr. Braude Hebrew Gymnasium of Łódź. He spent a few years there and groomed many students while not neglecting his literary and scientific work. Aside from several research works and critical articles in Hatekufa (see Bibliography, page 16), while residing in Łódź, he translated the book "The War of the Jews" by Flavius from its Greek original into Hebrew, with the addition of a preface, notes, and index. He also wrote a detailed introduction to the Hebrew translation of Tchernichovski's Gilgamesh, and authored three sections of a comprehensive textbook on Jewish history (of which only two were published).

In 1925, he was invited to the editorial board of the Eshkol Israelite Encyclopedia in Berlin to work on its two editions, in Hebrew and German. This work was to be the crowning achievement of his activities. He was an encyclopedist by nature, an overflowing wellspring of breadth of knowledge. Immediately after arriving in Berlin, he immersed himself in this work with wondrous diligence. He made his nights like days, and within a few months, he became one of the supporting pillars of this massive enterprise. The list of articles published in the first two volumes of the German edition (see bibliography, pp. 16-18) as well as the articles published in the Hebrew volume of the encyclopedia, testify to his work and influence.

He suddenly became ill at the beginning of Sivan 5685 [1925], and died on the day after Shavuot at the age of 42. Great honor was extended to him in the Hebrew Berlin and in the Berlin of Jewish wisdom.

(From the *Tzionim* anthology)

Translator's footnote:

1. The original has Msaismus in Latin characters, but I suspect it was a typo, and have corrected it.

[Page 105]

In the Place of Torah and Haskalah

by Dr. Aharon Domnitz

Translated by Jerrold Landau

In the Yeshiva of Rabbi Nechemia

At the age of twelve, I was exiled to a place of Torah, to the Yeshiva of Rabbi Nechemia in Slutsk in the *Beis Midrash* of Rabbi Isserke (Isserke's Shul). Rabbi Nechemia did not talk to his students a great deal. He was stringent on the meaning of a teacher, and he instilled bitterness in the student solely with the gaze of his eyes.

After I had been in the Yeshiva for a few weeks, a bad event took place, and I thought that I would be expelled from the Yeshiva because of it.

This is what happened: My father commanded me in one of his letters that my letters home should be written in the "Holy Language." For this purpose, he sent me via the wagon driver the Book of Jeremiah with the commentary of the Malbim, and the well-known *Maslul* Hebrew grammar textbook. He wrote, "You should learn the Maslul for a half an hour before going to sleep at home, and peruse the Tanach for a half an hour between *Mincha* and *Maariv*."

I perused the *Maslul* as I went to bed, and the Tanach with the commentary of the Malbim in the *Beis Midrash* between *Mincha* and *Maariv*.

Once, one of the prominent householders of the *Beis Midrash* passed by me, looked at me and the book, and raised his voice to me: "You are studying *shvarba* (the 24)[1] in Yeshiva? This leads to apostasy." He slapped my cheeks in wrath. My friends later told me that they saw the man who insulted me speaking with the head of the Yeshiva. I suspected that I would be expelled from the Yeshiva.

The next day, Rabbi Nechemia taught his class and did not react at all to the incident. After the class, he gestured to me to come to him, and he asked me a question unrelated to the "issue": "Do you have all your days taken care of?"[2].

"I am missing one," I responded.

"So what do you do?"

"My mother sends me bread and cheese with the wagon driver."

"O, o, that is good. But a hot meal, ah, a hot meal..." That is how the interview ended. I felt fatherly concern, warmth, and hidden love in his words and voice.

That day after the *Maariv* service, when all the householders as well as the Yeshiva head left for their homes, and only the Yeshiva lads remained, a young lad entered, approached the lad at the edge of the bench and asked him something. He pointed toward me. The lad approached me and asked me in a whisper, "Are you the one who was slapped on the cheek by my father?" I nodded my head to respond affirmatively. "Do you want to study the Holy Language?" He continued to look to the side. "If so," he added, "Please come on Friday afternoon to the home of so-and-so on Zareca street, next to the Baalei Mussar Yeshiva, but don't reveal this." I promised him, and I went to that place on Friday.

I entered a room full of books, piled up in heaps. A lad around the age of twenty, tall, with a long, thin face, approached me and asked me about my knowledge of Bible and the like. He pointed with his finger to an open book and asked me to read it to him. I looked and was amazed: A Hebrew book such as this I am seeing for the first time. There were words with square letters and the vowel diacritics, but without the Biblical trop signs in the middle of the page. There were smooth pages on both sides, without *Rashi* and without *Tosafos*. The short lines on the long page were organized in sections, four lines per stanza. I read one stanza. "Do you understand what you read?" he asked me. "Not everything," I responded, "but I do know isolated words." "If that is the case, come here on every Sabbath eve, and we will help you learn Hebrew."

I came every Sabbath eve. One other lad was connected with me, and together we learned reading, the ordering of nouns and verb, and how to express thoughts in writing.

That man who slapped my face for my iniquity with the Bible between Mincha and Maariv was named Lifschitz. His son, who brought me under the wings of Hebrew, was Feitel. That Feitel Lifschitz escaped from his parents' home to go abroad. He graduated from universities and became a professor in Switzerland. He published a series of articles on economical matters in *Hashiloach*, titled "Economy and Politics in its Theories and Streams," in which he analyzed well the foundations of the subject of economics, from the physiocrats and mercantilists in England, to the theories of Adam Smith, David Ricardo, and Maltus. He was unable to continue his research on the Marxists due to the censor.

As I peruse serious research works, I see the image of Feitel Lifschitz and his father who slapped my cheek before my eyes. Even that slap is recalled positively.

The Ridva'z

In the latter part of the 19th century, the personality of the rabbi of the city of Slutsk, Rabbi Yaakov David, was prominent. He later became known as the Ridva'z. Here are some sections of memories of his personality.

He was then occupied with his writings - his commentary on the Jerusalem Talmud - and he required technical assistance in finding required books for study, in copying the bibliographies, and the like. For this purpose, he used the services of the Yeshiva students of the area, who came to him in turn, with the permission of their rabbis for several hours a week.

I too was among them. With time, I was given a special task - to copy from his handwritten rough draft. This work was interesting, albeit somewhat difficult. His handwriting was very difficult to read. The letters were joined to each other, and were not sufficiently precise: the *zayin* looked like a *gimel*, and the *ches* like a *shin*. He also used many half words and acronyms, as is the custom among rabbis. I immersed myself in this matter and succeeded in fixing it up and improving it a great deal. I also found some errors in writing, such as interchanging an *aleph* with an *ayin* and a *tes* with a *tav* - slips of the pen. At first, I hesitated to show him my fixed out of fear of embarrassing the Gaon.

When I was forced to do so, his face became serious. Then he turned to me with a heartwarming smile and said: "You did well! You are a smart lad! Fix! Fix! I believe I can rely on you." As he was talking, he pinched my ears strongly. Thus, I became his private secretary for a period of time.

The Ridva'z and Doctor Schildkraut

On a cloudless morning on a hot summer day, the Ridva'z invited us to go with him to bathe in the river. Along the way, he discussed Torah matters with us. He asked questions and posed difficulties on the Talmudic discussion in which we were studying at the Yeshiva. Everything was lighthearted and playful, for he loved to joke with our group. Those who knew how to respond and what to answer earned a loving pinch. Whoever did not know was given the punishment of having to remain in his *Beis Midrash* for a week, until he knew his studies.

[Page 106]

The river in Slutsk passed through the city, and there were changing booths for the bathers. When we arrived, we only found Dr. Schildkraut, who had just come out of the water and was starting to get dressed. Dr. Schildkraut spoke Yiddish with a Russian accent. He was known as an excellent physician. The two men recognized each other, greeted each other, and exchanged a brief conversation with mutual respect, as befits two great people, each in their own field.

We young people jumped into the water immediately. The rabbi also jumped into the cool water after taking off his clothes. Dr. Schildkraut looked at the rabbi and said, "O, honorable Rabbin, one should not do this. It is harmful to the health. One should first get wet up to the chest, and only then enter." The rabbi smiled and responded, "My sir the doctor, if everyone paid attention to the words of both of us, the world would not exist," and he laughed heartily. The doctor remained standing open mouthed and uttered, "Rabbin! *Eto Zamechatelno!* [Awesome!] This is wonderful, I never would have imagined!... This is the wisdom of life that only a great rabbi could say." - and they both laughed.

Translator's footnotes:

1. Twenty-four refers to the 24 books of the Tanach.

2. This refers to the rotation of days for the local householders to host Yeshiva students for their meals.

Gleanings

Translated by Jerrold Landau

Rabbi Yerucham Dobrow was a native of Slutsk. After he left the rabbinical seat in Keidanov, he was appointed as the head of the Yeshiva in Slutsk. He left that post in his old age and sat in the synagogue of the hatmakers (Der Kirznenere Shul), occupying himself with Torah day and night. When I was studying in the Eitz Chaim Yeshiva, the name of Rabbi Yerucham enchanted me, and I went to see him. I found him sitting alone next to the oven. I approached him, but he was so immersed in his studies that he did not notice me. When he interrupted his studies, he looked at me and started a conversation with me, but to my great dismay, I did not understand his words.

My eyes filled with tears. I bowed me head so that he would bless me, and he did not refuse. I visited him several times a week, until I became accustomed to understanding his words, more or less.

I would bring to him everything that was difficult for the scholars in the Yeshiva. He would respond in brief, and straighten out the difficulties.

When my visits to Rabbi Yerucham became known in the Yeshiva, other of the finest students of the Yeshiva began to visit him and disturb him with their questions. It was difficult for them to understand his conversation, for he was careful with the minutes that were precious to him. Therefore, they refrained from visiting him often.

(Told by Rabbi Aryeh Levin of Jerusalem)

b.

The elderly rabbi, Rabbi Yehuda Leib Setzer of blessed memory, formerly the honorary president and director of the Union of Orthodox Rabbis of the United States, spent time during his youth in the shadow of the aforementioned Rabbi Yehuda.

He spoke a great deal of the praiseworthiness and modesty of Rabbi Yerucham. The following is one of his stories: A *melamed* with many older daughters lived in the neighborhood of Rabbi Yerucham. A proper match was made for one of them with a lad from a well-off family, and the groom demanded a dowry of 300 rubles. The *Tenaim* [premarital agreement] was arranged in Rabbi Yerucham's home. To the question of the father of the groom as to when the dowry would be paid, the *melamed* replied, "In a month." The in-law did not agree, and asked that the dowry be paid immediately. He grabbed his coat and prepared to leave the party.

Rabbi Yerucham could not bear witnessing the agony of the *melamed*, so he stood up and said, "I will be his guarantor."

The *Tenaim* were written at a propitious time, and the date of the wedding was set. The *melamed* promised Rabbi Yerucham that he would travel afar, and with the help of G-d find what he needs, and collect the money for the dowry. Since the *melamed* did not succeed in this endeavor, and was unable to fulfill his words, Rabbi Yerucham approached Hirsch Natzov, the well-known tycoon of the city, to borrow 300 rubles, which he gave to the father of the groom. Despite the promises of that melamed, the debt has not been repaid to this day.

c.

Rabbi Aryeh Levin of Jerusalem relates:

When I was in Slutsk, I went to the cemetery on Tisha B'Av (as is brought down in the Code of Jewish Law), and I tarried next to a gravestone: "Here is buried, the G-dly Tzadik and Kabbalist, Rabbi Gedalya HaKohen from the village of Kuzmitz."

To my question as to who was that *Tzadik*, I was answered that it was known to the elders of the generation that he was nicknamed "Der Leiventener Tzadik."

Later I found out that he had lived in the village of Kuzmitz. The answer was in his external appearance. He wore linen clothing, and a rope around his waist. At times, he would bring firewood to sell in the marketplace. When he came to the city, he would go at night to the homes of the renowned rabbis Rabbi Yossele Feiter in his time and Rabbi Yosef Dov in his time, and discuss Torah thoughts with them.

There is a tradition from the elders of the generation that at the funeral of Rabbi Mendele of Slutsk, who became ill at the conclusion of the Sabbath, Reb Gedalya was among those who attended. Several people testified that on that Saturday night, they visited Reb Gedalya in the village of Kuzmitz. There is a distance of about ten miles between Slutsk and Kuzmitz. This was a wonder.

d.

Rabbi Mendele, the head of the rabbinical court of Hlusk, left the rabbinate and settled in Slutsk, where he gave a class for students in the *Kloiz*.

The Gaon Rabbi Yosef Dov Soloveitchik was among those who attended his class during his youth. After time, when the write of the rabbinate for Rabbi Yosef Ber reached Slutsk, he responded to the *parnassim* [administrators] of Slutsk: "A lion dwells in your midst, so why are you turning to me?" (He was referring to Rabbi Mendele.)

e.

Rabbi Shmuel Leibowitz from the village of Podlivcha near Slutsk, the father of the Gaon Rabbi Baruch Ber, the rabbi of Hlusk and later a Yeshiva head in the Yeshiva of Kamenetz Litovsk, was great in Torah.

Every Sabbath, he would deliver a class in Mishnah in the Tailors' Beis Midrash, which was full to the brim.

When I studied with Rabbi Baruch Ber in Hlusk, I saw with my own eyes the honor that Rabbi Baruch Ber extended to his father when he visited him from Slutsk.

[Page 107]

Hillel Dubrow

by Sh. N.

Translated by Jerrold Landau

Hillel Dubrow was born in the year 5637 [1877] in the town of Stushin, district of Mohilev.

He was orphaned from his mother during his childhood, and was sent to his father's relatives in Slutsk.

During his early years, he already became known as a genius. When the bounds of the Yeshivot were too small for him, he went to the large *Beis Midrash* and diligently studied on his own Talmud with its commentaries, and the early and latter rabbinical decisors. He was from a well-off family, and was a scholar. He fraternized and befriended veteran studiers, and discussed matters of halacha with them, as one of them.

A few years passed, and that pleasant youth discovered a new light in a different arena. Hillel Dubrow, the pioneer in Hebrew teaching in Slutsk, appeared. He was the living spirit in the Zionist organization and the dissemination of Hebrew culture. These were the early days of political Zionism, the era of the first congresses, and the sprouting of the new Hebrew literature. Hillel Dubrow, alert and vibrant by nature, left the bounds of the *Beis Midrash*, acquired secular knowledge to a certain degree with wondrous speed, and dedicated himself with all strands of his soul to the Zionist movement and the revival of the Hebrew language. He was young, and his small room at the edge of the city became a gathering place for everyone interested in Zionism and Hebrew culture. The finest of the intelligentsia of the city, with nationalist consciousness, would come to his door morning and evening. He was graced with a wonderful power of attraction. The youth, lads and girls who knew Hebrew, gathered around him. Through his influence, the echoes of the living Hebrew language were heard in public gatherings, in parties for issues of the new and old literature, and even on the street and in private homes. He knew how to encourage literary talents that were exposed within the youth close to him. No small number of those were close to him during their youth, in time became leaders in our literature. (Among the most well-known, we recall the prominent researchers and writers, professor Simcha Assaf and Abraham Epstein, may their memories be a blessing; and, may they live long, Y. D. Berkowitz, and in the United States, Dr. Meir Wachsman.)

Dubrow left Slutsk at the beginning of 5665 [1905]. At first, he settled in Yekatrinoslav, and occupied himself with teaching the Hebrew language. Later, he worked alongside Yechiel Halperin of blessed memory in Warsaw and Odessa, in the seminary for kindergarten teaching. During the latter part of the First World War, he moved to Bessarabia for family reasons, where he founded a modern Hebrew school. He groomed hundreds of students with nationalist consciousness. Many of them were among those who actualized the pioneering in the city. He was known in Bessarabia as one of the diligent activists of the Young Zion movement. He worked greatly for *aliya* to the Land. His family home in Bessarabia was a Hebrew-Zionist home by all perspectives: the spoken language was only Hebrew, and his children were educated in the pioneering spirit.

He made *aliya* to the Land with his family at the beginning of 5696 [1935]. He was already close to sixty when he arrived in the Land. He moved away from his wide-branched activities in communal affairs (aside from his activities on behalf of the Jewish National Fund at the school). He continued to work in the teaching and education profession for another seventeen consecutive years, until he reached old age.

He died on 2 Tevet 5716 [1955].

Hillel Dubrow's personal and communal image during the period of his nationalist activity in Slutsk is described in sharp, cutting, comical style in the letter of the young writer Y. D. Berkowitz, who was working then as the literary editor on the editorial committee of *Hazman* of Vilna.

Hillel Dubrow fulfilled the adage, "Say little and do much"[1]. Furthermore, he did not write many letters, and he often neglected responding to his letters that he received from his friends.

The following letter focuses on that matter.

Takanat Agunot[2]

I seek my husband!

It has been five months since my husband [i.e. my master], my honorable teacher Hillel the son of Reb Moshe, may he live, Dubrow, left me to my groans, and I do not know where he is. Before he went, he told me that he would be in Katrineslav, and also sent me several postcards from there, but it has been a long time since I have received any communication from him. And I am a weak, poor women with young children. Since he was handsome, and I have been told by reliable witnesses that all the single women in our city were literally hanging from his neck, and I did not know that he found favor in the eyes of all who saw him, princes have seen him and praised him, queens, and concubines, etc.; and he was also a cynic and went around with all the Maskilim and young people, and even the women an madams in our city in general – therefore I present my petition to the Jews, merciful ones the children of merciful ones, have mercy upon me and save me, and I, if I am lost, etc.[3] For I am not considered by the Jews as a weak woman with children at the breast, so tell me where he is, why he does not write, and why he has forgotten about me and his children. Then the blessing of G-d will come upon you, and it will be a great mitzva.

The signs: he is of average height, and he wears a white, linen cap, a black rubashka shirt with black kotas in the summer. In the winter, he wears what is called a dizhurke in the vernacular, and had great enjoyment from it. His hair was white (yellow-blond), his lips were small and thin, and when he talked he sprayed with his nose and mouth. There was always a thick pencil sticking out of his pocket to prevent any mishap. He always had a small booklet in his chest pocket, in which he wrote every piece of trivia. The main thing was that my husband was very handsome, and all the women said that he was Krasovetz, etc. The virgins follow after him, leaving me and my son in great danger. I will forever remain as an aguna with little children, Heaven save us.

Send the response to the rabbi, Gaon, rabbinical judge, and teacher of righteousness of this community, and save a daughter of Israel from descending to the netherworld.

Thus speaks the unfortunate woman pleading for her life and the life of her children, and wandering about in great want.

Yitzchak Dov Berkowitz

I testify to the truth of this woman's words.

Signed: E. Singalovski[a]

Living here in Vilna

Translator's footnote:

a. Later Dr. Aharon Singalovski, president of the ORT organization. At that time, he was living in Vilna as a flatmate of Y. D. Berkowitz

Translator's footnotes:

1. *Pirkei Avot* 1:15.

2. A difficult title to translate. It refers to the halachic concept of finding solutions for women stuck in an unworkable marriage – in modern times primarily due to a husband's refusal to give a get, and in older times, primarily due to the disappearance of the husband during a journey or a war. It could also refer to cases, such as during 9/11, where a husband is presumed dead, but this cannot be proved. There is extensive rabbinical literature inf finding a solution for such women so that they can become unstuck from the previous marriage, and therefore remarry.

3. "If I am lost, I am lost" from Esther 4:16.

[Page 108]

In memory of Dr. Nathan Klotz

by Dr. Meir Waxman

Translated by Jerrold Landau

Dr. Nathan Kotz
of blessed memory

The city of Slutsk merited renown in the Jewish world, not only due to the fact that its rabbinical seat as occupied by Torah greats who achieved fame in the world of *halacha*, but also because it succeeded in raising and educating writers and wise people whose contributions enriched Hebrew literature and the wisdom of Israel in many subjects. Among them were Y. N. Simchoni, the historian and researcher of literature of the Middle Ages; Y. D. Berkowitz, a storyteller with talent and a wonderful style; Lisitzki the poet, who earned a place in the Hebrew poetry of our nation Dr. Avraham Epstein, who excelled in his penetrating, deep criticism.

I wish to erect a monument to a wise man of Slutsk with great knowledge in the wisdom of Israel, who excelled in particular in Biblical research. However, due to his modesty, or perhaps due to his great thirst to absorb knowledge and wisdom, he did not give off much. This is Dr. Nathan Klotz.

This wise man, who was my childhood friend, excelled further with his great enthusiasm for the wisdom of Israel. The names of its builders: Zunz, Graetz, Shada'l, [Shmuel David Luzzatto] and others never left his lips. In every meeting with a friend, he never ceased praising and lauding their important contributions. A desire was hatched in his heart to leave the city of his birth, to travel to Germany, and to register as a student in the Breslau Rabbinical Seminary in order to become a disciple of the sages and to quench his thirst from the wellsprings of their wisdom and their vast knowledge.

This aspiration was realized after he spent a few years in the famous Yeshiva of Odessa headed by Dr. Chaim Chernovitz of blessed memory, in which Dr. Yosef Klausner and Ch. N. Bialik taught. There, he also engaged in general studies , including European languages, especially German language and literature. In Breslau, he delved deeply into the Bible and its commentators, and became export in all their corners and hidden areas. He received his Ph.D. for his German story about Rabbi Shmuel David Luzzatto as a Biblical commentator, which is to be published soon.

He came to New York a few years after the First World War, and was immediately appointed in a professor at the teachers' seminary of the Yeshiva of Rabbi Yitzchak Elchanan[1], where he taught for 24 years, until the day of his death in the year 5706 [1946].

In that school, he found the opportunity to disseminate his great knowledge among his many students, if not in writing then orally. He educated an entire generation with sharp, deep knowledge in the holy writings. He especially attempted to instill in the hearts of his students the love of Jewish wisdom and its builders, and to encourage them to delve into their books, to appreciate them and revere them.

As his students and friends in the Beis Midrash have told me, he excelled in his speeches, whether in the teacher's seminary or in the Dr. Revel graduate school of Jewish studies, both in their comments and in their style. They left a deep impression upon the hearts.

This sage of Slutsk merited to be a guide to hundreds of students in the knowledge of Bible, and in implanting the love of Torah and the wisdom of Israel in their hearts. These students, many of whom are rabbis or schoolteachers, will imbue the spirit of their rabbi upon their congregations and students during the course of their holy work. This is the important contribution of Nathan Klotz to American Jewry.

Translator's footnote:

1.   Yeshiva University.

Rabbi Shachna the Shamash [Sexton]

by Rabbi Dr. Moshe Chiger

Translated by Jerrold Landau

To his face they called him Rabbi Shachna, but he was called "Rabbi Shachna the Shamash" when not in his presence, in any case, with the title of rabbi. He was a great scholar, with a sharp mind. Aside from his great expertise in Talmud and halachic decisors, he had great knowledge of Bible and literature, and was considered to be one of the special people in whom Torah and wisdom were blended.

However, the source of his livelihood was neither from Torah nor wisdom. He did not make them a crown with which to aggrandize himself of a spade with which to dig[1], but rather to enjoy and provide enjoyment to others through them.

He was not a rabbi, but rather a *shamash*[2]. He was the assistant and secretary of the rabbi of the city. During the era about which I am writing, 1912-1920, he was the assistant and secretary of the Gaon Rabbi Isser Zalman Meltzer, may the memory of the righteous be a blessing.

Those years were the years of the First World War, as well as a few years before and after. There was difficulty and tribulations for the Jews of Russia. From time to time, he had to publicize proclamations for the community, telling them to avoid and refrain from certain activities. Rabbi Shacha was both the author and the announcers of such decrees.

Rabbi Shachna was a great writer. His vocabulary was rich, and he always found the appropriate words with which to give proper and precise expression

[Page 109]

to various intentions and reasons that made it necessary for the leader of the community to issue the proclamations. The style of the proclamations excelled in their simplicity and clarity. Every person, and even children, could understand them despite their great brevity. There was no dual meaning, unclarity or misunderstanding in the world. No additional commentaries were required. The proclamations were skillfully constructed, and testified to the talents and intelligence of their author.

There were approximately twenty synagogues in Slutsk. Approximately one third were in the center of the city, and the rest were scattered along various roads. Almost every Sabbath during the time of the morning prayers, one could see Rabbi Shachna go from street to street, hurrying from one synagogue to the next, tired and weary, breathing heavily and sweeting. He would ascend the *bima* [podium] of the synagogue and begin to proclaim. His voice was clear and resonant. Every word and phrase was uttered with appropriate expression. His voice and bodily movements would change according to the content and the meaning of the words, without any outside input, but rather with understanding and deep feeling for the seriousness and importance of the matter. The faces of the audience testified that all his words made a deep impression, and did not miss their mark.

Thanks to his clear style and clear expression, he was also good at telling popular jokes. He had a joyous spirit by nature. Sadness found no place in his heart. There was a light smile on his face, and his eyes sparkled with calm and joy. He never missed an opportunity to tell a joke, appropriate to the time and place. He wanted to enjoy and be glad, and also bring joy and happiness to others. When he told any joke, he used descriptions and similes that attracted the heart, stemming from his good personality. The audience would stand around him open mouthed, swallowing his every expression. When he reached the punchline of his joke, he would end suddenly, and mirthful laughter would burst forth from the depths of the souls of his audience. The laughter of the teller of the joke would join with the laughter of the audience, for enjoyed telling jokes and making others happy.

After many years, the Gaon Rabbi Isser Zalman Meltzer, may the memory of the holy be blessed, would tell over the jokes of Rabbi Shachna during moments of mirth for the enjoyment of the listeners. He would add, "Had you heard this joke from the mouth of Rabbi Shachna himself, you would have enjoyed it sevenfold."

With his great love for his fellow, and especially from scholars, he took it upon himself to care for the Yeshiva lads who streamed to Slutsk from all corners of Russia to hear Torah from the Gaon of the generation Rabbi Isser Zalman Meltzer, may the memory of the holy be blessed. At the end of the vacation period after Passover and Sukkot, one could meet Rabbi Shachna in the company of groups of lads, going around and looking at houses on the sides of the street, to determine whether it would be possible to host one or two of the Yeshiva lads there. During those years when the Yeshiva lads took their meals in rotation, Rabbi Shachna would also arrange the rotation system.

Since this institution was called a *komitet*, one can surmise that a special committee of the town notables was set up to conduct the matters of the institution and tend to its needs. However, in actuality, the entire concern and burden fell upon Rabbi Shachna. He bore the entire burden of the great work without complaint. He did everything out of the joy of fulfilling a mitzva. His righteous wife, who was in full agreement with all his deeds, sewed a special sack of white linen, which she used to collect loaves of bread and other food items from the residents of the city for the *komitet*. Every morning, Rabbi Shachna could be seen on the streets of the city with his short stature bent over under the weight of the heavy sack, which reached his ankles. He hurried in the direction of the dining hall to provide breakfast for the Yeshiva students as early as possible.

Rabbi Shachna's house on America Street was poor and meager on the outside, but clean and warm on the inside. The name "America" requires explanation. This street was not one of splendor, luxury, and wealth, as the streets of the new world. On the contrary, the street was noted by its puddles of mud and slime, and its shaky houses. This street was the place of residence of the poor people and the "underworld" of Slutsk. All the corruption and licentiousness, all the boisterousness and drunkenness, all the indigents and paupers found their center on that street. The residents of the street would give two reasons for the splendid name of America for their street. Those who belonged to the group of licentiousness and drunkards would say that the road symbolizes free America, where everyone is permitted to do whatever they desire. However, the paupers and indigents gave the reason as the irony in the name, which contrasts the bitterness and disappointment in their life conditions with the life of wealth and excess in America, the land to which they desired. Rabbi Shachna set up his home specifically on that dirty, filthy street. It is possible that this too was influenced by the love of his fellow, with his readiness to help them and benefit them. Indeed, his house was like a grassy lawn in a large bog, like a shade tree in a sandy desert.

Since he was known as a man who was expert in world events, with some business knowledge, at times, merchants and businessmen would come to his home to write an agreement or a contract. When such people came to his home, they would bring with them a better atmosphere to the forlorn street. This was especially noticeable on Sabbaths and festivals. Rabbi Shachna used to invite guests to his home for Sabbaths and festivals. Preachers, orators, authors, emissaries, and ordinary scholars would stream to Rabbi Shachna's house to benefit from his words of wisdom and the handiwork of his diligent wife, who would prepare treats and delicacies, and would relate politely to all guests. The clean *kapotes* and sparkling hats of the guests were a complete opposite of the filthy street.

The fact that Rabbi Shachna and his household did not suffer from the filth and corruption of the environment is interesting. The residents of the street, both Jews and Christians, honored and revered Rabbi Shachna, and not only treated he and his family with respect, but also his house, yard, and garden. They did not throw stones at his windows, his fence was not broken, and his garden was not trampled. It seemed that the drunks and rowdies of the street apparently accepted upon themselves to grant extraterritorial immunity to Rabbi Shachna, his household, and everything belonging to him.

During his free time late at night or early in the morning, Rabbi Shachna would sit in his room and study Torah.

He would study out loud with a melody at the time that the songs of the drunkards, the loud voices of discord and shouting, or an argument between a drunkard and his wife, would permeate outside. The pleasant voice of Rabbi Shachna would echo and attract the hearts of the neighbors.

Rabbi Shachna died at an old age several years before the outbreak of the Second World War. He was eulogized appropriately. However, most of his family was murdered by the Nazis, may their names be blotted out. There were only two survivors of his large family, one in America and one in Israel.

Translator's footnotes:

1. Expressions referring to utilizing the Torah for earning one's livelihood, based on *Pirkei Avot* 4:5.
2. Usually referring to a sexton or a beadle, but here referring to the assistant of the rabbi.

[Page 110]

From the Recent Past

by Rabbi Moshe Yissaschar Goldberg, z"l

Translated by Kadish Goldber

1. The Yeshiva After the Revolution

The Rabbi of Slutsk, the illustrious Rabbi Isser Zalman Meltzer, zt"l, with the brilliance of his Torah and his congenial character, enlightened the eyes of his congregation and of the thousands of pupils who flocked to him from near and far.

The overwhelming majority of the people of Slutsk were *mithnagdim*. They avoided the Chassidic practice of exaggeratedly lauding the miracles and wonders performed by this *tzaddik* or that saintly *Rebbe*. Despite this, the masses believed with perfect faith that there was some power inherent in their rabbis and righteous men; whatever they blessed was blessed – "He [the Almighty] fulfills the will of those who fear Him."

I remember how, as a child, I heard my mother tell of an event that amplified the greatness and righteousness of our Rabbi Isser Zalman Meltzer in the eyes of all the community. A Russian policeman had come to the home of the Rabbi with orders from the Chief of Police to carry out some act; refusal to do so would result in incarceration. The Rabbi was not intimidated and he refused to obey the order. The policeman forced the Rabbi to accompany him to the station, pulling him bodily. The policeman had seven sons. Soon after the outrageous event, his firstborn son suddenly took ill and died. After a few days, most of his other sons took ill and died, leaving only one son hovering between life and death. The bereaved policeman believed that the holy "*Rabbin*" was responsible for the tragedy, and came to beseech forgiveness. He entered the Rabbi's home, prostrated himself on the floor, wept, and pleaded that the Rabbi forgive him and pray for the recuperation of his young son. The Rabbi forgave him, and the son's health returned.

During the First World War, the joy of the Sukkot festival turned to melancholy. The number of battlefront casualties grew daily; the front moved closer and closer to Slutsk. The synagogues were full of worshippers, but a cloud of sadness enveloped the congregation – was not a single *ethrog* in the synagogue. Because of the disruptions in travel, the Slutsk community had managed to acquire only two *ethrogim* that year, and these were placed in the homes of the rabbis. The Jews flowed to the homes of the two rabbis in order to fulfill the *mitzvah* of the four species. Father, of blessed memory, took me with him – how we looked forward to observing the *mitzvah* of holding of the *lulav* in the home of Rabbi Isser Zalman Meltzer z"l!

With the dethronement of Tsar Nicholai II, all the citizens, Jew and gentile alike, believed that a new order of total freedom and equality would replace the rotten regime. Young Jews burst out joyfully into the streets of Slutsk and conducted enthusiastic demonstrations, giving public voice to that which had been repressed in their hearts during the old order. In the processions marched the different Zionist organizations and the members of the Jewish Socialist "Bund." The former marched arm in arm, the blue and white flag leading the companies, all singing with great fervor "Shum BeEretz Chamdat Avot" – "There in the Fathers' Beloved Land" and "Se'oo Tsiona Nes VaDegel" – "Raise the Banner and the Flag to Zion." etc. The Bundists also marched proudly, their red banner waving, singing the Bundist "Vow" and the "Marseilles."

Never had the Jews enjoyed such good days. The city elders were fearful lest the youth be swept up in the currents of the revolution, distancing themselves completely from the tradition of their parents. As a preventative measure, it was decided to establish a modern, religious high school. In order to attract the youth, it was decided that the pupils would wear special uniforms, with bright brass buttons embossed with a Jewish emblem. These pupils would not be inferior to their companions in the Russian gymnasium, neither scholastically nor in appearance; they would even surpass them, thanks to their Jewish studies.

The idea quickly won adherents, arousing the envy of youth like myself who had been brought up exclusively on the knees of Torah. I confess without embarrassment, that even during the days of the Tsar, I was envious of my friends who studied in high school. I was comforted with the projected establishment of the school for Torah and science, in which I would be able to study both Torah and science, and in my school uniform I would externally resemble the gymnasium pupils. I revealed my secret desire to my revered father, and his face took on a somber look. "We're going to talk to the Rabbi." *Abba* told the rabbi of my intentions. The Rabbi lovingly stroked my cheek and said: "Such a school is a necessity for boys whose Judaism is threatened by the wave of the revolution. It is to be feared that, because of the new freedom, the boys will grow further apart from the bosom of their parents, and it is important to draw them close and to keep them in the framework of traditional life. But a boy such as yourself, educated and raised in a home marked by Torah and fear of God – why should you desire such a school, in which the Torah studies are limited, and the holy and profane are intertwined? Go back to the Yeshiva, and there you will find your world."

These simple and heartfelt words, lovingly spoken in a concealed vein of worry, penetrated deep into my heart, and I ceased to dream about gymnasium, about uniforms and brass buttons. (Incidentally, tremendous effort was invested in the establishment of this school; unfortunately, the tumultuous events that suddenly blackened the skies of Russian Jewry prevented realization of the plan).

The honeymoon of the revolution witnessed great fermentation in the Jewish community. During the Tsarist regime, because of fear of the police who kept track of the behavior of the community leadership, it was difficult to realize the yearning for free personal and communal expression. No sooner was the arm of oppression broken and the last of the Romanovs gone down in defeat, then great forces burst forth onto the Jewish street. I remember how the city was in tumult at the approach of elections to the "Kehillah" and the "Founding Meeting." "Agudath Yisrael" appeared as an organized body. The "Zionists" and the "Bund" also conducted vigorous campaigns. The air was full of slogans; posters were plastered on walls and pillars. In the center of the city, on the "Shosai," the Orthodox raised a large poster which described the aged and the young carrying a Torah scroll in their arms, marching up a path to the light of a new sun, which shone in the skies of Jewry. Hundreds of men and women, taking their Shabbat noon walk, would stop and stare in wonderment, impressed by the religious campaigning, or perhaps just surprised by the very fact that eligious Jews publicly take positions on political issues which had previously been considered unimportant.

The synagogues also provided platforms for the masses during the campaign. I see, as though standing before me and alive, in front of the Ark of the Law, Reb Zelig of Starobin (Rabbi Zelig Portman), one of the Slutsk Yeshiva's finest students (He eventually died in New York). He spoke with fiery enthusiasm, holding his audience spellbound. Rabbi Avraham Yitchak [M?], z"l, spoke with polished style, with sweet and clear intonation. The Yeshiva Head, Rabbi Aharon Kotler, may he be set aside for long life, stands on the pulpit, words of flame shooting from his mouth.

[Page 111]

The Rabbi of Slutsk, Rabbi Isser Zalman [M?]eltzer, zt"l, his noble appearance radiating gentleness, would occasionally appear among the speakers.

I remember how, on a winter night, a large crowd gathered in the Great Beit Midrash to hear the speakers – or to heckle. The rabbi had barely ascended the pulpit and begun to speak when a few arrogant young men began to harass him with interruptions. The rabbi answer softly, as though reciting the Talmud before his students: "Let them disturb all they want; this will not harm us," and continued with his speech.

The First World War, which brought in its wake severe problems and great destruction in all branches of life, hit the yeshiva "Etz Hayyim" of Slutsk very hard. Military conscription, damaged roads, and the dangers characteristic of emergency situations, diminished the number of pupils.

The authorities expropriated the spacious yeshiva building, and the yeshiva was forced to go into exile, first to the Tailors' Synagogue, then to the synagogue named after Reb Isserke. I recall those moments of exultation that beat in our hearts when the yeshiva building was later evacuated and we were able to return to our 'home.' The number of pupils increased, but there was a dearth of Talmud texts; without texts, how does one learn Talmud? The inventory of the booksellers emptied out; the connection with publishers of religious books was severed; pupils rushed to the city's synagogues to try and obtain Tractate "*Gittin*" from the *gabbaim*. Some were lucky enough to obtain a tome – whether on loan or by full payment – from private sources.

My companion, Yitchak Sochalitsky (currently in Israel), and I went from synagogue to synagogue, searching unsuccessfully. Suddenly an idea! The volumes of the Lyakhovichi refugees! When the Jews of Lyakhovichi fled the terrors of the approaching war, they took their Torah with them; tomes of Talmud, *Poskim*, and *Responsa*. The books were loaded on wagons and brought to Slutsk. Since there was lack of space in private homes to house this large and valuable treasure, the refugees agreed to store all the books on the windowsills of the "Cold Synagogue."

We set our eyes on the "*Gittin*" volumes of this treasure, but two obstacles blocked our way. One, how does one climb to so great a height? Two, may one take books without authorization? For a response to the second question, we approached the rabbi. He walked back and forth, sunk in thought, and, after consideration, rendered his decision: It is permissible to take them, on the proviso that we intend to return them. The serious look on the rabbi's face indicated that it was very difficult for him to decide on his own. It appears that he suggested that we also confer with Reb Moishe, one of the senior yeshiva students; he certainly would understand the pressing need.

Reb Moishe was an outstanding scholar and a noble personality who was later, in the beginning of the 20's, appointed rabbi in Kletsk. Rumor has it that the Nazis murdered him.

I recall my transgressions. We looked for Reb Moishe of Lyakhovichi that day, but could not locate him. We got to work, assuming that we would receive *post facto* approval. The mission had to be executed on Shabbat, because on weekdays the synagogue was closed. We entered the synagogue during the afternoon *Mincha* service, opened some side doors and left them slightly ajar, so that the *shamas* would not notice them. When the congregants finished *Mincha* and entered the side rooms in order to chant Psalms and the *Maariv* service, we left the synagogue, sneaking in later through one of the opened doors. Now we had to overcome the main obstacle. We placed bench upon bench, *stender* upon *stender,* and then scaled our wobbly ladder. Finally, right before dusk, we found two volumes of "Gittin," Vilna edition, beautifully bound. We descended safely, and returned the benches and *stenders* to their places.

The Gaon Reb Aharon Kotler

The next day we returned, ashamed, to the Rabbi's home. Fortunately, Reb Moishe of Lyakhovichi was present. We told him the whole story. Reb Moshe listened with a smile on his lips and approved our action. Our consciences were relieved of a heavy burden.

On the morrow, the noble figure of the Rabbi appeared in the Yeshiva entrance. He entered unhurriedly, exchanged words with a few of the students, as though he were one of them; he then walked back and forth, engrossed in thought. When he sat down, my companion and I, with hearts full of both fear and joy, approached, and our entrance exam began. The Rabbi did not ask difficult questions, nor did he indulge in intricate *pilpul;* he decided that we were capable of independent self-study.

Well do I remember that winter day, when the Slutsk yeshiva went off to exile, to Kletsk. A treaty between the Bolsheviks and the Poles transferred Slutsk to Soviet rule. Reb Aharon Kotler, may he live to long and good years, and our family, assisted by a few of the senior students, loaded their belongings on the wagon. They, themselves, went on foot, heads bowed, souls sad. The Yeshiva "Etz Hayyim" of Slutsk went into exile, but the exile was not total. A substantial minority of students remained. Supervised by the city Rabbi and the spiritual mentor, Rabbi Asher Sandomirsky, they remained to continue the holy work in the city, despite the foreseen difficulties and dangers. Thus was the body of the Yeshiva cleft in two.

Before long the Slutsk students began to feel the pressures of the Soviet regime, and they found it necessary to "steal the border" and move to Kletsk. Thanks to experienced smugglers, this was not an involved operation, but it did entail dangers.

[Page 112]

The Yeshiva "Etz Hayyim" of Slutsk going off to exile, to Kletsk

Some boys were apprehended by the Bolshevik Border Police and accused of counter-revolutionary activity. Rumor had it that some of the students were arrested by the Polish Border Police, sentenced to incarceration, lashes, and torture.

When my time for departure arrived, I was afraid of being caught, and shared my fears with the Rabbi. My apprehension touched his heart, and he considered what could he do for me. Finally he decided to give me a letter, written in Polish, to the effect that he knew me to be an honest young man, a student in his Yeshiva. The Rabbi thought that such a document might lighten my punishment should I – God forbid – be caught by the Polish Border Police. A scribe proficient in Polish penned the document in a clear cursive script, and the Rabbi signed.

At the time, I did not appreciate how much the Rabbi had endangered himself by giving me this letter. Had I been apprehended by Soviet guards with the letter in my possession, they certainly would have accused the Rabbi of aiding young men to flee from Russia to Poland. As it was, the Soviet authorities had already set their suspicious sights upon him. (He, was, in fact, forced to escape into Poland a month later). Yet, despite his precarious position, he gave me the document with a blessing that I succeed in safely reaching my destination.

Until this day, I am amazed. Is it possible that he was not aware of the danger, and endangered his own life in order to save a Jewish soul? Perhaps he was well aware, but still he put his life in danger. He was certain that, with God's help, no evil would befall him.

2. Reb Kaddish der Melamed

My grandfather, Kadish Kraines, best known as Reb Kadish the Melamed (teacher), was weak and thin, his face framed with curly sideburns and wispy beard, his large eyes expressing gentleness.

He taught Talmud and Bible to the fourth grade of the city Talmud Torah, instilling the fear of God in his pupils, along with the other teachers in town. My friend, the poet Ephraim Lissitsky, told me that he obtained his knowledge of Hebrew grammar from Kadish the Melamed. In addition to his work in the Talmud Torah, Reb Kadish taught adults in the Kapashker Synagogue.

Mother told me that he used to teach the children of Reb Shmuel Leibowitz in the neighboring village of Podelipseh. (One of them, Reb Boruch Ber, z"l, served as rabbi in Halosk). He owned a farm in the middle of the town and paid Grandfather in part with various crops –

[Page 113]

including a wagonload of potatoes, which provided food for a long time. Mother and her brothers once transferred potatoes to the cellar by the light of a kerosene lantern that hung from a wall. Unfortunately, the lantern fell and the kerosene spilled on the potatoes. But the family ate the potatoes down to the last bite, despite the foul kerosene smell – so great was the family's poverty.

Grandfather used to walk by foot to and from the estate of Reb Shmuel. Once, in winter, the ice broke beneath him, and had farmers not heard his cries and rushed to his rescue, he would have drowned in the river.

His last years were difficult ones. The city passed back and forth a number of times – Russians to Poles, Poles to Russians. Once, during Soviet rule, he was discovered by a Jewish renegade teaching Torah to two grandchildren in the Kapashker Synagogue, and was arrested. He stood trial but was soon released because of his very old age. In the town it was said that both the informer and the judge were former pupils of his.

When our family emigrated to the United States, we urged him to come along. He deliberated, but finally declined, preferring to spend his final years in the city of his birth among other family members.

In his letters to us, he never complained. His youngest daughter and her husband provided him with respectable support. He was happy in the knowledge that his children and grandchildren continued to engage in Torah and *mitzvot* even in America.

On the seventh day of Pesach, 5686 (1926), he died, at the age of 75. The Jews of Slutsk paid him great honor, eulogized him as he deserved, and brought him to eternal rest among the most respected members of the community.

3. My Father's Life

Abba, of blessed memory, Rabbi Chayim Ze'ev Wolf Goldberg, was born in Kolna, Poland, to poor parents who eked out a meager survival from carpentry. Even though he was a young adolescent, he learned in the yeshivas of Lomza and Slobodka. Later he moved to the Etz Chayim yeshiva in Slutsk. His wife was Hod'l, daughter of Kadish der Melamed. When he was ordained as a rabbi, he acceded to the request of the illustrious Reb Moshe Mordecai Epstein to travel to America and raise funds for the Slobodka yeshiva. The New World and its democratic institutions found favor in his eyes, and he almost decided to remain there and serve as a rabbi. But he returned to Slutsk.

He chose not to make the Torah his means of livelihood. He did not return to the rabbinate upon coming back to Slutsk. He tried his hand at business, but since he never really understood the ways of commerce, he made nothing. Most of his time was spent in the study of Torah and books of Jewish ethics.

The outbreak of World War I opened many opportunities for massive assistance to Jews in distress. Abba took upon himself the responsibility for helping unfortunate co-religionists who suffered effects of the war. This was the acme of his activities during those "days of awe." The large local population of paupers was swollen by refugees who fled border towns – entire families lacking all necessities, some of them affluent Jews who had lost their fortunes, women whose husbands had been conscripted into army service, leaving them and their children destitute, without means of support.

Infectious illnesses swept through the town. The problems of providing food, clothing, shelter, and medicine for the refugees occupied the energies of the triumvirate which devoted itself to public aid: Dr. Shildkraut, father and patron to all the inhabitants of the town, Reb Yeshaya Mendel Deretzin, an energetic public figure with a noble heart, and my father and teacher.

Daily they would supply flour or bread to the needy. Every Friday morning they would distribute two *challahs* for *lechem mishneh* for the Shabbat meals. (If my memory does not deceive me, the distribution took place in the *Linat Tzedek* office in the Cold Shul.). Father would 'hide' a few *challahs* to give secretly to householders who had lost everything, or to scholars and members of prominent families, so as to spare them the embarrassment of waiting in the queue.

Although father was rigid in religious matters, he valued the study of the Hebrew language and Jewish literature, and did not prevent me from studying *Tanakh* and reading modern Hebrew literature.

With the Bolshevik revolution, the situation in the city took a turn for the worse. The war between the Bolsheviks and the Poles brought ruination. When the former advanced, the town faced the danger of starvation, illness, and fear for the future of religious life. When the Poles advanced, life itself was threatened. The troops of the "*Lerchikim*" and the "*Poznatchikim*" molested Jews, killed them, wounded them, and plucked beards. Jews were hurled from trains. Many were murdered by hooligans in neighboring villages and brought to Slutsk for burial. Father fled to America. After three years he was able to bring over his family. But his connection with Slutsk did not cease; he helped support the yeshivas in Slutsk and in Kletsk. This is attested to by letters in my possession written by Reb Aharon Kotler and Reb Asher Sandomirsky, who was spiritual mentor in the Etz Chayim of Slutsk.

The following is a portion of a letter from the latter, dated 24 Tammuz 5683, after Reb Isser Zalman had been forced to leave:

"There are about 100 Torah scholars who sacrifice themselves, just as did our great leaders and sages of old in the days of the evil decrees. We can say of them, '*Should a man die in the tent...*' [Midrash exegesis reads this as referring to "the tent of Torah", i.e., one who devotes his total self to the study of Torah]. This institution is the largest and most important, the sole remnant, which remains in all our land... God forbid that this holy institution be destroyed because of material causes."

Father died in New York in 1935.

[Note by Kadish Goldberg, grandson and translator: "After a short period as rabbi of Derby and Ansonia, Connecticut, my grandfather served as rabbi for the Orthodox synagogues in South Brooklyn, New York."]

4. Dr. Leo Shildkraut, of blessed memory

Tall and broad-shouldered was he, and of noble spirit. He sought neither wealth nor honor. He acted for the public's welfare and for the good of the individual, in times of peace and in times of emergency. When he entered a house, he brought a spirit of respect, and he was received with great admiration and affection.

In winter he would appear in the patient's home, dressed in a fine fur coat, with a fur cap on his head. He looked like a Polish nobleman, but actually there stood before you a Jew who loved his poor brothers, and rushed to their aid in times of distress. In education and appearance he differed

[Page 114]

from the Jewish masses, but he understood their feelings and psychology; he spoke their lnguage, and he came close to them.

The poet, Ephraim Lissitsky, told me in New Orleans, how he fell ill with malaria as a youngster. He visited Dr. Shildkraut before the 9th of Av. The doctor commanded him not to refrain from eating meat.

For the welfare of the city's indigent, Dr. Shildkraut placed a closed contribution box in his waiting room, into which patients inserted the doctor's fees, each according to his ability. Sometimes, after examining a poor patient at his home, he would slip – unnoticed – a coin beneath the pillow. Upon leaving, he would say: "I left a prescription under the pillow, and I wish the patient a full recovery."

He liked to jokingly say that one should believe in *"techiyas hameisim,"* the resurrection of the dead. "If a Jew can eat a large serving of *cholent*, take a deep nap – and still rise healthy and whole – is this not veritably a resurrection of the dead?"

Dr. Shildkraut was not a synagogue goer. But on Yom Kippur, he would come to the synagogue for the closing *Neila* service.

After the October Revolution, a plague of dysentery erupted. The situation was difficult. Many fell sick. Few doctors and little medicine were available. Medicines that were available were expensive. The gravest problem was lack of food to strengthen the body, and starvation claimed many victims. Dr. Shildkraut worked day and night without stop, not caring for his own health.

One morning, pairs of soldiers spread throughout the city, conducting searches. Officially, the searches were for contraband, but once set loose, the brigands did not differentiate between forbidden and unforbidden; they took all that came to hand. A great tumult arose; there was no one to halt the plunder. Suddenly, as if a miracle had occurred, the searches ceased. Rumor had it that Dr. Shildkraut had rushed a telegram to the authorities in Moscow, and from there an order was issued to stop the searches.

The above incident is deeply engraved in my memory, because a few days later, I went with Mother to one of the warehouses, where we signed a declaration that two sacks of flour had been confiscated, and the plunder was returned.

The battles between the Russians and the Poles over Slutsk left the community totally impoverished. There was no choice but to turn to our brothers across the ocean with pleas for help for looted, suffering Slutsk. The three heads of the community – the two rabbis and Dr. Shildkraut – sent a "Plea To Our Brethren In The United States." Published in "*Hatsfira*" on 24 November 1920, it read:

"A Call For Help –From the Jewish Community of Slutsk"

"Our brothers, hear us! Throughout the years of war, we suffered greatly, many misfortunes passed over us; we passed from regime to regime, our situation changing again and again. All sorts of disaster befell us. Our lives were in danger, and the fear of death was upon us. Stores were closed. The past four months brought great poverty. Travel came to a stop; we remained unclothed; we were all plundered. Recently we saw with our own eyes the blade of the two-edged sword, for the war was waged within the city itself. Arrows flew overhead, arrows of death, explosive arrows. Houses were destroyed, many people were wounded, many killed. Fires broke out throughout the city. The wall of the bathhouse was consumed by fire. The wall of the community and stores went up in flame. All institutions of charity, the orphanage, the old folks' home, and the hospital – all are in a deplorable state, without food, without clothing. Aged and young stretch out their hands for help. We have not the strength to meet their needs, not even with bread and water. The schools have closed down, for lack of salaries for teachers and of firewood for heating. They walk the streets, hungry, barefoot and unclothed, seeking help. But who can help them? For we lack everything. Householders whose hands were once open to help those who ask and beg, now themselves have become those who ask and beg.

"Now, our brothers, our own flesh and blood in America, our eyes are turned to you, our hands outstretched: Help us in our distress. You know what you must do. Hurry, tarry not, for we have no strength to do anything. We lie before you like a stone that has no one to turn it over; it is your obligation to save us.

Sunday, 27 Cheshvan 5681, Slutsk

Dr. L. Shildkraut

Rabbi Isser Zalman Meltzer, Head of the Beth Din and the Yeshiva.

Our Rabbi and Mentor, RabbiMeir

Funds should be sent to the Slutsk Community through the Community of Warsaw."

The news that Dr. Shildkraut had suddenly fallen critically ill spread rapidly. That morning became sevenfold more painful when word came that Dr. Shildkraut was no more. Crowds flowed from all corners of the city to accompany him to his final rest. His coffin was brought out to the street, and a great silence hung over all. Thousands of spectators stood, silent and grieving. The huge mass stirred, the procession began. His coffin was carried on shoulders to the large modern hospital, and from there to the old "*Hekdesh*," where lay sick indigent Jews, whom he had treated for decades.

At the cemetery, he was eulogized by Rabbi Avraham Yitchak Shisgal, z"l, a student of the yeshivas of Slutsk and Kletsk. He had barely begun to speak, with great emotion and sad voice "… we had a precious pearl, and it is lost to us…" and immediately all groaned and wept. On of the speakers, Rabbi Yosef Peimer z"l, praised the deceased and said that in his life he sacrificed himself upon the altar of his brothers and fellow citizens, and now he was like a "*korban olah,*" a sacrifice offered totally to God. Upon hearing this, one who "denied the covenant" jumped up, as though bitten by a snake, and publicly insulted the rabbi. A scandal almost erupted at the graveside, but the Rabbi, despite his humility and shyness, was not deterred by the insolent fellow, and continued to eulogize the saintly doctor.

[Page 115]

Portraits

by Baruch Domnitz

Translated by Jerrold Landau

How much splendor is exemplified in this name – Slutsk – for me. How numerous are the memories that are evoked within me when I hear that name. In the eyes of my spirit, I see its gardens and alleyways, people and rabbis, synagogues and yeshivot full and bustling from morning to evening, worshippers and studiers; pure, dreamy Yeshiva lads who streamed not Slutsk from the nearby towns to learn Torah from the great Torah sages who lived there: the Kldba'z and Rabbi Melike, Rabbi Issei Zalman Meltzer and Rabbi Nechemla, Rabbi Yosha and Rabbi Michla, Rabbi Beil from the Karnaim, and others.

That city was filled with merchants, shopkeepers, tradespeople, and intelligentsia. It had strong active movements: Bund, S.S. [Zionist Socialist], Poalei Zion, as well as Zionist parties: General Zionists headed by Leibush Gutzeit, with Alter the Shochet, Reuven Altman, the Ratner and Lifschitz families, and others. Some succeeded in making *aliya* to the Land and others did not. There was Tzeirei Tzion [Young Zion], including Avraham Yitzchak Shpilkin, who signed his name in short as "Ish," Avrahamele Ratner, Yosef Eliyahu Rubnitz, and Shmuel Noach Landau, whose black eyes sparkled with wisdom, and who had a heartwarming smile on his lips. In addition, there was the lone teachers for Hebrew: Chazanovich, Gutzeit, Katznelson. That groups also included the older youths who studied in the gymnasja, including the dear female members who worked with dedication and at times wit risk to their lives: Fania Karpach, Eshka Leb, Sonia Zimering, Henia Arenbaum, Ruchama Itzkovich, as well as girls of the youngest age, such as Rachele Bergman of blessed memory, who died in her youth at the age of 18 from a cold and pneumonia. She got sick while running in the cold and rain to collect money and provisions needed for our members who were in jail, and from standing for many hours next to the jail to give over the packages in person to our members. How bright were her blue eyes from happiness when she told me every detail of her mission, how she managed to slip notes into the biscuits and bagels, etc…

View of the landscape atop the bridge to Kolonia

* * *

Slutsk – a city of Torah, labor, and commerce, all together. It is situated on the Sluch River that passes through Polesye and reached the Pripyat, passing through forests and bogs for a distance of hundreds of kilometers. Who does not remember its beauty? The nighttime sailing of boats on the river to Kolonia, and from there onward; the laughter, singing, and mischief, spiced with youthful charm, the secret longing for love, the secret kissing, caresses with a soft, delicate hand, and quiet conversation in the moonlight on spring nights.

At a distance not to far from Kapolya, as it continued on, there was a small agricultural farm called "Shulka" that wholly belonged to a Jew, Reb Yisrael Shulker, and was called by the name of the Land of Israel. On Sabbaths, festivals, and during evening hours, we loved to stroll in that area, which was fully traditionally Jewish and was only working on weekdays. Its trees, pathways, wide pastures with flocks of cattle walking peacefully and eating the pleasant soft grass for enjoyment would imbue you with a sort of special pleasant, calm mood that is hard to forget even at this point. There, we also wove our dreams for Zion and Jerusalem, for the fields of Israel in the valley, the Galilee, and on the Jordan, that is a hundredfold more beautiful than the Sluch.

[Page 116]

We loved to stroll in the quiet alleyways, with fruit trees on both sides – cherries, pears, and apples – with their intoxicating aromas in the spring, and whose leaves turn yellow in the pleasant autumn days, suffused with sadness and silence.

From there, the roadways to Kolonia, and Vigoda spread out, with expansive vegetable gardens, almost extending to the nearby village.

There – is the main road in the center, the highway, with two broad sidewalks, which served as a separation, one for the Bund on the right side, and the other for the S.S. and Poalei Zion on the left side. In the center of the street was the café of Solomiak, with his large belly. It was bustling until midnight with people eating ice cream and layer cakes, drinking cold beer – as well as just a general group of "loafers" who were chatting and joking about Slutsk and its *gabbaim*, about "America" street and its harlots, about its crazies, wagon drivers, and porters.

On Sabbath and festival days, the street was bustling with people strolling, men, women with their children, brides with their grooms, people walking arm in arm, cracking seeds, as the brides were glancing in every direction. The group of "barefooters" was also not lacking, who would stick pins into the backs of the single girls, to their great laughter and joy. That group was organized by Benny Manyuk the tailor, who had seven sons, left to themselves in a wanton manner, for the parents did not have enough energy to supervise them. They were called "the ten sons of Haman," which caused no small among of pain to the elderly Manyuk, who was almost half blind at the end of his days.

Vilna Street, also called Charpashker Gasse (meaning Street of Shame[1]) on account of its crosses and icons that were situated not far from the old synagogue with thick walls built of stone and brick, was also well-known. Torah scholars, wise people, and the religious intelligentsia worshipped in that synagogue.

The Street of the Smiths, di Shmideshe Gasse, also had a unique appearance and a characteristic way of life. It was an alleyway that included most of the smiths of the city as well as the various wagon manufacturing workers. From early hours in the morning, while all the city was still resting with their sweet morning sleep, that street was already bustling and noisy. The trotting and neighing of horses, the sounds and echoes of heavy anvils hitting the hot iron, the crackling of the sparks, and the blowing of the bellows could all be heard. All this created a unique, encouraging harmony, the song of work, instilling hope into the person, into the Jewish energy. There, you would meat the Jewish worker, earning his living from his toil, the broad-boned, muscular Jewish worker. These were pure, simple, people, who often stood on guard to protect the honor of the city and Jewish honor from hooligans.

We remember the days, every year, during the months of the drafting of new recruits in October and November. This when the youths of the nearby villages who were designated to join the army would gather in the city. They would wander through the streets of the city and the market, and pilfer merchandise from the stalls of the grocery stores and confectionaries without paying. They would also attack old, weak people on the side alleyways.

Then the lads would come: the smiths, the wagon drivers, the tanners, and the carpenters, the group of beaters [*klapers*], and would take revenge upon these villagers, show them the force of their arms, and teach them a bit of respect and fear of the Jews, so that they would know and remember.

The following are words about interesting, characteristic personalities in our city of Slutsk:

Reb Leibush Gutzeit

He was a communal activist and an enthusiastic Zionist, who loved the Hebrew language.

With his wide heart and generous hand, with the Jewish pain in his dark eyes, that serious Jew, openly and secretly assisted the individual and the public without seeking honor, without any haughtiness. His large quantity of property was confiscated by the Bolshevik government, and he remained only as a director of his large Chipley estate and director of the alcohol distillery and large sawmill, in which only Jews worked, numbering a hundred or more. He greatly helped out friends who were imprisoned in the jail for the crime of Zionism and teaching Hebrew. He generously supported the community, which had become impoverished during the time that the switch from the Polish to Bolshevik regime.

Reb Leibush Gutzeit

I will never forget the moments that I took leave of him as I left Slutsk. When I told him the "secret" of my *aliya* to the Land, the man wept from a combination of great joy and pain. "If only I could" – he spoke quietly and with emotion – " If only I could escape and wander, even as an indigent, and go to the Land, I would be happy. For what has been perpetrated against me, and what is left for me from all my great fortune… You are fortunate that you have merited this. Go up and succeed, and do not forget me."

His words were spoken in Hebrew, with strength and a stormy soul. They shook up the strands of my heart, and I took leave of him with agony and great pain. When his property, the flourmill and large sawmill, were confiscated, the workers granted him a good turn, and due to them, he remained as the director of work. They left him a horse and buggy for his needs, as a memory that the world is a revolving wheel…

[Page 117]

Reb Chaim Yehoshua Friedman

He was a scholar, and knew Russian, German, and Polish. He was expert in the Talmud and Zohar. Every day after the Maariv service, he would read lesson of Talmud with great proficiency and astounding simplicity. His proficiency in world literature was very great. He would frequent the house of rabbi Abramsky when he was in Slutsk. He was the mouthpiece of the community before the authorities. The elderly man merited that at least one member of the entire family, his grandson Shmuel Friedman, made *aliya* and lives in Tel Aviv.

[2]Itze Nota's the Melamed was known as an expert scholar. For the most part, he could be found in the home of Rabbi Isser Zalman. He concerned himself with the needs of the studiers. He took care of the Yeshiva students with love, and arranged for them to partake of their Sabbath meals in the homes of various householders. Itze Nota's brother was Rabbi Yosha Tritzaner, the head of the Yeshiva in the Kloiz.

Itze Nota's wife Tila Grozowski was considered to be a righteous woman. She would collect money and supported anyone in need. During the time of the Soviet regime, she would bake bread secretly, with danger to herself, and transfer the bread to the Yeshiva students.

She continued her blessed work even after she arrived in the Land. She collected money and supported anyone in need of assistance. She was the gabbai of Heichal Hatalmud and the Or Zoreach Yeshiva. She also founded Gemilut Chesed in Tel Aviv.

Michael Wilenchok

He was a flour businessman. He was expert and sharp. He loved to ask many questions and delve into didactics with his learning. He was an upright man, and a zealous Zionist. When I was already in the Land, he wrote me a letter, asking me to send a certificate [for *aliya*] to his daughter. To my great sorrow, however, I was unable to do so.

Yosef Rekiner

He was Shpilkin's son-in-law. He was a modest, upright man. He was a scholar, a Zionist, and he knew Hebrew.

Yeshyahu Mendel Derechin

He was a haberdasher. He was a Yeshiva student during his youth. He was diligent. He partook of his meals in rotation [yamim] and suffered, until Feigele came along, with the warts on her face. She was a businesswoman, the daughter of a family of merchants, and she turned him into a man. Derechin's name went before him, for he was trustworthy, upright, open hearted, and generous. He set aside times for the study of Torah, and he occupied himself with charity. He discreetly collected money for the poor and for scholars who suffered from lack. On Mondays and Thursdays, he would distribute food to poor Yeshiva students and to all who were hungry: bread, cheese, salted fish, and hot tea in the morning; potatoes fried in duck fat without meat, and lentil soup in the afternoon; and five kopecks for a meal in the evening. He did this as a remembrance of the verse: I recall the days of my poverty and suffering. Later, he moved to Baranovich and became a large-scale merchant. There too, he organized assistance activities: Gemilut Chesed, Small Credit. He helped Jews in their time of need. He was a sublime Jewish character.

All this was during the times of his wealth and greatness, until the Bolsheviks came and afflicted his life.

Leibe Yoich

The elderly smith Leibe was a unique character. He was known as Leibe Yoich – i.e. Soup. He was given this name because on every Sabbath eve, he tied a leather sack on his back, carried a large pot in his hands, and made the rounds to the doors of the wealthy people to request "*challa mit yoich*" (bread and soup) for poor women who had just given birth, or for regular poor people who were unable to "make the Sabbath" in the manner of the householders.

He was a strong Jew despite his great old age. He was broad boned, with warm, good, penetrating eyes. His face was adorned with a thick, straggly beard, which was, apparently, never combed. His peyos were curly. He wore a black, oiled kapote that went down to his heavy boots, polished with tar, exuding an aroma in honor of the Sabbath.

His sons lived together with him with their families, and worked together. They honored the old man, and waited for him on Sabbath eves until he had finished his rounds, and sat down to recite *kiddush* on a cup of wine. The elderly Leibe loved the drink, the cholent, the kugel, and the Sabbath hymns. He would enjoy spiritual contentment on the Sabbath, which quietly descended upon him on the street of the smiths, from the eve of the Sabbath until Sunday morning, when the street once again woke up to regular weekday work.

Dovidl "Kvartalner"

Among those who cared for the needs of the poor was Dovidl, a unique character. He was a beggar the son of a beggar for generations. His mouth was crooked on the right side. Four teeth protruded upon his thick lower lip. He was half blind in one eye, and the other one squinted sometimes to the right and sometimes to the left. His nose was closed and red. His mucus dripped both in the summer and the winter, and he would wipe it with his sleeve or the corner of his wormy kapote.

He had a red cane, which he used at night. During the day, the man would run. He would run as if someone were chasing him. He held a red handkerchief in his left hand, spread out to the sides, "A donation, a donation, dear Jews, a donation."

Poverty and lack pervaded in his home. There was a great deal of mildew and rot with him, but all this did not stop him from being concerned about others. He was especially concerned about the Yeshiva students, who partook of their meals in daily rotation. Everywhere he went, he would receive [a commitment for] a set day of food for lads suffering from want.

Among the righteous women, it is worthwhile to mention Rachel, the wife of Yankel Poliak. Two sisters sold milk, Esther and Malka, as well as many others. The charitable organizations were Bikur Cholim [tending to the ill], Hachnasat Kallah [tending to poor brides], Lechem Aniyim [providing food for the poor], Kimcha Depischa [providing Passover supplies], and others. Tens of men and women gathered around them, not concerned about their time, doing good for the public. Rebbetzin Margolin, who concerned herself with Jewish prisoners in the city, continued to concern herself with Jewish prisoners here in Tel Aviv as well as in Jaffa.

The police already know her, and always permit her to freely enter the prison yard and give over the kosher food and money that she collected for the prisoners.

[Page 118]

Leizer the *Shamash*

He was a short Jew, with a thin face and inquisitive eyes. He served as the *Shamash* of the large *Beis Midrash* for decades. He was careful with his words and mannerisms. Everything happened in accordance with his word.

He was the *Gabbai* of the Linat Tzedek organization. When he would borrow utensils for the indigent ill, such as bloodletting vessels, icepacks, etc., they told him, "Reb Leizer, you are indeed the Leizer – the redeemer of all tribulations."[3] He was goodhearted, and when his cheerful daughter Chaya Reizel became involved in Zionism, he said, "You will bring full healing and redemption to the People of Israel, and me – to the individual. The public is composed only of the individuals."

The Soviet regime that became entrenched in the city mercilessly oppressed the Jewish population, and imposed harsh decrees and heavy taxes. The Kalte Shul [Cold Synagogue] was confiscated and turned into a grain warehouse. The holy utensils from the synagogues, the crowns, the silver letters atop the curtain, the silver reading pointers, and the copper basins were confiscated. Foreclosure was imposed upon the treasury of the Chevra Kadisha, and they demanded money from the funds raised from synagogue honors [*aliyot*]. *Melamdim* [religious teachers] were banned, and the property of the Hebrew schools was confiscated. Only a few Hebrew teachers remained, who taught Hebrew clandestinely and privately to Jewish children. The teacher Chazanovich was forcefully drafted, and was forced to teach in Yiddish.

I was removed from the ranks of the Red Army and sent to the Pedagogical Teknicum in Minsk, where I studied for a full year and then returned to Slutsk. I worked as the supervisor of the Yevsektsia and principal of the trade school for carpentry and sewing. They also gave over to me the large civic library, which was supervised by Efron Meisel. Thanks to the trust they placed in me, I took advantage of the opportunity to the extent possible to remove Zionist literature in Russian, Yiddish, and Hebrew from the library and distribute it to our members, friends, and acquaintances. The books that I did not succeed in removing remained hidden away in the archives. It was only possible to obtain Hebrew books with a special permit. The supervision was strict, but nevertheless, I knew how to make arrangements with Efron, for he knew Hebrew and appreciated its literature. He still had a Jewish spark within him, even though he was a former member of the Bund, and then transferred to the Yevsektsia.

Necha (Nechtzka) Shapira was the main superintendent of the schools. We suffered many tribulations from her. She was a hardened, strict woman. The teachers wept secretly over their bitter fate. She related well to me, for I would visit her father's house, and also had served as a soldier in the Red Army for two years.

In 1925, I requested that they release me from all my tasks, and I made *aliya* to the Land. My personal documents remained with the G. P. U.[4] because they thought that I would still return to Russia. They confiscated many of my books on the pretext that they are superfluous, and I would have no need for them in Palestine.

Despite the oppression and spying, clandestine Zionist activity took place specifically among the youth. They arranged meetings during the day and night, in the fields and in the cemeteries, where they divided themselves into small groups of five or six individuals. The spying also did not pass over me, but thanks to my strong personal connections between me and one of my students, Avrahamele Hertzman, I was saved and did not fall into the hands of the authorities.

There were several other Communists who did favorable things for their friends and acquaintances. They were Communists externally, while secretly adhering to Judaism its traditions.

One of these was the red haired Vofka, the son of Malka the milk woman. When his eldest son was born, he came to me to ask for advice as to how to arrange a circumcision. I arranged the circumcision in my house, at night, behind closed shutters and windows covered with curtains, in the present of several trustworthy individuals. Malka beamed with great happiness and wept tears of joy as she prayed silently for the welfare of the baby who had been entered into the covenant of Judaism.

This Malka was goodhearted in an unparalleled fashion. With her last coin, she helped everyone in trouble or with a bitter soul.

Slutsk merited to give its portion to the Second, Third, and Fourth Aliya. Many Slutsk natives can be found in Tel Aviv, Haifa, Jerusalem, Petach Tikva, and various kibbutzim. Among them are teachers and writers who are well-known within the community.

We also had a great share among the victims who fell in the founding of the State. There is no comfort other than building our young, dear country, and in our great hope for a brighter future of a life of happiness and peace.

Translator's footnotes:

1. *Cherpa* means shame.
2. It seems that a heading for **Itze Nota's the Melamed and his wife Tila** is missing here.
3. A play on words. In Yiddish, the term can be construed to mean "the reliever."
4. See https://en.wikipedia.org/wiki/State_Political_Directorate

The Clandestine Hebrew Teacher

by Tzvi Chazanovich

In memory of my revered father

Translated by Jerrold Landau

The Hebrew School, the "Modern *Cheder*" had great value in the realm of Hebrew and Zionist education. It had a good, dedicated teaching staff. Some were writers, or at least people who knew how to write. They invested great energy in imparting to their students a love of the Hebrew language, a connection to Zionism, and a longing for the Hebrew homeland. Their efforts bore fruit to a large degree: Many of their students tied their lot to Zionism, the Land of Israel, the pioneering movement, and clandestine work. Some were imprisoned, deported to desolate places, or even expelled from the country. Many rebelled and rejected the doctrine that they had studied. Nevertheless, the fire still smouldered in a few of them, who maintained their faith with the Hebrew language, albeit in secret. However, the flame was completely extinguished in many of them. They turned their backs upon what they learned, regarding it as nationalism, reactionism, and opposition to the essence of the great Russian Revolution, acting as a brake to its wheel. Therefore, they felt it their duty to fight against it and extinguish it.

The fate of the Hebrew teachers was bad and bitter. With the strengthening of the Soviet government and the rise of the Jewish Yevsektsia that persecuted with anger any Zionist and Hebrew manifestation within the Jewish population, the Hebrew schools were closed, and teaching of Hebrew was prohibited. The source of livelihood of the teachers was broken. However, there were still some teachers who endangered themselves and clandestinely taught Hebrew. Such teaching was fraught with great danger and deep difficulties.

[Page 119]

* * *

And now, the image of my revered father, Mordechai Chazanovich, floats before the eyes of my spirit. He was the principal of the modern *cheder* for many years, and he taught students of the Russian high schools on a private basis. He was strongly tied to Hebrew culture and literature, and he educated his children and his children's friends to Zionism and love of the language.

I recall the gatherings of Hebrew teachers in our house next to the steaming urn, as they discussed various topics. I also recall Father's visits to the teachers Avraham Epstein, Zeev Gutzeit, Berger, Katznelson, and Nachamovich (Nachmani).

The atmosphere was warm and homey. In the latter period, it was suffused with silent sadness, with hints and foreboding of the approaching disaster[1] that was about to take place over the heads of the Hebrew teachers.

Indeed, that which the teachers suspected did come:

A ban was imposed on the Hebrew language, and arrests began. A Yiddish school was founded in place of the Hebrew school. My father was enlisted against his will to that school due to a shortage of experienced teachers.

He was forced to teach Yiddish according to the new Yiddish orthography, with his heart dripping blood as he saw the purpose of his life – teaching Hebrew – liquidated.

This weakened him. He expressed this in his letter to me in the Land.

* * *

In 1924, I was imprisoned for the third time, and deported to the Land. There was a constant mail correspondence between Father and me until his death at the beginning of 1948. His stormy spirit was recognizable in sections of his letters. He expressed his longing for the Land, for Hebrew, and for a life of freedom. The political viewpoint that he had to express in order for his letters to pass through the censor also stood out.

He was precise, made points, asked about new words, fixed expressions, pointed out my mistakes, and also tried to sneak in conspiratory facts in concealed language regarding the fate of my friends who were arrested and deported to far-off Siberia.

In his first letters, he writes:

"It has been many years since I have seen a Hebrew newspaper, a new Hebrew book. A Hebrew word has not been written to me, nor have I written to others Now, for the first time in a long time, I am writing in Hebrew: To who? Not to a friend, not to an acquaintance, but to you, my dear son! Can I describe my joy, my emotions to you?

"I drink with thirst any information, any news from the Land. Everything interests me, enthuses me, and involves me. Everything is new, for in truth, I do not know what is happening in the Land. I do not know was a *kvutza*, a *kibbutz*, a *moshav*, or a *moshava* are? What is a *pluga*? I do not know the many factions in the Land or their plans? I wish to know the population of Tel Aviv and of the entire Land? How many new immigrants are there every week, what is the harvest of the fields, do they grow fine wheat? How many dunams of Land do the Jews possess in the Land? What is with the new Hebrew literature and the authors? How is Bialik, and does he continue to write?

"And how can I know all this, if I have been cut off from everything for so long? Here, there are no factions, there is no Purim, there is no Passover, religion is dying. In general, you yourself know the situation here. From the time you left, the order of things has not changed."

He began to dissect my expressions in several letters, and make notes:

"Regarding punctuation, punctuation was not given from Sinai. It was created, if I am not mistaken, during the Geonic period, in a later time, and therefore it is not holy for us. It is open to correction, and it is permitted to tamper with it. How much more so are we required to make efforts to ease the reading and study for young children.

"However, the researchers, linguists, writers, and teachers will decide on this question. They will seek ways to improve the language. Efforts should be made that the changes should be appropriate to the principles of punctuation and morphology. Who am I to be so brazen as to place my head into the thick beam?

"Regarding the recommendation of Itamar the son of Ab'y to transfer to the Latin script, this recommendation seems strange in my eyes. Do we not have a unique alphabet? It is an imitation. It is liable to lead to a loss, and I do not know who can justify such a recommendation?"

In one of his letters, he writes:

"There are multiple benefits in my Hebrew writing. My soul that has become naked finds its rectification. My style is renewed, sharpened, and strengthened. Many expressions, formulations, adages, and verses that were forgotten and have been removed from my essence have come to haunt me: How can you not be embarrassed, o son of man, how many years have you tended to us, and now, you have turned your thoughts away from us. I clearly see that from the time I began to write in Hebrew, I have recalled its ways. Indeed, there are many words that I find difficult, especially the new words in your letters, but I am happy that I can still remember that which I have forgotten.

* * *

N. N. left the Land and returned to Slutsk in 1928. He brought with him bad reports about the Land. Father walked around confused. He wrote me: "N. described the situation to me in black colors, to the point that my hair on my head stood on edge: 'In the Land they are dying of hunger. There are no possibilities that the situation will change. The labor is backbreaking. People only earn a bit of bread and a meager amount of water. The Slutsk natives in the *kibbutz* do not eat to satiety. They look like skeletons.'"

These words had great effect on those whose children were in the Land. Many did not believe his words. Baskin (Shabtai's father) said he would be satisfied if he were able to obtain a visa for his son. Father asked that I write him the truth to refute the false words.

* * *

After the first group of Slutskers made aliya to the Land, many of the members of our movement remained in Slutsk. Some were imprisoned. Father responded in an elusive manner to my question about their wellbeing and their deeds. When he wrote about the wellbeing of my relatives, he would also include the friends, as follows:

"The situation of the rest of the relatives, such as Moshe, Feivel, and Eidelman of Minsk[2] is very bad. This is an unfortunate family. It seems to me that it numbers about 15-17 people. They do not work, they do not study, they are sick."

And in another letter:

"For Shraga[2], they purchased a fur already before the Passover holiday,

[Page 120]

fine and long, so that even in the 40 degree cold, I am sure that if he wears it, he will not feel the cold. Regarding the wellbeing of Uncle N.[3]: that which he earned from shechita, he earned into a bundle with holes. I was told that there is discord and conflict, hatred, and grudges among the family members. One like to eat such and such a food, and N. likes to eat Kurtza[4]. Therefore, many family members battle with him, curse and blaspheme. There is confusion, perplexity, and discord in everything.

"I am happy that you are not in prison, that you are living a life of calm and peace in the Land."

* * *

Father wrote often about political matters. He was forced to praise the regime of Stalin. However, it was possible to read entirely different things between the lines.

This is what he wrote in 1946:

"Apparently, I am close to 70 years old. I have already become old. Many of my 248 limbs[5] have been afflicted. I am now reading 'The History of the World' – ancient and modern history. I am making connections, forging links, coming to conclusions, and making logical comparisons, a fortioris. In no way can I understand how the Jewish problem can be solved in the Land of Israel. It can only be done through the doctrine of Marxism or international politics. It is easy to solve the problem in accordance with the doctrine of Lenin and Stalin. However, until the ideal is clarified, 'and the wolf shall lie with the lamb'[6], it is possible that the wolves and the leopards may maul the lambs."

* * *

In 1947, he writes from Leningrad:

"I went to the synagogue on the last day of Passover. I saw many Slutskers there. I stood the whole time at the threshold of the *Beis Midrash*, and cold not move from the place, for the house of worship was full to the brim. I found an old Gemara, and peered into it. I reviewed a certain Talmudic section, and it interested me more than the service. I cold not read *Ki leolam Chasdo* [for His mercy endures forever][7] at the time when Hitler and his friends have murdered approximately six million Jews, the elderly, women lads, and children. Let people read the prayers and pour their words out to the Omnipresent, but I do not believe that 'prayer alone' can avert the evil decree."

* * *

Father did not merit to be alive when the Hebrew state – the desire of his life – was founded. He died a few months prior. I still succeeded in writing to him about the vote at the United Nations, the decision regarding the establishment of the State, and I described to hi the joy of the Jewish community and its successes.

My teachers at the modern *cheder* and the Hebrew teachers in general did not succeed in reaching the Land, other than a few who left Russia before and after the First World War. They did not merit to be present for the wonder – the creation of a Hebrew state. However, their toil was not for naught. Many of their students set up deep roots in the Land. They we always recall with gratitude their alma-mater, the modern *cheder*.

Translator's footnotes:

1. The word used here is *Shoah*, but it is not referring to the Holocaust, but the upcoming disaster for Hebrew culture.
2. There are two footnotes in the text here: * These are my friends that were arrested after I was deported to the Land. ** This refers to Feivel Efron, who was deported to the district of Neris.
3. There is a footnote in the text here: A friend of ours who became a provocateur.
4. In Talmudic language, "eating *kurtza*" refers to starting disputes.
5. According to rabbinic tradition (Mishna *Oholot* 1), there are 248 limbs in the human body.

6. Isaiah 11:6.
7. The refrain of Psalm 136.

Personalities

Translated by Jerrold Landau

Avraham Yitzchak Shpilkin

From right: Dr. Yaakov Tzvi Lifschitz, Avraham Yitzchak Shpilkin, Nachum Chinitz

He started off as a *Sofer Stam* [A scribe of Torah scrolls, *tefillin*, and *mezuzot*]. For the most part, his friends would find it at his worktable, bent over parchment folios of a Torah scroll. The aspiration of his soul was Zionist and cultural work. His personality and external appearance aroused attention. He was modest and unassuming, but sharp with his speech. He published sharp feuilletons and poetry on issues of the day in bulletins that appeared in print. He used the signature I'sh. Indeed, he was a fundamental man, an autodidact who developed and obtain communal stature in time.

His father Reb Ben-Zion was a *Sofer Stam*, an upright man. His mother Esther Malka, the daughter of the renowned Tzadik Reb Rafael-Yosel, inspired him from the womb.

Their house was a gathering place for Zionists, and clandestine Zionist activity. The man suddenly stopped his work as a *Sofer Stam* and began teaching Hebrew in Tymkovich and later in Slutsk. He was active and vibrant in the Tzeirei Tzion movement.

The Soviet authorities remembered the sins of his youth: Zionism and Hebrew teaching. He was imprisoned for a certain period. He was a craftsman from his youth. When he was freed, he worked as a shoemaker, having no other options. His heart always pined for Zion. In his letters to his friends in the Diaspora and the land, he shook up the hearts of the readers with his sublime longings.

As the Nazis approached Slutsk, he wandered off to Soviet Armenia. His wife Keila the daughter of Reb Yosef Jaronson was killed along the way, and he died in the Diaspora. May his memory be a blessing!

Reuven Altman

He was educated in the Yeshiva of Slutsk. He was a Zionist activist, faithful to the Hebrew language and its literature. Hebrew was the spoken language in his house. He opened the second modern *cheder* in Slutsk together with the teacher Katznelson. It existed until the outbreak of the Soviet revolution.

His letter from 1932 that he sent to his brother Eliyahu Altman in America testifies to his experiences during the time of the Soviet regime. During the Holocaust, his fate was the same as that of all the Jews of Slutsk, who perished at the hands of the Nazis.

May his memory be a blessing.

[Page 121]

Next to the grave of their father. Reuvke Altman is in the center.
Minka and Eliyahu (Zeidel) are on the sides.

The gravestone reads:
Here is buried a dear, honorable man Yehuda Leib the son of
Reuven Altman. Died on Sunday 12 Shevat 5676 [1916]. May his
soul be bound in the bonds of eternal life.

May 3, 1932

My dear Eliyahu!

I received your last letter, and I thank you for it. In general, the day I receive your letter is a holiday for me. It arouses in me forgotten memories, memories of my childhood and youth. I am now writing you a letter as if life is passing before all the times that we spent together in the home of or parents, and all the events. Here it is your birthday. Do you know where you were born? In some ruin. This was after the fire. Our house was burnt. We found a ruin in which people had not lived for years because of the danger. You were born there. We made some sort of canopy in the yard, and your circumcision took place there.

Another image passes before me: I am in the "Storeve" as a teacher of Jewish students. I go outside and from the distance, I see some young lad in yellow clothing. I was surprised. It seemed that these were the clothes of my young brother, but how did he get here? I drew close, and indeed it was true. He had come to some wedding with the musicians.

Now they are taking me to army service, to fight against the Germans. I was in the middle with other prisoners, and we were surrounded by soldiers. I looked back, and our late father was accompanying me with tears in his eyes. I fought, I returned, but I did not find him. I did not merit to be present at his death.

In general, the image of our late father is etched very deeply in my heart. He was of the character of Bonche Shveig[1], or those who are miserable but not miserable. I too have many of the traits of our father. I, along with you and Minka, are standing next to the gravestone of our father, photographing ourselves. The photo came out fine. I still have it, and whenever I wish to forget about the present a bit and turn to the past, I take out the photo and pass it before me.

All the days of my life have passed like a dream. Now I am looking at the picture of my children and seeing how big and lovely they are. My Yitzchak is already 22 years old, and Yeshayahu is almost twenty. It was just yesterday that they were small children, and I carried them in my arms. In previous days, I walked to the synagogue with them and talked to them in Hebrew. I wanted Hebrew to be their spoken language. Now, they are men with different concepts, men who have taken upon themselves the goal of destroying the old and building a new world. They are building a new life, and I see how small I was with the idea that I bore in my heart of building a home for the Jewish nation. My children desire to build a full world, a new world, and a new life!

I sent you a photo of my children. Why have you not written me that you have received it, and what it was like before your eyes? We now have sadness in the soul. It has already been two years since my Yitzchak has not been at home. We waited impatiently for him to come this summer. Now they have sent him to work in the city of Khabarovsk. Look on a map and see how far away it is[2]. A letter from there takes about three weeks to arrive. I already considered Leningrad as his second home, and then they came and destroyed my nest. Thus, our family members are scattered in all directions, to the four corners of the land, and I have already become old. I already have white hair on my head. I am a man without energy or initiative, and I still have to toil with physical labor to earn a loaf of bread.

You wrote in your letter that I am angry at you. I do not know why you suspect this? Is it because I do not write that much. If so, that is because I do not always have time. You remain the only one with whom I can speak what is in my heart. For all my acquaintances have scattered in all directions. Different people with different ideas are around me, and I cannot mix with them. When I am in their company, I am like a mourner among bridegrooms. I wanted to write to you about your acquaintances, but there are barely any. Only Shpilkin remains. He is a shoemaker, and works in the Artel. The sins of his youth, as well as mine, cannot be mentioned or verbalized. The destruction and ruin in our spiritual lives is much greater than in our economic lives. Not even one child can be found who knows how to read Hebrew, or who can understand even one word of Hebrew. Only the Kloiz and the Karnaim remain of all the synagogues and *Beis Midrashes*. So, it is enough for now. Be well, and see good things.

Your brother who wishes you well,

Reuven

Henia and Liba inquire about your wellbeing, and the wellbeing of your wife Sara. You have asked about our sister. Do not worry about this. Her situation is strong. He[3] is no longer a worker. He is the director of a large cooperative store, and she has everything.

The aforementioned.

[Page 122]

Moshe Yericho

My father was an upright, goodhearted man. The residents of Slutsk loved him and called him lovingly – Mosheke the Feldscher.

He was a medic by trade. He was dedicated and faithful, dedicating all his energy and strength into his patients. He cared for them with love, comforted them in their illnesses, and eased their pains with a pleasant countenance. He did not differentiate between the rich and the poor. He did not consider their status, as he concerned himself with them.

He was the assistant of Dr. Schildkraut. They were cousins, and they enjoyed good relations. They worked together for 25 years.

Reb Moshe Yericho (der Feldscher) and his wife Gittel

They both got married in the same year, and they also both died in the same year. Schildkraut died three days before Passover, and father died three days after Shavuot. Indeed, they were not separated during their lives and their deaths.

Reb Yosef of Tshernichov of blessed memory

Reb Yosef Tshernichov of blessed memory was the son of Reb Yehuda Leib and Rivka, the daughter of the praiseworthy rabbi of renown, Rabbi Yossele Peimer the first.

He was born in Slutsk in 1868 and perished in the Minsk ghetto. He studied in *cheder*s, and continued to study Torah throughout his life.

He was a well-known grain merchant. He was close to the common person and easy to get along with. He distributed charity generously. He had an adage: "If a person knows how much he distributes, his deeds are not for the sake of Heaven." Before Passover, he would amass full warehouses of flour for Passover [matzo] and potatoes, which he would distribute to anyone in need.

He would sit in the synagogue on Kapolya Street every day until noon and study Torah. The landowners of the area already figured out where he was sitting, and would come to the synagogue courtyard with wagon hitched to four horses to clarify and conclude various business matters with him.

He had a business sense, and a special understanding of the grain business.

He would export grain to Germany for large sums of money until the First World War. He exchanged letters in Hebrew with the well-known agents (commissioners) in Koenigsberg, Ephraim Rosenberg and Lifschitz.

He lived frugally[4] and spent time in the tents of Torah in suffering and difficulty. When his son complained: why does he suffer and not benefit from life? Is it possible to sit secretly and suffice oneself with secret gifts? His response was brief: "G-d commanded those who fear Him to make their soul like dust." "Behold I have dared to speak to G-d, and I am but dust and ashes."[5]

Indeed, he made his soul like dust. He endured various tribulations. He was imprisoned in 1931. He moved to Minsk in 1932. His property was confiscated. He wandered to foreign places, and was deported to far-off Kazakhstan. When he returned to Minsk, the hand of the Nazis came upon him and his family, who went up on the pyre along with the martyrs of Minsk. "Make my soul like dust" was fulfilled with him.

"And I am but dust and ashes."

May his memory be blessed!

"Der Salanter"

That is what the second rabbinical judge in Slutsk was called. He worshipped in the Karnaim Synagogue. He was of average height, and a shiny black beard adorned his face. His pure eyes expressed uprightness and wholesomeness. He did not speak much, was taciturn by nature. He nodded his head and uttered some sort of a silent prayer with every tribulation. When there was good news, his eyes brightened and his entire being expressed joy and gladness, as his lips uttered: everything is in the hands of the Dweller On High, Who is capable of everything!

May his memory be blessed!

Shimshon Nachmani (Nachaminovich)

He was born in 1885 in Horozava. He studied in *cheder*s and the Yeshiva of Slutsk. He was a student of Gershuni of Minsk. He was one of the founders of the modern *cheder* in Slutsk fifty years ago, one of its first teacher, and the instiller of the Zionist spirit.

He was injured and beaten over the head by a Bundist ruffian while he was selling Zionist stamps in the Slutsk cemetery on Tisha B'Av.

He moved from Slutsk to Lyubar, where he taught in the Hebrew school together with his friend Kagan.

After a few years, he made *aliya* to the Land. He taught in Poria in Tiberias and Safed. After that, he transferred to the Neve Tzedek school in Tel Aviv.

He merited to be one of the layers of the foundation of a Hebrew school in the Diaspora – one of those who revived the language in the Diaspora and the Land – the educator of an entire generation.

After he left Slutsk, he taught Hebrew in the *Mafitzei Haskalah* school in Rozhichov and Kyiv. He translated twenty books from Russian: *Haseara* by Ilya Erenburg, (workers Library), "Far from Moscow" (*Am Oved*), and others. The book *Πιιιμγας Πμκιια* was not translated, but only translated by Sh. Nachmani as is noted in the inner cover.

He participated in *Kuntrus* and *Davar*.

He was the chairman of the organization of natives of Slutsk and its environs.

[Page 123]

Eliyahu Yarkoni (Greenfeld)

He was born in Slutsk on 24 Elul 5646 (1886).

He studied in *cheder*s and the Yeshiva of Slutsk. He moved on to *Haskalah*. He was examined in the government gymnasja and was certified as a public-school teacher. He taught in the modern *cheder* of Slutsk for about a year. He made *aliya* to the Land in 5672 [1912], and was accepted to the teaching staff of the Neve Tzedek girls' school. He also taught evening courses in Hebrew.

He had the good fortune of coming across the mother of settlements, the oldest school in the land, which is the Pik'a[6] school.

Eliyahu Yarkoni (on the right) and Sh. Nachmani

The First World War broke out before he was able to strike roots in the Land. Many at that time "went down to Egypt" and did not return to the Land. Mr. Yarkoni remained. He suffered hunger, wandering, and deportations during the final years of the Ottoman government. With the liberation of the southern portion of the Land by the English and the establishment of Hebrew brigades, Mr. Yarkoni changed from a man of the book to a man of the sword. He left behind the staff of the teacher of young children and took up the gun in order to actively participate in the liberation of the Land from the Turkish oppressors.

He stood on guard of that elementary school for more than 45 years with boundless faithfulness and dedication, with the exactitude that was typical of him, and with the diligence that few in the modern times can even conceive of.

It was clear to him that he must also teach nature and agriculture along with all the other subjects that he taught, so that he could bring the students close to the soil and landscape of the native Land. He was one of those who laid the foundations for the education of the generation.

The disturbances in Petach Tikva during the 1920s shook him up to the depths of his soul. From that time, he took the duty of broad defense of his Moshav upon his shoulders. His days were dedicated to Torah and education, and his nights – to communal affairs and local defense.

Mr. Yarkoni educated generations of students who are spread out today in all areas of the Land. They include teachers, guiders of the youth, government officials, and those who conquered the homeland. Many of his students, including senior army captains, participated in his retirement party that was hosted for him by the veterans of the defense in Petach Tikva,

Yarkoni merited to be one of the founders of the modern *cheder* in Slutsk, and to stand by the cradle of Hebrew education in the Land. He was among the builders and forgers of the image of the elementary school.

Not only this, but with his many tasks, he was the director of the teachers' division in Petach Tikva, and he was active for the Keren Kayemet [Jewish National Fund]. He visited the school daily and took interest in everything that happened there.

Congratulations to him!

Dr. Shraga-Feivel Meltzer

He was a teacher in the Mizrachi teachers' seminary, a school principal, and a member of the leadership of the community council in Jerusalem. He was born on 25 Adar 5657 [1887] in Kovno. He was the son of the Gaon Rabbi Isser Zalman Meltzer. He moved with his family to Slutsk. He was educated in the Yeshivot of Slutsk and Slobodka, the University of Berlin, and the Mizrachi teachers seminary in Jerusalem. He was a communal activist, and a member of Young Zion in Poland.

He was in the Land from 1921. He was a Mizrachi activist in the Land, and active in various communal committee. He served as the emissary of the Keren Hayesod to Eastern Europe in 1935. He lectured in the Rabbi Yitzchak Elchanan Yeshiva[7] in New York. He was granted the degree of Doctor of Literature at the university of the Yeshiva of Rabbi Yitzchak Elchanan [i.e. Yeshiva University]. He currently lives in Jerusalem, and lectures at Bar Ilan University.

Rabbi Dr. Moshe Chiger

He was born in Slutsk, and was the grandson of Reb Shachna.

He studied in the Yeshiva of Slutsk and then in Kletzk and the Yeshivas of Mir and Slobodka.

When he arrived in the Land, he studied a page of Gemara daily privately with the Gaon Rabbi Isser Zalman Meltzer.

He was in Africa[8] for several years as a teacher, and was granted the degree of Doctor.

He lives in Jerusalem and serves as a (Torah oriented) lawyer.

Translator's footnotes:

1. Bonche the Silent – a character in one of I. L. Peretz' short stories. See https://teachgreatjewishbooks.org/resource-kits/i-l-peretzs-bontshe-the-silent
2. A city near the Chinese border, not far from Birobidzhan.
3. This must be referring to her husband.
4. Literally, as a Nazirite.
5. The second quote is from Genesis 18:27.
6. Palestine Jewish Colonization School.
7. The rabbinical school of Yeshiva University.
8. I assume this refers to South Africa.

[Page 124]

Hassidim in Slutsk

Translated by Jerrold Landau

The Baal Shem Tov in Slutsk in the year 5500 (1739)

Rabbi Uri Natan Nota was one of the *Gaonim* of Brisk. In his youth, he was called the *Illui* [Genius] of Krinik [Krynki]. One of the wealthy men of Slutsk took him as a son-in-law and gave him all his needs throughout many years, while he devoted himself to Torah for its own sake. When his wife died, his father-in-law married him of to his second daughter. He became a widower once again. One of the *Gaonim* of Slutsk who knew him married him off to his widowed daughter, and he settled in Slutsk. His first father-in-law had no children other than his two daughters who had died. With his love to his prodigious son-in-law Rabbi Uri Natan Nota, he gave him a field and a vineyard that he had leased, from which he was able to earn his livelihood in an ample fashion.

When the *Gaon* Rabbi Uri Natan Nota of Brisk moved to Slutsk, his first father-in-law did not agree that he sell his field and vineyard. G-d granted him success as a leaser, and he maintained the field and vineyard for many years with a good income from the lease.

His son Rabbi Shlomo was educated in the home of his father the *Gaon*. At the age of fourteen, he moved to a place of Torah, from there to Horodno, and from there to Krakow. There, he met one of the *Gaonim*, Rabbi Menachem Aryeh, one of the group of hidden *Tzadikim*. He cleaved to him, and studied the doctrine of Hassidism from him under the condition that nobody should know about this. Rabbi Shlomo returned to his home in Slutsk at the age of twenty-two. His father the *Gaon* derived joy from his Torah and concerned himself with a match for him. He was matched with [the daughter of] one of the owners of the settlement adjacent to Slutsk. About a half a year after his marriage, his wife lost her sanity, and he became an *agun*[1] for about six years. At that time, in the year 5500 [1740], the Besh't [Baal Shem Tov] came to the city of Slutsk. All the *Gaonim* of Slutsk and the region greeted the holy countenance of the Besh't with holy awe and great honor, among them the mighty one of the elderly *Gaonim*, Rabbi Uri Natan Nota. He complained to the Besh't about the lot of his son who has been in a state of *agun* for approximately six years. The father of the woman who lost her sanity also came to ask for advice and a remedy for her daughter, the wife of Rabbi Shlomo.

The Besh't invited the in-laws, the *Gaon* Rabbi Uri Nota, the tax collector Reb Eliyahu Moshe and Rabbi Shlomo, and asked them if they have any grudges in the heart one against the other. Rabbi Uri Natan Nota talked about the praises of his in-law Reb Eliyahu Moshe, saying that he set times aside for the study of Torah, he hosted guests, his home was open wide to any Jew, and he supported Torah scholars in a generous fashion. Aside from this, when they became connected through marriage, he supported his son-in-law as if he were his own son, providing all his needs with love and great honor, and from time to time, he also provided support for himself. – – – Reb Eliyahu Moshe was effusive in the praise of his son-in-law, with his fine traits in addition to his diligence in study and comportment in the fear of Heaven. He said that throughout the time that he lived in the settlement, he drew the simple folk near, and studied with them *Chumash* with *Rashi*, and *Ein Yaakov* on a daily basis . On the Sabbath he would recite *Midrash* and *Pirkei Avot* to them. He would inculcate in them love to each other, for before Rabbi Shlomo came, there were times when the residents of the settlement would quarrel with each other, which for the most part was due to jealousy and thoughts that they were impinging on each other's livelihood. However, since his son-in-law arrived, not only did the disputes stop, but love and honor began to be shown among them. – – – He became beloved by the entire settlement, and they all were saddened with his agony, and prayed to G-d that his daughter should return to health, and her husband, my son-in-law Rabbi Shimon should return to my house, study with them, and guide them as before.

The Besh't listened to the words of the in-laws with special concentration, and said, "With the help of the blessed G-d, I am able to heal the sick woman, so that she will become healthy with a clear mind as previously, but the condition is that when she is cured, they should not live together, and a few days later after she regains her health completely and she is able to receive a *Get* in accordance with the laws of the Torah, she should be divorced willingly and with a joyous heart."

The in-laws were quite astounded at this. The *Gaon* Rabbi Uri Natan Nota presented several reasons from the Torah that it not be permitted to divorce her. Reb Eliyahu Moshe claimed that his daughter would be very distraught regarding this, for she honored her husband greatly, and that his son-in-law would also be distraught that he is forced to divorce her and separate from her.

The Besh't responded that if they do not agree to the condition that he stated, he would be unable to help them.

After a few days, the in-laws and Rabbi Shlomo came to the Besh't and stated that the three of them accept the condition, but they cannot guarantee that the woman would be willing to be divorced from her husband. The Besh't agreed with this and told Reb Eliyahu Meir that he should go to his house and tell his sick daughter that the Besh't, known as a worker of wonders, has come to Slutsk, and summons her to come to him, for he has an urgent matter to discuss with her.

The in-laws looked upon this with surprise. At the end, Reb Eliyahu Moshe girded his soul and stated that she had not uttered a word from her mouth for about three years now. She has chosen a place for herself between the oven and the wall, and they feed her with great difficulty. It is the same with all other human functions, for she has no intellect at all. The Besh't did not answer anything. – – – Now when Rabbi Shlomo merited to see the Besh't and hear his Torah, he has become bound to him with his whole heart and essence, and he told his father-in-law that in his opinion, he must act in accordance tithe command of the Besh't, for is he not a renowned worker of wonders. Rabbi Uri Natan Nota also said that since the agreed to the heavy condition before them, they must certainly act in accordance with his statement.

Reb Eliyahu Moshe returned to his house and found his daughter sitting in her usual place behind the oven. He told his wife what the Besh't said, that with the help of the blessed G-d, he can cure their sick daughter. He spoke effusively about the wonders that people talk about the Besh't, and how greatly amazed they were to hear these stories about the Besh't. Suddenly, their daughter came out from behind the oven, approached them, and asked who is this worker of wonders. They were surprised to hear her voice, for they had not heard it for six years. They saw that her face changed, and that the light of her eyes returned to as it was before. Since the sick woman heard

[Page 125]

that the man about whom they were talking was a *Tzadik* of renown, she said that she first wishes to wash up and purify herself. Her father and mother were astounded to see the complete change, that she had turned into a healthy person. They did not believe what their eyes saw and what their ears heard. Throughout the entire time, they thought that their daughter's illness was due to the evil eye. They felt this was due to the fact that they told someone that due to her great merits, she succeeded in marrying a scholar with fine traits, who loved his fellow Jew and drew the simple folk near, to learn with them and guide them in good traits. A few days after this conversation, their daughter became ill and lost her sanity. Therefore, when they saw that her sanity had returned, they closed the door so nobody would come in, and the matter of her recovery would become known.

That night, she ate in the manner of all people, and she lay down in her bed to sleep. However, she was especially weak. In the morning, she spoke like a healthy person, but a great weakness overtook her. On the third day, she became ill once again, not with a mental illness, but rather will a fever. Due to the high fever, she spoke at times incoherently, and at times about the stories of wonders that she had heard from her father about the Besh't. She wept and said that she wishes to see the *Tzadik* who works wonders. When Reb Eliyahu

Moshe heard the words of her daughter, she remembered that, due to the great astonishment from the great change, he had forgotten to inform her that the Besh't had invited her to come to him. She was very happy, and on the second day, she traveled to Slutsk with her parents.

When Reb Eliyahu Moshe and his wife saw that she had returned from insanity to sanity within almost a moment, the sent a special messenger in the morning to inform their son-in-law Reb Shlomo and their in-law the *Gaon*, and wrote to him in detail about all that had transpired. When the emissary came to Rabbi Uri Natan Nota, he was very astonished. His son Rabbi Shlomo, in addition to his great joy about the recovery of is wife, was happy about the impression that this event had upon his father, who had been one of those who stood distant from the doctrines of the Besh't. – – – He found it to be a propitious time to speak to him about the doctrines of the Besh't: a) Understanding of Torah for the matter of G-d is only knowledge and not complete understanding, and the Torah is similar. For even with *halachot* that are explained before us, we only have knowledge and not complete understanding, since their internal meaning is endless. b) Divine providence: Not only does this mean that it is on every being in exacting detail. The intention is to live from what has been created through His efforts. c) The positive character of Israel: Even a simple person of Israel is sublime in the essence of his sublimity, literally as the *Gaon* of *Gaonim*. – – – d) Love of Israel: The trait of love of Israel according to the doctrine of the Besh't and his Torah is not only from the side of the trait of good and benevolence, but that every person of Israel must work with himself to expel the bad traits of pride, deceit, jealousy, hatred, and the like. – – – The sigh uttered by a Jew over the agony, Heaven forbid, of another breaks through all the iron partitions of the accusers. And the joy and blessing that a Jew rejoices with the joy of another Jew, and he blesses him, is accepted by the blessed G-d as the prayer of Rabbi Yishmael the High Priest in the Holy of Holies.

When the elderly *Gaon* Rabbi Uri Natan Nota heard from his son about the Besh't and his doctrines, he pondered it all day and all night. He went to the Besh't and told him what he had heard from his son about his doctrines. He concluded that he wishes to connect with him. He informed the Besh't about the good news that he received from his in-law, that his sick daughter has returned to her sanity. The Besh't then said that his daughter-in-law had become ill again today, and then when her father Reb Eliyahu Moshe fulfils the mission, she will become well, and she will come. When the sick woman and her parents all went to the Besh't, the sick woman, her husband, and her parents all together, the sick woman entered to the Besh't with her husband, and the Besh't told them that they should accept upon themselves to get divorced. The sick woman told the Besh't about the fine behavior of her husband, and if the *Tzadik* has decreed that she must get divorced, he certainly knows that that she is not fitting to be the wife of a *Tzadik* of the caliber of her husband, and she is forced to fulfil this. She wept greatly. The husband also talked about the praises of his wife in all fine traits, and if the *Tzadik* decrees, it must be fulfilled. He too wept greatly.

The Besh't told them that he gives them three days, and they should come on the fourth day to arrange the Get in accordance with the law.

The woman, her husband, and the parents were immersed in deep sorrow. They fasted for three days, prayed a great deal, and recited Psalms. On the fourth day, they all went to the Besh't as mourners with broken hearts. The woman and her husband were weeping with tears.

When they entered to the Besh't, the rabbi, the scribe, and the witnesses were already present. When the Besh't asked them if they wish to get divorced willingly, they responded that they both believe in the Tzadik, and that this must be for the benefit of both of them. – – – The Besh't entered his room and tarried there for some time. When he returned, he told them, "Six years ago, there was a great accusation[2] against you, may such not befall us. A decree came from On High that the woman will be punished with the illness of insanity, and the man will be punished with the tribulation of *igun*[1]. When they took it upon themselves to get divorced based on faith in *Tzadikim* and dedication of the soul, in the merit of the faith in *Tzadikim* and simple faith, they received a positive verdict from the Heavenly court, and the negative decree[2] was revoked. The Besh't blessed them with children and length of days.

Rabbi Shlomo remained in Slutsk for three years. After that, he moved to Minsk upon the directive of the Besh't, and G-d blessed them with sons and daughters. He traveled with his wife to the Holy Land in the year 5556 [1796] and lived there for about fifteen years.

(From the booklet 18 Elul 5703 [1943], from the holy writing of the Admor Rabbi Y. Y. Schneerson may the memory of the holy be blessed, his soul in the Garden of Eden, of Lubavitch[3]).

About the Besh't

Two wealthy brothers lived in Slutsk. They had come from Galicia and leased all the estates of the Polish prince Radziwiłł. These main lessees, who were known to Shlomo Maimon, a Lithuanian member of their generation, by their Polish name Derzowcki, ruled over masses of village Jews, who leased small farms or taverns from them. The strong-handed brothers oversaw the small-scale lessees with a vigilant eye to ensure that they were not negligent in their work, and that they pay their lease fees. They did not pay attention to the outcries of their poor brethren who cursed them with the name *aritzim* (tyrants).

A Hassidic legend states – once, the wife of one of the wealthy brothers invited the Besh't, who was from her native area, to come to a dedication of a large house that her husband had built in Slutsk. The *Tzadik* spent about three weeks there, but he felt that the Lithuanian environs was looking upon him with suspicion, and that they do not believe in his "portents." As he was leaving, the Hassidic woman asked him how long their period of success would be. She received an answer: twenty-two years. That prophesy was fulfilled, after twenty-two years, the prince became angry with his prime lessees and put them in prison.

(An excerpt from "The Annals of Hassidism" by Shimon Dubnow.)

[Page 126]

A Story About the Besh't

When the Besh't was with the Derzowckis (prime lessees) of the holy community of Slutsk, the name of one of whom was Reb Shmuel, and the second was Reb Gedalia – Reb Shmuel's wife Tovale urged her husband to send for the Besh't for they had built a mansion and were afraid to live in it. They invited him and he came to them. There was nobody in the house; he wished to make a meal, and he said that one must inspect the knife. The *shochet* had to come and show him the knife. The people of the city were extremely vexed as to how he saw fit to show the knife to the city *shochet*, especially in a large city, but they could not do anything about it, for the mistress of the house commanded thus. At *Mincha*, when they heard that he worshiped in accordance with the Sephardic rite, they became even more vexed. When Reb Shmuel returned to his house, they slandered him, and he responded that it is not proper to do anything to him without a complaint. Even before *Mincha*, they took him to all the buildings, and in several places, he made gestures as if he saw something. They suspected him of deceit, for the entire city was present. He said to his wife that he wants to test him in one matter (and I have forgotten the matter). The Besh't heard in his guestroom what the man was telling his wife in the bedroom. The Besh't summoned the maid to come immediately, and to pay no attention to all the guards standing there. She immediately got out of her bed and set out, but the husband prevented her from going. However, she paid no attention to him. When she arrived, the Besh't hinted to her that "The fool wishes to test me." She became greatly afraid and assured the Besh't to the point that he was calmed When she came home, she told this to her husband, and she became important in his eyes. The next day, they made a big feast for him, and spoke to him about the ways in the Holy Land, for he wanted to be sent overland. He asked the Besh't how much that might cost, and the Besh't responded that he needs a thousand of expenses. He responded that this is a small matter for him, and promised to send him money every year for his livelihood, for the main thing is that he should merit to live there in the Holy Land. The Besh't remained there for three weeks.

Once, the aforementioned Tovale asked the Besh't how long her the times of good fortune would ask. The Besh't scolded her and told her that one is not to ask such things. She urged him greatly. He closed his eyes for a moment and said that they would last for twenty-two years. When her husband heard this, he became very angry at him. Another thing happened, that one of the wealthy men had a sick child and came to the Besh't to ask that he live. Then he saw that he would die. He understood that they wish to shame him, so he left in the middle of the night, travelling approximately fifteen parasangs in a speedy fashion, until he left their bounds into a different realm. They[4] came to the village, and as he went through a village or a city he went as all people did. After exiting one village, they immediately entered another village. Rabbi Tzvi Sofer asked him what was this about, and he did not answer anything, for he was not permitted to stop. He only pushed him off with his hand. This is what I heard from the aforementioned rabbi several times, that one must not stop him. When they came to one border, and he stopped to rest, he wrote a letter.[5] Know in faith that I was able to give him advice and he would not be able to do anything to me, but I was afraid that this might damage me in another place. Therefore, I have turned away from you, so that not one of the things that I said should befall you, that after twenty-two years, you will have a downfall from one of your servants. He signed at the end: signed by Yisrael Besh't, the servant of G-d. He sent that letter with a special emissary. Rabbi Shmuel became very vexed. Rabbi Shmuel was embarrassed to show the letter to anyone. He only showed the signature.

I heard about the end of the Derzowcis from Reb Yitzchak Izik of blessed memory as follows: The duke of Slutsk was Radziwiłł. He borrowed a large sum of money from them, and they could not collect from him. They were worried lest he ask them for another loan of money. They decided to move to the city of Breslau. They spoke to the king to take them under his protection to the community of Breslau, and they transferred the aforementioned debt to him as a gift, so that they king could collect it from him and his possessions. That is what they did. The travelled by ship over the water, and passed through the community of Slonim, which was the place of residence of the duke. They took with him three barrels of money to place in the community of Breslau. Their official also traveled with them. As they approached the port, and Reb Shmuel went to his inn with his official. He dressed himself up to go to the minister. While he was still preening himself and getting dressed, the official left him. He became very frightened, and ran to the duke. When he saw him, and saw that the official was standing with duke in a room inside a room and speaking to the duke, he approached the official and smacked him over the cheek. The duke responded, since you hit him in my presence even though it is not proper, I nevertheless forgive you for this, because you trust, from my great love to you, that even if you hit my son in my presence I would forgive you. He responded to this statement, but he did not have what to respond. The aforementioned duke sent for the ship, and found what the official had said. He was immediately put in prison, and he ordered that infantry soldiers be sent to the mayor of the community of Slutsk. He ordered the mayor to seal off all their money and property. When the letter from aforementioned duke arrived, the mayor became very afraid. He was concerned lest the wheel of fortune turn toward the good, and he would then become their enemy. He pretended to be drunk, and he slept a great deal until the night. When he saw that everyone in the city was asleep, the mayor himself went to Tovale, Reb Shmuel's wife, and informed her of this, to empty and destroy everything possible, for in the morning everything would be sealed off. She sent her son-in-law, who escaped with the ornaments and jewelry. He later became the head of the rabbinical court of the community of Breslau. He became vey wealthy from this. – – – That Mrs. Tovale requested from the people of their city to send for the Besh't, for perhaps he could help them with his prayers. The people of the city hated them. Even so, they sent a special emissary, but they told him in complete secrecy to ask the Besh't to not help them. It was two or three days before the request of the city people became known. The Besh't said, "I have looked for some path to help them, but since Israelites ask me to not help them, I will not help them." This happened after twenty-two years had passed, as the Besh't had written to them.

Rabbi David, the rabbi of Makow tells in his book *Torah Hakenaot* – – – The famous tycoons known as the Derzowcis who had greatness under the duke (Radziwiłł), there is barely any essence to their greatness. They requested to know what would happen to them later on, and they sent for him… He told them that their greatness would last only twenty-two years… And that is how it was in truth.

(From the book *Shivchei HaBesh't* [praises of the Besh't], published by Dvir)

Activity Against Hassidism

During the days of uproar in Lithuania and Reisin [White Russia] at the border of the 18th and 19th centuries, the preacher of the *Misnagdim* Yisrael Leibel passed through these states and reached the district of central Poland, Galicia, and Germany. He shook up the winds with his sermons and stories. We already saw him arming himself for war, threating the leader of that sect, to bring them to a court case with the state.

Rabbi Yisrael the son of Reb Yehuda Leib was apparently a native of the Lithuanian city

[Page 127]

of Slutsk (a colleague of the ranks of *Misnagdim*, author of the book *Zamir Aritzim* (5551 [1791], always known as Reb Yisrael of Slutsk). He played the role of preacher in the community of Mohilev in Reisin until the year 5547 [1787]. That year, he came to the city of Novogrodek and was accepted as the preacher of righteousness and a permanent judge.

His opposition to the cult of Hassidm grew when he was still in Mohilev and saw the deep influence of Reb Zalman upon the youth, who streamed by the hundreds to the holy city of Lozna. Rabbi Yisrael's younger brother was also caught up in the net of instigators of the sect. All the efforts of the preacher to turn the misguided one away from his dangerous path were for naught. He had already gone far along that path, and there was no hope for him. Then the preacher sent a letter to the *Tzadik* in Lozna full of reproof. He threatened him that a public rebuke against him and against all members of that sect would be forthcoming if they do not return his displaced brother. When this too was to no avail, Yisrael role and traveled himself to Reb Zalman for a debate.

According to his words, the *Tzadik* received him in anger and reproved him for his thoughts to protest against the sect in pubic, thereby exposing the internal dispute before the eyes of the gentiles, the enemies of Israel. The preacher responded that he finds a fundamental principle of Hassidic doctrine to be damaging to Judaism and the principles of religious morality [*mussar*] in general, and that he feels that the good people of the nations of the world will see the positive side of rabbis who expose the rot in the minority of the nation, in order to rectify the entire nation.

When Reb Yisrael began to clarify the details of the rot, and prove that Hassidim chase after pleasures, love monetary gain, and dispense a vain craft, Reb Zalman got angry at him and sent him away. Then he wrote "The Book of Debate" against Hassidism, and traveled to Warsaw to publish it there. This was in the year 5557 [1797], after the *Gaon* had issued his well-known decree against the sect to the leaders of the communities in each and every Gubernia. Reb Saadya, the emissary of the *Gaon* who was in charge of the hosts of the *Misnagdim*, gave the Lithuanian preacher permission and authority to preach against the sect in every place, and he wrote an approbation for the publication of his book (Sivan 5557).

In the month of Av, Leibel moved to Israel via Slutsk, and received an approbation from the *parnasim* [administrators] of the community.

The "Book of Disputes" [*Sever Havichuach*] was published in Kirov (approximately Kislev 5558, December 1797).

A booklet *Taava Tzadikim* by Rabbi Yisrael Leibel was also published in Warsaw in the year 5558.

The people of the sect purchased the copies of the book and burnt them, so that only a small remnant remained of everything that had been published. Zealots would ambush the preacher Yisrael Leibel, beat him, and curse him in the outskirts of Warsaw and other cities that he passed through.

His essay in *Milchemet Hamitzvah* testifies as follows: (*Zamir Aritzim*, 5558 1798): "And the wonderful scholar, our Rabbi Yisrael of Slutsk, already aroused in his book of debates, he who is zealous for the G-d of Hosts, and he gave himself up to be killed by the accursed Hassidim who spilled blood like water – they threw stones after him – – They tore up his books and trampled him as mud outside. They nicknamed the author "Preacher of Foolishness.""}

The Involvement of the Russian Government with the Dispute (1800-1801)

From the responsa of Reb Zalman regarding *Sheelat Avigdor* [Questions of Avigdor] only two of the letters regarding the government were preserved, questions 18 and 19, as follows:

"The people of the holy community of Slutsk hate us, for they have greatly persecuted the Hassidim of Liachovitz. The issue is well known, for a decree was issued by the authorities of Minsk, as has been clearly heard."

(This is an innuendo to the persecution of the groups of Hassidim, headed by the *Tzadik* Rabbi Mordechai of Liachovitz, by the *Misnagdim* of Slutsk).

(From Sefer Hachasidut)

Hassidic legend tells that the Baal Shem Tov of blessed memory, as he was "going into exile" came to Slutsk, and its residents did not receive him politely. Then he cursed the city, that Hassidim should never be found there. The curse was fulfilled, and Slutsk remained one of the four cities known by the name Karpa's[6]: Khosova, Ruzhany, Pruzhany, and Slutsk, in which no Hassid had any inheritance. These cities never heard their residents recite *Hodu* before *Baruch Sheamar*[7]. Many generations passed, and a *Nusach* Sephard Siddur was never found in Slutsk.

* * *

During that period, there were lone Hassidim in Slutsk, headed by Reb Pinchas (Pinie) Kantorovich, but they never found a place to conduct organized prayer services in a synagogue. After the Mishnayos Synagogue was built, they were given the *Shtibel*, where a *minyan* took place. If they were one or two short of *minyan*, *Misnagdim* would join in the merit of the drink. (They would drink liquor as a *Tikun* [spiritual rectification] on memorial days.)

The great crowding in the *Shtibel* was on the evening of Shemini Atzeret. The Hassidim would conduct the *Hakafot* ceremony, in contrast with the custom of the *Misnagdim*, and there would be appropriate drinks.

When I passed by the Hassidic *Shtibel* in the Mishnayos Synagogue, the Hassidim asked me to enter to complete the *minyan*.

When I asked them, why are you still waiting when you already have a *minyan*, one of them pointed out: "One must specifically include two *Misnagdim* to fill the place of a tenth Hassid.:

* * *

Two Chabad Hassidim from Rechitsa came to Slutsk and stayed in the Nekritz Hotel. This took place on the 19th of Kislev, and they decided to conduct a public prayer service and a celebration of thanks in memory of the release [from prison] of the Rebbe, the author of the *Tanya*.

Since it was difficult to gather a *minyan* of Hassidim in Slutsk, they placed a flask of liquor and all sorts of treats on the table, to treat anyone who entered the inn. There was one short of a *minyan*. At 12:00 midnight, a Jew entered in a commotion and called out, "Is there a doctor here?" They responded, "First, let us treat you with a drink, and then then the doctor will appear." The Jew was enticed. He drank himself to the point of intoxication, and they were happy with him that he completed the *minyan*. His wife waited for the doctor, and when she saw that her husband had not returned, she went to look for him. Along the way, she heard the voices of celebration and joy from the inn. She peered through the window, and noticed her husband among those dancing.

She burst into the room in anger, and shouted at him, "I am waiting in fear and trepidation for the fate of the sick child, and you are dancing here."

The drunk man apologized and responded, "You fool, why are you shouting? Tonight is Nitl Nacht[8] and it is a mitzvah for me to rejoice and dance.

(Noach)

Translator's footnotes:

1. The *halachic* term for someone trapped in a marital situation that is not working, but is not eligible to be broken with a *Get* [religious divorce]. It is the masculine form of the more well-known term *aguna*. The term is based on the Hebrew root of being bound. A woman not of sound mind is not able to accept a *Get*.
2. The term *kitrug* refers to a spiritual accusation.
3. The second to last Lubavitcher Rebbe, Rabbi Yitzchak Yosef Schneerson.
4. There is an intermixing of singular and plural in this story, making it quite confusing. I suspect that the plural refers to those accompanying the Besh't.
5. What follows seems to be the content of the letter.
6. *Karpas* is of course the name of section of the Passover Seder where vegetables are eaten. Here it is an acronym for the four cities.
7. *Nusach* Sephard (which is used by Hassidim) and *Nusach* Ashkenaz have various differences, one of them being the location of where the *Hodu* prayer is recited in *Pesukei Dezimra*. Another difference between *Nusach* Sephard and *Nusach* Ashkenaz is that the *Hakafot* [Torah processions] ceremony of Simchat Torah is also conducted on Shemini Atzeret night in accordance with *Nusach* Sephard, as is noted in the following paragraphs.
8. A term for Christmas.

[Page 128]

Folklore

Translated by Jerrold Landau

Reb Mendele

Reb Mendele was one of the giants of the generation. He hated [i.e. shied away from] the rabbinate, and never sat on the rabbinical seat in Slutsk. He set up a Yeshiva in the home of the tycoon Isserlin, where he would sit and occupy himself with Torah, study and teach, disseminate Torah to the *Treisar* – the twelve students who were supported at the tycoon Isserlin's table. He had the custom of going every day with his students to Isserlin's house to drink tea. He himself would stand and serve them. He would fill each one's cup, two or three times according to the will of each person. After they all drank to satiety, he would sit and drink his portion.

Once, a representative of the Mir Yeshiva came to Slutsk. He entered Isserlin's house saw the important ones of the generation sitting around the table with a cup of tea, and a short, old man was standing and serving them. He said, "It must be that he is one of the servants in the home of the tycoon." He sat among them, and ordered the old man to serve him. The emissary was corpulent, and flooded with tea. He emptied cup after cup, as he treated Rabbi Mendele as a servant. Those around the table looked at each other and did not say anything. The tycoon Isserlin had the custom that on every Sabbath prior to the daytime meal, they could come to his home for a *Kiddush*. When everyone was sitting around the table, the tycoon entered with Rabbi Mendele, and everyone stood up and greeted those who had entered with Sabbath greetings.

The emissary was among those who came to the home of the tycoon for *Kiddush*. When he sat among them, he saw that the tycoon had entered with an elderly man, and all those seated stood up and called out, ", our rabbi, *Shabbat Shalom*!"

"Who is that old man?" asked the emissary.

"Indeed, it is Reb Mendele," they responded.

His eyes became dark. He had treated Rabbi Mendele like a servant. He immediately stood up, ran to Rabbi Mendele, and began to plead before him, "Forgive me, our rabbi, I did not know…" "And what did sir do to me?" Reb Mendele looked at him with eyes full of surprise, "That I should forgive him?"

"I did not know our rabbi," said the emissary with a broken heart, "and I troubled him…"

"I do not know," said Reb Mendele innocently, "what sir did wrong to me, that he is trying to appease me. He asked for a cup of tea, and I gave him. On the contrary, I must thank sir, that he bestowed me with the opportunity to perform a good deed."

Reb Yosi Ber Soloveitchik

When Rabbi Yosi Ber of Brisk occupied the rabbinical seat of Slutsk, the poor and indigents of the city would come early to his door and pour the agony of their hearts out to him. He knew how to deal with the poor and save the souls of the indigents. Once, as the Passover festival approached, a wagon driver came to him and wept before him, "Rabbi, tribulation after tribulation has come upon me. All winter I have sat idle, not earning a penny. Now, close to Passover, when there is work and I might be able to earn something for the needs of the festival, my horse had died."

Rabbi Yosi Ber did not hesitate for a moment, and said to him, "Go to my cowshed, take my cow, bring it to the market, and exchange it for a horse."

The wagon driver did not demur. He went to the barn, took the cow, and walked with it. A few minutes later, the Rebbetzin entered the cowshed to check on the cow, and the cow was gone. She hurried to the house and screamed, "Yosi Ber, our cow has been stolen!" "It has not been stolen," said Rabbi Yosi Ber calmly. "Then where is it?" asked the Rebbetzin. "If that man has not exchanged it yet," answered Rabbi Yosi Ber gently, "Then it is with him." "That man? An exchange?" the Rebbetzin looked at him, "What are you talking about?"

Rabbi Yosi Ber told her about what happened, that he had given the cow to a poor wagon driver whose horse had died and who had no source of livelihood.

"What have you done?" The Rebbetzin became angry. "We had one cow. Where will we find a drop of milk?"

"Figure out for yourself," Rabbi Yosi Ber told her, "Is it proper that we should have both milk and bread, and that unfortunate indigent should not even have bread?"

* * *

When Rabbi Yosi Ber occupied the rabbinic seat of Slutsk, there were two *shochtim* [ritual slaughterers] in the city, Reb Tzvi and Reb Nocha, a father and son. Reb Tzvi was not afflicted by old age. He looked like his son and was the same height of his son Rabbi Nocha. When Rabbi Yosi Ber went to get married for the second time, he took Rabbi Nocha with him, for he would only eat of his shechita.

When Rabbi Yosi Ber returned to Slutsk with his new wife, Rabbi Tzvi entered to wish him Mazel Tov. After he left, Rabbi Yosi Ber's wife said, "It seemed to me that Rabbi Nocha was here."

"No," replied Rabbi Yosi Ber, "that is the father of Rabbi Nocha."

[Page 129]

"His father?" his wife said in astonishment, "It seems that the father is the same age as the son."

"That is the way it is," Rabbi Yosi Ber smiled and said, "It is like this. Rabbi Tzvi is married to his second wife, and a second wife takes half of the years off her husband…"

* * *

When Rabbi Yosi Ber occupied the rabbinical seat of Slutsk, the tax collector of kosher meat came and complained."

"Rabbi, they are bringing in meat from the outside to the city!"

"What is the problem with that?" asked Rabbi Yosi Ber.

"Apparently?" the tax collector stated in surprise, "It is meat slaughtered from the outside. We do not know the *shochtim*." "Calm down," smiled Rabbi Yosi Ber, "This is an a fortiori: And just like the meat of the *shochtim* of Slutsk, who we know, is kosher for us; how much more so is meat slaughtered from outside, where we do not know them…"

There was another story with that tax collector who sent a fine cow as a gift to Rabbi Yosi Ber, which produced a large quantity of milk.

Before long, the tax collector came to him and asked him to declare a ban on outside slaughter. Rabbi Yosi Ber did not respond. During that visit, he called his wife and said to her, "Return the cow to Rabbi Avrahamel immediately, and pay him the money for the milk that it has provided…"

* * *

When Rabbi Yosi Ber occupied the rabbinic seat o Slutsk, the first buds of the *Haskala* [enlightenment] began to appear in the city, and many people started to have heretical thoughts.

Men of virtuous deeds in the city approached Rabbi Yosi Ber, "Our rabbi, heresy, Heaven forbid, is increasing. The hand of the heretics is strong." Rabbi Yosi Ber said calmly, "There is no surprise with this, truth will prevail."

"What is our rabbi saying?" they said in surprise, "That heresy is truth?" Rabbi Yosi Ber replied to them, "What I am telling you is that the heretics are promoting heresy in truth, so they are succeeding. The G-d fearing people among us are not true fearers of heaven, so they are weaker."

* * *

When Rabbi Yosi Ber occupied the rabbinic seat of Slutsk, there was a certain householder in the city, Shmuel Simchovich, who knew Torah and was caught by the *Haskala*. Rabbi Yosi Ber said of him:

"Shmuel would have already given up this attitude if the fear of Heaven as upon him…"

* * *

The Rogochover *Illui* [genius] studied during his youth with Reb Mendele in Slutsk (later known as one of the great ones of the generation, the rabbi of Dvinsk). When he was young, Rabbi Yosef Ber did not allow him to look into the Rambam before he came of age and not filled himself up with the Babylonian and Jerusalem

Talmuds. However, the young *Illui* could not control his spirit, and secretly began to study the *Mishneh Torah* of the Rambam.

At that point, Rabbi Yosi Ber entered and found him in his dishonor. Rabbi Yosi Ber smiled and scolded him, "You *shegetz*[1], why did you go against my word?"

"Rabbi," exclaimed the *Illuy*, "Is this not an a fortiori: If I, who only perused the Rambam, am already a *shegetz*; then our rabbi, who studies it constantly and does not move from it, how much more so is he a complete gentile…"

* * *

When Rabbi Yosi Ber left Slutsk, he did not find a rabbinical position appropriate for him, and he went through several years without a rabbinical position and without a livelihood.

Once, while riding on a train, one of the *Parnasim* [communal administrators] of Brisk was sitting in the wagon with him. The *Parnas* told him that the community of Brisk was looking for a rabbi who would be appropriate to occupy its rabbinical seat.

Rabbi Yosi Ber responded, "My advice is to send a rabbinical contract to Rabbi Yehoshua Leib, for he is fitting and qualified to serve as the rabbi of Brisk." That is how it was, Rabbi Yehoshua Leib was invited to Brisk and sat on its rabbinical seat. After some years, when Rabbi Yehoshua Leib left Brisk, Rabbi Yosi Ber was invited to take his place.

Rabbi Yaakov David (the Ridba'z)

When Rabbi Yaakov David, the Ridba'z, occupied the rabbinical seat in Slutsk, there was a certain man who observed the commandments and conducted himself normally, but Rabbi Yaakov David knew that his insides were not like his outside[2]. He was G-d fearing on the outside, but a transgressor in secret.

Rabbi Yaakov David said of him:

"How indecent is that man. He is cleanshaven. Would it be that he shaves off his beard, and everyone would see that he is cleanshaven…"

* * *

A certain Hasid was talking with Rabbi Yaakov David of Slutsk:

"Before, I was in the cemetery in Brisk. I went there to supplicate at the grave of the *Tzadik* of Turisk. I saw and was surprised: the grave of the *Tzadik* was clear on all sides, whereas the grave of Rabbi Yosi Ber was surrounded by graves upon graves."

"This comes to teach you," responded Rabbi Yaakov David, "What is the difference between Hasidim and *Misnagdim*? With Hasidim, as long as their Rebbe is alive, they draw close to him and cleave to him. When he dies and exits the world, his grave is holy, and nobody approaches it due to the honor. It is the opposite with *Misnagdim*. As long as their rabbi is alive, everyone escapes from him. When he leaves the world, everyone seeks the merit to be buried near him…"

[Page 130]

* * *

When Rabbi Yaakov David of Slutsk occupied the rabbinical seat of Bobruisk, there were another two rabbis in the city: Rabbi Shmarya Noach, the rabbi of the Hasidim, and another rabbi, who did not have a good relationship with Rabbi Yaakov David. The two rabbis would go out wearing streimels on their heads. Rabbi Yaakov David di not wear a streimel on his head. Rabbi Yaakov David used to say, "There are three types of rabbis of Bobruisk, the rabbi with a streimel, the rabbi without a streimel, and the streimel without a rabbi."

* * *

When Rabbi Yaakov David occupied the rabbinic seat of Slutsk, he was not satisfied with the residents of his city. He would complain that the people of Slutsk denigrate his honor and afflict him financially. The city notables asked him, "Our rabbi, if indeed you are not satisfied with Slutsk, why do you live here and not go to another city?"

Rabbi Yaakov David responded to them, "I say to you, I have accepted the seven levels of hell. Why so much? For are there not difficult tribulations at level one, the tribulations of hell, to punish the evildoer? However, I tell you, when the evildoer becomes accustomed to his level and his tribulations, they are no longer difficult for him. Therefore, they transfer him from level to level, and at each level there are new tribulations." Rabbi Yaakov David concluded, "I too am like that. Slutsk is like hell to me, but I am used to it and its tribulations. That would not be the case in different city, where I would have a new hell with new tribulations…"

* * *

The Ridba'z once said to Binyamin the crazy person: "It is better that you come into the synagogue and peruse [a book] rather than wander through the streets." Binyamin responded, "That makes sense rabbi, but bless me that the spirit of folly shall depart from me." The Ridba'z blessed him and asked him, "And how do you bless me?"

Binyamin replied, "Would it be that the number of people who listen to your Talmud class grow and reach the level of the number of people who run after me in the streets of the city…"

* * *

There is a story about Rabbi Yosi Ber of Brisk and Rabbi Yaakov David of Slutsk, who both met on a journey and traveled in the same wagon. As they were traveling, the discussed words of Torah, and debated matters of Jewish law, as is the custom of rabbinic scholars. Rabbi Yaakov became upset, left the passenger compartment, and sat on the platform with the wagon driver. They entered the town in that manner.

The townsfolk saw this and were surprised: Two rabbis in one wagon. One is sitting in the passenger compartment and his friend is sitting on the platform. They greeted the one sitting on the platform and sked him, "From where and to where? And who is the rabbi sitting in the passenger compartment? Rabbi Yaakov David responded, "I am Rabbi Yosi Ber coming from Brisk, and the rabbi sitting the passenger compartment is Rabbi Yaakov David of Slutsk. And since it is not appropriate for the honor of Rabbi Yaakov David that I sit together with him, I ascended and sat on the platform."

"Don't believe him," Rabi Yosi Ber stuck his head out of the compartment, "I am Rabbi Yosi Ber of Brisk, and he is Rabbi Yaakov David of Slutsk." Rabbi Yaakov Dvid said to him, "Our rabbi, your efforts are for naught, everyone knows our rabbi and his iniquities…"

* * *

Rabbi Yaakov David of Slutsk, the Ridba'z, used to say: "Come and see how many measures of haughtiness this generation took. If you ask a person: What re you learning? He responds and says: *Bavli* [The Babylonian Talmud]. If he does not have extra haughtiness, he responds and says: *Nezikin*. If he merited and leaned modesty, he responds: *Bava Kama*. I am surprised: How can a person study the entire Talmud at once, or an entire Order, or even a complete Tractate? I know: a person studies a single page, then another page. If this is the heart of the generation, that they are only satisfied to study the entire Talmud at once, an entire Order, or an entire Tractate…"

* * *

The Ridba'z came to Bobruisk in the year 5652 [1892] from Slutsk to eulogize the Gaon Rabbi Yosef Dov Soloveitchik. After the eulogy, he was invited to the home of the tycoon Boaz Rabinovitz for dinner. During dinner, he asked the Ridba'z: "Rabbi is not there a direct road from Bobruisk to Slutsk, and one can travel from one city to the next in one night. Why, rabbi, did you go from Bobruisk to Slutsk via Vilna, Plotzk, and Vilkov, which is very far?" He asked and he answered: "When Israel left Egypt, G-d did not lead them through the Phillistine route, even though it is close, but rather lead them through a far route, lest the nation have regrets if they see a war and return to Egypt. You too rabbi, G-d led you from Bobruisk to Slutsk on a long route, lest you have regrets when you see a war in Slutsk and return to Bobruisk…"

* * *

When the dispute regarding the rabbinical seat broke out in Slutsk between Rabbi Meir Peimer (the son of the Rabbi Yosele the first) and the Ridba'z, it grew stronger and divided the city into two factions for many years.

The following words of folklore testify to the denigration and discord: They told the Ridba'z – why are you denigrating Rabbi Meir, for is he not great in Torah? He told them: "If I state that I am greater than him in Torah that is haughtiness. If I say innocently that he is great in Torah, is it not written 'distance yourself from words of falsehood.'…"

* * *

They told the Ridba'z: "Our rabbi, is it proper to denigrate the honor of a rabbi, for he is like his name, Rabbi Meirke, and he illuminates[3] the eyes of the residents of Slutsk with Torah

"If that is the case," notes the Ridba'z, "there is also a village in our area called *Raav*-Zevitz."[4]

* * *

The daughter of the Ridba'z made efforts to obtain a divorce from her husband, who refused to fulfil her request. The Ridba'z said to someone close to him who intended to slander his daughter that she is promiscuous, and her husband must divorce her. They said to him: "If that were the case, nobody would want to marry her even after she gets divorced." The Ridba'z answered that he would latter place his head in the Holy Ark and swear before the people and the community that the slander is fundamentally false.

When the matter reached Rabbi Shmuel Simchovich, he reacted sharply: "Now I understand why they honor Rabbi Yaakov David

[Page 131]

with *Shlishi* [the third *aliya*] when he goes up to the Torah. It says in the Torah: Kozbi the daughter of Tzur the head of the people (Numbers 25, 15). Rashi notes on this that Tzur was one of the five kings of Midian, as it is written: Evi, Rekem, Tzur. He was more important than all of them, but since he disgraced himself by letting his daughter go loose, they counted him third."…

* * *

Rabbi Meir, the rabbi of Slutsk was great in Torah and pious in deeds. He occupied the rabbinic seat of Slutsk for several years. He set up a Yeshiva and groomed many students.

When his granddaughter joined a strange crowd and entered the gentile school, Rabbi Meir retired from the rabbinate.

His reason was as follows:

"I could not guide the members of my household on the straight path, so how much more so can I not do so to a Jewish community…"

Others said that after the large fire that took place in Slutsk, Rabbi Meir looked into the deeds of those acting for the benefit of those who suffered from the fire, saw things that were not in accordance with his spirit, and left the city.

* * *

There is a story about Rabbi Isser Zalman Meltzer of blessed memory, who was asked by his student Shmarya , one of the veterans of Deganya regarding the ways of the kibbutz. When he heard what he heard, he said, "It is fine and dandy, but you are not conducting yourselves in accordance with the commandments of the Torah and its details, and this is a black mark upon you." Shmaryahu responded, "How, can you, honorable rabbi, see black upon us, when our entire essence is the white group."

* * *

Rabbi Moshe, the *Maggid* [preacher] of Slutsk, the author of *Moshe Yedaber*, was a man of stature. His beard was full, he wore the garb of a scholar – he had the appearance of a rabbi.

Once, when he was riding in a train, he entered a certain car full of Jewish travelers, and there was not even room to stand, and certainly not to sit. When he entered, a whisper went through the travelers: "A rabbi! A Rabbi in Israel!" The standees squeezed themselves and made room for him. On of those seated stood up, clearing a seat for him: "Let our rabbi sit." Rabbi Moshe sat down. As is customary on journeys, a conversation began: "From where are you, our rabbi? To where are you going? In what city do you serve as a rabbi?" Rabbi Moshe replied: "I am not a rabbi in Israel, but rather a *Maggid*. I am the *Maggid* from Slutsk." As he said this, the one who gave up his seat for him told him to stand up, for the seat is taken.

Rabbi Moshe stood up and remained standing for the entire journey.

* * *

Rabbi Yitzchak Hochmark was travelling to the Unite States as an emissary of the Slobodka Yeshiva. Along the way, he stopped in various countries in his course of duties. He was once speaking to Rabbi Zeltzer, suggesting that he come to Hamburg and travel to the United States together. When Rabbi Zeltzer arrived lacking everything, and with worn out clothes, Rabbi Hochmark had to delay his departure on the Alba ship, ostensibly because he had to concern himself with purchasing tickets for Rabbi Zeltzer, and also to get clothes for him. Rabbi Hochmark was very dismayed, especially because their departure was delayed for more than three weeks on a commercial ship, and they suffered the tribulations of the journey. When they reached Ellis Island, they were surprised to see black flags waving for the rabbi.

When they asked for an explanation, they were told that the Alba ship had sunk on its way.

Rabbi Hochmark raised his hands in gratitude to the Dweller On High that he was saved from drowning in the ocean in the merit of Rabbi Zeltzer.

* * *

Shapira, the government appointed rabbi of Slutsk, was not chosen again because of his age. Ashman was chosen in his place.

They said that Shapira had become very old. When he came home and knocked on his door, his wife would ask through the corridor: "Solomonchik, is that you?"

As a sign of agreement, he would nod his head from behind the door.

* * *

In the bathhouse, the disabled people would bathe with aprons over their waist. When the numbers of such disabled people increased, the city decided that all those who enter the bathhouse, even those fully able, should wear aprons over their waists – "so as not to embarrass those who do not have."

From Yehuda Grazovski (Gur)

- Slutskers had crooked fingers.

- Slutskers have a dimple below their chest: because they stick their finger in that place saying: "I am a Slutsker."

- If Krupnik[5] is a food, Slutsk is a community.

- Slutskers are trusting, they trust and count.

- The butchers conferred and decided to build their own *Beis Midrash*. They hired workers and began to build. The city crazy passed by them, stood, and called out: "And all humans will call in your name"…

- A Jew from Slutsk places his right finger on his left pinky and said: "First I am a Slutsker! And second… There is no second to the first. It is the beginning and it is the end.

(From M. Lipson of blessed memory and various sources)

Translator's footnotes:

1. A derogatory term for a gentile, but also use as an insult to a Jew whose behavior is not in accordance with religious expectations.
2. I.e. he was insincere or hypocritical.
3. The Hebrew for illuminates is *meir*.
4. Apparently referring to Rubezhevichi, 112 km northwest of Slutsk. *Raav* means hunger or famine. Return
5. A sweet alcoholic drink.

[Page 132]

Unfortunates

by Baruch Domnitz

Translated by Jerrold Landau

Yudel

He was from a good family. He enjoyed eating a piece of pork in public. They asked him: "Can this be? Eating pork, and furthermore, in public?" He responded, "I have permission for this. At the time of the giving of the Torah on Mount Sinai, all souls, including mine, were present. I agreed to each and every negative commandment. When they declared 'Do not eat pig,' I rebelled. I went to Moses our Teacher and whispered in his ear that eating of pig is literally a case of life and death, and I cannot exist without it. Moses our Teacher grabbed my leg and whispered to me, 'For you, Yudel, it is permitted!'…"

David

He was a scholar. When his sanity departed from him, he was sitting and sermonizing on Jewish law and lore. He went barefoot both in the summer and in the winter. He wore tattered pants, with his bare flesh exposed through the holes. He would run and speak out loud, as if he were debating with someone. He erected a cross with icons at some distance from the synagogue. A farmer traveling into the city once saw him bowing down, making the sign of the cross, and worshipping aloud in Russian. "Oh Mr. Person, what are you doing? You are a Jew," the farmer said to him. "You understand," responded David, "Perhaps the old man does not hear. I said, come, I will exchange him for a young person, perhaps he will listen to me. But I realized that someone completely young would not succeed. It would be worse than the old man." As he was talking, he rose up and spat on the cross. "To hell," David uttered out loud and left. The farmer crossed himself out of fear and uttered: "Our father in heaven, forgive him, for that man is crazy."

One winter day, someone saw him running barefoot outside the city with a knapsack on his back. "To where?" they asked him. "To Kapoli," answered David, "A crazy person died there, I am hurrying to take is place, for a city without a crazy person cannot exist."

David the crazy man once caused mischief and grabbed cakes from the stalls in the marketplace. "Is this proper, Reb David, to grab. Have you gone mad?" "There is nothing strange about this," he responded, "It is written 'For David when he feigned insanity [Psalms 34:1]' If David the king could be insane, how much more so can I…"

Veve

That crazy man had two good traits: He loved cleanliness very much, and he knew all the *Haftarahs* of the Sabbaths of the year by heart with their tunes. At times he would run in the outskirts of the city, approach the courtyards and houses, and say with his stuttering voice, "Give Veve a clean pair of long underwear." Early on Sabbath mornings, he would go out like a bridegroom from his wedding canopy, wander through all the streets, and chant the *Haftarah* for that Sabbath very loudly. This awakened the householders from their sweet sleep, which they wished to elongate a bit for their benefit. However, who can insult a simple man whose sanity was not full? When they approached him from time to time – "Veve!" he would respond, "No, Velvel."

Yankel Mashe

That Yankel Mashe was a caustic man who hatched pretexts on how to provoke and insult people. His desire was to have a seat in the *Beis Midrash* on Zaretza Street, and from there, to cast his sharp arrows of mockery. I heard the following story from an eyewitness: On the Sabbath of Rosh Chodesh Nissan, Yankel Mashe ascended the *bima* and declared: "Since it is a good sign for a Jew to die in the months of Nissan, to whom is that fine portent fitting if not to the tycoons? I hereby declare that today, on the Sabbath of blessing the new month[1], and say: It is now time for the tycoons to begin to get ill."

Avraham Sakovitz

Avraham Sakovitz took pride in his own craziness, for he was a millionaire. He would haughtily count all his millions out loud. When they pointed out to him that the biggest tycoon in Slutsk was Reb Leibush Gutzeit, who himself does not have millions, he responded, "Therefore, what did you prove to me, that he is a tycoon and I am a millionaire. My name is Avraham Sakovitz, who is like me and who can be compared to me."

He was short and clumsy. The silvery hairs of his head and beard added some sort of splendor to his appearance. He did not wander from place to place very much, for in his insanity, he was "extremely wealthy" – literally a millionaire. His lips moved all day uttering, "millions, billions, gazillions,"repeat over and over. At times, he marveled at his words, and at times, he got mixed up with his accounting, and woe to anyone who disturbed him. He was present at wedding and circumcision celebrations and imagined that he was among the invited guests due to his "millions." He muttered about his partnership with the wealth of the king, and the sugar groves of Brodski, Poliakov, and several wealthy Jews of Peterburg and Moscow. It was as if the millions of franks of Rothschild were in his pocket.

Reb Binyamin the Crazy

There is a story of an elderly woman who owned a dairy shop. She closed her shop in the middle of the day, and on her way back, she found the shop open with a gentile inside. She began to scream: "A thief has broken into my shop." The gentile countered, "Jewess, I found the shop open, and I entered." The woman continued shouting, "Thief! Thief!" The gentile struck her with the wooden stick in his hand. "Jews, save me! Save me!" the woman continued screaming. Many people gathered on account of her screams, including Binyamin the crazy man (who was a scholar).

To the question about what happened, Reb Binyamin pointed out, "The matter is quite simple, there is a discussion in the Gemara. He claims I found an open door, and she claims, I have been smitten by a piece of wood…"[2]

Translator's footnotes:

1. There is something mixed up in this story, as *Shabbat Mevorchim* (the Sabbath before Rosh Chodesh when a prayer for the upcoming month is recited) occurs before Rosh Chodesh, and not on it. When Rosh Chodesh is on the Sabbath, *Shabbat Mevorchim* is the preceding Sabbath.
2. Based on Talmudic references regarding a dispute over the virginity of a new bride.

[Page 133]

Native Authors of Slutsk and the Vicinity

Translated by Jerrold Landau

Shalom Yaakov Abramowich (Mendele Mocher Seforim)

He was born around the year 5595 (1839) in Kopyl. That date is only an estimate, since Mendele himself only described it as "as accepted in his family."

His father Reb Chaim Moshe was an upright, G-d fearing man, a scholar with good traits, beloved and honored by all the people of his city. He earned his livelihood from leasing the meat tax in his locale. When he was free from work, he would occupy himself with communal affairs, deliver sermons in public, and give a class in Talmud and rabbinic decisors to the youths of the town.

Reb Chaim Moshe was an expert in Talmud and rabbinic literature. He was also fluent in Bible, and conversant in the current world events. The people of the city would bring every difficult matter to his attention. His mother Sara Nisi was a refined woman, with a pale face and a humble heart. She was also erudite in her ways – she knew the techinot [women's petitions], and was a great expert in the popular books *Tzena Urena*, *Menorat Hamaor*, and *Kav Hayashar*, which she would read aloud to the women in the synagogue.

Shalom Yaakov was an exceptional child – with a good intellect and sharp grasp. Within one year he learned how to read and started the study of *Chumash*. Everything that he learned was immediately etched in his memory, and bore fruits. Aside from that, the child had quick impressions, and everything that his eyes saw and his ears heard in his environs, every characteristic movement or unusual mode of speech, he was able to imitate faithfully. Everyone who entered his father's house recognized the good traits of this child who was more intelligent than the peers of his own age. His father especially recognized that his young son was destined for greatness. He was diligent with his education, sparing no effort or monetary expense to find good teachers for the lad, who would not only teach him Gemara and rabbinic decisors, but also the Bible with the Metzudot commentaries, and even grammar to a significant extent – which was a complete innovation in those days.

The luck of the lad was that he had a certain teacher (Yosef Hareuveni – in those days Lipa Hareuveni) who also had the artistic spark. He was a unique persona – a poet and an artist, with wonderful handwriting, who knew every artistic craft and was especially loved by his students. There is no doubt that this teacher-artist nurtured in his students, primarily, a sense of beauty and an aspiration of mastery in every craft. It is possible that he [Mendele] learnt from him while still a lad to "forge and form" until a finished object comes forth from his hands.

The receiving of this Torah study from Lipa Hareuveni exposed the light and song of the Torah of Israel to the lad. However, the greatest enthusiasm and dedication to Torah for its own sake came at age eleven, when he began to study with his father, who used to teach his older sons himself. The lad who was dear to him was already considered as an adult in his eyes. From that time, the study of Torah was not a duty to him, but rather a sort of service from love. When he would arise before dawn and walk with his father to study Torah, he felt the secrets of the night, the song of the night. At that hour, he felt the song of the Torah. "His spirit went forth and became emotional, and his heart was filled with song and holy longing, as he arose and studied Torah for its own sake with a calm spirit and a melody." ("In Those Days") – – –

In his twelfth year, the lad with a poetic sense started to become disgusted with the lack of childish matters which the Mishnah deals with and the Gemara focus upon. Then he began to take breaks from his learning and turn his heart to "vanity" – strolling through the streets of the city and outside of it, visiting the smithy and carpentry shops of his father's two neighbors, witnessing simple, healthy work, listening to sharp, easy words, and seeing the "inventions" of "faithful" artisans, in the manner that was endearing to the simple masses from their childhood. When Reb Chaim Moshe's material situation faltered, he became ill and died in his prime, at the age of 42 or 43 (around 1849), leaving behind a widow and orphans without anything.

Shalom Yaakov was then a thirteen-year-old lad of Bar Mitzvah age. The relatives of the family decided to send him to a place of Torah in the nearby city so that he would not go about idle and would not become a burden upon the widow. In his autobiographical letter, Mendele said, "Then I was immersed in the stormy sea without a guide or counselor." He writes about that period of his life, "The ways of Torah were fulfilled with me[1], and the painful life of scholars, along with eating my meals on a rotation basis [*yamim*] in all the details and minutiae."

At the beginning, he went to Tymkovich, a small town near Kopyl, where he sat and studied in the *Beis Midrash* and partook of his meals on a rotation basis. There he got to know Hassidim for the first time (Kopyl was a city of *Misnagdim*). Their enthusiasm during prayers stuck to him. However, longing for his home overtook him, and he returned to Kopyl.

However, the intense poverty in his house forced him to wander again away from Kopyl. He went to Slutsk, where there was a famous Yeshiva. At first, he studied in the first class, which was designated for young lads. He studied Torah there from "the rabbi of renown, Rabbi Avraham Baruch." After he succeeded in his studies, he "went up" to the highest class, where "The sharp Rosh Yeshiva Rabbi Michael M's" taught. From that Yeshiva, he transferred to "the *Beis Midrash* of the tycoon Reb Yona," where he attended

[Page 134]

the class that the great rabbi, Rabbi Avrahamele, gave to the top students.

Reb Mendele's daughters say that they heard from their father that in Slutsk, the lad Shalom Yaakov would accompany the elderly midwife Sara at night with a flashlight when she had to attend to a birth at night. In return, he had a place to sleep in her house.

When he left Slutsk, as was the way of lads in those days to not settle in one place, he wandered to various towns, and studied Torah in Yeshivas or *Beis Midrash*es in each place. This continued until his wealthy relative Reb Nachum Chaim Broida called upon him to come to Vilna.

In Vilna, he studied in the *Kloiz* of Rabbi Meila, which was famous in those days. He studied in Zhitomir, served as a teacher in Kamenetz, lived in Berdichev, and moved to Odessa.

His first Yiddish story was published in the name of Mendele Mocher Seforim, which became his penname.

His Yiddish stories that were translated into Hebrew include: "The Abridged Journeys of Benjamin the Third," "The Book of Paupers." "In Those Days." In Zhitomir, he wrote "The Nag" [(1873, "My Horse"), as well as "The Travellers of Benjamin the Third" (Yiddish 187, Hebrew 1896), "The Book of Paupers" (1901), "Fishke the Lame."

The characteristic Kavtziel of Mendele appears in his book "The Vale of Tears." Mendele discusses the memories of his childhood and youth in his autobiography "In Those Days."

The Complete Works of Mendele was published seven volumes in Tel Aviv, 5689 [1929], and in one volume in Tel Aviv, 5707 [1947]

Yehuda Grazovski

He was a translator and writer. He was born in Pohost, Slutsk District on February 28, 1862. He was the son of Yeshayahu Reuven (a merchant). He was educated in *cheder*, and the Yeshiva of Volozhin. He was one of the first of Chovevei Tzion. He was in in the Land of Israel from 1887. He was active in Rishon LeZion, and an official in the store there. From 1899, he was a teacher in Ekron, and from 1891 in Zichron Yaakov. He was one of the first to teach Hebrew in Hebrew [*Ivrit beIvrit*], and he was an enthusiastic fighter for the full Hebrew school. In 1891, he made efforts and founded (with D. Yudelevich) "the first teachers' organization," and he was one of the authors of the first curriculum of studies for the Hebrew school. In 1893, he was a secretary of the B.M. headquarters that had moved to Jaffa. He was one of the editors of "Letters to the Land of Israel," a founder of the Hebrew school for boys, and a Hebrew teacher and significant personality there. From 1899, he was a teacher in Mikve Yisrael. From 1905, he was a member of Merkaz Hamorim [Teachers Headquarters]. From 1906-1911, he was vice director of the Anglo Palestine Bank in Beirut, and from 1911-1921, one of the directors of the Anglo Palestine Bank in Jaffa. In 1918, he redeemed the first plot of land on Mount Carmel (for the Ango Palestine Bank and the Organization for Preparation of the Yishuv). He worked a great deal in the literature of teaching and Hebrew agronomy. He authored articles from the Land of Israel to Hebrew newspapers in the Diaspora on a regular basis, especially in *Hashiloach*. His textbooks included: "The Hebrew School" (3 parts), 1895-6. He produced many translations of world literature (Dickens, Jules Verne, Mark Twain, Andersen, and others), especially for youth. He wrote a pocket dictionary (with the participation of Klausner) in 1903; the Hebrew dictionary (with the participation of D. Yellin), 1920; The Dictionary of the Hebrew Language, 1934-5.

Avraham Epstein (Abba Aricha)

He was a native of Slutsk, born n 1877. His literary work began with letters in *Hatzofeh* of Warsaw, which were written in in good form, juicy language, vibrant expression, with a vibrant, lyric style. Indeed, after a few years, his pen began to produce stanzas of poetry. He even had a story printed in several installments in the renewed *Hatzefirah*. He displayed his talents in feuilletons of criticism in *Hameilitz* and *Hazman*, which excelled in their sharpness and beauty of expression.

His literary activity broadened especially after the First World War. He published feuilletons and articles of criticism in the *Aretz* anthology and the *Barkai* newspaper that appeared in Odessa during the time of the Bolshevik revolution, in which his unique talents as a critic were demonstrated. However, he acquired his permanent place in literature when he came to America. He lived in the United States for thirty years, where he disseminated Torah in one of the fine educational institutions in New York and groomed tens of students, full of love for the holy matters of Israel and continuing our cultural traditions. He became vibrant there, and was one of the forgers of the image of Hebrew literature. He also merited to be one of the revealers of Hebrew America, as he dedicated his pen to evaluating the creations of Hebrew writers and poets who sprouted on American soil. These articles and essays were collected in his book "Hebrew Writers of America" which was published by Dvir in Tel Aviv in two volumes.

He died in New York in the year 5713 [1953].

Zalman Wendroff

This was the nickname for Zalman Vendrovsky.

He was born in Slutsk on November 5, 1879. His father was a *shochet*. Until the age of thirteen, he studied in Yeshiva, as well as with private tutors for Hebrew and Russian. He moved to Łódź at the age of eighteen. He worked in a factory, and authored poems and stories. He moved to England where he worked in a soda factory. He lived in Glasgow. He published in *Der Yiddisher Zeitung* a large story about the travels of a young Jew throughout the earth and his longings for a Jewish environment. He settled in London and published stories in *Arbeiter Freind*, the journal of Rudolf Roker. He earned his living by teaching at the Talmud Torah, peddling in villages, and typesetting in a publishing house. He returned to Moscow in 1905, and earned his livelihood by giving English classes. He went to America and travelled through its length and breadth. He participated in *Morgan Journal* and *Americaner*. He was sent to Russia in 1908 as a journalist for *Heint* and *Yiddishes Tag-Blatt*. He lived in Warsaw until June 1915, where he directed the "Jewish Cities and Towns" division of *Heint*. He wrote feuilletons and published articles in *Morgan Journal*, *Americaner*, *Freie Arbeiter Shtime*, and *Yiddish Wachenscrift* of Peretz. He left Warsaw in 1915. He worked in Moscow as the executive representative of the committee for aid to those affected by the war. He participated in the Mafitzei *Haskalah* [Disseminators of Knowledge] group, Az'e [Children's Aid Society], and the society for Jewish historical ethnography. After the March revolution, he was invited to be the Yekopo [Jewish Relief Committee for War Victims] emissary for Ural and Siberia.

He was an official in the Natzminden [Nationalities] Commissariat. He directed the division for journalism and literature in the communications Commissariat He participated in Russian newspapers, specially in Зкономнческая Жизнь [Economic Life].

[Page 135]

He sent his articles to *Tag*, *Forverts*, and *Tzeit* in London. His book "Humoresques and Stories" was published by Shimin Publishing in Warsaw in 1911. His two-volume book of stories *Pravozhitelstvo*[2] was published by Yehudia in 1912. His two volume books of stories "The Wide Smile" and "Laughter Through Tears" were published in 1914, and "Work and Need" was published in Moscow in 1919.

Yaakov Cohen

Uncaptioned. Yaakov Cohen.

He was born in Slutsk, Minsk Region (Russia) in 1881.

He lived in Zgierz, Łódź, Moscow, and Warsaw. He was educated in regular school, and he obtained a Ph.D. from the University of Berne. He edited *Haivri Hechadash* [the New Hebrew], *Haogen* [The Anchor], *Sneh*, and *Hatekufa*. He made *aliya* to the Land in 1934. He was one of the editors of *Knesset*. He translated the following works of Goethe: *Iphigenie auf Tauris*, *Torquato Tasso*, and *Faust*. His works were published in twelve volumes in a jubilee publication by Masada. He won the Bialik prize in 1938, the Tchernichovsky prize twice (1946, 1957), and the Israel prize twice (1953, 1958).

He died in Tel Aviv at the age of eighty on Saturday, 29 Cheshvan 5721, 1960.

Dr. Yaakov Naftali Simchoni

He was born in Slutsk in 1884 and died in Berlin in 1926.

He was a historian and a Hebrew translator. He published several research works on the history of literature during the Middle Ages, and he authored a textbook of Jewish history from ancient times until the crusades. He translated "The War of the Jews" by Josephus Flavius from Greek, with the addition of an introduction and commentary.

Dr. Meir Wachsman

He was an important scholar, writer, and researcher. He was known in the Jewish and general works for his four-volume English book on the history of Jewish literature. The books consist of more than 3,300 pages about the spiritual creativity of the Nation of Israel after the finalization of the Bible: the Talmud, rabbinical decisors, rabbinic literature, Kabala, parables, Hassidism, *Haskalah*, Hebrew literature, Yiddish literature.

Dr. Wachsman served as a professor emeritus in the *Beis Midrash* Latorah in Chicago, and played a significant role in Jewish education from 1925.

In *Beis Midrash* Latorah, known by its English name: Hebrew Theological College, he taught Bible, Jewish history, and philosophy.

Dr. Meir Wachsman was born in Slutsk, and studied in the Yeshiva of Slutsk and other Yeshivot. He was ordained at the age of 18 He graduated cum laude from the famous Columbia University after he came to America. He graduated with an M.A. in 1912, and with a Ph.D. in 1916. He was busy with the preparation of a fifth volume on Hebrew literature during his final twenty-five years.

The writings of Dr. Wachsman include: "Parables of Israel," a translation of "Rome and Jerusalem" by Moshe Hess, "Selected Writings" by himself in several volumes, and a new anthology of his essays "In the Pathways of Literature and Hebrew Thought" published in Tel Aviv.

Dr. Meir Wachsman wrote a great deal in Yiddish and published a series of articles in Yiddish newspapers.

He participated in *Haolam*, *Hatekufa*, *Hadoar*, *Bitzaron*, and many English publications and important encyclopedias.

Dr. Feitel Lifschitz

He was born in Slutsk in 1877.

He published the following important articles:

1.   "What is Political Economics" *Haolam*, year 1, 1912, issue 32.

2.   "Political Economics in its Theories and Streams" Chapter I: The Mercantile Theory, *Hashiloach* 12 (5663-64 1903-04); Chapter II; The Physiocratic Theory; Chapter III: Adam Samet; Chapter IV: Robert Thomas Malthus, 5665 [1905].

Dr. A. Domnitz

He was born on 20 Tevet 5644 [1884] in the town of Romanova. He received his education in Talmud and *Haskalah* literature from his father Reb Asher, a Torah scholar. He studied in the Yeshivot of Slutsk and Minsk. When he left there at the beginning of the century, he became the head of the Zion and its Language society in Minsk, which legislated the speaking of Hebrew amongst its members. When he came to America in 1906, he continued with his Hebrew-Zionist activism. He was the first secretary of the Hebrew league in the United States, which was founded in 1908. He settled in Baltimore from 1919 and worked in his profession of dentistry. For several years, he was the examiner for Hebrew at the University of Maryland. His first literary works appeared at the beginning of 1906. His first poems were published in the first booklets of *Hameorer*. He assisted in the establishment of the first literary endeavors in America during that period. He participated in various publications in America, and in several newspapers in the Land of Israel. Aside from poems, he published literary criticisms and stories. After some time, he edited a Yiddish newspaper in Baltimore dedicated to Zionist publicity and local affairs.

[Page 136]

Yitzchak Dov Berkowitz

He was born in Slutsk on 7 Cheshvan 5646 (October 15, 1885) to his father Ezriel Zelig the son of Dov and his mother Dvosi the daughter of Reuven Rivin. His father was descended from the Chinitz family of Starobin, known at that time of the scion of upright, straight-pathed people, some of whom were great in Torah. He too was erudite, and he engaged in teaching during his youth as well as his old age. For most of his life, he earned his livelihood from manual toil, at first in Slutsk and later in Brooklyn, New York, where he settled in his middle age with his family, and managed a small shop for cleaning and dying clothes. His mother was the native of a village near Slutsk, from a family of cattle merchants and farmers.

He studied in *cheders*. He began to study Gemara at the age of seven, at first from the *melamdim* [teachers] of the *cheders*, and later from the expert Gemara teacher Reb Yosel the Parush in the Synagogue of the Householders. There, he made acquaintance with the future poet Eliahu Lissitzky. They both cleaved to each other in friendship. Later, they both transferred to study in the Yeshiva of Rabbi Nechemia Immerman, by request of his father who sought to turn him into a "complete vessel." During his childhood he studied Hebrew grammar privately from one of his teachers from Hamaslul, and with the influence of his uncle the Maskil Lipa Berkowitz. While he was still a student of the Yeshiva, he was attracted to *Haskalah* books.

He began teaching at the age of fifteen. This was the time of the first Zionist Congresses, and since he was enthusiastic about the vision of redemption and the revival of the Hebrew language, he participated along with other youths, including Avraham Epstein and Hillel Dubrow, in the founding of a Hebrew-Zionist organization called *Dovrei Ivrit*, in which he served as secretary. He even read his first literary attempts at its meetings. As a result, he published, along with his friends, Avraham Epstein and Meir Wachsman, both future writers, a hectographic newspaper called *Hatzair*. He also participated along with his aforementioned friends, in the founding of a public Hebrew library and in giving evening classes for the study of the Hebrew language and history for Yeshiva students in their city.

At the age of seventeen, he was called to Łódź to teach the children of a certain estate owner near the city. There, he connected with love and brotherhood to Yitzchak Katznelson, who became famous in those days for his first poems, and he moved to live in his parents' house. Through the recommendation of Katznelson, his first stories were published in the *Hatzofeh* daily newspaper in Warsaw at the beginning of the year 5664 [1903], in its first competition for Hebrew literature. The judges were Y. L. Peretz, A. L. Levinsky, and Dr. Yosef Klausner. (Twenty-five years later, the hero of his book *Moshkele Chazir* served as the topic of his play "He and His Son" that was adapted for stage in New York by Maurice Schwartz and in Israel by Habima.)

During his first visit to Warsaw, he made acquaintance with Z. Shneur, who was then beginning to publish his first poems. Both of them forged a bond of friendship that never stopped even in the later times.

From Łódź, he was called by his friend Avraham Epstein to Ekaterinoslav, where he worked in teaching. When he returned to Slutsk, he invited Yitzchak Katznelson to be a guest in his parents' home. Then, they both went to Warsaw, and the stopped on the way at the summer home of Dr. Yosef Klausner, where he met Ch. N. Bialik for the first time – one of the great experiences of his childhood years.

In the winter of 5665 [1904-1905], he was called to Vilna as the full-time assistant in *Hazman*. For a half a year, he edited the fine literature in the *Hazman* monthly and wrote for the daily *Hazman*, aside from stories, a weekly feuilleton "In the Cities and Towns," with the signature "Barak." He got to know Sholem Aleichem in Vilna, and during Chanukah of 5666, after the pogroms of October 1905, he married Esther, the oldest daughter of Sholom Aleichem, in Kiev, and moved to Galicia with the family of his father-in-law. He lived in Lvov for a half a year, and moved to Switzerland. He lived in Geneva for a year and a half, where he got to know Mendele Mocher Seforim and M. Ben-Ami. After Sholem Aleichem returned from his first trip to America, he too went there to visit his parents and his family. He remained there for about a year, and published stories and feuilletons in Yiddish newspapers. Then he returned to his family in Geneva, and moved to Italy. He lived with the family of Sholem Aleichem in Nervi near Genoa, and then in the Black Forest.

When he returned to Russia, the first volume of his Hebrew stories was published in Odessa, and an anthology of his Yiddish stories in Warsaw. In 1910, he began to translate the writings of Sholem Aleichem to Hebrew and was called to be the literary editor of *Haolam* (Vilna-Odessa). He lived in Berlin in 1913-1914.

With the outbreak of the First World War, he sailed to America with the family of Sholem Aleichem. In 1915, he founded the *Hatoran* weekly in New York with the assistance of Shmaryahu Levin, and also became its editor. In 1920-1921, he edited the *Miklat* monthly, published by A. Y. Shtibel. In addition to translating the letters of Sholem Aleichem, he prepared and worked his plays for performance in Hebrew and Yiddish. He published "The Sholem Aleichem Book" in New York in 1926. He made *aliya* to the Land in 5688 [1928]. In 5689 [1929], he edited the *Meoznaim* weekly along with P. Lachover. That year, he was chosen as a member of the committee for the Hebrew language, which became the Academy for the Hebrew Language with the founding of the State of Israel. He won the Bialik prize in 5714 [1954], and the Tchernichovsky prize twice for his translation of the works of Shalom Aleichem. He won the Israel prize at the decade of the independence of Israel.

From the time of his *aliya* to the Land of Israel, he moved on from stories about the town and immigration to America to descriptions of the Land. Aside from short stories about life in the Land of Israel, he published his two large books: "The Days of the Messiah" and "Menachem-Mendel in the Land of Israel." During his latter years, he wrote and prepared for publication stories of his first impressions of the Land of Israel, called "Yesterday that has Passed."

Ephraim A. Lissitzky

He was born in Minsk on 15 Shevat 5645, 1885. His mother died when he was seven years old. He moved to Slutsk when his father remarried. His father sailed to America from there, while he and his stepmother remained in Slutsk for about eight and a half years. He received his education in *cheder* and Yeshiva during those years. He came to America when he was about fifteen years old, and studied in the Yeshiva of Rabbi Yitzchak Elchanan[3] for some time. Later, he began to teach Hebrew. He lived in a remote town in Canada for about three years, and served as a sort of town teacher. Then, he moved to Milwaukee, where he entered Marquette University and graduated in pharmaceutical chemistry. However, Hebrew teaching attracted his heart.

[Page 137]

From that time, he worked in teaching in Buffalo and Milwaukee, until he moved to New Orleans and settled there.

His first poem was published in Berner's *Hameorer*. In 5688 [1928] an anthology of his collected poems was published in Tel Aviv. His book *Naftulei Elokim*, a great dramatic vision, was published in 5694 [1934]. His book "Dying Campfires," a poem of accusation regarding the life of the Indians [i.e. Native Americans] in America, was published in 5697 [1937].

His poetry is suffused with despair and cold disappointment. From that pessimistic perspective, Lissitzky set out to deal with his life of oppression within the world in general. He was on one side, opposite the group that destroyed its order; and the Jewish people in general was on the other side, opposite its oppressors and disturbers. Lissitzky knew how to equalize the strength of his poetry with the pathos of his idea. His inclination to search for the obligations of life and find its meaning stands out.

His last books include: *Naftulei Elokim*, Tel Aviv, 5694 [1934]; "The Annals of Man," "Man On Earth," New York, 5706 [1946]; "In the Tents of Kush" Jerusalem 5714 [1954]; *Bemaalot Ubemuradot* [On the Ascents and Descents], Tel Aviv, 5714 [1954]; *Negohot Bearafel* [Illumination in the Fog] Tel Aviv 5717 [1954]; *Anshei Midot* [People of Stature] Jerusalem 5718 [1958].

Baruch Katznelson

He was born on December 21, 1900 in Slutsk. He was educated in *cheders* and Yeshiva, and he also was involved in secular studies. From 1919 until the end of 1924, he wrote and published poems and works of criticism in Yiddish. From that time and onward, he wrote in Hebrew. He came to America in 1922 and worked in teaching. He made *aliya* to the Land of Israel in the year 5695 – 1934, and settled in Kfar Saba. He worked in his orchard until the end of the Second World War.

He is currently a teacher of Hebrew studies in the Kfar Saba high school.

He was a member of the local council and its leadership from 1939-1943.

His books include: *Leor Haner* [To the Light of the Candle], published by Ogen, New York 1930; *Bechor Demama* [A Silent Firstborn] published by Neuman 1948; *Milev El Lev* [From Heart to Heart] published by Agudat Hasofrim, Dvir, 1954.

Reuven Wallenrod

He was a Hebrew writer, born in Vizno.

He studied in *cheder* and Yeshiva, and later in the Real School in Slutsk. He came to the Land of Israel in the year 5680 [1920]. He worked in paving roads in Tiberias and later in Kfar Yechezkel. From the Land of Israel, he went to France and then to the United States. In America, he earned his livelihood from factory work. At the same time, he studied in New York University and Columbia. He authored research works at the Sorbonne University in Paris. He was a teacher of Hebrew literature at Brooklyn College.

His stories are dedicated to portraying the realities of Jews in Jew York, and describe the new life in America. Wallenrod primarily attempts to describe the change of fate of the immigrants from Eastern Europe who were seeking to strike roots in their new country.

His books include: "In the Third Diota" Tel Aviv 1937; "In the Family Circle" New York, 1939; "Pathways in New American Literature" New York, 1940; "For the Day has Declined"[4] Tel Aviv, 1946; "Between the Walls of New York" Jerusalem 5713 [1953]; "With No Generation" Tel Aviv 5713 [1953].

In the Margins of the Section

1. History of the writers who were from Hlusk, Lyuban, and Kopyl appear in the sections of those towns.

2. All the material was edited in chronological order, from encyclopedias and lexicons.

Translator's footnotes:

1. A reference to *Pirkei Avot* 6:4: Such is the way [of a life] of Torah: you shall eat bread with salt, and rationed water shall you drink; you shall sleep on the ground, your life will be one of privation, and in Torah shall you labor. [Translation from Sefaria].
2. A term for the legal right to live outside the Pale of Settlement.
3. Yeshiva University.
4. *Ki Panah Yom* – For the Day has Declined – is taken from the *Neila* service, where it stresses that the day of Yom Kippur is rapidly coming to a conclusion.

[Page 138]

Rabbis and Authors of Rabbinics

Translated by Jerrold Landau

Baruch the son of Reb Yaakov Shklover

He was a scholar, a doctor, and a transcriber of science books. He was born on 7 Adar 5512 – 1752 in Shklov, and died on Rosh Chodesh Adar 5570 – 1810 in Slutsk. His family was sometimes called Shi'k, which is the acronym of Reb Shmuel Yehuda Katzenelbogen, for Raba'sh [i.e. Rabbi Baruch Shklover] was related to him. He was also known as "doctor" for he was a medical physician. Toward the end of his life, he was the physician in the home of Prince Radziwill. The descendants of Raba'sh were called "Baruchin," named after their father Reb Baruch. He studied in Shklov and then in Padua, Italy. He excelled in in his studies. In 1764, he was ordained by Rabbi Avraham Katzenelbogen the rabbi of Brisk, and was appointed as a rabbinical judge in Minsk. He later moved to England, where he studied medicine.

He was in Berlin in 1777, and published the book *Yesod Olam* [Foundations of the World] by Rabbi Y. HaYisraeli, with his addition of brief notes. He authored the book *Amudei Shamayim* [Pillars of Heaven], an explanation of the laws of the sanctification of the New Moon by the Rambam, with *Tiferet Adam* [Glory of Man] at the end, about the science of pathways (Berlin 1777); and *Derech Yeshara* [The Straight Path] on preserving health (Hague, 1779).

He returned to Russia, and was received lovingly in Vilna by the Gr'a. He supported him in transcribing books of wisdom and science into Hebrew. Raba'sh translated six volumes of the books of Euclid, published with three tables (Amsterdam, 1780). He authored the book *Kaneh Hamida* [The Measuring Rod] regarding the science of triangles. He settled in the palace of Reb Yehoshua Zeitlish near Cherkov in the region of Mohilev, and studied together with other scholas who occupied themselves with Torah. He conducted chemistry tests in a special room. He came to Slutsk a few years before his death and was accepted as a rabbinical judge. He was a physician in the house of Prince Radziwill, and lived in Slutsk util his death.

The Gaon Rabbi Eli Zuta

The Gaon Rabbi Eliyahu Zuta died on the first day of Passover 5556 [1796]. The following is inscribed on his gravestone:

Here is buried the author of the book *Tana Debei Eliyahu*. He diligently produced ten works on the Talmud and the Four Turim. He was a rabbi of renown. Our teacher Rabbi Eliahu the son of Rabbi M' Aharon, died on the first day of Passover 5556 here in Slutsk.

May his soul be bound in the bonds of eternal life.

Rabbi Avraham Moshe HaLevi Shevelov, the head of the rabbinical court of Svislach

He was born on 7 Adar 5606 [1846] to his renowned father Rabbi Menachem. At the age of thirteen, he studied with the Gaon Rabbi Yosef Dov-Ber Halevi, and was ordained at the age of 22.

He was accepted as the rabbi in Svislach in the year 5636 [1876]. He died suddenly in his prime on 19 Tevet 5642 [1882] after serving in the rabbinate for six years.

He left manuscripts of responsa and commentary. He printed articles in Halevanon under the name of Emesh.

Rabbi Tzvi Masliansky

He was born in Slutsk in the year 5617 [1857]. He appeared on the preacher's podium along with the awakening of the national idea. To this day, he remains the lion of the group, and the chief of the Zionist preachers. His speaking talents and enthusiastic emotion while delivering a sermon were amazing. His sermons were full of life, with wonderful illustrations from the lives of the fathers of our nation and their events, from which he surveyed the life of the nation in the Diaspora. He aroused the spirit of national might and pride amongst his brethren through the strength of his words.

In the year 5655 [1895] he visited the Jewish communities of Germany, Belgium, and England where he encouraged the spirit of the nation through his words. He preached in New York for several decades.

He was rightly considered as the chief of preaching and a first-class national spokesman. He dedicated his talents to raising the spirit of his nation.

He authored *Drashot Masliansky* [Masliansky's Sermons] in three volumes. The first two volumes include sermons for all the Sabbaths of the year, as well as the festivals. The third section is "sermonizing material." He also published the book *Zichronot Udrashot* [Memoirs and Sermons] in three parts.

Rabbi Aharon Heiman

He was a rabbi from 1885, as well as an author and researcher. He was born in Slutsk in 5623 [1863], the son of Mordechai (a merchant from a rabbinical family). He was the father-in-law of the philanthropist Harry Fishel of the United States. He was educated in cheder, and the Yeshivot of Bobruisk and Volozhin.

He was a rabbinical judge in Londin from 1885-1932. He founded the Etz Chaim Yeshiva and the Chevra Shas [Talmud study group] there, and was its gabbai and principal for ten years. He founded the union of shochtim in England.

He was a member of the Zionist Center and the vice president of Mizrachi in England. He wrote articles in scientific and Torah newspapers. He authored; *Beit Vaad Lachachamim* [A Gathering Place for Sages], 1901; *History of the Tannaim and Amoraim* [History of the Mishnaic and Talmudic sages] (3 volumes), 1911; "Letters of Rabbi Sharira Gaon" and the *Patshegen Haktav* commentary, 1911; "A Treasury of the Languages of the Sages and their Adages" 1934; "The Written Torah and Tradition."

[Page 139]

Personalities of Israel
Part I
Tractate Shabbat

Novellae and Explanations on Order Moed of the Gemara
Yisrael Isser the son of our teacher Rabbi Mordechai, may he live Isserlin of Slutsk
The author of the book Shem Yisrael on Order Zeraim of the Mishnah
Published in Vilna 5624, 1984
(From the front page of the book)

Rabbi Yaakov of Tomaszów

The great rabbi, Rabbi Menachem Nachum the son of the Gaon Rabbi Meir Katz, the brother of the Gaon the Sha'ch. He was the son in law of the Gaon Maharsha'k, and served the rabbi and Gaon Rabbi Yaakov of Tomaszów in his high-level Yeshiva in the holy community of Slutsk. (*Birchat Hazevach Menachot*, chapter 6). He went out along with the exiles. He published the book *Birchat Hazevach* of his father-in-law the Gaon in the year of *mishpat* (5429) [1669].

Kiryah Neemana, Vilna 5620 [1860], page 26.

Yaakov Tzvi Brodotzki

He was born in Slutsk on May 14, 1873 to a clerical family. He studied in Yeshivot. He was a *shochet* [ritual slaughterer], a *maggid* [preacher], and a *melamed* [teacher]. He moved to Irkutsk, Siberia, where he was a teacher, and the *shamash* [sexton] in the synagogue from 1908.

He published the book *Midrash Tzadikim* in Hebrew in the year 5659 [1899], a refutation against Parisian fashions. He published articles in *Hameilitz*, *Hatzefirah*, *Hazman*, *Haderech*, and *Hamodia*. As an addendum to *Hamodia*, he listed Talmudic aphorisms --- 300 adages worked into verse.

He was dedicated to the research of Jews in Siberia and Ural. His works were published in various newspapers.

He was active in communal institutions and in the Zionist Organization.

Rabbi Reuven Maharsha'k,
the author of the book *Dudaei Harab's*

Rabbi Shmuel Dov the son of Rabbi Shimon Yitzchak Maharsha'k

The rabbi was pleasant in his mannerisms and wondrous in his wisdom. He was born in Pohost on 9 Adar 5637 [1877] to a family of good pedigree, descended from the Maharsha'k, may the memory of the holy be blessed.

Uncaptioned. Rabbi Shmuel Dov.

He studied with his maternal grandfather Rabbi Avraham Rabinovich (the rabbi of the city of Pohost). When his father the *shochet* died, he learned the craft of *shechita*, and took his father's place. He served as the *shochet* in the city of Slutsk and was an enthusiastic lover of Zion. He arrived in America in the year 5683 [1923] and was accepted as a *shochet* in Rochester. He published works of Torah and participated in Hebrew newspapers. His book *Hegyonei Shmuel* on *Aggadah* (Talmudic lore) was published in 5694 [1934].

Rabbi Leib Neumark

He was tall with a long beard and intelligent eyes. His entire presence exuded splendor, and he dressed finely. He was a rabbinical judge and rabbinical teacher [*Moreh Tzedek*] in Slutsk. He was an intelligent man and calm in his manner. He would straighten out matters and he was ready for any case of arbitration or dispute.

His hand was involved in everything. His mouth exuded pearls, and he would rend hearts with his eulogies. They would say about him, "Reb Leib – he is the lion that roars, and who is not afraid?"[1]

He was a preacher, a scholar, a pursuer of peace, a Yeshiva head, and rabbinical teacher in Slutsk. He authored the book *Even Yaakov* on sermons and moral lessons from Tractate *Avot*.

Rabbi Moshe Binyamin Tomashov

He was a sharp rabbi, the son of Rabbi Yehoshua Sender. He was born in Slutsk on 7 Adar 5638 [1878]. He studied in the Yeshiva of Slutsk, and when he was still young, he became known as an *Illui* [genius] for his talents, his wonderful memory, and his great expertise in Talmud and rabbinical decisors.

He married the daughter of the Gaon Rabbi Tzvi Yaakov Aspenheim of Kelm at the age of nineteen. He opened a printing house in Slutsk, and earned his livelihood in a comfortable fashion. He moved to New York in the year 5673 [1913]. He published a Torah anthology titled *Yagdil Torah* in Slutsk along with Rabbi Isser Zalman Meltzer of blessed memory. The great rabbis and scholars of renown participated in it.

[Page 140]

Many of his novellae appear in that anthology. He authored various books (see the list by Rabbi Nissan Wachsman in "Slutsk, the Host of Torah.")

Translator's footnote:

1. Based on Amos 3:8.

Rabbis Who Were Born in Slutsk

Translated by Jerrold Landau

(Who are mentioned in the book "The City of Vilna" by Steinschneider, 5660 [1900].)

Aryeh Leib Aharonovich, a rabbi of Slutsk, mentioned in the list of Lithuania (6) 472 (March 3, 1720).

* * *

Rabbi Yekutiel the son of Rabbi Yaakov Zusman HaKohen Kaplan, head of the rabbinical court of Starobin, born in Slutsk in the year 5599 (1739).

* * *

Rabbi Menachem Mendel Aharonson, 16 Cheshvan 5635 (1875).

* * *

Rabbi Alexander the son of Rabbi Alexander, a *parnas* [communal administrator] and leader in Slutsk.

* * *

Rabbi Yoel Chefetz.

* * *

Rabbi Shmuel Maltzman, known as the Maggid [preacher] of Slutsk. The greats of the generation testified regarding him that he was "great in Torah and the fear of G-d." He was the author of the book *Even Shleima*, an anthology of the words of the Gr'a, may the memory of the holy be blessed.

* * *

The rabbi and Gaon Rabbi Naftali Tzvi, head of the rabbinical court of Starobin, son of Rabbi Moshe, son of Rabbi Naftali Tzvi, son of the Rema, who was the author of the *Mapa* on the Code of Jewish Law.

* * *

Rabbi Tzemach the son of Rabbi Yosef rabbi and head of the rabbinical court in Slutsk.

* * *

The Rabbi and *Nagid* [leader] Rabbi David Kreines.

* * *

The book of Rabbi BenZion Eisenstat tells of Rabbi Avraham Yitzchak Masliansky of Slutsk. He lived in London for twelve years, and came to New York during his old age.

* * *

Rabbi Asher Sandomirsky (son-in-law of Rabbi Shachna, the well-known *Shamash*). He was a Yeshiva head and *Mashgiach* [Yeshiva supervisor and guide] in the Etz Chaim Yeshiva of Slutsk during the years 1913-1920.

* * *

Rabbi Yechiel Michel the son of Rabbi Mordechai Yona Rabinovich. He was born in Slutsk. He was the rabbi in Szuszczyn in 1928. He authored a two-volume book called *Afikei Yam*.

* * *

Rabbi Yehuda Tzvi Meltzer, the son of the Gaon Rabbi Isser Zalman of blessed memory. He was the rabbi of Pardes Chana and Rechovot. Today, he is the head of the rabbinical court in Rechovot, and head of Yeshivat Hadarom.

Rabbi Moshe Yissachar Goldberg

Uncaptioned. Rabbi Goldberg.

He was the grandson of Kadish the Melamed. He was born in Slutsk on May 15, 1905. He studied in the Etz Chaim Yeshiva of Slutsk and the Yeshiva Rabbi Yitzchak Elchanan in New York. After he received his ordination, he served as a rabbi in New Orleans, Louisiana, for twenty years.

He died on 9 Kislev, 5720 [1959].

[Page 141]

Between Governments

by Tzach

(In the wake of an event that occurred.)

Translated by Jerrold Landau

A period of great upheaval passed over Russia following the October revolution.

Endless bitter battles took place between the Bolsheviks and their opponents. One regime followed the other: Bolsheviks Germans Poles, Ukrainians. Hetmans [field marshals], generals and ordinary captains formed factions. Jews were the scapegoat during this battle.

A wave of disturbances against the Jews of Russia ensued. There was murder, slaughter, and pogroms. Man turned into a wild beast. Leaders arose for the man-beast, encouraging and inflaming him to deeds of murder. Let the following names be remembered for eternal contempt: Petliura, Denikin, Kolchak, Wrangel,

Balachowicz, Makhno, Semesenko, Grigurov, and Zliunov along with the names of Bogdan Chmielnicki and Gonta.

The cup passed through Slutsk as well. The regime changed and everyone pursued their predecessor with fury. Gangs of Belorussian murderers arose who took out their anger upon the Jews.

The Jews of Slutsk who traveled from city to city for business were captured by one of the gangs, whose members tortured them, murdered them, and then set them on fire. They brought the charred corpses to the city. All the Jews gathered around, and when they saw the slaughtered corpses, a cry burst forth from their throats: "L-rd G-d, please save us." The place turned into a place of fear, weeping, and grief. A sense of atrocity and fear peered forth from their eyes. The youths made fists and gritted their teeth: Shall we fall to the perpetrators as guilty people?

* * *

In 1920, White Russia was in the hands of the Poles. However, the Poles began to retreat from the entire front after maintaining their regime throughout the Minsk region for a year. The Red Army opened a strong attack and expelled the Poles from Russia. They broke through the expanse of Poland and reached Warsaw while called out their fiery motto: We will advance to Warsaw.

The Poles displayed their heavy arm against the Jewish residents of Slutsk already during the first period after their entry. Previously, however, they displayed some sort of restraint, expressing themselves only with cursing the Jews, trimming their beards, cutting off their *peyos*, and uttering disparaging words. Things did not get more serious at that point, but along with their retreat, they began to pour out their wrath and anger against the Jews.

The front approached Slutsk, and the Polish soldiers became crueller. They began with looting. They would enter a shop and take what they wanted without paying. At first, the Jews tried to protect their property, but there were several cases where they paid a heavy price for daring to stand up to the pillagers. In one shop on Zarcha Street, the soldiers took the entire stock. The shopkeeper who was left emptyhanded pleaded with them, implored and begged. When none of this helped, and seeing that they were preparing to take his money, out of despair he grabbed the soldier who was holding the money in his hand and dragged him by force. The coins scattered on the ground. Both the Jew and the soldier crawled on the ground and started to collect the scattered coins, one from one side and the other from the other. The soldier became infuriated, grabbed his revolver, and within a moment shot a bullet through the heart of the shopkeeper.

This incident instilled fear and terror upon the entire city. Complaints to the authorities were to no avail. The high captains looked with hatred upon the Jews who came to complain, and would say: "There is no problem, you must be Bolsheviks, and it is no big deal if they flay your skin a bit." The soldiers, however, spewed forth the entire venom from their mouths and began to perpetrate a wave of organized attacks. They would go from street to street and house to house with nobody to stop them. In the best case, they would only pillage what they saw. They would respond to any resistance with death blows. Their fear was especially great with the young women, and several cases of rape took place.

When the soldiers entered the houses, the Jews would abandon them, and burst forth outside shouting loudly: "*Gevald! Pazshar!*" [Alarm! Fire!]. There were cases where the screams were effective. The residents of Bobruiskai Street perfected this. When the soldiers came to a house on that street, all the residents would gather around and begin to shout: "*Gevald, Pazshar, Ratevet.*" [Alarm, Fire, Save us]. The screams were already well organized, and it was as if they had already mastered them, and their voices spread through the entire street. They would heed with their ears, and the accompany and chase the soldiers everywhere. The soldiers were left without recourse to fight against them, and they would scatter and administer beatings to the crowd. When they entered another house, the Jews would again gather and start to scream, until they [the soldiers] were forced to leave the street. In fact, that street suffered relatively less than the other streets.

In particular, a great fear would fall upon the residents of the city at night, when the pillaging reached its pinnacle. They would sleep in their clothes, ready to escape. They had already hidden their valuables some time previously. They would pack the rest of their belongings for fear of a fire, but it would be easier for the hooligans to pillage them.

Slutsk endured several days of fear and trepidation in this manner. The Jews went about as shadows. Nobody was certain of their lives and property. Despair increased. Only by acting with caution did the hope remain that the Bolsheviks might arrive in town while there was still time.

* * *

The Bolsheviks advanced continually, and already afflicted the city. The Poles prepared to retreat. Valuables were packed quickly and sent outside the city. Anything that they could not take was given over to be consumed by fire.

[Page 142]

The entire neighborhood was lit up at night: villages and farms were on fire. The horizon was always red. Then Slutsk itself was engulfed in flames. Bridges were blown up and warehouses were set on fire. The large, three-story business school that rose in splendor at the edge of the city, went up in flames, as did other houses. The sound of the shooting of cannons could already be heard from close by, and explosive cannonballs reached the city. Houses were ruined and destroyed… Within this upheaval, the Polish soldiers still found time to torture the Jews, even though they knew that they would have to leave the city within a short time. They would hasten to their prey.

Then, three tall, thin soldiers entered a certain house at the edge of the city near a wide field. Their faces were fiery and their eyes exuded fury. They were carrying in their hands some packages that they had still managed to pillage from several houses. A Jewish family with their only daughter Mirele lived in that house. Despite the urging of the neighbors, they did not want to leave the house under any circumstance. The young daughter did not want to part from her parents. By chance, the soldiers had skipped over that house all the time, but this time, the cup was passed to them as well.

"Mirele, escape quickly from here," the distressed mother managed to shout. But the soldiers had already sealed the door. They had not yet been able to see clearly who was in the house. "Give money, Jew," shouted one of the soldiers to Mirele's father in a scary voice, as he waved his fist toward his face. They spread out to the rooms, with one searching through the closet and the second dealing with the drawer.

Mirele stood in her place in shock. Her thoughts raced through her head. One soldier shut the door and stood next to her, as two of them grabbed Mirele and tossed her on the bed. At the first moment that they touched her she was in shock, and she lost consciousness and was not aware of anything. However, when a heavy hand began to grope her body hungrily, she regained consciousness and clearly realized what was about to happen to her. A shudder went through her body, and without uttering a word, she used her remaining energy to protect her life and her honor. She bit with her teeth and mauled with her nails, but what is the strength of a weak girl against two healthy soldiers who were overcome with lust, and whose strength was doubled due to the victim being in their hands?

One soldier grabbed her hands and the second began to rip off her shirt and dress. Mirele continued to struggle, but her resistance weakened. She felt heavy breathing next to her. She saw a fearsome face near her face, black, covered with ash from the fire, and with a layer of mud, and as if overtaken by spasms. With amazing clarity, she saw a shaggy head of hair, large, yellow teeth bared like a wolf ready to maul its prey, a large, broad nose making a cruel gesture at her. She felt that her legs were exposed, and a heavy body hovering over her… Her energy left her, her breath stopped. In despair, she placed her two hands on the soldier's neck and attempted to strangle him… At that moment, the shutter of one of the windows opened, and a scream was heard from many mouths: "*Gevald, Pazshar!!!*" The scream was mighty and frightening. Various different voices were heard: the heavy voices of men, crying out and shouting; the voices full of wailing and sobbing of women; as well as the thin voices of children. Great fear, terror and despair were sensed from these voices – the end of all the ends…

The soldiers were shaken by the suddenness of this scream, and they flinched. Suddenly, Mirele gained a huge amount of energy. She pushed away the soldiers with force, jumped toward the window with the open shutter, shattered the windowpane with her two hands, and stood before the crowd of Jews that had gathered next to the house. Her hair was disheveled, anger came forth from her mouth, and her eyes rose from their sockets. Her dress and shirt were ripped, and the cleavage of her body could be seen through the holes in her clothes.

She raised who two hands that had been cut from the glass shards toward the Jews. She stood in her place, with her face overcome by fright and terror. When the Jews saw her, they renewed the screaming and wailing with greater intensity. Some of them spread their hands toward her. They banged their hands together, and women began to tear out the hear of their heads. Suddenly… noise and panic were heard, the sound of shooting approached, the rattle of cannons. The galloping of horses could be heard, along with shouts of "Hurrah, Hurrah"… the Bolsheviks had penetrated the city.

The Polish soldiers who were still standing in shock from the screams of the Jews recovered their composure, burst forth from the house, and tried to escape through the fields. However, the Jews surrounded them from all sides. "Capture them, grab them," they shouted. It was as if the fear had departed from them. A single feeling pervaded the crowd: revenge for the atrocities, for the honor that had been disgraced and degraded, for the life that was snuffed out, for the women who had been raped. People lay their hands toward the soldiers from all directions. All the suffering and bitterness that were enclosed within the soul burst out in new paths. They began to grab the soldiers, remove their armored helmets, beat them with clenched fists and with the broken sticks and boards that were rolling about, with anything that they could get their hands on.

The soldiers, who could not imagine such brazenness from the Jews, were subdued. It was as if the expression on their cruel faces had melted. They stood without any recourse against the large crowd who surrounded them. Their faces exuded despair. Their faces quickly turned into a pile of puffy dough. They fell to the ground. People trampled over them, beat them, and slapped the mercilessly…

In the meantime, shouts of joy were heard in the streets. The Poles fled from the city, and the few who did not succeed in escaping were subject to the justice of the lynching crowd. Bolsheviks appeared from all directions, with smoking guns in their hands. They were drunk from victory.

The Jews greeted the soldiers with shouts of joy. They hugged them, wept from joy, with their faces beaming. What awaited them in the future did not matter. They did not care that they had not experienced contentment during the time of Bolshevik rule. The main thing was to be free of the terrible nightmare that they had endured, and not to think too much about the future. For at the current moment, the entry of the Bolsheviks was a sign of liberation, and the protection of life and honor.

[Page 143]

The Holocaust

The Jews of Slutsk During the German Occupation

by Steiman

Translated by Mira Eckhaus

Reported by Daniel Mlodinov, 17 years old, the son of Binyamin Mlodinov, the shoemaker. He was born in Slutsk and escaped from there during the liquidation. He lived as a Christian and hid in the forests around Slutsk and arrived in Bialystok.

At the outbreak of the war, approximately 13,000 Jews lived in Slutsk. Among them were refugees from Poland, who arrived in 1939.

On July 5, 1941, the German occupiers entered Slutsk. Rumors were spread that they would exterminate all the Jews. There were also cases where the Germans shot Jews who uttered words that displeased them.

For seven months the Jews lived in their apartments. The Germans required them to work in all kinds of hard work, in the construction of roads, in the construction of buildings and barracks, etc.

A Nazi tank division advances from the direction of Minsk, Slutsk goes up in flames, fire and smoke according to description of a German from Berlin.

(photo-radio from "New York Times", July 22, 1941)

[Page 144]

During the work, they beat them to death with whips, rifle butts and tortured them with unusual cruelty. The tombstones of the cemetery were moved from their place and laid as foundations for four German residences.

One Sunday, in November 1941, a Lithuanian regiment arrived in Slutsk to exterminate Slutsk Jews. Some of them surrounded the city and the rest went from house to house looking for Jews. A Jew who happened to be on the street, or was found in a house, was shot on the spot, the property of the Jews was looted.

In just a few hours, about 500 Jews were exterminated that day. The majority managed to hide and escape. After this action the Lithuanian regiment left the city.

In January 1942, Slutsk Jews were imprisoned in two ghettos. In one ghetto, children, the elderly and the unqualified for work were put. A total of 1,000 Jews. This ghetto was outside the city. The other ghetto, where 5,000 people and their families were put, was in the center of the city and surrounded about 40 houses. Both ghettos were fenced with three electrified wires.

In May 1942, the first ghetto was liquidated. It was surrounded in one of the days, all the Jews were put on trucks and taken outside the city, to a place where they were shot, according to the information received from the local population.

Half a year later, on November 8, 1942, the second ghetto was also liquidated. On November 7, the ghetto was surrounded by a reinforcement guard of Lithuanians. On the morning of the 8th of November, the Lithuanians entered the ghetto and began to take the Jews out of the city in trucks. They abused them. Small children were taken out of their mothers' arms from their hiding place and were shot. Many were thrown to the ground and brutally murdered. At the same time, a group of ten Jews (who had hidden weapons in their hands) opened fire on the Germans.

The Germans, wanting to prevent a Jewish uprising, decided to set the ghetto on fire and burn the Jews alive. They poured gasoline on the houses and set them on fire. Almost all Slutsk Jews perished in this fire. About 25 Jews managed to break through the wired fence and joined the partisans around the city. Among the survivors were the 18-year-old Galansan and his mother who was 35 years old.

Written by Steiman

Signature of the witness Mlodinov from, Bialystok, 31.5.1945. Written and recorded in the protocol by the chairman of the historical committee.

(Translated from Yiddish to Hebrew, from the Yad Vashem Archives, no. 11/317 m).

Slutsk after World War II

by Morris Hindus

Translated by Mira Eckhaus

Morris Hindus, writer and journalist was born in Slutsk and was the first American Jew, who was allowed in 1944 to travel as a journalist, with the Red Army and to enter Slutsk after the Nazis withdrew from the city. At the same time, he printed his reviews and impressions in a series of articles in the "New York Herald Tribune". This article was written by Mr. Hindus especially for the Slutsk's book.

In the middle of November 1944, I made my way in an old and squeaky Ford from Minsk to Slutsk. Some Soviet officials from Minsk, who knew Slutsk, joined me on this journey.

We passed through desolated areas. From both sides of the road, black smokestacks stood out, crushed and sooty parts, remnants, which were left from the towns and villages, which were previously inhabited by masses of residents. In their retreat, the Germans destroyed everything and set on fire everything they encountered on their way.

We drove for hours and never saw Slutsk again. When my companions to the journey noticed that I was impatient, the comforted me and told me all the time that we will arrive soon, because there is no way to skip it. Slutsk was a big city and even though the landmarks and traffic signs were destroyed, they were sure, that we will see it stretched on both sides of the road.

But we didn't see it. We continued our journey, unaware of the fact that we were already far away from our destination. We delayed a villager, an old bent woman, who was carrying heavy load of firewood and we asked her what was the distance between us to Slutsk. We realized that we had already passed the city by 10 kilometers.

I mention this event in order to point out that during our journey, we could not get to know the city for a simple reason: the destruction and devastation were terrible and horrible, more than all the ruins I saw in ruined and desolated Russia. And I, after all, also saw Stalingrad in its ruins.

We drove first in the direction of the former Gutzeit flour mill. On the way to the market, I saw only a few buildings. The market, as I remembered, was crowded and noisy in the fall and now – it was deserted and empty. There was no squealing of geese, croaking of chickens, snorting of pigs, as it was accustomed during November in Slutsk on market days. Not even a single farmer carrying a full sack on his back, or holding in his hand a basket full of apples and pears, for which Slutsk and its surroundings were famous, was seen.

I will remember for the rest of my life the shock and grief that accompanied my steps on the broad street. I couldn't recognize that favorite street in the city. The avenue has disappeared completely. Out of revenge, the Germans cut down all the beautiful trees and left protruding roots and bushes with wild grass. The beautiful houses in the city were destroyed and demolished. The Lutheran church, which stood out with its Gothic spire and its ancient shape, was cracked and unstable - a collapsing building. The playground, that was nice and great, turned into a deserted wasteland.

Kapoli Street should be called the "Slaughter Street". No traces of a street were seen at all, because all the houses were ruined. On this street, behind wired fences and corrals, Jews were rounded up and exterminated. No one was able to tell me how many Jews were murdered. The only thing I could find out was that out of a population of 23,000, a third of the residents were Jewish, and only a few escaped and survived the

[Page 145]

extermination. Tangled and rusted barbed wire, which they did not have enough time to remove, were silent witnesses to the terrible killing place it was.

Slutsk was occupied by the Germans three days after the outbreak of war. Several Jews fled on the first day of the war, when they heard the noise of the German planes, which flew over the city. With the silencing of the transportation of trains and automobiles, as they were recruited for the needs of the army, the only means of escape was walking. Three of my cousins: Raphael, Gershon and Shlomo Gindelwitz, gathered their families and walked from here to Russia. Gershon came to a village on the Volga and settled there. Raphael and Shlomo, who were members of the kolkhoz in Slutsk, arrived in a village near Kostroma and joined the kolkhoz there.

By escaping they saved themselves from certain death.

According to reports from Soviet officials, no more than a hundred Jewish families left the city and they managed to reach safe districts throughout Russia by walking. They could not tell me clearly who they were and where they sat down.

The rest of the Jews stayed in Slutsk. They could not imagine and believe that the Germans were corrupt and such cruel murderers. They hoped that they could somehow continue their lives even in the difficult conditions. It did not occur to them, that the Germans would organize a massacre of the elderly, women and children. This was the fatal mistake of our brothers and sisters of the people of Israel, not only in Slutsk but also in all of White Russia.

The Germans showed no signs of hatred with the occupation of Slutsk. The Jewish community received an order to choose a representative, who would appear as its proxy before the German commandant. Attorney Chipchin was chosen for this position. For several weeks it seemed that he was doing well with the new city masters. However, one day the Germans called a Jewish assembly, to give them an opportunity, so to speak, to express their claims and demands in public. Chipchin was the first speaker. But before he could say a few words, a German officer drew his pistol and shot him dead. He was the first victim in Slutsk.

The Jewish community was filled with fear and horror. For the first time, the Jews realized, that the devil is blacker than black and more terrible than they could have imagined. Again, they felt that they were helpless and had no power to prevent them from doing evil. Only a few of them planned an escape. One of the women, called Mishlov, risked her life and left the city with her two children. Her light hair and blue eyes, along with a fake passport, assisted her to escape from the hands of the Nazis.

Three old men, the Neimark brothers, managed to reach the Russian positions. A few more managed to escape, but none of those I talked to could call them by name. Slutsk was surrounded by strong partisan battalions and the Germans were so afraid of them that they rarely dared to travel and wander on the roads.

I visited the villages around Slutsk. Even the geese of the village farmers were not touched by the Germans. Those villages were far from the main road, and the Germans left them. They did not even risk themselves by taking geese, whose meat was very tasty. Other Young Jewish people from Slutsk managed to escape from the city and joined the partisans. During my stay in the city, these young men were recruited into the Red Army and were at the front and I did not have the opportunity to talk to them.

Why didn't the Jewish youth as a whole join the partisans? Common sense dictated that if they were among the partisans, their lives would be safe, except for the risk of being killed on the battlefield, or from an anti-Semite partisan bullet. And indeed, the residents said that a few anti-Semites were found among the partisans. The mayor of Slutsk, who was the chief commander of the partisan battalions at the time, told me that the Jews did not suffer from anti-Semitism under his command and he rebuked the anti-Semites and punished them severely. Besides that, the Jewish partisans were armed like Christians and could also defend themselves.

It was a fact that not only in Slutsk, but in all of White Russia, relatively few Jews joined the partisans. My friend Meir Hendler, a reporter for "Unites Press" in Moscow, visited the Pinsk district during my stay in Slutsk. When we met, we compared our lists. He brought from Pinsk the same horrifying and heart-wrenching news as from Slutsk, Minsk, Pohust and other communities. The question that arose was why?

In Slutsk I met a Christian carpenter called Popov. He told me that on one of the evenings during the occupation, the wife of a Jewish hairdresser named Melnik, entered running to his workshop and asked him to save her children. Popov went with her to her house and took her three children and brought them to his house. They were at his house for a week. Since he was afraid to keep them in his house, the mother came and wanted to take them home. Popov begged her to go with her children to the partisans. He was one of their secret agents. He offered to help her with the transfer to the partisan territory. She refused. Had I been alone, she emphasized, I would have tried, but with the children, I will not succeed and without them I will not go». She ignored his solicitations and pleas and kept with her refusal. A short time later, she was murdered with her children.

There were many cases when mothers, fathers, sons and daughters, could save themselves, had they transferred to the partisans separately, but they did not want to be separated one from the other. This is how parents perished together with their sons, sons and daughters with their fathers. The German horror united Jewish families until the last moment. They ended their lives behind the barbed wire fences on Kapoli Street.

Addendum by Rabbi Nissan Waxman

In a personal conversation with Mr. Hindus, after receiving his article, I asked him to remember and tell me something about the synagogues in Slutsk and especially about the large synagogue known as "Di Kalte Shul".

This ancient synagogue was famous in White Russia and many legends circulated among the residents about it. I also asked him about the fate of the Jewish cemetery, the place where geniuses and famous Torah sages were buried.

Mr. Hindus told me, that he saw the cemetery and its stone fence abandoned and breached, but the cemetery was not completely destroyed. He did not have enough time to hear from the residents anything about the synagogues during the one day he stayed in Slutsk.

[Page 146]

Later on, I had a conversation with Rachel Picholtz, who was born in Slutsk, that was under the Nazi occupation from June 1941 to July 1942. She managed to escape from the city and joined the partisans. She told me about the fate of the synagogues. She said that even during the Soviet rule, before World War II, the synagogues were used for various purposes. The cold synagogue building was used as a bakery. The younger generation forgot their God and neglected the houses of prayer.

In June 1941, when the Germans bombed Slutsk with fighter planes, the synagogues were among the first buildings to be destroyed. It is possible that in Mr. Hindus' stay in Slutsk after the retreat of the Nazis, he did not have the opportunity to see the remains of synagogues.

The picture was drawn by the boy Haim Rusak, one of the
survivors of the Holocaust (now lives in Kfar Avihayil). (His father,
Avraham Yitzhak, was an officer in the Soviet army and was killed
in a battle with the Nazis in the vicinity of Bobroisk).

From the Partisan War
(Excerpts from Moshe Kahanovitz's book)

On April 10, 1942, a group of twenty or more people, led by Israel Lapidot, left the ghetto (in Minsk) to the Slutsk forests.

The combat organization in the Minsk ghetto sent two groups to the Slutsk forests in April 1942.

* * *

Misha Otsar (Maustrog Wahlin), a platoon commander in the "Zashukov" company, took a few Germans captive on the Minsk-Slutsk Road and killed them.

* * *

The young woman Falye Weinberg from Lodz, escaped in January 1943 from the labor camp in Swierzshani to the Zashukov company in the Kapoli district. She went to Slutsk several times, disguised as a farmer, to spy and find out a way how to blow up the large sawmill, which provided building materials for the front. She excelled in the performance of her duties and returned with a detailed plan of the sawmill.

In May 1943, she received the task of blowing up the electricity station in the sawmill in Slutsk. Dressed as a farmer, she hid a gun in her bag and among all kinds of vegetables she put a loaf of bread with a mine inside.

5 kilometers from the town of Haresk, one of the farmers recognized her and handed her over to the Germans. After suffering and various tortures, she was hanged in public in Slutsk.

Excerpts from the newspapers

The Central Office for the Investigation of War Crimes in Ludwigsburg, West Germany, turned to the World Jewish Congress and asked for its help in finding witnesses who could testify about the actions of the Nazis in Bialystok and Slutsk, in connection with an ongoing investigation against Nazis suspected of murders there.

* * *

The investigation of two people, who served as senior police officers during the Nazis regime, was opened today by the General Prosecutor of Kassel.

The suspects are a retired police lieutenant-colonel Franz Lechthaler, 70, and a police inspector Willy Papencourt, 52, who are accused of being responsible for the killing of 500 to 700 Jews in the city of Slutsk in White Russia on October 27, 1941, by two German police companies and a unit of the Latvian Guard.

The two suspects have been in custody for several weeks.

* * *

The chief prosecutor of this country, Afka, announced today that Franz Lechthaler, who was a police officer, and Willy Papencourt, who was a "Nazi chief commissar", the former aged 69 and the latter aged 51, confessed to the shooting death of "several hundred Jews" in Slutsk, which is in White Russia, on October 27, 1941, claiming that they did so, "according to orders".

[Page 147]

Slutsk in the Hebrew Literature

Mendele Mocher Sforim
(Mendele the Book Peddler)

Excerpt from the book "Of Bygone Days"

Translated by Mira Eckhaus

The childhood of Mendele Mocher Sforim (Shalom Ya'akov Abramowitz) and his early youth were spent in his hometown of Kapoli and in the nearby cities, mainly in Slutsk and Timkovichi, and in his autobiographical story "Of Bygone Days" he also dedicates a considerable part to the description of these surrounding cities. Here are excerpts from chapters describing the lives of the students of the Yeshiva in Slutsk in those days. Mendele indicated the names of the cities in their initials and endings and wrote: S-K (Slutsk), T-I (Timkovichi). We publish here, for ease of reading, the name Slutsk in its entirety and write it as follows: S[luts]K

Mendele Mocher Sforim

A

[On the way from Kapoli to Slutsk]

- - - And one day after the holiday, in the early morning, when the sun was seen beyond a shroud of clouds, like someone who fears change, covering his moustache, Shlomo secretly left the city to make his way to

S[luts]K, and in his backpack was nothing but a tefillin, a slice of bread and the cloths he was wearing. And the road was not good, it was made of ridges, mud and clay from the rains, and Shlomo'li was not familiar with it. So, what shall he do? He decided to wait until a cart comes across him on the road and throw himself into it without payment, or to sit cramped, bent and hanging behind it. Just like a poor traveler who was not like the others – and so he would stand and wait until the coming of the Redeemer but to no avail. - - - Shlomo'li ponders and ponders, he stands and his heart goes to S[luts]K, his spirit aspires to his destination, so he can prepare for him all his needs there ahead, lest someone else will arrive ahead of him and he still has to pass the bumpy road. Finally, he made up his mind and went on his way. His feet are drowning in with mud, his shoes are soaking up water, his overshoes are torn, the soles are exposed, his heels are ruined and his capote is all worn out, from the bottom to the neck. He becomes weak, and he hesitates, he walks a little longer, and he falls on the road - at that moment, a curse and the sound of a whip was heard, and here, he sees a beaten and oppressed horse before his eyes, all filthy and dirty with mud, and a figure of a man wrapped in front of him, his brown hat hanging down to his eye brows, the collar of his coat is raised up and a worn-out handkerchief is wrapped around it. And here a muffled voice, as if the voice is coming out of an empty barrel, calls to him from the rag: Hey, boy! What are you doing here, the son of Rabbi Chaim? On such a cloudy day, even a fool dog is not seen outside. - Oh, Rabbi Michal! Shlomo'li shouted and spread his hands, but his speaking ability disappeared and he felt as if something is stuck in his throat and he can't speak. And here, the voice is calling him again: Come on, boy, climb on the cart!

Indeed, it was the talkative Michal Ba'ar Bar Hana Yentil.

- "Some by car and some by horses," - - - The "governor" Damta fell ill last night. It can be because he went to sleep just after eating Arvit. They rushed to bring the expert and he came with all his tools - blood-letting tools and with the Micromeria fruticosa, with a razor and scissors, but to no avail. And the governor said at once: Send someone to S[luts]K and bring me the doctor Hirschili, he is the expert and there is no one else better than him! And now, here he goes on this gloomy day, on a mission for the sick governor. And he swore, so help him the blessed God, the creator of all reasons and the master of all the happenings, that his heart is very happy that God caused a stomach ache to the governor and he granted Michal the right to lead in his cart the son of Rabbi Chaim to the Yeshiva in S[luts]K. - - -

B

At the Yeshiva in S[luts]K

The city of S[luts]K is one of the towns in Lithuania, that served as a place of the Torah in the Yeshivas there. It is the Yeshiva that gives this city its reputation among all the Jews around it, and if it weren't for it, the city would have been

[Page 148]

forgotten and there was no memory of it in the world. One can dare to say, that the Yeshiva is a kind of livelihood, similar to the learning in the university, which brings abundance for the residents of the place it is located in - God forbid! On the contrary, not only that it does not bring benefit to the people of the city, but it takes from their money. The professors that teach in it are poor Yeshiva heads, and their students - poor guys with not even a penny in their pockets. They come to the city neither by car nor by horses, but on their feet, poor and with no belongings, except for their bundles of tattered and worn-out shirts, and a pair of dirty shoes with scuffed heels, and so, the people of the city have to take care for all their needs. And the people of the city themselves are in need and the needs of the poor of their city are already taken care by them, and now they also take on themselves to take care of the needs of others, of these young men, and they do it willingly. The poor man in the city shares his bread with a wise scholar - all in honor of the Torah!

The Yeshiva scholars learn in two classes, one above the other, each class and its melamed. The melamed of the upper class is the great head of the Yeshiva, and the melamed of the lower class is his deputy who is subordinated to him. This deputy teaches every day after the morning prayer his lesson in the Gemara with its interpretations according to the Pshat, when he sits in the middle of the table and his students surround the table in front of him like a crown. And by the way, he tests them with his questions about the same matter that he teaches, to know if they learned it properly yesterday. And when he is not satisfied with the knowledge of one of his student, he embarrasses him with his words, and sometimes even with a slap on the face, so that he knows that the Torah needs study. Most of his students are new faces, students who came only short time ago. And the head of the Yeshiva teaches his daily lesson to his older students and discusses with them questions and the words of the sages. And at the same time, the wise students start to argue and discuss and negotiate with each other with shouts and loud voices, while straightening their hands and pointing their fingers and rubbing their foreheads and frowning, to emphasize and explain the deep meaning of "that is" and where the argument of "one has to settle" ends. When the day's lesson is over, the big students are dismissed and they go to study and do their homework for tomorrow wherever they want. And the little ones, most of them, must prepare their homework in the Yeshiva house under the supervision of their Rabbi, who is a regularly present there. Sometimes when he comes and they don't notice him - while the young students are tired and weary from their Talmud and they put down the Gemara and get up of the tables to make some fun - he tells them exhortation and proves to them with moral books, how great is the offense of canceling the Torah and how severe is the punishment for those who cross it. And he adds his own perspective, that it is forbidden to the people of Israel to make fun in this world, and that the joy of this world is not their goal... But there is no wisdom, no morals, and no exhortation that can prevent the youth from laughing in order to forget for a moment about all their studies, as they are flesh and blood. This is how the young men rejoice all year round, in chastity; And during the "in between days" until they start their studies at the Yeshiva, and while the horror of the rabbi is not yet upon them - the boys want to laugh in public.

The days are the "in between days" after the Sukkot holiday, the time for the people of Israel, from the youngest to the oldest, to start learning wherever they are. The S[luts]K Yeshiva is crowded with young men, some are new, some are returning from their home, where they went by foot, some are residents or residents' sons, that the Yeshiva is their permanent Yeshiva and it is their home. The time is the time of the great fair in the Yeshiva, and the "days" - that is, the fixed days for eating at the house owners. The eating arrangement is the goods, which is the desire of all the Yeshiva students. The first important thing for each of them is the eating. And there are searching and running, competition and jealousy, quarrels and fights over the fixed days, and not all the students get to fill the entire days of the week with eating arrangements. The young man that managed to fill the entire days of the week with eating arrangement is very lucky; The young man who managed to fill five days of the week with eating arrangements is also lucky; And miserable is the young man whose most of the week days lack an eating arrangement! The status of the young men that are residents of the place among their fellows is as strong as the status of the great merchants with money among the small merchants and peddlers in the market at the time of the fair. After all, they have a lot! They have a place to eat for the entire days of the week, and they have easy income, part of it is from Yeshiva students, and therefore their minds are free to deal with others' needs, to do favors for the poor boys who come anew, to guide them and lead their leadership over them high-handedly - with a hand strike on the cheek, on the side and on the shoulder in order to educate them in the Yeshiva life and the way of the Torah in all their details and tortures.

As soon as a young man comes to the Yeshiva, just as a little one who is born, he enters the covenant and the naming. He will no longer be called by his birth name, but he will be named in a new name after his city, such as Nisoizi, Kalitskyi, Salonimi, Lechvizi, etc. The boy will forget his name and his past, as well as his home and his childhood days. - - -

And at the time of this fair for the Yeshiva students, the business of benches and tables is also done there. The possession of the benches for overnight stays is bought and sold from hand to hand. A bench that is closer to the oven is more expensive, and the one next to the oven is the best, and lucky is the student who wins it and rests on it at night. Above it is the oven itself, which lying on it is a kind of taste of heaven, but there are only few who deserve it.

And there are two kinds of easy income which do not involve trade, and they are: the Minyan and the wallet. What is the Minyan? These are Yeshiva students who are assigned to pray at a Minyan (ten people) in the evening and morning at the mourning house during the seven days of mourning, or throughout the entire year, and receive a reward for their prayer. And what is the wallet? This is a wallet of charity from the donations of homeowners for the maintenance of the Yeshiva, which the deputy head of the Yeshiva with one of the guys that accompanies him, collects every Thursday and Friday. And in addition to the great honor in going with his rabbi and collect money from the houses, he also receives a salary of 18 pennies. These two good gifts are reserved for the elders of the yeshiva, or for those who excel in the Talmud, and the young Yeshiva students, who just arrived to the Yeshiva, do not have rights in them.

A young man, who just arrived to the Yeshiva, is similar to one who has come to a new world, a kind of world to come with all its mortification and tortures. Because he arrived, he immediately feels the sorrow of the beating - a beating behind him and in front of him, plucking and beating from all sides. His friends - damagers and angels of destruction - they greet him with cheers, welcome and jokes, starting with supposedly good things, and while talking they change

[Page 149]

and turn to words of laughing, and from laugh they start to push, and from a blow to a punch and a kick and a crushing of bones, all seems incidentally and by mistake, until they finally reach the part of putting incense in his nose, and several damp rags on his head. The torments of the Yeshiva student in the first days of his arrival are difficult, similar to the torments of hell. He will eat only a little bread, he will sleep on a hard bench which will hurt all his bones, he will place his capote under him as a linen and his hands under his head, and will be rubbing and rolling a lot until he becomes tattered and turns into a kind of new person and a kind of a "soul" that is strangely connected to the souls of the other students, who are known and marked by the name of "Patrons"; And the experience of guys in this hell is not the same for everyone. The suffering period of those who are arrogant and rude in spirit, last longer than the period of those who are humble and miserable, who listen and do not answer. The braggart students are the most hated ones. Since you came here, they say to him, follow the path of Torah like all your friends, and don't say I am a great man!

This fair, which began to be a frequent event "in between times", is usually more crowded in the evening, while the young men, both new and old, come back from their wondering in the city, after being busy all day with their affairs. So, at one of the evenings, the students of the Yeshiva were talking one to another about daily matters and about the things that are necessary for eating and all their needs. One said he hopes he will manage to fill all the "days" with eating arrangements. Another student despairs and worries and complains about his bad luck, that all his eating arrangements are at poor families, that offers only bread and a grits stew, and his friend brags how lucky he is, that the Holy One, blessed be He, arranged for him a wealthy householder for the holy Friday and Saturday, which are known as days of eating and drinking well among the Yeshiva students all over the world. He is busy there on Shabbat evening cooking fish and scraping horseradish at the brewery, and Haema, a good woman and a kosher Jew, gives him a loaf of bread when she takes it out of the oven, so he will have something to eat on Sunday. Another gang of guys would beat each other by loud growling and singing of the Mishnah and Gemara, and the voice of the leaders of the gang rises above everyone, shouting and arguing and doing whatever their heart desires, and there at the back of the house in the dark, one of the boys prostrates himself and lies down like a king in a regiment on a bench, his left under his head and intending to take a nap.

- - -The ancestors' merit was by Shlomo'li, not only for his coming safely to the Yeshiva, but also for finding eating arrangements for all the "days" and being liked there and on more for good things there. - - -

Shlomo'li was brought to Slutsk to the same inn, where the people of his town and Michal Ba'ar Bar Hana Yentil stay regularly, and there he realized that his ancestors' merit helps him from beginning to end. The owners of the inn, both good and kosher people, who respected Rabbi Chaim, agreed to feed his son on their house on every Shabbat evening and on Saturdays, and the two brothers, the aforesaid intercessors, also remembered his father's kindness and provided him with eating arrangements for the other week days, and also arranged a place for him to sleep in a house of an honorable man, a man from their community. And so, he had all he needed - daily meals and a hot oven to sleep by in his bed at night, which is not the share of every Yeshiva boy.

From all the days of Shlomo'li's yeshiva in the city of Slutsk, which lasted two years with a break in between, only a few of them are worth noting, most of them were days of nothing but dealing with day-to-day matters.

The evenings of the rainy days left impression on Shlomo'li. In these evenings he would spend with the gang of young men in the Yeshiva --- Outside, the ice was getting stronger and, in the house, there was darkness. One by one, the young men come back from their places of feasting, shivering from the cold and rubbing their hands. The oven is burning - bonfires and lots of wood. Two guys, one with no eating arrangement for that day and one who brought a few potatoes from the house owner that feeds him for the Arvit meal, sit on their knees near the oven and watch over their cauldron there. The cauldrons are boiling and the boiling grits move inside them, rising and falling and knocking bang, bang!

And the rest of the guys sit in semi-circle and warm themselves against the light, cheering and joking, mocking and joking, and their faces are full of excitement. And one piece of wood gets excited and dodges among the other woods, extends the tongues of fire, moves here and there and shoots sparks and fireworks, making pif paf sounds and finishes with a big blow! The potatoes and the grits are ready to eat. They take out the cauldrons from the oven and a voice comes out from one of the guys that were sitting, and he announces and says: Stand up friends, the time for reading the Shema has come, the Cohanim, the owners of the cauldrons, get inside to eat their potatoes and grits.- - -

[Page 150]

Y.L. Gordon's Letters to *Maggid* Reb Zvi Dainow of Slutsk

Translated by Mira Eckhaus

Edited by Jane S. Gabin

Y.L. Gordon's letters to *Maggid* Reb Zvi Dainov of Slutsk testify to the mental distress, persecutions and great suffering to which *Maggid* Dainov was subjected. Ninety years ago, Dainov advocated to *Haskalah* and love for Zion. On the recommendation of Y.L. Gordon and his advice, he settled in London and was somewhat relieved.

Telz, Rosh Hashanah Eve 1868, 5628, 5th of Tevet.

Honorable Rabbi, the *Maggid* of Slutsk, the famous preacher, our teachers Rabbi Zvi Hirsch Dainow, may he live long.

His letter, as long as the length of the exile of the Jews, with 24 pages, written only on the face on the page and not backwards, came to me on the fourteenth day after it was written. - - - My heart was happy to hear from his second letter that he acclimatized well in this city (Kaunas) which was full of gentlemen, benefactors and wise and well-known people. I knew that he would be successful even without recommendation letters, because his name was already widely known. And I do not yet know what the focus of his new sermons would be about, and therefore I will be brave and ask him to stir up the hearts of the people of Israel for these two issues in his sermons: a) Little by little, to leave these districts, where many thousands of people of Israel are living in crowdedness and density, cruelly to each other, and each generation deteriorates even more due to this tight pressure, which they push one another, and to move their home to the middle districts in the land of Great Russia. As he has now given a license to the artisans, and this thing is good and beneficial to the whole nation, he should also awaken the hearts of the benefactors to form societies in every city and collect alms to support such wanderers. b) To expel from the hearts of the people of Israel the soft heart and the fear of working in the army, until in every city the heads of the community are trying with all their might to pay ransom money to free the people from the army, and by this their pockets are emptied and poverty increases. And why wouldn't the poor people who know lack and poverty and are bloated with hunger go with willing hearts to work, so they will be able to heat their homes and buy clothes to wear. - - - Search and find some nice *midrash* to sweeten these things when you say them, maybe you will find suitable the words of *Chazal*, a man will always run towards the kings of the world, maybe we will be privileged and able to distinguish between the war tactics of the world's nations and our war tactics for the future, and we will wait day by day for the coming of the Messiah, and why don't we prepare for him an army of soldiers, - - - and you, go with your power to save Israel from the burden of superstitions and the suffering of stupidity; and God with your help in your mission. And do not be afraid of the governors and rulers, who are flatterers and people of intrigue, who pounce like dogs on passers-by. Do your actions with wisdom and knowledge and they will not be able to harm you, and all the wise people will bless you and remember your good deeds. - - -

Your friend who respects you as your value, Y.L. Gordon.

Telz, Tuesday, 5630

Greetings to you, a very wise man, a knowledgeable, brave and strong man!

- - - The correction of our material nation is combined with a religious correction, I have no doubt about it. And you, my friend, if you are a true man and do not speak with us deceitfully, you will remember the status of our brothers in our land, through their negotiations and through their upbringing and livelihood, will come up before you, and you will remember that about 80% from all the multitude of the House of Israel in our land don't have livelihood, in every city and city we will still find *cheders* of horror where a new generation of the desert is educated by foolish and completely ignorant *melamedim* - and the rabbis and the community leaders pay attention to falsehoods and chattering words. - - - Raise your hand to the supreme God, to a good and beneficent God, who does not desire the corruption of the world and say to him: indeed, the status of the material, moral, temporal and religious House of Israel is not standing and shrieking like a crane: fix me! And why should we loosen the hands of the few who sacrifice their souls to forbid war against a large and hard-backed people who destroy themselves?

- - - Peace be upon you, be strong and strong to enlighten the eyes of those in the dark and may God will privilege us to see the redemption of our people and the consolation of Zion and Jerusalem.

Your friend who is only concerned about your health and benefit.

My friends H. Dainow!

The gentleman Ginzburg did not want to send a telegram, but he sent a letter to Rabbi of the holy congregation, the letter that I read you while you were here with us, signed by his father, the gentleman Yuzil Ginzburg, and let us hope that the words of that letter will enter to the heart of the reader, and he will not disappoint us.

- - - And you, do not fear of the crowd that surrounds you, and speak everywhere wisely and with great knowledge as much as God will give in your heart for the benefit of our brothers who are sick and do not feel their sick, and do not be angry and bring your cry before the ministers who sit on high; for why will the ignorant of heart say, "Dainow has become an obstacle and an informer"! Guard and be quiet, because just as they dance against the moon and are not be able to touch it, so they will not be able to touch you in a bad way; And if they kill you, we will worship you and sanctify you after your death and place your name among the saints who are in the land - who were killed for the sanctification of God. Isn't that enough for you?

Your friend, Y.L. Gordon

June 5 (22 Sivan 5633)

My friend H. Dainow!

You are waiting for my advice and I am helpless; Because who I am that I can instruct someone about his path in life? Am I so unimpeachable person that I can advise you what to do and what to avoid? But I'll ask you one thing: if you find it difficult to live in Slutsk, if you find around yourself dangerous people, why don't you change your place of residence to change your luck? Are you so connected to this city that wants to throw you up? In my opinion, it would be good for you to move your house, your wife and your children to one of the big cities where, even if there are many bad things, there are also many educated people who will protect you when needed, such as the city of Vilna, Kaunas and the like; And if there is still any money left in your hands, create to your wife some kind of living or livelihood that she could manage, so that you will be engaged only in preaching and it will be your pride, and you will not be focused only on the reward you are paid for your sermons, and your wife will deal with the

[Page 151]

trade and you will be diligent on your work and your way onward; And you will no longer fear the slander of rabbis and their blasphemy; And you revealed their real characters and their disgrace and their failures to all the people of Israel in all your journeys and all the people will flock after you and it will also be your reward when they see your action.

This is the advice I advise you from someone who is not knowledgeable, because I do not know much about you, your family and your conduct.

I wrote today to the director H. Pursau and asked for mercy for you as well, and if it will be of benefit to you, it will make me very happy.

June 26, 1873 (13th of Tammuz 5633)

My friend, Zvi the *Maggid*!

The one who tells you that I incited H. Pursau in the people of Israel and I told him that according to the law of Israel it is permissible to write on *Shabbat* and according to the law of the kingdom to force them to do so is nothing but bearing false witness in me and he will be held accountable for that. It never happened! H. Pursau did what he did according to himself and according to the instruction of some Palhedrin rabbis who did not hold back the power to tell him the truth. And I, on the contrary, I strongly argued with him and advised him to deviate from this way of forcing the boys to violate *Shabbat* in public, because by doing so he delays the redemption of the people of Israel and prevents them from redeeming their souls. And the words were already published then by the *Daan* and by the *Maggid*. And here I am willing to fulfill the request of the people of Slutsk and I will write to H. Pursau in a few days, even though I am almost sure that my words would be of no use, because you also know the way of that man, that he is very stubborn and no one can change his mind. In the meantime, please send the following letter to those who wrote to me, because I do not know their address and I would like to send my letter to them directly. Goodbye and do not speak falsehood about your friend who honors you Y.L. Gordon.

20th Kislev, 5634.

To the people of Israel community in Slutsk, my honorable brothers!

I received your letter and your honest and righteous complaint about the director came to my ears and entered my heart. I am willing to fulfill your request and write to H. Pursau to remove an obstacle from the path of your children's education, although I am very sorry if I will not succeed, as I know the man and his way of conduct and his stubbornness; And I already had a discussion with him about this while he was in Shavel but without any luck. But I haven't written to him for many days, and if I come to him all of a sudden about this matter, which as important it is for us, it looks immaterial to him, I am afraid he will not listen to me; Therefore, I will wait a few more days until I have another issue to him and my words to him will also include your request and I will try to convince and persuade him and I hope he will listen to me.

Be blessed from your brother who honors and cherish you, Y.L. Gordon.

20 Kislev 5634.

To H. Zvi Dainow, my dear friend!

I cry your kindness all the days. In all the places where you have been, from Slutsk to London, that your tumult always rises above your enemies, and as I always was, I am skeptic and I do not believe, that they really did to you all these terrible things and that the persecutions concern yourself and to your relatives. However, if you are wise, you will not be able to bear the sting of death flies, and if the stings of the hornets in Lebanon will hurt you - how will I comfort you and what will I be of use to you? If I said that I would say to your words to the members of the committee, I knew their answer in advance, because they will not interfere in a quarrel that is not related to them; And if I write to him, who am I that he will hear my voice? Is it possible to convince such a man? He will probably say his allegory: did not the starling go to the crow in vain? That's why I decided in my heart to ask Dr. Neiman to write about you to Dr. Adler and ask him not to listen informers and to take you under his protection; And if my words enter the heart of Dr. Neiman and his words into the heart of Dr. Adler, then you will be saved. And in the meantime, I thought I'd write these few words to you in response to your letter of the 15th of Kislev, so that you may know that you will not find your help in me, not because I am not willing to help you but because I can't. Farewell and bless upon you from your friend who cherish you and shares your sorrow and wishes to comfort you.

Y. L. Gordon

(21 Kislev 5635, on the day I turned (43) (44) years old).

To the above

My dear friend!

- - - I am happy as the joy at the *Simchat Torah* on Sinai, that you finally reached a safe place, and switched Slutsk with London and the status of a passes *Maggid* by the status of an existing *Maggid*. Now you can rest from your sorrow and your anger and from all the tribulations that you and your family have encountered and you all will be able to live peaceful life, and may you find among the people of your community people with big hearts, who know and who will desire to repay a man according to his deeds, to provide you with a livelihood and a remnant in their land, and God will provide you peaceful and respectful life, and you will dwell with no anger and pain.

- - - The great thing that the community of the people of Israel in London thought about our brothers sitting on the holy land was known to us from the writings in the holy language and in the Ashkenazi language, because the writings is the Russian language did not say anything about it.

- - - I thought of the great thing and its results, and the power of imagination that was strong in my childhood, awoke and showed me in this thing not only a stone of remembrance for the honorable Reb Moshe

Montefiore, but as a foundation stone to re-establish the home for the people of Israel, - the very burial of our scattered bones that will be gathered together one by one, and there they will become one flesh and a skin will be put on them from above and they will live and stand on their feet by God giving his spirit to them. If only my wish will come true before my last day come. - - - And I went up and came down to the mountains of Israel with a Shofar in my lap, to prophesy and call with a loud voice, a voice that outrages the ruins of the worlds and mischievous wastelands of sixty-seven generations. But to reach this goal we need to start from another place, we need to purify the land and expel from it all the Jews who live there, there will not be a horseshoe left, and sweep away with a broom the cobwebs that have been woven by these millipedes and pass a fresh wind over the land and air of the Land of Israel, which was spoiled with their filth and stupidity. If all these will not be done to them, then all our efforts were in vain. - - -

And I am your truly friend in all times and ages,

Fast of Esther, 5635

Y. L. Gordon

[Page 152]

Israel Behmer

by A. Y. Papirna

Translated by Mira Eckhaus

Edited by Jane S. Gabin

One of the pillars of the Lithuanian rabbinate in the last century was the brilliant rabbi from Slutsk, the *Gaon Reb* Yosef Faimer (a distorted last name under "Behmer", because he was born in the state of Behmin), known to this day in Lithuania by the honorable and affectionate name "Reb Yosili Slutsker". He was the distinguished student of Reb Chaim (a scholar of the HaGra), the founder of the Volozhin Yeshiva, and a friend of the *Gaon Reb* Yitzhak of Volozhin. He was a great opponent of Chassidism, which was successful in those days and captured many hearts in several kingdoms of Russia. Only in the districts of Vilna and Minsk it encountered a hard war on the part of the rabbis who were scholars of the HaGra (headed by Reb Yitzhak of Volozhin and Reb Yosef of Slutsk), and for many days it could not find a place there. But it did not last long, and to his dismay, when Reb Yosef was very old, he saw that one of the "righteous" had settled in Kuidanov and found many followers there. A few more years passed and God challenged Reb Yosef with another disaster that came from within his house. And this challenge was: Israel, his only son[1], was excellent in his talents and perseverance, and was very successful in learning the Torah, and Reb Yosef was certain that he would be great in the people of Israel and will replace him when the time comes, but - so great was the power of doubt or, to speak in the language of the *Chassidim*, the power of the "shell" in that generation in the heart of the people of Israel. While he was still young, he had many and enormous doubts in matters of faith and knowledge, for which he could not find solutions in rabbinical literature, and these doubts did not give rest to his spirit, and he decided to try and ask, maybe he would find solutions to them in Chassidism, and he ran away from his father's house and went to Kuidanov. The Kuidanov *Chassidim* considered the coming of Israel, the son of Reb Yosef, their main opponent, to ask for the Torah from their rabbi, a great victory for Chassidism in general and the Kuidanov Chassidism in particular, and they were very happy about it and accepted him with love. Israel stayed for about two months in Kuidanov, in the house of the *tsaddik* in the company of his followers and close associates, observed their actions, heard their stories, and especially paid attention to the *Tsaddik* himself, his ways of life and his "Torahs" (the *Chassidim* called the *tsaddik's* sermons

"Torahs"). But even in Chassidism he did not find what he was looking for - rest for his turbulent spirit - and he planned to turn to the third party that had arisen in Israel at the time, the party the educated.

And Israel thought about a way to get rid of the company of the *Chassidim*, as he was tired of them and their antics. One day, the *tzaddik* preached his sermon or his Torah on *Shabbat* after the third meal in front of a large crowd of *Chassidim*. This time his Torah was regarding the counting of *Tif'eret shebatif'eret* (glory of the glory). This Torah, spoken by the rabbi with great enthusiasm, was very deep and no one understood it. The large crowd of *Chasidim* neither hoped nor paid attention to understand the riddles and hints of their rabbi. It was enough for them to see the face of the *tzaddik* and his movements , but among the *Chassidim* from among the close associates of the *tzaddik*, there were also those who aspired to know the basics of Chassidism and to get to the bottom of it, and this time they too did not understand anything from the rabbi's Torah, and so they turned to Israel, as they who knew the depth of his mind, and asked him to interpret the Torah of the *tzaddik* to them so they will finally know what is the matter of *Tif'eret shebatif'eret* (glory of the glory). And Israel said to them: Let me explain this matter to you in a tangible and visible way, and he led them to the window and pointed his finger at the hole in the mezuzah and asked: What do you see in it? - "A hole" - they replied. "Yes, a hole", - Israel said, - and if I take a drill and drill a hole inside this hole - what will it be called? it is "the hole in the hole", do you understand? And this is similar to *Tif'eret shebatif'eret* (glory of the glory). The *Chassidim* tried to understand the meaning of his words, but they quickly realized that he was mocking them and in Chassidism, and they prepared to flog him, but he fled for his life, and ran away from the rabbi's house and left the city.)I heard this episode from the late writer Israel Bernstein, who before his arrival to the *Beit Midrash* was one of Kuidanov's *Chassidim*, just as was his father, the great rabbi Reb Chaim Haikel from Minsk).

From Kuidanov, Israel returned to Slutsk, and his father, seeing his son's spiritual condition was very bad, took hold of the well-known trick (which was used by parents at that time in the cases of their sons' departure to a bad culture) - marriage: he will have to support his wife and family and will not have time to be engaged in nonsense. This is what Rabbi Reb Yosef imagined for his son, and so his son married a woman from an Orthodox family in Bobroisk. He lived for a few years in this city at the house of his father- in- law with his wife and children, who were born, and engaged openly, during the day, in the study of the Torah, and secretly, at night, in the books of philosophy (the *Rambam*, the *Kuzari*, and the *HaIkkarim*) and in the new literature. This literature was then young and very poor in the poetic part and even more so in the scientific part. It could not bring its readers into the rich and wide world of science, but it had enough power to take them out of their narrow and meager world, and the newspapers like *Kerem Hemed*, *HeChalutz*, and books like *Ary Nohem* (a lion growls), *Kol Shachal* (a lion's voice), *Bchinat HaDat* (the religious examination), *Kin'at HaEmet* (envy of the truth), *HaTorah VehaPhilosofia* (Torah and Philosophy), and *Moreh Nevochei hazman* (The Guide for the Perplexed), had the power to awaken a lot of the foundations of the *Massorah* and *Kabbalah*. And this is what happened to Israel. And I heard from the elders of Bobroisk that one *Shabbat* night, when Israel planned to sit and read his books, he walked with a lamp from one room to another. He thought that his wife was already asleep, but she saw what he had done, and she was terrified. She thought that he was struck with madness, as a "wise man", a man with a clear mind would not do such a strange thing. He did try to calm her, telling her that he did what he did with a clear mind. But in doing so he only further increased her disaster, for he was a complete heretic. The next day the unhappy woman told her parents about her grief and a great commotion broke out in the city. Then the question arose: What is he - a madman or a heretic? The people were divided in their opinions, some leaned this way and some that way, and finally, after a long discussion, they came to an agreement that he was a heretic and not a madman. First, because of his confession, and second, because it was clear to them that even a madman would not commit such an abomination, and only a heretic can do that, and the third, and this is the main thing, that by such an agreement they could get rid of him by a divorce, they would force him to divorce his wife, which can't be done if he was a madman, as in such case, his divorce was invalid. And since they came to this agreement, they demanded that Israel to divorce from his wife, and he fulfilled their demand.

[Page 153]

And since then, the days of Israel's wanderings began. To stay in his city, in his country, after the sin he failed in, that was beyond the bounds of possibility. He had to run away. But where to? There was only one answer to this question: to Berlin. To this place of Torah and wisdom, for more than a century, the great spiritual men of our nation, "God- seekers", seekers of truth, seekers of resourcefulness and wisdom, have moved. At the time, the philosopher Shlomo Maimon of Nesvij moved to Berlin, where the *Gaon* Rabbi Menashe Ilir and the *Gaon* Rabbi Israel Salanter went (the latter two went and sat down, or rather - were set up). From Vilna to Berlin also came the yeshiva scholar Daniel Havolson, and many more. Israel Behmer desired for quite a time to move there, so he was not sorry for the "impure" incident that had happened and he moved to Berlin.

In Berlin, Behmer found someone of his kind, Schneor Zakash. I say "his kind", because these two were very similar in their origin, education, ambitions and the events of their lives. Also, Schneor Zakash was the son of a great rabbi (Reb Tzemach of Jagar) and he was also one of those who fled to Berlin to seek wisdom after various obstacles, tribulations and adventures. When Behmer came to Berlin, Schneor had already settled there, and his name was already known as a writer and engaged in the wisdom of Israel, and in those days, he renewed the publishing of the *Kerem Hemed* newspaper, which had been discontinued before that. Through Schneor Zakash, Behmer was introduced to Ashkenazi sages - Tsuntz, Geiger, M. Zacks, and they recognized his worth and brought him close, and they guided him with their advice and showed him the path leading to his goal. However, his new acquaintances could not give him material help, and he arrived to Berlin empty-handed, and so all his years in Berlin were spent under stress and oppression, and out of poverty and sorrow, as is "The Way of the Torah". He read and repeated and studied wisely, studied Ashkenazi language and ancient languages, heard history and philosophy lessons from professors at the university, and together with the great sages of Berlin, engaged in the study of Israel's history. The profession he chose was the study of the sects in Israel during the Second Temple period and he published the results of his investigations in print, in Hebrew and Ashkenazi newspapers as well as in special pamphlets. And in my youth, I read two of his notebooks: *The Writings of Israel Behmer and How to Evaluate*, the latter included, if I remember correctly, critical comments to Rashi Rappaport's book *The Value of the Words* (*Erech Milin*).

Reb Yosef mourned for his beloved son for many days, and after dozens of years, in his old age, he addressed him in a letter and asked him not to let him die mourning and asked him to return to Slutsk. Reb Yosef apologized before of his associates for reconciling with his heretic son and excused it on the fact that he wished to learn from his son the *Halacha* of the holy month of *Rambam*, this is the only halachic, which he cannot understand completely without any knowledge of arithmetic and astronomy, and the son fulfilled his father's request.

On his way to Slutsk, Israel Behmer passed through Kapoli, my hometown, and stayed there for a few days. Then I saw him, and his appearance made a sad impression on me. He was then about fifty years old, but he looked much older, a cloud of sadness settled over his beautiful face, his stature was stooped and on his high and broad forehead he had deep wrinkles, the signs of all his sadness and irritation, toil and hard work in the days of his wanderings. Broken in heart and body, depressed and hunched, Behmer returned to Slutsk and lived there for another five years and died before his father, who had lived longer.

I may have gone on too long in this chapter, as I wanted to give a picture of the life of the first educated people, their great aspiration for wisdom and the great sacrifices they made on their altar. And Behmer's name - his typical personality and the description of his image and lifestyles - is to a known extent the description of the image and lifestyles of the majority of the educated in that generation.

(From records)

* * *

Supplement

It is a mistake, what some writers thought, that David Gordon was the editor of this newspaper from the beginning. Silberman himself was certainly not qualified for this job and always was assisted by others in this profession.

The first editor of the *HaMaggid* was the distinguished philologist Israel Behmer, the author of the small notebook in quantity but much in quality *How to Evaluate*, his books *Israel's writings on the sect of the Essenes* and a small book *God's Finger* also appeared. Every time I remember that this great man, who has almost no equal in his wonderful philosophical sharpness, served for a while as a journalist, I get angry and gnash my teeth. I always say: poor nation, that this is what happened to it. Israel Behmer did not live long, and on his way to his homeland, to see his family members, he died in the city of Slutsk. Then, Silberman decided to call Gordon, who was then living in London, to come to him and assist him in the work of the *HaMaggid*. This was approximately in the year 5620 (1860).

Shimon Bernfeld (*The World*, 23rd Iyar 5686, 1926)

Editor's note:

1. Here Papirna was wrong: Rabbi Yosili had another son, Rabbi Meir, who superseded him as the head of the rabbinate in Slutsk

[Page 154]

Avraham Epstein
(Excerpts from "Records")

Translated by Mira Eckhaus

A

Grandma Rivka

That's how everyone in the city called her, from the smallest of the babies to the oldest. They were all her grandchildren, they were all born on her lap and her laughing face welcomed them on their way out into the air of the world.

She was a midwife. For more than eighty years she was on duty, from the thirteenth year of her life until the day of her death. Thousands of children received the first treatment, the first warm caress from the blessed hands of this lovable little grandmother.

Every day she would pass through the streets of the city, full of joy, her steps are light and fast, and she seemed to be floating and flying towards the new life that awaits her arrival through the labor pains.

Her face was wonderful then: small, laughing and glowing from within. Something of the brightness of the sunset was reflected from them - a distant hint of an earlier unknown majesty.

As she walked, she would bother her "baby" grandchildren, whom she came across on the street, and give them from her pocket - that same deep and wide pocket, which was always full of all kinds of sweets - leftovers from the refreshments from the "circumcision" (Brit Mila) of a male child, and the elders would look after her fondly, and a happy laugh would spread across their faces like a shadow of a pleasant memory from days gone by.

The women were devoted to her, loving and adoring her immeasurably. She would spend two or three weeks with each woman giving birth, and all the days she spent with them were days of celebration and joy to them. She knew how to make them endear the agony, sweeten the labor pains, comfort and encourage them in moments of crisis.

As soon as she entered the room of a woman giving birth, she immediately affected her with her calmness and confidence, she took care of all the necessary preparations quickly and with the joy of a mitzvah. And during the process she consoled, soothed, persuaded and reconciled her while combining in her words proverbs and words of advice, wise conversations, jokes and anecdotes, which she had many. The patient began to smile out of agony and on her face, which were distorted by pain, a kind of light was being spread, a light of hope and consolation, and she was happy for the happiness that awaited her in a few moments.

Most of the women who she served were poor and destitute, and she took care of all their needs during their illness. The doctors were always ready to go on her errands, the medical warehouses would provide her with every object she needed, and from the gentlemen's wives, that she was their midwife, she asked to prepare for the poor women poultry soup, semolina cakes, and sweets, everything necessary for their economy and the arrangement of a "Brit Mila" (circumcision). And there was no one who dared to refuse her request. Everything was given to her generously, willingly and happily. They all knew that to the extent that she took from others, she was also taking from her own, and needless to say, she would not have taken any fee from the poor new mothers for her much trouble for two weeks or more. She was philanthropist, she was the first to volunteer for every charity. Scholars and yeshiva students ate at her house regularly. Among the diners at her house was also S. Y. Abramowitz (Mendele Mocher Sforim), when he studied at the yeshiva in Slutsk.

Avraham Epstein

Her home was open to anyone who was downtrodden and asking for help. And many of the dignitaries of the city would come to ask her advice. Because who else like her knew everyone's soul, their speech and their stuttering, their afflictions and harms? She nurtured them all and all their hearts were visible to her.

She performed her work for more than eighty years, the holy work, unceasing work without rest and without sleep at night. And with all this, her strength was the same, she was quick in her movement and fast and she was happy towards every mitzvah until the last moment.

A spring of life was within her. Her mind was not impaired even when she grew up. The life experience she accumulated added to her a kind of clarity of wise forgiveness, good and sweet as old wine. She knew the blessed peace, the peace of mind that comes from the love of life and the love of humanity. Her heart was burning with a bright light and overflowing with the light of faith and confidence. And perhaps this is the secret of her wonderful freshness, which did not leave until her last day, despite the many and severe injuries she suffered during her long life.

She had a life full of work and trouble. All her loved ones died and perished before her eyes. Her husband died in his mid-life, her only son, Reb Avrehemel Shevliov, who was a rabbi in Swisslotch, died of tuberculosis in his thirtieth year, leaving behind a wife and sons, whom she took care of. Her eldest daughter also died and her youngest daughter, Sarah the midwife, the mother of the writer of this article, was buried one week before her death.

The details of her death are wonderful, a tragic majesty poured over them.

On the evening of that day, when my mother passed away, after we returned from her funeral, they rushed the old woman to my sister, who was then in her ninth month, because she had to give birth unexpectedly. The old woman came and gave birth to a daughter. And after the delivery of the baby girl, she fell down next to the maternity bed and did not get up, because she had a stroke.

[Page 155]

Her dying lasted about a week, until she passed away. And the baby girl was called by her name and by my mother's name: Sara Rivka.

A large crowd followed her bed and the rabbi eulogized her near the synagogue. The number of candles that were brought to her home at the time of her death - memorial candles - reached to thousands. She was ninety-five years old when she died, and left her heirs only an apartment and a good name.

Editor's note: In Slutsk, grandmother Rivka was called: "Di alte babka", and her daughter, Sara the midwife, who also reached an old age, was called: "Di yonge babka".

B

Reb Kuti (Yekutiel Isaac Golda's)

With sounds and lightning this man appeared to me, out of both silence and sound. I remember: it was the night of Kol Nidrei, a sea of candles in a sea of heads wrapped in tallit, shivering wicks, stormy hearts, a glowing silent prayer, consolation of sorrow, empowerment, holy trembling, to the depth of the soul. The prayer was said in enthusiasm, the voices were united, flowing like the sigh of the sea, as a stormy moan. And in the midst of the storm he stood, Reb Kuti Isaac Golda's, silent, frozen, without moving - a block of silence amidst the noise of waves. The prayer was over. They began to read the Shir Hayichud. And suddenly he shook himself, all ablaze with flame, his hands reached up into the air, his tallit fell on his shoulders, his face burnt, his eyes – were as steel fire and his voice – as the roar of a lion. Like a thunder, the voice rolled over the heads of the worshipers and they were all swept away after him, swallowed by the flow of his roars. He called and the audience answered after him. A symphony of mighty voices, a prayer of thunder that reached the heaven and plowed under the throne of honor. And suddenly, he became silent and once again stood in his place like a still statue, like a mountain that the fire that caught it was extinguished. That's how he stood all that night and the entire morning of the day after, his tallit was covering his head and face and his tears were burning the pages of his Machzor book. The time of Musaf prayer has arrived. They read the order of work. The audience woke up, their eyes were directed towards him, to Reb Kuti Isaac Golda's, the hearts were beating, vibrating; Everyone was silent with awe and expected, and suddenly he moved from his place and the sound of a terrible roar, an inhuman roar, escaped from his mouth; And the Cohanim and the people who were standing in the Ezra (aisle)... kneeling and bowing down and falling on their faces..." And he fell on the ground with his whole body and groaned with sobs, and the whole crowd followed him. And when he got up, everyone got up after him. The Chazan (cantor) became unimportant, no one watched him and his curls; Reb Kuti was the conductor, according to him they will kneel and according to him they will get up. And so, it repeated until the end of the work order.

Reb Kuti Isaac Golda's

And another story I remember.

It was the night of Tisha B'Av after the mourning. Anxiety was all over and a heavy sadness rested on my heart. I was still a boy and my soul was full of pictures of destruction. As I had sleeping disorder, I was wandering in the old Beit Midrash and black shadows were all over me. Everything was engulfed in darkness and only the platform next to the Holy Ark was lit by the flickering light of a candle. A group of old men were sitting on the steps of the platform and Reb Kuti was reading before them about day-to-day matters. His voice pierced my heart: the voice of a sick person, a small weak voice, the groan of a torn soul lost in poverty. I will never forget the picture; The mourning of all the generations suddenly reflected to me from this face. At this moment I saw the exile face to face.

And I remember more.

A dispute arose in the city, and the people split into two parties, one party was composed of the gentlemen, the leaders of the community with all of their assistants gathered around Rabbi Reb Meirke Faimer, the son of the late Reb Yosili, and the other party was composed of the students, the scholars and the multitude of the people headed by Rabbi Ridbaz (Rabbi Yaakov David ben Ze'ev, known for his great work on the Jerusalem Talmud, at the end of his days he headed a yeshiva in Safed, and died there). Two sides, two worlds. Here - an old tradition, noble manners, ancestral attitude, and there, genius and sharpness together with mass simplicity. And the agitation was getting bigger and whistleblowers were passing on rumors from one side to the other, spreading slander and causing conflicts between the two sides. The scourge spread and the division between the two parties grew, and only R. Kuti Isaac Golda's was still standing in the middle. As one of the scholars, he tended to follow the Ridbaz, but he also respected Rabbi Yosili and he was a visitor to his son's house. And suddenly he changed his mind and did something that caused a storm in the city: he got on the stage and began to demand in front of everyone against Rabbi Meirke. He said very severe, difficult, terrible, amazing things: He is an evil person, who brings troubles to the people of Israel...

Vast fear fell upon the audience. The next day he went to Rabbi Meirke to ask for his forgiveness. He prostrated at his feet, kissed the flounce of his coat and cried like a baby...

This is who he was and how he acted. His appearance was always amazing, his proximity aroused both curiosity, anticipation and anxiety. His image had sharp, intense lines: he was not tall, his body was solid, he had a large head, prominent and stubborn forehead, and his face were tormented as if it was the face of a monk; There was something heavy, restrained, a sort of self-conquered effort in his bent form and his sloppy movements. Beyond his downcast eyes was a fiery storm and beyond his frozen silence - a silence before the storm.

He was an enigma to the people, an enigma full of contrasts and contradictions. Enthusiasm and ecstasy of an ascetic and recluse aside from grumpiness and dissatisfaction

[Page 156]

of someone who is dealing with public affairs. He was a lenient person and a friendly man in his own business, but very zealot and strict in everything that was related to public affairs. However, all these contrasts derived from one source, from his soul, which was all temperamental and furious.

His soul was always tense, his heart was full of sparks and stubbornness. The smallest thing made him burst out like a thunder.

Life brought him face to face with the twilight of modern times. They damaged one after the other in the wall of old Judaism. The young people of the generation started asking for corrections and changes and new winds were blowing and coming. Reb Kuti immediately felt the impending danger and with religious fanaticism he went to war with all his anger.

He was a man of war all his life. He had many opponents and enemies. Some called him fickle; The others called him hypocrite and disingenuous. However, it was enough for him to appear among them in a people's assembly, in the Beit Midrash, in the seat of sages, and immediately everyone became silent, submissive, everyone stood up and waited anxiously for the sound of his words.

Sometimes he would sit in his shop, a shop for processed leather. It seemed that here, in his shop, among the simple farmers, the buyer of his goods, he would rest from his other matters. Here, he was immersed in secular things, sunk in the crass lifestyle and the centers of his heart turn off for a moment between one ascend to the other.

I saw him again after ten years. I returned from the big world, I missed my little city and the distant legends of my childhood. I went to the synagogue and found out that Reb Kuti Isaac Golda's was still alive. He was the only one among all the elders of his generation who was alive. His appearance was terrible. A bundle of agony in a rotting and old body, a rickety tombstone on the grave of his life.

He seemed to me as a symbol - the symbol of the dying of a lifetime.

C

Crazy Binyamin

Every day he would walk through the streets of our city with his tall and upright stature, his white and wild hair and his undone clothes are hanging from him in tatters. A wave of dirty rags is wrapped around his neck and a thick rope is tied around his waist. He would walk slowly in the middle of the roads, his eyes hidden under their thick eyebrows. He didn't look to any side. If a person struck him, he did not turn away from him, if a cart passed on the road, he stood in his place and did not move aside.

In one hand he held a long pipe just as the farmers did and with the other hand he waved threateningly in the air, as if he was quarreling with an invisible rival. His mouth was like an overflowing spring. Thousands of garbled and confused words would erupt from his mouth with shards of mucus and foam. Voices and combinations of voices, but the ear did not catch a single word from them.

In the few moments of silence, he would stick the pipe into his mouth and he would suck and gulp very quickly and with extreme rigor, when frequent, panicked circles of smoke bursting out of his mouth and nostrils. A terrible secret was hanging over his head and an old legend was woven around his name and hung on his long and difficult life path.

And this is what the people of our city would say.

Many days ago, Binyamin was a rabbi in one of the cities and his name was known all around as one of the great geniuses, whose power grew in the open and in the hidden, and all the great men of the generation would turn to him with their questions. However, to the extent that he was great in the Torah, to that extent his strictness increased. He was a hard man, stubborn and opinionated, and many wise people were offended by him. It happened that once, one of the rabbis, who was living in the nearby town, happened to come to his house. They immediately started talking about Halacha and had disagreements: one wept and the other wept, and both of them did not change their opinion. It was a furious debate which broke out the limits of a debate for the sake of heaven and turned to be about strictness and leadership. They started teasing each other and didn't move away until the guest rabbi was hit hard and rudely. Immediately the guest rose on his feet and said: "You have a stubborn mind, Rabbi Binyamin, I wonder if you will not go crazy!" Rabbi Binyamin looked at the guest and answered: "If it is a decree, I will accept it, but you will not see it!"

And so it was: Reb Binyamin went crazy and the guest rabbi did not awake from his sleep.

In our city there were many jokes attributed to the crazy Binyamin. Once the butchers in the city wanted to build for themselves a prayer house. They hired laborers and started with the construction. Crazy Binyamin passed there and called over them the scripture: "And all flesh shall be called by your name".

To light his pipe, he would go specifically to the town of Rozova, which is far from Slutsk. When he was asked: Why did you go specifically to Rozova? Is the fire in Slutsk not enough for you? He would answer: The fire in Slutsk is too cold.

Once in the cemetery, he passed by the grave of one man, a well-known miser in the city, stood in front of the tombstone and pointed his finger towards the letters PN (here is buried) and said the initials straight and upside down in the Russian language:

Пойдеш Назад ? Не пойду!

Почему Нет ? Не Пускают!

A strange combination: these jokes and this tiny and tragic personality!

[Page 157]

Excerpts from "The First as Humans"

by Y.D. Berkwoitz

Translated by Mira Eckhaus

Edited by Jane S. Gabin

A

With Pesach Karon, known as "Pesach Ezra's"

I was a Bar Mitzvah teenager, I studied in my hometown at a small yeshiva, I filled my soul with studying the Gemara with Tosafot (additions) and from the Maharsha. And here, in my great thirst for a refreshing word, the smell of the secular books sneaked to me and I pounce upon them as if they were a spring of living water, I thirstily read one book after the other. I first read everything I could find in a dark basement of a remote book store, then I moved to the shelves of a more important bookseller, until I finally found my way to the Hebrew library, which was well known among the educated people of my city. The owner of the library was a very old Jew. He was actually a Melamed, but a wonderful man of his kind, short and with a long and strong beard, always combed, wearing shiny dark glasses under his thick and strict eyebrows, God-fearing and educated and a lover of Zion at the same time, who would teach the Torah all day in a house full of young children, guiding them with a soft hand and harsh discipline, singing with them on Shabbats evenings the Haftara in a pleasant melody that draws the heart. He sent his sons far away to study in a gentile agricultural school, so that they could immigrate to Eretz Israel to work the land in the colonies. In his bedroom, which was always extremely clean and was separated from his students' room by a dark hall, there was a large cabinet, full of Hebrew books. I always felt from this room an absolute silent of a mysterious storehouse, a place where precious world treasures are kept, and he himself, the long-bearded little Jew, with the bundle of keys under the hems of his immaculately clean capote, always seemed to me as the careful and strict keeper of the wonderful treasure, who would bring me every day to his room to enjoy a little bit of the precious light.

In the yeshiva I read the books, of course, in hiding. The Gemara was open above the page of the book, and below, in the darkness of the box, was open the book of Smolenskin, "The Wanderer in the Ways of Life", or "Religion and Life" by Broides. From the bottom up, small and terrible flames were burning, plotting in the darkness to become a great blazing fire, which would burn and consume everything. If only the head of the yeshiva had watched and seen this! But he didn't pay attention and didn't see anything. I was among his loyal, humble disciples, how can he suspect kosher like me? Only my friends knew that. But my friends did not discover my secret, because they themselves did even a worst thing than mine: they played cards. Although not with real cards, but with cards "Lamed-Alef". However, they would play like real habitual gamblers, with money.

In the yeshiva I would only do the beginning of my reading in the book, as a short-tempered nervous person I would taste secretly of the precious delight only a first taste. I would leave all the pleasure of reading for the evening, upon my return home. I wouldn't go to sleep until I finished reading the entire borrowed book. As a result, my mother's expenses for oil increased. But she felt comfortable about it, as she figured her son is very persistent in Talmud Torah and sits on the holy books until midnight. And only the old librarian was not the most favorable about it.

Y.D. Berkowitz

At the beginning, he praised me for my great diligence; However, with the passage of time, he saw and witnessed that for a salary of twenty pennies a month I read almost thirty of his books, and between times, during the Passover and the Sukkot holidays, days when the yeshiva was closed and the students went to their homes, I would come to change my books twice a day.

- Did you come to diminish me?! - He would say as if from irritation, when he looks at me through his dark and shiny glasses and moves his long, strong and thick beard, which was a mix of black and white. I couldn't understand his meaning completely: was he mocking me, or was he simply angry, that he made a bad deal with me?

However, due to my excessive diligence, another trouble was expected to me: the books that were left for me to read were decreasing day by day. And the anguish in my heart was greater each day. What will I do after I read all of them? Where will I turn and what else will I find in my world? My life will be Empty and desolated!...

And here the calamity came. I have already read all the big and small stories. I also read all the new and old collections, also the books dealing with the Chronicles of Israel and the Chronicles of the World, the Natural History and the Paths of the Land. And more than that, when all hope was lost, my benefactor and spiritual provider brought me down from a hidden place in his attic the large and heavy volumes of the "HaMelitz", which I put in a sack and took on my shoulder to my house (I would be ashamed to carry them openly, lest I draw the curious eyes of

[Page 158]

passersby). From the stories of Mapo and Smolenskin, Broides and Brandstetter I have no hope, I have already read them three or four times. What will become of me? Where will my help come from?

- I am afraid that today you will leave empty-handed! The old librarian told me once, after he reviewed the shelves of his closet with his shining glasses and did not find any more consolations for me in them. My heart failed. I saw it as the end of my life. A dark abyss opened before me. I stood dreary and could not move from my place.

Please wait a moment, - the old man suddenly turned to me, who was also standing worried next to his closet, and from his dark glasses a glimmer of hope glimmered at me. - Do you want to read jargon?

Pesach Karon,
known as "Pesach Ezra's"

"Jargon", I knew, was a fancy name, a sort of scientific definition to the simple Jewish language, the Ivry Teitsch language, that the common people and women would read. For a Gemara guy like me, who has already smelled the smell of education and filled his heart with words of vision and thought, to come down from the peak of the poetic Hebrew to the poor pleading language - such a solution to my difficult situation was not to my liking. But since my guide in education called this language by the honored name "Jargon", it must have something to praise, and it is also worth a guy like me to figure it out. I went out with the old man from the

Hebrew treasure store to the dark corridor, where a cabinet full of Jargon books stood in a distant corner. I began with one of the novels of Shomer (Nahum Meir Schaikewitz), which I encountered first.

I felt that this was a big drop for me, and even so, I pounced on Shomer's novels out of a new hunger and swallowed them one by one. But I did not bring them to the yeshiva - I was ashamed of my friends, that even though they were all diligent about playing the game of "Lamed-Alef" in the boxes of their dark lecterns, many were found among them, who on the fifth day of Shabbat, this is the test day before the head of the Yeshiva, showed a surprising sharpness in the in-depth study of the Maharsha or "Pnei Yehoshua". How light I was then in my eyes with my wife's pleas compared to the harsh "Pnei Yehoshua"!... And so, I read Shomer's novels in secret, late at night at home. However - I was not relieved at home either, where it was soon discovered, that the books, which I read all nights, are not holy books at all, but a kind of empty fairy tales in the Ivry Teitsch, with which servant girls delight their souls on Shabbat days. Is it possible? Do I use up all the oil in the house on that? And is reasonable at all that the yeshiva boy, whose parents have high hopes for him, to be engaged in these vanities? What is the purpose of this?...

Even I myself did not derive much pleasure from Shomer's stories. Indeed, I read many of them, but after reading them I had the feeling as if I had swallowed into my stomach with spoilt fruits After such reading, I always felt a great discomfort and a heartbreak. All these clumsiness stories about bad and sinful Jews, cruel in heart and evil persons, who always harm righteous, holy and pure souls like the angels of heaven, did not touch my heart and did not excite my imagination. Their voices and words came out of an empty space, without an origin and without a purpose, and did not evoke any echo in my soft and deluded soul, which was centered in its loneliness and looking for its paths in the world. How far were these creatures, in the crude imagination, from that lofty spiritual atmosphere that surrounded the heroes of the stories of Smolenskin and Broides, from that sublime pathos in their fiery speeches, which in my eyes elevated them to the upper echelon of prophets, warriors of the holy war and redeemer of the people!

And yet, I willingly immersed myself in this heavy fog and filled my head with bad fumes. I was afraid to exclude my soul from the world of imaginations, beyond its gates I was expected to face a terrible fate, only the boredom of the Gemara. And so, I read novel after novel, I moved from Shomer's stories to the American novels, at Passover time I got involved in a great tangle of "Man-Eater", a novel in twenty-four volumes, which I exchanged in the library, as I do on my days off, twice a day - and thus I provoked the old librarian's anger.

- I want to tell you something - He told me once in the early evening, when I came to him to exchange my books for the second time that day. - I don't find it proper at all, that a young man like you chose these vain ways!... What will this "Man-Eater" give and add to your life? You will only harm yourself forever!

- But what will I read? asked the "young man", that was in the lowest level, almost with tears in his eyes. - Afterall, you don't have any better books than these for me!

- Be quiet, you know what? - He told me. If not don't tell anyone, I'll try to give you some kind of a thing that will revive your soul! And he takes me and brings me back to the quiet and silent archive, it is the Holy of Holies from which I have been distanced for many days. He takes out the bunch of keys from under the hems of his capote, bends down with his long beard to the lower part of the Hebrew bookcase and opens a hidden drawer there, from which shines before my eyes a row of great books in good, strong covers.

- These books, which you see here, - He tells me with a warm glow in his dark glasses, they are all hidden precious delights.

[Page 159]

I don't take them out to anyone. I have encrypted them here as an inheritance for my son after my death... But with you I will make an exception because you are in a difficult situation - because I see that your soul is dying... but only make sure to keep them as the apple of your eye, lest even a light dust stick to them!... Here are the volumes - Do you see? These are the "Dawns" volumes of Peretz Smolenskin. Now they can't be found anywhere, no one will sell them to you for even a thousand carbons, unless he is bankrupt... and this book, which I will give you to read today, is also very expensive. Only on one condition will I give it to you - Don't read it all at once! It is not equal to "Man-Eater"!... Read them little by little, and listen to every word you read, because it is the precious treasure of all. It's true that this is also a jargon, but a jargon of a completely different species!... You will find in it precious things, and I am certain that you will remember this mercy of me forever!...

With bated breath, I opened the precious book, which my elderly benefactor handed to me after such a solemn introduction - it was the annual collection of Shalom Aleichem "Di Yudishe Folks- Bibliothek" (the popular Jewish bibliography).

* * *

What was the reason that Shalom Aleichem's "popular Jewish bibliography" was so valued to my old literary guide, who singled out a place of honor for it among Smolenskin's "Dawn" volumes, and what was its value in general in the eyes of the educated of the previous generation - this became clear to me many days later, when I got to know Shalom Aleichem closely and learned to know his first steps in literature.

* * *

Not for nothing did the old librarian prophet, that I will remember his kindness to him forever. Every time I remember the Shalom Aleichem's collection, I will remember him too. His name was Pesach Karon, and he was one of those who appeared as the signatories, which was printed in the second volume of the collection - the only signatory in Slutsk, my hometown.

B

With Mendele Mocher Sforim's childhood friend

In the meantime, I left the yeshiva and I started an independent life. My father's authority was no longer on me (my father migrated to America), so I was able to persuade my mother to hire a Russian teacher for me, and I started studying secular studies. And in order to win her mind, lest she think of me that, God forbid, I deviated from the straight and narrow, I promised her that for half a day I would study Gemara by myself in the synagogue on our street. Our synagogue was already empty and desolate in my time, on weekdays only one old Jew studied there, called "Moti the Kapoleshchik", named after his origin, as he was born in a town nearby Kapolei, - so I chose lunchtime for me, when the Kapoleshchik would go to his house to eat and take a nap for a while, and I walked around the stage and memorized the rules of Russian grammar and the names of the heroes of Russian history. The gloomy walls of the Beit Midrash may have heard the sounds of the foreign language and the foreign and strange names for the first time, such as "Sviatopolk Okaianni", "Vladimir Monomakh", "Dmitry Donskoi"... I felt pangs of conscience at the sight of the ancient Holy Ark, lying in the shadow of the wilderness, which looked at me as if in rebuke, but the Holy Ark was silent. And against this I was not saved from the Kapoleshchik's criticism.

- Listen, you, handsome guy! He turned to me once in a soft tone. - Indeed, you are not a bad boy, with a not bad perception, - but what is the nature of these gentile books that I found in your lectern? Huh?...

- These are kosher books, I try to ease his mind, - textbooks for language and arithmetic.

- For language and arithmetic? What a boy who studies Torah has to do with such matters? Do you intend, God forbid, deviated from the straight and narrow?

- On the contrary, - I spar him with my words, - I intend to go to a good culture, with proper behavior. After all, it is written in Pirke Avot: "Tova Torah im Derech Eretz" (Torah should be combined with proper behavior).

- Oh, - He said, - You are already talking as one of the people of society, damn them! You bring me evidence of your despised matters from Pirke Avot!... I should discuss it with your mother. I am afraid that you will end up like one of my past friends.

- Who was your friend? - I am filled with curiosity.

- A famous criminal. If you deal with these little books, you must have heard his name. He belongs to the same print company. He writes stories in Ivry Teitsch.

- What is his name? I was eager to know.

His name? wait a little and I will tell you... - He has a little difficulty with this and rubs his forehead with his hand. - Blessed is the reminder of oblivion!... Yes, his name was Shalom, Shlomke!...

My heart was thrilled. Indeed, the Kapoleshchik was a native of Kapolei!

- Shalom Yaakov Abramowitz? - I asked almost anxiously.

- Abramowitz! - Says the old man, waving his hand dismissively. - In our day we didn't know any Abramowitz, his name was Shalom, and after he became a heretic, he wrote a book of tales in the Ivry Teitsch, a kind of nonsense, a joke, about a horse or a mare there... Women's wisdom, nothing important that should be talked about!...

- He is Mendele Mocher Sforim! - I jumped out of my seat in admiration.

- Which Mendele? Why are you struggling with me? - The old man got angry. - Why you say Mendele when I tell you his name is Shalom!... And where did you get the idea that he is a book seller? He is not a book seller, but just a feckless person, an empty person, and also desecrates the Shabbat...

I did not move from the old Kapoleshchik and I longed to hear from him new things about the life of Mendele.

- See - He said - How this little boy is all excited as if I told him about a famous teacher, about the greatest of the generation! And the old Kapulshchik told me that this Shlomke was not at all a wise student in his youth. Both of them studied in Kapolei in the same Beit Midrash, except that Shlomke was an empty person in his eyes.

[Page 160]

As the old man continued to the studies of the Gemara and the Tosafot, while Shlomke studied the anecdotes and legends, light things. And this would not have been so terrible, if he had not left Kapolei and travelled far away, to Vilna or Warsaw, and there caused his destruction!!... The rumor that he writes on Shabbat is indeed true. He married a kosher, God-fearing wife, and she takes the pen out of his hand on Shabbat and hides it until after Havdalah...

The story of Mendele Mocher Sforim in his youth strengthened me and excited my dim hope: Well, it's not impossible. Mendeley too was a regular boy among the boys in Kapolei!... But from then on, it was no longer convenient for me to continue my studies in the empty synagogue, because Mendele's friend watched over me carefully, lest I dishonor the holy place. That's why I left the synagogue and worked hard on my studies at home.

C

Mendele about Slutsk and his childhood friend

I met Mendele Mocher Sforim by chance, and became one of the regular visitors in his home. - - - When he heard from me that I was born in Slutsk, he was overjoyed:

- Indeed? A real Slutsk native? Do you have a bent finger?...[a] Then, we are somewhat relatives! In the days of my youth, I spend a few years in Slutsk, I studied in the Beit Midrash of Rabbi Yona, the Slutsk gentleman, I ate my lunch meals in the houses of the other Slutsk gentlemen... Listen to a nice story! If so, why are you silent? He is from Slutsk - and he sits there silently!...

And Mendele, all awake and smug, with a fresh redness in the skin of his thin and tanned cheeks, sits and interrogates me about Slutsk and his friends from long ago, all of whom have already passed away and in my childhood, I heard only the echo of their words and deeds. He draws for me on the palm of his hand the paths of the city of Slutsk and its streets: here is the market, and from the market you turn to Kapolei Street, and from here you turn sideways and turn to Rabbi Yona's Beit Midrash and to the courtyard of the synagogues' yards, and inside the city runs the road, this is the King's Road, which leads to Ostrova... There, in Ostrova, lived his good friends, gentle people, with great genealogy, they and their excellent sons, all well-educated, ... He rubs with his hand in his handsome, tall, forehead that is plowed wide dense wrinkles, and says: Oh, Lord, what were their names?... Wait a minute... No, he forgot their names! After all, this was several years ago!...

How many years ago, the grandfather did not mention.

* * *

Mendele's childhood friend from his hometown Kapolei comes to my mind, the one who used to watch over me in our synagogue and comments me about morality, that I should not follow his friend's ways and not go out like him into a bad culture. I tell Mendele about him.

- Really? - Mendele says as if out of curiosity. - From Kapolei? And my friend? what was his name?

- His name was Moti, and we called him the "Kapulshchik".

- Moti - says Mendele - it is a weak sign. There was a whole lot of "Moti" in Kapolei. What was Moti's personality type?

- I know that in the past he used to travel to the villages to buy linen from the farmers, and in his old age he retired to the Beit Midrash to study Torah. He used to study the entire Shas during the year.

- This is also one of the weak signs! - Says Mendele and rubs his forehead with his hand. - Moti, Moti... well? What, you say, Moti did tell you about me?

- He was saying a lot of things. For example, that in your childhood, when you studied together in the Beit Midrash in Kapolei, you were more attracted to the legend than to the halacha.

I assume this Moti followed the halacha? - Says the grandfather with a witty sneer, and I feel that he has already bitterness in his heart against that Moti. - Well? And what else did he tell you about me?

- Just stories that were told in Kapolei, after you left it.

Well, come on! Tell me, please tell! Why do I have to pull the strings from you one by one?...

I regretfully reflect on the whole act. If I will tell him the things like they were, that his friend was disrespecting him, talking about his "mare" as a foolish thing and an act of shame, portraying him as someone who desecrates the Shabbat, whose wife had to take the pen out of his hand and hide it until after the Havdalah, - I am sure that I will upset the grandfather and bring him to anger. Therefore, I am trying to soften the story as much as possible, and nevertheless I see that this matter has tainted Mendele's spirit. He sits for a few moments afterwards silently with a gloomy face.

- No! - He suddenly says and shakes his white and handsome head. - The whole thing is difficult for me... How did he become to be my friend?... I don't remember at all that I had a friend named Moti actually!...

* * *

On my third visit, Mendele asked me to join him for a walk outside the city. We set out on the road leading to Mount Salivo, walking under the bright and pleasant sky of a fresh and encouraging summer morning. The cautious Mendele, with his upright, brave and noble elderliness, was wearing his tall straw hat, which made him look as an old, arrogant and confident nobleman, that everyone must clear the way for him and bless him with the removal of their hat. He walked with young and firm steps, walking and talking, without getting tired in both actions together. And only when we went out of the city, towards the mountains, passing between scattered villas, with grassy yards, shaded by green oaks, did he stop walking and present his stick in front of him, he turned his head back and forth, widened his nostrils

[Page 161]

and breathed deeply into his body the smell of the harvested hay, that was drying under the sun here and there in the yards. "Oh, what a reviving smell in here - there's no need at all to go out to the village for a summer meeting!..." And suddenly he turned to me, as if from the combination of his thoughts, turned his face and said with a little anger:

-Listen... that Jew of yours, who used to travel between your villages with linen, the same Moti himself... I then pondered over him all night... Yes, it was true that there was one in Kapolei's Beit Midrash... But he was with a clumsy soul - not from the circle of my friends... How did it come to me?... Yes, I remember him. He was just stupid... stupid!...

A roasted pigeon flourishes in the air

Grandfather Mendele Mocher Sforim said:

After my father's death, my widowed mother sent me to the ancient city of Slutsk, which is close to Kapolei, my hometown, to study Torah there in a yeshiva. I was a poor boy, but from a good family, I also excelled in my talents and diligence from all my fellow yeshiva students. The people of the city noticed me, praised me, and differentiate me favorably than all the boys of my age, and there they called me: "the prodigy from Kapolei".

One day, the city's rich man, who was famous all around for his wealth and generosity of spirit, made a feast in his house for the dignitaries of the community, the rich and the Torah scholars, and among the rest of the guests I was suddenly invited to his table. I - the poor orphan, who has never set foot on the threshold of a rich man's house! All my friends talked about this great event and were jealous of me, because I was honored so much. And the clowns among them sent the arrows of their tongues at me and said: "the rich man invited you because he intends you to marry his daughter in the future!"

The day of the feast came, and my heart was full of anxiety. I wore my Shabbat clothes, but I was not sure that I would know how to behave in the rich man's house according to all the rules of etiquette, accepted in the homes of the rich. I was not a foolish boy, and therefore I decided in my mind: I will observe and see the actions of all the other guests, and I will act similarly to them.

When I came to the feast in the evening, I was amazed at what I saw and I was like a daydreamer. I have never imagined that there is such wealth and such glory in the world! The house was like a palace of kings.

High and luxurious rooms. A sea of light poured all over. Silver and crystal lamps, golden chairs and sheets of velvet and silk. In every corner I turn - gold and silver, blue and crimson. And my wretched feet step on expensive carpets, softer than butter.

I entered all anxious and ashamed into the large splendid feast hall, among the other guests. The rich man and his wife received me with a beautiful welcome and seated me at the head of the table, that was prepared for the meal - in the place where the dignitaries sat. All the people turned their eyes on me and were surprised. Each turned to the other and asked in a whisper: "Who is this boy?", - "Don't you know who he is?" - "He is the prodigy from Kapolei!" - "Is he a son of a rich man?", - "No, he is a poor orphan". - "And why did he deserve to be invited to the feast?" - "It is said that the rich man he intends to marry his daughter to this young man in the future". - "Indeed, he is!? Then this is a boy of valor! Blessed is his mother!"... And I hear all these conversations, I feel the eyes of the guests staring at me, and I sit in my honorable place with a face burning with shame and afraid to move a hand or a foot.

Then the feast began. Servants run back and forth, bringing the best food and drinks to the table. All the guests ate and drank and enjoyed themselves. Everyone was talking, laughing, clinking spoons and forks, and the noise is great and the joy is great. And I was the only one, who sat still among them, as a captive among the hunters, and did not touch the food given to me. Overwhelmed by my emotions, I forgot my soul and my appetite was gone.

And here they served roasted pigeons to the table, a pair of pigeons for each of the guests, and I suddenly hear the lady's voice speaking to me: "Why don't you eat, boy? Do you intend to leave this feast hungry?" - There was a great silence in the hall, and all eyes turned to me. I was very ashamed so I took the knife and fork in my hand, but I did not know what to do with them. Until that day, I never had a chance to use such utensils, because my food in the yeshiva was only dry bread with cold water... I remembered my decision and looked here and there as if stealthily, to see what the rest of the people were doing with their knives and forks. However, due to my excessive excitement, I saw only heads moving in the mist and mouths busying themselves with their work. So, I decided to try to handle the roasts pigeons on my own. I started to touch them with my knife and fork, I turned them in the bowl from side to side, I abused them mercilessly. And while I was doing this and that, alas, a disaster happened! - One of my two poor pigeons, who could not bear my antics anymore, picked up her wings and flew out of my bowl and into the face of the lady who owned the house, who was sitting in front of me...

* * *

That night I made a vow: I would never again come as a poor man to a feast of the rich. And one more vow I made in my heart then: not to eat roasted pigeons for the rest of my life!...

Original footnote:

a.   It was acceptance in our places, that the Slutsk people are extremely proud people. When you ask a Jew who comes from Slutsk, who he is, he bends one finger and begins to count his virtues: "First, I am from Slutsk..." And since he has nothing else to add and count besides this virtue, he remains standing with his bent finger.

[Page 162]

Yitzhak Katznelson in Slutsk

by Y. D. Berkowitz

Translated by Mira Eckhaus

Edited by Jane S. Gabin

From right to left: Hillel Dobrov, Yitzhak Katznelson, Avraham Epstein, Y.D. Berkowitz

In the summer of 1904, when I returned from the place where I lived abroad to spend the summer months in Slutsk, I invited my friend Yitzchak Katznelson, who was already well known for his first Hebrew poems and songs, and to whom I became attached with a great love when I lived with him in his parents' house in Lodz. Katznelson willingly accepted my invitation and came to stay with me for a few weeks at my parents' house. Yitzchak Katznelson, the great lamenter of the last terrible destruction, who was murdered, together with his wife and sons, along with millions of our brothers, by the hands of the corrupting Satan's soldiers, and left behind him "the lamentation over the Jewish people who were killed", which agitated the Jewish world, - was in those days a nineteen-year-old boy, handsome, cheerful, nice and pleasant to the people. At that time, the Zionist youth in Slutsk would gather at the well-known Zionist "teahouse", and in the evenings they would gather at the private home of the midwife Abigail Karon (Pesach Karon's daughter-in-law), who had a reputation in the city as a kind of an intelligence committee house, and Yitzhak Katznelson made a great impression there, he was liked by everyone, and in particular he won the hearts of the young girls in Slutsk.

A memory of those days is this photo, that was preserved in my archives. Before we parted from Katznelson, the four of us went out in the "Khila" to tour the towns around Slutsk, of which Neswij and Timkovitz are remembered (the latter greeted us with a large fire and almost all

[Page 163]

the town caught fire). When Katznelson later wrote his book "On the Borders of Lithuania," he also incorporated something from his notes, which he perceived in Slutsk and the surrounding area.

Episodes from
"These Are the Generations of Adam"
(Eleh toldot Adam)

by Ephraim E. Lisitzky

Translated by Mira Eckhaus

Edited by Jane S. Gabin

A

Slutsk's Jews

It is said of a Jew from Slutsk that his little finger is always bent. What is the reason for that? Nine tenths of pride went down into the world and all of them were taken by the Slutsk Jews, and when a Jew from Slutsk is asked: Why did you take upon yourself this excessive pride? he places his right finger on the little finger of his left, bends it and begins to say his praises: First of all, I am from Slutsk! And secondly... there is no second to his beginning, it is its beginning and its end - and his little finger remains bent.

Slutsk was famous for its poverty, the same Israeli poverty in the cities and towns bordering the moshav area, and of which it took a leading part. Most of its Jews were destitute poor people living in misery, wearing rags, living in ruins and eating bran bread and grain soup, called Krupnik in a foreign language, - a kind of a stew in Slutsk's style, which was nothing more than distilled water with a few potatoes and grains floating far from each other. Slutsk was a poor city - but it was a Torah place that accepted its poverty and its path in a life of sorrow. Its rabbis were a chain of mighty and great in the Torah people and there was an abundance of outstanding scholars in it, and they set times in its Beit Midrash houses to study and teach the houseowners and the common people in the population, and even vacuous people of Israel enjoyed it. Slutsk had yeshivas for the young and the old, and poor boys and young men flocked to them from near and far, and they come to study Torah in them, and the Jews of Slutsk, who were themselves poor, shared their bread and grain soup with them, and the synagogues offered them a place to sleep. The glory of the Torah and its respect were preserved in Slutsk and it was the Jews' pride.

I spent eight years, years of childhood and youth, in which the image of a person's being is shaped, in Slutsk, and it was the one which shaped my spiritual being and embedded in me its nature. From studying the Pentateuch and the Prophets I moved to studying the Gemara, and the world of nobility in the Pentateuch and the Prophets was replaced by the practical world of the Gemara. In this world there is no discussion in the act of the creation or in a very complex matter, as it is done is the world of the Bible, but a discussion in the existence of the world and the reality, and yet its power strips them of their reality, while the faces of the Tannaim and the Amoraim that discusses these issues are clothed with realistic portraits, in the form of the elders of Slutsk's Beit Midrash houses. I can see them clashing over the interpretation of a difficult issue, with frowning faces, frowning brows and sparking eyes, debating with each other while pointing their thumbs ups and giving shrugs, as they are about to interrupt each other's lives. But these Tannaim and Amoraim treated me with grace and pleasantly explained me the secrets of Torah, and my loneliness is sweetened in their company.

Ephraim E. Lisitzky

I had a desire to be tested in my studies, if not in the presence of my parents – then at least in the presence of my grandfather. And not by my Rabbi, towards whom I had bitterness that I was discriminated compared to the rest of his students - but by one of the scholars of whom I had heard.

Those days I studied in the cheder the issue of "Tigray Lod," and I decided to memorize it for the exam. When it became understandable, I began to forcefully ask my grandfather to take me to be examined by Rabbi

Hischa - an old scholar, a former Rosh Yeshiva, who used to pray in the synagogue of the yeshiva that my grandfather attended. My grandfather initially refused my request: his place in that synagogue was on a bench behind the bimah, among all the other poor and inferior people like him. How would he dare to approach Rabbi Hischa, whose place of honor is next to the Holy Ark, and to discuss the act of creation or very complex matters? Where it was customary to stand up at his entrance and exit, and discuss this issue with him? Finally, my grandfather gave in to my pleas and took me to Rabbi Hischa on one of the Shabbat

[Page 164]

afternoons. With great fear and trepidation, he approached the place of honor in the synagogue, and I followed him with a great fear, and Rabbi Hischa– 's head and most of his body were in the Gemara open before him and he did not notice us. My grandfather coughed a few times and Rabbi Hischa stopped his studying. I began lecturing in front of him the "Tigray Lod" issue orally, with my eyes lowered in shame and awe at his sullen face. When my lecture was over, he began asking questions, both relevant and unrelated, and I answered correctly, and my eyes were slightly raised and I caught a glimpse of him and saw a contented expression on his face.

"He is blessed," he told my grandfather. "he is a wise scholar! Happy is his mother in the world of truth and his father in America."

Tears were in my grandfather's eyes, and I felt discomfort in my heart and my throat choked. And my grandfather turned his grumpy face towards him, saying: "What is your wish, Jewish Rabbi?" "My wish," my grandfather said hesitating "my wish, that is, his wish... this is my grandson, the son of my dead daughter... his father is in America... he is a young Torah scholar... he wants... he wants... that is, he asks to be tested in his studies, Rabbi."

When Rabbi Hischa asked me the name of the treatise and the issue which I studied, he ordered me to go to the bookcase and take it out.

"My son," Rabbi Hischa said to me, "study persistently, and may your father be happy with you in America and your mother be happy in the world of truth, as it is written: Your father will be happy." A cry burst from my mouth, and every insult about my loneliness was concentrated in one whimpered word: Father! father!

B

My friends Berl and our Rabbi, Rabbi Nehemiah

A rabbi does a lot and a friend does a lot, and sometimes the influence of a friend is greater than the influence of a rabbi. My friends influenced me a lot in those days of my loneliness, and I became much closer to them, especially to Berl, just Berl, without the addition of his last name by which he was famous in our Hebrew library. For about a year and a half we studied together with Rabbi Yossel at the "synagogue for the homeowners" and for a year with Rabbi Nehemiah at his yeshiva, and from the moment we got to know each other, we were bound by bonds of love and brotherhood that never stopped until we parted from each other.

His image is preserved in my memories, as it was then in his youth: his face was white, tense and rigid, and his look was rather sadness or sullen, that was sometimes softened a little with a suppressed smile, his eyes were black and dreamy, and the flickering of grief was in their pupils. His hair was black and shining and brightened his white face even more. I keep in my memory very clearly the sight of his fingers: nobility prevailed in the whiteness and gentleness of their shape. There was a kind of heaviness in him, which was not a heaviness of body or sloppiness of movement, but a seriousness of behavior and burden of thought, which was expressed in his walk, which was balanced and moderate. And his mindset was similar to his walk. He was gifted with scholastic talents, and they distinguished him from the rest of Rabbi Yossel's students, and in addition, he was gifted with the talent of imitating actors. When he was amused, he would imitate, with the cutting of his speech and the grimaces of his face, big and small, and hitting their weak points with banter, which was mainly a poignant and sharp humor. Every day we would repeat together the Gemara lesson that we learned from Rabbi Yossel, and between Minchah and Ma'ariv, we would go to a corner in the synagogue, put aside the Torah issues and turn to a daily conversation, mostly about things in the heart, we would talk and tell stories to each other, I told him my memories of the days of my mother's life and the time of her death, and he told me miraculous stories he read in Hebrew books that he received, such as "Emek Arazim," "Shlumat Reshayim,"and "Kur Oni." Sometimes we would sail in our imaginations to distant lands and reveal hidden treasures there, shake hands and make an oath of friendship for eternity.

One day, the days between times, Berl persuaded me to join him going to Rabbi Nehemiah to be examined by him for entry into his yeshiva. I did not believe that our Gemara knowledge would suffice to enter Rabbi Nehemiah's yeshiva, which was a well-known yeshiva in Slutsk and its surroundings. Nevertheless, some of the degree of confidence in Berl was also conferred on me and I agreed to join him. We entered Rabbi Nehemiah's house, he was at the head, in a bit of awe, and I followed him, full of fear and trepidation, and when we entered, Berl spoke for us and told Rabbi Nehemiah of our wish. Rabbi Nehemiah accepted his request and gave us two pages in the Gemara, for him a page in tractate Baba Metzia and for me a page in tractate Baba Kama, and ordered us to go over them ourselves and come to him tomorrow for an examination. We immediately went to the synagogue where we studied and began to study these pages of the Gemara, he separately and I separately, and we helped each other in difficult places, and we did not move from there until everything was clear and understandable to us. The next day we came to Rabbi Nehemiah, and upon finishing our exam he ordered us, after he learned from us that both his father and my father were in America, to send our mothers to him. We knew the meaning of sending our mothers to him: we were accepted into the yeshiva. We hurried to our homes, Berl's walk also became reckless this time. We rushed to Rabbi Nehemiah with our mothers - he his mother and I my stepmother - and when they entered his house we stayed outside silently, in this moment that was so important to us! After a little while, both of them, his mother and my stepmother, came out shining, and told us the good news: we were accepted to Rabbi Nehemiah's yeshiva, and he even told them that if they are unable to pay the tuition, he intended to appoint us as helpers to two of his lagging students, so that their parents would pay him the tuition in our favor. That day was a real Yom Tov for us, a real Simchat Torah.

A tangible symbol of Shammai's portrait was that of Rabbi Nehemiah: a very sharp man, refined in halacha and sharp in appearance - his facial features were pointed, his sideburns and beard were pointed, and above all were his eyes – prominent and staring eyes, which pierced like sharpened spears. His yeshiva was famous not only for the quality of the studies but also for the quality of the manners: its students had a great fear towards him, similar to their fear of God. It was his sharp appearance that helped him intimidating his younger and older students. After he finished his daily lesson in both of his classes, he used to move around the bimah, round after round, hammering while perusing an issue and his eyes were wandering and watching his students that stood by their lecterns and repeated the lesson he taught today and prepared themselves for the lesson he would teach tomorrow. Woe to the student who stopped learning or turned to small talk with a nearby friend - he would stare his pointed face at him

[Page 165]

and became annoyed. He responded willingly to the students who asked whenever they encountered difficult issues and explained to them thoroughly, but he never spoke with them a daily conversation, even if it was just about courtesy and good behavior. He treated his students as if they were babies, when the left side was rejected, he added to the rejection on the left half of the rejection on the right side. Nevertheless, he was loved and respected by his students: he was eloquent and knowledgeable and had the power of explanation, and reciting his daily lesson enlightened their eyes with the Gemara, solved their issues and brought it closer to their intellect.

For half a year we studied together, Berl and I, in the small "small table" class at Rabbi Nehemiah's yeshiva, and even before we ended the first half, I noticed a change in him: he was no longer open with me, the frown on his face was more than his sadness, his desire to study had loosened and the love and brotherhood towards me decreased materially.

For the second half of the year, Reb Nehemiah separated me from the rest of his students in the "small table" class and transferred me to the "big table" class. I counted this great honor as a loan I should repay and I devoted myself to my studies with all my might. Rabbi Nehemiah's eyes were softened whenever they looked at me and I was proud, while Berl - his heart was no longer with me and our friendship broke up! Finally, Berl withdrew from the yeshiva and we were distanced. We became citizens in two worlds that were differentiated and distant from each other: I delved deeper in the gardens of the Torah, and he, who peeked and was hurt, uprooted himself from it and began to delve in the garden of education. Our relationship ended.

We met by chance one day in the hallway of the house owners' synagogue, he had a book of songs of Judah Leib Gordon under his lap, and I had a thick Gemara in my hand. We started a conversation, I spoke about my studies and the Gemara pages I reviewed and the glory of "Maharam Schiff" and "Pnei Yehoshua," and he spoke about the Hebrew literature and the books he read and the glory of "kotzo shel yud", and "the religion and life" and "the sin of youth" and the like, wonderful names that I have never heard of. We did not hear each other's language - we were relatives at a distance. From that time on, we did not meet again in Slutsk. Berl disappeared from my life and I didn't know where he was and what he was doing.

Six years later, when I was in America, I also replaced the garden of Torah with the garden of Hebrew literature. I met with one of my friends who studied with me at Rabbi Nehemiah's yeshiva. We began reminiscing about the past and when our conversation turned to the rest of our friends and Berl among them, an exclamation of astonishment came out of his mouth: "Who could imagine then that Berl is about to occupy a place of honor in our Hebrew literature and will be among its leading narrators!" In a flash, my memory put before the young people the Hebrew narrators that I knew, and I said: "He is Y. D. Berkowitz!"

C

Rabbi Pesach

A new yeshiva was founded in Slutsk, and it was founded and headed by Rabbi Pesach, known as Rabbi Pesach the Moshi, after Mosh, the city of his residence from which he came to Slutsk. My heart swept after this new yeshiva and I considered moving to it after spending one year in Rabbi Nehemiah's yeshiva.

Just as Shammai's portrait was reflected in Rabbi Nehemiah, so was Hillel's portrait reflected in Rabbi Pesach, and just as the title "A man who is sharp in everything" well suited Rabbi Nehemiah, the same way suited Rabbi Pesach the title "A man who is smooth in everything" - a kind of silky smoothness was in his body and within him. His face was pure and shone with the light of the Torah and the light of an exceeding soul (neshama yetira), and the tiny clefts in them, the traces of a former smallpox disease, looked like dimples. His eyes were black, glowing and producing good faith and pureness of the soul; Also, the hair of his head and his beard, every hair and hair a thread of glory. He had a beautiful soul, used to care for himself and was meticulous in his clothes, which should be ironed, and in his shoes, which should be polished, and in his walking, which should be upright and one step at a time, and the like in those outwardly minutiae. And this behavior was free from pride, even from that eighth of the eighth that was commanded on a wise scholar. He was not arrogant; He loved the simple and poor people and treated them with brotherhood.

That is why he chose the synagogue of the blacksmiths to house his yeshiva. The blacksmiths in Slutsk were considered the inferior among the craftsmen. They were clumsy Jews, and it was easier for them to wrestle with a rebellious horse when they put his horseshoe to his hoof and with a reluctant wheel that requires an iron hoop, than to handle the letters in the siddur. Due to the disdain on the part of the Torah followers for the artisans, they also withdrew, as did the tailors and hatters and butchers, from the synagogues where the Torah snobbishness prevailed and built synagogues for themselves - the Blacksmiths' Synagogue.

The synagogue of the blacksmiths housing Rabbi Pesach's Yeshiva in it, became a place of Torah for those artisans as well; From time to time, Rabbi Pesach would preach in front of them, and he would recite a lesson in "Chayei Adam" (the life of a person) in front of them every day, between Minchah and Ma'ariv." This lesson that he recited in front of them included written things, which he recited and explained to them, and oral things, which he added, words of admonishment and things that were intended to carry away the hearts and encourage the soul, with a melody that yearns the heart and brings tears to the eye. He was sitting at the head of the table and they were sitting around it, their calloused and charred palms under their beards, and their eyes looked at him with murmurs of thanks and blessing for this hour of joy that they have with his grace - a taste of the world to come, and it is more beautiful to them than all the life of this world.

Rabbi Pesach minimized himself with the simple and humble people and with his disciples. He did not impose authority on them, he was their friend, a great friend who minimized himself and glorified them. Nevertheless, its yeshiva was privileged from this friendship: he did not impose a great fear on them but great love of a rabbi for them, and they rewarded him with doubled love for the rabbi and love for his Torah.

And here is a story that happened one day:

It was the season "between times" and the time of the melting of the snows, when the ground of Slutsk's streets and alleys became muddy and swampy, and I and three of my friends went to visit Rabbi Pesach at his home, to discuss a matter that he wanted to consult with us about. A festive whiteness overflowed from the walls of his house that were whitewashed in honor of Pesach. Torah nobility was reflected from the

[Page 166]

bookcases of the thick books with the elegant covers that were inside them, and his wife, a young lady, who was all grace and pleasantness, instilled in it a gentleness of soul. We sat before him, just as students sit before their rabbi, and he, our rabbi, discussed with us, as with his fellows, the matter for which we were asked to come to his house and he asked for our advice. When we finished, he turned the conversation to the story of his life, telling us a story of adventures that happened to him until he reached teaching, and what he saw that caused him to replace the rabbinate in which he served as the head of a yeshiva, and turned to teaching Torah to the people of Israel. And his wife occasionally entered into his words with a beautiful folk parable or a story that happened in her hometown.

Suddenly a shriek of indignation was heard from outside, and when we looked out the window, we saw a farmer standing next to his cart stuck in the mud and whipping the horse, cursing and snarling, and his poor horse pulling with all his might but the cart did not move from its place.

"Let's go," Rabbi Pesach hastened us, "let's go out to fulfill the mitzvah that has reached us!" Rabbi Pesach hurried and went out into the street and we followed him, wallowing with him in the mud and getting closer to the cart, and pushing with our shoulders and pulling with our hands, together with the trembling and frightened horse, to get the cart out of the swampy mud. As we left the cart, we gazed at Rabbi Pesach and did not recognize him: our rabbi, who has always worn clean and ironed cloths, from his feet to his head, was covered in mud, with mud marks on his face and puddles of mud in his beard. Awestruck we stood before him: From the dirt on him, we felt the light of his noble soul. The farmer also stood awestruck before him, his mouth open, astonished and silent, and finally he took off his hat and crossed himself.

Rabbi Pesach influenced me and instilled in me his nature more than my other teachers and rabbis. He was my rabbi and like a father to me, a rabbi in Torah and my father in guidance. I loved him a profound love, and because of my love, I dedicated myself to my studies with extreme persistence. My mind did not cool down until I began to sit "Mishmar" (learning Torah at night) once a week, on Thursday night. I was weak in my body, and the sleepless nights of Torah studies exhausted my strength, and more than once Rabbi Pesach would rebuke me for the sin that I was committing by studying nights at the yeshiva and disrespecting the health of the body, as the people of Israel were warned to guard their body equally to guarding their soul.

Rabbi Pesach rebuked me, but I continued with my study nights: physical torture in them, but the pleasure of the soul is on the other side. I enjoyed adding a study night to my days of study, and had even more enjoyment in actually studying in the dark silence that filled the space of the synagogue. I was blessed to engage in the Torah, in the future I hope to be a teacher in Israel, and my father would be exalted by me and would receive glory and honor, reparations for his sufferings and insults. Only a few days passed and the students of the yeshiva raised me to be their "chozer" (repeater): every day, after Rabbi Pesach finished reciting his daily lesson, they gathered around me and I would lecture them, in great details, all the innovations of the Torah that he recited in his lesson, his innovations as well as innovations of others, and he, Rabbi Pesach, would sit aside, and from the smile on his face it seemed that he enjoyed listening to his "chozer".

After we finished two years at the yeshiva, I and one of my friends decided to leave Rabbi Pesach's yeshiva after the celebration of the end of the tractate we studied that season and to move to the higher yeshiva from which we could later go to teaching. We held this graduation celebration with great splendor and with a large crowd - the students' parents and their relatives, including the owners of the "Blacksmiths' Synagogue." The synagogue seemed as if it was the night of Simchat Torah: its lanterns and chandeliers were lit and it was full of joy, and the crowd filled its space with joy and happiness - happy and cheerful in this Simchat Torah that they celebrate on a secular day. They were happy and Rabbi Pesach was doubly happy. He was the "Chatan Torah" in this Simchat Torah celebration, and his joy shone in his face and sparkled in his eyes. There was also joy in his voice when he said the "Hadran" (the concluding reading in the final study of a tractate in the Talmud) in front of us in which he bound together a halacha and a legend, but there was a note of sadness encapsulated in it. We knew what this sadness means: saying this "Hadran" is saying a farewell blessing for him, a farewell blessing to his students who were retiring from him, and this sadness was absorbed in us as well: We were sorry to retire from our beloved rabbi!

After saying the "Hadran" and eating some sweet delicacies, we held each other's hands, with Rabbi Pesach in the middle, and danced around the bimah with joy and happiness and later we went outside and danced in the square in front of the synagogue in the open air. The days were the days before the eve of Passover. The winter passed by with its snows and ices, storms and colds. A bleached moon, as if it was ready for Passover, floated in the azure of the sky, and its white light was woven in the puddles of water that flowed in the canals towards the street. A warm wind soaked with fresh moisture blown through the air, patted our faces with affection, curled our hair and whispered in our ears a whisper of good news, good news that spring is about to affect the world, and the branches of the bushes near the synagogue that have begun to burst out the first buds, moved and responded amen to its good news. In addition, from a bakery came the sound of the ladies who were rolling matzah cakes - a sound that heralded good news: the spring holiday was approaching and it was time for joy! Also, the croaking of the frogs somewhere and the chirping of the crickets on the wall of the synagogues - their grief had turned into happiness, they were chanting for the good news of spring that was being heard in the world. It seemed as if the whole world was dancing with us, dancing and singing: Sisu vesimchu beSimchat Torah (rejoice and be happy in Simchat Torah)! Rejoice and be happy with the joy of spring!

[Page 167]

Rabbi Rafael Yosel

by Ephraim E. Lisitzky

Translated by Jerrold Landau

a.

He was a tailor in his youth: for the work
In Torah he was designated while still a lad,
His Torah was restricted: the reading of the Siddur,
Prayer from it to the G-d Who awakened his soul.

One day - when he was already married -
He decided and said: I will separate from work
And to Torah, study Torah, to its study
He dedicated himself with his entire soul, his entire means.

His wife agreed, and her neck
Took upon itself the yoke of a livelihood - her husband imparted to her
A half of the recompense for Torah - he left his work
And sat studying Torah day and night.

The studiers of the *Beis Midrash* acceded to him,
For he urged them, and they set times for him
They volunteered to teach him: this one a portion
In *Chumash*, and this one a chapter in *Mishnah*.

This one a page of *Midrash*, and this one a folio of Gemara -
He added day to day and night to night, he did not depart
From the *Beis Midrash* - the study was difficult to him
But his will was ironclad, may the flint rock forgive!

After years of toil, he was ordained for teaching
Rabbi Yossel the Gaon, he was the rabbi of the city
And the heads of the nearby community gave him a writ of rabbinate
Urging him to accept it.

But he refused to serve as a rabbi: His Torah will be disseminated
To his brethren like him, the simple masses,
To the tailor, the shoemaker, the smith, the woodcutter
And the water drawer, his trust was with them.

They gave him space in the wing of the *Beis Midrash*
So he separated. He studied Torah there, and he
Taught Torah to his brethren of his type
To them he cleaved, and he imbued his light upon them.

He imbued his light on them through the illumination of his countenance
Through which his noble heart shone,

And the words of his mouth dripped out, as medicine drips
To those who are hurt, he bandages their afflictions.

He paid attention to the downtrodden and those with a lowly spirit
Saying G-d will be with them. He granted a blessing
To those who were encountering difficulties. Hope to the despairing heart,
And comfort to the groaning soul.

Anyone who had a bad dream would hasten to his door
And tell it to him with a palpitating, trembling heart.
He would interpret it in a positive way, and as he left -
With a crestfallen spirit, he would encourage him.

He would extend his benevolence to the crazies of the city
Peering at him like fungus and mushrooms,
Wandering about on the streets during the day, and at night
Hanging out in the synagogues.

If a crazy person played a prank
And the one without mercy urged him to have mercy!
And at times, those brazen ones who heard his reproof
Were sullied by the sin of the crazy ones.

He would corner them and haul them to the bathhouse
Until they started to scream, like those dragged
To slaughter there. He would wash them, and they would exchange
Their worn-out clothes with donated clothes.

If he heard that a quarrel had broken out between a man and his wife
He would go to them in the morning, and make peace between them -
He would plead with them, and would not leave
Until they made up with each other.

It once happened that a certain person was angry with his wife
Before the seven days of
Marriage celebration had passed - as he got angry
With his father-in-law for tricking him, and a dispute broke out.

Rabbi Rafael Yosel would demand from their neighbors
To inform him of the reason for the dispute, and he would
Speak with the person, he would speak at length
And in his voice was soft with moans of mercy:

"No my son, abandon the dispute! Did you find something wrong
With your wife?" "No but," he answered,
"I found something wrong with her father, Rabbi,
For he did not come through with what he promised to give:"

"He promised to give a Ritonda but a cloak
He gave her instead, and she was silent!"
Even though he had formerly been a tailor
He made male clothes, but not female clothes --

And he will ask him: "My son, of what use are these clothes
That he promised to give, that you call Ritonda?"
- "This is an outer garment made without sleeves
For beauty and splendor of a bedecked woman."

"My son" - he innocently said to him - "There is a remedy,
You can fix it with her extra cloak:
Undo the sleeves and remove them
And this will be a Ritonda for splendor."

"Tear off a pair of sleeves from the cloak
But do not, my son, disrupt a united couple with discord.
Make peace with your partner, and may it be His will
That you shall merit to sew her a Ritonda yourself!"

b.

And remember him, Rabbi Rafael Yosil
Positively also for me, for he stood to save me
When I was in difficulties, in the bathhouse, in the boiling water
For my grandfather was going to judge me on Friday.

On the eve of that day, the evil people snuck out of
Gehinnom [Hell], and their punishments stopped.
For me, Gehinnom was prepared: the bathhouse, my grandfather
Was going to drag me there by force.

He would sentence me to lashes first
For he would take me up to the upper balcony
With the section of rope in it, and he would bind me
As someone sentenced to have the verdict carried out, on the back.

And I would be whipped with a small bundle of twigs
My body would be flogged, not forty minus[1]
And the punishment of strangulation[2] is added to the verdict
For I will be tormented there by the mist.

I will fall apart without recourse from my suffering
When the flogging and the strangulation end
And I will cry out from the violence - and the sound of my cries
Will be stifled by the mist, hoarse and heavy.

And my grandfather will not tell you: the sentence of boiling water
On my body will make a mist, completely cleansing -
And it is literally boiling: if you put an egg into it
In a moment you will take it out cooked!

My flesh, the majority of it will be fried
It will be purged well in the bathhouse
With the boiling water drawn from a pail, and I in it will be disgusted
To me, it tastes like a burning pressure!

I will be cleansed in my pain, and my voice
Will scream out. It will not itch, and the mist will no longer be obscured

[Page 168]

And Rabbi Rafael Yosil
Will instill fear in my grandfather, for he has heard.

And he will beg him, "O, arouse your mercy
For your grandson. And mix cold water
Into the boiling water of your pail - G-d will also bless
You for blending the trait of justice with mercy!"

And my grandfather will agree - one does not refuse
The modest Rabbi Rafael Yosil! -
And he will cool the boiling waters for me - and in that way, his mercy
He will extend to me every Friday.

G-d will also not judge me from that time
With boiling water. I am filled with its shots
I supplicate, suffer from it, and in my prayers it seems like:
The voice of Rabbi Rafael Yosil I hear:

"Merciful Father, cool down your wrath,
O, mercy to judgment and merit to guilt
Come and join for him!" And when I hear his prayer
I am encouraged, and hope for salvation soon.

c.

And blessed is that Rabbi Rafael Yosil
Who saves me from the judgment of the boiling water of my grandfather, naïve
In the bathhouse I am on Fridays, for
My nightmare has been interpreted positively.

And I did not dream this dream about myself -
About someone else, my friend, the friend of my youth

From when we got to know each other,
We were bound in bonds of brotherhood and friendship.[3]

We were both students in the *Cheder* of Rabbi Yosil.
It was housed in the *Beis Midrash*, its anteroom was the Yeshiva,
And we were both diligent in the study of Gemara.
Rabbi Yosel paved our path for us

We both reviewed the lesson every day,
And prepared for the new lesson.
We helped each other, and in the evening we moved over to
The wing of the *Beis Midrash*, the secret corner.

We talked there together, a secret discussion
Yearning hearts and effervescent hearts,

We even discussed dreams while awake,
For we were both dreamers.

We traveled in our dreams to hidden places
Where wonderful treasures are buried,
And we made a covenant to divide them between us
The desired treasure would be split in half.

And that Beis Midrash in which we studied
Can be compared to a river. Old and young
During the comforting summer days
Went to enjoy themselves in bathing and swimming.

We too were both among the group of bathers.
We learned to swim properly with our arms and legs,
Even though we did not put a great effort into swimming,
It is a very serious issue!

And one night I dreamt: We are both swimming
In the river. Floating in splendor like the splendor of light gold
And suddenly my friend immersed himself
And before he came up - he sunk into the depths!

His body reddened in the depths for some time
But as it sunk deeper
It got covered up, disappeared, and was no more!
And I woke up, and my voice rose in a scream.

Sleepless the rest of the hours of the night
I tossed and turned in my bed, overtaken by trembling
I rose quickly in the morning, and hurried
To Rabbi Rafael Yosil, pacing quickly.

I met him in the wing of his *Beis Midrash*
In the early *minyan*, where he had
Concluded his prayers. And I told him my dream.
My voice was talking through a treasury of tears.

"Calm down, my son!" - he answered me. His voice
Was speaking pleasantly, with love -
"It is a good dream, my son, you saw in your dream
Only good and fine things you prophesied for your friend.

"For water is a sign of blessing. For a blessing
This will be to your friend. And water
Is compared to Torah - he dove to its depths
And dredged up from there unique pearls.

"However, today, my son, your friend
Should avoid bathing in the river!
G-d will have mercy on you, and cast his shadow at your right hand
Through his Torah. It will protect you from all evil."

And that day my friend asked me
To go bathe. His desire for it
Was sevenfold. With a strong force
The river attracted him! - and I followed after him:

When he was still a lad, the reading of Hebrew books
Took hold of his heart. He swallowed them as his birthright.
From them, as we talked as friends,
He would tell me wonders and secrets.

And within a few days, good news
He told me. He was happy as if he found a hidden treasure:
He had the opportunity to read a book of wonders
From then he would seek it, "*Emek Haarazim.*"

With this book, I used a pretext
To turn his mind away from bathing: I asked him: What are
The wonderful adventures in this book of wonders?
Tell them to me, so I can enjoy them and know them!

I opened a concealed faucet in the midst of his soul
And precious things came from his mouth, from the recesses
Adventures from days of yore - the vibrancy of his soul
With his voice in wonder and his eyes shining

He told me about adventures from old times
His wellsprings and senses were swallowed up
He was alert to them when the time of our studies stopped
And we returned to study for the second half of the day.

However, a river can also describe the suburb
In which my friend lived. And before the end
Of the day, for it was long, when our studies finished
We would go there for dangerous bathing!

I accompanied him when he returned
Home in the evening, and I tarried
In his house, I talked with him a great deal
Until the danger passed: the sun set!
- -

- -

Dreams follow after the mouth - the holy mouth
Interpreted the dream well to me: I was a blessing
For my friend. Many special pearls
Did he dredge up from the depths in which he swam -

The depths of Torah and also the depths of literature,
The light of Torah illuminated from its perplexity -
And perhaps in the merit of Rabbi Rafael Yosil
A writer was raised in Israel!

Translator's footnotes:

1. The Biblical punishment of lashes is 40 (Deuteronomy 25:3), but it is in actuality reduced to 39. It is the custom in a bathhouse to be whipped by a bundle of twigs for health reasons – and the author is comparing this to the Biblical edict of flogging.
2. One of the four types of capital punishment in the Torah. (The author clearly does not like the bathhouse to which is grandfather takes him - although he is using the entire experience as a simile for extrication of the suffering of the Jewish people as a whole).
3. There is an editor's footnote here: The author is referring to his friend Y. D. Berkowitz.

[Page 169]

Excerpt From the Book
"When There is No Generation"

by Reuven Valenrod

Translated by Mira Eckhaus

The main street in the provincial town of Slutsk is paved with stones and is called "Shusey". Horses' hooves are tapping with rapid sounds, carts and carriages are rattling on the edges of the stones, and new faces that he has not seen before, - perhaps he will never see them again - pass in front of the boy, who came from the town, and expand his world. Once in a while, a car belonging to one of the Polish noblemen passes in front of the hotel of Butnitsky (Bukshitsky); Grocers and homeowners go out into the street, arguing and estimating its price, and children run after it in noise and commotion.

Isaac walks down the street with a crowd of high schoolers, his uniform ironed and his buttons shiny. Isaac wouldn't run after the car, even though he wanted to run like those boys. He will be laughed at if he does so. He misses and does not miss the wide market of his town, where he used to run fast from the Beit Midrash to the low fence of the House of Awe.

It's good that he found here in the high school (gymnasia) Alyosha Yaakobovitz, the son of the owner of a remote and tiny estate. One of the visitors of his father's house, who reminds him of oblivion. Alyosha's father is one of the poor Shlyachtits, that the "Polish noblemen", who own the big estates, see them as peasants, but they actually see themselves as nobles. That's why he was such a man, who usually lived at the edge of the village, or in a four-by-four estate, who loses out from both ways. Usually, he would connect with one of the wealthy Jews and tell him about his troubles.

This is how Yaakobovitz also socialized with Fayvel Halber. When he came from the village to the town, he would park his horse and cart in Fayvel's yard, enter the kitchen, put his things down, speak loudly to the maid and hand out hazelnuts, pumpkin seeds, apples and pears to the children.

Isaac's studies seem easy, the grades are good, and he would proudly await to the teacher calling him to the blackboard. It's nice to repeat the things he acquired during his studies. Speaking in front of the department summarizes his knowledge and, in this manner, he clarifies himself the subject. It's quiet in the department and he hears the sound of his voice. The theorems in geometry are placed on top of each other and the conclusions come from each other. "Quod Erat Demonstrandum" …(what should have been proved). Even these words themselves, heavy and strong, are a nice taste of the victory... "Quod Erat Demonstrandum" - metal scraps are ringing... Sometimes these words seem like the trees of the great forest, that was seen from the window of his father's house.

The boy with the light hair stands by the blackboard and speaks Russian with the rustic intonation of Policia residents, and the teachers smile at him, at this excellent boy, with sympathy. And so do the students, thanking Isaac for bringing the skinny little Alyosha close to him, even though they themselves did not express any closeness to him. Apart from that, Isaac serves as a sort of middleman between the Russians and the Jews in his department. Those and those speak to him with excessive closeness, although he has not yet become friends with one group or another. - - -

The first years of the war did not bring with them a noticeable change during the life of the boy studying at the high school in the district city: the paved road of exams and grades, sailing on the river that flows to the Prift, and sitting in the evenings on the hotel's balcony, continued. It seems as if the war broke out in another country and it did not reach the hotel or the high school, except for dull echoes.

Isaac read the newspapers every day and knew what was going on: somewhere in the Galician towns the wounded and the dead rolled in, in East Prussia thousands died in the swamps. Isaac heard about this horrible death from an eyewitness soldier: the swamp soil slowly pulls and absorbs the man and he sees his death with his eyes, tries in horror to pull out one leg and the other sinks deeper. After that, the despairing man stops his war on his life and helplessly waits for the impending death. From the refugees, Isaac also knew about the acts of the Cossacks in Galicia and Poland. But all these were nothing but stories, such as he read in books: the stories of Versayev about the war with Japan or Tolstoy's descriptions in "War and Peace". - - -

Over time, the heavy, threatening feeling also spread to the district city. Near Bukshitsky's balcony, the noise and commotion grew significantly. Horses' hooves and carts wheels now rattled day and night. The front drew closer, the soldiers multiplied, and the "Shusey" was filled with convoys of deportees from Poland and Galicia: Jews in long clothes, wearing small hats, who spoke in a soft and prolonged tone. Isaac heard their stories and the events became closer to him and touched his heart.

* * *

The winds blowing during the war also broke through the walls of the school. The one who was a high schooler some time ago was now an officer, who goes around freely for his pleasure and does what his heart desires. The boys and girls looked enviously at these young officers and looked forward to the day when they too could get rid of their books. As the prices increased, the salary of a respected teacher, dressed in uniforms, was not enough for them, and restlessness was imposed on their faces and movements. You should now smile at the boy, whose father is rich and you can get a favor from him, and you should be wary of a cheeky boy, because who knows how the boy will act the next day. The mood of the boys is also changing for the worse from day to day, and the paved roads to their heart are weakened. And when a student is called to explain a theorem in geometry to the department, he stands and answers boldly and arrogantly, and the students smile in anticipation. One must therefore overcome regular and accepted habits and smile. At a time when the house is being destroyed, what is the point of taking care of every tool and tool, that it be standing in the place designated for it in advance?

Isaac did not feel and did not know how and when this happened. Suddenly he realized that his knowledge had become an obstacle.

* * *

In the midst of this chaotic laxity, which is felt within the walls of the school, Isaac's diligence is weakening. The excitement that accompanied the writing of the essays faded due to the tensions. The visions no longer accumulate to a single point, but rater wander here and there.

[Page 170]

A Symphony of Generations

by Baruch Katznelson

In memory of my city of Slutsk

Translated by Jerrold Landau

The symphony of generations suffering in exile, longing for life and redemption
Enters my heart like strong wine of agony in the loneliness of night;
Illuminating me and causing me to have tears, and refusing to die
Of them only it remains.

The symphony of generations, the progeny of the funeral of an elderly, faithful person;
The violin of their soul during their wanderings in the hallways of time –
It is still in its sadness with refreshing, flowing clearness
As it was born in sadness.

Like a ray of light shining forth from the heart in the darkness of the netherworld
In it shines the faith and bereavement smiles.
A ray of anguish opposite G-d, calling out loudly,
And dancing with the melody.

A wonderful symphony, moving every heart without words
Imbued with sweet suffering, pride in the depths.
And it is a ladder, in it is a ladder on which those who thrust off the yoke ascend
To the heights of "One."

Generations raised the symphony, and it raised them
In the depths of despair, in the hopeless agony, the seed of the holiness of the age
Dancing on pyre with them, pouring out nauseating joy
And it is burned with them.

Now, old and childless, flowing over the graves –
A silent violin with no hand to move the strings.
It is silent and will be silent: no more will the generations of singing be heard.
Their voices have been silenced forever – – –

The symphony of generations suffering in exile, longing for life and redemption
Comes into my heart like strong wine of agony in the loneliness of night;
Illuminating me and causing me to have tears, and refusing to die
Of them only it remains.

Natives of Slutsk and its environs in Tel Aviv at a memorial ceremony for the martyrs of the community on 3 Adar

[Page 171]

Avraham Epstein[a]

by Y.N. Adler

Translated by Mira Eckhaus

Avraham Epstein was a personality studded with charming gems, some bright and some modest. He was an esteemed and humbled man with God and people and a noble man in his manners - to the point of weaving a thin partition between him and the other person - while his heart was a heart that listens, in fact, to every heartbeat of the other person; He was tired of wanderings and tribulations, he was uprooted and exiled from place to place - while his spirit was not turbid and the character of his nobility was not blurred in any way.

I remember that once, when Epstein returned from his wanderings and tribulations all over the "settlments area" to his beloved city, he was in total despair and gripped by doubts from various sources, about the way he captured himself - he was half a Hebrew teacher and half an external - swifts in the stream of the detached people, without a visible safe harbor. In this mental crisis Epstein found himself surrounded by enthusiastic followers, who followed him in the evenings during the group walks along the road and listened passionately to his words, which were seasoned with witty intelligence and a touch of forgiving wisdom. While the little ones, his students in the "reformed cheder", would also, upon the completion of the study, follow their admired teacher. And why should it be surprising? Their teacher was then a children's poet; A modest and unknown poet – he was of high quality and comprehensive. However, these little ones found with the power of intuitive achievement peculiar to them (and to the poets) - the spring of poetry that was repulsive in their teacher's soul; they found it and drank from it thirstily, to their pleasure and the teacher's pleasure as well. To the appearance it seemed that the little followers had finally brought a cure to the sad soul of the teacher and the mental crisis has already passed. After all, there was a brightness on the face of a teacher. But who can understand the spirit of a poet? And even more so when it comes to a children's poet. And indeed, one day Epstein got up and took his walking stick and his cape and went to an unknown destination and he never again returned to his beloved city, if I'm not mistaken.

The last stop on Epstein's life path was America. And this is where Epstein was "discovered". And this is also where one enigmatic issue is revealed, as precisely here, in loud America, Epstein, who is humble, found himself as a critic writer who earned him the right of citizenship in Hebrew literature; Unexpectedly here, in the material and feverish America, Epstein was able to praise with thin and pleasant explanatory threads and heartfelt words of praise for the poets and writers who conquered Epstein's heart. Admittedly, it is to be regretted that Epstein for some reason did not write about the issues of Hebrew education in America that he himself debated about - at the time: in that first and difficult period at the Etz Haim Yeshiva, in Borough Park, and later at the Flatbush Yeshiva and finally in Herzliya. Indeed, this is also an enigmatic issue. Here are the necessary signs: an observing eye, a listening heart, hard trials and a writing talent. And why does his educational canvas remain empty, most of it intact? It is an enigma. However, who can understand the spirit of a man full of inspiration? Whether it is one way or another - this chapter, the Avraham Epstein chapter, is one of the most beautiful chapters, even if few in number, in the tractate of Hebrew America.

Original footnote:

1. This list (printed in " HaDoar" (The Post)), was received late and due to its importance for the evaluation of the personality of the late A. Epstein, we print it in this section.

[Page 172]

In the Fight for Independence

Those Who Were and Are No Longer Alive
(The deceased during the events in Israel)

Translated by Mira Eckhaus

Reb Noah Imerman

He was the son of Tema the baker. Everyone knew her and heard Tema's name in Slutsk.

She was a woman of valor, who would support the poor and distribute charity openly and secretly. Her son Noah studied at the Slutsk and Slobodka yeshivas. He later moved to the Hebron yeshiva and excelled as one of the yeshiva students, who was deeply involved in the study of the Torah.

He was murdered in Hebron during the events of 5689 (1929) at the age of 32. He left after his death a wife and three daughters in Jerusalem.

The Baruch Domenitz family

In 1925, Baruch emigrated to Israel with his family from Slutsk. They were from the first members in the "HaChalutz" and the "Zifzif" group in Acre. Later they moved to Rehovot and in 1932 they settled in the village Gibton.

On the 2nd of Adar 5699, the Arabs from the village of Al-Qubayba attacked the village. The house of Baruch Domenitz, that was located at the edge of the village, was marked as a target by the attackers and they murdered with terrible cruelty his wife Mina, the daughter of Reb Yaakov Poliak of Slutsk, 42 ??years old, his son Yerachmiel, 17 years old, a member of the Haganah, Chaim, 10 years old, and Emanuel, 8 years old.

May their memory be blessed.

The only survivors of the whole family were his the daughter Hadassah, who happened to be in Givat Brenner that night, and the father Baruch, who was staying at the "Hadassah" Hospital, after being injured in a car accident.

Avraham Voskoboynik

He was the son of Yitzchak and Ida and Voskoboynik from the Fleischtsik house in Slutsk, who emigrated to Israel in 1925. He was a very handsome and hard-working boy. At the age of 17, he graduated from the high school "Ahad Ha'am" in Petah Tikva. In the riots of 1936, he enlisted to be a guard in the British police force (ghaffir) and in one of the orchards he was murdered by Arab murderers while he was on guard duty.

Nathan Zeldes

He was born in Slutsk in the year 5657. His parents were Fayvel and Haya Zeldes. They were wealthy people (they owned an iron materials shop), well-educated and their sons were educated in the spirit of the tradition as well as the general education. Since he was a child, Nathan dreamed to travel to Eretz Israel and study at Gymnasia Herzliya, and his ambition came true. In 5662, he was accepted as a student at the Gymnasia Herzliya.

His friend Hillel Landsman wrote the following list after he died in the battle for the defense of Jerusalem:

I first met Nathan in Odessa, on his way to Israel, in 1913.

Nathan was familiar with the paths of this coastal city in southern Russia. Back in 1911, he was sent here by his parents from Slutsk, his hometown, to study at the yeshiva of Rabbi Tchernowitz (a young rabbi).

[Page 173]

He became our guide, toured the city with us, led us to the club of Zion lovers, introduced us to the poet C. N. Bialik and he was all fresh and lively, his body was firm, his cheeks were flushed and his eyes were smart and intelligent. In the ten days of our trip by boat, we became closer to each other and together we made a plan to arrange our lives for entering Gymnasia Herzliya.

In Neve Shalom, the Jewish neighborhood that was adjacent to Jaffa, we rented a room and we prepared for the exams, and the more I was in his presence, the more the feeling of respect for him grew. He was full of life wisdom and knew the ways of life and was independent and responsible. All these gave him the impression of a much older man, although he was only two years older than me.

With the outbreak of the First World War and with the joining of Turkey to it, the land and the settlement were in distress and under siege. The settlement was required to enlist in the Turkish army. The Gymnasia was an Ottoman institution, and as such, a large part of its teachers had to recruit to the Turkish army. There was a danger that the Gymnasia would be closed and some of the high school students recruited to the army and were sent to the officers' school in Kushta, Nathan was among them. After ten months of hard and arduous life in a military base, in a foreign land, far away from the Land of Israel - the young officers were sent to the different fronts of the Ottoman Empire, according to the lottery method. Nathan was given the fourth front (Syrian-Land of Israel) under the command of the well-known Djemal Pasha. Others of us were sent to Macedonia or the borders of the Black Sea. And some were jealous of those who went in the direction of Israel.

We met again after the occupation of the country by the English when we returned to school. Nathan returned to continue his studies without any financial support, on his own account. He traveled abroad and finished his studies there as a road engineer. Since then, we parted ways. Each sank into his own corner. In our temporary meetings, a note of dissatisfaction could be heard in Nathan's words. It seemed that he was not in the right place for him. In our conversations about the village and the city, he expressed longing for village life and agriculture.

He told me about all the hardships and struggles in the war of existence in the city during the unemployment period, etc. Even now, just like in our first meeting in Odessa, I saw in Nathan every time I met him, the same knowledge of life and a realistic approach to problems. He was always vibrant, full of energy and a desire to create and build.

I'm sorry that our meetings were rare and short. And I regret his untimely death even more. He died in the defense of Jerusalem at the beginning of the year 1948.

Ezra Sperling

He was killed in the explosion of the "King David" hotel in Jerusalem, on 23rd of Tamuz, 5706, July 22, 1946. He was born in Slutsk in 1889. When he was 15 years old, he left to America. He volunteered for the Hebrew Regiment during the First World War. After his release from the army, he started working as a government official. He was an amateur journalist. He wrote and printed his words in America and also in local newspapers, especially in "Palestine Illustrated News".

He left after his death two sons and two daughters. One of the daughters served in the army during World War II. One son served in the American army and was wounded.

The deceased was a friendly man, with a subtle sense of humor. He was a loyal Jew. He was about to retire from his service due to seniority but the cruel death came earlier.

May he rest in peace!

[Page 174]

Those Who Died in the War of Liberation
The sons of the Slutsk residents
Translated by Mira Eckhaus

Ethan Meisel

Eitan, the son of Yehuda and Hanna Meisel, was born in Jerusalem in Adar 5691 to a family of laborers from the pioneers of the third Aliya.

At the age of six he entered the public school "Tachkemoni". Studies were easy for him and he attracted the attention of his friends due to his intelligence and vigilance. When he finished his studies, he joined the youth club of "HaShomer Hatzair" and proceeded to a training at Kibbutz "Shaar Ha'amkim".

During the two years he spent there, he adapted to the social life and organized a circle of music lovers. He even turned out to have a great sense of humor and at friends' parties he exuded joy and happiness.

He finished his training at "Shaar Ha'amkim" when the war of liberation was already ongoing and together with his fellow trainees he was sent to the aid of Kibbutz "Lehavot HaBashan" on the Syrian border, in the Upper Galilee. There he was wounded in the hand.

Six months later, he moved with his fellow trainees, who formed a group of settlers, to Mishlat Harel in the occupied Arab village of Beit Jiz, which is in the Jerusalem Corridor.

In Emunim, he distinguished himself as a guide and organizer, and after passing a squad commander's course, he held military positions in the Negev Guards. Through his guidance he became beloved on his apprentices who were from the new Aliyah. With his cheerfulness and loyalty to his destiny he captivated people's hearts.

On the 14th day of Elul 5710, during a tour in the Beit Govrin area, a commander's car drove up to a mine, which had been buried by terrorists. Ethan and three of his friends died there.

May his soul be bounded in the bundle of life of the heroes of Israel, who scarified their lives for the homeland.

Biller Ilan

He was the son of Patchia and Nechama. He was born on May 12, 1930 in Tel Aviv.

He studied at a public school, and later on he continued until the sixth grade at the Montefiore Real School. He became known as one of the best athletes in the Aguda of "Brit Maccabim Atid", among the best swimmers in Israel, a youth backstroke champion, one of the best water polo players, one of the representatives of our country in international swimming competitions, and in one of them he won a trophy. The day after the revelry of Lake Success and the beginning of the war operations in Israel, he enlisted for service and was accepted into one of the Palmach battalions (Yiftach Brigade). As a fellow well-liked by his comrades, he also pushed them to enlist for full service in his battalion. After short training, he went on patrols and scouting operations as a raider and saboteur. He served in escorting convoys between Tiberias and the northern Galilee, in battles in the Galilee, in the mopping up of Arab villages, in the occupation of Ein- Zeitoun and was one of the first two Hebrew soldiers to penetrate the Arab part of Safed in the battles to liberate the city. In the battle of Nebi Yosha, the steel helmet on his head was hit by a bullet and his head was also scratched from the force of the blow. He was transferred with his battalion to the central front, for the "Dani" operation, and participated in the occupation of Lod and Ramallah and the surrounding villages.

On the brink of the second truce, he was with his company in Kfar al-Borj, on the road Latrun-Ramallah and participated in the effort to cut off Latrun for its conquest. And here there was a counterattack by the Arabs with five times more forces and with armored people. Being a second machine gunner, he hid and when he saw the threatening enemy movement, he shot constant fire on the armored vehicles. When his comrades warned him of the danger in his action of revealing their location and drawing the enemy's fire towards them while they have no barrier against it, he said: "It is fine, the main thing is that the armored vehicles will be stopped". He achieved this goal, but he was hit by the enemy's fire in his spine and refrained from crying out in pain when he was transferred to the gathering point, so as not to weaken the spirit of his comrades. Only once did he ask why he wasn't being evacuated, and when it was explained to him that the ambulance could no longer arrive because of the enemy's fire, he did not talk about it anymore, he restrained his suffering and joked that after being wounded he would finally get a vacation. He died of internal bleeding on July 16, 1948. He was buried in Nachalat Yitzhak on July 18, 1948.

Baskin (Beit Zvi) Zvi

He was the son of Shabtai and Karina, he was born on January 8, 1930 in Stalingrad in the Soviet Union, the place his father was exiled to because of his Zionist activities. About a year and a half after Zvi's birth, the family settled in Nikopol, Ukraine, where Zvi's father got a job in a factory. Zvi's parents aspired to emigrate to Israel, but had to hide this aspiration even from their children. Only later did they reveal the secret to their only son, Zvi. In 1941, the Baskin family fled from the Nazi invaders to the North Caucasus. There Zvi continued his studies at school. On February 20, 1942, he disappeared. It turned out that under the influence of the stories about the heroism of the children, the 12-year-old boy decided to go to war against Hitler's armies. Only a few days later he was found at one of the train stations near the front and was returned to his home. With the advance of the Germans,

[Page 175]

the family abandoned its temporarily place of living in the North Caucasus and migrated to Armenia. There, the family went through a period of famine and serious illness. In the city of Yerban, Zvi finished his studies at the public school and entered a high technical school in 1945, but in October of that year his parents decided to emigrate to Israel. After many upheavals, the family arrived at the Jewish camp in Landsberg, Germany. Zvi studied at the camp electrical engineering and joined the United Pioneer Youth Organization (Naham). In July 1947, he emigrated to Israel with his parents and lived for several months with his mother and sisters in Kibbutz Ein HaShofet. He expressed his desire to learn seamanship while he was still in Germany. His parents promised to help him with this. However, he did not accomplish this desire.

The war of liberation broke out. Zvi worked for a while as a simple laborer in "Solel Bone", then he volunteered to escort convoys in the Galilee. After his friends from Naham arrived in Israel, he moved with them to "Dorot" in the Negev. In May 1948, he enlisted in the IDF Transportation Corps. He was sent to a drivers' unit in Tel Aviv. From there he volunteered for the Armored Corps and participated in the battles on Beit Naballah, Lod and Irak al Manshiya. He was hit several times; However, he remained in his unit.

He died in the battle of Be'er Sheva on the 18th of Tishrei (October 21, 1948). He was buried in Mishmar HaNegev and on October 21, 1949, he was transferred to the cemetery in Nachalat Yitzhak.

Madutsky Yaakov ("Yankale")

He was the son of Israel and Dvorah. He was born on the 13th of Shevat 5690 (February 11, 1930) in Tel Aviv. From the age of 12 he lived in the Meged neighborhood in Pardes Hanna. After graduating from the agricultural school in Pardes Hanna, he moved to Ein Shemer and learned there welding. Upon his return, he worked with his father in the installation of water pipes. In his spare time, he prepared for the entrance exams to the Technion. He was one of the best athletes in swimming (he was an instructor and a lifeguard, he was qualified to teach swimming at the Pardes Hanna pool, and according to the regulations, the certificate was delayed until he reached the age of 18 and it was sent to him after he died in the war). He also excelled in football (he was the head of a team) and in high jump and received awards and certificates of excellence. At the age of 14, he was sent to a squad commander course of the Gadna, and later he served as a guide at the Gadna in Ein Shemer of immigrants and local youth in Pardes Hanna.

On November 25, 1947, before the partition decision, he received permission to transfer to the recruitment at the Palmach. He served as a guard in Beit HaArava, Kalia and Sodom. He finished a squad commanders' course. He participated in the operations of the "Breaking Battalion" in the opening of the road to Jerusalem, in the occupation of Katamon and Mount Zion, and was among the first who broke into the Old City. He encouraged the wounded and devoted himself to alleviating their suffering. In the second attack on the radar station, he was the first who broke into the building and there he died on June 1, 1948. He was buried in Mount Herzl in Jerusalem on November 17, 1948.

Simbol Yosef

He was the son of Shlomo and Yehudith. He was born on the 21st of Shevat 5681 (1931) in Tel Aviv. Immediately after that, the family moved to settle in Ein Ganim near Petah Tikva. He studied at Pika school and Ahad Ha'am high school in Petah Tikva and later at the District School in Givat HaShlosha. From his childhood he helped his parents with the farm works. At the age of 15, he joined the "HaNoar HaOved" (Working Youth) and stood out as an instructor, and in "HaPoel" he excelled in gymnastics, games, light and heavy athletics and was a coach for games. He was liked by the members and alert for the urgent and important duties and from a young age he participated in the war for organized Hebrew labor. He was among the first to join the "Hapoel" companies and served as an instructor for useful sports. At the same time, he also joined HaHaganah and was sent to work in the establishment of the barbed wire fence on the northern border during the Arab riots.

In 1942, he enlisted in the Palmach, and this service was more important to him than enlisting in the British army, as he foresaw the necessity to fight for the liberation of the homeland. He contributed his part bravely in bringing to Israel illegal immigrants and in underground operations against the British, which was in his opinion, the main national front. In the British siege on Rishpon, he also fought with 5 soldiers who were guarding the chain of siege and burst out to help the besieged. In 1945, he was released from the Palmach, began working at the Electric Company in Petah Tikva and continued to work in youth guidance. On his 25th birthday, he married his girlfriend, Malka.

When the Arab attack began after the declaration of Lake Success, he immediately returned to service in the Palmach, without considering the release that his parents had obtained for him, being their only son, and his wife being pregnant. He participated in the patrols and in operations against rioters and with his machine gun he shot down a lot of enemies, but in an operation against one of the villages, when Arab women entered the surrounded house, which Yoske was firing on, he directed the shots to the height of the roof so that the women wouldn't get hurt. Later, he was assigned the role of intelligence in the department, and just as his comrades in the Palmach filled with dedication the lack of equipment and weapons, so he filled the lack of means to fulfill his role and he completed it with great success. He was later on promoted to the position of deputy regimental intelligence officer. Considering his family circumstances, his commanders and friends tried to keep him away from extremely dangerous military missions. Although his service was very important to the war effort, he could not accept service on the "home front", and he was not pleased until he was allowed to participate in the break-in operation of the road to Jerusalem.

His friends told wonderful stories about his coolness and devotion and his quickness in handling the machine gun, when he would wait until the enemy approached a safe range (even though it was more dangerous for him), then he would achieve a maximum output with a minimum of bullets. He stayed away from command positions, but his very presence instilled confidence in his friends. From Huldah to the strait of the valley

[Page 176]

beyond Shaar HaGai, he worked wonders with his machine gun and in capturing posts to ensure safe passage. There, in the narrow valley, when the enemy cut off part of the convoy, he stopped it with his machine gun, allowing the wounded and dead to be collected and preventing the enemy from pursuing the main part of the convoy, which managed to cross the small bridge before it exploded, but he himself was killed in this battle on April 20, 1948. He was buried in Kiryat Anavim on April 22, 1948. His daughter was born after he was killed.

Kotzer Arieh

He was the son of David and Ruth. He was born in 1924 in Slutsk, White Russia. In 1932, he emigrated to Israel with his family which settled in Tel Aviv. He graduated a public primary school and a high school. He learned the profession of turnery and worked at it. From his youth he devoted himself to "HaHaganah" organization. As a youth movement trainee, he joined the Gadna, started in the liaison service, completed courses and promoted to the rank of a squad commander, and later on to a platoon commander. It soon turned out that he was born to serve as a commander. He was brave, directed his action according to the purpose of the operation and he was capable of instilling with simple and short words the feeling of duty in the heart of his subordinated. He later transferred to Hish (Haganah corps), and there he continued training and commanding with great dedication. The day after the decision in Lake Success he enlisted to the defense system of Tel Aviv and at the beginning of March 1948, he took command of a company of one battalion in the "Givati" brigade, which was then stationed in the besieged Ben Shemen. In the middle of that month, the company was sent to "Camp Yona" in Tel Aviv and he was involved in its training. At the same time, he would go out with the company's divisions for mining and sabotage operations in the area, without the knowledge and without the consent of the battalion commander. In April, he was attached with his company to the headquarters of "Nachshon" operation, and he did very well as a commander in the defense of the large convoy of 250 freight cars full of supplies to Jerusalem, when he managed to transfer it safely, despite Arab attacks and British "order enforcement".

When 4 of his comrades were killed near Tel-a-Rish, he entered with some of his subordinated into enemy territory and removed the dead bodies. In "Barak" operation his company captured the villages of Sheyat Batani, Sharki and Barka in a few days and he was very stricter in preventing his people from looting. He moved to Ramallah - Latrun Road and captured the villages of Abu Shusha and Al Kubab, and when the great Egyptian invasion began, he operated with his company against it.

In the battles near Ashdod, he worked and worked his men beyond the limits of human ability. Fatigued to death, falling and getting up and passing over dead bodies while the enemy keeps shooting continuously, they stood with supreme bravery against the enemy's armor and their many soldiers, and the resistance of Arieh and his men in this battle played a very significant role in stopping the enemy's march towards Rehovot and Tel

Aviv. It was the decisive delay, which made it possible to prepare the counterattack. Again, he stood with his reduced company in front of the Egyptians advancing to Nitzanim pass. At the beginning of the truce, he was transferred to the battalion headquarters, and from the start of the planning of Operation An-Far (anti Faruk), he returned to the front line. On his way to help the jeep company "Shualey Shimshon" (Samson's Foxes), he was killed near Beit Afa on July 16, 1948.

He was buried in the cemetery in Kfar Warburg on December 29, 1948.

In the order of the General Staff of September 29, 1949, he was awarded the rank of captain.

Kersik Yaakov

He was born in Nahalal; He was the third son of Michael and Nechama Kersik (from the Fleischtsik family in Slutsk). From his childhood, he was an independent child, and when his mother was busy every day with the morning wakening in the chicken coop and in the dairy barn, he would get down from his bed, slice himself two thick slices of bread, spread jam and leave the house for the field. All searches after him were to no avail.

He would only return in a late hour. Over time they realized that he was a man of the field and got used to his escapes. He walked around the fields and knew all the types of grass, and when he was hungry, he ate edible grass. At the age of eight, his mother died during the birth of his twins' sisters. His father was left with five children, he married a wife and Yaakov was very unhappy. His suffering was great and he tried to stay away from home. Nevertheless, he developed nicely. From his childhood, he was active in "HaHaganah" and at the age of eighteen he got married. After his father died, he dedicated himself to farming and was successful, until the Sinai War came. He left his wife and his two young daughters. He enlisted as a scout and was among the first who were killed. He was only 25 years old in his death.

Rivin Yechiel

Yechiel was born on the 23rd of Elul 5685 (September 12, 1925) in Tel Aviv. When he was only one month old, he moved with his parents for the occupation of labor in the Arab Acre. Hie parents' goal was to settle down in the Zvulun Valley. But for the sake of financial support until the settlement is realized, the candidates founded the "Zipzif" group, which was the foundation of a Jewish settlement in Arab Acre.

The occupation of labor and the competition with the Arabs for years, the move to Herzliya and the constant struggle with the lack of work, the bloody

[Page 177]

events of 1929, 1936, the constant aspiration to hold on to the right of agricultural settlements on the land of the nation and to maintain a social life without exploiting others - these were the conditions and the atmosphere in which Yechiel grew up and was educated. From his childhood, he absorbed the love of manual labor, and especially for agriculture, the appreciation of the working man and the admiration of the Hebrew protector. How happy was the eleven-year-old boy, when he participated in the preparations for the settlement in Moshav Rishpon and with what affection and dedication he took care of the animals and plants. It once happened that he was late for the bus after he finished his studies at the school in Herzliya and he had to move seedlings from the nursery, which he built by himself, to the new settlement. He was sad about the soft seedlings, and having no other connection with the point, he gathered the seedlings into the basket, put it on his shoulders and walked about ten kilometers on foot along a rough road that was full of murderous enmity (this was during the events of 5696). The events of 1936 started. The young moshav, which had only a small number of inhabitants, served as a target for the enemy's attacks every night. The members did not know what a quiet sleep was and the child helped as much as he could, to the protectors - in guarding and to his parents - in the farm work.

He finished his studies in Herzliya public school and in the continuation classes, and then he continued his studies at the district agricultural school in Givat Hasholsha. During this period, he joined "HaNoar HaOved" (the working youth), because this organization was non-partisan and he did not support any party or any certain political view, until he grew up enough and understood the matter deeply. At the same time, he was also attached to the Palmach; He had already belonged to the ranks of HaHaganah organization before that. In 1942, when the Nazi enemy approached the Egyptian border, he enlisted in the British army, and he was only sixteen and a half years old at the time. When they asked him to postpone his enlistment until the following year, he replied: "How can one sit and study while European Jewry is being destroyed and the enemy is after our walls? And if my father is already prevented from going to war now, because of his age and the family situation, then this duty falls on me". IIe was attached to the water supply battalion where he served throughout the war in the Western Desert. This battalion performed hard tasks in the brutal conditions of the desert. Yechiel fulfilled his service with devotion. He was loved and respected by his friends. He maintained connections with his friends in Israel and abroad.

When he was released, he aspired to a life of productive work. And indeed, he found a cooperative work in the paving stone industry. However, he left his job for fear that a trace of exploiting others would stick to him. He went looking for another job and did not reluctant from any arduous work. He was attached to his family with all his heart and helped his parents in their farm and in the building of their house.

When the war of liberation broke out, he once again showed up to fulfill his duty in the fateful struggle for redemption. During his service in the Defense Forces, he was one of the first to join the Artillery Corps at the beginning of its organization and was one of its first drivers. Day and night he drove in his car to all the fronts in the valley and the Galilee, on impassable roads, until he was wounded very seriously near the village of Zarin, when his car stepped on a mine on the 20th of Iyar, 5708, and on the 23rd of Iyar (June 1, 1948) he died in the hospital in the valley. His young life was sacrificed on the altar of the liberation of the people and the homeland, and his name will forever be preserved among the heroes of Israel, who sacrificed their lives for the redemption of the people and the land.

He was a native of the country, but it seems that none of the flaws that are instilled in the "Tzabar" (native Israeli), stick to him. He listened with appreciation and admiration to the words of the great and old and absorbed into him the devotion to the nation and its sanctities. It was therefore natural when one day he disappeared from his father's house and enlisted in the British army while he was still a young boy. And even then, he knew how to justify this step: "I will not fight for the English, but for European Jewry, which is bleeding".

The world war ended, and he returned refined and pure, full of passion and a deep recognition of his purpose and duty only a short time before the establishment of the state throughout fights and sacrifices.

And in the battle for Jenin, he was killed. He was only 23 years old in his death.

(The lists of the fallen were collected from the Book of "Yizkor")

Those Who Died in Israel
The sons of the Slutsk residents

Translated by Mira Eckhaus

Zev Gluskin

He served as "Redemption" manager from 1924. He was one of the best activists in Zionism and one of its elders, both operationally and spiritually, in several institutions. He was born on the 9th of Elul 5619, in Slutsk. He was the son of Eliezer (merchant in Königsberg, from a family of rabbis). He was educated in the cheder and in high school. In the years 1882-1896, he served as the director of a high school in Warsaw.

In 1882, he was one of the first Hovevei Zion in Warsaw and one of its activists. In 1890, he was one of the founders of the Beit Midrash in Warsaw, he was a member of "Menucha Venachala" in Rehovot. In 1893, he was one of the founders of "Achiasaf" and one of its directors. On 1896, he was one of the founders of "Carmel" in Russia (in 1899 in the USA, in 1902 in Israel under the name of "Carmel Mizrahi") and one of its director. In 1903, he was one of the founders of "Ha'Tzofeh". In 1904, he was one of the founders of "Geula". From 1906, he lived in Israel (he visited Israel in 1900 in the affairs of Rehovot, in 1903, on a mission of Hovevei Zion, with Ussishkin, Ettinger and Droyanov, and for the opening of "Carmel Mizrahi"). In the years 1906-1922, he served as the director of the wineries in Rishon Lezion and Zichron Yaakov. He participated in several local and cultural enterprises. During the first World War in Egypt, he served as the Vice-Chairman of the aid committee for the exiles of the land of Israel and was very active in it.

He donated and founded a library at the municipal school in Tel Aviv on the name of his wife, Vela, and also donated his home to the municipal library "Shaarei Zion" in Tel Aviv.

[Page 178]

Y. L. Garzovsky

Yehuda Leib Garzovsky was born in Slutsk on the 1st of Nisan, 5656 (1896), to his father Yitzhak Hillel, a Hebrew teacher and melamed, educated and Hovev Zion, uncle of the linguist writer Yehuda Gur-Grazovsky, and his mother Tehila. He studied in cheders and yeshivas in Slutsk and Slobodka.

In 1910, he moved to Vilna and studied general education and the profession of optics.

He was an enthusiastic Hovev Zion and from a young age he was in "Tze'irei Zion" (Zion youth). In 1925, he emigrated to Israel and founded the first professional optical business in Tel Aviv. He was an activist in various associations. He was also a member of Bnei Brit and one of the founders of "Yitzhak Yelin" Chamber.

He passed away in Tel-Aviv, on the 3rd of Tamuz, 5718, 21.6.58.

Michael Polyak

5624 (1864; Slutsk) – 5714 (1954; Haifa). He visited in Israel on 1908, 1914, 1920 and from 1922, he lived permanently in Israel. He was an industrialist, a pioneer of the largest industry in Israel. From his youth he lived in Nizhny Novgorod (now Gorky). He completed his studies (mathematics) at Petersburg University. Since then, he was involved in the business. He was one of the pioneers of oil plants in Russia (Baku). From 1898, he was a partner of the Rothschild family in the "Mazut" company. After emigrating from Russia after the revolution, he learned that he owned shares worth 2 million Pound in the Shel company, to which the Rothschild family had sold its oil wells in Baku even before the revolution. Since then, he has directed his energy and money to the Land of Israel and founded the great cement factory, "Nesher" in Yagur, near Haifa. In 1946, he sold the factory to the "Solel Bone" company. He secretly donated large sums to charitable and educational institutions in Israel.

Yitzhak Elyashiv

El-Yashiv Yitzhak ben Meir. His mother was known in the city as Tila Elyashiv, owner of a merchandise shop.

He was born at the end of 5631 (1871) in Slutsk. He left the city at a young age.

In Warsaw, he was a member of the association "Hovevei Zion", the director of the Achiasaf publishing house (1901-03), the publisher of the "HaTzofe" newspaper (1903-05).

He was the founder and chairman of the association "Lovers of the past language" in Lodz. He also served as the Vice Chairman of "HaZamir" Company.

He was the Lodzer writer "Tag Blat" at the congresses in Hamburg and in Vienna.

In Moscow: he was a member of the Zionist Committee, a member of the "Tarbut" Committee, a member of the Center of Russian Zionists.

He participated in congresses in Basel, The Hague, Hamburg, and Vienna.

In 1931, he received a permit to leave Russia.

He passed away in Tel Aviv in 1954, on the 1st of Iyar.

Eliezer Zeldas

He was born in Slutsk (1874) and was among the first Hebrew teachers there.

He emigrated to Israel in 5668 (1908). His first job was in Gaza, in which, at that time, there were only few Jews, around 12-13 families. He stayed in Gaza for two years and from there he moved to Har-Tov to Mr. Goldberg's farm. He taught at a school for Bulgarian Jews and stayed there for two years.

Afterwards, he moved to Castinya and stayed there the entire period of the First World War.

At the beginning of 1921, he moved to Beer Ya'akov and that was his last place of work.

Later on he retired and lived in Tel Aviv and Ramat Gan.

He was involved in literature from time to time and these are the pamphlets he printed:

Historical library: the ancient Arabs, 5683; India, 5683; Ancient Egypt, 5684; Assyria and Babylon, 5684; Persia and Medes, 5684; From the ancient Egyptian literature, 5684; Canaan, 5690; The days of Zerubbabel and Nehemiah, 5690; **From the Babylonian literature:** published by "La'am", 5690; The culture in the Land of Israel, according to Prof. McCallister (5673); "Practical history A, B, C, (5695, 5696)

He wrote various articles in the "Haaretz" newspaper, criticisms of history books and sometimes signed under the name "Eliezer". He was 80 years old when he passed away in the year 5714.

[Page 179]

Reb Aharon Ratner

He was born in 1878, in the village of Dobi near Slutsk. He married the daughter of Reb Shimon Kotzer, a salted fish merchant.

A short time later, Reb Aharon became famous as a retail merchant and a wholesaler of butter and all kinds of cheeses, which were sent all over Russia and abroad. He was a Zionist with all his heart and soul. He raised his sons and daughter in the spirit of dedication and Zionism. His eldest son Israel was banned and deported to Israel in 1924. After his property was confiscated by the Soviet government, he finally managed to emigrate to Israel with his family members in 1925 and settled in Tel Aviv. He started his business all over again and opened a grocery store.

But in his old age, he was drawn to village life. He moved to Hefer valley and settled in "Havatzelet HaSharon", and took care of a small farm and a small orchard. He lived there for twenty years.

He passed away in Tel Aviv, at the age of 77, in 5715, 1955.

Reb Chaim Ratner
He was the father of Reb Aharon Ratner. He passed away
at the age of 80

Sara Zlata Kotzer
She passed away at the age
of 83 in Tel Aviv in the year
1936

David Kotzer
He Passed away at the age
of 70 in Tel Aviv in the year
1955

Reb Shimon Kotzer
He passed away at the age
of 84 in Tel Aviv in the year
1935

[Page 180]

The Rebbetzin Beyla Hinda Meltzer

The Rebbetzin Beyla Hinda Meltzer was the daughter of Reb Fabel Frank. He was a wise scholar, a merchant and of the dignitaries of Kovno. She was born in 1873.

Even in her youth she was famous for being versed in the Bible. While she lived in Kovno she had a leather shop. When she moved to Slutsk, she took over the management of the yeshiva's physical affairs.

She used to say: In one verse I sin by changing the word leather in the word light, "a leather for light" and a person should give everything they have for their soul. She meant that she replaced selling leather with the light of the Torah and she was ready to devote her whole soul to it.

She was particularly famous for her constant work of copying the innovations of her husband to the Torah in her clean and orderly handwriting and preparing them for printing. All seven volumes of "Even Haezel", which were published during the lifetime of her husband (the late Reb Isser Zalman Meltzer) were written in her handwriting. She would point out to her husband about mistakes and things that could be corrected.

She passed away in Jerusalem at the age of 86, in the year 5719.

Malka Ila the sister of Zeev Gluskin, she emigrated to Israel in 1925. She passed away at the age of 88

Reuven Gross -Passed away at the age of 60 in Tel Aviv in the year 5719

Aharon Baruch Becker He was born in 1883. He was from the second Aliya. He passed away in Tel Aviv in the year 1934

From the pioneer movement

Avraham Yitzhak Nozik

He was born on 1899 in Slutsk, to an Orthodox family. His father was a Torah scribe, who also processed parchment into Torah scrolls.

However, this did not prevent him from being an enlightened Jew who tended to general education. He also educated his children in this spirit, blending Torah studies and general education together. Avraham attended first the cheder and then spent sometime in the yeshiva. Along with this, he also received a general education and entered the high school of commerce.

His family house served - with the complete sympathy and support of the parents - as the committee house for every public action in the city, in which the family members and Avraham among them, participated. With the awakening of the Zionist movement at the end of the First World War, he was an activist in "Tze'irei Zion" and to every act, in which he participated, he added enthusiasm, joy and jokes, as such was his characteristic.

He emigrated to the Land of Israel with the great wave of the third Aliya. First, he was wondering on the road, he was active everywhere and carried any burden. In 1921, he came to Israel with a group of members and joined the work battalion, the Rosh Haayin company. With the organization of the jeep battalion, he was one of the first volunteers. From there he moved straight to Tel Yosef.

In the first months he worked in draining swamps and was engaged in agriculture. From there he moved to carpentry, where he worked until his last day.

When his terrible disease was discovered, a tumor

[Page 181]

in the brain, there was no option but to send him to Vienna for a surgery, which was considered as one of the most dangerous surgeries.

After the surgery, his condition improved considerably, and he returned to Israel. He continued his life, but from time to time, signs of the disease appeared again and he began X-rays and radium therapy.

And again, his condition worsened and he travelled to Jerusalem for treatment. His condition seemed to have improved and he prepared to return to his home. And suddenly, the final disaster came.

Mosia Katznelson – Harkavi

Mosia Katznelson was the daughter of Reb Yosef Harkavi. She was born in 1902, in Slutsk. Her father, from the well-known Harkavi family in Russia, was a merchant for the export of cheese and butter. He was a businessman and a Torah scholar.

From her childhood, Mosia was educated in the national spirit and joined the "HeChalutz" and "Tze'iri Zion" movements. She was a member of the community committee in Slutsk, active in the movement and participated in the "Tze'iri Zion" assembly in Minsk. During the occupation of White Russia by the Poles, she was sentenced to death on charges of her activities and the discovery of hiding a gun that belonged to the "Haganah". She was saved from death under the influence of the late Reb Isser Zalman Meltzer.

In 1921, she emigrated to Israel and worked on the pavement of roads. She initiated the establishment of cooperative dairies.

She passed away in Tel-Aviv, on 24th of Tevet, 5688.

Yocheved Hinich Agranov

Yocheved Hinich Agranov was born in Starovin (in White Russia) in the year 5662 (1902). In her youth, she joined the Zionist movement and "HeChalutz", and in 1923 she went to Tel-Hai which was in Crimea, with two loyal members. She was of the first who were trained in this training point. She devoted herself with all her heart to work and society. She was loved and accepted on all the members.

She was among the opponents of, at that time, the well-known decision of the majority of the members of the "HeChalutz" Center, to turn also the "HeChalutz" farms into a collective conceptual training. With the split in the "HeChalutz" in Russia, she moved to "Mishmar", a training point in the Crimea that she was one of its founders, and from there, she emigrated to Israel in 5686 (1926).

She was a short time in Acre, where occupation groups of members of Hapoel Hatzair were concentrated, especially among the Russian immigrants whose goal was to settle in the Acre valley. From Acre she moved to Rehovot and worked there as an agricultural laborer until she and her boyfriend (may he live long life), Gershon Agranov (who was also one of the pioneers of Russia and one of the founders of "Mishmar"), moved to the settlement in Gibton (auxiliary farms). But her desired goal was full settlement, and she achieved this only by moving to the village of Warburg - in the early years of its establishment. They settled in the place and hit deep roots in it with hard work, despite her frail health, and reached a well-developed farm.

She raised her two sons with her spirit. One of them, the eldest, was seriously injured in the War of Liberation and the other is currently in the IDF; Both are involved in the work in the Moshav - the eldest has an independent farm and the youngest in his parents' farm. She did not get to enjoy the fruits of her hard work for a long time.

May her memory be blessed among the conquerors and builders of the Hebrew village in the homeland.

Misha Efrat

Misha was born in Slutsk, to a wealthy and honorable family. He grew up and was educated on the spirit of Zionism. He was inspired of it since his early childhood. It served as a beacon for him, that illuminated his path in life, he attached to it forcefully and found in it solutions for his troubled and trident soul.

He received a Hebrew education in his childhood. His first school was the reformed cheder. There, the foundations for his path in Zionism, in the Hebrew language and to the Land of Israel, were laid.

The days after the Russian Revolution were prosperity days for the Zionist movement. In these days, a group of children was organized, who founded a Zionist Children's Histadrut called "Pirchei Zion". The head of this Histadrut was Misha. He was the living spirit of it, the permanent chairman. He was vigilant and active, calling assemblies, developing different activities and building this Histadrut as the format of the Histadrut for adults.

The boy turned into a young man. He studied at the Russian trade school and at the same time continued his studies in Hebrew.

During this period in his life, the reconstruction of the Bolshevik Russian state began. Persecutions against Zionism began and the movement went underground. An apolitical Zionist youth organization called "Kadima" was founded. Misha was among its organizers and its founders. Its action was making waves among the Jewish youth and it was expanding and prospering.

Misha moved to Moscow. In the capital city he was familiarized with the busy and intense life. He found his way in a youth organization called

[Page 182]

A.S.Y.P. (Yidisher Socialistishar Yugent Perain), was in touch with the members of "Kadima" in Slutsk, and made every effort to join Kadima to the A.S.Y.P. and succeeded in it.

He emigrates to Israel and immediately joins the kibbutz and the party (Achdut Ha'Avoda, before it was united with "Hapoel HaTzair"). He never ceased to take care of the members who stayed in Russia and were thrown into prisons, or deported to the far north. He demanded help for the movement. When a group was organized in the kibbutz (which was then named "Kibbutz Ein Harod") that was given time off to work in the city, in order to earn money and send it to the movement, he was one of the first in this group.

When the group dispersed, he returned to his farm in Yagur. In the kibbutz he was vigilant, he was involved in the social life, he was sensitive to any injustice and opposed against any discrimination; His heart was open to the suffering and distress of the individual; His treatment of people was just, impartial; He had a good and realistic intuition.

He loved his farm and was attached to it, but at the same time he complaint all kinds of shortcomings he noticed. He was gentle, cordial, and polite, and a look of sadness spread across his melancholic face. Out of love for the truth he could not hold back and sometimes he would lash out against some injustice caused to one of the members.

His life was not easy and his death was also difficult.

Yehuda Mas

Yehuda Mass was an exemplary husband and father, kind to people and did not know what anger was. A man who was both educated and simple in his relations with others. He filled his roles quietly and without any arrogance.

He was born in Slutsk, in August 1906. He was from the family of the well-known preacher Reb Zvi Hirsch of Slianski, who was among the Hovevei Zion. He was the third generation of a family of farmers.

He emigrated to Israel in 1926 and was one of the founders of "Afikim". He went through all the difficulties of the establishment of the kibbutz and its managing in its early days, and he accompanied its development until his last day.

During the events of 5696, he was among the defenders of Hanita. He fell ill and had to go to work in the bookkeeping of the farm. He took on himself many duties after his working hours, mainly in sending a "soldier gift" to members of Kibbutz Afikim, who served in the army.

The news that reached him from his family in Russia was extremely unfortunate. During the reign of collectivization, his parents' farm was destroyed and they were forced to leave their city of residence and flee to the Urals. In the days of the hard persecution during Stalin's time, his brother and brother-in-law disappeared. According to an official announcement, they were sentenced to ten years in prison, but at the end of their prison term they did not return.

This news had a negative effect on him, and his body, which was already weak, weakened even more, until he fell ill and didn't recover.

In his last days, he continued to talk about the many jobs waiting for him, but the cruel fate did not fulfill his wish and he passed away, being 54 years old.

Eliezer Rivin

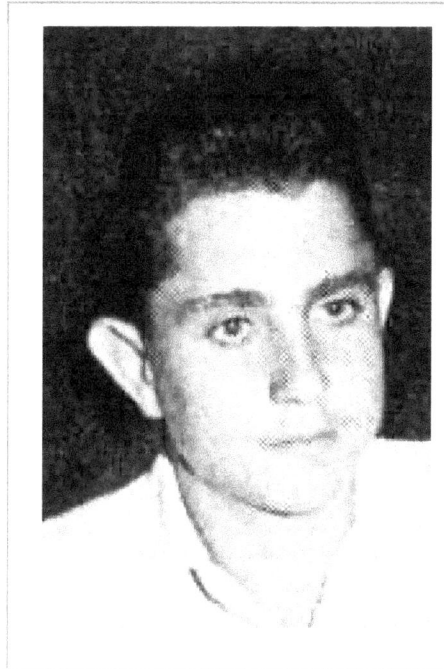

He was born at the end of the Second World War, on Av 5699 (21.7.1939).

He attended the kindergarten and then the elementary school. The first crisis in his life was the death of his older brother Yechiel, who was the ideal character to him, and he became more serious and closed.

When he finished the elementary school, he started having doubts. He didn't know exactly how to continue, whether he should study a profession or continue to high school. He chose the second option. He studied at the high school in Herzliya and was an excellent student in almost all subjects, especially in the real subjects. He had his own opinion and when he received an answer from a teacher that did not agree with his opinion, he did not hesitate to point it out to the teacher and express his opinion.

After two years of studies, he reached a turning point and he decided to go to the kibbutz, where he saw his path in life. In order to be ready for a life of agriculture, he moved to a school in HaKfar HaYarok, where he received the guidance of the working youth branch in Ramat Hasharon. He devoted to guidance with his whole heart and soul. He invested in it all his energy, initiative and time and really succeeded in establishing a large and cohesive branch that was the glory of Ramat Hasharon. His apprentices respected and admired him and saw him as an ideal guide, but due to this guidance he neglected his studies. His teachers did not agree that he would divide his time between studies and guidance. So, he decided to abandon his studies, but not its society, and he remained within it until his last day. This group established the settlement of Yotvata, the youngest settlement.

He was a handsome young man with blue eyes and a curly forelock. He was loved by everyone and was pleasant and devoted to his friends. When one of his friends was wounded in the army and later died of his wounds, he came to the grieving family of the deceased and offered them his help in place of the son who had died.

May he be of blessed memory!

[Page 183]

The Vicinity of Slutsk

Uretshe

Hlusk

Hrozova

Vizne

Verchutin

Timkovich

Lyuban

Starobin

Stary-Dorogy

Pahost

Kopylia

Romanova

[Page 184]

[Blank]

[Page 185]

Urecz
(Urechcha, Belarus)
52°57' 27°54'

by Nachum Chinitz

Translated by Yocheved Klausner

The little town of Urecz was located at a distance of some 25 km. from Slutsk, on both sides of the main road and the dirt road that stretched from Slutsk to Bobroisk. The houses were made of wood and some of them were covered with straw. Over 200 families lived there and most of the residents were shop owners, laborers and Jewish peddlers, who walked through the towns in the neighborhood and sold everything. Most of the merchandise was flour, leather, flax, petrol, herring and the like.

The connection between Slutsk and Bobroisk was maintained by the local wagon owners, who provided the town and surroundings with all that was needed, including letters, newspapers, books and religious objects. The rabbi of the town was an old and modest man, R'Avraham Aharon Peshin. There was in town a *Bet Midrash*, several *Minyanim* [*minyan* = prayer quorum of at least 10 people] and several Hadarim [religious Torah teaching class for little children].

The rabbi R'Avraham Aharon Peshin

In town there were also some "enlightened" and Zionist Jews, like Avraham Baruch Epstein, the teacher Leibowitz who lived in Bobroisk but came at times to his birth-town and brought with him light. When the railroad was continued to Urecz and, during WWI to Slutsk, the town revived. A post office was opened and a new *Bet Midrash* was erected in the place of the old one that was burned down, near the train station and green trees. Two rows of new beautiful houses were built, forming a brand new street more than one kilometer long. A gas station, managed by the Zionst Jew Shmuel Reznik, provided fuel for the entire region.

With the new trains, a fresh new life began in town, and new faces were observed at times. Commerce bloomed, Hebrew, Yiddish and Russian newspapers were on sale, a bookstore was opened. When the old rabbi died, there was a conflict in town concerning the election of a new rabbi. The town was divided in two: The simple folk and the workers elected the young rabbi Appelman, who excited them with his simple sermons and the Intelligentsia including the wealthy (lit. *house-owners*) elected Rabbi Ben-Zion Zwik, a respected man of an imposing appearance. The conflict reached such a stage, that the wagon owners and their followers poured petrol on the flour sacks of the merchant Epstein, one of the followers of Rabbi Zwik. But finally all simmered down and the town had two rabbis, both living a life of poverty and stress.

Yet, a new spirit spread in town and a "modern *Heder*" opened, in Hebrew. The respected teacher Glinik, who had come from Eretz Israel, won the hearts of the parents and they sent their children to the two classes of the new *Heder*. The second teacher was Elta (Sara) Assaf (the sister of Prof. Assaf z"l). The rich man in town, Dobrobovski, also opened a new *Heder* for the children of his own family and other rich families in town. He hired a young teacher by the name of Gurewitz.

With his help, and by the management of Mechl Reznik, a "Hebrew" man and an enthusiastic Zionist, a Zionist Association was founded. Lectures were given on various subjects, and sermons on subjects of Eretz Israel were heard in the synagogues. Yet there were also Bundists and others who disturbed the activities, but the general Jewish public did not listen to them. On the eve of Yom Kippur, collection bowls of the "Odessa Committee" were placed in the synagogues, Zionist stamps were sold and Zionist assemblies were held on the Balfour Declaration day or 20 Tamuz, Herzl's Memorial Day. A "literary circle" also existed where lectures on literary subjects were given.

As the regime changed, all this Hebrew and Zionist activity stopped. When the Poles retreated from the town, it was set on fire and it almost entirely burned down. When Hitler's soldiers appeared, the Jews in town met the fate of their brothers everywhere, and only very few managed to reach a safe shore.

[Page 186]

Halusk
(Hlusk, Belarus)

52°53' 28°41'

Translated by Yocheved Klausner

As far as it is known, in 1847 the Jewish community in Halusk numbered 3,148 souls. I the past, the town, located near the river Petitz, was named Halusk Dombrovitzki.

In 1897 the number of residents was 5,328, including 3,801 Jews. The town had 2 Pravoslav (Orthodox) churches, one Catholic Church, one synagogue and 5 prayer houses, a general elementary school, a Jewish school, a school for girls.

There were 3 tanneries and 22 shops.

Halusk is mentioned in documents from the XV century. It is mentioned that in 1508, the Prince Michael Galinski held negotiations with various emissaries.

From the Brookhaus-Efron Jewish-Russian General Encyclopedia.

The Rabbi of Halusk

by Rabbi N. Waxman

The rabbi R'Baruch-Ber Leibowitz was born around 5630 (1870) in Podlivtza in the suburbs of Slutsk and married the daughter of Rabbi R'Avraham Yitzhak Halevi Zimmerman, the rabbi of Halusk.

When his father-in-law was appointed Rabbi of Krementchug, R'Baruch-Ber took his place in Halusk. Although during his young years, as he studied with Rabbi Soloveitchik at the Volozhyn Yeshiva he was already famous as a great genius and a deep thinker, when he became rabbi and obtained the right to make decisions he was very fearful and strict with himself in matters of prohibition and permission. When a woman came to him with a "question" [*she'ela*] he would try to evade the question and postpone it for a day or two, finally sending her to the other rabbi, R'Shmuel Paritzer, the rabbi of the Hassidim in Halusk.

Many legends were told in town about R'Baruch-Ber's boundless innocence and his remoteness from the facts of life; here are two of the most famous and characteristic: at the beginning of his service in town, a woman came with a chicken in her bag and asked him what to do – a needle was found in the gizzard [*pupik* in Yiddish] of the chicken – was it kosher and fit to cook and eat? R'Baruch-Ber, who knew all the laws by heart but didn't know the names of the innards of a chicken, didn't understand where exactly the needle was found. He asked one of the students and received the correct answer. The Rabbi said Ah! and solved the problem.

One of his students went to see someone's daughter for the purpose of a *shiddukh* [match]. As he returned, the rabbi asked what he thought and the man answered that she was not beautiful and elegant enough. R'Baruch-Ber wondered and said: As far as I know, only the *Etrog* [the citrus-fruit, used on the holiday of Sukkot for blessing] should be beautiful and elegant [*mehudar*] – for a woman the Torah does not say that she must be so…

There was no limit to his love of the Torah and he became famous in that respect, and a group of young men gathered around him and drank his words with thirst.

The Rabbi R'Baruch-Ber Leibowitz,
head of the Yeshiva Knesset Bet-Yitzhak

Their sustenance came mostly from "Eating Days" [a custom by which poor Yeshiva students were eating each day of the week in the home of one of the wealthy families in town; for the students it was real support, and for the families it was an honor, mostly]. R'Baruch-Ber himself, who was also the Rabbi of the town, ate the food that his parents brought him every week from their village, on a cart. His meager means did not allow him to seek out excellent young men and make them study the Torah in the Yeshiva, and whenever he discovered such a young man he made every effort to take him in.

[Page 187]

In his nature, he was very talented to teach in the Yeshiva. But it turned out that he was also an excellent guide and leader of his community as their rabbi. He was loved by the people, hated greed and had a soft character, but was never biased toward anyone.

Halusk became a center of learning. From near and far people came to study with R'Baruch-Ber and his Yeshiva became famous. The Knesset Bet-Yitzhak Yeshiva in Slobodka appointed him Head of the Yeshiva. The Yeshiva thrived in his time.

During WWI, the Yeshiva relocated to Krementchug and R'Baruch-Ber went with them. In 1921 he went with some of his students to Vilna. He didn't like the life in the big city; he was of the opinion that it distracted his students and kept them away from learning Torah.

After some time, he relocated again, to a quiet corner in the small town Kamenetz, near Brisk. During 18 years, the Yeshiva remained there, flourishing. With the outbreak of WWII, Kamenetz came under Soviet rule; R'Baruch-Ber and the Yeshiva returned to Vilna.

He aspired to make Aliya to Eretz Israel with his Yeshiva, but he died in Vilna. May his memory be blessed.

Some of the Well-Known Halusk Rabbis

Rabbi R'Yosef of Halusk, gave in 1772 an approbation to the book *Tif'eret Israel* by Israel Yaffe of Shkalov and signed "Yosef son of the great scholar Menachem-Mendel head of the Religious Court in Slutsk and Halusk."

R'Shmuel Landa.

The rabbi R'Shmuel Zimmerman.

R'Shmuel Paritzer, the rabbi of the Hassidim in Halusk.

The rabbi R'Baruch-Ber Leibowitz.

Avraham Regelson

He was a Hebrew poet and critic. He was born in 1896 in Halusk. At the age of 11 he immigrated with his family to the United States. By profession he was a teacher. His first poems were published in *Miklat* (New York, 1930). He also published essays in newspapers and periodicals in Eretz Israel and America. His poem *Kaiyn veHevel* [Cain and Abel] was printed in 1932. After he made Aliya he was member of the editorial board of the daily newspaper "*Davar*" (1934) and *Davar Liyladim* [Davar for Children]. In 1936 his book "*The Dolls' Journey to Eretz Israel*" was published. In 1936 he returned to the United States and remained there until 1949. Upon his return to Eretz Israel he worked first at the Publishing House *Am Oved* and later was member of the editorial board of the newspaper *Al Hamishmar*.

Regelson was knowledgeable in English and American literature, as well as Hebrew poetry. In relation to poetry he was very self-demanding, concerning form as well as content. ----- So he was as a critic and essay writer, in particular in poetry. A considerable part of his essays is devoted to Hebrew and English poets. In the poem Cain and Abel Regelson presents his view on the powers that fight over human experience. Cain's victory over Abel is a symbol of the powers that control the world. Yet his conclusion is optimistic – faith in a new man, freed from Cain's curse.

His books: "A Shawlful of Leaves" (essays and discussions), NY 1941; "There the Crystal is" (sights and legends), NY 1942); "Non-Being and Was Cleft" [*El Ha'ayin Venivka*] (poems), Tel Aviv, 1945.

Translations: Poems by William Blake, William Cullen Bryant,Walt Whitman and others. Stories by Kipling.

[Page 188]

Hrozava [Grozov]
(Grozovo, Belarus)

53°10' 72°20'

Translated by Yocheved Klausner

Grozov – a small town; population 211. The town received "permission" (to exist) in 1693. There were two monasteries, Nikolski and Johann Bogoslavski, 2 Orthodox Churches, one Catholic Church, a Jewish prayer house, one synagogue, 11 shops and one beer factory.

From the Brookhouse–Efron Encyclopedia

Hrozava. On Saturday, 5 Iyar a fire broke out and burned the entire town, rendering it a heap of ruins. The synagogues and the holy books, except the Torah Scrolls, were burned. Almost all residents remained naked and hungry; we hope that our brothers the Jews will feel pity and help this burned town.

The writer with a broken heart, Eliyahu Yona Kitayewitz. To Rabbi Epstein, address: Hrozava, Minsk District.

Hatzefira, 18, 1881. 18 Iyar 5641

Hrozava

by S. Alexandroni

The town of my childhood, small as the palm of one's hand, was located on a wide area – on one side mountains and on the other side a swamp. Next to it was a narrow rivulet flowing from the mountain and being swallowed by one of the Niemen tributaries.

The story of the beginnings of the town is not very clear. According to one opinion, a Polish nobleman in the 16th century thought that it was important to establish an urban center for the estate owners and the villagers. He allotted a certain area from his estate Grozobok, divided it into plots, built houses on 4 streets and rented them to Jews, who owned inns and pubs in the villages. They populated the houses with young couples who established families. The town was named Hrozov (Hrozava).

The Jews of the town were called by the name of the village they had come from: the Balawitz people, the Baslutzi people and so on. The last of the Polish rulers in the area was named Lagouda. I remember when he died and was buried on the top of the mountain. After his death the estate became the property of Kriyakov, a high ranking officer.

A few Christian families settled in town as well. A Pravoslav church was built in the Central Square of the town; it had gold plated bell towers and was surrounded by a tall and wide stone fence.

Near the church, a number of shops were built for the Jewish settlers, as well as a *Bet Midrash* [house of study and prayer] and a "cold synagogue" for the summer. In my childhood days this synagogue did not exist anymore, since it had been burned during one of the fires and was not rebuilt. During the year (summer and winter) the *Bet Midrash* contained all the Jewish residents of the town. Only during the "Days of Awe" (*Rosh Hashana* [New–Year] and *Yom Kippur* [the Day of Atonement]), when the Jews from the nearby villages came with their families to pray, was the synagogue really full. Among the village guests who came to pray on these days, I remember in particular the famous Hirshel Verbiaver (the miracle–worker R'Zvi–Hirsh Wiener), who was remarkable with his tall stature and beautiful looks.

The Jews opened shops where they sold various things; they had a 'market day' every week and several fairs during the year. Commerce bloomed in town. The peasants would sell the produce of their land and buy in the shops their necessary things, according to their needs. Soon many craftsmen also settled in town, and had an honorable sustenance. Most of the craftsmen were Jews, but there were a few Christians as well. The Christians cultivated mostly fruit orchards, for which the type of local soil was favorable. Sometimes the Jews would rent an orchard from the Christian owner and cultivate it.

The town was situated far from important crossroads and from the main roads, and most of the residents had not seen a railroad all their lives. Since Slutsk was also far from a railroad station, big covered wagons would pass through town every Sunday afternoon on the dirt road, on their way from Slutsk to Minsk, carrying produce to the main city of the district. Such wagons would go also from Hrozava to Minsk, carrying goods and passengers. On Fridays they would return from Minsk with passengers and goods needed in town.

Many families in town were called by the names of their first grandmother in the family: they were "the sons of" Riva, Khiyuta or Rusha. These have been, apparently, exceptional women, who had built the town. Rusha (I am one of her descendants) was probably a very courageous woman: all her sons had the fingers of their right hands cut off. The story was that she had done it herself while they were babies, in order to avoid their recruiting to the army, the fate of the poor. The sons of the wealthy and respected Riva and Khiyuta were released from army service by other means – bribes or dividing the family into small units and registering each son as an only child.

[Page 189]

A street in Hrozava

By the way: any person whose surname is Grozovski (or Rozovski, for the purpose of camouflaging the name) is probably a descendant of a family from Hrozava.

The first ancestor of the Grozovski family, Feivel Hrozover, was a great scholar, All the Grozovski's and Rozovski's, from the Diaspora and Eretz Israel, stem from him. In my memory, this surname is connected to my first years of secular education. As I was visiting often the home of Fruma Horowitz, sister of the well–known linguist and writer Yehuda Grozovski (Gur), I found there a treasure of "enlightenment" books: a complete series of "*Hashakhar*" by Smolenskin, poems by Yehuda Leib Gordon and more.

When I was ten years old, I had already completed my studies of the Bible and the Talmud, with the greatest *Melamed* in town R'Beril Chaim Grozovski, and for the winter I was sent to study in the Slutsk Yeshiva, my sustenance coming from "eating days;" only the autumn vacation I spent in my parents' home in our town. The above–mentioned books – which were hidden from sight and I discovered only with the help of my friend, member of the family – produced the crisis in my spirit. After reading "The Crucible of Affliction" (Robinson Crusoe) and "The Love of Zion" I read all the pamphlets of *Hashakhar* and Smolenskin's novels, and even the writings of Spinoza. All these books were my companions day and night – at home as well as at the *Bet Midrash*, on top of the pages of the Talmud…

Livelihoods in Hrozava

Almost every home was a tiny farm. In the courtyard one could see chicken, which, during the cold winter days were walking inside the house and for the night were gathered in a place near the stove. In the summer they were warming the eggs under the bed, to the joy of the children when the little chicks were seen. Most of the chicks were sold, helping the sustenance of the family. There was one cow – part of the milk was used at home and part was made into butter and various cheeses, for sale. Sometimes all the milk was sold and the children drank only leftovers.

In back of the cow shed there was a large vegetable garden, providing for the family potatoes and other vegetables, but mainly cucumbers, which, during the summer market days were sold in masses to the farmers in the neighboring villages. Many of the Jews in town had a cart and horse and were visiting the houses of the peasants in the village and sell them haberdashery, in exchange for much needed food, produce of the village: eggs, chicken, grains, flax seeds etc. All this merchandise was then sold to the wholesale merchants and to the salesmen who went every week to Minsk.

There were many bakers in town. They would bake special cakes and sell them to the people who came to the church on Sundays and Christian Holidays. In their own villages they ate only meager food and white bread was considered Heavenly food.

[Page 190]

The Jewish families would bake regular bread for weekdays and special bread for Shabat and Holidays. The craftsmen in town worked for the villagers, for the townspeople and for the wealthy farmers, and sometimes even for the estate owners.

Among the craftsmen it is worth mentioning Nachum the cobbler, a respected house–owner, whose place in the synagogue was at the honored Eastern wall. Every week he recited the Torah Portion during Shabat *Minkha* prayer [afternoon prayer] and on Mondays and Thursdays – it was his "right" for many years. He taught his children the profession of shoe making, after they completed their study in the *Heder*.

R'Shmuel the tailor served as cantor at the Morning Prayer [*shaharit*] of the High Holidays, Shabat and Holidays. At the time of my childhood, he was no more a tailor; he cultivated a special fruit orchard, but the title "tailor" remained. There were other tailors in town.

The "Sons of Arye" family were builders, butchers and cattle traders. They were strong men; the villagers feared them and did not dare rioting during the market days while drunk. Much was told about that family, but I shall keep the story short.

The wealthy people in town were mostly innkeepers, accommodating the estate–owners who had business in town, like negotiations with forest cutters, tax collectors and the like. The wholesale merchants in grain, flax, leather etc. were different from the others in town: they had large and beautiful houses and large warehouses and barns in their courtyards.

The wealthiest in town were the sons of Riva and Khayuta. The big inn in town belonged to Avreimel Riva's (R'Avraham Vigodski). There was another inn, a smaller one, owned by Ar;e the bartender (Are Khrinover). In his cellar he has many barrels of various wines, and he prepared also raisin wine as well as a drink made of honey and hops. His son was a big man, the fear of the peasants in the neighborhood and a soldier in the Russian Army. His story is told in Yiddish, in one of Zeide's articles.

The wholesale merchants in town were: Mechl Epstein (Mechl Chayute's) named after his mother–in–law; his fortune was estimated at hundreds of thousands of rubles, and even his sons did not know where he kept it.

The same Chayuta had a daughter, a "woman of valor," who sold textiles. Her husband, R'Pesach Greenwald, who had come from Lithuania, was a great scholar. He was a handsome man, and died young. His picture, which hung on the wall of Mechl Epstein's living room, was painted by his childhood friend Feitel Schwarzbord. As a child of ten he excelled in painting landscapes and portraits; it was said that his mother was the sister of the well–known sculptor Antokolski.

Of the famous merchants in town I shall mention Leibel Shimon's, (Leib Segalowitz, of the Riva sons), who was the competitor of the aforementioned Mechl Epstein.

The town was surrounded on all sides by thick forests that covered large areas; this was the reason why famous forest businessmen, from far and near, resided in town. I remember the Poliak family. They were "enlightened" Jews and did not resemble the regular residents of the town. Forest traders lived in the neighboring villages as well. They were acquainted with the Polish noblemen, who became impoverished due to their wild life and had to sell their forests.

One day, a big argument about money erupted between the Poliak family and a Jew from a neighboring village. I don't remember who was the accuser and who was the accused, but the matter was quite complicated and the sum of money involved was tens of thousands of Rubles. The argument was brought before elected arbiters, religious judges from neighboring villages – Kapoli and Blyakhowitz – presided by the Hrozava Rabbi, R'Shimon Zvi Skokolski. These people were remarkable in their handsome appearance and their beautifully adorned prayer shawls. The children would look at them with respect and admiration. Such people were rarely found in a small village like ours.

When the verdict was issued, a new conflict arose, and R'Shimon Zvi was forced to leave the local Rabbinate.

The *gabay* of the synagogue, R'Shmarya the judge, was a great scholar, righteous and modest. He did not use his knowledge to make a living; his sustenance came from the labor of his hands, working day and night as a baker. Only during the period that they had no official rabbi, did the townspeople turn to him for advice and guidance, in matters of religious commandments as well as in matters of finance. When he passed away he was given a great honor – his coffin was placed in the synagogue in front of the Holy Ark, he was eulogized and then the entire town went to his funeral and accompanied him to the cemetery.

R'Shmuel Epstein was a son–in–law of the Arkowitz family. I remember him as a very old man, righteous and honest. As a child of 4 or 5 I often went with my grandfather to his house – as they had some business together – and he would hold me on his knees and play with me.

His son–in–law R' R'Shimon Zvi Skokolski was a great scholar and an ordained rabbi. He had a big business and was renting lakes for fishing, but later he became mixed up with unsuccessful business and lost his entire fortune. Anyway the old rabbi intended to leave his business and go to Eretz Israel and suggested that his son–in–law take his place. The "simple folk" in town agreed, since he was a smart and pleasant person and a good preacher, but the scholars, led by R'Pesach Grunwald and the judge R'Shmaryahu opposed this step. If the old rabbi wants to go to Eretz Israel they will not oppose him, but it should be announced that the rabbinic office was free and hold elections, as in other communities. But they did not win the argument. The old rabbi went indeed to Eretz Israel, but for an unknown reason he returned before reaching it and was rabbi of one of the little communities in the neighborhood, and his son–in–law served as the rabbi of the town for a period of about ten years.

The rabbi was loved by all for his wisdom and his pleasant ways, as was fitting a rabbi. Every day after the Morning Prayer [*shakharit*] he learned Talmud with a group of young recently married men

[Page 191]

who still lived with their in–laws, and he preached in the synagogue for the entire community on the Shabat before the Pesach Holiday [*Shabat Hagadol*] and the Shabat between *Rosh Hashana* and *Yom Kippur* .

As a result of a new conflict he was forced to leave the town and R'Chaim Fishel Epstein replaced him. R'Chaim Fishel was loved by the people, thanks to his heart–warming sermons, in spite of the opposition of the town's "respected" headed by R'Shemaryahu Shullman and the synagogue *gabay*, because he had once participated in an important Zionist Congress and in his youth he had published Zionist poems and songs. But the greater public won, after a difficult struggle.

Yet, as time passed, the young rabbi found it necessary to get closer to the wealthy and respected people in town, despite the opinion of the simple people.

And here is another thing that happened… One of the salesmen received from the merchants in town a considerable sum of money for merchandise that he was supposed to bring from Minsk. The money was stolen from his home, and one of the "folkspeople" was the suspect. The rabbi, in order to find out who was the thief, performed a ceremony of "excommunication" [*herem*]: he assembled the people in the synagogue, lit black candles, blew the *shofar* and declared the *herem*. This ceremony angered the people, and the women would later tell that the number of babies who died in infancy rose since then.

And yet another story: On the night of the *Simchat Torah* Holiday, a conflict occurred in the synagogue concerning who will be honored with the reading of the prayer "*Ata Hor'eita*". The conflict ended in blows, broken benches and broken lamps. The prayer stopped, the festivity ended and the children were sad, and the rabbi had to look for a post in another place.

As he finally was accepted as rabbi in a town in Lithuania, he left. During WWI, he was deported with all Lithuanian Jews, reached Slutsk among the other refugees and was helped by R'Alter Maharshak z"l. Later he came to America and served as rabbi in the communities of St. Louis and Chicago, where he died.

The youth in Hrozava

There was a difference between the very talented young people and the "ordinary folk". These would complete their education in the *Heder* at the age of Bar Mitzva and continue the occupation of their father: in the shop, in the workshop, with the horses on a wagon and so on, and the more gifted would go to a place where they could continue the Torah study. In most cases it was Slutsk, where several small *Yeshivas* existed. Some of the students stayed for a while and left as soon as the life of poverty, "eating days" and sleeping on a hard bench began to upset them; then they joined again the way–of–life of the small town.

The most talented went straight to the big *Yeshivas*, in Mir, Telz, Radin etc. Those who returned to the town worked mostly as apprentices in the workshops, but some, from "the better families," chose another occupation, which was just then established in town: the easy and clean occupation of scribe [*sofer STA"M*] – writing *Tefilin*[phylacteries], *mezuzot* and Torah Scrolls. Every Jew needed *mezuzot* and *Tefilin*; a young man in town was making them and also teaching others. But later, another young man, from Slutsk, who was a certified scribe, married a woman from Hrozava and went to live there. He opened a business and exported his products to America; the scribe products of Hrozava (R'Chaim–Leib the Scribe, R'Hillel Nozik, R'Mordechai Yakov, R'Ben–Zion Shpilkin and others) were famous. The young man mentioned above rented a spacious apartment, placed in it long tables and taught young men how to write Torah Scrolls for export.

Finally these young men became tired of that work, for several reasons, among them the many religious rules and restrictions involved. Winds of change were already in the air; as the population grew and means of sustenance became scarce, the need to emigrate (to America) reached Hrozava as well. Many did, and some became rich there.

The Hrozava girls did not go to the *Heder*. Some of them learned privately to read the *siddur* [prayer book] and write in Yiddish. Those who came from poor families usually became cooks or maids in Slutsk and other towns.

In the time of my childhood, there was no doctor or certified pharmacist in town. The sanitary situation was very bad. The only person who knew something about giving medical aid was R'Avraham (Fikos) "the doctor." He was a handsome man with a white long beard, and was helped by his wife. On the market day, his house was surrounded by villagers in carts and wagons, and he treated them for various ails and pains. He also gave vaccines against smallpox.

The death rate in town was high, in particular from tuberculosis. The doctor himself died of the disease.

The Secular Rule in Town

The only ruler in town was the "Urdanik" – he ruled in particular over the shop owners. If he was good at heart and also received a good bribe, he would inform the shop owners about the arrival in town of the "Revisor," and they would take off the shelves all the restricted ware for which they had not obtained permission to sell. But if the "urdanik" was strict and the "revisor" came unannounced, their fate was bitter – they received fines and other punishments. I was told that in the days of the revolution in 1905, the urdanik was particularly cruel – his name was Kulak – and he was murdered; the murderer was not found.

The Jews of the town had a form of independent rule: residents elected (by secret elections) R'Chaim Zisel Krigstein as the "community elder" [Staroste].

[Page 192]

Avreim'l the *Hasid*

The Jews of Slutsk and surroundings were not *Hasidim*; only one of the Hrozava Jews was known by his loyalty to his ADMOR. Every year, before "The Days of Awe" he would leave his home and family, take his walking stick and walk to his Rabbi, to spend the Holy Days with him and his *Hasidim*.

The man was a *Melamed* of little children, loved by all his friends and acquaintances. He had joyful disposition and used to rejoice with the public on the Holiday. He wore his *kapota* wrong–side–out, held a broomstick in his hand and danced in the streets, children running after him.

His "occupation" was to strengthen cooking pots with wire; on vacations, when he was not in the *Heder*, he would visit the villages and perform this task – which added a little to his meager income. He was very poor, but happy, and he brought happiness to his fellows as well.

The old Rabbi R'Shmuelki

He died in Hrozava in 5653 (1893). The same year died also the cantor and ritual slaughterer of the town, R'Naftali Rabinowitz.

I heard a joke about the two people mentioned above:

Once they both traveled on a sleigh from Slutsk to Hrozava. Once as they were on the road, the sleigh turned over and the cantor remained under it, his face down in the snow. The other passengers called for help. The cantor R'Shmuelki, whose wit was famous, silenced them, saying: hush, you know it is forbidden to talk when the cantor is repeating the prayer."

R'Israel Perlman

In addition to R'Berl Chaim Grozovski, mentioned above, there were several other *melamdim* in town. Among them I would like to mention the Talmud teacher R'Israel Perlman, from the "Sons of Baruch" family. On Shabat and on the Holidays he would recite in the synagogue the Torah Portion and was one of the leaders of the Community; his opinions on public matters, as the election of a rabbi or slaughterer, were respected by all. When a conflict occurred, his voice resounded and he was listened to.

This was Hrozava in my days, about sixty years ago. The hand of fate, which hit the entire Jewish settlement, did not spare it. At the present, we do not have clear news about it.

One of the immigrants to Israel told us, that in 1946 a young man, who had been in the Soviet Army, visited Hrozava, looked for Jews and found only one Jewish woman, by the name of Wandrof. I think that she was one of the descendants of R'Shmuel the tailor.

May these lines serve as a memory to the Jewish town, the cradle of my childhood, which existed and is no more.

Mendele Mocher Sforim [*MO"S*] / In Those Days (Section)

It happened once, that one hot summer day an old man visited our own. He was short, a little fat and good looking, and everyone said: a nice visitor came to town, Reb Nachum from Rozovi, let us go welcome him, and then say "good–bye!" All knew what "let us welcome him" meant. When Reb Nachum from Rozovi married off his youngest daughter and remained a widower at an old age, he agreed to make Aliya to Eretz Israel and die there. And since a man needs sustenance, even when he is old, and is also taking a wife, he needs money – so what would he do? Reb Nachum did what other Jews used to do. He went from town to town, said Hello and then Good–bye. And when one parts from his friends, he would usually receive a gift, mostly some money, especially when it became known that he was going to Eretz Israel. In time, it would become a regular custom, and people would use this method to make some livelihood. A person like that would be honored and invited for breakfast or supper, and when he left he would receive some money and food for the journey. Reb Nachum would promise that he would pray for them on the grave of Rabbi *Meir Ba'al Hanes*, and send them some of the soil of Eretz Israel.

One day, Reb Nachum went to "say good–bye" to the Jews of Kapoli. During summer nights, the Kapoli people used to eat supper in the moonlight, and when the moon was covered with clouds they ate at the light of a cheap candle. The meal did not take long, and right after the blessing after the food they would recite the prayer of "Shema before sleep" or take a short break and go for a walk under the sky. One summer night of a beautiful full moon, at the home of R'Chaim, the order of things changed: the table was beautifully set and candles were lit, as on a Shabat or Holiday. This change was made in honor of Reb Nachum from Rozovi. R'Chaim had invited him for supper, and they were sitting for a long time and had long discussions about the *Western Wall* and the *Cave of Machpelah*, the Mount of Olives, the tomb of our Mother Rachel and other holy graves and buildings in Eretz Israel, and conclude with sweet talks about dates and figs and pomegranates, grapes sand carobs. The people around the table felt as if they were eating all these sweet things and their eyes were shining with pleasure. Rabbi Nachum was a great talker –he talked and talked as if he had just come from those places and had seen everything with his own eyes. All listened with great respect and love, and deep in their hearts envied him for having been privileged to go there. Can one think of Eretz Israel and Jerusalem as simply words? On the surface, it is a land and a city: soil and dirt, stone and clay as in all other places. But it only looks like that – in reality it is something else entirely. And what is that "something else?" Not something that the mouth can describe, it is felt in the heart only. Strangers cannot understand this – only Jews can feel and understand.

From discussions on holy matters the people around the table went on to discuss worldly matters: Rabbi Nachum had traveled in the world and visited many Jewish homes; he would leave accompanied by a blessing and some charity; he heard and learned much in all the places he had visited.

[Page 193]

Vizno
(Chyrvonaya Slabada, Belarus)

52°51' 27°10'

Translated by Yocheved Klausner

The village Vizno belonged to the heiress the Princess Witgenstein, Papenlala. The estate measured approximately 5,000 Disyatins, had 958 residents, 2 synagogues, a hospital, 5 shops.

From the Brookhaus-Efron Encyclopedia

The Rav Moshe Yakov Mendelowitz
(Died in New-York)

Vizno, a small shtetl, contained 150 Jewish families, two synagogues, a rabbi and a ritual slaughterer [*shohet*]. Most of the residents were orthodox Jews and scholars, and even the so-called secular residents observed most of the commandments and traditions. The synagogue had a *Hevrat Shass* and a *Hevrat Mishnayot* [groups dedicated to learning Talmud and Mishna] and a fund for lending money to the needy. How pleasant it was to see Jews working for their sustenance and also learning Talmud and Mishna.

The people in town, as those in the neighboring towns, earned their livelihood from shops, peddling, working at the forest dealers etc. They sent their sons to study at the Yeshivas in Slutsk, Mir, Volozhin and sometimes to the High-Schools in the cities. Some of the rabbis, grown-up and educated in Vizno, occupied posts in other towns, as for example Rabbi Menachem-Mendel and Rabbi Moshe-Yakov Mendelowitz.

The name of the first Rabbi in Vizno was *R'Shabtay-Ozer from Vizno*. The second, called R'Yechiel Michel Yazgur z"l, was famous in the entire neighborhood. The last rabbi was R'Moshe-Meishel Weiner.

Many of the Vizno Zionists, former residents of Vizno, live in Israel and in the United States, among them the writer Dr. Reuven Wallenrod. During the invasion of General Bulak-Balakhowitz and his army in 1921, the Jews were tortured and Jewish women violated. In 1940, the town was totally destroyed and almost all its Jews were murdered by the Nazis.

Fragments from "*Be'ein Dor*"

Reuven Wallenrod

When he came to Vizno for the Holidays, he felt the big change that had occurred in the place. The town looked empty and sad. During the reciting of the Torah in the Synagogue, the joking voices of the Yeshiva students and the sounds of the slow "negotiations for the prices of the Torah portions to be recited" were missing. Changes were felt among his own age-group, as well. Most of the young men had left the study of the Talmud [*Gemara*], some of them went home, their arms full of secular books, some became merchants or peddlers, looking happy and confidently walking the streets. They did not notice his High-School uniform, and the older generation stopped talking to him respectfully. - - -

He was told about people with whom he had grown up, who fell in the war and he would never see them again. He will never see "Hirshel the long one" or, as he was called since he returned from America "Hirshel Attaboy," who was sitting at the entrance of his shop at the market, opposite the low green fence of the Church and tell stories, or was playing ball with the school children. In Aizik's imagination, the people of America looked like Hirshel Attaboy: tall and good-hearted, with big yellow shoes and colorful coats, narrow pants and shining golden teeth, standing in the street and throwing colorful balls to one another. On both sides of the street were big houses with open windows, where fathers and mothers, men women and children stood watching and urging the players loudly: Attaboy!!

When the war broke out, was "Hirshel the long one" one of the first in town to defend Russia during discussions and arguments. "You don't know what patriotism means" – he would shout angrily to his opponents: "When the homeland is calling, its sons must go and fight – all the reckoning and side-observations should be done after the war comes to its end. And indeed, when it was his turn, he left his young wife,

[Page 194]

who always looked at him with love and admiration, left his two small children and went to war – and disappeared. His friends related that he was killed in the fields of Eastern Galicia. Another townsman who was killed in the war was Pesach ben Shmuel the butcher, who used to inspect every wagon that came to the market. Pesach Shmuel's was about twenty, had a boyish face and would run around with the little boys as they left the synagogue during the Memorial Prayer and join their mischief. On Yom Kippur he would be among those who handed to the fasting adults the "smelling bottle" to ease their fast. And Moishele the rabbi's son, a handsome and elegant youth, who had organized "The Intelligentsia Club" in town and was a walking with the girls carrying books and newspapers under his arm – now was bent and limping... he would walk as fast as he could, not talking to anybody. Moishele had mutilated himself, by the advice of his relatives, in order to be released from the army (as many young Jews did) and he was certain that everybody knew his secret. - - - -

*

One event remained forever etched in my memory: Meir the blacksmith, small and thin, standing near the dead body of a polish soldier, his hand holding one of the shafts of his winter carriage. Only later it became known how it has happened: as the Polish rider entered the town, everybody hid in their houses. Lipa the short-sighted *shames* went to draw water from the well, and suddenly the soldier jumped at him: "Water my horse!"

R'Moshe-Yitzhak Kantor (SHU"V [ritual slaughterer]), born 1860,
died 1915. Scholar, enthusiastic Zionist, brother-in-law of
Professor Meir Wachsman
(Died in New-York)

As Lipa approached the horse with the pail of water, the soldier hit him with his whip, and as he tried again to give water to the horse he jumped on him and pushed him to the ground. The heavy pail turned over and the water poured on poor Lipa. The drunken soldier enjoyed the sight of the man crawling on the ground and kicked him:

- Get up and stand on your feet, despicable Jew! Dog's blood!!! – shouted the drunk Pole, kicked again the *shames* and whipped him, then he pulled out his sword and dragged Lipa by his beard.

The Jews, hidden in their houses, saw this from behind their windows. Compassionate and merciful as they were, some of them tried to find their way through the alleys, until they found Aizik. When Aizik and his friends came, they saw the wounded soldier and near him Meir the blacksmith, frightened and holding the big rod in his hand; Leibl was standing near his father and looking at him with admiration.

One by one, people began to crawl out if their hiding places, and Leibl said angrily: - What are you standing? Let's take the corpse to the garden and bury it. Are you waiting for his friends, or for the minute his friends will get the news about him? -

A typhoid epidemic was raging in town, and many were its victims. We would carry the dead through the gardens and white alleys, to the cemetery, situated near the big pine-forest. Not a day passed without a funeral. Most of the time there were two or three deaths a day and the funerals were performed together, the coffins carried in a row. The mourners would walk in the deep snow and it was difficult even to shed a tear, out of the fear of falling into the ditch alongside the road. They were also worried about the children, who had remained home – who knows what calamity could happen there, while the parents were away, who knows who could enter the town through the main road, while they were fighting with the snow on the way to the cemetery?

This was how the Jews were walking together after the black coffins, in the deep snow, stopping every once in a while, with the defense groups in front of them and behind them. - - - - - -

One day, Leibl's father and Aizik's mother died. One funeral was held for both. The two young men followed the coffins, and other men, guns in their pockets, walked in front, at the sides of the coffins. - - - - - - -

Under Lipa's guidance, the ceremony was performed according to the rules. The voice of Aizik's father was heard, as if coming from a distance: - Aizik, say "Kadish…"

- - Aizik was not aware that he was replying – the syllable came out as if by itself:

- No.

Father is begging:

- Aizik, Aizik'l….

- You know I don't believe …. Why "Kadish?"

He felt the words only after he had pronounced them, and only then they gained weight. They were heavy and menacing. But it was possible to cling to them stubbornly.

It was hard. But at the same time it gave him strength: Piercing and desperate was father's question:

-Aizik… you won't say Kadish, Aizik?

[Page 195]

Verkhotin
(Verkhutina, Belarus)

52°58' 28°03'

by Khen

Translated by Yocheved Klausner

In 1906, a Jewish settlement appeared inside a thick forest, full of fresh air and pleasant, soul refreshing winds. In a hidden corner, enveloped in grass and trees, the princess Gogin-Logy decided to live, in a beautiful house on a large hill. Not often did she come to visit the place to have a rest in the midst of Nature. The estate was managed by her agent and his workers, who lived near the house.

Suddenly, everything changed. The forest was sold to the "Fritz-Schulz" Company in Leipzig, which established a saw-mill and a laminated-wood factory. The railroad from Stari-Dorogi was extended to Verkhotin.

The whistles of the locomotive and the factories introduced new life in town. Houses were built for the workers who came to live in town, working in two shifts. The tall trees were cut and taken to the saw-mill. New faces were seen in town, which became full of people, among them agents and buyers of wood for heating and wood panels. A fence was built around a large area, and it served as a storehouse. There was also a small factory of coal and tar, owned by R'Zelig Khinitz and David Dobrovorski.

Hinda Rachel Khinitz

R'Azriel Zelig Khinitz

Jewish merchants arrived from Minsk, Vilna, Warsaw and even from Koenigsberg and Berlin. Tens of Jewish families built beautiful houses and settled in town; they were merchants, laborers, office employees, hotel owners.

A small community was established, with two *minyanim*, one of *Hasidim*, the other *Mitnagdim*. A Modern Heder existed in the Community, where the language of instruction was Hebrew. A small group of "intelligentsia" was formed. During the summer, many tourists visited the place, enjoying the shade of the trees, the pine groves and the dry climate. The days were sunny, and at night the streets were lit by electric lights, thanks to the saw-mill, which worked day and night and provided cheap electricity to all houses.

Through the local post office, almost every family received newspapers in Russian, Hebrew and Yiddish. Parents sent their children to study at the "Lida" and "Etz-Chayim" [Tree of Life] Yeshivas in Slutsk. With the change of regime in the country, the Jewish leadership changed as well, as did Jewish life in the Community. In 1942, they were all sentenced to destruction and annihilation.

[Page 196]

Where are you, dear Jews, who served as an example in your education, with your good faces and merciful hearts? I remember many, many of you.

R'Azriel Zelig Khinitz, former ritual slaughterer, a scholar among the students of the Volozhin Yeshiva – refined, educated, Zionist and lover of the Hebrew language. His house was a meeting place for scholars – a place of both Torah and enlightenment.

R'Levi-Yitzhak Halperin, who always set aside time for the study of Torah, a good cantor and a pleasant conversation man.

Mordechai the butcher, a friendly person, loved by all.

R'David Katzenelson, a Hebrew "enlightened" [*maskil*], a man of culture and a Zionist.

The brothers Fisch, working as office employees, intelligent, full of the spirit of enlightenment.

Goldman, a plump Jew, a strong forest-man and a good worker. His daughters were famous – they were very intelligent and had a good education.

R'Noah Weinstein, a Torah scholar. He was an accountant; this was his livelihood and Torah was his pride.

The brothers Dobrovorski. The elder became rich and famous and made a fortune, the younger, David, was a good Jew, of simple ways and a big good heart.

Leiba the tailor – everybody knew him. He had a big beard and many children. He would say: "Blessed be the Lord, day by day. He bears our burden" (Psalms 68:20) – and indeed Leiba was burdened with children, but also with many wise sayings. He was guided by faith and confidence. On Shabat and Holidays his children would follow him to the synagogue, and would say: "we are a full *minyan*!"

Eliyahu Bodenitz, baker and innkeeper. He had beautiful daughters and his house, which was situated near the train-station and the post-office, was always full of joy and singing; it was the stopping place of many passers-by.

The brothers Binyamin and Efraim Vinnik, sons of R'Pinye "Rossayer," – faithful and honest Jews, one was a grocer and the other a broker.

R'Binyamin Shinderman, came from Vholyn, an honest and righteous Jew, owned a grocery store. His family charmed the residents, with their simplicity and honesty.

The Radonski family, pleasant and honest.

The Glinik family, the father a Hebrew teacher in the United States, a true scholar. His house was a place of Torah and learning.

Where are you, the holy and pure?? A cruel and wicked hand has put an end to your lives.

May these lines be a memorial for you, and the others that I did not mention by name. May their memory shine for generations and generations.

[Page 197]

Timkowitz
(Tsimkavichy, Belarus)
53°04' 26°59'

My Shtetl

by Rabbi R'Moshe Paleyev

Translated by Yocheved Klausner

My shtetl is standing before my eyes, as if alive. There I spent my childhood years, in my parents' home, in the *Heder* and in the *Bet Midrash*. I remember my Father-and-Teacher R'Israel z"l and my Mother who has given me life Mrs. Chana z"l, whose only wish was to raise their son to study Torah and be suited for study at the Yeshiva and maybe, as the townspeople hoped as well, become the town's rabbi.

There were 3 synagogues in town: the Big *Bet Hamidrash*, where the rabbi and the respected residents prayed; "The Cold Synagogue" for the summer days and a small *Bet Midrash*, called "*The Hassidim Shtiebl*" where prayer was conducted in "*Nusach Sefarad.*" On Sabbath they had the *Se'uda Shelishit* [the Third Sabbath Meal]

The Rabbi R'Moshe Aharon Paleyev

with singing, as was customary among the Hassidim. I should mention that this was the only *minyan* in *Nusach Sefarad* in the entire region. In all the other towns and villages, most people were part of the respected well-to-do house owners and the intelligentsia, who read the *Hatzefira* and the *Hamelitz* and Russian newspapers. The local rabbi prayed there only once a year, on Simchat Torah, when they danced with the Torah according to the Hassidic custom. The rabbi would be invited to give a sermon and speak about current affairs.

The Timkowitz Jews, as the Jews of the other small towns in Belarus, were far from being rich. Many of them were artisans, working mostly for the village peasants. Most of them went during the weekdays to the neighboring villages, with their wagons and horses, and traded with the villagers. They bought from them the produce of their land, their cows and their chicken, and sold them soap, salted fish and haberdashery. On Fridays they would come home and stay there over Sabbath, until Sunday morning. The shopkeepers in the market place provided the villagers with all their needs in the house and in the field. What they had in common, with a few exceptions, was that they were very poor.

Sundays and Tuesdays were the market days; the peasants from the surrounding villages would come and sell their produce and buy what they needed.

This was the source of livelihood of the townspeople. However, in spite of their constant distress, their spiritual life was interesting and fulfilling: all Jewish residents were God fearing people and observed the *mitzvot* [religious commandments]; every morning they went to the synagogue and joined the early Morning Prayer [*minyan vatikin*]. The elderly among them, who did not have to hurry to work, after the prayer would sit around the table and learn Torah, or Mishna, or one of the books. Between *Mincha* [the afternoon prayer] and *Ma'ariv* [the evening prayer] the Bet Midrash was full of artisans, who left their workshops to their wives and hurried to the Bet Midrash to learn. The looks on their faces testified to the fact that their spiritual enjoyment from the study was far greater than the pleasure of keeping shop.

R'Eliyahu Govizinianski (Elie Yesels)

This is how it was on weekdays. On Sabbath, when the *Shekhina* [Divine Presence] was in every person's house and family, even the needy and passers-by would join the table.

[Page 198]

Every respected family made an effort to invite a guest for Sabbath. As they ate the festive Sabbath dinner and sang *zemirot* [Sabbath songs at the dinner] the poor forgot their poverty and troubles.

Most of the Timkowitz Jews were learned in Torah – some more, some less. Among them were also scholars and ordained rabbis, but they did not use this as a profession to make a living. I remember R'Avraham Moshe Perlin, when he was already a very old man. In his youth he studied at the Volozhyn Yeshiva and was a good friend of the great scholar Rabbi Elie Feinstein from Pruzhin. Several times he was offered the position of rabbi in Timkowitz, but he refused and remained a shopkeeper. He was very learned, and when one of the rabbis left the town, he would replace him until a new Rabbi was appointed. All the time he studied Torah.

Another great scholar, who worked as a shopkeeper all his life, was R'Aharon Ratchkewitz. He had a special quality – he loved the Yeshiva students who came home after completing their studies. On free days he would invite them to his home, discuss with them religion and encourage them to study constantly.

R'Pesach Kamshitzer lived all his life in the village Kamshitz, near Timkowitz, and in his old age he settled in our town. He was a great scholar of the Torah, knew several Tractates of the Talmud and was a friend in study of

R'Avraham Moshe Perlin. R'Yitzhak Shapira, called Itche the *Shohet* [slaughterer] was an expert in slaughtering laws and all local rabbis trusted him. The *melamdim* [teachers in *heder*] were R'Yosef Yudel the *melamed*, R'Leizer, R'Nachum Borech's and R'Shlomo Perles. The latter was an excellent preacher. When he would eulogize a person at a funeral, all listeners would cry. When he gave a lesson in *"Ein Ya'akov"* he would sweeten his words with stories and fables. All the *melamdim* in town were scholars, who knew how to explain to their students a "page of the Talmud." Some of them were erudite in the Bible [*TANACH*] and knew Hebrew perfectly; among them was my father-and-teacher z"l.

There were many activist people in town, who ignored their livelihood and their family and worked all their life for the public needs. One of them was my father-in-law R'Elie Yesils, as he was called. He was a public worker and all decisions in town were made after his suggestions. He would see to it that there was always firewood to heat the synagogue and the bathhouse. He also took care of needy orphans and women who gave birth, and collected money for the dowry of needy brides. R'David Reuven the butcher would, during the week, knock on the doors of the charitable people and collect bread and other food for the needy in town. Many of the residents sent their sons to study at the Yeshivas – in time many of those students became ordained rabbis.

The Rabbis in Timkowitz

a. The Rabbi R'Efraim (I forgot his surname) served as rabbi from 5615 (1855) until approximately 5625-5630. I heard that he never abandoned the study of the Torah and was loved by all residents of the town. They called him lovingly R'Efroyke. He died at a ripe old age in Timkowitz. I met many townspeople who were called Efraim, after him.

b. The rabbi R'Noah Rabinowitz, who was called R'Noyech'ke, served as Rabbi until approximately the year 5640 (1880). He was a great Torah scholar and an excellent speaker. He left us two books: *"The Waters of Noah"* and *"The History of Noah,"* – commentaries on Law and Legend. He was the father-in-law of the great scholar R'Baruch-Ber Leibowitz, the head of the Kamenitz Yeshiva. After he left Timkowitz he was appointed rabbi in the town Shadova (Lithuania).

c. The rabbi R'Aharon Michael, son of rabbi R'Moshe Zvi Hakohen Dvoretzki, was called R'Arye. He served as Rav in Timkowitz until approximately 5655 (1895). He was a wonderful preacher, and knew the language of the country. After he left Timkowitz he served as rabbi in Ivenitz. In 5664 a great fire broke out in Timkowitz and all the houses, including the Bet Midrash, burned down. When a new Bet Midrash was built, R'Arye from Ivenitz was invited to the inauguration ceremony (at the time, Timkowitz had no rabbi of its own). R'Arye and various other important people were part of the procession with the Torah Scrolls, headed by a music group. Among them was also the Polish nobleman who was the owner of the land, and had donated wood and other building materials for the synagogue. As thanks, he was honored with opening the gate of the new synagogue. R'Arye gave a speech in perfect Russian. I was then about 16 years old and I heard his speech. Later I met his son R'Yehoshua at the Yeshiva in Slutsk.

d. The Rav R'Menachem Krakovski was the rabbi of the town until approximately 5666. He was a Torah scholar, knew how to explain a page of the Talmud and was an excellent modern speaker. He was firm and rigorous in his opinions. Due to his efforts, the Authorities allowed to hold "market days" on Sundays and Tuesdays. All Timkowitz people appreciated his important activity and he was respected by the "Pristav" and the Judges of the Peace in the Province and he helped many of the accused for political reasons. He knew well the language and did not need translators. From one of the elders I heard an interesting story about his appointment as Rav in Timkowitz: R'Menachem was the son-in-law of the scholar R'Elie Feinstein, the rabbi of Pruzhin. When R'Arye left Timkowitz, Elie came to Timkowitz and visited his old friend the rabbi R'Avraham Moshe Perlin and said to him: If you agree to accept the position of Rabbi in Timkowitz, do it and I am going back home; if not – I would ask you to help assigning the post to my son-in-law R'Menachem. R'Avraham Moshe replied: I do not accept the position of Rabbi. R'Elie said: If so, I am going home and for the coming Sabbath I will return with my son-in-law. And so it was: Next Sabbath R'Menachem gave a sermon in the synagogue and greatly impressed all people, and in the evening the community leaders assembled and decided unanimously to assign the position to him. Suddenly they noticed that R' Moshe was not present, and without him, no one wanted to be the first to sign the decision. R'Elie hurried to the home of R'Avraham Moshe to find out why he didn't come; the latter first used several excuses, then declared: "I have asked you if you wanted to accept the position and you replied negatively; now I command you to go back to the assembly and be the first to sign the assignment." And so it was. Rabbi Menachem was given the position of Rav in Chaslawitz. I heard that after he died; his sons published his book about the RAMBAM [Maimonides].

e.   The rabbi R'Gershon Moshe Gelbard was rabbi in Timkowitz until the year 5682. Before that he was rabbi in Starabin. He was a great scholar and wrote many new commentaries. I was very happy about his assignment.

[Page 199]

Once, as I came to visit my father, I visited him and showed him some of my Torah commentaries. He made some remarks and treated me as a father.

He was a great speaker, and although he was sick he wrote commentaries and I, with God's help, helped him a little. In 5680 (1920), when I prepared to leave Russia and go to America I went to him to say farewell, he burst into tears and said: I wish I and my family would also be able to go to America (it was at the time of the Soviet rule). When I left he was still Rabbi in Timkowitz, later he was appointed rabbi in the town Oshmina. To this day I cannot forget him, his exceptional qualities and in particular his greatness as a Torah scholar.

f.   The rabbi R'Yakov Kanterowitz was appointed in 5683 (1923) and I corresponded with him, through my grandfather R'Elie Yesils. I wrote to him novel commentaries of the Torah and he replied, and so we got to know each other. When the Soviet rule strengthened, he decided to go to America and I helped him. When he arrived, he was appointed rabbi in Trenton, New Jersey. He was one of the great rabbis of our time. He excelled in the knowledge of the Talmud and *Tosfot*, knew by heart almost all of the early Sages [*Rishonim*] and he knew perfectly all four parts of the *Shulkhan Arukh* [The Codex of *Halakha* (Law)]. He was very modest. For a short time he was teacher at the Brooklyn Yeshiva *Torah Vada'at*. He wrote a book, and after his death his sons published another book written by him, about the Tractates of the Talmud (New-York 1948).

g.   The rabbi R'Shmuel Yitzhak Meizus, the last rabbi, was appointed in 5684 (1924). I corresponded with him on Torah subjects. He was diligent and studied Torah day and night, and his family suffered from hunger. Once I received from him a letter with some new commentaries, and Rabbi Moshe Yissachar Goldberg from New Orleans was at my house at the time. I asked him one of the questions that were in the letter of R'Meizus. He asked to see the letter. Sometime later, R'Goldberg wrote a long article about this and sent it to "*Pardes*" in the name of R'Meizus. From that time I heard nothing about him, since our correspondence ended.

People Born in Timkowitz who Became Rabbis

The rabbi R'Yudel Garfinkel was the son-in-law of the rabbi of Vendzigala and after his father-in-law died he took his place. I remember when he once came to Timkowitz to visit his mother, my father took me to him to examine me – I was then about ten years old. I heard that later he settled in Eretz Israel. In America I met rabbis who knew him, they told me that he was a great scholar and he wrote many novel commentaries on the Torah.

The rabbi R'Israel David Ratchkewitz, son of Rabbi Aharon Ratchkewitz was the son-in-law of the rabbi from Lekhewitz in the Slutsk Province, and after the death of his father-in-law he was appointed rabbi.

The rabbi R'Yitzhak Aharon son of R'Nissan Koifman served as rabbi in one of the small towns in Lithuania. He was a scholar and a great speaker. He died before the last War.

The rabbi R'Elie, son of R'Binyamin Starasta, was rabbi in Shinyavka near Slutsk, after WWI.

The rabbi R'Avner son of R'Yakov Zvi Nankin-Aklianski, son-in-law of the great scholar R'Yosef Leib Bloch, was head of the religious court and teacher at the Yeshiva in Telz.

The rabbi R'Avraham, son of R'Aharon Reichlin, was rabbi in various communities in New York and New Jersey, now he is rabbi in the Bronx. His brother, called Ritch, is serving as rabbi in Chicago.

The rabbi R'Moshe Yehoshua son of R'Mordechai Halevi Shragewitz, studied at the Yeshiva in Slutsk with the great scholar R'Aharon Kotler SHLITA [May he live long and good years Amen]. When he came to America he was appointed as Rabbi in Dorchester.

The rabbi R'Zvi Dov Kontofski, born in America, son of R'Meir Kontofski from Timkowitz. He was teacher [RA"M] in our Yeshiva in Brooklyn.

The brothers, Rabbis R'Baruch Cohen and R'Pinchas Cohen, sons of Rabbi R'Yitzhak Cohen, came to America with the refugees of the Mir Yeshiva. Now they are known rabbis in the Bronx, NY.

The rabbi R'Moshe Aharon Paleyev, born in 5649 (1889) in Timkowitz. Studied six years in the Yeshiva of R'Isser Zalman. He was a merchant, in 5681 (1921) he came to America and was teacher at the Yeshiva in New York. His books: Mahane Israel (New York 5690 [1930]), Beer Avraham (New York 5699 [1939]). He also contributed to two Collections.

The rabbi R'Yehuda Leib Perlman, born in 11 Tishrei [Tzom Gedaliahu] 5604 (1844). He studied at the Yeshiva in Bobroisk and then in Slutsk and Vilna. In 5652 (1892) he published his prayer book [siddur] Minhat Yehuda with added remarks Minchat Milu'im. The scholar Rabbi Reines wrote: "It was a good thing he did for his people – to translate the prayers into the language spoken today, so that those who do not know our ancient language would understand."

A Passage from "In Those Days"
[Bayamin Hahem]

by Mendele MO"S

Translated by Yocheved Klausner

Situated on a large plain about ten miles from Kapoli, it looks from afar as a small settlement. But as you enter it, you smell immediately that it is a Jewish town, by the signs: the market with its shops, the alley of the synagogue and the bathhouse – those three things are for the Jewish community as is water for the fish, even when the community is small and includes only ten people. The name of the town is Timkowitz. The town is small and its Jews are few. To these few Jews another soul was added: a young man who came to town in the early summer. All day long he sat in the Bet Midrash and studied, although Timkowitz was not a great Torah center. Its Jews needed to make a living: right after the prayer, the Bet Midrash and the entire alley was empty. Everyone went to take care of his own business – his work at home or his shop in the market place. The young man who arrived in town – he did not come to study Torah but to look for food. He was expecting to receive his daily meals in one of the houses. And he did not come of his own free will, but was forced to do so. His mother, a poor widow, had mercy on her beloved son, the eldest of her young children, and sent him to this town, hoping that her acquaintances there will help him. Shloime'le was the name of the lad, son of R'Chaim. Oh, how sad was his fate! - - - - - The *shames* [attendant] of the synagogue came and pulled him by his coat, saying:

[Page 200]

Come, young man, don't stand outside, it is time for the *Minkha* prayer. For Shloime'le the prayer was a ray of light, which pierced the fog of sadness in his soul and lit up the darkness. Maybe there was not much Torah in Timkowitz, but there was indeed prayer – Hassidic prayer. Shlomo had never in his life seen Hassidim; in his hometown there were none. The *Mitnagdim* [opponents (to Hassidism)] would criticize them, and he imagined them as some strange creatures, whose religion was different and prayers were odd. But when he met them he realized that they were Jews like all others, and was excited by their prayers that were full of enthusiasm and joy; his heart was attracted to them. Most of all he was excited by their singing, filled with love and longing for the Presence of the Holy One, blessed be His Name; he loved in particular the prayer *Yedid Nefesh*.

- - - - - - From the Timkowitz Hassidim Shloime'le learned to turn his prayer into a prayer of compassion, and he was pouring out his soul in front of the Creator. The prayer became a ray of light, but his soul was still desolate and veiled in a fog of sadness. - - - - Yet, sometimes Shloime'le was excited and his heart woke up. He would see in his imagination a red fat figure with one blind eye, and then a hot current would pass through his body and his face would burn. This was the figure and the eye of the family's fat daughter – the family where he lodged and ate on the Sabbath. Shloime'le has never paid attention to her – blind and fat as she was – but one day he heard secretly that they intended to take him as her husband and this made him very sad. - - - - Sometimes Shloime'le felt that he missed his home and his town - - - - and one day during *Selikhot* his imagination took over and he burst out, frightened, from the empty and desolate *Bet Midrash*, and his feet took him in the direction of his hometown. He met his mother and both cried – it was the poor tears of a forsaken widow and her beloved son, who, because of her poverty, was forced to live far in exile.

From the Press

A Christian woman came out of the Church, took off her overcoat and began to run, shouting that a Jew had done that and that he intended to kill her. Immediately many Christians gathered around and threatened that they were going to destroy the town. A Jewish boy, a student at the Talmud Torah passed there, and she pointed at him saying that he had stolen her coat. The "destructive angels" caught him and took him to the jail. Several days later it was revealed that one of the peasants in town did it, and the coat was found among his things.

(*Hamelitz*, No. 4, 1882)   **Shlomo Matzkewitz**

The governor of the province visited several towns, including our town. The leaders of our Community welcomed him with bread and salt. He received them willingly and discussed with them our situation. In Church he spoke to the people, urging them not to harm the Jews.

(*Hamelitz,* No. 31, 1882)   **Shmuel Grunem Rabinowitz**

There were indications that the Christians were preparing a pogrom. The Pristav called a meeting of the neighboring villagers and elders of the Councils and warned them to take measures of protection. In town, a "Fair" took place.

(Voskhid, 23, 1882)

A *Maggid* [preacher] came to give a sermon about Zionism and went on the stage without the permission of the head of the community. The public began to shout "Down!" and the scared preacher left the stage. Zionism was of no importance in Timkowitz, and its young people were shedding tears and complaining about the situation.

(Hatzofeh 137, 1903)

*

Major-General Kapustin demanded from Giltchik 30 men for the purpose of carrying out a command: to sabotage the Timkowitz Police. By contact with a Jewish partisan who was also a spy, thirty Jews and forty Russians were given the task to kill the Timkowitz policemen. At night, they approached the police building and cruelly killed 22 policemen in their sleep. They left one of them half alive, to tell the Germans how partisans take revenge on spies and traitors. Following that, thousands of Germans arrived from Minsk and killed many of the townspeople, accusing them of helping and collaborating with the partisans. Tziganov's unit fulfilled successfully its task: They derailed six enemy trains between Baranowitz and Minsk and on their way back to their base they burned over 200 tons of grains and a large alcohol factory near Timkowitz.

(From **The Book of the Partisans** by Moshe Kahanowitz)

[Page 201]

Lyuban
(Belarus)

52°48' 28°00'

Translated by Jerrold Landau

[Note: Area of Lyuban. Bobruysk is the bold type city in the center. Minsk (on the left) and Mohilev (on the right) are the bold type cities at the top. Mozyr is the bold type city at the bottom. Slutsk is shown west and slightly south of Bobruysk, and Lyuban southeast of Slutsk.]

Our small town was the estate of the Prince Wittgenstein. In earlier times, we would pay a set tax to him, each person in accordance with his property. However, twenty years ago, an official of the overseer of the prince's property came to us and harshly demanded that each of us should pay double. A few residents of the town did not with to obey his words; however most of the residents, out of fear, signed the book indicating that they agree to pay the double tax, as was demanded of them. However, later they regretted that they did this. So-and-so the expert [1] wrote requests to lower and higher ministers. He also traveled to Minsk and entered into negotiations with lawyers. The official did not accept the requests, and insisted that they pay double.

The years passed, and it is now twenty years. A few days ago, the *Pristav* (Police Chief) of Hlusk (Glusk) came and informed us that a final decision has been reached, and that we are required to pay the entire tax that was due over the past twenty years, the sum of 2,000 silver rubles. We were told that if the sum was not paid, our houses would be sold. Each of us had to pay 40 or 50 rubles or more. From where would we obtain the money? We were given a term of thirty days. The situation is bitter and difficult.

"*Hamelitz*", volume 54, 1884
Written by a resident.

Translator's footnote:

1. The name is not given here, it is signified by dashes. Given that this section is a direct quote from a newspaper, the name was perhaps sensitive at the time.

My Town That Is No More

by Rachel Feigenberg

Translated by Jerrold Landau

During the 1890s, Lyuban was a far off corner at the edge of the bogs of Pinsk, surrounded by forests and ponds. A distance of more than 100 *verst* (and old Russian unit of measure) over poor roads separated it from the nearest train station. Nevertheless, even at that time, this small town displayed an exceptional vitality as a creative and working Jewish settlement. It provided its wares to larger cities of the region.

Lyuban was well known for its fine carpentry products, especially chairs. The regional capital of Bobruysk and its environs were a safe market for these.

Lyuban fattened ducks for export. These were sold in the choice marketplace of Bobruysk.

The residents of Lyuban fried duck fat for the Passover holiday. This won acclaim throughout the region.

The town also had a primitive manufacturing enterprise for Sabbath candles, which were sold locally as well as in nearby communities.

We should not neglect to mention the home made products of this sort, such as the braided *havdalah* candles [1] made of appealing colors, which were home produced by Reb Yedidya the teacher. These were works of fine craftsmanship with an expert religious-popular motif. They were popular with the surrounding communities as presents for homes and families.

Similarly, there were two brothers who conducted an enterprise for the manufacture of pipes. These pipes were of fine form and easy to use.

These handcrafted products of Lyuban had a guaranteed market among the farmers of the nearby villages. The merchants of Bobruysk served as the middlemen and distributors.

Traditional and isolated Lyuban of those days also supplied domestics who were expert at home economics. The notables and rich people of Bobruysk valued their services. They paid appropriate salaries and also provided nice gifts. A girl from Lyuban served Jewish homes in the city faithfully and honorably. The members of her community honored her as well when she returned home after several years with her sack of money – i.e. her dowry – in her hand, as well as a large suitcase of clothing and linens to enhance her parents home.

Lyuban also supplied workers for the estate farms of the region during the harvest season.

Lyuban, isolated between forests and bogs with tortuous roadways – this Lyuban of the 1890s, kept mainly to itself. During the days of fairs, its residents only reached the markets of the cities and towns

[Page 202]

of the region. They worked and conducted business there, and then they returned to their homes and families. The entire town was enwrapped in its communal and local bounds.

During those days, there was only one Jew of Lyuban who was so brazen as to break forth from the bounds of the town. This was the pampered young man Nachum Epstein – my maternal grandfather – who was an only child. By his luck, when he was a youth, he once hid in the attic. After many difficulties and attempts, he managed to construct an apparatus for the grinding of pepper that he gave to his mother as a present. From then on, he began to regard himself as an inventor of grinding equipment. To this end, he left his home and his parents, and wandered throughout the cities of Ukraine – which had the most important mills of Russia – where he attempted to introduce his inventions. For this purpose, he entered into imaginary business deals and went into debt until he was forced to work hard in the field of teaching in order to pay of his debts.

He repeated this chain of events several times until he ended up in Odessa. Only there did he abandon his milling machines. He dedicated himself to teaching religious subjects. Rich Jews hired him to teach these subjects to their children, over and above their general education.

Then came them time for his family as well to jump forth from the bounds of Lyuban. They left the town in the summer of 1876, and did not return again. They left there only their eldest daughter, who was married to the son of the local rabbi. This was my mother.

This single emigration did not have any influence on the Jews of Lyuban of the time. They remained closed off and shut in within the bounds of their town, as was usual.

* * *

As well, very few people came to the town from outside.

Sometimes a *Maggid* (itinerant preacher) came to deliver his lecture on the Sabbath. A rickety wagon laden with wandering beggars would unload in the synagogue courtyard, and the group of beggars, men women and children, would spread through the town to solicit donations.

At times the town would awaken from its slumber by the arrival of Dr. Schildkraut, who was specially invited from the city of Slutsk to tend to a seriously ill person. At such a time, the entire community of Lyuban would wait on the street for the arrival of the young doctor of Slutsk, who loved to joke and jest as the Jews asked him for cures for their many ailments.

At times, Lyuban would hear the sound of joyous bells, when the splendid caravan of the wealthy area landowner would pass through. His estate included the civic jurisdiction of Lyuban. At that time, the Jews of the town would stand at the doors of their homes, overtaken by submission and reverence. They would look at his splendid chariot harnessed to three pairs of horses, with thin backs and beautiful decorative saddles. The driver, wearing a purple cloak, would drive the chariot while standing. The entire sight instilled honor for his high position. To the residents of the town, this appearance of the *poretz* (landowner) was like a wonderful theatrical performance. They did not move from their places until the sound of the bells of the chariot could no longer be heard. Even the next day, the children of the town would tell stories of this splendorous appearance of the landowner and his "gentile" frivolousness.

Then, the town would return to its somnolence, frozen in its usual tradition.

From time to time, there would be a wedding in Lyuban. A Lyuban wedding in those days would be an experience and cause for joy for the local residents, particularly the women, for the task of making the bride happy with dancing was entirely in their hands. For dancing with women was forbidden to the men.

The children, who were uninvited guests, enjoyed the wedding to an even greater degree. They would always make a great deal of noise and shout at the time of the festive procession through of the couple through the streets. They were also given the privilege of holding up the poles of the *chuppa* (marriage canopy) in the courtyard of the synagogue. Their mischievous joy would be all the greater if the wedding was delayed due to a dispute between the in-laws over the dowry.

At such a time, the children of the town would be awake until very late in the night, along with the adults. At times, the dispute between the sides would last for many hours. Sometimes, it would even get more serious as midnight approached, and the bride and groom still remained in their fast [2].

Then they would call the wife of the rich person of the town, who was very meticulous with the *mitzvah* (commandment) of facilitating weddings (*hachnasat kallah*). She was Sheina Leah Moshe Neshes, a small, thin woman with a wrinkled face; however with blue eyes that sparkled with an eternal fire.

She would be wearing her weekday clothing, with a large embroidered scarf over her shoulders. This was a sign that she was not invited to the wedding as a guest, but rather as an arbitrator, judge, and facilitator of compromise. At such a time, before she left her home, she did not forget to don her earrings that were set with precious stones, which testified to her high rank among the wealthy residents of the area. These also testified to the social status of her husband Moshe Neshes, who was already far removed from the small scale weddings of forlorn and parochial Lyuban, for his eyes were turned to the forestry industry, to great riches, and upward mobility.

Indeed, the diminutive Sheina Leah, with her sparkling earrings, would hold influence over the disputing in-laws with her appearance alone. Immediately, the fervor of the dispute would calm, since both sides were already weary from the useless dispute. After a short practical deliberation conducted by Sheina Leah, the well-to-do woman of the city, they would reach a compromise. In accordance with her command, they would bring a pen, ink, and a piece of paper. She would write a promissory note, witnessed by herself, testifying that those signing the note would fulfil their obligations.

After the note was signed, the noise and rejoicing resumed. The wedding procession would then proceed on its way towards the synagogue courtyard. Everyone would be amazed that the young children were awake all night. They would accompany the celebrating couple with rapturous joy. They would hold lit paper lanterns in their hands, as they were wont to do each evening as they returned from their *cheders* in the darkness of the streets of the town.

After such an important communal event, Lyuban would return to its mundane life, with great boredom. A cow that was late in following its flock to pasture would lie crouched down for an entire day, along with an emaciated dog whose strength was exhausted due to hunger. Below them, a filthy hog, which had escaped from the streets of the gentiles, would crouch down. Yakim, the drunk from the gentile settlement on the outskirts of town would sleep innocently in the middle of the street, and nobody would move him. He did not disturb anybody, for they were all caught up with the worry of their livelihoods.

The town was poor, but the people were not starving for bread. The Jews of Lyuban of those days earned their livelihoods for the most part from the large vegetable gardens that they kept near their homes; from the produce of their milk cows that were kept in a creaky, cracked barn; and from their two or three laying hens

[Page 203]

who toiled for days on end in the garbage heaps in the streets and the courtyards in search of morsels of food. They also ate the kitchen leftovers of the dairy and vegetable dishes of the weekday fare. Meat and fish were only eaten on the Sabbath.

There were also residents of town who lacked those natural sources of livelihood. These included weak people, including lonely elderly people. The community looked after such people. Aside from two pious women of the older generation who went about from door to door on Thursdays with sacks over their backs and flasks in their hands to collect something for the Sabbath meals of the poor, there was also an organization "*Matan Baseter*" ("Discreet Giving") to support the poor in an honorable fashion.

The residents of Lyuban of that time knew want and lack when they required cash for purchasing clothing, shoes, and work implements, for repairing their dwellings, and particularly for redeeming their sons from army service and providing dowries for their daughters.

Working Lyuban was used to putting forth constant, diligent effort, for it always was seeking out its narrow sources of livelihood, and therefore was frozen due to the expenditure of energy.

This was the Lyuban of days gone by, when the Jews of the town did not even have their own cemetery in which to bury their dead. A heavy farmer's wagon, hitched to muzzled horses, carried the dead Lyubanite along muddy roads to bury him in the cemetery of the community of Slutsk.

This was still before the row of stores was built, which uglified the beautiful Town Square. At that time, satyrs [3] still sang danced at night in the "Cold" synagogue [4], and the good wife of Mota the smith would chase away any ailment and evil visitation with her wonderful incantations.

This was the innocent Lyuban, the Lyuban that believed in G-d and Satan together.

* * *

However, at the threshold of the 20th century, everything changed almost at once. New times came. News reached Lyuban that a railway line would be built nearby. Merchants and industrialists from among the Jews of Minsk had already begun building the line to connect the Bobruysk road with the man railway that ran between the eastern and western parts of the country. They designated the new station next to that road, which was called "Old Ways".

News faces appeared in town. Jews of stature, wearing fur clothing with splendid krakol hats arrived. They settled in town as permanent guests, and were involved in the businesses of the towns of the region. They were generous. They fixed the roof of the synagogue. They gave the rabbi of the town unusually large gifts of money at festival times, and they donated generously to the poor of the community.

Nevertheless, the Jews of Lyuban did not rejoice at these new situations that they had been blessed with.

* * *

At the same time, towards the end of the 1890s, the residents of Lyuban did not feel at home. The town moved, became uprooted, and Jews streamed, as they did from all of the settlements of the area, towards the desirable shore that was called America. Lyuban was emptied of its younger residents. Only people of the older generation remained in town. These people did not have the energy for the long journey abroad. The mothers and children who were set to emigrate also were among them [5].

These people were joyous.

Most of the women were already called "Americans" – a very honorable title. When the wagon drivers returned from the cities of the area, these women gathered around in order to received their large bundles of letters and valuable bank statements.

Money flowed into the town via these letters.

Among the noisy stream of prospective emigrants in Lyuban at that time, there were also some "Returned Americans", who were full of disgrace and perplexity. You could recognize them by their sparkling clothing. Such a "returnee" would bring with him a few hundred dollars. Using the double amount of Russian rubles that he received in exchanged, he would open a store in the city. He and his family would support themselves in this manner for a year or two, and then he would be ready to go again.

There were those who tried their luck in this manner two or three times. The money that they earned from the backbreaking work in the sweatshops of America of those days was dedicated to an attempt to ensure that they would not have to emigrate with their entire family. However, the struggle was for naught.

The young women of Lyuban ceased serving as maids in the homes of the wealthy people of Bobruysk. They also stopped hiring themselves out as harvesters in the local farms. The eyes of everyone looked across the ocean.

Every local worker and artisan was material for emigration. The sweatshops of America of that time devoured the town with a wide-open mouth.

* * *

Despite this, Jews remained in Lyuban, and a new generation arose. This was the generation of the revolution (the Russian revolution of 1917), but we don't know much about the lives of the people of that generation.

We only know the frightful fact that, during the stormy years of the revolution, the residents of Lyuban drank from the cup of agony along with all other Jewish communities in that land. The murderous gangs of Balachovich, who perpetrated atrocities in the Jewish communities of the region, slaughtered approximately thirty people in Lyuban, parents and children.

Only very few of the youth of Lyuban of that era reached the shores of the Land of Israel during the 1920s.

In 1942, the Jews of Lyuban were murdered – men, women, and children. This was a complete annihilation by the German murderers, with the decisive participation of the local murderers from among the gentiles of the region. These treacherous people took revenge against the local police and the Jews, for they regarded the Jews as their loyal servants.

They killed the Jews with cruel and unusual deaths, just as was done to the rest of the millions of our people.

Translator's footnotes:

1. *Havdalah*is the ceremony marking the end of the Sabbath, which consists of a blessing over wine, spices, and a multi-wicked candle.
2. It is customary for a bride and groom to fast on the day of their wedding, unless the day itself is a festive occasion (e.g. *Chanukah*, *RoshChodesh*, etc.).
3. Mystical demons.
4. There is a footnote here in the text, as follows: "The very old synagogue, which was built without an oven for heat. Therefore, they only worshipped there on summer Sabbaths and the High Holy Days."
5. The husbands generally emigrated prior to their wives and children, bringing them over when they had made sufficient money to pay for the passage.

[Page 204]

Rabbi Yaakov Elya

by Zalman Epstein[a]

(One of the personalities of Lyuban)

Translated by Jerrold Landau

A great and valuable change took place in my life. I had waited eagerly for this change, and it was very precious and honorable in my eyes, for it would uplift me and place me on the seat of honor. This was that I left the teacher of young children and entered the *cheder* of Reb Yaakov Elya...

Rabbi Yaakov Elya! Though you did not know of him or his greatness, I knew him very well. I know that he was the choicest of teachers in our town, and his good name was known throughout the city and its environs. The best of the children would be his lot. I know that it was a special privilege for me that I was able to join his *cheder* and be numbered among his students. All of the students were older than I in years, and they were already studying *Gemara* and *Tosafot* (a commentary on the *Gemara*). A few of them already put on *tefillin* [1], and I was a young child of eight years...My former friends still remained with the teacher of young children for some time. Only I was raised up and merited to be accepted by Reb Yaakov Elya... On what account? Because, I, Shlomo the son of the Elkoshite, was a good and pleasant boy, a boy with fine talents, diligent in my studies, and finding favor with all that saw me... I could now look down disparagingly at the young children who remained in their lowliness in the *cheder* where I had studied up until this time. These were my friends in days gone by, but what about now? I no longer have anything in common with them! They would still sing *"mahapach pashta"* [2] each winter, recite their prayers in the *cheder* morning and afternoon, with their *rebbe* standing over them and guarding their mouths. I would worship in the *Beis Midrash* along with the adults. I was free in my soul, for an respected teacher such as Reb Yaakov Elya would not concern himself with such trivial matters; he would only care about teaching the students, for that is the main thing.

When I recall the images of my childhood, the portrait of Reb Yaakov Elya my teacher stands before me as if alive, with his thin face, his shriveled cheeks, his long *peyos*, and his *tallit katan* (four cornered fringed garment) with its long *tzitzit*.

To me, how dear is this portrait! How much light and warmth did he instill in the hearts of his young students, the young of the flock, who surrounded him! Oh, how he knew how to win over the hearts of the children with words of lore and ancient commentaries... On Thusdays, the *rebbe* would sit with his group of students, reviewing their lessons that they had studied during the week. The *Gemara* that they had studied that week, you should know, was difficult, extremely difficult. The sea of the Talmud boils like a cooking pot, it builds up and is torn down, asks and answers. Reb Yaakov Elya worked very hard during the week, many drops of sweat dripped from his face, until he succeeded in imparting understanding to his students, and guiding them in peace through this storming sea. His work was not in vain. This young child, sitting at the edge of the table, with the face of a cherub, white, soft and pure like the heavens, with the eyes of a dove, long *peyos*, a forehead as smooth as small, with his small hat covering the top of his head, was sitting bent over the large *Gemara* that was in front of him, chanting with his thin, pleasant voice the discourses of the Talmud... It is now the time of the exam, to see if his *rebbe* succeeded in his efforts. From the first glance it was possible to discern that both the *rebbe* and the student were satisfied, and that everything will work out properly. With a joyous face, a strong voice, with emotion and melody, this young, tender child will go along his way with confidence. He will not stumble, and his tongue will not be heavy. The words of the *Gemara*, interwoven with *Rashi* 's commentary, were uttered by the mouth of the child as if alive, enlightening, and joyous, and would hit their mark. This entire time, the *rebbe* would be sitting opposite his student, and would listen with full concentration to every utterance... A faint smile was on his lips, and rays of joy sparkled from his eyes. On occasion, when the child would stumble for a small moment, and become perplexed because he did not find sufficient words to explain the concept fully, Reb Yaakov Elya would utter two or three words, seemingly unintentionally, and the child would be encouraged and would get back on track… This would continue until, praised be G-d, the lesson would end and the child would leave in peace, in an exalted manner. The face of the child was burning from joy and internal and external emotion. "Rebbe, did I know the *Gemara* today?" the child would say, half asking and half making an assertion about which there was no doubt. "You knew, you knew, my son! You are a good boy, a very good boy", the *rebbe* would answer, holding the cheeks of the child with love. Both of them were happy. The child was happy because he would be honored by his friends, and also because his father would be happy to hear about the praises that Reb Yaakov Elya gave to the child. But why was Reb Yaakov Elya so happy? Do you know the source of this joy? He was so happy when he saw that the divine labor was not for naught, he was happy to see that his sapling was bearing praiseworthy fruit. This impoverished man could forget about his poverty for a moment, and he could take joy in his love for his young student, in whom he saw greatness, and foresaw that he would be a rabbi of the Jewish people. For he, Reb Yaakov Elya would not receive the reward if this child would wax great and be the first among the greats. He would not be freed from all of his difficulties for this, and he would not receive a monetary reward from the parents, for they were also very poor. He loved this child with a love that was not dependent on material reward. He loved him because he was his student, because he was a good an pleasant boy, he loved him as a father loves a child…

You must not forget that this day was Thursday, and Reb Yaakov Elya did not have sufficient money for the many expenditures needed for the Sabbath. At evening when he returned home, his wife greeted him with her usual request of Thursday: to give her some money so that she can prepare for the Sabbath. Reb Yaakov Elya answered her in a vague manner, for he was afraid to reveal the truth to her. Finally, when he was forced to tell it as it was, he would tell her with a low voice and eyes towards the ground that he had no money at the time, but tomorrow… His wife chastised him and yelled that tomorrow, he would not have enough time to purchase flour, to kneed and bake. Reb Yaakov Elya stood and listened, but had no answer. His wife continued to storm on and said: "Why do you stand as a tree stump and be silent? Go to one of the "householders" and request the tuition money…" She did not know that all of the householders had already paid more than was owing at the time.

[Page 205]

His wife cried out loudly, "I do not know, I will leave you the children to do with them as you please, and as for me, if I am to be lost, I am to be lost" [3].

Reb Yaakov Elya could not bear her words anymore, and he went out… Where could he go, who could help him?… To whom can he go for help in his difficult straits…Perhaps to the wife of the Elkoshite?

Suddenly, the door opened, and here he was in our home… My mother, the children, including me, and two or three other acquaintances of ours were sitting around the long table. Without grace, with stumbling feet, Reb Yaakov Elya approached the table. My mother asked him to sit down, but he continued standing dejectedly… Several minutes passed in silence. Those gathered around, particularly the children, look at him in astonishment… Finally my mother asked him: "What is it, Reb Yaakov Elya? Why did you come?" "I have nothing, I have nothing" muttered the poor man, and he stammered to my mother that he has no provisions for the Sabbath, and he does not know how to extricate himself from his difficult situation…

Translator's footnotes:

1. A Jewish male begins putting on *tefillin* (phylacteries) at the age of bar mitzvah (i.e. 13).
2. *Mahapach* and *Pashta* are the names of two of the cantillation (*trop*) notes of the bible.
3. "If I am to be lost, I am to be lost" was the statement that Queen Esther made to Mordechai when she agreed to risk her life by going to King Achasverosh to plead on behalf of the Jews.

Original footnote:

1. "from his writings." From the context 'his' refers to Epstein and not the rabbi.

[Page 205]

Rabbi Nechemya Yerushalmi

by Tzvi Asaf

(His character)

Rabbi Nechemya Yerushalmi (Jeruzalimski)

One of the well-liked personalities who is still remembered by Lyuban natives with love and reverence was Rabbi Nechemya Yerushalmi of blessed memory.

He was born in Novogrudok in the year 5613 (1853), and was an only child. His father was an expert scholar, and was close to the Gaon Rabbi Yitzchak Elchanan Spektor [1] of holy blessed memory, who served at the time in Novogrudok.

His talents were evident already in his youth. He studied Torah diligently in well-known Yeshivas, and was ordained by the Gaon Rabbi Yitzchak Elchanan and other greats of the generation. His Torah novellae were printed in the commentary to the Mishnaic Order of "*Nashim*" [2] that was published by the "Ram" publishing house.

They loved him and respected him even though he was strong willed, and conducted his rabbinate with a high hand. His intelligence and his many activities in communal affairs made gave him renown, and people would come to him for judgement from far away. Even Christians would come.

Czarist government officials, and later on Polish government representatives (during the First World War) took heed of him. He appeared before them without fear on behalf of his community.

By nature, he pursued peace. He was very hospitable with guests. He was honored and appreciated by all segments of his community. The youth especially found in him an enthusiastic spokesman. He loved them so much that he organized a Sabbath prayer quorum (minyan) in his home especially for the youth. He believed in their traditional education, and would say: "A Lyubaner *Bundevetz* [3], if a pair of *tefillin* fall down near him, he would give them a kiss."

The youth of Lyuban were Zionistic, even though most of them studied in Yeshivas. Lyuban excelled above all the towns of the area in the number of students who went to study in far off Yeshivas.

All his life, the rabbi longed to make *aliya* and settle in the Land of Israel. He was fortunate that, in his old age, he succeeded in coming to the Land. He arrived in the year 5682 (1912), and settled in Jerusalem, where his son-in-law Rabbi Simcha Asaf already lived.

He held the new settlement in esteem, and played a part in organizing "*Knesset Yisrael*". He did not follow after the isolationist rabbis, despite their pressure upon him [4].

He would explain the situation as follows: "It is possible that the *chareidim* are correct in their isolationist stand, for they are concerned about the education of their children and are concerned lest they break free. However my children (he refers here to the youth who grew up near him) already are part of those circles – and I cannot separate from them."

He would look out for the *chalutzim* (Zionist pioneers) in Jerusalem. He would especially keep in touch with workers' kitchen and members of the work group to ensure that kashruth was kept. He would appear on Sabbaths at every workers' gathering in Jerusalem, with his full rabbinical garb including his cylinder (rabbinical hat) and flowing white beard. His appearance was sufficient to ensure that they would stop smoking [5], for he conducted himself pleasantly, and everyone respected him.

Once when I was on route by bicycle to the printing house in Tel Aviv to give over corrections to one of the books, I saw him. I approached him. He was happy to meet me and extended his hand. I said to him: "Rabbi, my hands are dirty."

He asked "Dirty from what?"

"From work," I answered.

He said: "Work is never dirty, give me your hand."

In the midst of the conversation, he said: "I like Tel Aviv, with its new settlement. Here, there are proud Jews who are building up the land, and the stores are closed on the Sabbath.. But in Jerusalem with its *Tzadikim* - and we cannot imagine their great piety. In truth, the Orthodox have made a great mistake. I refer to

[Page 206]

how they wake up with G-d, and go to sleep with G-d, while the *Apikorsim* (heretics) are around 24 hours a day. However, this is not correct, for you are dear Jews, very dear Jews, despite the fact that you trample on the Torah with the soul of your foot."

His will is also very interesting. It also is true to his path:

…"C. Immediately after my death, the society for *Hachnasat Orchim* (providing for guests), the organization for Sabbath observance, and the funds for the building of Jerusalem, the *Beis Midrash, Hachnasat Orchim* and my friends in the Talmud Torah, should be informed that they should be careful to fulfil my request. For I am a member of their group, and they must fulfil the wishes of the departed. They should fulfil the commandment of *"skila"* [6] with my body. It is good that I receive pain and embarrassment in this world, so that I should not suffer in the World To Come, for my sins are always before me, and I am not exempt from the law of the four death penalties. Therefore I accept upon myself the most stringent of them.

D. No embellishments should be made in the eulogies, for every embellishment contains some exaggeration, and this causes a punishment. I do not wished to incur punishment due to any of the eulogizers. They should only say that he served in the rabbinate for forty years. If the eulogizers cannot see any benefit in discoursing on Sabbath observance or the love of peace, etc., it would be best if they do not eulogize me at all. If they can see benefit in doing so, then I permit them to deliver eulogies for me in public, and if not, I request that they do not eulogize me. They should weigh every word carefully, to ensure that it is has benefit for the audience.

Those who occupy themselves with matters of the funeral and burial should inform the workers' kitchen and the work group that if they wish, they should take precedence to anyone [7], for I toiled greatly to improve their spiritual life. If they will grant me kindness and recognize their debt, I grant them precedence. If not, those storeowners and barbers with whom I worked to ensure that their stores would close on the Sabbath, should take precedence in dealing with my bier, and they should recognize their obligation. If even these do not recognize their obligation, then you should follow the custom that is followed in this place."

He died suddenly. On the night of the 24th of *Shvat*, 5690 (1930), he was sitting and studying Torah until 9:00 p.m., and then he went to bed. He woke up with pains in his heart at 10:30, and his soul left him in purity a short time thereafter. May his memory be blessed.

Translator's footnotes:

1. The rabbinical seminary of Yeshiva University in New York is named after Rabbi Yitzchak Elchanan Spektor – the Rabbi Isaac Elchanan Theological Seminary.
2. There are six "Orders" of the *Mishna*, each dealing with a major category of Jewish Law. "*Nashim*" (literally: women), deals with issues of marriage, divorce, levirate marriage, vows, etc.
3. I am not sure of the meaning of this term – it may be a reference to a member of *Bund*, an ardently secular socialist organization. If that is the case, the rabbi would be saying that even such people have a reverence for what is holy.
4. This brief paragraph refers to the tensions between the more isolationist, non Zionistic rabbis of *AgudasYisrael*, and the *EdahHachareidit*, who did not participate in the modern communities being founded in Israel at the time (although after the state was founded, *AgudasYisrael* did start participating to some degree); and the more Zionistically inclined rabbis of the *Mizrachi* movement who participated fully in the new communities. I cannot do justice to this important historical (and current) conflict in a brief footnote. The word "*chareidim*" in the next paragraph refers to those Orthodox people who were more on the isolationist side. The word is used in modern Israel to denote those people as well – and is often translated as Ultra-Orthodox, although that is not a very useful term. The word "*chareidim*" literally means "those who tremble," i.e. those who tremble in fear before G-d.
5. Smoking is forbidden on the Sabbath.
6. This is a very strange request. "*Skila*" literally "stoning" is one of the four categories of humanly administered death penalties in the Torah (there are also death penalties by the hand of G-d). These penalties would be administered under certain very restrictive conditions at the time that the Temple existed and the main court (*Sanhedrin*) was functioning. *Skila* involves pushing the criminal over a precipice, and then throwing heavy rocks down at him. "*Skila*" is considered to be the most stringent of the four death penalties. The others are

"Sreifa" (burning), *"Hereg"* (beheading with a sword), and *"Chenek"* (strangulation). I have never heard before of this being done to a corpse for the purposes of expiation until I translated this segment.

7. The implication here is apparently that they should take precedence in the funeral procession, and the carrying of the bier.

[Page 207]

Rabbi Professor Simcha Asaf (Osovski)

Translated by Jerrold Landau

He was the son of Yehuda Zeev the merchant, and Feiga the daughter of Tzvi Yaakov Epstein of Bobruysk. He was born in Lyuban on the 9th of *Tammuz* 5649 (1888).

He received a traditional education in cheder, and in the Yeshiva of Slutsk from Rabbi Isser Zalman Meltzer, and in the Yeshiva of Telz (from the years 5665-5668, 1905-1908) from Rabbi Eliezer Gordon (Reb Leizer Telzer). He received his ordination. He served as a rabbi in Lyuban in the years 5670-5671 (1910-1911).

From the years 5674-79 (1914-19), he served as the Rosh Yeshiva of the Yeshiva of Odessa that was founded by Rabbi Chaim Chernovitz (Rav Tzair). He began his scientific-literary work in Odessa, and published his first articles in *"Hashiloach"* and *"Reshumot"*. He had already become a Zionist in the Yeshiva of Telz, and there he worked to disseminate the Zionist idea. In Odessa, he joined the Zionist movement, and was elected as a member of the Zionist council of the city.

He married Chana, the daughter of Rabbi Nechemya Jeruzalimski (a rabbi in Semezhevo and Lyuban, who made *aliya* to the Land of Israel in his old age). He made aliya at the end of 1921, and was appointed as a teacher of Talmud in the *Mizrachi* seminary in Jerusalem. He published many investigations and books on classroom surveys in Israel, teaching methodologies, court proceedings, and relations between Torah centers in the Diaspora and Israel.

At the time of the founding of the Hebrew University (5685 – 1925), he was appointed as a lecturer, and later a professor in Gaonic and rabbinic literature [1].

He was one of the veteran *Mizrachi* activists, and he represented *Mizrachi* in the national council and various meetings. He was a member of the honorary court of the World Zionist Organization, as well as the honorary court of *Mizrachi*. He served as the chairman of the honorary court of the teacher's union of Israel, as a member of the advisory committee for the Hebrew Organization for Research of the Land of Israel and its Antiquities, as the vice chairman of the educational committee, as a member of the active council of the Hebrew University and its rector, as the chairman of the "Awakeners of the Slumbering" organization, as a member of the council for the Rechavia neighborhood of Jerusalem, and as vice president of the B'nai Brith organization of the Land of Israel.

* * *

We cannot be too verbose regarding Rabbi Simcha Asaf. It is most unfortunate that he went to his eternal rest in his prime (at about age 64) in Jerusalem. He was indeed a Renaissance man, and he wore many crowns. He was an excellent writer and researcher. At the establishment of the State of Israel, he was appointed as one of the five first Judges of the Supreme Court of Jerusalem.

[Page 207]

As a researcher, he stood out because of his easy and pleasant style, and his clear explanations. He published important books during his life: "Sources on the History of Education in Israel," "Punishments after the Closing of the Talmud," "Court of Law and their Proceedings," "Responsa of the *Gaonim*, and Excerpts of the Book of Judgement," "An Anthology of the Letters of Rabbi Shmuel the son of Eli and his Generation," "The Book of Documents of Rabbi Hai Gaon," "From the Gaonic Literature," "The Library of the *Rishonim*, " "Responsa of the *Gaonim* from the Cambridge Library," "In the Tents of Jacob," "Sources and Research in Jewish History," "The Book of Professions," and others.

Writers and Hebrew readers were very pleased with his work "The People of the Book and the Book" (printed at first in one volume of the *Reshumot* anthology, and collected with additional material in his book "In the Tents of Jacob") until this day, this serves as a reliable source for all of those who are seeking plentiful and valuable material

The text was written by the writer Sh. Y. Agnon, and the engraving
was by the graphicist Y. Shechter.

[The inscription is as follows (the photo is unclear, and some lines cannot be made out):
Rabbi Simcha Asaf
Professor at the Hebrew University
And Judge of the Supreme Court
A writer of books with wisdom and knowledge
Disseminating Torah in the Diaspora and in the land
(line cannot be made out)
9th of *Tammuz* 5649 (1889) – 10 of *Cheshvan* 5714 (1953)
(3 lines on the foot stone cannot be made out)
May he be remembered for eternal life]

[Page 208]

on the Hebrew book in ancient sources and in the eyes of the *Rishonim* and *Acharonim*. He left behind unfinished manuscripts and material for several books, including a book on "The Era of the *Gaonim* and its

Literature." He had hoped to finish these books shortly, and he promised to write his autobiography when he reached the age of seventy. He did not attain this age – and the song of his life was cut off in the middle.

I remember when he came to New York in the year 5711 (1951), and was hospitalized in the Mount Sinai Hospital. I visited him there, and I found in his room Professor Boaz Cohen and the researcher M. Lutzki. I was astonished to find Rabbi Simcha Asaf happy with life, and in a humorous mood. He discussed with me his two years of study in Minsk (5671-5673 – 1911-1913), the city of my birth. There he studied in the *Kolel Avreichim* [2]"Prushim." He was also appointed by the chief rabbi, Rabbi Eliezer Rabinovitch, as a teacher in his home. He related to me his memories of personalities and well-known events from the time of my youth. His memory was wonderful, and his descriptions were full of minute details. Later, he told us jokes, so that the room was filled with waves of laughter. He was happy because the doctors had determined that he did not require surgery. Later, we learned from them the secret that the hardening of the liver has no cure at all.

By his nature, he was a man of action, and he fought for the Zionist idea. During his youth in the Yeshivas of Slutsk and Telz, he was very active in Zionist activities. He lectured and spoke, and entered into debates with representatives of *Bund*, the S. Z. (Socialist Zionists), and other disputants. Later, he became one of the leaders of *Mizrachi*, a position he held until the day of his death. He always took upon his shoulders public, educational, Torah and literary assignments. He expressed everything with exactness, order, faith, and joy, as is testified by his first name, Simcha [3].

By D. P.

Translator's footnotes:

1. The period of the *Gaonim* in Jewish History extends from the closing of the Talmud (approximately 600 C. E. until about 1050 C.E.). The period that follows the *Gaonim* is known as the *Rishonim* (The earlier generations of sages – as opposed to the *Acharonim*, the latter generations of sages – extending from about 1500 C. E. to the modern day). The Terms *Rishonim* and *Acharonim* come up in subsequent paragraphs.

2. Kolel, or Kolel Avreichim is an institute for advanced Talmudic study, primarily for married students who wish to continue their studies for several years.

3. Simcha is the Hebrew word for happiness.

[Page 208]

Memoirs

by Reb Moshe Gershon Finkelstein[a]

Translated by Jerrold Landau

Reb Moshe Gershon and his wife Sara

My maternal grandmother lived in the village of Kuzmichi, near Lyuban. Her name was Fruma Batya, and she had three brothers, Reb Tzvi Noach, Reb Efraim Yitzchak, and Reb Gedalya. They were all upright men. Their neighbors and all of their acquaintances respected them due to their vast knowledge of Talmud and their good heart. Reb Tzvi Noach lived in Kuzmichi, and Reb Efraim Yitzchak and Reb Gedalya lives in the vicinity of Lyuban. Reb Gedalya occupied himself with business, and he studied Torah when he was not busy with his work. They said of him that he knew the six orders of the Mishna by heart [1]. At the time of his old age, he gave over his business to his children and he occupied himself with Torah. His neighbors and all of his acquaintances regarded him as a holy man. When a bad incident occurred to any of them, they would go to Reb Gedalya to ask his advice and request his blessing. Being of good heart, he tried to fulfil their request, and became known as a wonder man. People came from near and far, and gave him no rest. He pleaded: "What do you see in me? I am as one of you, and if I am in trouble, I pray to G-d." However, his words were of no avail. People begged him with bitter tears, and some also tried to honor him with monetary gifts, which he refused. When they advised him to give the money to charity, he told them to do so themselves, for "a *mitzva* is greater when done by a person himself than by an emissary." [2] When he saw that the multitude of petitioners continued to grow, and that he could not free himself from them, he decided to leave his home and to go to his brother Reb Tzvi Noach in order to hide from his fans. That is what he did.

When he came to his brother and told him all that had happened to him, his brother said to him, "Live with me as long as you desire, and we will enjoy our brotherly company." Reb Gedalya said to him, "You should certainly know, my brother, that I cannot accept my bread as a gift, so if you allow me to cut wood, to light the oven, and to care for your produce, I will live in your house." Reb Tzvi Noach answered him, "You can do as you say, but do not push off my servant; let him also chop wood and watch over the produce." After about half a year, people found out where Reb Gedalya was living, and they began to come to him in greater numbers than previously. Perforce, he made his peace with his lot, and no longer hid. Even the local farmers bothered him with their requests. One of the farmers came to him and said, "Do good for me, oh you man of mercy, sit in my wagon and traverse the length and depth of my field, so that my produce will grow."

My grandmother Fruma Batya remained as a young widow with five children. She sustained herself and her children from her meager business, but when the time came to teach them Torah – and she was the only one in the town who had need of a teacher – she decided to raise calves. She would sell a calf every half year, and with the proceeds, she would be able to pay the tuition of the teacher that she hired from Lyuban. One summer when the flock was out at pasture, a wild animal came and preyed upon the calf of Fruma Batya specifically. When the time came to pay the teacher, she took two pillows and four Sabbath candlesticks, and went to her neighbor Frakof and said to him, "You of course know that my calf was torn up, so please lend me 20 rubles, and I will leave these objects as security.

[Page 209]

" Frakop said, "Leave these on the table" and he gave her 20 rubles. Approximately a half year later, Frakop took the pillows and candlesticks to her home. She asked him, "Why did you take the security at first, and now you are returning it?" He answered, "I did not take them from you, I only told you to put it on the table, so that you would not have to carry them yourself."

* * *

How was the Lyuban cemetery founded? There were approximately 200 Jewish families living in the town, and they did not yet have a Jewish cemetery. They would bring the deceased to the cemetery in Slutsk, an entire day's journey. One of the residents of Lyuban moved to live in Bobruysk. In the home of Boaz Rabinovitch, the well-known rich man of Bobruysk, there was private rabbi, who taught him and his sons. That rabbi was very careful about distancing himself from the sin of the evil tongue, and therefore he desisted completely from speaking. His voice was only heard with regards to the study of Torah or prayer.

When he wished to express something, he would write down his request on a piece of paper. The Lyubanite who settled in Bobruysk told that rabbi that the Jews of Lyuban had no cemetery. One morning, when the residents of Lyuban entered the synagogue to worship the *Shacharit* (morning) service, the well-known rabbi of Boaz Rabinovitch was standing outside the synagogue with a note written in large letters: "It is urgently necessary to set up a cemetery near Lyuban so that they will not be forced to carry their deceased to a far off city." After the morning service, he wrote another note: "I request that the leaders of the community remain in the synagogue for a meeting regarding the above mentioned matter." My father-in-law, Reb Yaakov Chasid, who was one of them, promised the rabbi that they would act in accordance with his wishes. He told him that the *poretz* landowner of the town already set aside a plot of land from his estate for a Jewish cemetery, and all that was missing was 200 rubles to build a fence. The rabbi wrote an additional note: "I will not move from here until the required sum is raised." The money was raised that very day, and the rabbi returned to his place.

* * *

After my marriage, I joined the *Chevra Shas* (Talmud Study Society) of Lyuban. The members of the society would split up the tractates of the Talmud among themselves. One would study the tractate of *Berachot*, a second *Shabbat*, etc. The teachers of young children would always choose the same tractate that they would be teaching to their students, and the rest of the members chose whatever tractate they desired. Most people did not jump to take the tractates from the Orders of *Kodshim* and *Taharot* [3]. These tractates only had three redeemers, Rabbi Nechemya Jeruzalimski, my father-in-law Reb Yaakov Chasid, and their friend Reb Halulenchik (the incense maker). These three made Torah their prime occupation. Each year on the holiday of Chanukah, all of the members would gather together for a general meeting where they divided up the tractates anew, and partake of a banquet.

During one of these meetings, I was elected as the *gabbai* (trustee) of the society. The tasks of the *gabbai* were to concern himself with all aspects of the society, to invite the members to the meeting, and to organize the banquet. All those who wished to join the society would turn to him, and the *gabbai* would present the names of the new candidates to the members. A few young people requested that I bring them in to the society, including one young person with a shaved beard. In my innocence, I discussed the names of the candidates with my father-in-law. "The shaved one is not fit to be a member of the *Chevrat Shas,*" he told me in anger.

The days of Chanukah approached. The issues surrounding the meeting and the banquet had to be organized. I went to Feiga the baker and ordered wheat flour rolls in accordance with the number of attendees, and I also prepared fish. On the night of the meeting, all of the members came with the exception of Reb Binyamin Halulenchik, who felt that the study of Torah should take precedence over the banquet. Reb Nechemya turned to me and said: "I thought that Reb Binyamin would have come to the banquet this time, for is he not trampling [22] and you are the *gabbai*." I took it upon myself to bring him against his will. Three young men assisted me in bringing Reb Binyamin. The entire assemblage greeted him with applause, and seated him next to the rabbi. I went to bring him his portion, but, alas, the roll had disappeared, and it was impossible to obtain another one. The rabbi said with laughter, "If we merit to have Reb Binyamin partake of the banquet, it is fine, provided that one of us forgoes his own portion."

The New Synagogue that was built after three splendid
synagogues burnt down

Translator's footnotes:

1. There are six "Orders" of the *Mishna*, each dealing with a major category of Jewish Law. "*Nashim*" (literally: women), deals with issues of marriage, divorce, levirate marriage, vows, etc.
2. The members of this group obviously split up the entire Talmud (or Mishna – it is not clear if the study was of Talmud or Mishna), so that the entire Talmud would be covered. Of the six Orders of Mishna (or Talmud – the orders are the same, the Talmud consisting of a great deal of rabbinic discussion on the terser Mishna), the final two, *Kodshim* and *Taharot*, dealing with the Temple service and ritual purity respectively, and more difficult and less studied, primarily due to their content being not applicable to the post Tempe era, for the most part.
3. The term here seems to imply "impolite" or "trampling upon custom".

Original footnote:

1. The writer is 85 years old, and in his time, he was the first teacher of the rabbi and professor Simcha Asaf of blessed memory – the editor.

[Page 210]

Reb Dov Ber Katznelson of blessed memory

by Shlomo Katznelson

Translated by Jerrold Landau

The community of the town appreciated Reb Dov Ber Katznelson, and he faithfully fulfilled any task that he took upon himself. He was not a native of Lyuban, for he was born in the village of Bapolsia. He studied in the nearby town of Kopatkevichi from the best teachers of *Gemara*. He married a Lyuban native when he was seventeen years old. He continued to live in the village even after his marriage. He would bring his merchandise for sale in nearby Lyuban or Slutsk. He did not wish to be supported by his father-in-law or charity, so he was forced to seek his livelihood from afar.

He served as a teacher at the home of one of the wealthy people of Kremenchug, and he spent a year in Poltava.

He returned to Lyuban after a few years. He searched for an appropriate livelihood, and when he ran out of money, he returned to teaching for want of other options. He was one of the superb teachers of *Gemara*. His students aspired towards the *yeshivas* of Slutsk and Mir.

He was appointed as the *gabbai* (trustee) of the Talmud Torah in Lyuban. He brought in a teacher who taught the students to write letters in Yiddish, as well as in the vernacular. Zecharia the son of Hershel the hat maker served as a teacher in the Talmud Torah at the same time. The students of the Talmud Torah were for the most part orphans or children of poor people, so he had to concern himself with providing clothing and shoes for them. The town was impoverished, and my father Reb Dov Ber Katznelson had to find a source of income.

The forestry traders near Lyuban and its environs donated money to the Talmud Torah. Donations came in from outside the bounds of Lyuban, from as far as Starye Dorogi. The officials of the "Poliak-Visbram" sawmill also donated.

When the Yeshiva of Slutsk was founded by the Gaon Rabbi Yaakov David, the son of Zev known by the acronym Ridbaz, he himself would visit the towns that were close to Slutsk to request donations for the Yeshiva. He came to Lyuban as well.

My father was once present at a conversation between the Ridbaz and Rabbi Yerushalmi, the rabbi of the town. The Ridbaz turned to him and said, "Reb Ber, your students of today will later be students of the Yeshiva of Slutsk, and therefore you have the duty to collect donations for the Yeshiva."

Father's desire to establish a Yeshiva in Lyuban similar to Slutsk was not actualized.

The following incident should be remembered for good, in that the writer of these lines and his brothers assisted in the fulfilling of this *mitzvah*.

A fire broke out in town, a very common occurrence. Among the houses that were burnt down was the house of the Widow P. They only succeeded in salvaging her cow and a few of her moveable belongings.

Father of blessed memory and Reb Yisrael Leib took it upon themselves to rebuild her house. They began to collect donations from the residents of Lyuban and its environs. This diligent effort lasted for over a year, and despite this, they only barely succeeded in purchasing a ready-made house from a gentile from a nearby village. The gentile was obligated to transfer it to the town and set it up.

The house was erected as was agreed upon with the seller, but there was a need for sand to be put on the roof to stick it together. The seller was not obligated in this task, and there was no money to hire a worker. Father of blessed memory enlisted my brother and me for this task. Each morning, we would wake up early and go to help Father carry the sand to fill in the roof. We continued with this work until it was finished. Father of blessed memory himself participated in the plastering effort. When the widow returned from her sister's home and came to live in her new house, she complained that the plaster caused her nausea. Father was disturbed, and told her that the worker who plastered the house considered himself to be an expert, and that he invested a great deal of effort in it.

* * *

The widow ran out of sustenance, and she went to ask for bread from the neighbors. In the event that they could not give her anything, involved as they were with the care of their own children, she would come to us and turn to my father. Father immediately went to the pantry, took out the last loaf of bread, and gave it to her. Towards evening, when Mother went to prepare supper for her children, she saw that there was no bread. My brother told her what had happened. Mother informed Father that it is not fitting to give away the last loaf of bread from the house. Father's answer was characteristic, "There is an explicit verse 'Spread your bread to the hungry, and in particular to a widow who is caring for hungry orphans.'"

When Father took ill with his final illness, his Gemara did not leave his hands. When the family members urged him to take a break from his learning to rest a little, he answered with an adage from the Sages: "If someone has a headache, he should occupy himself with Torah."

Father served as a prayer leader for approximately forty years, and he served as a successful and fitting *Baal Mussaf*[1] on the High Holy Days.

For over thirty years, he gave a regular class in the Beis Midrash on "*Ein Yaakov*"[2] on weekdays, and on the weekly Torah portion on Sabbaths. He concerned himself with the needs of the Talmud Torah for about thirty years, and he was one of the leaders of the *Chevra Kadisha* (Burial Society).

He died at the age of 64. May his memory be a blessing!

Binyamin (Benny) Katznelson of blessed memory

Binyamin Katznelson was born in 1888 in Lyuban to his father, the well-known teacher Reb Dov Ber.

He studied in well-known Yeshivas, and was one of the intelligentsia of the town. He and his wife Musia, nee Harkaby, were among the first *chalutzim* (pioneers) who made *aliya* to the Land in 1921. He worked in building and paving roads for his first years, and later was appointed as an official in the Tel Aviv city council.

He died in Tel Aviv on the 13th of *Adar*, 5721 (1961). May his memory be a blessing.

[Page 211]

R' Binyamin Wolfson

by Zivia Ostrovsky

Translated by Phyllis Schulberg and Michelle Schulberg

Reb Binyamin (in the center) among the staff of the *Talmud Torah* teachers in Kfar Ganim

In 1922 my father crossed the Russia-Poland border alone, and reached Baranovitz. He was accepted as a teacher in the Yeshiva and decided to settle there. The news that reached us illegally encouraged us, and he looked for ways to bring the whole family to him in Poland.

Our family then was made up of five people: Mother, three daughters and a son. The married daughter, Taibel (may her memory be a blessing), with her husband and their 2-year-old son, had previously succeeded in crossing the border, and settled temporarily in Baranovitz, with the hope of emigrating from there to the great world. Father's message, that he had succeeded in contacting a certain person in order to bring us across the border, was received gladly. But it was impossible to implement the departure of the whole family at once. Mother suggested that I travel first, but I did not agree to this, and on the pretext that it would be easier for her, I took the boy with me and she remained, temporarily, with the two girls. But, sadly, my brother and I were stopped by the Polish border police; we remained in prison for three weeks. Father succeeded in freeing the boy and I was returned to Russia.

One night I decided to try to flee from the police station. In one of the small towns on the border, I knew some people and I hoped they would help me. Indeed, the escape went well, and after two weeks I was brought to Baranovitz. The meeting with my father was fraught with danger, because he had sworn that he did not know where I was. With the help of good people, I received a certificate that I was a native of a small town near Baranovitz.

After three months, I received from America 'greetings' (perhaps an official invitation to come) and money.

At that time the Polish government announced the expulsion of foreign subjects, except for those who were planning to emigrate and they were permitted to remain a set time within the Polish borders. Even Father was ordered to leave Baranovitz, but the leaders of his school received permission for him to remain at his job.

My sister and brother-in-law and their child left Baranovitz, and after many moves over a period of a month, they arrived back in Luban. Their first letter made us very sad, because they found Mother ill, in critical condition, and after three weeks she died. I decided to forego my trip to America in order not to leave Father alone in his mourning. I suggested to him that we travel to the Land of Israel; he agreed in spite of his decision to return to Russia to reunite with his family. Father turned to Jerusalem, to Rav Yeruslumski (may his memory be a blessing) with a request for help for Aliya. After a short time we received an offer from Yeshiva Torat Haim, to be a teacher and to bring his son and his 'servant girl' (it was forbidden to mention his daughter).

At the end of the summer of 1924, we prepared to make Aliya to the Land of Israel. We knew the hardships that awaited us, as we were lacking resources. Good friends loaned us money, and on a Friday the boat reached the port of Yafo. We were brought to a hotel on Nachlat Binyamin Street and Father was happy to welcome the Sabbath in the Land of Israel.

During that Sabbath day, I found people from our town in Tel Aviv. They were surprised to see us and welcomed us warmly. They guided us, at the beginning, as good brothers. We settled in Petach Tikva and registered in the labor office. We received several days of work in 'tobacco' (fields? factory?). Even Father did physical work and he was happy. After Passover, Father was accepted as a teacher in the Hebrew school, Shearit Yisrael (Remnants of Israel); his salary was 4 lirot per month but he signed a confirmation saying that it was 12 lirot, so he would be able to prepare an application to bring the two girls from Luban.

Several months passed and he received entry permits for them. Ten months from the day of our arrival we went to the port to welcome the girls, who had traveled with another family. Father settled in K'far Ganim, bought a small piece of land, planted fruit trees, and built a small cabin in which to live.

In the Hebrew school he acquired a good name (reputation) and many friends, and was happy until his last day. In the village he devoted himself to community matters and was active in all religious matters, especially the building of the Synagogue.

He was privileged to see during his lifetime the establishment of the State, and he also sacrificed on the altar of this statehood his grandson, my son Avner (may his memory be a blessing), who died serving in a Palmach operation.

My father reached the age of 77. On Rosh Hashana he prayed in the Synagogue and (six days later) on the 6th of Tishrei[3], he died. The residents of K'far Ganim appreciated him, and in his memory, the Synagogue was named Tiferet Binyamin (the Glory of Binyamin).

[Page 212]

Rabbis Who Came From Lyuban

Translated by Jerrold Landau

Rabbi Yerucham Halevi Leibovitz
(5633 / 1873 – 18th of *Sivan* 5696 / 1936)

He was one of the greats of Torah ethics in our day.

He was born in Lyuban to his parents Avraham and Chasha Leibovitz and was educated in the Yeshivas of Slobodka and Kelm. He served as the spiritual guide[4] of the Yeshivas of Radun (The Yeshiva of the Chofetz Chaim), Slobodka, Panevezys, and primarily in the Mir Yeshiva until the day of his death.

After the First World War, his influence in the Mir Yeshiva increased. The Mir Yeshiva was a center of Torah, and had about 500 students, including about 100 students from the United States, England, and Germany. Most of the leaders of the Yeshivas of Poland were the students of Rabbi Yerucham Halevi. They would come on occasion to visit him, and take counsel with him on various matters.

He died at the age of 63.

The Rabbi and Gaon Shimon Starlitz died in Jerusalem. He was a member of the editorial board of the Talmudic Encyclopedia, and one of the primary students of Rabbi Kook of holy blessed memory.

He was known as one of the Torah leaders of Jerusalem, and the prime movers of the efforts behind the Talmudic Encyclopedia.

He was born in the town of Lyuban and studied in the Yeshivas of Klyetsk and Slutsk. He studied at the Merkaz Harav *Yeshiva* in Israel, where he found favor in the eyes of Rabbi Kook[5] of holy blessed memory. He remained his faithful student. He published articles on the writings of the Rav. Over and above his greatness in Torah, he was also very articulate. He wrote in a very deep fashion about the philosophy of the Rav of holy blessed memory.

He was a member of the editorial board of the Talmudic Encyclopedia from its initiation. He was very diligent, and occupied himself with Torah day and night. He had a fine character, and loved Zion with his entire soul. He was a Gaon, and produced innovative ideas like an overflowing well.

He left behind many innovative Torah thoughts in writing. His Torah novellae were published by Machon Harry Fishel[6]. He published the commentary of the Meiri on the tractates of *Avot* and *Moed Katan*. He was beloved by all of his acquaintances and friends. He died of a heart ailment at age 49.

Rabbi Chaim Kabalkin Of Blessed Memory

Uncaptioned. Rabbi Kabalkin or Rabbi Starlitz[7]

He was born on *Rosh Chodesh Adar* 5658 – 1898 to his father Rabbi Yehuda Leib and his mother Nechama Lea the daughter of Reb Binyamin Epstein.

He was educated in Lyuban and transferred to the Eitz Chaim Yeshiva of Slutsk. He excelled in his Torah study, his talents, and his fine character.

At the beginning of 5681 (1921), the Yeshiva Knesset Yisrael returned to Slobodka[8] from its exile in Kremenchuk, Ukraine. Reb Chaim Kabalkin was among the 300 Yeshiva members who returned. He succeeded in escaping from Slutsk, which was under Communist rule, and arriving in Slobodka.

He became active in the life of the Yeshiva within a short period of time, and he became well-known despite his modesty. The situation of the *Yeshiva* was very bright at the time, thanks to help from America.

In the middle of the summer of the year 5681, Kabalkin attempted to collaborate with several Yeshiva students to found a charitable organization.

Many books had been torn and destroyed due to the wanderings. The books were purchased again; however there was no source of loans for the Yeshiva students during their times of difficulty.

One Friday, a discreet notice was posted indicating that anyone who wishes a loan for a short period should turn to either … or Mr. Chaim Kabalkin, every Friday in the house of … next to the Yeshiva.

The Yeshiva passed through a crisis during the year 5682. Then it became obvious that Chaim Kabalkin prepared the balm prior to the wound, since there were more than 1,000 lira in the charitable fund

His activities were not restricted to within the walls of the Yeshiva. In the year 5683 (1923),

[Page 213]

the year of the famine in Russia, he organized a group of Yeshiva students to collect donations and send food packages to save Jews.

Rabbi Yehuda Leib Kabalkin of blessed memory

Chaim Kabalkin was among those who made aliya in the year 5685 (1925), when the Slobodka *Yeshiva* transferred to the holy city of Hebron with the support of the Jews of America.

Chaim Kabalkin implanted the idea of founding the T.T. foundation (*Tomchei Torah Lanitzrachim* – Supporters of Torah for the Needy) among the Yeshiva students. The directors of the Yeshiva set aside a monthly allocation for the T.T. fund.

In the month of *Adar* of the year 5689 (1929), after he married Chaya the daughter of Reb Yitzchak Zelig Slibkin of blessed memory from Riga, he moved to live in Tel Aviv. His brother-in-law Noach, may G-d avenge his blood, was killed during the unrest of 5689. He then returned to Jerusalem so that he could take care of the education of his nephews.

Reb Chaim Kabalkin made efforts to establish a Torah-oriented village in the mountains of Jerusalem (in the place that Kfar Etzion was later built). He also established a foundation called "*Neta Emunim*" ("*The Shoots of the Faithful*") in the name of the Elder (Saba) of Slobodka—The shoots of the faithful for G-d and His Torah.

That year, he established a Beis Midrash for Torah called Ohel Torah for young men who do not require support. This organization was to ensure that the strengthening of the Torah and Mussar (religious ethics) from the Slobodka Yeshiva. This Torah institution turned into a high level Torah academy. The mantle of leadership of Ohel Torah passed to Rabbi Sh. Y. Hilman of holy blessed memory, the son-in-law of Rabbi Y. A. Herzog[9] of holy blessed memory. During its years of existence, it graduated Torah and Mussar giants, who today serve as religious judges, rabbis, and heads of *Yeshivas* in the Land.

In the year 5702 (1942), at the height of the Second World War, when the danger of famine afflicted the inhabitants of the Land, Reb Chaim established a charitable fund for *Yeshiva* students called *Keren Palman* (*Peilat Lemaan Mishpachot Nitzracho*—Action on Behalf of Needy Families), as well as a fund to support the needy.

In the year 5704 (1944), he served as the right hand of Rabbi Y. A. Herzog of holy blessed memory, according to the recommendation of Rabbi Moshe Epstein and Rabbi Isser Zalman Meltzer of holy blessed memory in actualizing his idea of anthologizing the literature of practical *halachah*. Thus was founded the splendid institution of *Otzar Haposkim* (Treasury of Halachic Decisors), which published five volumes on *Even Haezer* [10] up to this time.

He died after a serious heart ailment on the 20th of *Adar* I, 5711 (1951). May his soul be bound in the bonds of eternal life.

[Page 214]

Lyuban As I Remember It

by Tzvi Asaf

Translated by Jerrold Landau

The Cheder Hametukan in Lyuban.
Among the teachers were Yosef Feiges and Tamara Katznelson.

Lyuban was a typical Jewish town. It was turned in to itself, and earned its livelihood in the neighboring villages and forests. The lumber was exported in barges on the Orossa River[111]. Lyuban was built up along its banks.

Lyuban was far from a train station. The only regular mode of transportation between it and other civic centers such as Slutsk and Bobruysk was by the wagon drivers.

Despite its distance from modern transportation, merchants would come to the town from afar to purchase the produce of the villages, such as butter, honey, dried mushrooms, lard, wax, various seeds, grain, wheat and cattle.

There were no wealthy people in Lyuban, and for the most part, the people earned their livelihood with great difficulty. Nevertheless, it seems to me that nobody was starving in the town.

The main sources of livelihood in town were as follows: merchants, shopkeepers, carpenters, shoemakers, and tailors. Most of them spread out to the neighboring villages on Sundays and returned on Friday. There were also teachers, scribes, Yeshiva students, a rabbi, a *shochet,* and *shamashim* in town. The town was not lacking of a "fool." His name was Shlomoke, a spoiled lad, whose "craziness" was that he did not wish to work. The community supported him. One of his antics was that he would suddenly approach the members of the "more beautiful sex" and give a kiss. The women did not complain about this because, after all, he was a fool.

Approximately 200 Jewish families lived in Lyuban. Communal activities were centered around various charitable organizations such as: *Linat Tzedek* (providing of lodging for the indigent), *Matan Beseter* (Discrete giving of charity to the poor), *Chevra Kadisha* (the Burial Society), *Makabei Eish* (the firefighters), and groups for the study of *Mishna, Shulchan Aruch* (Code of Jewish Law), and *Ein Yaakov.* The sounds of Torah echoed from the many *cheders* and from the synagogues, where not only did the *Yeshiva* students study, but also the *Perushim,* older men who separated from their families and dedicated their lives to the study of Torah. Aside from these, there was a *Cheder Metukan,* which was innovative in its time, and where the finest of the intelligentsia of the town gathered.

There were also secular groups in Lyuban. Particularly notable were *Tzeirei Zion* and the *Bund.* It is worthwhile to mention that Itza the son of the rabbi of the town was forced to flee to the United States because of the fear of the Czarist government on account of his Socialist activities.

The synagogue served as the center of communal life. Every travesty in communal life found its answer in the synagogue, where the main "weapon" was a delay in the reading of the Torah on the Sabbath until matters were settled.

I remember only once occasion where a ban of excommunication was issued on someone who was suspecting of informing. The black candles that were lit on the weekday evening, the sound of the *shofar,* and the entire ceremony of excommunication made a deep impression on me. Not too many days passed before the guilty party repented, and the ban of excommunication was lifted.

There was not one household of Lyuban where at least one of the sons did not dedicate himself to the study of Torah in the *Yeshivas* of Slutsk, Hlusk, Mir, or Shklov. They even reached Telz and other Torah centers, in order to study to the point of being ordained as a rabbi. There were also young people who studied in the *gymnasia*of Slutsk. On vacation days, they adorned themselves with the uniform of the *gymnasia,* replete with shiny buttons.

The Yeshiva students ate their daily and Sabbath meals on a rotation system with the householders of Slutsk, who for the most part treated them with respect. Aside from this, they received packages of food and clothing from their homes, sent to them by their families via the wagon drivers. The wagon drivers received no benefit from this, for they saw it as their donation

[Page 215]

to help the *Yeshiva* students. However, they did not bother to remember who sent to whom. It was a characteristic scene to see how the *Yeshiva* students would search through the thick layer of hay in the large wagon in order to find their package, and how great was their disappointment when they did not find it. For despite the short distance, a trip home would only take place around the High Holy Days and Passover, in order not to neglect the study of Torah.

Lyuban excelled over all of the other towns of the area in its level of knowledge and Jewish learning. It was a very interesting scene when Avraham Noach the shoemaker delivered his lesson on *Shulchan Aruch* or *Ein Yaakov* between *Mincha* and *Maariv*, for most of the workers of the town were Torah scholars or at least lovers of Torah.

Itza the doctor

Berl Feitel, his wife Nechama, and family

* * *

There were no times of joy in Lyuban more so than on Simchat Torah at the time of the *Hakafot* (Torah processions). Chaim Yosef the teacher gathered together all of the children of the town after services, and joined with them in song and dance in the streets. He would dance before the most prominent householders.

The joy was also very great on Purim. There was the reading of the *Megilla* (the Scroll of Esther) accompanied by *graggers* (Purim noisemakers), and the sending of food portions (*Mishloach Manot*). There was the coronation of a "Purim Rabbi." They selected a Yeshiva student, brought him to the rabbi's house, and dressed him in fine silk, a belt. A white beard flowed down over his cloak. They sat him on a large chair and presented him with questions and problems. Despite the scoffing, this indicated their sharpness in learning, and served as an escape from day to day life.

* * *

There were three synagogues in Lyuban. The Great Synagogue was where the communal leaders and influential householders worshipped. The rabbi of the town also worshipped there. The Tailors' Synagogue was for members of that trade. (Of course, you could also find various artisans in the Great Synagogue and important householders in the latter synagogue, but for the most part, there were divisions in membership between them.) The third synagogue was "The Cold Synagogue", which was built by the landowner (*poretz*), and did not belong to the civic property. It stood out for its unique architecture. It was only used during the summer. Many legends were passed along about this synagogue, since it did not have Torah scrolls and *mezuzahs*. Everyone told about the corpses who would gather to worship there, etc. The hearts of the children pounded out of fear as they passed by it during the nights.

The synagogues burnt down in the great fire that overtook Lyuban at the eve of the First World War. One modest Beis Midrash was built in their place.

Lyuban was known from afar on account of its physician Dr. Spiridonov. He was a good-hearted Christian doctor who loved Jews. He was expert at curing trachoma, and all those who were preparing to immigrate to the United States and were afraid that their entrance would be impeded by eye diseases would turn to him to be examined and cured.

There was also a Jewish doctor, known as Itza the doctor. He was one of those who were "snatched" for army service during the time of Czar Nikolai I. He completed his medical degree while he was serving in the army for 25 years. Later he returned to town. He continued serving as a doctor until his old age, when he was already completely deaf.

His son-in-law Berl Feitel was the local pharmacist, and one of the heads of the intelligentsia.

[Page 216]

* * *

The last *shochet* of Lyuban, Reb Yaakov Moshe
Kostanovitz, who perished on the 10th of Av, 5701 / 1941

Reb Itcha Yaakov Malin (on the right) and his family

Reb Yaakov the *shochet* was a unique personality. He also served as the *mohel* (ritual circumcisor) in the town. He had a bright countenance, and a smile never left his lips. When a butcher stormed angrily that his fingernails were guilty in the removal of a "*sircha*"[12] and therefore rendered the meat non-kosher, he would retort "You are a fool (*shoteh*), you are a fool," pronouncing the 'sh' as an 's'[13]. In truth, he was concerned with the money of the Jewish people, and he was anguished by any animal that was rendered non-kosher. He wore a long *kapote* covered with fat stains, and his livelihood was earned in particular from the stomachs and intestines that he received in return for the slaughter. His children also studied *shechita*. One of them Reb Nechemya, is a rabbi in Toledo, United States. His two daughters were married, the first to Reb Reuven Leibovitz, and the second to Reb Moshe Feinstein[14]], the final rabbi of Lyuban. Both of them are in New York.

My pen is too poor to portray a complete picture of life in the town and its events. However, I wish to present one episode that caused a ruckus in the town.

Itcha Yaakov the butcher was considered to be a well-to-do person in Lyuban. He was one of the large-scale cattle dealers, and he would travel to fairs in far off places for that purpose. He took great pride in his beard, and took great care of it.

At every opportunity, his friends urged him to sell his beard, and of course, he refused. However on one occasion, when his heart was merry with wine after a good business deal at a fair, he agreed to sell his beard for the sum of 100 rubles, a large sum at the time. He was required to give over his beard when he returned home.

When he regained his sobriety he realized that he would be the laughing stock in town if he fulfilled his promise, so he attempted to get out of it. However his friends did not forego, and he was required to do so. They went to Rabbi Yerushalmi for a judgment. The rabbi adjucated that the sale was not a valid sale, since a Jew is not permitted to sell his beard, which is his "Divine Image". He imposed a fine of several fast days upon Itche Yaakov, and he required him to donate ten pounds of candles to the synagogue.

His neighbor was my uncle, Mordechai Kikayon, who toiled in Torah, while his wife Batya Malka supported the family and took care of the needs of the household. She was widowed at a young age, while she was caring for many children. She earned her livelihood from her store. She purchased fruit from the villagers prior to the harvest, while they were still unripe. She made excellent preserves from them. She also took care of the baking of matzos, both *shmura* and regular[15].

She was a woman of valor, full of energy. Her heart was open to charity and good deeds. She merited making aliya to the Land, and she lived until an old age. May her memory be blessed.

[Page 217]

Sitting from right to left: Rabbi Yitzchak Eizik Small, Rabbi Yechiel Michael Feinstein (in the center a young member of the family), and Rabbi Reuven Lebovitz
Standing from right to left: Rabbi Nechemya Katz, Rabbi Zelig Furman, Rabbi Nisan Wachsman, the Gaon Rabbi Moshe Feinstein, his son-in-law Rabbi Eli Moshe Shizgal, and the latter's father Rabbi A. Yitzchak Shizgal

(Photograph from New York, 5703 – 1943)

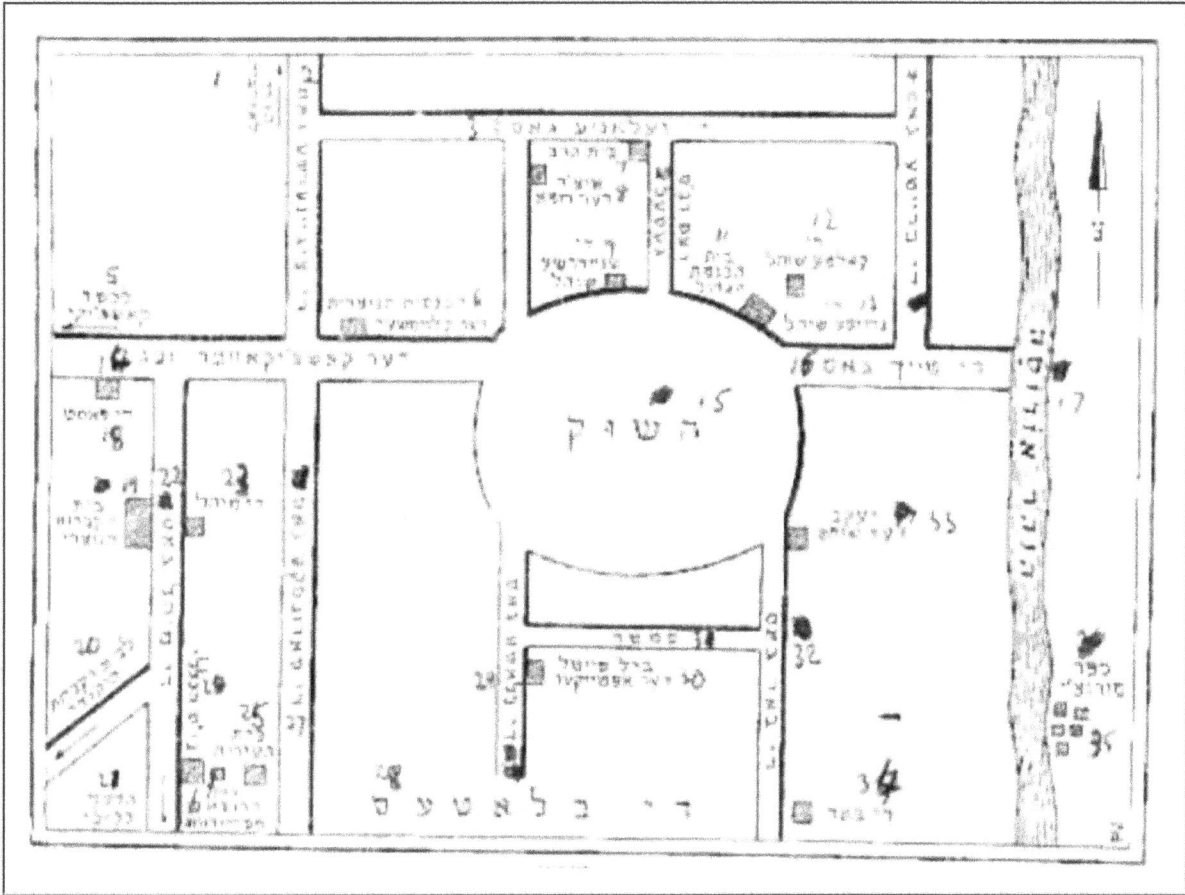

A map of Lyuban

The arrow on the right points north. The initials at the bottom right are M. B. The key is as follows:

1. The Route to Urecca
2. Tzigeinershe Street (Gypsy Street)
3. Zelonia Street (with a question mark beside)
4. Breite Street (The Wide Street)
5. To the village of Kostyuki
6. The Christian Church
7. The Rabbi's house
8. Itche the doctor
9. The Tailor's Synagogue
10. The Rabbi's Lane
11. The Great Synagogue (Hebrew caption)
12. The Cold Synagogue
13. The Great Synagogue (Yiddish caption)
14. Kostyukover Street
15. The Market
16. Teich Street (River Street)
17. Orussa River
18. The post
19. The Christian Cemetery
20. To the Jewish Cemetery
21. The route to Luchi
22. Mill Street
23. The Mill
24. Public School
25. Town Hall
26. The house of Dr. Spiridonov
27. Padovska Street
28. The Marsh
29. Blotte Street (Muddy Street or Marsh Street)
30. Berl Feitel the pharmacist
31. a lane
32. Bod Street (Bath Street)
33. Yaakov the *shochet*
34. The Bath
35. The village of Sarachi

[Page 218]

Reb Yehuda Zeev Osovski

My father Reb Yehuda Zeev Osovski

Finally, I wish to write about my father Reb Leib Wolf[16] of blessed memory. He was one of the important householders of Lyuban. He was G-d fearing, and he honored scholars. He did not leave the synagogue on Sabbath eves without inviting a guest or two to eat at his table. The Sabbath hymns during the meal, shouted out by my brother Chaim David, attracted an audience, particularly from among the youth. *Yeshiva* students ate at our house on a rotational system, as was customary in those days. Our house was full of guests, including emissaries and preachers who came from the land of Israel, and spoke at length of its rebuilding and renewed settlement.

My father of blessed memory was particularly fond of leading the synagogue services. Since he was an excellent prayer leader, who did not drag out the service with extraneous melodies, the young people would often urge him to lead the service.

Our home was spacious, one of the largest houses in town. In the cowshed, there was a barn that was filled with grain, barley and wheat during the time of harvest. This was a place of enjoyment for my friends and me on Sabbaths and festivals.

My father's field of business was very broad, including forestry dealing, the leasing of ponds for fishing, lands for planting potatoes, etc. He would provide these fields at half price for the residents of the town, and it would be a *mitzvah* to bring a sack or two of potatoes or a wagon of wood to a destitute widow. Everything was done with a generous hand.

He had good relations with the regional government. He served as an intercessor and advocate for all types of difficulties. He knew how to approach the Russian regional representatives, who were not among those who were fond of Jews.

My mother Feiga of blessed memory, who oversaw the house of the pious RebYaakov, died before her time, leaving behind young children. My father then married Slova, the daughter of the *shochet* Chaim Zelig Kaplan.

His dream was to make *aliya* to the Land of Israel and to join his children. But to all of our great dismay, he did not attain this.

My brother, Professor Simcha Asaf of blessed memory, in his letter to the meeting of Lyuban natives here in the year 5708 (1948) in the home of Yosef and Bluma Kikayon, proposed the proposition that "It is worthy to think about making a memorial for that wonderful town called Lyuban, which excelled in its love of Torah and charitable deeds." He expressed his desire to donate his share towards the establishment of a literary monument, memorializing the names of those who were sublime in Torah and wisdom all of whom were raised in that town. His work far and wide in other areas did not permit him to fulfill his duty, He comforted himself that he would do this when he retired, but death caught up with him. A large piece of Lyuban was buried away with him.

The Library of Lyuban

by Yosef Kikayon

Translated by Jerrold Landau

When I was still a child, the library captured my heart, at first as an avid reader and later as a librarian, dedicated with a full heart and soul to expanding the library.

To my good fortune, my advisor and guide was my dear teacher Reb Heshel Trushkin of blessed memory, one of the best of the progressive teachers in the town, who himself "gazed and was injured"[17]. He instilled a love for Hebrew poetry in his students. When Bialik's poem "*Al Hatzipor*" (About the Bird) reached our town, he read in before his students with a special enunciation, and commanded them to learn it by heart.

The library in Lyuban filled an important need among the students of the *cheders* and the Yeshiva. It made it possible for them to complete their knowledge in general and to read more Hebrew literature.

The works of Mapu, "*Ahavat Zion*" (Love of Zion), "*Ashmat Shomron*" (The Guilt of Samaria), etc., had particular influence on them. These books portrayed imagery from the *Chumash* and the Bible. The first book that made a deep influence upon myself was "Between the Hammer and Anvil," about the pogroms of Uman.

The library developed under the directorship of my relative Chaim Asaf, and reached the size of 2,000 books, a significant number of a small town such as Lyuban.

After he went to the United States, I took the directorship of the library upon myself. I attempted to collect donations for the library, and I approached the artisans and horse dealers.

Once, I found myself in the home of Shalom Baruchke, a well-known horse dealer. I requested that he donate to the library. He looked at me, and then said his statement, "A gift to the library, from me? I am very far from these matters!" I noted to him, "Indeed this is known, but I had hoped that it would be your will that your sons not be boors as you are." I awaited his retort, but to my surprise, my answer hit the mark, and he gave me a large donation.

Many of the *Yeshiva* students participated in *Tzeirei Zion*. I was also active in that organization and I still have my membership certificate with me today.

[Page 219]

Chalutzim (Zionist Pioneers) from Lyuban on their way to the Land of Israel

From left to right, seated: Yosef Kikayon, Yisrael Yaakovi, Yemima Katznelson Bar-Natan, Beilka Kikayon, Sara Kustanovitz-Shenkman, and Eliezer Shenkman
Standing: Reuven Kustanovitz, Eliezer Tepper, Chaim Ostrovski, Naomi Vaskovoyinik-Rabinovitz, Shlomo Kaplan

Batya Malka Kikayon

Membership card of the Zionist group *"Tzeirei Zion"* in Lyuban

Editor's note: the text of the card is as follows:

Zionism aims to acquire a safe haven
For the Jewish people in the Land of Israel
The *Tzeirei Zion* Zionist Organization
Card Number: 15
Member's name: Yosef
Family name: Kikayon
Chairman of the committee (name not given)
Secretary: Yosef (cannot make out last name of signature)

Note: At the time of entry, the member is required to present his card

Editor's note: the circular stamp reads as follows: The *Tzeirei Zion* Committee of the city of Lyuban, Minsk region.

Even the Orthodox in our town had a supportive attitude towards Zionism. Rabbi Nechemya Yerushalmi particularly supported us. He himself later made *aliya* to the Land of Israel.

Just prior to my *aliya* to the Land of Israel, my mother of blessed memory took ill and went to complain before Reb Nechemya of blessed memory that I was about to leave her in this situation. His answer was: "*Oy* Batya Malka, you are an intelligent person, if he does not go, and I do not go – who will go?"

People began to make *aliya* from our town even during the time of the Second *Aliya*. Those who made *aliya* included the brothers Zalman and Yitzchak Epstein, as well as Efraim Epstein from Kuzmichi, who was among the conquerors and guards of Sharona and Merchavya, and one of the founders of Kfar Yechezkel. Chanan Yaakov Feiges went to study in the Herzliya Gymnasia. When he returned due to an serious illness, he told wonderful stories about the Land and its blessed fruit. As an example, he brought a coconut (a fruit that does not grow in the land). The inside was eaten by the family, but the shell was passed around from hand to hand by us children, with longing for the Land and the time when we would also merit to eat this fruit.

Many natives of Lyuban reached the Land during the Third *Aliya*. During this time, the parents of several of them also arrived, such as my mother, my father-in-law Reb Chaim Katznelson and his wife, David Itzes and others.

Translator's footnotes:

1. The *Mussaf* service is added on to the regular morning service (*Shacharit*) on Sabbaths and festivals. On the High Holy Days, the *Mussaf* service is particularly lengthy and elaborate. Baal *Mussaf* is a term used for the prayer leader of the *Mussaf* service.
2. *Ein Yaakov* is an anthology of the *aggadaic* (lore) sections of the *Talmud*.
3. Rosh Hashanah is on the 1st and 2nd of *Tishrei*.
4. The position of spiritual guide (*Mashgiach*) is a very important official role at a *Yeshiva*. The *Mashgiach* is responsible for the spiritual development and wellbeing of the students.
5. Rabbi Kook (1875-1935) was the leading spiritual force behind religious Zionism. The *Merkaz Harav Yeshiva* in Jerusalem was founded by him. Rabbi Kook is often affectionately known as The Rav.
6. A publisher of Torah works in Israel.
7. This photo is under the section dealing with Rabbi Kabalkin. However, on the next page, there is a captioned photo of Rabbi Kabalkin, which looks quite different. Therefore, I suspect that this earlier photo is not of Rabbi Kabalkin, but rather of Rabbi Starlitz. (This makes sense as well, as the photo is that of a younger man, and Rabbi Starlitz died at 49.)
8. lobodka, the location of one of the most famous *Yeshivas* of the era, is a suburb of Kovno (Kaunas), Lithuania, and would have been under independent Lithuanian rule at the time.
9. A former chief rabbi of Israel.
10. *Even Haezer* is one of the four main volumes of the Code of Jewish Law (*Shulchan Aruch*). It deals with marital and family law.
11. There is a footnote in the text here: The river was also known as Rusa – and since the name was ambiguous, Lyuban was not fitting for organizing *Gittin* (religious divorces). End of footnote, Translator's comments begin: On a *Get* (Jewish bill of divorce), the locale of the issuing of the *Get* is identified by the city name, and the rivers which are adjacent to the city. There are various technical *halachic* details why this is so. Thus, in a city that is adjacent to a river with an ambiguous name, a *Get* cannot be written. The divorcing couple can go to a different city to have the *Get* written, as the locale does not depend on the place of residence, but rather on the place of the divorce proceedings.
12. A *sircha* is a blemish on a lung that is not severe enough to render an animal non-kosher (an animal's lungs are examined after ritual slaughter to ensure that there are no blemishes, and certain blemisher do render an animal non-kosher). A *sircha* is a removable blemish, and if it can be successfully removed, it does not render the animal non-kosher.
13. Lithuanian Jews often pronounce the 'sh' sound as 's'.

14. Rabbi Moshe Feinstein was recognized as one of the leading rabbinical authorities of the United States, and some might even say of the entire world. He died in New York in 1986 at the age of 91. His voluminous writings are used as precedents for current rabbinical decisions. His two sons Rabbi David Feinstein and Rabbi Reuven Feinstein, and his son-in-law Rabbi Moshe Tendler, are leading rabbis today. His son-in-law Rabbi Shizgal, pictured in the photo below, predeceased him by many years.

15. Matzo *shmura* is specially prepared matzos that are used on the *seder* night. The wheat used for matzo *shmura* is guarded from water from the time of harvest, whereas for regular matzos, it is guarded from the time of grinding into flour.

16. Leib Wolf is the Yiddish form of Yehuda Zeev.

17. This is a Talmudic reference to people who "investigate into mysticism", and if they look too hard, they might become spiritually damaged. The Talmud related the story of four people who became involves in deep mystical thoughts: one came through intact, the second became a non-believer, the third went crazy and the forth died. Here the reference is to someone who became involved in modern culture and became enthralled with it.

[Page 220]

Lyubanites of my Mother's Family

by Rachel Feigenberg-Omry

Translated by Jerrold Landau

A Memorial light to my brother Yitzchak, who died in Lyuban in his prime.

A.

I lost my father when I was four years old. We were three children—me and my two younger brothers Yitzchak and Nachumke, the baby. Later, only two of us remained, me and Yitzchak, for Nachumke died suddenly at age two and a half after drinking vinegar instead of water.

The medic in our town did not know that the child's stomach should have been pumped. He writhed in difficult suffering all night, and died in the morning in his mother's arms, just as she arrived in Slutsk to seek help from our relative Dr. Schildkraut, in an attempt to save him.

Dr. Schildkraut looked at the mother with her dead child and spoke harshly. He was shocked at the stupidity of the medic in our town.

This tragic event left a terrible shadow on our small, bereaved family, and many days passed until we slowly began to recover.

I do not remember my father, Ber Feigenberg. From my childhood, only his many books remain in my memory. These were large and heavy, finely bound with brown covers, with decorations and white letters on the spine. My mother was widowed in her prime. She then sold her husband's books to a wealthy Jew from Slutsk in order to be able to open a store in our house from the money she received in exchange. From this, she sustained her young children.

However, it was as if the books of father remained in our house even after my weeping mother packed them up in sacks and sent them to the wealthy Jew of Slutsk. She would always tell us—me and my younger brother Yitzchak, the story of our father's books. She also had a share in these, for they were purchased with her dowry money. She deprived herself of her bread and paid the bookbinder for the fine bindings. She had further plans for these books in the future. The rich Jew who purchased them promised her in his righteousness that when her children would come of age and have the ability to redeem the books of their father, he would ensure that they would be able to do so.

My father was certainly not a Lyubanite, for he was always involved in teaching outside the town.

My father's father, my grandfather Rabbi Yaakov Feigenberg, appeared very strange and foreign to me during my childhood. He served as the rabbi of the community for more than thirty years, yet he did not strike roots in the community until the day of his death. He did not look at all like a rabbi, but rather like a villager. He loved to sail in a boat on the river in order to catch carp for the Sabbath. He often traveled to the city, for his origins were from well-to-do and honorable stock in Slutsk. Some of his relatives were large scale merchants who were fluent in the language of the country, and who would travel on business to Gomel or even to the large city of Kiev.

Perhaps he was fleeing from the poverty in his house. Even his two wives did not strike roots in the town because of the severe poverty in the house of the rabbi. The first, who was the daughter of well-to-do people from the village, died quietly just as she had suffered quietly throughout her life. Her relatives from the village, who were the leaseholders of estates and ponds in the area, certainly helped her to feed her hungry children. His second wife, the *rebbetzin* of Lyuban, was from the city, and she enjoyed dressing herself up and reading love stories. She despised the poverty in the home of her husband, the rabbi of Lyuban, and she would spend months on end pampering herself in the home of her rich daughter from her first marriage, Chana Pesha Zinda, until her husband would come to request that she return home. When his request was fulfilled and his *rebbetzin* returned home, only a brief time would pass, about two weeks, until she would again travel to Slutsk to enjoy the pampering in the lovely home of her daughter.

Uncle Yehoshua, my father's brother, also had an impact on me. It was as if he was in Lyuban by accident, by force, even though he was a local native. He was always seeking out news from outside the town. Every day and every hour, he would search out new people with whom to discuss politics. He was always looking for a newspaper in the language of the country so that he could find out what was going on in the capital of Petersburg. At times, it appeared to me as if he were a prisoner in the hands of his wife Nechama, the daughter of Reb Chaim Zelig, a veteran Lyubanite. She was proud of the scholarship and intelligence of her late husband. It was due to the haughtiness of her and her sister that they were given the nickname "The readers" in the town. In Lyuban, people did not like relationships that imposed themselves upon the community, for there was no differentiation in status among the residents of our town. The level of living of the well-to-do was not that much higher than that of the poor.

My Aunt Nechama, who tried to assert her status due to her pedigree, which was not in accordance with the local custom, was indeed one of the well-rooted Lyubanites of my mother's family. She was a member of our faithful family.

There were already those who had broken boundaries in our family. The first to break the boundaries was my maternal grandfather Nachum Epstein. He was the one who had left the town in his youth due to his illusory plans to build mills. After many difficulties, he reached the large city of Odessa. He brought his family there as well.

My mother, Sara Feigenberg, nee Epstein, passed up on the riches of the city of Odessa. After the death of my father, her brothers advised her to come to them along with her children, and they would help her to sustain and educate them. However she decided not to leave our home in Lyuban. She decided not to seek her livelihood from her good brothers, but rather from the hand of G-d.

Grandmother especially expressed her dedication to the town. Even when she was in Odessa, on account of her actions, Odessa seemed to us so close, as if Lyuban was one of its suburbs.

Our grandmother Feiga Beila Epstein, nee Shapira, was not a native of Lyuban. She came from the city of Bobruisk to the forlorn town that was filled with mud. It was not for naught that her young brothers mocked her before her wedding, saying to her that in Lyuban people wear wooden shoes like the non-Jews, and that in the town there is only one pair of shoes that stand near the door of the synagogue. Anyone who has to approach the Holy Ark would put them on. She wept greatly when she heard this.

However, after her wedding when she arrived in Lyuban, she immediately adopted the way of life of the town, and became a merchant among the gentile population, as was the custom

[Page 221]

of the astute local women. She tried to teach her three daughters reading and writing. She taught them the reading the *siddur* (prayer book), the ability to write letters in Yiddish, and also the first fundamentals of the Russian language, so that they would be able to write their address in the vernacular.

My grandmother knew poverty and want in our town. She worked very hard with her own two hands, for she was forced to sustain the family herself. This was because her husband was always wandering afar, and experiencing endless setbacks. She remained rooted in the town. Even in Odessa, she only became acclimatized as a temporary resident. Her home remained virtually in Lyuban.

She married off her second daughter in Lyuban as well, after the youngest one was already in Odessa for four years. There, in the bustling port city that attracted a mixed multitude of immigrants, she saw no possibility of marrying off her daughter without lowering the Jewish spiritual level of the family.

She married her to Zalman, our relative from the village of Yaminsk. He was a villager from birth, but he knew his books. She set up her home in the nearby village of Troychani, an isolated village in the vicinity of Lyuban. Their home was the only Jewish home there.

Now, her soul was bound to Lyuban through two daughters, and she enjoyed her visits to our town.

B.

It was a holiday in our house. I was seven years old at the time. My mother baked an apple pie and butter cakes that spread their aroma throughout the house. Our curious neighbors stood at their doors with their babies in their arms. Young boys who returned from *cheder* peered through their windows. I and my younger brother Yitzchak already were dressed in our Sabbath clothing from the morning. We were happy.

Grandmother arrived. Grandmother arrived from Odessa. Her large, stuffed suitcase stood in a corner. This large, locked bag attracted everyone's eyes, and we children caressed it with love, and tried to move it from its place with great caution. We already knew that it was full of gifts that were sent by our aunt from Odessa. Grandmother told us news from the far-off big city to which she had immigrated. It was the eve of the Sabbath, and people were coming and going. One came as the other left. Men, women, and children were making noise.

At the onset of the Sabbath, the door of the house was closed to the curious crowd. Mother and grandmother made the blessing on the candles, recited the *Lecha Dodi* prayer with the traditional melody, and we all sat around the table for the evening meal. Before we finished eating, our many relatives from the town came to visit. My grandparents came, as well as my mother's aunts and uncles with their children and grandchildren. Grandmother continued with her stories, and spoke at length about that wondrous city called Odessa.

The candles had already gone out in the four copper candlesticks that were on the table. The visitors left one by one. The room was enveloped in shadows, as the light in the kerosene lamp dwindled. My younger brother Yitzchak was sleeping sitting down on the sofa with his head resting against the windowsill. He did not want to go to sleep. He wanted to listen to grandmother's stories until the end. I was sitting on the hassock next to the bed, still listening. Grandmother and mother were still talking, and I was making an effort to not miss even one word that was spoken between them. However, sleep overcame me. My eyes closed. I dozed off for a moment, and one moment later I was asleep.

When I awoke I found myself sleeping in bed. The house was full of light, and the sun was shining outside. Children were playing outside behind the window, and among them I heard the voice of my young brother Yitzchak. Mother and grandmother sat next to the table and drank coffee and milk. They continued talking, but this time they talked about family matters. Grandmother told about her two children. The oldest son, Zalman, had become a writer (he was the writer Zalman Epstein of blessed memory). He wrote in the newspaper in Hebrew. His younger brother Yitzchak was a farmer in the Land of Israel. This was not what she had hoped for. They had sharp minds, were very diligent at their studies, and astounded their teachers. She had hoped to see her two sons become rabbis, but G-d did not have this in mind for her. It was said that despite this, they were important men.

My mother sighed:

"Yes, they are important people, the entire town mocks me. Everyone knows that they eat bareheaded. Each gossipy woman throws her scorn about my brothers in my face. They say that they no longer say their prayers."

Grandmother dried her eyes. Her tears fell upon her wrinkled hand, but her voice was clear as usual:

"We did everything for them. I gave up everything in my life for my sons. You of course know that Father of blessed memory sent Zalman to Volozhin. Later, both of them studied in the Odessa Beis Midrash for three consecutive years. I watched over Yitzchak as the apple of my eye, even though he was already studying in the Gymnasia. Father of blessed memory interceded on his behalf so that he should be accepted as a member of the choir of the Great Synagogue, and thereby be exempted by the Gymnasia from studies on the Sabbath. I baked oil cakes for him so that he would not have to wash his hands in the Gymnasia[1]. However they jumped out of their skins. This is my lot, G-d did not grant this to me."

My grandmother burst out weeping. However she quickly regained her composure and said:

"Let us not violate the enjoyment of the Sabbath. It is time to go to the synagogue." My mother was very emotional.

"Forgive me, Mother, that I have caused you pain."

"I forgive you, my daughter."

C.

Approximately five years passed. I and my brother Yitzchak grew up. He already studied Gemara in *cheder*, and I studied Yiddish, Russian, and a little bit of arithmetic with a Jew who was called "the teacher." He came from a nearby village, but he acquired his education from some city, and he sought teaching positions for girls in the towns of the region. In the evenings, I studied bible with our neighbor Reb Yedidya the teacher.

One day, there was joy again in our home. A package came to us from my mother's far off family. It was before Passover. The wagon drivers returned from Bobruisk with a sealed crate, nicely bound. It was received in the post office there in my mother's name, and was sent from the Land of Israel by her brother Yitzchak Epstein.

The personal and social status of this Yitzchak Epstein grew among the people of Lyuban of that time so much that they forgot about his sins of eating with an uncovered head and neglecting his prayers, just like

[Page 223]

his brother, the Hebrew writer Zalman Epstein. For at that time, the new spirit of *Chibat Zion* had already reached isolated Lyuban, as well as the wondrous stories of the *Biluim* who went to the Land of Israel to be farmers there. Yitzchak of Lyuban followed in their path.

In the town and the region, people were very enthusiastic to read his letters from the Land of Israel that he wrote in Yiddish to his mother and sisters. Everyone discussed at length the letter that he wrote, describing his marriage to the daughter of farmers from Rosh Pina.

Everyone was particularly astounded about the fact that he did not receive a dowry, as our forefathers always had. They toiled in backbreaking labor for the wives that they married. Of course Yitzchak was happy that they did not require back breaking labor of him for their daughter that they married to him.

On occasion, his letter would make the rounds from hand to hand, through the city and neighboring villages, until it was in tatters, and the writing completely faded.

However, it was impossible to prevent the residents of the area from reading these letters. Now, they found out that he also sent a heavy present for the Passover festival.

Of course, people gathered together for that important occasion. The curious neighbors left their work of house cleaning and preparing for the festival. They congregated around the door of our house. The children of the town were scampering noisily around them. The package was opened in front of them all. Inside there was another package of glittering tin. When it was opened, it was filled with bottles of Kosher for Passover wine by the name of "Carmel"[2]—wine from the Land of Israel.

The crowd was astonished and curious. They looked at the sealed bottles and read their labels. The labels were in Hebrew, with the insignia of the Carmel company—"and they carried it on a pole with two people,"[3] a reference that everyone recognized.

Everyone became excited. These were indeed the same grape clusters that the spies had brought to Moses. These were actual bottles of wine. Wine from the grapes of the Land of Israel. Almost everyone was certain that this wine came from the vineyards of Yitzchak Epstein. At first he was a tiller of the soil, and now he already owned an estate, or he was a partner with an owner of a vineyard and winery, and now he was sending to his sister a gift from the fruits of his estate…Nice, very nice.

This particularly made an impression on the young school children. They were enchanted, moved, and enthusiastic. They ran home and brought their *Chumashim*. They leafed through them and found the Torah portion that tells about the pole with the cluster of grapes. They all read this aloud joyously, each one as if he had found a treasure in his *Chumash*. They pointed to the writing with their little fingers and stared at the bottles of wine with the drawn labels on their sides, enchanted labels straight from the *Chumash*.

My emotional mother counted the bottles in the meantime. There were twelve, and there, in front of everyone, she made an accounting as to how to split up the wine, how many she should sent to her sister in the village, how many she would need for the four cups of wine along with her children, and how many she would divide up with her local relatives. Of course, she would send one bottle to her father-in-law the rabbi of the town, and another one must be given to Reb Yedidya, the teacher of her children, who was also sitting in our house. According to her accounting, she would require eight bottles of wine, and she would keep the other four for Passover of the following year.

At that moment, there was a fierce protest to her allotment.

David, the cantor, who was also among the curious crowd who looked into our house to see the wine, complained. He spoke harshly, as was his manner.

Sarahke, it is not just to keep the Israeli wine in the cellar until next Passover, and not to let the Jews of the town taste it. If this wine was indeed sent here from the Holy Land, we should at least be able to taste a drop of it, at least, for the first Seder. Sell the rest, everyone will pay you honorably.

My mother laughed, "The four bottles of wine that remain will suffice for the first Seder of all of the Jews of the town? Besides, I do not want to sell my brother's gift."

"Whatever is missing from the *Kiddush* cup [4] will be made up with raisin wine as usual in order to fulfill the commandment, but at least, we will be able to recite *Kiddush* on the wine of the Land of Israel."

Mother agreed to this recommendation. She agreed to sell the rest of the wine cup by cup on the condition that the money received in payment will be given to the poor of the town, each in accordance with his wishes.

The community was very satisfied.

On the eve of Passover, they brought cups to mother's house, and she filled them from the four sealed bottles that she had given over to the community. Everyone received their share from my mother.

We children, me and my little brother Yitzchak, sat next to her and held onto the plate in which the coins for the poor clanged.

The three of us were happy with the job that we merited in performing.

This division of the Israeli wine for the festival of Passover in Lyuban had important results for the benefit of the community. My mother always chased after a *mitzvah*, but she was too bashful to start something new. Here, she had succeeded in dividing up the wine for the benefit of the poor of the town. This fortified her so much so that she founded herself, and with her own money, a charitable fund in the town. She did this with wisdom and good judgment.

She purchased the merchandise for her store from nearby Slutsk. Each week, the wagon drivers of our town would bring all types of merchandise to the store, in accordance with what she had ordered for the city. Twice a year, prior to Passover and prior to the High Holy Days, my mother herself would travel to Slutsk in order to arrange for her large scale purchases, and to settle her accounting with the wholesalers.

Each half year, she would give over money from the store to the community to be used for the charitable fund, on the condition that one week before her trip to Slutsk, the loan would be returned to her [5]

This condition remained holy for several years.

This private charitable fund of my mother's existed in Lyuban until she was stricken with influenza, and succumbed to it in her thirty eighth year of life.

D.

After mother's death, our grandmother from Odessa made various arrangements for us for one year. I was to continue on being the shopkeeper, as I had done during the time of my mother's illness. She wished, apparently, to make me into an actual shopkeeper. At the age of twelve, I already knew the principals of arithmetic. I also knew how to discuss purchases with the customers.

I was also obligated to be the tutor of my young brother Yitzchak.

With regards to the store, grandmother gave me ordinances upon ordinances. She especially warned me about dishonesty in weights and measures. Then she warned me with particular severity about my behavior with the gentile customers. If I were to be dishonest over weights and measures with a Jewish customer, he would say that I was an improper person; however a gentile would say that, just as the weights and measures of the Jews are false, so is their faith also false. Therefore, dishonesty towards a gentile is a desecration of G-d's name. Therefore, you should be wary, my daughter.

I listened to the honest words of my grandmother, and I attempted to remember them well in order to fulfill them.

About a year later, grandmother again came from Odessa, and she was disappointed. She did not recognize our beautiful store. The store that sustained our family in an honorable fashion for years had become impoverished and diminished under my hand. They laughed about this in the town. They told her that I divided up the store the poor of the town.

This was a bitter mistake. I would not have been so brazen as to "divide" up the store that was placed under my control by the family in order to support me and my younger brother. It was only out of fear of grandmother's admonitions regarding the sin of dishonest weights and measures that I always overdid the measures, and for poor people, I overdid them doubly. The gentile customers particularly benefited from my exaggerated measures, so that they would not be so brazen as to say that the dishonest weights and measures of the Jews are an example of their religion.

Grandmother realized that I would not be an appropriate storekeeper, so she liquidated the store. She decided, for family reasons, to take me to Odessa. With regard to my brother Yitzchak, there was the oral last will of my late mother. Her last will was that the lad not be moved to Odessa before he acquired his Jewish religious education in one of the important Lithuanian Yeshivas.

She fulfilled this wish of her daughter, who had been cut off in her prime, to the best of her ability. She chose the Mir Yeshiva. She traveled there with him, and arranged everything on her account, so that he would not feel any pressure with regards to his living conditions, his food, and clothing. She also arranged that he would have ready cash in his pocket, so that he could be dedicated to his studies. Everything would be provided for him from Odessa.

However, about a half a year later, my brother returned ill from the Mir Yeshiva to Lyuban ill. The doctors could not diagnose his illness. He simply wasted away. He was always a delicate child, and was not strong enough to handle all of the great changes that took place during his short life.

Odessa reacted to this with vigorous activity. The family asked my Aunt Chaya from the village of Troychani to take the lad to her home and take care of him until he would recover in the fresh village air.

However, my brother did not wish to live in the home of his aunt among the gentiles. He pined for Lyuban, where all of his *cheder* friends were. He particularly longed for his Rebbe, the teacher Berel, who would always discuss divine matters with him.

My brother Yitzchak died in Lyuban at the age of fifteen. My little Itchke. His memory always lives in my memory.

He died without an illness; he simply weakened and expired for lack of energy. He was, as it were, the most rooted Lyubanite from our entire family.

I also did not acculturate quickly in the city of Odessa. I longed for Lyuban so much that I wrote a book about it at the age of sixteen. This was my first book, and it was called "Childhood Years".

The Family of Nachum Epstein

Sara Feigenberg, nee Epstein

Feiga Beila Epstein with her family[16]

The father of the family was born in Lyuban and died in Odessa. He was the first person to leave the town for the wide world.

Feiga Beila Epstein, nee Lieberman, the mother of the family, was born in Bobruysk. She lived in Lyuban for most of her life, and she died in Rosh Pina.

Sara Feigenberg, nee Epstein, was the oldest daughter of the family. She was born in Lyuban and died there in her prime.

[Page 224]

Zalman Epstein

He was a writer from the year 1879. He was born on the eve of Rosh Hashanah 5621 (1860) in Lyuban, the son of Nachum (merchant, owner of a mill, and also a teacher). He was educated in *cheder* and in the Yeshiva of Volozhin from 1875. He was a bookkeeper in Odessa from 1878–1904. He was one of the founders of *Bnei Moshe*. From 1890-1900, he was the bookkeeper and the secretary of the Odessa committee. He was in Petersburg from 1904-1914 and 1916-1919, where he was active in Hebrew education and *chusha* [7]. He was a member of the communal council in 1918. He was a representative of the 11th Zionist Congress.

He was in Israel from 1925. He died in 1937 in Tel Aviv. He participated in newspapers, most steadily in *Haaretz*. From 1879, he published articles, literature, portraits, and memoirs in *Hakol*, *Hamelitz*, *Hatzefirah*, *Hashiloach*, and others. From 1881, he was a veteran journalist in the newspapers of *Chovevei Zion* and others. (On occasion, he also wrote in Yiddish and he wrote eulogies.) He published an anthology of letters in 1905, the Memoirs of Yitzchak in 1927, and a monograph on Lilienblum in 1934.

Yitzchak Epstein

He graduated from the University of Lausanne in 1905. He received a doctorate in literature in 1915. He was a writer, linguist, pedagogue, psychologist, and one of the first teachers of the new settlement. He taught in a teacher's seminary. He often lectured on the Hebrew Language on the radio in the Land of Israel. He was born in Kislev 5623 (1863) in Lyuban. He was the son of Nachum, and the brother of Zalman Epstein. He was educated in *cheder*, in the Real School[8] of Odessa, and from 1902-1905 in the University of Lausanne. He was in the Land of Israel from 1886. (He was one of the six who were sent by *Chovevei Zion* to the Land of Israel to study agriculture.) Until 1891 he was a student, gardener, and land surveyor in Rosh Pina and Metula. He pioneered the "*Ivrit BeIvrit*" teaching style[9].

He was in Switzerland from 1902-1915. He was the principal of a school in Salonika from 1915-1919. He was the principal of the seminary for teachers and pre-school teachers in Tel Aviv from 1919-1923. From then on, he taught in Jerusalem and Tel Aviv. He was one of the first to deal with the question of the status of our relations with the Arabs, and earning their friendship. (His article on this question, from *Hashiloach* in 1905, has disappeared.) He was one of the founders of *Brit Shalom*. He was active in the development of the proper Hebrew accent (he lectured and served as advisor in various theatrical studios in the Land of Israel). He was concerned with exactitude and nuances in language. He invented new words, particularly in pedagogy and psychology. He published research in education, language, and psychology, as well as many articles in the daily newspapers on practical issues of Hebrew. He published the book "*Ivrit beIvrit*" ("Hebrew in Hebrew") in 1901; "*Higyonei Lashon*" ("Studies in Language") 5707[10]; "Investigations of the Psychology of the Hebrew Language", Jerusalem 5700 (1940); "Thought and the Plethora of Languages" (in French), 1915. He translated "*Nefesh Hachinuch*" ("The Soul of Education") by William Stern. He died in Jerusalem in the year 1943, 5703.

Rachel Feigenberg (Omry)

The writer Rachel Feigenberg (Omry) was the third generation of the Epstein family on her mother's side. She was the daughter of Sara. She was born in Lyuban in 1885 and left the town at the age of 14. She made *aliya* to the Land of Israel in 1924 along with her husband G. Shapira of blessed memory and their son Yisrael. She is currently resides in Tel Aviv. The photograph was from the age of 25.

She is a popular writer in Yiddish and Hebrew. She wrote stores of the events of the Jews of Poland. She looks after the "*Hameasef*" library. She translated the following works from Yiddish: *Megilat Dobova* (A description of the destruction of Dubova, Ukraine); *Na VeNad* (Wanderings), *Biyemey Zaam* (In the Days of Wrath) by Mordechai Necher; *On the Banks of the Dniester*; and *For Two Years*. She wrote[11]: *A Romance Without Love* (on life in the land), *The Final Era* (of Jewish Life in Poland); articles on topical events and youth, the Jewish woman, and the building of the land; In *the Confusion of Days*; *Between the Barbed Wire Fence*, and others. She edited: The *Nation in its Land*, 5708-5709 (1948-1949). She translated the writings of the Jewish Russian writer Semion Yoshkovich into Yiddish.

Gruna Iskolski

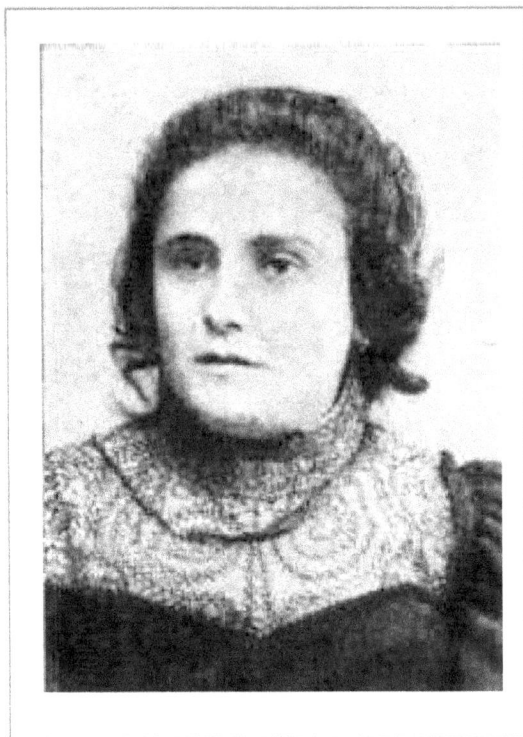

Gruna Iskolski, nee Micheikin, was the wife of Reb Yaakov Iskolski of blessed memory of New York. She was born in Lyuban and died in New York. The photograph from her youth is from the family archives of the Epstein-Feigenberg family.

Translator's footnotes:

1. It is a rabbinical commandment to ritually wash ones hands with a cup prior to partaking of bread. This hand washing is not necessary prior to partaking of other baked goods.
2. The Carmel winery is still one of the prime producers of wine in Israel today.
3. A quote from the book of numbers, describing the heavy clusters of grapes brought back to Moses by the ten spies.
4. *Kiddush* is the prayer of sanctification of the day recited at the beginning of the Sabbath and festival meals. It is also the first of four cups of wine drunk at the *Seder*.
5. Evidently, the charitable fund was a free loan fund.
6. The family is not in the picture – the caption must be an error.
7. I am not sure what this acronym is: *chet vav shin ayin*.
8. According to the Even Shoshan dictionary, a Real School is a secondary school with a natural sciences trend.
9. Hebrew in Hebrew: a teaching style, popular in Hebrew schools today, where the teacher uses the Hebrew language to teach Hebrew – i.e. a form of Hebrew immersion.
10. This date corresponds to 1947, which would be four years after he died. Perhaps it was published posthumously.
11. I inserted the two words 'She wrote'. It seems that the list of items translated from Yiddish ends here as there is a period in the text, and the rest are her own writings. However, this is not completely clear from the text. It is also unclear if Mordechai Necher is the name of the author of the translated works, or a work in itself (The Hebrew word *Necher* can also mean foreigner, so perhaps there was a work called *Mordechai the*

Foreigner). In any case, this is all somewhat ambiguous from the text. The list of edited items is not ambiguous.

[Page 225]

Starobin
(Starobin, Belarus)
52°44' 27°28'

Starobin – 3213 inhabitants, a church, a school, a post office. Surrounded by large swamps. In addition to trade, the inhabitants were engaged in various types of home industry, and rented tracts of hay and pits.

(According to the Brookhouse-Efron Encyclopedia)

About Starobin

by Eliyahu Chaim Chinitz

Translated by Irit Dolgin

Starobin, a little town with a small number of inhabitants, is located in the northern border of Polesia, a geographic region which is covered by deep forests and fettered by swamps. The town was stagnated in its development. A railroad did not pass through its territory and the roar of a locomotive [steam engine] and the rumble of its wheels did not bother its inhabitants. Nor was a road built in its area, and cargo and passenger ships did not sail over the Slutsk River, which runs along the length of the town; and therefore, the town was disconnected from trade and industrial centers and from administrative centers as well. Only twisting dirt trails, with prints of men's feet, wagons' wheels and hoofs, would lead to distant villages and small towns in the vicinity. And most of the year, those trails were also disrupted by mud and clay, or covered by snow piles during the winter. Transportation to and from Slutsk was difficult and exhausting. The ride from here to there, a distance of 35 kilometers, lasted eight to ten hours. Such a journey was executed twice a week, by a procession of wagons.

But, despite the difficult connection with the larger world, the town did not lack influence from the outside. Towards the end of the nineteenth century, our town was already considered to be progressive – it has been adopting new lifestyles and manners. The Enlightenment [movement] that had previously conquered the big cities, also reached it, and penetrated the hearts of the young Yeshiva students of the "homeowners" social class. "Hamelitz" and "Hatzefira" [nineteenth century Hebrew newspapers; Hamelitz was published in 1860-1904 in Odessa and St. Petersburg; Hatzefira was published in 1862-1931 in Warsaw and Berlin] attracted several subscribers. The Enlightenment books written by Mapu, Abraham Dob Bär Lebensohn, Kalman Shulman, Isaac Baer Levinsohn, and the like, found their ways to some of the households as well. The heralds of the Enlightenment, the ones that had brought the new movement into the town's households, were two people: Nachman Shweidel and Nissan Marmur, or Nissan *HaMelamed* [the teacher]. The latter was a grammarian and a major Hebrew enthusiast. His *Cheder* [*Cheder* literary means "room", but is also the name for a traditional elementary school, which teaches the basics of Judaism and the Hebrew language] was closer in its character to the *Cheder Metukan* [a *Cheder* of the Jewish Enlightenment Movement], which was established not long after. He taught not only the *Tanakh* and the *Gmara*, but also grammar and Hebrew; in his *Tanakh* teachings he was meticulous with regard to accentuation of the penultimate and ultimate stresses. His students were cautious over the correct stressing of the words during the prayer times as well. And if one of the students was called up to the *Torah* on a *Sabbath* or festival, during the reading of the *Torah*, he would read in a beautiful tone while keeping the melody, so that even the adults would envy his students and would imitate them, but, because they did not know the rules, they would switch between the penultimate and the ultimate stresses, and would become a source of ridicule in our eyes.

His method of teaching was as follows: he would orally read a sentence in Yiddish to us and we would have to translate it to Hebrew. And if the translation was not in accordance with to the essence of the language, he would correct us – and then we would write it in the notebook. He brought into the hearts of the students the love of Hebrew and the Hebrew writers; at this point in time, he already referred to the old lifestyle with criticism and allowed himself to make fun of its many deliriums and dull customs, in front of us.

The teacher Sh. N. tells that when he was a teacher in the girls' school in "Neve Tzedek", he had a reticent student; but despite the scarce amount of words she said, one could feel that she possessed a great knowledge of Hebrew, it was especially apparent in her written essays. She told that her grandfather was a teacher in a *Cheder Metukan* in Russia. Sh. N. asked her to invite her grandfather to visit the school, and when he came he was surprised that he [the grandfather] knew the teacher of the *Cheder Metukan* in Slutsk, in which he [Sh.N.] studied as well.

Nachman Shweidel (The teacher Nachman Shweidel died in Tel-Aviv.) owned a stand in Tel-Aviv, where he sold fruits and vegetables during the weekdays and on *Sabbaths* he would study at the Synagogue of the Americans. He was a *Torani* [classic observant Jew], with a beautiful soul and noble virtues.

Reb Zelig Milkavitzer (a Falx Mench), his wife and daughter

Nachman Shweidel was an educated person, he read and studied a great deal, and was proficient in all areas of Hebrew literature, including the new and old research and science books;

[Page 226]

it was rare for him not to have read a book about the Enlightenment. He would bring the books from Slutsk, from Shmuel Reiser's printer's workshop.

Both of them, Nissan *HaMelamed* and Nachman Shweidel taught many students who were knowledgeable of Hebrew and some of them later exiled themselves to places of *Torah* in Slutsk and Minsk, and continued educating themselves in the *Torah* and the Enlightenment. These two people deserve to be noted for future generations, in a Memory Book to a town that was destroyed.

* * *

The town excelled in that, that almost all the Jews were engaged in gardening. It was not their primary business, but a side business. Each house owner had a garden behind the house, in which people would sow various vegetables: potatoes, cabbage, turnip, legumes, beet and more, and especially pumpkins. The pumpkins were sowed not merely to feed the humans and animals, but, and especially, for a seeds trade. They would put them in flowerbeds until the end of the summer, until they grow and become properly yellow; they would collect them from the garden and place them in the sun, in rows, on the inclined roofs, so that they become more yellow and ripe. Afterwards, they would bring them to their houses, cut them in halves lengthwise, take out the soft part from the inside, together with the seeds, and filter them through a sieve. They would throw away the softness that would come out of the holes, and the seeds would remain in the sieve. They would dry the seeds in the sun again and spread them out on sheets. After the seeds would dry, they would store them in bags, until traders from Minsk would come and buy them for sowing.

Teme Chinitz

Aharon Baruch Chinitz

From Starobin

(the parents of the author of the article)

All the members of the household took part in all those tasks: the father, the mother, sons and daughters. It was a hard work, but the family worked enthusiastically and diligently. These seeds were of excellent species and called "*Manarim*" ("*Manastirsky*"), and had a great demand. Even those Jews, that did not own their own garden, rented land lots from non-Jews, and planted pumpkin in those lots. But, as I have already mentioned, this was a side business.

Overall, among the inhabitants, there were many craftsmen, tailors, shoemakers, carpenters, blacksmiths, goldsmiths, constructors, bakers, butchers and wagon-owners. The middle class was engaged in storekeeping; there were stores that sold fabric, grocery, crops, iron tools etc. The indigent were engaged in peddling. The peddlers went to villages in the vicinity, with wagons loaded with barrels of tar and different kinds of haberdasher [sewing goods, such as ribbons, buttons, thread, needles], and sold that to the peasants. In consideration for their merchandise they would get bundles of pig's bristles, calf, lamb or goat, stalks of linen, wool etc.

Also, there were tree traders in our town, who bought small lots in the forests from the big traders, they [tree traders] would cut down the trees and made beams for construction or railway sleepers of them. One of our tree traders had business with the father of Chaim Weitzman z"l [of blessed memory]. Due to his business, he would often go to Pinsk and Motal, and stay in the house of Reb' Ozer Weitzman, whose sons, and Chaim one of them, were already students and took an important place in the Zionist movement. When this trader, who was a *Chassidic*, uneducated Jew, came back to his house, and the conversation would turn to Zionism, he would say dismissively: Oh my to the Zionism that the "Sons" of Weitzman are its leaders!

Overall, the Jews of the town were poor, worked very hard to earn their bread, yet their poverty did not disgrace them; they were simple people, naïve and honest, and almost all of them were people of the *Torah*. The *Torah* was the aspiration of their souls; and those who peeked and had been stroked, their ideal was the Enlightenment. On *Sabbaths* and festive days the sound, the sound of the *Torah* would emerge from the synagogues and *Batei Midrashot* [houses of Talmud studies] and fill the town.

As in all places, in which the sons and daughters of Israel were of inferior status, likewise in our town there were important people who faithfully dealt with the public needs; people, who love doing good and kind deeds to others and helping them in time of trouble; people who could approach the authorities and make efforts on behalf of someone who encountered an unfortunate business, or to repeal a harsh decree imposed on people. Among those people, my father Reb. Baruch Chinitch [Chinitz] z"l

[Page 227]

excelled especially. He was a likable and easy-going person, took care of all the public needs, was always the messenger of the public, made efforts before the authorities in Slutsk and Minsk and had done a great deal for the benefit of the public.

Yet the life did not always run its normal course. A terrible disaster would fall over the inhabitants and turn the town into a pandemonium. The greatest enemy of the town was the fire, or, as it was named in our town, the red chicken. The houses in our town were built of wood and many of the roofs covered with straw; in the droughts of summer the houses were dry and could easily be ignited. And if it happened that either a fire was created, or so-and-so, intentionally or unintentionally, start a spark, and incited a stack of straw, hay, or a straw roof – at once a tongue of fire would be created and the entire town was in flames. People would lose all their property and the entire House of Israel cried over the fire that so-and-so initiated. The disaster was great, but after a while, a year to two years, the town would get a new face. New houses were constructed on the burned lots; those who mourned over the destruction of their houses got to see their new houses, and greater was the honor of the second one over the first. The non-Jewish neighbors saw the beautiful new houses, and were sure that Jews are extremely wealthy and that they hold great fortune, but, with due respect to them, they erred an error of a non-Jew. Jews ate dry bread with a salted-fish broth, combined a penny to a penny until saved the required amount of money for the construction of a new house.

And therefore the jesters of the generation would say that the Starobin Jew is a "house owner from the outside and poor in the inside".

And I remember, when I was a child, how a ban of *Cherem* [the highest ecclesiastical censure in the Jewish community, a total exclusion of a person from the Jewish community] was announced at the Synagogue, over the ones who started the fire. It was a terrifying spectacle, which left an unforgotten impression in my heart. A black rod was put on the pulpit, black candles were lit, the *prochet* [ornamental curtain covering the front of the holy ark in the synagogue] was removed, the Shofar [ram's horn] was sounded: *tekiah, teruah, shaevarim*, and the beadle of the community pronounced the curse, that on behalf of the place and the public, in accordance with the heavenly court and the mortal court, we impose the Yehoshua Ben Nun *Cherem* on the one who starts a fire; that this individual will be struck by all the curses of the biblical punishment and by all the curses that were pronounced on Mount Ebal; that this individual will be banned from the community, and that it will be forbidden to be in vicinity to him, and so on and so forth.

Our town was divided into two parts: the southern part, which was named the "Eretz-Israel" Street, and the northern part, which was called the "Slutsk" Street. The indigent lived on the Eretz-Israel Street: the peddlers and the simple craftsmen. These were simple, uneducated people, who were barely familiar with "*Chayei Adam*" "The life of a Man" – a work of the Jewish law written by Rabbi Avraham Danzig] and the *Mishnahs* [the first major written redaction of the Jewish oral traditions called the Oral Torah], but they were ruffians. As opposed to them, the grocers and the craftsmen of clean and effortless occupations, who could study a page of the *Talmud* with medieval commentaries, lived on the Slutsk Street. There was neither love nor comradeship between the two streets. The latter would act arrogantly toward the former, and there were always quarrels and disputes between the two on public matters. When the time to elect a new rabbi has arrived, the two streets were divided into two parts. Those wanted to elect one rabbi, the others – another rabbi, and there was a great dispute for the sake of heaven, which even lead to physical fights at the synagogue. And, surely, the ruffians would almost always win. On a market day, when a fight erupted between the peasants and the Jews, and the Jews were in great danger – the ruffians appeared and showed the non-Jews the power of their arm and saved the honor of Israel.

Among the ruffians were also horse traders. Two were partners in a business: one was Moshe, and the other – Yaakov. They would buy horses from the Gypsies that were staying in tents outside the town. Moshe was the head negotiator with the Gypsies. He measured the horse with his eyes, inspected its teeth, patted its back, and began the purchase negotiations with the Gypsy. One asks so and so, the other gives so and so; this cries and this cries. At first they have spoken softly, and later harshly. They tried to set an agreement to one another. They almost reached an agreement, but immediately backed off, and began speaking to one another with disrespect, and as the things got heated, they began struggling and hitting each other. The other Gypsies interfered and a great riot had risen, and in the heat of the moment, Yaakov (the other partner) jumped on the horse and escaped to the Eretz-Israel Street – and the horse disappeared. A jester that has been watching this entire spectacle came to the *Beit Midrash* [place of Torah study] and announced: People! I just saw a deed and recalled a Midrash P'lia [enigmatic Talmudic legend]: when Moshe [Moses] killed the Egyptian, Yaakov rode a horse and escaped to Eretz-Israel.

In this manner, the sons and daughters of my town, Starobin, had been living for hundreds of years: growing up and quarreling, working and trading, studying Torah, aspiring to Enlightenment, rejoicing at times of peace and quietude, suffering at times of difficulties, arguing with each other, giving to charity and doing good deeds, holding rabbis great in Torah on the Rabbinic Chair, joking and jesting – and there the reaper found them: a despised and sordid non-Jew, Hitler-the-evil – may his name be obliterated – cut their short-lived lives, gathered them into a slaughter house and burned them alive. *Hashem* [God] shall avenge their blood!

[Page 228]

My Town

by Rabbi Nissan Waxman

Translated by Paul Pascal

[This is a translation of pp. 228-234 in Hebrew with additions from the Yiddish article of the same title, pp. 460-465. The essay exists in the Slutsk Yiskor Book in both Hebrew and Yiddish versions. For the most part the two are very similar in content, but do differ occasionally in significant ways. The translation below is based on the Hebrew version, with additional or alternative passages from the Yiddish where these augment, clarify, or improve on the Hebrew text. The Yiddish additions are given in square brackets. Hebrew terms retained in the translation are rendered here with a Yiddish pronunciation, out of deference to those in Starobin who actually used the words, with this pronunciation, in their daily lives.]

[Starobin – 3213 souls, a church, a school, a post office. Large stretches of swamp land. Aside from trade and business, the Jewish townspeople devoted themselves to growing vegetables and cultivating large tracts of hay and grass. – From Bruckhaus-Efron's Encyclopedia]

A child of Starobin am I. My forefathers, simple and pure-hearted, were born within its borders and buried in its cemeteries.

I am a child of the twentieth century, oppressed by stormy winds and exhausted by the crashing waves. The cradle of my youth lay in Starobin and upon its ashes I took my first steps.

Many years have passed since I left you, my darling town. I have experienced events and adventures. I have crossed oceans and countries of the world and have seen large cities, but none is more beautiful than you.

You remain engraved in my heart and before my eyes [with all of your attributes and your flaws, with your forests and fields, your mud and bog, your simple folk and your luminaries, so noble in character]. Your radiant countenance and pure heart will never be erased from my memory, even with the poverty and illiteracy which also nested in you.

I will try to describe your appearance so that your memory might endure for generations to come.

* * *

My town of Starobin belonged to the Gubernya (province) of Minsk, the city of Minsk itself being about 140 kilometers (85 miles) away. However, most commerce was conducted with the District Town of Slutsk, about 35kilometers (20 miles) away. The town was divided into three parts: Slutsk Street [also known as "Town's End"] on the edge of town, the market [also known as the "Well-to-do Section"], and Eretz Yisroel Street. I could never understand the reason for this name and have never heard of its use in any other place. Each of these three areas had its own Beis Medresh (House of Torah Study and Prayer), with its own individual charm.

Three hundred and fifty Jewish families lived in Starobin. Some earned their income from the various trades in which other Jews of White Russia were also employed, such as shoemaker, tailor, and storekeeper. In addition to these, Starobin Jews had a unique "industry" of their own from which the majority supported themselves, based on their vast gardens of cucumbers. The cucumbers were overseen with great care all summer, and at summer's end they were taken from the gardens, sliced in half by hand lengthwise, and their seeds removed. These were washed and then dried in the sun.

Merchants from deep inside Russia would then come and purchase the seeds in order to do their own sowing, and they would pay about twenty or thirty rubles a pod (40 pounds), a substantial price. It was fair, though, when you consider how labor-intensive the process was. You can also imagine what sort of income this kind of business eked out.

But Starobin was rich in Jewish souls, rare Jewish characters in whom she could justifiably be proud, including the following:

Peysakh the Melamed (the Torah Teacher)

In the Beis Medresh on the edge of town there were no outstanding scholars, but within it the voice of the Bible could nevertheless be heard. This was where Rabbi Peysakh the Melamed prayed, a teacher of Rashi Talmud. [He would take only] ten to fifteen Talmud pupils into his heyder (one-room religious school), and he worked with them with all his might from morning until late at night.

He taught Torah to Jewish young people in this way for about twenty-five years, until his throat grew hoarse and he spoke [with the voice of a duck. In fact, the jokers in town gave him the nickname "Peysakh the Drake."]

Of course, the teaching profession did not sufficiently support his household. Therefore his wife also would keep a pumpkin garden. [As if it weren't enough that this particular Jew with the gravelly voice grew exhausted each day from his long hours of teaching, at twilight daily he would run to the Beis Medresh and complete his day's work teaching a chapter of Mishna (the first part of the Talmud) to the congregants, and it was not for the sake of monetary reward, God forbid.] On the Sabbath, prior to Minha (afternoon prayers), he would preach on the Torah portion of the week.

The Postmaster

A quarter to a third of the Jews who prayed in the Businessmen's Beis Medresh were of the educated class and teachers of modern children. [They tended to be a more intelligent group, both in worldly matters and in Jewish thought.] They argued that every Jew ought to be proficient in the Bible, including the grammar. Every Sabbath a congregation of twenty or thirty refined Jews sat and listened to a lesson in Talmud by their rabbi, a great Bible scholar, Rabbi Shleyma Landa, one of the brilliant students of the gaon (Torah genius) Rabbi Boruch Ber Leibowitz, the rabbi of Hlusk.

Berel Kasshes,
Astarabiner "Mishnayot Yad"

Aside from a squash garden, Reb Shleyma earned money from a horse postal business, a dowry gift from his father-in-law, [Yankl Itshe Chaim's, on behalf of Yankl's only daughter]. Reb Yankl had leased the business from the government, and promised to support Reb Shleyma with it for all the days of his life. Thus Reb Shleyma engaged in Torah and community work, while his father-in-law Reb Yankev ben Yitzhok Chaim [Yankl Itshe Chaim's] took care of the horses, harnesses and carriages, all the while taking pride in his son-in-law.

Hirshke the Shoemaker

In that same Beis Medresh prayed a Jew who was called Hirshke the Shoemaker because of his trade when he was young. He had a powerful and pleasant voice and would lead services in front of the Holy Ark on Rosh Hashona and Yom Kippur. However, the intellectuals of the town had misgivings about a cantor in their Beis Medresh who had been a man of a lower class, one who had been a shoemaker in his youth. Still, no one dared to say anything, for there was no one who could chant those heartfelt melodies as well as he could, especially his "Yaaleh" prayer on the eve of Yom Kippur and in the Musaf service of the next day.

His wife – Merka was her name [Khasha Merka's] – is a story in itself. This Merka was a saint of the highest order. [She did the work of ten women.] Whenever there was a need for charity and kindness, helping a poor family, providing a dowry for a poor [or orphaned] bride, staying with a sick person without family, [lending support for the funeral of a pauper], or other acts of lovingkindness, she was always there first, [organizing things quietly, so that no one would know who was responsible for the support. And when she could, she endeavored to hide her efforts from even people of means for whom she might be working, to avoid revealing how and through whom the help had come.]

In 1914-15, in the throes of the First World War, [when virtually all the Russian armies were passing through White Russia,] a regiment of Cossacks happened to arrive in Starobin exactly on Yom Kippur afternoon. When the Cossacks saw some Jews walking in the streets of the town they immediately taunted them, pushed them and knocked them down.

[Page 229]

The Jews fled frantically and rushed into the Beis Medresh crying: "Cossacks! They have come and are attacking the Jews!" In the Beis Medresh a panic arose and many of the worshippers fled to their homes. The officers of the Beis Medresh turned to Hirshke who was standing in front of the Ark and begged him to stop the service for fear of the danger, [so as to allow the congregants to get away.] But Hirshke paid attention neither to the words of the synagogue officers nor to the imminent danger. He [dismissed them with] his hand and uttered one word: "Service!" [as if to say, "How dare you suggest we break off our worship without reciting the central service, the Shmon'Esrey – the holiest part of the prayers?"] His strong stance made a great impression on the worshippers and they too remained in their places, to hear and join in the chanting of their spiritual leader.

The excitement had just calmed down when a group of Cossacks with long swords in their hands broke into the Beis Medresh. A great terror fell upon the worshippers. Yet, when the Cossacks saw Hirshke, shrouded in white, prostrating himself and chanting the prayer "The Priests and the People" in a melody which penetrated the heart, and saw too all the worshippers on their knees, a fear of this holy atmosphere fell upon them. For a few moments they stood as if petrified, then slipped outside, one by one.

The Great Beis Medresh and Moshe Nomi's the Shammes (Synagogue Sexton)

Rabbi Dimta and all of Starobin's religious leaders prayed in the Great Beis Medresh, the most important one in town. The building stood on the edge of a wide courtyard known as the "Shulheyf" (or Shul Hoif, "Synagogue Grounds), which served private and public life. At the other end of the courtyard was the rabbi's house.

Rabbi Moshe Chaim, the son of Rabbi
Yehuda Leib Kaptzitz, was known in
Starobin as Moshe Nomi's

In the middle of the Shulheyf there was a building called "House of Talmud Torah" (community Torah school for young children), even though no one in town could remember when school children had studied there. The house served as a storeroom for old objects and utensils and the Khevra Kadisha (Burial Society). This desolate building instilled fear in the children of the town and many frightening tales about it circulated in town.

It was in the Shulheyf that a khuppah (wedding canopy) would be set up, after the bridal couple had been led through the town. At a bris (ritual circumcision), the newborn infant would be carried to the Great Beis Medresh, and once he had been brought into the covenant of our Father Abraham, the community went to the home of the boy's father for a festive meal.

Sara Rivka Kaptzitz
(wife of Moshe Nomi's)

Pallbearers would carry the deceased in their coffins to the Shulheyf. Many of the townspeople took part in the funeral, and shops closed when the funeral procession passed them on its way to the cemetery. The life of every Jew in Starobin was tied, from birth to the last day to the walls of the Beis Medresh and its courtyard, where everything began, happened, and ended.

In the Great Beis Medresh, Moshe "son of the Woman Naomi" (also known as Moshe [Ed: not Moishe] Nomi's) made his home [and "kingdom"]. [Ed: Reb Meysha Chaim b'reb Yehuda Leyb Kaptshits.] He was a unique character, [the rare kind of Jew that hasn't been seen for many years now]. To all appearances, he seemed to be only the shammes of the Beis Medresh and the shammes of the Khevra Kadisha. But he was also called "Shammes of the Besdin (Rabbinical Court)". This was his official position, and the truth of the matter is in this role he was the only authority in all religious matters in the town – proficient in Talmud, religious arbitration, and in the wisdom of the Kabbala, which he studied when no one was in the Beis Medresh.

His dedication to Torah knew no bounds. He sat in the Beis Medresh and studied Torah day and night every day of his life. The elders of the town would say that for fifty years no one ever arrived at the Beis Medresh before he did nor left after him. He fulfilled his job as shammes faithfully and devotedly and did not rely on others. Every Thursday he went around to all the doorsteps of the homeowners collecting contributions for "Paupers' Bread" (food bank). All the people in town, from youngsters to elders, admired him. Many feared his glance, although he never looked "beyond his own four cubits" (never looked critically at others).

He also presented a lesson in Shulkhn Orukh (voluminous summary of Torah laws) every day between minkha and maariv (afternoon and evening prayers) to whomever came to the Beis Medresh. After the maariv prayers he taught a page of Gemora (Talmud) to the scholars of the town. [Regardless of the fact that in Starobin there were always great rabbis with world-renowned reputations, it was Moshe who taught the Gemora in the Shul, and Rabbi Dimta would sit and learn from him.]

The people of Starobin, like most of the Jews in the District of Slutsk, did not recognize the Hassidic movement. Everything to do with Hassidic "rebbes" and the practice of "personal blessings" and "redemption money" were foreign to their spirit. Yet people came from far and near to receive a personal blessing from Moshe Nomi's the Shammes. Not just the Jews—even Gentiles came to him with requests. He never took payment from a son of Israel. Only from Gentiles did he accept payment, in the form of candles and towels for the Beis Medresh.

[Page 230]

A yeshiva for advanced young people existed in town for a few years [prior to the First World War], founded and run by Rabbi Shimshon [Zelig] Fortman (more on him later). The yeshiva acquired a good reputation, and students from the entire Slutsk region flocked to it. I, too, was among the yeshiva's young students. Many of its students are now great and famous Torah scholars of our generation [Ed. note: this was written around 1959].

On one occasion, Rabbi Fortman had to leave town [for a few weeks] and asked Rabbi Moshe the Shammes to be his substitute. So it was, and once during a lesson, a peasant carrying a package came into the Beis Medresh. Rabbi Moshe apologized to us and went out to speak with him. When he returned he sensed our strange reaction and he responded with a smile, saying, "It happened that two cows had run away from this Gentile and disappeared. A week ago he stopped in to see me and asked me to "whisper a blessing" on his behalf.

I did as he wished, for why should it bother me if a Gentile believes in these things? And look, the cows returned safely, and this man has now brought enough towels for the Beis Medresh for an entire year. "When the Gentiles believe," added Rabbi Moshe, "this is a welcome thing, and it is forbidden to make fun of it. For if they stopped believing, it would signal a great danger to us."

Rabbi Moshe's wife was a woman of great saintliness. In addition to her squash garden, she also spun threads for the tsitses of the townsmen (tsitses, or tsitsit, are ritual fringes on the four corners of prayer shawls, perpetual reminders of God's presence and of a Jew's obligations). Everyone in town knew that Sora Rivka, the wife of Moshe Nomi's the Shammes, shared credit in their mitzvah of tsitses (in the fulfillment of their religious duty to wear tsitses). She also performed acts of anonymous charity.

[In the corner of the Great Beis Medresh there sat Reb Avrohom Reuven Hinda's (surname Rubnitz), reciting "Alshekh". He was the oldest of the brothers in his family, the others being Peysakh the Melamed and Elya Hinda's. In town they were known as the "Bney Ruvelekh" (the Little Sons of Reuven), probably because of their grandfather, whose first name is discernible in their surname – Rubnitz (Reuvenitz). They and the Chinitzes were the largest families in town.

As I picture him, Avrohom Reuven was already in his late eighties and had long ago stopped working. Previously he had been in the fur and pig-hair business, at which he was considered the greatest expert. But all of these "foolishnesses" were only sidelines. His real passion lay elsewhere. For over sixty years in a row he would "talk" Alshekh. That is to say, for half an hour between Minkha and Maariv prayers every day, he would teach a group of Jews the Torah portion of the week, using the interpretation of "Alshekh". [Ed. note: Moshe Alshekh, ordained a rabbi by the famous Joseph Caro, was a 16th century Sephardi halakhic authority, teacher, and preacher, whose published ethical and philosophical commentaries on most books of the Bible, supported by extensive Talmudic and Midrashic references, were widely disseminated throughout the Jewish world.]

Among those who were there to listen were Jews who had been attending his lessons since he started teaching: Motta Yankl the Wagon-Driver, or Moishe Berl the Glazier, who were themselves already old-timers. In the eyes of all of his students, who were basically drawn from the working class elements in town, Avrohom Reuven was the symbol of Torah and wisdom. His word was the epitome of astuteness, even though in his own mind he considered himself to be artless and simple, and would in fact often come out with indolent comments.]

[One of his comments that circulated around town had it that he didn't believe "on this Earth" there were such places, really, as Moscow and St. Petersburg. "Maybe Vilna and Warsaw, I'll grant you," he would say, "you can't deny their existence, since you see their names in black and white printed on the first page of the Mishna texts." As for Minsk or Smolensk, he himself had met with merchants from those places who would come to buy his fur and pig-hair, "but the others – it's all deceit and lies, made-up stories which good-for-nothings concoct to make mischief, since they are too lazy to attend my lesson in Alshekh and would rather gossip about stupidities!"]

[Nowadays who can deny what he said? Maybe he was actually right!…]

The Rabbis of Starobin

Rabbi Ahron Feinstein and his descendents served as the rabbis of Starobin over the course of the last century. Reb Ahron's son, Reb Eliyohu, in particular, excelled and became famous for his genius and wisdom. All his friends and acquaintances admired him, and his name preceded him throughout the Jewish world. (He died in 5689, or 1928-29).

Rabbi Reb Eliyohu Feinstein (known as
"Rabbi Elinka Pruzhaner")

Reb Eliyohu was born in the month of Teyves 5602 (winter of 1841-42) in Slutsk. His amazing talents were recognized while he was still a child, and although he was physically weak, his diligence knew no bounds. At the age of seven he was proficient in "Seder Nezikin" (fourth section of the Mishna). The head of the rabbinic court of Slutsk, the venerable gaon Rabbi Yoysef Peimer (or Pehmer), was strongly attached to him and loved him as a dear son.

When the youngster was ten years old, the old rabbi himself began to teach him and to speak about him to the outstanding personalities of that generation. When Eliyohu reached the age of thirteen, he became engaged to the daughter of the gaon Rabbi Yitzkhok haLevi Davidovitch, the Rabbi of Karlitsh. His future father-in-law gave him, as an engagement present, the book "Yad Malachi", whose pages the young groom soon filled with marginal notes. After the betrothal the groom went to the Volozhin Yeshiva.

Rabbi Reb Yitzchak Noach Vecherebin, may God
avenge him, from the village of Domanovitz near
Starobin

In those days there erupted in the Volozhin Yeshiva the famous controversy between the leaders of the NeTSiV Yeshiva (NeTSiV is an acronym for Rabbi Tsvi Hersh Leyb Berlin, head of the Volozhin Yeshiva), and Rabbi Yosef Dov Soloveitchik. The two sides decided to bring the dispute before the court of the great rabbis of the day: Rabbi David Tebli (Tevela?) of Minsk, Rabbi Yosela (Yoysef Peimer) of Slutsk, Rabbi Z'ev Volf, the head rabbi of Vilna, and Rabbi Yitzkhok Elkhonon Spector, who was then in Novogrodok.

When these rabbis arrived at Volozhin in the month of Kheshvan 5618 (1857), the leaders of the Volozhin Yeshiva came out to welcome them, and Rabbi Yosela asked the Volozhin leaders, "How is my Rabbi Elinka (affectionate form of Eliyohu)?" They heard his question and knew that Rabbi Yosela did not honor just any man with the title "Rabbi." But they were silent, saying they had not heard of him. Rabbi Yosela admonished them; he told them that not knowing the son of the rabbi of Starobin rather blemished the quality of their yeshiva administration.

From then on they began observing Eliyohu Feinstein and discerning his greatness, to which the NeTSiV himself testified, for the youngster already knew the works of Rabbenu Nissim (Ha-RaN, 14th century Talmudic commentator) and the commentaries on the Mishna of Rabbi Shlomo ben Adrat (Ha-RaSHBA, 13-14th century Spanish Talmud giant).

When he was nearing his eighteenth birthday, his marriage took place – on Rosh Khodesh Tammuz 5620 (1860), and he remained in his father-in-law's home in Karlitsh. The elders of the generation would say about him that during the time he was living in his father-in-law's house he studied every part of the Shulkhn Orukh forty times and knew every section of it by heart.

During Passover 5623 (1863) his father died and the people of Starobin unanimously decided that he should fill his father's place. But he refused because of his great desire to devote himself to Torah study, and also out of fear of the burden of rabbinic leadership when he was just twenty years old.

[Page 231]

His father-in-law tended to agree with him. But instead he respected the wishes of Rabbi Yosela who appealed to him saying: "I would like to see my Rabbi Elinka take on rabbinic leadership while I am still alive." Reb Elinka granted his request, but on the condition that the contract for his rabbinic appointment stipulated that he would not be obligated to render any rabbinic judgments or handle other rabbinic matters before midday, and that in general none of the townspeople would approach him except for teaching and for decisions on Jewish law.

In spite of those conditions, after he had taken the rabbinical seat he conducted his office on a high level, and was not intimidated by the powerful rich people who, in those days, ruled as they pleased in matters of land leasing from the Polish princes and in taking over other people's land. These people would get their sons released from army service at the expense of orphans and the sons of poor people who were sent against their will. Against these unethical people the young rabbi stood up and fought with uncompromising words and a breadth of spirit, until he became renowned throughout the country.

In the year 5627 (1866-67), when Rabbi Yehoyshua Rabinovitz from Kalish (probably either Kalush, near Lvov, or Kalisz, near Lodz), the rabbi of Kletsk, left his post in Kletsk for Nesvizh, the Kletsk community sent a rabbinic missive to Rabbi Eliyohu with a sum considerably greater than his salary. As soon as this became known to the people of Starobin the entire town was in a turmoil, and they tried all sorts of tactics to keep him. But the people of Kletsk would not give him up. Finally the two sides came before the rabbinic law court of Rabbi Arye of Eihumen (also called Chervin) and Rabbi Gershon Tankhum of Minsk. The court ruled in favor of Kletsk and so Rabbi Eliyohu went there in 5630 (1869-70).

This ruling greatly depressed the people of Starobin, and even after several decades had passed the matter was not gone from their memory. Generation after generation in the town would tell wondrous stories about their rabbi, who had grown up in their midst and been stolen from them.

To their joy, the people of Starobin were able to have their revenge on the community of Kletsk. For Rabbi Eliyohu did not stay long in Kletsk and moved from there to fill his father-in-law's place in Karlitsh in 5634 (1873-74). He then moved to Choslovitz (Khislavichi), and afterwards to Pruzhani, in place of the esteemed Rabbi Yerukhom Leyb Perlman. There Reb Eliyohu gained fame and was renowned as Rabbi Elya Pruzhaner, of blessed memory.

After Rabbi Elya moved to Kletsk, the people of Starobin elected his brother-in-law, Rabbi Yekusiel Zusman haCohen Kaplan as their rabbi. He wore this rabbinic mantle until the day he died, on the 8th of Iyar 5660 (1890). After his death a controversy broke out in Starobin over the issue of the rabbinate. Most of the people, especially the butchers, were tired of a reserved rabbi and yearned instead for a rabbi who would speak before the public from the bima (platform) of the Beis Medresh, at least on Shabbes Shuva (Sabbath between Rosh Hashana and Yom Kippur) and Shabbes haGodl (Sabbath preceding Passover).

Many rabbis, several of them famous, offered their services, in particular the R.Y.D.Ba.Z. (or R.I.D.Ba.Z., Rabbi Yankev Dovid Vilovsky/Willowsky) of Slutsk, for the sake of his son-in-law, the young Rabbi Yoysef Kahnovitsh (Kanovitsh?), who had made a favorable impression with his sermons. The RYDBaZ himself promised to come to Starobin from time to time to preach to the congregation. But the important people and the scholars of the town ultimately did not agree to hiring any of those who emphasized the importance of sermons over other rabbinic tasks. They chose instead Rabbi Gershon

Moyshe Helbord, who was known by the name "the Prodigy from Trok (Trakai, Lithuania)." Reb Gershon stayed in Starobin for seven years until he was chosen in 5667 (1906-07) as the rabbi of Timkovitsh, and from there he went to Oshmina, near Vilna.

Out of love for Reb Elinka, the community of Starobin then hired his young brother-in-law, Rabbi Dovid Feinstein, the rabbi of Uzda. Although Reb Dovid was shy and did not preach before the public, all the people in town loved and admired him. He became famous for his great proficiency and his talent for delving deeply into the Law, such that the gaon Rabbi Isser Zalmen Meltzer of Slutsk sometimes invited Reb Dovid to help him rule on matters of civil law in the rabbinic court there.

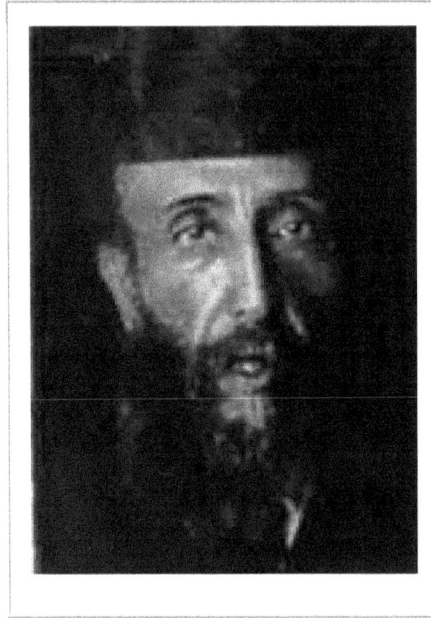

The late Rabbi Reb Shlomo Dov Landa, born in 5638
(1877-8) in Romanova - died in 5702 (1941-2),
served as rabbinate from 5687 (1926-7) in Starobin

Reb Dovid was distinguished for his nobility and outstanding character. He conducted his rabbinate with wisdom, prudence and utmost grace. His outward appearance also garnered respect. He was a tall man and cut an imposing figure. His home was always wide open to the needy.

According to the tradition of Starobin, then and always, no one was allowed to sell candles or yeast, for it was the customary right of the rabbi's family as part of his regular income. Of course, the rabbi himself was not involved; his wife, the rebbetzin, and his children took care of it. On Thursday evenings all the people of the town would stream to the rabbi's house to buy candles for their Sabbath blessing, and yeast for the challahs at the Sabbath meal, which most of them baked themselves.

On the eve of Yom Kippur, those who came to the Great Beis Medresh would stay awake all night, on their feet. Among them, of course, were Reb Dovid and his sons, who would read verses from Psalms. Around the middle of the night, Reb Dovid and his son Reb Moishe would study the entire Talmud tractate "Masekhet Yoma".

With the death of Rabbi Dovid Feinstein on 27 Tishrey 5688 (1927), the rabbinate in Starobin effectively ended. Rabbi Shleyma Landa, mentioned earlier, tried hard to fill the void and to protect Jewish values, but this ended when the Soviet government nationalized his horses and carriages, and he was arrested as a "bourgeois" and a reactionary. He was exiled to Siberia, and there all traces of him disappeared. (His son, Rabbi Grunam, was the son-in-law of the gaon Rabbi Peysakh Frank, and was one of the directors of Yeshivat haDarom in Rehovot, Israel).

Among the family of Rabbi Dovid Feinstein, of blessed memory, who perished, are the following:

His youngest son Yitzkhok, died while still in his prime. His son Rabbi Mordekhai, a Torah genius and a man of distinguished character, was the rabbi in Hrozov (Grozovo) and Shklov; he was exiled to Siberia and perished there. His son Rabbi Dov Ber, the sheykhet (shohet, or ritual slaughterer) in Starobin and Shemezova also died in Siberia. His son Rabbi Yankev and all his family perished in Riga, Latvia. His son-in-law, Rabbi Yisroel Shoel Yapin, the rabbi of Choslovitz, Smolavitsh, and Rechitsa (Rzeczyca), was in Latvia and perished there. May the Lord avenge their blood! (See Sefer Zikaron L'Yahadut Latvia, pages 391 and 406)

[Page 232]

Members of the Council of Rabbis in Lita (Lithuania, Latvia, and White Russia)
Rabbi Reb Yisroel Tankhum haCohen Fortman is standing in the first row, third from left to right

And may the following members of his family be blessed with long life: His grandson Rabbi Yekhiel-Mikhl Feinstein, the son of the above-mentioned Yitzkhok, who is presently in Tel-Aviv. His daughter Hanna, who is the wife of Rabbi Yitzkhok haLevi Smol in Chicago, U.S.A. One of his outstanding sons, the gaon Rabbi Moishe Feinstein, who was formerly the rabbi of Lyuban and is now in America. He is head of the Tiferes Yerusholayim Yeshiva in New York. He is one of the exceptional individuals, out of all the rabbis, who are accepted by every stripe of (religious) Jew in America. [Ed. note: Prior to his death in the 1980's, Rabbi Moishe Feinstein had become universally regarded as the single highest world authority on matters of Torah law of the Twentieth Century.] His wife, the rebbetzin Sima, the daughter of Rabbi Yankev the shoykhet of Lyuban, is renowned for her charity and kindness.

The Scholars and Yeshiva Pupils

Starobin was full of scholars, many of them with rabbinic ordination, qualified to teach, so much so that there was a standing joke in town: "Why is this shtetl called Starobin? It's because in Russian 'Sta-Rabin' means 'a hundred rabbis'." Nearly every youngster in Starobin who finished kheyder with a Gemora melamed (elementary level Talmud teacher) went on to Slutsk to complete his Talmud studies in Rabbi Nekhemia's "religious preparatory school", followed by Slutsk's renowned Eyts Chaim Yeshiva co-founded by the RYDBaZ (Ed.: see earlier reference; and Rabbi Isser Meltzer). From there they fanned out to the yeshivas of Slobodka, Mir and Telz (Telsiai), and the Khofetz Chaim Yeshiva in Radun.

At the beginning of this century, two rabbis – The "Brothers from Starobin" – were particularly well known. Yisroel Tankhum haCohen Fortman and his younger brother Shimshon Zelig both revealed a talent for preaching, even from their earliest years. They were the sons of Shimon the Melamed, one of the Gemora teachers of the town, a Jew who excelled in the clarity of his explanations.

Their mother, Henya Roshka, a mother of six boys, helped by selling fruits and vegetables, but after the death of her husband, the entire burden of supporting the family fell on her. Yisroel Tankhum and Shimshon Zelig were by then studying in various yeshivas away from Starobin. From time to time they would return home to give sermons in the synagogues and yeshivas of the nearby towns, for which they were paid. With these small sums they helped alleviate the burden on their mother. They continued their studies in the yeshivas of Mir and Radun, becoming famous as great scholars of Torah and as outstanding preachers. Whenever they came home for a festival or holy day, there was no limit to their mother's joy.

Now it happened that on market days she would be standing alone tending her shop. Peasants would enter in a flurry and, without her noticing, would surreptitiously snatch fruit from her shelves and slip it into their sacks. On one such occasion, a relative of hers happened to come into the shop and spot this happening. He told her about it, and asked: "Why do you stay here alone? Your sons are in town today, and certainly they would help you if you called them." At this she grew angry, and answered indignantly, "The fruit is mine and if the peasants are going to steal, let them steal. But my sons were given to me for safekeeping by my husband Shimon, and he did not entrust them to me in order for them to stand in my place in the shop."

[Page 233]

Rabbi Yisroel Tankhum haCohen Fortman became known afterwards as one of the outstanding rabbis of Lita (Lithuania, Latvia, and White Russia) in his capacity as rabbi of Shveksna and Zezmer (Ziezmariai). It was in Zezmer that he perished, with all the members of his family. His brother Rabbi Shimshon Zelig haCohen Fortman became known as a pre-eminent interpreter of Torah, and served as rabbi in the towns of Kopatkevichi, Osipovichi, and eventually, Far Rockaway, New York, during which time he was training students in homiletics at the Toyro veDaas Yeshiva of Brooklyn, New York. He died on 27 Shvat 5711 (1951).

Rabbi Reb Zelig Fortman

In the course of the First World War, most of the yeshivas of Greater Russia moved to the towns of Ukraine. By the summer of 5678 (1918), as the First World War was close to ending, Russia became calm for a short while, until the outbreak of the civil war that sparked the Russian Revolution. At that point, some of the Starobin students at the Mir Yeshiva, which was then situated in Poltava, Ukraine, returned home temporarily.

Rabbi Dimta met with them and told them that in Starobin there was a distinguished group of young students being taught by Rabbi Fortman and that it was important to hurry and move them to the big yeshiva before the roads became obstructed. Traveling from Starobin to Poltava was beyond the ability of these young boys on their own, particularly in those days of political agitation and fear. But they rose above the hardships, and accompanied by Rabbi Chaim Vetsherebin managed to make it to the Mir Yeshiva in Poltava.

A few years after the war, the yeshiva returned from Poltava to Mir in Poland. The head of the yeshiva, the gaon Rabbi Eliyezer Yehuda Finkel, told me that the group of boys from Starobin deserve utmost credit, for if not for them the Mir Yeshiva would not have survived. Remember well the names of those boys:

Zusman Tiroshkin, who died young at the Mir Yeshiva in 5685 (1924-25).

Herzl Domnitz, who perished with all the members of his family in the town of Stoypts (Stolbtsy) close to Mir.

Avrohom Pasmanik, the son of Hirshke the Shoemaker and his righteous wife, both mentioned earlier, who was the rabbi in the town of Rafalovka in Wolyn (Volynhia), and who died with all his family and members of his congregation. His younger brother Mordkha, who was an outstanding talent in his own right, was one of the students of the gaon Rabbi Shimon Shkop, and died on the Day of Slaughter in Kletsk.

Tsvi Hirsh, the son of Rabbi Moishe Ahron and Hinda Tsirin-Tehilim, an outstanding personality in Torah, wisdom, and in character, who was the rabbi in Kovaliev-Polesia, and was killed there. May God avenge their blood!

Yitzkhok Chaim Krasnitsh, presently in Jerusalem in the Council of Torah Scholars of the Rabbi of Brisk (Brest-Litovsk).

And the youngest in the group, the writer of these lines

There were three other boys, on a higher scholastic level than the aforementioned, who studied in Starobin and from there had also gone on to Poltava:

Yoysef Grozovsky-Rozovsky, known as "The Prodigy of Uzda (Byelorussia)." He later became a rabbi and teacher on the Council of the gaon Rabbi Chaim Oyzer Grodzinski in Vilna. When the Nazis entered Vilna, he fled to Russia, where he disappeared.

An article under the authorship of a "Rabbi R.Y.B.M." – the initials of "Rozovski, Yoysef ben Mordkha"—was included in Sefer haYovel [The Jubilee Book) of the gaon Rabbi Shimon Shkop, and published in Vilna, 5696 (1935-36).

Shimon Berenshteyn-Shapiro, the rabbi of Lipovka-Vilna, where he perished. (See "Yerushalayim d'Lita b'Meri u-b'Shoah" by Dr. M. Dvorzhitsky, p. 278). He was a Biblical scholar and wrote many original interpretations of the Torah from his young years on. His article on religious law, based on "Shi'budad'Reb Nossn" ("The Subjugation of Reb Nossn"), was printed in the collection "Ohel Toyro" ("Tent of the Law") by the gaon Rabbi Yekhiel-Mikhl Rabinovitch; his three-part article on "Tomei sheNikhnas laMikdosh" ("The Unclean Who Enters the Temple") appeared in the collection "KnessesYisroel," volumes 12, 13, and 14, published in Vilna, 5692 (1931-32). Grozovsky and Berenshteyn were the brilliant students of the gaon Rabbi Moishe Feinstein (mentioned earlier, in detail), who brought them from Uzdato Starobin. May God avenge their blood!

Yehoyshua Dovid Kustanowitz-Povarsky from Lyuban, author of the book "Yeshuas Dovid" ("The Salvation of David"), which deals with "Khoyshen Mishpot" (the fourth part of Joseph Karo's massive and seminal summary of Jewish law, the Shulkhn Orukh), published in Belogorye (Ed.: possibly Bilgoray), 5693 (1932-33). He is presently one of the heads of the Ponevezh Yeshiva in Bnei Brak, Israel.

Another who was an excellent Bible scholar was Yehuda Leyb Rakhmilovitsh. He studied in the yeshivas of Slutsk, Shklov and Amtzislov (Mtsislavl). A relative of Dr. Nakhmen Rakhmilovitsh of Kovna, Lithuania, he himself was from Starobin, and was the rabbi of the town of Ivatsevichi (Iwacewicze), where he perished.

Meanwhile the Soviet government was growing stronger. It closed the institutions of Jewish religious education and wiped out all Jewish community life. With that, the glory of Starobin was lost forever.

In the United States there are many families who came from Starobin. Among the better known ones are the following: Rabbi Avrohom Chinitz, and his sons, who also served in the rabbinate. His brother, Rabbi Dovid Chinitz-Chazanovitsh, who was the head of the Ostrog (Oistroh) Yeshiva in Wolyn, and who perished there. Rabbi Meyir Chinitz, whose melodious renderings of Jewish song was well known in the provinces of Lithuania, Latvia, White Russia, and Poland, and who served as cantor in Kovel, Lida, Nesvizh and Slutsk. Crowds flocked to hear his chanting and prayers. In his last days he served as cantor in Tshernigov. Rabbi Shakhna Chinitz served as rabbi in the Khevras Shas b'Talmud Toyro Tiferes haGRA (a rabbinical school named for the Vilna Gaon, Rabbi Eliyohu of Vilna) in Brownsville (Brooklyn, N.Y.). He died on 29 Iyar 5690 (1930). Others include: the soyfer (religious scribe) Mr. Chaim Lifshitz (Ed.: possibly Lipshitz), and his brothers – Rabbi Yankev Lifshitz, the shoykhet (ritual slaughterer), and Rabbi Binyomin Lifshitz – all grandsons of Rabbi Zelig (son of Z'ev) Chinitz, one of the distinguished individuals at the Beis Medresh on the edge of town; Rabbi Yitzkhok Yankev Mendelson (Ed.: possibly Mendelsohn or Mendelssohn) and his brother Simkha (Felix), who was one of the great Reform rabbis; the Hebrew writer Aharon Domnitz in Baltimore, son of Rabbi Asher the Melamed (religious teacher); and the teacher Dov-Ber Brodetsky in Chicago

* * *

Before the Second World War we had heard reports from Starobin that the Soviet government had drained the swamps in the area and had illuminated the town with electricity.

[Page 234]

But we also knew full well that it had drained the lifeblood out of our magnificent community and had extinguished the last sparks of the Torah's light in our little town until nothing remained.

A group of natives of Starobin in the Mir Yeshiva

Seated from right to left: Tsvi Hirsh Tsirin, Yitzhak Chaim Krasnitz, Rabbi Chaim Vecherebin, David Kostenovitz - Fobarsky and Hirsh Chinitz
Standing: Chaim Lifshitz, Chaim Grunam Landa, Nissan Waxman, Yekhiel-Mikhl Feinstein and Yerahmiel Lifshitz

(photographed in Mir, 17th of Adar B, 5688)

When the brutal soldiers of Hitler, may his name be blotted out, arrived in Starobin, they found only lonely shadows in the form of human beings; their soul, their essence, had already been taken from them. When the murderers brought these vestiges of humanity to their deaths, they did not destroy the mighty spirit of our beloved shteteleh, which was still alive and vibrant in the wings that carried her children to scattered shores, and which exhorted them to carry on their great inheritance and to perpetuate Starobin's name for all generations.

Postscript from the Editors of the Slutsk Yizkor Book

[The accompanying Hebrew letter was the last one received by Rabbi Yoysef Leyb Kaplan, from his father Reb Moshe Nomi's (Moishe Chaim Kapchitz) in Starobin. For reasons that are well known, the forwarded letter was long in getting to us and could not be included in the Hebrew section of the Yizkor Book. [Ed. note: The Yizkor Book was completed around the time of the Cuban Missile Crisis, a possible explanation for the disruption in mail service.] We have decided to break format and include it in the Yiddish section, because of its importance; it provides a last insight into the life both of the great Torah scholar, Moshe Nomi's, and of Starobin Jews in general, in the second decade of this century.

"With God's blessing "On the fourth day (Ed.: possibly, Wednesday) of Seder BiN'soa HaAron (Ed.: probably following the Feast of Shavuot) 5686 (1926)

"Great blessings and success and peace to my dear son and esteemed rabbi and teacher Yoysef Leyb, and the members of your household. May all of them merit God's blessing and may you draw nakhas (parental pleasure) from their accomplishments.

"First off, I want to let you know that last week I received your lovely letter, together with the lovely writings from my wonderful grandchildren. A heartfelt thank-you to all.

"What I will say to you, my children, is that your letters give life to my soul. I can't describe to you my joy upon reading your letter, for my soul longs to see you and to know how you are. May the Master of Rewards enrich you for your kindness.

"It will not be a great surprise for you to learn of a great dread that I have been feeling. I will tell you my story and then I will take final stock of its results: What is there that remains of all the efforts and toil of my life in this world? – First, concerning my son B.: it is something like two years that I have not heard from him, yet I have heard through others that he has wealth and property. I'll tell you the truth, I get no nakhas from his wealth. Thank God I don't have any need for his support or his gifts. Over my son D., I have anguish in full measure, for he has been cast out to a foreign land and cannot return home, and there he remains naked and penniless. From my son Elya I've experienced only pain till now. His wife fell ill about three years ago and he has gone into great debt, to the point where he has had to sell his livestock and fine clothing, and ended up in prison. He signed over his store with all its machinery and tools, and was left idle, earning nothing, until I managed to gather together 100 silver rubles, which I gave him to buy a machine so he could get back to work.

Despite all that, he remains deeply in debt. Who knows when he will crawl out from under his debts, for the outlay is great and the income minimal. The businessmen of our town have all become "have-nots" (Ed. note: literally, "descenders"; probably a biblical reference to the Israelites, Jacob, his sons and entourage, who were "descenders" into Egypt for handouts when drought enveloped their land). In Starobin, Elya is not alone in his situation; there are three others trying to patch things back together. (Ed. note: the phrase in Hebrew is, literally, "there are three other quilters." Either this is figurative, hence the above interpretation, or it is literal, in which case it refers to Elya's specific line of business, and his possible competitors; the Soviets' "New Economic Plan", initiated by Lenin, was still begrudgingly allowing such activity.)

"After all the accounting, I am left with nothing from all the fruits of my entire life's work. Only when I receive a letter from you do I experience any contentment, and for that reason I beg of you and of my lovely grandchildren – may they live long lives – not to hold back from doing the kindness of looking in on me with your letters, and describing to me how your studies are progressing, how your daily lives are faring. And may God grant you all the strength to learn and to do God's will with a full heart.

"Be aware, my dear son, that every day, up until now, I had looked forward perhaps to be able to travel to the Holy Land, or at least to America, so that the following words might be fulfilled for me: "And Joseph will set his hand upon thine eyes." (Ed. note: This quotation is now a second reference in the letter to the biblical story of Jacob and his son Joseph, and the descent of the Israelites into Egypt (Gen. 46:4). Its inclusion is poignant, for like Jacob, Moshe Nomi's has a son Joseph (Yoysef) whom he has not seen for a lifetime. In the quotation, God is giving comfort to a dispirited Jacob by promising him that he will see his son Joseph before he dies, and that Joseph will perform the tender and respectful act of placing his hand over Jacob's eyes upon the latter's death, as has been the custom from the time of Jacob and Joseph, and earlier. Through this quotation, Moshe Nomi's is revealing that, like the biblical Jacob, he has been longing only to be taken to his own son Joseph in that faraway land, that he might see him once more before he dies.)

"But now I understand that my hope was a deception and that I must remain in this defiled land without any mainstay. To obtain a "pass" (Ed.: probably "passport"), one needs to pay 300 silver rubles. My strength is diminishing daily, and my eyes are growing weak. After Passover I traveled to an eye doctor in Slutsk who did a number of tests and then told me I had no need of eyeglasses. Instead he gave me eyedrops. It has been four weeks that I have been using them, daily, and I see no improvement from them.

In addition, my speech has become disjointed and my voice weak, so that only with great effort can I stand before the congregation chanting from the Torah. There is no one to replace me.

" 'It is not given to man to know the day of his...' If it takes a full month until you receive news from here, by then the Days of Ultimate Judgment will have passed, and there will have been no one to plead my case (on high). Therefore I lay my supplication before you, that starting now you study a chapter of Mishna each day and lead synagogue prayers at least once a day – provided that, if possible, this mitzvah would not prevent other mourners from performing their own filial duties. (Ed. note: Judaism maintains that pious acts performed by the child of a deceased, such as the study of holy books or the leading of public prayer, reflect positively on the deceased and increase his or her chances of being judged favorably by the One True Judge. Timing is crucial for the deceased, inasmuch as stages of progress in his or her fate in the World-to-Come parallel the stages of mourning by those he or she has left behind: the first week [Shiva], the first month [Shloshim], the first year [completion of daily Kaddish].)

"Your father, who blesses you with every goodness – Moishe Chaim Kapchitz"

[Exactly four years after Reb Moshe Nomi's wrote this letter, he went to his eternal rest, on 15 Sivan 5690 (Spring, 1930) and was buried in the town cemetery. Reb Moshe's wife, Sora Rivka bas Moishe Dov, died four years later, on 9 Teyves 5694 (Winter 1933-4). Upon their headstones were engraved loving and respectful Hebrew inscriptions, sent by their son Rabbi Yoysef Leyb Kaplan, Pittsburgh, U.S.A.

The Three

by Raphael Rivin

(In memory of friends who had fallen and did not get to Israel)

Translated by Irit Dolgin

We were a united group of friends, the children of public activists intoxicated by the social discontent of the years 1914-15. The love for Zion, for the people of Israel and for the freedom of the working men, demanded us for action. We were engaged in selling Shekels and stamps of the Keren Kayemet LeYisrael [Jewish National Fund], in collection of money for the Keren Kayemet LeYisrael – in the evening of Yom Kippur and before the reading of the Book of Esther on Purim, in spreading the Hebrew language etc.

The first of the group of three was our unforgettable friend Eliezer Fortman, or as we used to call him "Layser Ha'ani Rashkes". He was orphaned from his father when he was only an infant, and at young age he quit his studies in the *Cheder* and became a tailor's apprentice with Gronim, his brother, the most famous tailor in the town. But this lasted only for a couple of years. His two older brothers, who were Yeshiva students, excelled in their studies, especially Israel, who became a famous rabbi in Lithuania. He excelled in his *Drashas* [a homiletic method of biblical exegesis] and he would teach in the great Synagogue when he was still very young, approximately fourteen years old, and he captivated with the pleasantness of his speech and with his explanations to all his listeners, who came especially to hear his *Drashas*.

His second brother Selig, who later became a rabbi in America, was younger than Israel, and he also was one of the most famous students in the Yeshiva. They influenced their young brother, Leyser, who was a child born to elderly parents, that he joined them and accepted upon himself the burden of the *Torah*. This is how from being a tailor's apprentice he became a yeshiva student. Layserke had many talents, a smooth tongue and a pleasant voice, he was intelligent and had sense of humor. He was good at making the time our group spent together pleasant, with his stories and conversations, his jokes, and with his songs. A special bond was forged between the two of us, because we were studying together and because I, too, was hit by the bitter destiny that he experienced when he was young.

We were the first among the preachers for the Zion and for action of settling the Land of Israel. In our house, the place of the group's meetings, we would usually stay up until very late at night, engaged in friendly conversations and in gatherings for the purpose of the *Tanakh* studies and readings.

[Page 235]

This happened at the outbreak of the First World War, we came back from *yeshivas* and stayed in town. We published a local newspaper called "Der ve Eker", for a short period. In the beginning of January 1915, Layserke was recruited to the army. I remember his letters, in which he warned me to avoid the army at any cost and even to become a cripple, because, in all likelihood, he suffered profoundly of the bad treatment of the Jewish solders in the Russian army. I could not accept this idea and I too was recruited to the army. I haven't heard of him since. He probably fell in a battle or was captured and his traces were lost. May his memory be blessed!

The second in the group was our friend Moshe-Herzl, a talented young man. During his childhood and his first teenage years he was sloppy and inflexible. Suddenly, he left the yeshiva at the "Karnayim" Synagogue in Slutsk and transferred to a secular school for Jewish boys. We envied him especially for wearing a special hat and a leather belt with a shining buckle. His studies at the school did not last long. After a year, Moshe-Herzl along with a couple of students from our town, appeared and joined the Amzislav Yeshiva, which was in the Mogilev region. He was a member of the commission of the "Zion Youngsters" in our town. He was also one of the first amateur actors in the drama class we established.

And suddenly, another deviation in his path: he devoted himself to trade and invested all his energy and time in it. His life ended in a tragic way. With the retreat of the Polish army from our town, and due to his fear of the Russian army, he and two of his friends, run away, and on their way he was captured and murdered by the "Balchovzim" gang.

The third, the youngest of the group, Yankale, a son of Rabbi Mordechay Margolin (a butcher and *chazzan* [a Jewish cantor] in our town), was an intelligent and agile guy. He joined the group in the later years and was the first of the group to get to the Land of Israel in the year 1921, with the third Aliyah. As all the pioneers, he worked in building roads for one year. However, he could not withstand it, and so he came back to Poland and settled in the town of Baranovich.

In all likelihood, he was killed with the rest of our brothers and sisters during the Holocaust.

First row (right to left): R. Rivin, Y. Margolin, Chana Feinstein, Chaim Zirin
Second row: Chaim Krizitzki
Third row (right to left): M. Bernetz, Malka Reznik, Fruma Dolgin, Mordechai Rubnitz

Eliezer Portman

Doubts

by I. N. Adler

I was one of the students of the Great Yeshiva ("HaKibbutz") in Slutsk, the youngest of the group, who "peeked" and was "infected" by the "doubts' worm". The question "to where" was burning in my mind. And this time, with the evening twilight – and I am, all of me, confused and excited, amid the turmoil of physical and spiritual doubts – I got up and escaped my little room and turned my steps toward the road, the place of the teenagers' hikes, and suddenly I found myself standing next to the inn of the wagon-owners, who would come here from towns in the vicinity.

Every Monday, since I came to study at the Slutsk Yeshiva, I would go to the inn to meet with Yiche the-wagon-owner, who brought me to Slutsk. He was a tall Jew, broad-in-shoulders, he wore high boots, and carried a grey leather bag on his upper back, because he was an agent for the grocers who had connections with the wholesalers and the governmental bank in Slutsk.

Then, in my eyes, this Yiche was a symbol of my strong longing to my village. From time to time, he would give me a paternal treatment. In answer to my question: "Reb. Yiche, maybe you have a letter for me, maybe?", he would open his leather bag, rummage through it, and take out a squashed piece of paper, he would hand it over to me and say: "Here you are, a note from your father".

Sometimes he would take out a coin of 10 kopeikas [10 pennies] from his pocket, and would say: "This is also from your father". This time, when I came there to see him, I did not find him. And a young wagon-owner was standing on his lot, ready to take off to Starobin. I asked him if he had a spare seat in his wagon. And, in an instant, I climbed up and found myself underneath a worn out and patched piece of stretched fabric, which was not comparable to the magnificent piece of stretched fabric of reb. Yiche.

With dawn, following a night long ride, we arrived to Starobin. The wagon owner stayed at the small market square for a while.

[Page 236]

Starobin natives in the Mir Yeshiva, 5688 [1928]

Standing (right to left): Tzvi Hirsch Zirin, Hirsch Chinitz
Sitting: Yitzhak Chaim Krasnitz, Nissan Wachsman, Avraham Posmanik

I got out of the wagon's covering, frozen and shivering of the night's chilliness. I glanced at the meager and low-rise houses around the market. With feelings of pain of loneliness and orphanhood, I turned my steps toward *Beit-HaMidrash*. To my surprise, I found there the relatives of Zalman from Igumen, a yeshiva student who was older than I am, and who also turned up in Starobin. They introduced me to the beadle, who arranged for me: the weekly Torah portion "The Weekdays", a celebration of the Holy Sabbath in houses of various house owners, and also a place for a night's lodging.

On one of these days, this Zalman "clung" to me, and told me of Reb. Zerach the paramedic, the only doctor in Starobin, whose house was the meeting place of the sages.

Not a long time afterwards, Zalman brought me to the house of Reb. Zerah the paramedic, and introduced me to him and his two daughters, Bluma and Reizel, who were the "pharmacists and the cooks" of Reb. Zerach, who at the time was a widower and blind.

I was charmed by his majestic appearance, his persuading voice and his fine words; everything about him spoke fatherhood, intelligence and respect. As to his daughters, Bluma the oldest was modest, pleasant looking and everything about her said yearning to life, whereas Reizel – a soft-looking, pale and delicate girl – was busy working in the pharmaceutical room of Reb. Zerach, the only one in Starobin.

One time, shortly before sunset, I was sitting at the Reb. Zerach's table, and saw the "Book of the Khazars" "The Kuzari"] was open before him. Reb. Zerach began by saying: "You must have heard of Rabbi Yehuda Halevi [1075-1141 a Spanish Jewish physician, poet and philosopher], the poet who wrote the poem "Zion *HaLo Tishali LiShlom Asirayich*" "Zion, thou art anxious for thy captives"], and Rabbi Yehuda Halevi is also the author of the "Book of the Khazars". In this book you will also find answers to all your doubts. Reb. Zerach spoke very concisely of the Khazars, of the King Bulan, who converted to Judaism, of the essay "The Kuzari"], and of the Hasdai Shaprut [Abu Yusuf ben Yitzhak ben Ezra – 915-990, a Spanish Jewish physician, diplomat and patron of science]. He had spoken and handled me the book, in the manner of an outstandingly talented educator, and asked me to read to him the letter of "Rabbi Hasdai ben Ezra to the king of "Al-Kozar". The following day we completed the reading of the above letter and began reading the "Answer of the Khazar King Joseph the Turk-may".

The tale of the Kisimanic Sage was engraved in the tablet of my heart, and became a balm and cure to my soul. When we finished reading the letters, we began reading the core of the book. I admit and confess, the words of the essay were not entirely comprehensible to me, despite the pedagogic explanations of Reb. Zerach. Yet, throughout the discussion, I saw myself standing beside the essay, praying for its wellbeing, so that it, God forbid, will not fail in its language, and so that the peacefulness of its voice will reach King Bulan, even though I had a definite feeling, that this essay does not need my prayer, and that all its words were logical, solid and spoke the *Torah* truth.

Not many days have passed and the doubts had disappeared from my heart, as smoke is driven away – and we haven't yet accomplished a third of the book.

In honorable and precious memory of Reb. Zerach the paramedic of Starobin, who wrapped the wounds of my heart with great love, experienced hand and fatherly kindness.

May his memory be blessed!

Memories

by Raphael Rivin

Translated by Irit Dolgin

Full of longings and grief, I reminisce of the Jews of my town Starobin, somewhere in Belarus, on the edge of Polesie, a place of forests, lakes and swamps. I would like to commemorate the souls of the martyrs, who were destroyed by the enemy, with its crossing the borders of Belarus. It imprisoned them in a slaughter house and sentenced them to death by burning, and as a sacrifice their pure souls had risen up to heaven. We must commemorate those who died before the Holocaust as well, whose sons and daughters are among the pioneers and builders of the State of Israel.

In my memory, I see lovable and admirable characters in their simplicity, honesty and innocence. Here is the rabbi of the town, Rabbi David Feinstein, whose face radiated purity and innocence, God-fearing and people loving, humble and pleasant to people under his leadership. Rabbi Reb. Shlomo Landau followed him [as the rabbi of the town], and he was great in Torah, pleasant in singing *Zemirot* [Jewish hymns] and a convivial person. As his predecessor, he also cared about the people of his community.

A prominent character, the lion of the group, was Reb. Mordechai Margolin, or as he was called "Motel der shochat" [Motel the butcher], who was a butcher and a permanent leader in the town. He would please the ears of the congregants with his singing, especially during the High Holidays. He was a devoted activist, a community leader, he was attentive to the spirit of the young people, and in every public deed – a devoted partner to us, the young activists.

A character respectable and admirable by all the townspeople, from the eldest to the youngest, was Reb. Moshe Nemis, a beadle of the Great Synagogue,

[Page 237]

of whom people would whisper, that he is one of the hidden *tzadiks* [righteous ones], and whoever he will bless, will be blessed, and he had chosen the profession of the beadle, so that to preserve the importance and the dignity of this occupation.

Reb. Abraham Nachman Kravchik the educator, first of his profession, punctilious and strict regarding the rules of the accentuation of the penultimate [next-to-last] and ultimate stresses etc. His clear explanations of the *Tanakh* and his heartwarming melody fascinated us. His house was the "lodge" of the "Zionists", and he, the elderly was active with the youngsters, participated in festive ceremonies and the balls of *Hanukah, Purim* etc. He was pleased and proud that his students were the leaders of the *Tehiya* [revival] movement in the town and that they were also leaders in the community matters.

Among the most important personalities was also my uncle Reb. Yosef Shlimovich [or Shleimovitsch], the first *Gabbai* [a person who assists in the running of a synagogue and ensures that the needs are met] of the Great Synagogue, and one of the most honorable people in the town; he loved Zion with all his soul, he sometimes came to out gatherings and took part in the discussions as well. He was killed somewhere in Minsk, with his son Shalom, who did not want to leave him. My righteous aunt Rivka, was fortunate to die before the Holocaust.

My uncle "Yiche", a well-known personality – was a trader, the son of Reb. Abraham HaZaken [Abraham the elderly] (he was the rabbi of the Jews of the Eretz-Israel Street), his house was the meeting place of the town peddlers; from this family people would receive advance payment on account of merchandise that will be brought here. My uncle Yiche was a convivial person, he would support the ones who needed help. The arm of the enemy reached him far away from his home and from his modest wife – aunt Genia. Outside Starobin, in an old house, covered by a straw roof, lived Avrahamel Leibeks [or Leibaks] and his wife Beila, and their son, of whom they took pride, who dedicated with his entire soul and entity to the studies of the Torah.

The visits of Reb. Kalman HaMelamed – whose son made Aliyah – were unforgettable, and he would come to my place from another part of the town to show me the letters of his son. When he read his letters to me, one could feel that he was tasting the flavor of the Land of Israel and smelled its odor.

A hidden love and longings are awakening in me, when I recall the house in which our family lived for many years and the people of the House of Moshe-Aharon "Der Shizkarner", which was named after his occupation. During the days of the snow melting on the evening before *Pessah*, the Slutz River, in its pride, would devour the pillars of the cowshed. He [Moshe-Aharon] was modest and naïve and his wife Hinda was a witty woman, all her sayings and stories were spiced by a common people's humor. Chaim-Leib the grocer and his wife Alte were busy with their trade with the villages. I did not forget his pleasant way of praying, and that he was a representative of the public on *Sabbaths* and Festive Days.

How can I not mention my father? Ephraim son of "Zelig *Der Sofer-Stam*" [a Jewish scribe who can transcribe *Torah* scrolls and other religious writings such as those used in *Tefillin* and *Mezuzot*], who was well-known in our town and its vicinity. Especially among the great in *Torah*, who would always be meticulous to buy the scrolls for *Tefillin* in the handwriting of my grandfather Rabbi Zelig. He would avoid from talking about nonsense, and would always send my grandmother Beile to negotiate. My father was a public activist, he established associations for reciprocal assistance, and helped the *SHaDaRs* [acronym of *SHelichah DeRachmanah* – a rabbinical emissary sent to collect charity funds], who came from *yeshivas* in the exile and in the Land of Israel. He loved Eretz-Israel and the holy language with all his heart.

I began reading Hebrew books from a very young age. Though in the eyes of very observant people it was considered improper, but my father did not object to that. At the same time, he was zealous as to the learning of the tradition, and wanted with all his heart that I persist with the yeshiva studies.

It is an honor and a duty for me to commemorate my mother Alte-Ephraim's. This is how people used to call her; she was fortunate to make *Aliyah*.

Among those who were not fortunate to come to the Land of Israel, but were drawn to it with all their souls, the personality of Israel-Leibke the shoemaker stands out in his greatness, innocence and his love for Zion. With immense excitement and with an open mouth, he would listen to the words of the *maggid* [preacher], or an advocate in the matters of Eretz-Israel; it seems to me that I too, watching him, was infected with immense love to the life's goal I have chosen for myself. I remember how offended he was when sometimes, during the collection of donations, we wanted to pass over him; he would follow us, run to us and reproach us for insulting him. His donation was above his ability.

Avraham Ostrovsky, or as he was called in the town "Avrahamel Elinkas"

Reb Avraham Nachman Kravchik of
Starobin

Reb Yosef Shlimovich. The Gabbai Rishon of the
Great Synagogue of Starobin.

[Page 238]

of the adult Zionists joined us, the youngsters, in year 1917 promptly after the first revolution.

Despite him being busy and occupied with trade and taking care of his family, he was dedicated to the Zionist work with all his heart and soul. His love for Zion had no limits, and he also served as a treasurer of the Zionist branch in the town.

He was loved and respected in the town by everyone.

Our town Starobin was blessed by fires, almost every year there were fires. We used to count the dates of the years according to a certain fire that began from a house of so-and-so on the street so-an-so. The count of happy times and the disasters was also related to the fires. One fire broke out on the "Great Sabbath", a short while after the *Shacharit* [Morning] Prayer service, only eight months after the great fire that preceded it. The fire is spreading and swallows everything in the blink of an eye, and in a little while it will reach the Great Synagogue. Reb. Moshe Nemis left his house and the concerns of evacuation to his wife, so that she would deal with taking out the house-wares, and saved whatever possible. And he was encircling the Synagogue, while holding a big rod to the head of which a red kerchief was tied, and whispering words of *sgulah* [supernatural cure], in order to stop the approaching fire, but to no avail. The Synagogue caught fire as well.

The *"Zionistishe Fabric"* is favorably remembered. We, the youngsters, volunteered to bake the *Matzas* [unleavened bread made from flour and water, eaten on Passover] free of charge, for the poor of the town. The preparations and the baking works themselves were done voluntarily. The *matzas* were baked by us at the *"Zionistishe Fabric"*, and, of course, without flour there is no *matzas*, so we obtained the Passover flour as well.

Peaceful was the town's life before the eruption of the revolution, much more peaceful than the waves of the Slutz River, which devoured the houses of the town. The social life was concentrated, mainly, among the walls of the *Batei Midrash* [House of Interpretation, or Houses of learning], during most of the day, except for the hours that were set for the studies of the *Mishnas, Gmara, "Chayei Adam", "Ein Yaakov"* [a compilation of all the Aggadic material in the *Talmud* together with commentaries] etc. If a quarrel erupted between individuals, or between families, or between groups, this would also, usually, take place among the walls of the house of prayer, especially during the Holidays, Sabbaths, and *Moed* Days [intermediate days of certain Jewish festivals]. A delay in reading the *Torah* was the only way to pave a road toward a solution and compromise.

The *"prizivnikes"*, the ones recruited to the army, demanded compensation from those who were dismissed, and if they could not get it in a peaceful way, they would suddenly appear prior to the taking out of the Book of *Torah* and would cry out and announce their demands with noise and tumult. After exchanging arguments on the subject, that lasted for a while, the dispute would be settled, with the intervention of the best people of the town.

The lasting peace in the public life and on the Jewish street was disturbed especially by the youngsters in years 1904-5, the years of the revolutionary unrest. Generally, they would gather in places hidden from eyes of many people, so that the authorities, God forbid, will not find out. There were plenty of such hidden places, since the vicinity of the town was blessed with forests. Among the bushes and the needles of the pine trees, the propagandists preached to freedom and liberty, and to improvement of the condition of a worker. They spoke heatedly against the craftsmen in the town, most of whom were abjectly poor as well, who exploited their apprentices and workers. They also emitted words of denigration and vexation toward the Master of the Universe [God] and the czar.

The town accepted the revolution in the year 1917 as an unbelievable thing, and many would ask in a whisper: is it possible that they took off the Cesar and all his entourage? People were afraid to pronounce it out load. At first public gatherings they would want to finish with the accepted hymn, the Marseillaise, but did not know it, until a savior was found – "Reuben der wagon-owner", a muscular Jew, who at the time, was one of the leaders of the revolutionists in the town. He was the one who put himself to danger in the days of the First Revolution, and dared to publicly announce the rejection of the authority, and he obviously was punished for that: he was incarcerated and penalized to exile outside the area of the town for a couple of years. He stayed far away among political exiles, learned the hymn from them, and now saved the situation.

Reb Moshe Aharon Zirin.
Born in 1868 and died in 1923.

Reb Mordechai Margolin.
The prayer leader and shochet in Starobin.

[Page 239]

While in all the cities and towns different Zionist organizations had risen: Jewish Labour Bund, the United Jewish Socialist Workers, *Poalei Tziyon Smol* "Workers of Zion Left-wing" – movement of Marxist

Zionist Jewish workers], our town was blessed by them as well. The Zionist Organization [*HaHistadrut HaTzionit*] was the dominant on the Jewish street. Starobin, that was stagnant throughout all its years of existence – except for the disputes over the appointment of that or another rabbi – had changed, cultural clubs were opened, there were heated debates, and attempts to convince one another. It seems to me that everything derived from people's internal faith in the righteousness of their views. After the Soviet Revolution, a small number of people were fortunate to make *Aliyah*, a bigger part immigrated to the United States. Many were scattered along the U.S.S.R., and of them only small number of individuals came back to the destroyed town.

Of all the past only memories have remained, which become more and more blurred. I am afraid that there will be no one remained to say: "We suffer a great loss for those who are lost and whose replacement cannot be found" [a saying in memory of a deceased person].

May the words I have put into writing become an eternal memory to my town and its dear and unforgettable people.

Title on the upper part the photograph, above the Star of David (in Hebrew):
The National Youth Zionist Fraction the Youth of Zion in Starobin

Dated: 4th Iyar, 5679, [May 4th, 1919].

People on the photograph:

First line (from right to left):
1. Yaakov Marmur
2. Zusia Kaplan
3. Breina-Rachel Pasmanik
4. Yaakov Rodgon
5. Chaya-Leah Rubanich/ Rubnitz
6. Leah Schwerin
7. Feige-Leah Rubanich/ Rubnitz
8. Reuven Rubanich/ Rubnitz
9. Yitzhak Rapaport
10. Aharon Yachnich/ Yachnitz

Second line (from right to left):
1. Kayle/Kaila Dolgin
2. Rachel Marmur
3. Chaya Dolgin
4. Chanah-Rachel Domnitz
5. Sarah Sadowsky/ Sadovsky
6. Sarah Chinitz
7. Kayle/Kaila Chinitz
8. Yaakov Feder
9. Shimshon Chinitz
10. Herzl Dolgin
11. Avraham Margolin

Third line (from right to left):
1. Natan Shlimovich/ Shleimovitsch

2. Shabtai Sadowsky/ Sadovsky
3. Shime-Rachel Kriwitzky/Krivitsky
4. Rachel-Leah Rapaport
5. Chanah Feinstein
6. Mordechai Brantz
7. Leah Rubanich/ Rubnitz
8. Aharon Duchovich/ Dukovich
9. Mordechai Strubinsky
10. L. Chinitz
11. Yerachmiel Duchovich/ Dukovich

Fourth line (from right to left):
1. Henie Shusterman
2. Feigl Chinitz
3. Shimke Schwerin
4. Hinde Chinitz
5. Chaya-Geeta/ Gita Chinitz
6. Shaina/Sheina Zarenin
7. Asterman
8. Rapaport

Fifth line (from right to left):
1. Avraham Domnitz
2. Berl Brodetsky
3. Chaya Domnitz
4. Yaakov Domnitz
5. Mordechai Rubanich/ Rubnitz
6. Raphael Rivin

[Page 239]

The Partisans

(From the book "Jewish Partisans of Eastern Europe" by Moshe Kaganovich)

Translated by Irit Dolgin

In February 1943 the Germans initiated a pursuit over the concentrations of partisans in the vicinity of towns Starobin, Zhitkovitz [Zhitkovich], Hlusk. Hundreds of villages in the forests' areas, in which the partisans were staying, were completely burned. In several of the villages they assembled all the population in buildings and set those buildings on fire from every direction.

After encountering with many hardships and dangers, the survivors reached the vicinity of towns Glusk, Starobin, Zhitkovitz, Bobruisk, and were integrated into the various partisan divisions that were operating there.

Moshe Shulman (Lenin) had risen due to his fighting initiative and his bravery, from the rank of a private to the rank of a commander of the sappers' group, and was later appointed the commander of a company [a military unit], in the Russian Battalion "Shwiakov" (Starobin area, Glusk).

Almost all Jewish partisans, who were part of the dozens of battalions that acted in the areas of Glusk and Starobin, were Jews from the towns Lenin and Pogost-Zagorsky.

[Page 240]

Staryye Dorogi
(Staryya Darohi, Belarus)
53°02' 28°16'

About the Town
by Ch. N.

Between virgin forests and untamed surroundings, there was an isolated village in a concealed corner by the name of Staryye Dorogi. When the railway tracks from Daraganovo were laid, a train station by the name of Staryye Dorogi was built and the intention was that a settlement be established at the crossroads between ancient, desolate and forsaken roads.

Jews from Minsk by the names of Poliak-Weisebaum founded a sawmill there for the milling of planks and plywood and a vibrant and busy lifestyle soon emerged in this place.

On both sides of the railway track a blooming settlement of 200 families sprang up. Houses were built, shops opened, inns, a small community of "Mitnagdim"[1] and "Chassidim"[2] was established, and two synagogues were built, one for each faction. Rabbi Herzl Mahorki prayed "Kol Nidre"[3] and "Ma'ariv"[4] with the "Mitnagdim" and "Musaf"[5] in the Chassidic synagogue.

In this town there was a rabbi and a "shochet"[6]. It is worthwhile noting, that the rabbi also traded in coal and timber. It was said of him that if he didn't live from his Torah, he lived well from his trading and the maxim "Tova Torah Veschora [7]". (He was later known in Minsk and in Israel as the Red Rabbi Pesachovicz who for the Soviet regime). The "shochet", Rabbi Zadok, was known to be an intelligent and well-groomed man.

Wagon owners raced along the Staryye Dorogi road to Slutsk bringing various supplies from the train station, there and back with produce from the Slutsk district. The stagecoaches and the double-decker bus made their way along the road, there and back, from Staryye Dorogi to Slutsk, since a railway track to Slutsk had not yet been laid.

The town did well from travelers coming and going from everywhere in Russia: merchants, laborers, wholesale shopkeepers who sold their goods to the locals. The Jews of the area were scholarly, who knew Hebrew, for example Rabbi Yashiya Chaim Chinitz, Be'er, Fryd, the Weinstock family, Reznik and others were virtuous and dedicated Zionists, who worked for the love of Zion and the revival of the Hebrew language.

Fryd, Ravkin, Herzl Garatzikov were well known in the town as timber merchants. There were three hotels situated here belonging to Rabinowicz, the "Barazina" Hotel and one belonging to Ravkin. Notable amongst the workers of the "Poliak-Weisebaum" mill were Hanichov, Berger and Sheykevicz.

There were some large stores belonging to Sara Kazkovicz's husband, to Lipa Wasserbein and to Lankricz - a store for the retail and wholesale selling of fodder.

Sander Reznik, Kopel Simchovicz and Dobrovski were Jews who held important positions in the town.

The town's people subscribed to Yiddish and Russian newspapers. The teacher, M. Chaznovicz began as a Hebrew teacher for the children of the Staryye Dorogi businessmen, Leyb Berger, and later moved to Slutsk where he was amongst the founders of the "Cheder Hametukan"[8]. One of the first Hebrew teachers in the town was Chorgin and also served as a bookkeeper in the communal welfare office and was the driving spirit behind it.

The town was successful in opening a Hebrew school with the assistance one of the best teachers of the time by the name of Chaim Rabinowicz, who published quite a variety of stories in "Prachim" and other publications. Rabinowicz was dedicated to opening the school, which had two faculties. He was well liked by all of the town's people and thanks to him the sound of Hebrew speaking could be heard in the town. (He went to live in Israel in 1925 and passed away around 1931.) The teacher, Moran, continued on with this blessed work after his departure.

This town was different from all the neighboring towns, in its vibrant lifestyle, its residents' generosity, their level of education and their response and affinity with many of life's phenomenon. A casual visitor was amazed by and cherished this small blessed and isolated island.

There were also Jews who came from old ways and who found new content and a contemporary and blissful life in Staryye Dorogi. New times had arrived, and the roads remained deserted and the new-old vibrant life disappeared. Zionism was outlawed; the exemplary Hebrew "cheder" was closed. Jewish life was drained of its essence under the Soviet regime and the roads stood silent and abandoned in the absence of comings and goings.

The Nazi regime destroyed and annihilated all that remained.

Translator's footnotes:

1. A movement in opposition to the "Chassidic" movement.
2. Sect of pious Jews.
3. Opening prayer of Yom Kippur (Day of Atonement).
4. Evening prayer.
5. Additional prayer.
6. Ritual slaughterer.
7. Learned in Torah together with being a good trader.
8. Standard religious elementary school.

[Page 241]

My Town

by Shaul Bernstein

The town of Staryye Dorogi was established between the years 1900 to 1903 in a forested region, and its character was determined in the main by the timber trade on which it was founded. It was due to this fact that the town was linked to the railway, which continued from Asipovicy to the town of Urechcha.

The town was built near the main Moscow-Warsaw road. This road linked the cities of Bubruysk and Slutsk. Staryye Dorogi was about 60 km from Bobruysk and 40 km distant from Slutsk.

This city did not have a railway connection yet. Travelers to Slutsk would stay in Staryye Dorogi and would reach Slutsk by carriages and in later years, by bus.

Representatives of the Poliak-Weiscbaum company bought forests around the town of Staryye Dorogi and three kilometers from the village a town was established that was also called Staryye Dorogi.

The company built a large sawmill, and a plywood plant, that was burnt down in 1909, (many years after the fire, children were still collecting pieces of ply and converting them into rulers). A large flourmill was also built there.

The town's founders built themselves two grand villas and planted a fruit tree garden to be used in their families' summer holidays. A sports ground with all sorts of equipment stretched out in front of these villas and it was open for the town's children in the summer season and, in particular, on Saturdays.

Located near the mill, special houses were built for the factory's regular workers (mainly Russian) and special houses for the clerks, who were mainly Jewish.

It was said of the general manager, Katz that he did not like employing Jewish workers, and because of this the Jews were not involved in physical labor.

The branch of the railway line connected the company warehouse to the main line; large quantities of various shaped, processed timber would lie on both sides of the railway line.

The company's main office was situated in the mill area and a synagogue, which was financed by the company, was built there.

This development led to an influx of people from surrounding towns and villages, and a town was built on the western side of the railway line with all its facilities, according to a modern design - wide streets with wooden pathways. Wooden houses were built, since this was the cheapest and most common building material in the region.

Trade expanded and developed. Timber merchants appeared who purchased forests in this region. Following them came all sorts of dispatch agents, tree commissioners, shopkeepers, butchers, various tradesmen: bookmakers, bakers, tailors, porters and blacksmiths.

In addition, there were liberal professions: Doctors, medics and so forth. A small hospital, which contained 15 beds, was also built there.

A committee meeting of the "Kadima" youth movement
From right to left: S. Bernstein and the speaker - S. Mahrshek

[Page 242]

In Zelda Pavzner's inn, when two non-Jews would get drunk and would begin brawling, her two well-built brothers would appear, and in an instant the brawlers were silenced.

Amongst the wagon owners of the town, who would carry loads from Bobruysk to Slutsk there was a famous man named Yezze. In the main though, the wagon drivers excelled in bringing goods there and back from Slutsk to Bobruysk. The following was told about them: On the road, just before Bobruysk, there was a glass factory, "Galusha" and it's workers would set out at night to rob travelers. The travelers were frightened to go past this place, but the wagon drivers of Slutsk did not accept this situation. There were eight brothers called the "Dey Yaten". One night they organized an ambush and soundly beat up the robbers. From that time onward, they didn't dare coming near the wagon drivers.

In our town there was a volunteer fire-fighting unit, which had special uniforms, that was financed by donations from wealthy citizens, but woe to the miser who didn't give generously. After a fire drill was carried out on his roof, he quickly ran to give his donation.

A savings fund was opened in the town, and was run by the teacher, Chorgin.

A narrow railway line, seven kilometers in length, connected the sawmill with the town of Isibicz. It was intended for the transport of lumber to the sawmill and even for sightseeing trips, for which purpose a carriage with seating arrangements was prepared.

The youths of our town took frequent advantage of this line, particularly on Sundays and in the evenings.

There was "Skipider" factory for processing pine roots, located 9¼ kilometers from the town and another one at the edge of the town. In this second factory there was a long series of fires.

It should be pointed out that in 1910, the writer, Shalom Asch, visited Klatzkin and it is here that he wrote his work "Motke the thief".

In the year 1908, our town had the honor of having Berl Katznelson, who had relatives in the town, as a teacher but this was for a short time only.

Two synagogues sprang up in our town: one for the "Mitnagdim" and one for the "Chassidim".

There were two drama groups: one in Russian and one in Yiddish. A few people took part in both these classes. A large public library was also established and work was undertaken there on a voluntary basis.

The firefighting hall (where the firefighting equipment stood), was used for exhibitions and balls, and in a building closer to the mill there was a "cheder" with the following teachers: Simchovicz, Chorgin, Yosef Maron and Rabinowicz (the later managed to reach Israel and was a teacher in Ramat Gan). Some of the studies were carried out in Hebrew.

A further suburb by the name of Slobodka was founded close to the town where there were tens of houses belonging to Russian workers.

The town was built at a hectic pace and all the amenities that I have mentioned were established within a few years. This town was truly unique, unlike the other towns that were described by Mendel Moss and Shalom Alecheim.

It should be noted that in our town there were no poor people though, of course, there were differences in income between the local people.

The relationship between the Jews and the non-Jews was fairly normal. Youths grew up without fearing the "Shajgets"[1] and strode the streets with pride.

* * *

However, this idyllic situation was destroyed with the breakout of World War I. Tens of family heads were conscripted to the war and many families were deprived of their breadwinner. Many ate from food that they had accumulated in stores in better times. The tradesmen's situation was better, since they served the towns in the area to a certain extent.

The town's sawmill was the only one operating in the region and many residents to earned their living from it. Under the leadership of Ya'akov Lipshicz, a woman's group was organized, and they were responsible for loading timber on wagons. The men worked in the forests as lumberjacks.

The revolution came in February 1917. The Jewish population received this news with mixed feelings: joy of freedom, widening of horizons, new opportunities that were opened and this together with fear - will this be good for the Jews? There was great excitement amongst the youth. Assemblies and party conferences took place. Jews freely went out into the street waving Zionist and Bund flags. The following VIPs took part in the Zionist assemblies: Rytov from Usifovicz, Dubkin and Berger from Minsk.

In the beginning of 1918 the Germans conquered our region, though they didn't burden the Jewish population.

During the same period a corps of the Polish Legion, going by the name of Duber-Musnitski, was organized in Bobruysk. The Germans did not remain in our region for long. In the same year they left our town and were immediately followed by the Bobruysk legionnaires.

In the same year, despite the difficult economic situation, the Zmaskaya Gymnasia [high school] was founded with three faculties with the aim that each year a new faculty would be added. The educational standard was high. Shimon Merashek, who in 1923 was expelled from the Slutsk high school because of his Zionist activities, joined our school and completed his education with honors.

At the beginning of 1919 the Polish legionnaires withdrew and the Red Guard took their place. The Jewish population in all the towns of our district found itself between "hammer and anvil" and fell victim to every conqueror. As the Red Guard established themselves in the town, Jews began to be arrested and were accused of aiding the Poles.

There was also a case, that a farmer killed a Polish estate owner by the name of Bolhak and in the same year, the Poles again conquered the town after fierce battles. The Poles reacted immediately to Bolhak's murder, and hung the farmer who had killed him. They also caught two Jews and wanted to hang them. The nooses were already around their necks but at the last moment they were released.

The town suffered greatly, as did other villages in our region. Those people wearing light colored clothes were sent to unload coals and those wearing dark colored clothes were sent to unload flour. The Poles maltreated the people, cut off

[Page 243]

In the summer of 1920 the Red Army began an extensive onslaught on all fronts. As the Poles retreated they burnt bridges above the road and that of the railway track that connected to Slutsk.

Remnants of the retreating Polish army looted everything they could lay their hands on and there was a concern that they would burn the town down. With the arrival of the vanguard of the Red Army, the population breathed a sigh of relief.

I remember how hundreds of people tied together with ropes helped to move armored cars across temporary bridges; hundreds of farmers came of their own free will to put up the destroyed bridges. They worked day and night and the project was completed in a short time.

The Red Army wore torn and tattered uniforms, however they made steady progress and their slogan was "Onward to Warsaw".

However, as they progressed towards Warsaw, as they reached Warsaw's suburbs, they were fleeing with the Poles on their tails. Thus it occurred that they reached a distance of 15 kilometers from the town and the Poles had already conquered Slutsk.

We heard the thunder of the cannons day and night. Every day an armored train would stood in Staryye Dorogi and travel to Verkhutina where it's payload of shells would be unloaded on the enemy and then it would return. The settlers were starving. In spite of the unrelenting battles, they would go to the forest to collect berries, mushrooms and strawberries and this is how they sustained themselves.

The Red Army soldiers began emptying the villages of food commodities. The farmers tried resisting. The opposition continued to grow. Soldiers who were residents of the local villages began deserting the Red Army. Armed farmers grouped up in the forests. And who suffered the brunt from this situation? Naturally - the Jews. Despite this, when a peace treaty was signed with the Poles, our town had been under siege for months and those who had dared to leave, paid with their lives.

The same situation existed in all the towns of the region. In Gorki, tens of Jews were killed. There was also a rumor that the Day of Judgment was approaching for the Jews of Staryye Dorogi, and the population was anxious, tense and anticipating.

More than once my father's house, (Leyser Bernstein) had served as a refuge for our neighbors. We had a six-chambered, Smith & Weston pistol and a sufficient quantity of hatchets. In our house there was an atmosphere of battle. As the security situation worsened, we approached the local Soviet authorities to allow the organization of a self-defense organization and to supply us with weapons. After numerous efforts, we were given forty rifles and a defense force of experienced fighters was organized and which trained daily. The weapons improved the morale of the town's residents, since we also had a quantity of illegal weapons.

Guarding at night took the form of ambushes with four to five people in each position. I remember how one night an ambush squad managed to disarm half a platoon (15 men) of Red Army soldiers, since they didn't identify themselves. When they were led to the defense headquarters they became very angry and gnashed their teeth, on learning that a mere five Jews had managed to disarm them.

The authorities slowly began to eradicate dissidents' hideouts.

The fire fighter's orchestra in Staryye Dorogi

[Page 244]

Many of them were arrested and also shot. Hence, the essential calm was returned to this area.

The fate of the Russian Jews, in the main the fate of the youth, is vague and imprecise, since the Jews were mainly shopkeepers and traders and were counted amongst those in an "unproductive" status. A rebellion began amongst the finest of our youth, who organized themselves into underground Zionist youth movements, in order to productively prepare themselves and that when the time came, they would make "aliyah"[2] to the Land of Israel.

The Zionist youth movement "Kadima" was founded in our town and in other nearby towns, in the year 1922. Its center was in Minsk, and it published a monthly underground newspaper – "Kadima".

However, the authorities began to persecute us and in 1923 the first arrests began taking place in our region.

Seven of our comrades were arrested in our town and sent to Bobruysk and from there to Minsk. We were incarcerated for months in an attic belonging to the G.P.A.

When we were released, we continued on with our activities with rekindled fervor.

In 1925 the arrests were renewed and several comrades and myself were imprisoned for five months in the Slutsk jail. After interrogation we were exiled to Siberia and the Urals, where we spent five years.

We were not alone there. Thousands of the finest Jewish youth were sent to the Siberian deserts. Many of them managed to reach Israel, many perished and others even reconciled with the authorities and made peace with them.

From their places of exile the people of Staryye Dorogi managed to reach Israel: Shaul Bernstein (writer of this piece), Sara Katz, Sara Rosmocho and Nechemia Leibovicz.

* * *

What was the fate of Staryye Dorogi after the German occupation in 1941? There were rumors, that the Germans killed most of the residents and a few escaped to Russia. Others claimed that the town was burnt town and with the return of the Soviets it was rebuilt.

The bus from Staryye Dorogi to Slutsk

Translator's footnotes:

1. Yiddish for non-Jews.
2. Immigration to Israel.

Pahost
(Pahost, Belarus)

52°51' 27°39'

by Nachum Chinitz

Translated by Mira Eckaus

Pahost, which is near the river Slutz, is remembered in history in the
15th century, with a population of 500. It has a Prevoslav church, a
Jewish synagogue and two fairs

From the Brookhouse–Efron Encyclopedia

About two hundred Jewish families and about sixty Christian families lived in Pahost. Most of the town's residents were artisans and farmers, but there were also small merchants, shopkeepers, and peddlers. Wagon owners maintained a regular service from Pahost to Slutsk and nearby towns transporting passengers and goods.

Almost every resident took care of his own garden, had a dairy cow and raised poultry for his own needs. Two fairs were held in the town each year. On Sundays, the market was especially crowded. There were two synagogues in the town - Beit Midrash and Ker Synagogue. In the past, there was one butcher in the town, and later two, one rabbi and one shamash, who, in addition to his work in the synagogue, also served as a burier. There were also two pharmacies and a Christian medic. Until 1920, there were cheders, two government schools, one with four classes and the other with eight classes.

There are a few families from Pahost that live in Israel, among them: the Gur family (Grazovsky), the family of S. Ben-Zvi (Ratgon), the mayor of Givatayim, the Batia (Ginzburg) family and Azriel Shalev in Degania Alef, the Haim Kuntzer family.

Shimon Ben-Zvi (Ratgon)

He was born in Pahost in 5650 (1890). He received a traditional education in the cheder, at the Slutsk and Mir yeshivas. He was among the organizers of the students' group at the yeshiva, that demanded from the management to teach also general studies. The group's members were expelled from the yeshiva. He returned to Slutsk and studied there as an extern student. He made a living from teaching.

In 1914, he emigrated to Israel. He joined the labor movement, worked for a short time in Tel Adashim with HaShomer group. He worked as an agricultural laborer in Ein Chai, Ben Shemen and Petah Tikva. He was one of the first settlers in Kfar Malal (Ein Chai).

He served as the secretary of the Agricultural Workers' Histadrut (union) in Judea and ran the first workers' kitchen in Petah Tikva. He also served as the secretary of the Agricultural Workers' Histadrut (union) in Jerusalem and when the central institutions of the union moved to Tel Aviv, he also moved there.

He was the chief bookkeeper of the "Nir" company. With the foundation of the "Borochov" neighborhood, the first workers neighborhood, he was drawn to the involvement in the municipal public affairs as a resident of the place.

As the head of the council (now he serves as the mayor of Givatayim), he managed the affairs of the neighborhood for about two decades. He worked together with a number of members to unify the nearby neighborhoods called "Givatayim". He was a member of the Haganah, one of the founders of the cooperative consumer association in the Borochov neighborhood (the first consumer association in Israel), active member in multiple institutions, a member of Ort's management, he wrote articles in ÷HaPoel HaTzairø booklet and in the book "t;The Second Aliyah".

Pahost (Slutsk district), June 23, 1888.

Not long ago, Reb Noah the Persian, known to "HaMelitz" readers by the letters printed about him in the passing year, passed through our city; And when he opened his register to show me the testimony of the rabbis of the Minsk district, about his passing there that summer, I discovered the newspaper edition number 208 of "HaMelitz", which included the letter attesting that he is a trustworthy person and a faithful agent to his senders. As my question was not answered properly, I thought to open a discussion with him. Anyway, the matter was already published in the Beit Midrash, and Reb Noah showed all his courage there. And it was known to all that the rabbi from Priluk wrote about him in "HaMelitz" (170-5647) that he was a crook and a swindler.

Therefore, I decided his matter should be discussed publicly. He speaks in the holy language, while during his stay in Russia for the past seven years he must have already learned the spoken Jewish language. His register is not connected with a thread from page to page. He recorded in his register only part of the more decent donations (the smallest of them in the city of Starovin, 5 Rubal), and did not record the smallest donations at all. According to this, it seems that he acted with the donations as a man who acts for his own benefit. It is surprising, because in his register he mentioned only the cities in the Minsk region and none of the other cities from which he has received money for ten years. Therefore, it is appropriate that the rabbis will investigate this man, so that the public will know whether this man acts were kosher or not.

Avraham Levin

Reb Mordechai Finkelstein and his wife Batia

[Page 246]

Kopyl
(Kapyl, Belarus)
53°09' 27°06'
Translated by Jerrold Landau

This place was populated from early times. Implements of stone and bone were found there. Kopyl was designated as a city in the 14th century. Along with Slutsk, Kopyl was a unique duchy during the period of Lithuanian rule. It passed to Duke Radziwil at the beginning of the 17th century.

The town has 338 residents, 41 courtyards, a Christian church, a Catholic church, a Reformed church, two Jewish houses of prayer, an elementary school, two Beis Midrashes, a brewery, two water mills, and six stores.

From the Brookhouse–Efron Encyclopedia

The area of Kopyl is a civic settlement, 12 kilometers from the Timkovichi railway line (on the Osipovichi Baranovichi line, 186 kilometers from Bobriusk). Kopyl had a factory for the production of butter and cheese. In 1952, there were two high schools (Russian and White Russian), a library, and a movie theater. Various types of agricultural activities take place in the area, including potato cultivation, and the raising of chickens and cattle. It also had 2 *sovkhoizes* [state farms], 3 stations for machinery and tractors, 2 alcohol stills, a brick kiln, and 7 electrical stations.

According to the Soviet Encyclopedia

From the Newspapers

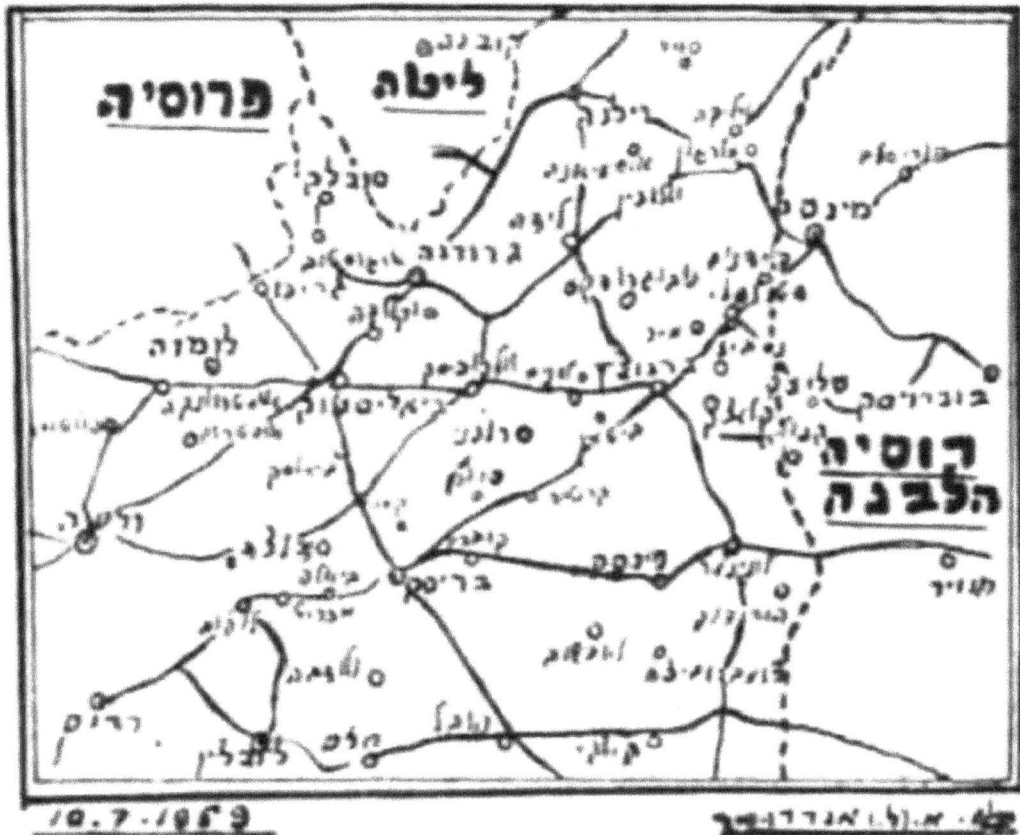

[**Note:** a hand drawn map of the area of Slutsk. Borders are pre World War II.]

On April 11th, a fire broke out in one barn and consumed the city. Approximately 300 houses, 4 Beis Midrashes and the Great Synagogue that had been standing for about 300 years and had been recently renovated were all consumed by the fire within two hours. The residents were not able to save the treasures and valuables from the Beis Midrashes and the synagogues. Thirty-seven Torah scrolls were burnt in the Great Synagogue, over and above the Torah scrolls and the many books and other items that were consumed in the Beis Midrashes. Kopyl became a ruin. Only 20 houses in the higher points of the city remained. On April 13th, the fire returned to consume that which remained. It destroyed fifteen of the remaining houses, including one Jewish house. We are hereby publicizing our great sorrow to the public, and requesting assistance and kindness from the neighboring towns, that they should have mercy upon the poor people of Kopyl, and offer them support so that they can rebuild, and a city among the Jewish people shall not be wiped out.

An upright man, a resident of Kopyl. From *"Hakarmel,"* Volume 8, Tammuz 2, 5626 – 1866.

* * *

On Sunday 28th of Iyar, a fire broke out in the house of one person, and speedily became a conflagration. Approximately 100 houses, including large storehouses filled with grain and other foods, as well as many lumberyards, went up in flames. In addition, all of the property that was in those houses was consumed by fire. The damage was great.

Ben Zion Kalman Rubinok, *"Hamelitz,"* 110, May 20th, 1887.

* * *

Yitzchak Berger, the principal of the private Jewish school in our town, was murdered with a block of wood by unknown murderers.

"Der Yud," Number 33, 1902.

* * *

[Page 247]

Rabbis of Kopyl

The Gaon Rabbi Yomtov Lipman, the author of "Kiddush Yom Tov" was a friend of the Gra [Acronym for the Gaon Rabbi Eliahu, known as the Gaon of Vilna] and the friend of Reb Chaim of Volozhin and Rabbi Yitzchak Davidovitz. He died in Karelitz.

Rabbi Avraham Yudelevitz, who died in New York. He was the author of books on homiletics and Jewish law.

Rabbi Yaakov Meir Krabchinski. He was the father of Rabbi Zeev Gold (the Mizrachi leader), and Dr. Rafael Gold, the son-in-law of Rabbi Dov Katz, the author of the "Mussar Movement" and the director of the office of the rabbinate in Israel [unclear if 'son-in-law' is referring to the rabbi who is the subject of the paragraph, or his son].

Afterwards, the rabbinate was divided, and two rabbis served there: Rabbi Shimon Rozovski and Rabbi Yisrael Yaakov, the son of Rabbi Chaim Yosef Lider. Both of these rabbis served in the rabbinate of Kopyl until the year 5684 or 5685 (1924-1925). They can be numbered among the final rabbis of Kopyl.

Rabbi Yitzchak Yechiel [The ordering of the rabbis here does not seem to be chronological, as from the context, it would seem that Rabbi Davidson was from an earlier period than those previously mentioned. Incidentally, Rabbi Eliahu of Pruzhan is the maternal grandfather of Rabbi Joseph Ber Soloveitchik, the head of Yeshiva University in New York who died a few years ago, as well the uncle of Rabbi Moshe Feinstein, one of the leading sages of the past generation of American Orthodox Jewry], the son-in-law of Rabbi Eliahu Feinstein of Pruzhan. He was the son of Rabbi Yissachar Davidson, the head of the rabbinical court of Kopyl. He was the fourth generation (son after son) on the rabbinate in Kopyl. He was the great grandfather of the famous doctor Yehuda Davidson.

Rabbi Yitzchak Yechiel was the great-grandfather of the poet Yitzchak Katznelson, may G-d avenge his blood, who was named after him.

The father of the poet was Yitzchak Binyamin Katznelson, a genius at the Yeshiva of Volozhin.

There was a communal administrator (parnas) in Kopyl whose name was Isser. He was very rich, strongly opinionated, and would give harsh retorts. During the controversy between the rabbi and the community, Isser said about the rabbi: It appears that our rabbi has no stature in our community, for if he did, we would be spitting in front of him…"

Reb Eliahu Moshe Karan. He was a Torah oriented person, one of the Jewish benefactors in east New York. He was a native of Kopyl. He supported Torah institutions with a generous hand. He studied Torah on a regular basis. He died on the 12th of Sivan 5688 (1928) at the age of 80.

Writers who were Natives of Kopyl

Reb Yehuda Leib Davidson. He was born in Kopyl into a rabbinic family. Four consecutive generations sat on the rabbinic seat of Kopyl. His father Reb Ber Kopylier excelled in the depth of his delving into Divine knowledge, in the area of the philosophy of Maimonides, and in the fields of mathematics and astronomy. His father had an extensive library, including modern works.

Reb Yehuda studied with a teacher (*melamed*) who was knowledgeable in the fields of grammar and bible with commentaries. The teacher was a thoroughly European person by the name of Shmurk who came from Kiev and spoke a clear Russian. This man was expert in Russian and Hebrew literature. He was a sharp orator and critic. His words made a deep impression on Yehuda Leib. When Yehuda was twelve years old, he went to the Yeshiva of Mir, later to Karelitz, and to then Minsk, whose noisy life had an impact on him. His first article "Before the Face of Evil" was published in four installments in "Hakol." Afterwards, he moved to Warsaw in order to earn his livelihood from giving Hebrew lessons. During the two and a half years there, he passed his exam and received his certificate of matriculation.

He was accepted to the faculty of medicine in university. In accordance with the advice of the Polish writer, Kalmanis Junosza, he translated the Third Travels of Benjamin [famous medieval Jewish traveler, Benjamin of Tudela], and called it by the name of Don Kiszut the Hebrew. His translations were not pleasing to the Poles. These books were sold, and distributed to the public. This served as his source of livelihood. In the meantime, he completed his course of studies and graduated as a doctor.

Reb Avraham Yaakov Zinger. He was born in the year 5624 (1864) in Kopyl. He studied in the Yeshiva of the Gaon Rabbi Ben-Zion Katznelson of Kopyl. He also studied in the Yeshivas of Slutsk and Minsk. He participated in "Hamelitz" in the year 5645 (1885), in "*Knesset Yisrael*" and in "*Haasif*."

He published a long story in "*Hamelitz*" called "The Trouble of the Daughter".

He settled in Warsaw in the year 5648 (1888).

Reb Avraham Yaakov Papirna. He was born on Elul 2nd 5600 (1840) in Kopyl. He studied Talmud and the halachic decisors. He went to the Rabbinical Beis Midrash of Zhitomir in 5623 (1863). He participated in "*Hakarmel*" and "*Hamelitz*" by publishing poems and investigative works. He served as a teacher in the city of Zakracyn and later in Plock. His books on education included the following:

    a.   "The Teacher of Russian Language" (Warsaw, 5629 – 1859);

    b.   "Pathways of Teaching for Males" with Russian Translation (5631 – 1871), in six volumes;

    c.   A Short Hebrew Grammar in Russian (5633–1873);

d. *"Merotz Agarot"* ["Course of Collections"] in Hebrew and Russian (5635 – 1875);

e. *"Lehrbuch der russischen Sprache"* [Textbook of the Russian Language], according to Olendorf's method (5636 – 1876);

f. *"Vollständiger Jüdischer Briefensteller"* ["Complete Collection of Short Works"];

g. On the Cheders in general and the Cheders of Slutsk (1884). He participated in the newspapers *"Dyen"*, *"Knesset Yisrael,"* and *"Haasif."*

The Poet M. Frankel. The Jewish American poet and researcher Michael Frankel died at the age of 62. He was the grandson of Mendele Mocher Seforim.

He was born in Kopyl (Lithuania) [in broad sense of the term], and immigrated to the United States at the beginning of the century. He toured the world a great deal, and in 1926, he lived in Paris for a period of time. There, he encouraged Henry Miller, who was taking his first steps in writing, to devote all of his energies to writing. Together with Miller, he published a book on the philosophical meanderings of Hamlet. He moved to London after the Second World War. He visited Israel a few times. His widow is the French educator Dafna Moshos.

[Page 248]

From "Those Days"

by Mendele Mocher Seforim

Translated by Jerrold Landau

The Decree of the Schools

The town of Kopyl was perplexed, and the Jews there were in deep mourning: they were disturbed by one of the *maskilim*, named Valilnatel, who along with his friends was the cause of this evil. This person would go around, at the behest of the king and his ministers, to all the cities with a Jewish population. He would gather crowds together and preach to them about the benefits of the school [a modern school]. The Jews of Kopyl would curse him, as did their brethren in all other places. They took council together to decide what to do. They decided to decree a public fast upon the community, to recite Psalms, and to implore the dead in their graves to request mercy on their behalf. The faces of the *melamdim* [teachers] were blackened like the bottom of a pot, for they were worried to the depths of their souls. These schools would destroy their livelihood, and if there were no salvation and respite coming to them from the Blessed G-d, they would become bloated with hunger, and would go to their graves before their time. From here you can learn why the *melamdim* were so concerned, and why they complained so vociferously against that decree. The townsfolk were standing in prayer, fasting, and reciting chapters of Psalms in the synagogues. The women were prostrating themselves upon graves, and were shedding rivers of tears in the synagogues. Even the schoolchildren were fasting. Shlomole fasted for the first time in his life during this fast of the schools.

The entire summer was a time of mourning and lamentation, and even the few gentiles in town looked like mourners. The gentile and Jewish residents of the town earned their livelihoods together and lived in peace. Everyone participated in the grief and joys of each other. If there was a wedding feast in a Jewish home, the gentile acquaintances would send gifts: this one a fattened chick, and that one a few dozen eggs, this one a loaf of bread, and that one a loaf of honey, fruit and vegetables, each according to his means. The

Jews did the same to them. Therefore, the weeping of the Jews at that time affected the hearts of their gentile neighbors. They wondered, why and to what end is this weeping?

The Jews, even though they were fasting and tearing open the heavens in prayer and supplication, did not rely on a miracle. Until such time as the merit of their forbears would have effect and G-d would have mercy upon them, they did what they could and married off their young children – and the time was a time of great "confusion!" The *shadchans* (marriage brokers), emissaries of G-d, labored on behalf of the Children of Israel with love, and made haste to bring the young boys and girls to the marriage canopy. Why all this? So that, if Heaven forbid, the decree of the schools should be fulfilled, there would not be found even one child among all of the Jews, for everyone would be married, all of the "young Jews!" To insure that the dowry of the young girls would not be inflated, a rumor was spread in the city that the young girls would be taken away for work in far off colonies.

The Kopyl Fair

Here is the fair! The marketplace, which was quiet on all the days of the year, took on a different appearance and nature during the time of the summer fairs. At such times, the marketplace was teaming with people. New people, and various characters and faces came from villages and towns, all types of noses could be seen – elongated, out of place, sharp, witty, crooked, and peaked. Wild heads of hair were seen, as were various locks of hair, thick beards, thin beards, and people wearing headdresses, caps and frightening hats. There were people wearing linen cloaks, skin coats, wide cloth pants and pantaloons. There were people with *lafi*[1] shoes, and nailed sandals. There were people covered with tar and smelling of kerosene. These were the villagers. They came with their wives. The "ugly" wives, with outstretched arms and bare chests, with necklaces of glass and coral around their necks, wearing embroidered and woven linen dresses. They would be sitting on wagons filled with bunches of onions and baskets of eggs. At their feet would be a young two-week-old calf, with all four legs tied up, fainting from thirst for its mother's milk. The spotted cow would be tied to the back of the wagon by its horns, waiting to be sold along with its child – she for milk and the child for slaughter, woe unto both of them.

From the valley, from below the mountain, a camp of horses with rolled back tails and straight manes, approach with a noisy, angry gallop, as they bump into each other in the crowd. Their drivers goad them on with a whip and foot, as they urge them on with a roaring call and a scream towards the horse marketplace, and line them up there! Immediately, the merchants come one after another, testing and examining the teeth of each horse, evaluating their beauty, debating the price, slapping the horse on the back, and passing their hand over the hindquarter. And could it be possible to have a fair without a gypsy? – He too, Grishka, the gypsy, was there! His face was flushed and sweaty from overwork, his hat was tilted to the back of his head. His quiver and his utensils, a knife, pins and iron hooks were attached to his belt. Grishka would walk along, and a tall horse, led by a halter, would go along with him, its skin smooth, with torch-like eyes – it appeared literally like a lion! Leizer Hirsch, the town water drawer, saw the horse in all its beauty and was astonished. He sighed and said to himself: "Oh miser, do not covet what you cannot afford." But his desires got the better of him, and he opened up his mouth and said: "Oh Grishka, what is the price?" They would converse, and the gypsy would continue with the conversation as he rode easily on the horse, running to and fro. The buyer and seller would haggle, one zuz [2], two zuzim. Both would plead with each other, literally in a weeping voice, take oaths, shake hands, and each one would take hold of the corner of his cloak and bring it to the nose of the other to consummate the deal. Finally, the deal would be established, and they would congratulate each other and share a drink, as was customary! Leizer Hirsch got a bargain. He took hold of the horse and led it home, joyous and glad of heart!

Large crowds of people, young men and women, mothers and children together, would gather together and come. There would be the sound of laughter and the sound of conversation as the eyes were raised upwards. The circus tent was there in the market, with amazing pictures posted on the outside. There were pictures of man-eating beings [3], frightening pictures of animals, flying dragons and various winged beings, photographs of magicians and sorceresses, as well as images of demons, and wild haired, naked spirits. On top of them, on the roof of the tent stood the clown, like one of the nonsensical [4] clowns of the world, a renowned clown, with large multi-colored curls on his hair, dressed in colored clothes with sparkling glaze. He would toot a trumpet, play around, and take a bow before the mothers and girls, daughters of the uncircumcised [5], whose mouths would be filled with laughter. He would continue to clown around, as he enticed them

[Page 249]

to come into the tent to see the performance.

Music could be heard from all corners of the land. One man, who considered himself to be a musician, would turn the organ [6] wheel with his hand, as it played a song to the audience by itself. A young girl, wearing boys cloths and pants, would dance and leap with all her might through the round opening of a barrel. Next to her, a sickly young boy would do gymnastics, spreading himself out completely, and standing on his head with his feet in the ear. The loud noise of the crowd could be heard on the opposite side of the marketplace, as people were gathering in confusion and with the sounds of strife. Leizer Hirsch and Grishka were fighting in the middle of the crowd and arguing as a horse stood in front of the gypsy, annoying him. The horse was old and weak, without stature and without splendor. The gypsy cheated me!" shouted Leizer Hirsch, as he turned over his case to the crowd – this cheater, may his spirit be crushed, inflated his horse under its skin in order that it should look like an inflated ball, and he even fixed up its teeth with a mouth file. He had given it a wine and spirit spiked potion to drink, so it became drunk, and was able to display the strength of an eagle and run like a deer! The crowd accused the evil gypsy, knocked him down, and beat him profusely in accordance with his evil.

Sources of Livelihood in Kopyl

The largest source of livelihood of the Kopyl community, which gave it fame in all of the towns of Lithuania, was a form of textile for women's headdresses. Astrakhan was a thick cloth, colored dark green, rolled up and folded into many pleats and served as clothing for the poor. The cloth of the headdresses was thin and ironed, with the dimensions of a napkin. The weavers of the town made both types of cloth. The women would put this white headdress on the hairnets atop their heads and position it so that its two ends flow down their back like two heart shaped droplets. Each one had a small, short heart on its side. A kerchief would surround the hatted head, round like the opening of a jar. The ends of the kerchief would be tied up in one knot, and each loose end would go over the side towards the ear, and be hidden there. The older, more modest women would have this knot in the front between their eyes, while the younger women would place it more towards the back. The wives of the rich people would wear a silk, Arab or Turkish style kerchief on Sabbaths and festivals. Each kerchief had an embossed, colored design on it.

The parents on the groom's side would send as gifts to the bride a Turkish kerchief and an embossed kerchief. The bride's family would send a *streimel* for the Sabbath to the groom. The mothers would be very careful to ensure that the headdress was always clean, ironed and smooth. Two women, homeowners, who were partners in this enterprise and supported themselves, did the smoothing of the headdress. The smoothing was done as follows: these two women would stand opposite each other at the distance equivalent to the length of the headdress. Each one would stand in her place, holding the widthwise edges of the headdress in her two hands. In this manner, the headdress would be stretched out between them in the shape of a gutter. They would place a large stone, glass or iron ball into the trough. One would raise her arms slightly, and the ball would roll from her towards her partner. Immediately, the partner would raise her arms, and the ball would roll back. Thus did the ball roll back and forth in the headdress until it was very smooth.

The gentile weavers in the town would weave these headdresses in their homes, and local Jewish travelling merchants would purchase them with money and with balls of thread that were needed by the weavers. The merchants of Kopyl were for the most part young married men being supported by their fathers-in-law, who were not yet penniless. Even the married sons of Reb Chaim engaged in this business. The headdresses would be passed over to large-scale merchants, who would distribute them throughout the cities of Lithuania. The headdresses of Kopyl were well known in the world, and many purchasers jumped upon them. Livelihood was found in the town, and many people were supported by the headdress business. This business was passed down from father to child.

Partisans in the Kopyl Region

From among the partisans of the Kopyl region, the following were well known: Glichik, a Jewish commander by the name of Zhokov (Brigadier Chapayev, of the brigade of General Major Kapustin).

After the slaughters in Kopyl, Nesvizh, Kletsk, Lyakhovichi, and Stolbtsy, many Jews went out to the surrounding forests. Many of them were unfit for battle. Kapustin ordered Glichik to round up all of those Jews and to set up a special Jewish brigade. The biggest problem was the lack of arms. Bozhanka (this was the real name of Kapustin) did not distribute arms to the Jews, but he rather imposed upon them to acquire arms themselves. The brigade, consisting of sixty people, had in total two guns, four bullets, and had a single aim. After some time, the brigade numbered approximately 200 people – 130 Jews and 70 Christians.

Glichik acted diligently in obtaining arms. He obtained arms in a variety of ways, and in January 1943, the brigade owned 11 machine guns, 23 automatic guns, and 130 guns. The "Zhokov" brigade suffered greatly from the persecutions and searches that the Germans conducted in that area. However Glichik, a native of Kopyl, was astute, and was able to lead his brigade safely through the danger. Only a very small number of members went missing.

* * *

During a hunt that the Germans conducted in the forests of Staritsa in the region of Kopyl on November 7th, 1942, Glichik's brigade excelled in its bravery and successful activities.

For the attack on the Khominka-Hancewicze train that transported railway ties and building materials to the front, Glichik chose 40 armed partisans, under the command of Wiener. He commanded them to bring back the weapons of the killed Germans. The partisans waited in ambush for the train to appear. As soon

[Page 250]

as the train arrived at the trap that was set, the partisans opened up with deadly fire upon it.

* * *

Prior to the war, the Jew Glichik served as the director of Zagotskot (a government economic agency for the provision of meat) in Kopyl. At the outbreak of the war, he fled to the forest of Rayovski and joined a small group of Russian partisans and Soviet activists from Kopyl. Later, he served as captain of the Jewish Zhokov brigade (the Chapayev brigade, the brigade of Maior Kapustin).

There were also many Jews who did not enter the Ghettos, but rather went out to the forests at the time of the invasion of the Nazi soldiers, or hid with farmers that they knew. For the most part, these were the rural Jews, who lived in villages that did not obey the order of the Germans to concentrate the Jews in regional cities, as if they suspected the impending disaster. These also included Jews who worked in the Soviet administration and the Communist party, who knew what was awaiting them at the hands of the cruel invader.

* * *

The brigade of General Maior Bozhanka also took along several light cannons and battalion mortars during its operations of incursion from the Kopyl region to the Grodno and Bialystok areas.

Zhokov's brigade, headed by Glichik, disbanded the end of 1943. The Jewish partisans separated into smaller groups among the Russian brigades that operated in the Kopyl region.

* * *

Commander Glichik, who was very familiar with the area for he had lived there for several decades, knew that the Germans, upon their entry to Kopyl, took out many Russian prisoners to be killed, and buried them with their arms (near the town of Staritsa). Along with the group of partisans, he removed the rusty arms from the communal grave, and thereby obtained 33 guns, 4 machine guns, and thousands of bullets. Afterwards, the brigade conducted an attack upon the families of guards that were on German service, confiscated their property and purchased arms with the help of farmers with whom they were acquainted.

Eight Jews from the above mentioned brigade, who worked in the armament storehouse in Stolbtsy prior to their flight into the forest and remembered the building plan and its passageways, went there in the darkness of the night and removed 12 guns and 200 bullets from the attic of the storehouse. Thanks to the arms that they obtained, they were able to accept additional young people into the brigade, who were trained for battle.

(From "The Book of Jewish Partisans" and the story of M. Kahanovitch.)

Leiwik Peker and his wife Roza

Footnotes:

1. I am not sure of the meaning of this.
2. A zuz is a Talmudic term for a coin of a certain value. It is best known from the Chad Gadya song at the end of the Passover Haggadah "One kid, which father bought for two zuzim".
3. The Hebrew is Lodaim. I am not sure of the meaning.
4. The term here is 'bokin mokin'. I am not sure of the meaning of this expression.
5. A derogatory term for gentiles.
6. The term here is Katrina, which is apparently a reference to some sort of musical device.

[Page 251]

Romanova
(Lenino, Belarus)
53°03' 27°14'

Working the Land in Romanova

Translated by Mendel Y. Spalter

The Jews in our small town worked by the sweat of their brow on land they had leased from for the local squire, Prince Wittgenstein, for some twenty years. The squire leased it to them for only six years at a time. Each time the lease was renewed, the Jews were prepared to leave the lands if he decided to raise the rent to the point that they would be unable to pay.

Nevertheless, when they could pay what he wanted, they did not slacken in their work. Twenty families from our small town, who each rented up to ten "*desyatin*" of fertile land, went out to work until evening. Just like the Christian peasants, who owned their own land, the Jews too farmed the land responsibly, and fertilized and cleared it. They treated it as though they were farming their own land.

Had the people of our town been able to afford purchasing the fields for themselves, they would truly have been fortunate. Instead of the substantial amounts they now spent on annual rental, they would be spending for whatever they might personally have needed.

Large numbers of people in other cities wanted to leave their business, (for many were doing badly in their businesses,) and begin working the land. Indeed, it seemed that only with that would they have enough to live. Proof of this desire is the charity of philanthropists among our people. They willingly distributed large sums of money to this end; and even greater proof are the small donations that were reported to be coming from all corners of our blessed land. One may further call to mind the Rabbis in the small cities, whose number is great in our land, who called upon the leaders of each city to awaken to truly rescue the thousands of the wretched, to establish for them a hopeful solution for living tranquilly in the places they resided.

(Ish Yehudi Safra (A Jewish scholar) / "*Hatzfirah*," #31, 10th of *Elul* 5640 – 1880)

Concerning the matter of the Jewish farmers, on December 26, 1844, an addendum was added to the law of April 13, 1835, giving rights to those Jews wishing to be farmers, as well as practical means to subsidize the farmers' needs. These were the first rights and subsidization given by the government.

1. Permission was granted to Jews who had reached the age of military service, to be able instead to farm the land.

2. Those who would settle on government land in the western provinces, would receive a plot of about twenty "*desyatin*," as well as be exempt from meat taxes amounting to 100 silver rubles per family. Additionally, the government would build them houses and provide them with everything necessary for the work, as well as many other rights.

According to reports received, it seems that from among 144,465 Jews living in the Minsk province, 2727 of them were considered farmers.

Despite all the benefits and subsidies provided through the government

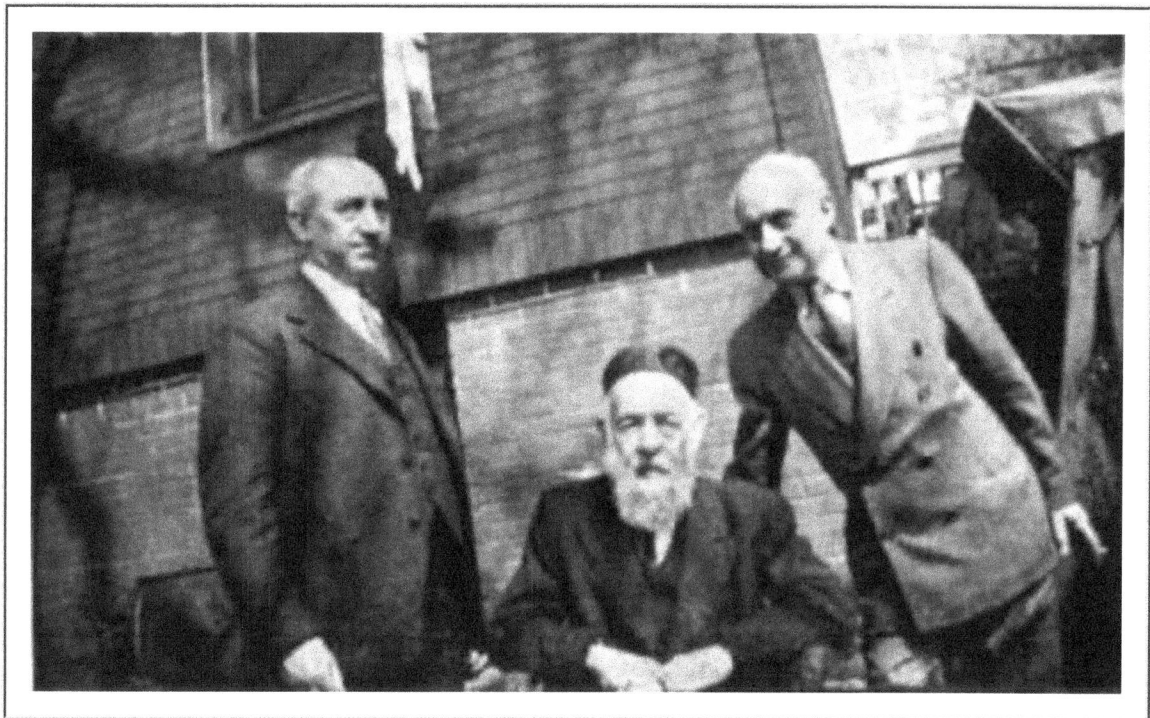

Shmuel Dumanitz (in the center - their father Reb Asher the teacher) and Dr. Aharon Dumanitz in the USA

Baruch Dumanitz and his daughter Hadassah in Israel

[Page 252]

to Jewish farmers, not many were stirred, and they did not decide to change from being city people, to villagers and full-fledged farmers.

According to reported figures, we reckon that around 15 of every 1000 Jews worked as farmers in this province. However, only a third of them worked on their own, in the fields, while most sufficed with working the patch around their homes, and they would rent out the fields [they had from the government,] to the peasants. They [1]would say, that according to Jewish belief, one may not work on land in the Diaspora, and it is therefore impossible to appeal to them to become farmers, for it is not in the spirit of their beliefs.

It says in the book[2]: "If Jews were to rent patches of land and larger plots, they would endeavor, with all their energy, to hold on to them permanently. And if it would not be worthwhile for them to do so, they would destroy every piece of wood—cut down every tree in the forests, neglect fertilizing the earth. The land would become barren; rich, fertile land would become a wasteland. They would destroy every good, worthwhile structure and not leave even one stone in place." One of our, so to speak, sympathizers, distanced himself from that group and said, ("The Voice," fourth year,) as in the "book of records," that many obstacles in the belief of the Jews prevents them from dedicating themselves to working the land.

(From the "record book" (the section on statistics, Minsk province, p. 69 – 1878)

Translator's footnotes:

1. The non-Jews of the area.
2. An anti-Semitic publication – see the end of the section.

[Page 252]

My Town, Romanova

by Dr. Aharon Dumanitz

The town of Romanova is nearby to Slutsk. The distance between them is around twenty kilometers. Most of its inhabitants, around two hundred families, are Russian peasants, and there are a number of Jewish families. Our home was in the yard of one of the peasants, and the rent was eight rubles a year, as well as an additional two rubles for the shed where we kept our cow.

R. Itsheh Gittes, teaches Gemara in Romanova. (In the days of Nicholas I, teachers were required to take a photo without a hat for a teacher's certificate).

All the yards and the houses were built in a specific pattern, as in a colony: There was a long row of houses, with straw-thatched roofs, and two rooms each; one to live in and the other for storage. Behind the house were a shed, a stable for horses, a pig pen [1], and a barn for the wheat. Behind the property was a range of vegetable gardens and fields of wheat, as well as orchards with different types of trees belonging to the owner. Aside from this, there was one cherry tree, which the wife of the owner allowed me to climb with my satchel in tow, from which I could cut fruit for my mother, to my heart's content, so long as the owner did not know of it.

After the harvest season, the peasant would give us some of the produce of his gardens and fields. The peasant-woman would also sell us during the winter, at a cheap price, something from the pen for our needs. We thus lived on good terms with our neighbor – a peasant family and a Jewish teacher.

After Passover [2], my father arranged for me to begin studying with a teacher of children beginning school, although I already knew well how to read in the prayer book. In the second grade, they learned, besides to read from the prayer book, also *Chumash*[3] for beginners, where each lesson included several verses of the *Chumash*. Each Thursday, every student would have to read his verse aloud, but only some of us knew how to recite and translate it correctly. I moved around from one study group to another, and by the time I reached seven years old, I was already learning the *Talmud*. At a certain point during this time, I was in my father's group, where my father taught *Tanach*[4], with the commentary of the *Malbim*, as well as two pages (a *daf*) of the *Talmud* each week. My father had a talk with his friend Reb Itsheh Gittes, who was a great scholar and who had left teaching, and they decided to establish a *Yeshiva* for younger students. This school drew several youths who were younger than I was, and Itsheh Gittes served as the *Rosh Yeshiva*[5]. Another three years passed for me in this manner, the years of the end of my youth in my birthplace, the town of Romanova.

The rabbi of Romanova, named Reb Pinchas Goldberg, was known only as "The Miracle Worker of Romanova." He was born in Meltz, near Pruzhni [6], from where he came to Romanova to assume the rabbinical post until his passing.

From the entire area, people came to him in droves with *Halachic*[7] questions, for advice, and to ask for his blessing.

He was also well respected by the non-Jews of the town and of the surrounding villages, and upon meeting him in the road, they would remove their hats to him in respect and give him their blessings. Throughout his lifetime, he made do with little, and from his meager livelihood from selling salts and yeast, he also gave to the needy. He passed away in the year 5685, at an age greater than ninety years old.

The rabbi of Hadera (Israel), Rabbi Yoseph Dov *HaKohen*, is his son-in-law.

* * *

Rabbi Moshe Mordechai Fras was a great scholar, and a well-known communal worker in Warsaw.

He was born in Romanova on the seventh of Adar 5620; excelled in his abilities, possessed a vast knowledge of the *Talmud* and its foremost commentaries, and was widely read in books of philosophy and Judaica. At the age of sixteen, in 5636, he contributed to "The Voice."[8] He then moved to Warsaw, where he became known as a national figure, and he published essays and articles in " *Hatzfira*[9], and various other news periodicals.

(Pictured in this section is Reb Itsheh Gitte's, a teacher of *Talmud* in Romanova. He is pictured without a hat [10].)

Translator's footnotes:

1. Some poultry etc
2. Of a specific year not mentioned in the article, when the writer was a young boy of around five years old.
3. The Five books of Moses, the Torah.
4. The entire scripture, including the Five Books of Moses, the Prophets and the Writings.
5. The position of dean of the *Yeshiva*, who would teach the older students.
6. Was unable to verify the names of these places.
7. Questions in Torah law.

8. Apparently, some publication in Romanova.
9. (Literally, the Dawn.) One of the first Hebrew newspapers of the 19th century.
10. During the reign of Tsar Nikolai I, teachers were required to have a photograph taken without a hat, although religious Torah teachers would generally wear may ho be without a *Yarmulkeh* (a head covering), and that may be why it explains his not wearing a hat.

[Page 253]

The Rabbi of Romanova

by Baruch Dumanitz

I wish to add several facets to the general picture: Everyone recognized him as a miracle worker, and all were therefore respectful in his presence, because everything he expressed, whether a blessing or a curse, became fulfilled.

There were several occurrences related about him:

Chaim Simcha Miezel had an argument with the rabbi concerning wheat for Passover, and he insulted the rabbi in public, saying he was mad. The rabbi replied: "If so, may <u>you</u> indeed become mad." The argument happened in the synagogue on *Shabbat*. That night, Saturday evening, Chaim Simcha traveled to Slutsk, to obtain more wheat for Passover without the rabbi's consent. During the trip, when he stopped to water the horses, a wild dog attacked and bit him. After about a week of terrible suffering from his wounds, Chaim Simcha died.

In one of the villages between Romanova and Kapyl there lived a Jew with a large family, who rented a flourmill from one of the local princes. At one point, a certain gentile conspired against the Jew and had the mill taken from him. The Jew came to the rabbi to pour out his bitter heart. The rabbi summoned the gentile and cautioned him to return the mill and he would not be punished from heaven, but the gentile did not heed his words. A short time later, the gentile got himself trapped in the millstone, and was injured and died. The prince returned the flourmill to the Jew, and he was again able to support his family.

Two Jewish youths were traveling to Timkowitz by way of Romanova. They passed Romanova on Friday, just before sundown, before candle-lighting time. The rabbi was standing at his door gathering Jews for a *Minyan*[1], (this was during the Bolshevik era). As they passed, upon recognizing them as Jews, the rabbi invited them to stay with him for *Shabbat*, but they refused. He then said to them, "You will spend *Shabbat* with me regardless," but they laughed and continued on their way. Twenty or so minutes passed, and they were brought back, injured, to the rabbi's house, where they spent the entire *Shabbat*, and afterward were taken to the hospital in Slutsk What had happened, was that as their wagon was crossing the bridge, the horse died, and they fell into the river. They were rescued by peasants who brought them to the rabbi's house. They begged the rabbi's forgiveness, and promised never to travel again on *Shabbat*.

A neighbor of the rabbi, a devout, kindhearted Catholic woman who had often presented the rabbi's wife with the best of her produce from her garden and fields, was having great difficulty while giving birth. The rabbi sent his wife, saying "Reizel, go to her, help her out; it is a pity on these fine gentiles." Indeed, everything did turn out well.

During the great fire that occurred around sixty years ago, the gentiles of the area came to rescue the synagogue and the rabbi's neighboring house. The rabbi said to them, "Go and save your church. Instead, I will watch over things here." As known, the entire village burned in that fire, aside from the synagogue, the rabbi's house, and the church.

There was a child who had received a slap in the face from his teacher, and he had problems with his ear as a result. The rabbi blessed him and said: "This is not of much consequence, it will save you from something much worse.". When the time of the draft came, the young man was released from duty as a result, and a short while later, his ear healed as well.

The rabbi married at the age of twenty-five, and continued studying Torah away from home for three years, without seeing his wife. He was a colleague and student of the known "great one" from Minsk. On the night the "great one" [2] from Minsk passed from his world, the rabbi rose at midnight, washed his hands, lit a candle, and sat barefoot on a low stool[3] for an entire hour, not uttering a word. However, he did not explain his actions. The following morning, Motteh the wagon-driver arrived from Minsk and brought the news that "great one" from Minsk had passed away. The rabbi uttered, "That is it…" Until his last day, he was able to read, without glasses, the small print of scholarly works. He was also able to easily crack open nuts with his teeth, like a young man.

He had penetrating green eyes, bushy eyebrows and a deep, compelling voice. I remember him well, as though I have just seen him. The storehouse [4] was just across from his house. He liked to take walks late in the afternoon, with my father of blessed memory, down to the river that flowed pleasantly on the outskirts of town.

Yitzchak Leib Dumanitz, (son of Reb Asher Dumanitz, the melamed in Romanova), an ardent Zionist, and a soldier in the Jewish regiment. He passed away in 1960, in San Diego Ca.

Translator's footnotes:

1. A quorum of ten, essential for prayer.
2. One of the greater Torah scholars of the time, who resided in Minsk.
3. In mourning.
4. Perhaps where the Dumanitz family kept their food.

[Page 254]

Additions

Translated by Mira Eckhaus

Edited by Jane S. Gabin

We were forced to open a section in the book called "Additions," since after ending the printing of the Hebrew part, we received important and valuable material, in which excerpts from the newspapers were supplied to us by Rabbi Reb Nissan Waxman from New York, that reflects the life in Slutsk seventy years ago (among the senders of the correspondences, is Feitel Lifshitz, who was later a professor of economics in Switzerland).

Also included are details which were received later by the members of the Baruch Domnitz family, who were murdered in Kfar Gibton in 1939, and lists about two of our townspeople, who died in Tel Aviv with the closing of this edition.

The editorial staff

From the Newspapers

Slutsk, January 1, 1897.

An amusing situation happened in our city in the last days of 1896. It was said in the city that from the beginning of 1897, the customs duty on schnapps will increase even in the regions that are not yet under the governmental monopoly, up to seven ruble per hin (liquid unit), hence everyone who pays the customs before the New Year according to the old law, will benefit from it.

A wise man will easily understand, that this news raised the panic level to the same level that was at the "grain gate" in 1892. Everyone who had money rushed "to make good deals" with the local people, to buy the schnapps from them, to pay the customs in advance, so that he could avoid the increase in the customs after Rosh Hashanah. And as only the persons who had schnapps were able to pay the customs, a competition arose between our brothers of Israel regarding the purchase of the schnapps from the local people, and as a consequence, its price was more than double its regular fixed price.

In addition, a competition about the loans arose, as there were many borrowers who borrowed money in order to pay the customs according to the old law. Soon our rich brothers, who are usually away from the sight, opened their bundles that were full of money. The artisans and laborers also wanted to benefit from the situation and to get rich as much as possible. The cobbler threw away the awl, the tailor his needle, the builder the meter, because their hands were full of the borrowing and lending "work."

And how great was the commotion and embarrassment in Slutsk at the Cash Gate, when they found out that for every hundred rubles, they paid two gold coins per day! The Treasury house was filled to the brim with those who were in advance to pay the customs of the schnapps on the eve of the Civil New Year.

But how much their embarrassment increased when they were informed that there would be no change in the customs! Everyone left the place, some left upset as their plot to benefit did not succeed, and some left happy because they managed to exploit the borrowers. In any case, it became the talk of the day in Slutsk.

Recently, the "Musar people" from Slobodka established here a permanent yeshiva with their faithful leader. Although this was to the dismay of our dignitaries, and nobody asked for their opinion on the matter, apparently, they relied on the words of Chazal: "It is possible to perform an action in favor of a person even without his knowledge" (*zachin le'adam shelo befanav*).

P. Lifshitz
("HaMelitz", No. 5, 16th of Shebat 5657).

Slutsk, January 12, 1897.

It has already been announced in "HaMelitz" No. 5, about the settlement of the Musar people from Slobodka here. It is no wonder that the readers were surprised to hear that the musar people came to live in Slutsk, even though the opinion of most of our dignitaries was not favorable about them. But be patient, dear readers, and you will hear and know what led to it.

In the last few days, the "Musar people" have multiplied in Slobodka, until there was no place for them to sit there, therefore their leaders searched for another city that would be privileged to house their disciples, who increase the "Musar" in the world. These leaders wrote letters to many cities, asking them to house their disciples; but apparently, their words did not find sympathetic ear. Therefore, they were forced to turn to some of the best of our city, but they did not receive an answer from them either.

When this became known to some of the people of the city of Slutsk, who thought that the yeshiva of the Musar people would be a good business opportunity for them, as they were hoping to be appointed among the ones who would assist them, they called an assembly to discuss what can be done to bring the "Musar people" into our city. (The reader can understand how great is the number of those who living in ignorance from the fact that on the eve of Yom Kippur 5654, they all gathered in one house to discuss how to prevent the evil Cholera disease, God forbid, and they could not find a more proven remedy to stop the plague, but to forbid the youth from reading books from the past). Of course, the assembly resolution was sent to the leaders of the Musar movement, to hurry to come to Slutsk, as the idea was liked by many –

[Page 255]

so they wrote - and for the rest whose opinion is not comfortable with them, they convinced them until they said, "We want it!" On the basis of such letters, the "Musar people" built their nest here, in the Zaretza lot, which stands at the edge of the city.

A wise man will easily understand how many disputes and quarrels will be caused here among the people of our city due to this issue. Don't we already have enough disagreements, quarrels and fights that we need to add to them these as well? After all, their yeshiva in Slutsk is to the dismay of our dignitaries and not in the best interest of the material and spiritual condition of our city, so why were they so urged to come here, against the will of the majority of the residents of our city, but only based on the will of some Jews, despised people, that their entire desire is to earn money? After all, there is no great blessing for Israel than peace among the people, and if it will be disturbed by the presence of the "Musar people" here, then for what reason should they come here.

These days an impure case happened in our city. In one house a mother and her daughter became ill. The doctor prescribed a medicine for the daughter to be taken orally, and carbolic vinegar for the mother to be used to bandage the wound, but the maid in the house replaced the prescriptions and gave the girl to drink the carbolic vinegar. The girl died that day in severe agony.

Last week, one insane Jew froze in the street of the city. He wandered the streets of the city all night and no one bothered to carry him to his home.

HaMabit
("HaMelitz", 30th of Shebat 5657).

Note, to remove slander,

As it is well known, the late Rabbi Reb Moshe Binyamin Tomshov signed many of his articles, or in his comments on the words of others in the Torah collection "Yagdil Torah" in Slutsk, in the name of "Mabit,"which is comprised of the initials of his name.

I was interested in finding out about this and spoke with him on the above letter, if he wrote the above words. He told me firmly that he did not write them and that he was one of the closest friends of the Gaon Reb Isser Zalman Meltzer, who came with his yeshiva from Slobodka to Slutsk, and he could have not written such rude things. Apart from that, he even assured me that all his life he signed his name "Mabit" and never "HaMabit".

Rabbi Nissan Waxman

Slutsk, January 24, 1897.

The members of the "Craft Lovers" esteemed association will not rest from renewing good and useful things. In these days, the members gathered at a house to discuss how to improve the moral condition of the boys who are learning a craft under their supervision. And they decided that they would teach the boys Hebrew and another foreign language. After it became clear that the association's fund could no longer finance teachers' salaries, the members turned their requests to many of the enlightened young people who would be willing to dedicate their time to teaching these poor children for free. These requests found sympathetic ear and many of our boys agreed to take part in this mission.

One of the esteemed and the largest associations in our city is "Linat HaTzedek," which was founded on the third of Tevet 5649, through the intercession of the preacher Reb Zondil Maccabi Shalita, when he came to our city to preach his sermons. This association, who number about a thousand people, does all kind of good deeds, such as supporting the patient when they become ill, helping them to heal, staying with them at night, serving them and fulfilling their desires. In addition, the association has all kinds of tools and medicines that are necessary for various diseases, and it lends them to anyone who wants them. This is intended not only for the poor, who cannot afford to buy them, but also to the middle-class people.

The reader can understand the extent of the association's success in our city from the account that it has now issued and pasted on all the doors of the prayer houses in our city. This account lists of the association's income and expenses for the years 5649-5657:

From the 3rd of Tevet 5649 to 19th of Shebat 5650 the association's income during all these years - from individual donations, from Midrash schools, from the Eve of Yom Kippur and from the members' contributions - amounts to a total of 1952.65 rubles. The expenses for all these years for medicines and doctors, wine for the sick, purchase and repair of tools, stationery and notebooks for regular use and fixed costs amounts to 1849.85 rubles. Only a total of 103.50 rubles remains in cash in the association's treasury. We hope that the members will continue with their blessed work in the association and they will be a blessing to us.

A resident of the city
("Hamelitz", 7th of Adar B, 5657).

Slutsk, 17th Adar B, 5657.

Today, after a long illness, the Dayan Rabbi Reb Meir, the Gaon Reb Pesach, passed away. He served as a Dayan in our city for fifteen years. The stress and distress, and a bitter life led the deceased to his grave. Only after his death, as is customary in Israel, did the community know how to cherish the deceased; they collected a sum of money for the support of his family, lest they collapse. A number of mourners eulogized him and the whole nation came in tears.

Ben David

"The Torah and the musar", Rabbi Reb Meir Faimer of Slutsk wrote an article in this name against the "Musar people" and stood by their opponents in the great dispute that flared up between the great rabbis of Lithuania. At the end of the article, he came out with very sharp words against the class leaders in Slobodka and Slutsk.

("Hamelitz", No. 56, 17th of Adar B, 5657).

Once again, Rabbi Reb Meir Faimer repeated his firm opposition to the Slobodka boys who were brought here without the "agreement from several important leaders and dignitaries of the city."

("Hamelitz", No. 57, 18th of Adar B, 5657).

Slutsk - during Chol HaMoed Pesach (the intermediate days of Passover), there were elections for collectors and leaders for the Association of "Craft Lovers."But the elections were without order and regime and they did not lack cheating. For example, the election balls that are always picked up secretly, so that everyone can express their free opinion, were missing this time, and here they only asked the voters for their opinion. It goes without saying that not everyone revealed their true opinion, and it became a mockery in the whole city. Such elections will not bring much reward for the "Craft Lovers" Association.

Feitel Lifshitz
("Hamelitz", No. 91, 3rd Iyar 5657).

Slutsk, June 10.

These days, a heartwarming case was discussed in the office of the magistrate's court: an old father complained before the local magistrate's court judge, for his honor

[Page 256]

that was desecrated by his beloved son, and he also demanded that his son would give him a monthly allowance, as he is old and does not have strength to work anymore.

The judge ruled the son's sentence, "properly," to be imprisoned for three months in the prison for insulting his father, and the son would give a monthly allowance of 6 rubles to his father from this day forward. This ruling became the main conversation's topic in our city. This ruling will be an example for all the rich sons, who do not agree to support their parents when they grow old and cannot work and make a living. And there is hope that peace and tranquility will be upon the poor fathers in our city.

An eye witness
("Hamelitz", No. 135, 30th of Sivan 5657).

Slutsk, 25th of Av 5657.

Last week an event happened here that became the talk of the town, and here is the event:

On Wednesday, Parashat Akev, a man in fancy clothes came to the city, wrapped in long clothes and a silk hat on his head with long sidelocks, with an average height and a small yellow beard. His appearance and the expression of his face showed that he was a man of faith. And he introduced himself to the people of the city as the chief manager of one of the large trading houses in Lodz, and when they asked him what prompted him to come here, he answered that his lord, who trade in manufactured goods, had sent goods to Bobroisk for a total of eight thousand rubles to various groceries, and as the goods were halfway there, he received a telegram, that the receivers of the goods on credit are about to go bankrupt. That's why his lord sent him urgently to the Liachowitz station to delay the goods. And meanwhile, he came here to prostrate himself on the graves of his ancestors, which he had not visited for many years.

To clearly prove that he runs a large trading house, he took out many promissory notes in the names of different people, checks, and also a promissory note on the name of a famous gentleman from Bobroisk, who bought goods from him for fifteen thousand rubles.

He planned another ruse in order to extract from the merchants information about where each of them buys and for what amount he buys and how much he owes to the merchant from Lodz. The swindler did not lodge as a guest in a hotel, but in a private person's house, saying that he brought a lot of money with him and he was afraid to spend the night in a guest inn.

Many merchants wanted to make a trade alliance with him, and paid him for doing successful business. And the people who trade in fabrics flocked to him to enter into a trade alliance with him, and in a short time the swindler collected a decent sum and on the evening of the holy Shabbat, he disappeared and his traces were not known.

Feitel Lifshitz
("Hamelitz", No. 186, 2nd of Elul 5657).

A very noble and honorable guest, the Gaon Reb Meir Faimer from Slutsk, is now staying in our city (Minsk).

Last week he consulted with the great men of Minsk, its dignitaries and scholars, with H D. Pines, B. Zeldovitz, H. Ettinger, A. Rappaport, Bernstein, and more, regarding the Musar people, and the above-mentioned Gaon expressed his opinion, which was already known to them. After everyone agreed with the opinion of the Gaon, they gathered and agreed to ask from the Gaon Rabbi Reb Eliyahu David Rabinovitz, who is one of the members of the associations of the "Musar people,"to hear his opinion, and argue among themselves.

("Hamelitz", No. 251, 1st Kislev, 5658).
M.

Slutsk - These days, a school for Jewish girls has been opened here, with the permit of the Minister of the Vilna district, and the tuition fee for a girl is 4 rubles per year. The rent was paid by the City Clerk's Office. All sixty places in the school were quickly filled; many girls who were eager to learn were not accepted due to lack of places. After all, what is one school for girls in a city that has about twenty thousand Jewish people? And even though this school is intended only for poor girls, whose parents cannot afford to pay a teacher's fee, nevertheless a large number of middle-class girls was found among the students, because this school was the only one in our city, while the boys have here a beginners' school that has two departments, apart from the preparatory school. Therefore, our enlightened people would do well if they would try to establish a large beginners' school for girls, similar to the beginners' school for boys. And the blessings of the girls who are eager to gain knowledge shall be upon them.

The "Craft Lovers" association, which was founded here about ten years ago by distinguished women, is very successful, and its financial situation is better than ever. During the year, the association handed over thirty boys to various artisans, and the association does not only give wages to those who learn the craft, but also supports the boys who need it with food and clothes. The association also hired a Russian and Hebrew teacher for them, who will teach them for two hours in the evening. May the name of the founders and the inspectors be blessed.

A resident of the city
("Hamelitz", No. 273, 27th of Kislev 5555).

Slutsk. - With the efforts of the honorable Dr. A. Meltzer, the "Bnei Zion" Association was founded in our city, with two hundred members, and the "Bnot Zion" Association, with one hundred members.

Now the association is trying to open a library for books with a place to read them. A decent amount has already been collected for this purpose.

Last week, the "Bonei Zion" association merged with the "Zionists" association, which was founded nine months ago, and has 40 members. It was thanks to the great efforts of the honorable H. Feinberg. Now they will have a central committee that will spread the idea of nationalism and make it the property of the people and not just for privileged individuals. It will also arrange the holiday of the Maccabees and will also consider the order of education in our city.

Our congregation is now like a widow, because its rabbi left (the Ridbaz) and went to America to sell his book there, and the rabbi on his behalf is also busy now, because the days of the elections are near.

A. Zislotsky
("Hamelitz", No. 254, 1900, 10th of Kislev, 5661).

Slutsk, January 25, 1901.

Anyone who has not seen the "Tu BiShvat" celebration that was held on Monday of this week, by the "Bonei Zion" Association, has not seen pure, inartificial national joy in our city.

The governing body of the association did not send invitations to the residents of our city, of course, but the rumor was enough that the Zionists would celebrate a national evening and already gathered at the designated time multitudes of people from everywhere, from all the parties in our city, until the hall was filled to the brim. Several speakers gave their speeches in honor of the evening and told the listeners about the cold-hearted people of many of the citizens of our city, and taught them to know their national duty. A choir of the association sang a selection of Zionist songs and also read national songs

[Page 257]

full of emotion, holiness and love of the nation. After that, there was a table of delicacies from the fruits of the land.

About one hundred rubles were collected for the construction of the association's library. The evening left a strong impression on those gathered.

Fondly remembered are the hardworking activists Dr. Meltzer, Mr. Yitzhak Feinberg and the association's secretary Mr. S. Beilin, who have worked diligently since the foundation of the association until now.

They are a blessing to our people!

Yehuda Leib Rabinowitz
("HaMelitz", No. 25, 23rd of Shebat, 5661).

Slutsk, Holy Shabbat Eve, Parashat Va'era, 5663.

Yesterday, on Thursday, an honored guest, the Gaon Reb Yitzchak Ya'akov Reines Shalita, came here. He gave a wonderful speech about Zion at the Beit Midrash and his words penetrated the hearts of the listeners and they decided to found a Mizrahi association here.

The next day he appeared at the "Etz Chaim" Yeshiva and gave a lesson in the Torah's innovations, which was also seasoned a little with legend. Here too his words made a great impression among the two hundred listeners and he was also very excited by his visit there.

("Hamelitz, No. 22, 1903).

Slutsk - The "Mizrachi" in our city is doing well, and has already gained more than a hundred members of the city's orthodox and its dignitaries. The head of the yeshiva Achmark was elected as the chairman of the committee. The "Mizrachi" should soon establish Shas and Mishnayot societies. The other Zionists also excel in their actions. The "Kadima" Association opened lately a warm banqueting house where you will find more than ten newspapers. Many people from all the different parties visit this house. The "Hebrew Speakers" Association is also doing well, and the number of its members is growing day by day. The girls of our city, who had been standing at a distance until now, woke up from their slumber and several associations of "Bnot Zion" were founded lately and many girls began to learn the past language.

Y. Ganiandski
("HaMelitz", No. 69, 1903).

Slutsk - In the name of the "Mizrachi" association and in the name of all the residents of our city, we thank and bless the rabbi and the preacher, Reb Mordechai Meir Zilberman, Av Beit Din, for the eulogy of the Gaon and the Tzadik, Reb Yosile of Slonim. He also lamented and reflected on the Kishinev victims. He spoke a lot about the situation of the people of Israel in general and about the idea of Zionism in particular. His words made a strong impression on the listeners and everyone burst into tears. May the Lord and all our rabbis lift up the miracle of Zion and let the hope of the people of Israel come from the Lord who dwells in Zion and Jerusalem.

Head of the committee, **Avraham Abba Raskin**
The treasurer of the committee, **Yosef Harkavi**
("HaMelitz", No. 110, 1903).

Moshe Fleischtsik, a soldier in the "Tsar's army," the son of Shimon Leib, the head of The Jewish folk musicians' band in Slutsk

A group of soldiers from the Hebrew regiment in 1918. Among those sitting from right to left the second Shlomo Simbol, now in Yad Eliyahu (the son-in-law of Shimshon Leib Fleischtsik of Slutsk)

[Page 258]

The Bereaved Family

by Hadassah

Translated by Mira Eckhaus

Edited by Jane S. Gabin

The mother, Mina Domnitz

She was the daughter of Reb Yaakov Meir and Rachel Golda Peliak. Her father was known in Slutsk as "Yankel Dichtyarnik," a grocery store owner and a Torah scholar. Her mother, Rachel Golda, was known as a charitable woman who helped poor families, and Mina inherited this trait from her mother. She helped anyone who needed help.

She was a motherly figure and took care of all the housework and raising the children. She worked from dawn to dusk in the house, in the garden, in the chicken coop and in the barn, and at the same time she always found time to listen to what was going on in the village and at public gatherings. The difficult life in the village of Gibton affected her health, but she was full of hope for the future: "soon the children will grow up and help support the household." Among the families who registered for settlement in the village of Warburg was the Domnitz family, but suddenly disaster came and destroyed everything.

The eldest son Yerachmiel

He was two and a half years old when he immigrated to the Land of Israel with his parents in 1925.

He was educated from the age of 3 in the kindergarten in Acre. He learned in a school in Rehovot until the age of 14 and then started working. He worked as a packer in an orchard, at a factory for trees, "Pri Pri," in addition to his much work at home, in the garden and in the barn. He was among the outstanding children in his class and among the best gymnasts in "HaPoel." He was a member of the "Haganah" in the signaling and communication company. He read and wrote stories and lyrical poems. His teachers predicted greatness for him.

He was quiet and modest, he did not stand out and was not boastful of his qualities and talents. He carried the burden of the family with love, understanding and responsibility and thought about the bright future expected to him in the settlement.

On the night of the disaster, Yerachmiel was in one of the guard posts. When he heard the sound of the gunshots, he hurried home to see how his mother and brothers were doing. When he reached the balcony of the house, he was hit by the murderers' bullets and fell covered in his blood. He was brought to Hadassah in Tel Aviv with severe injuries. He asked not to inform his father, who was lying in the next room in the surgical ward, nor to grieve him. After 4 days of terrible agony, he died. He was buried on the 13th of Adar 5699.

The sons Chaimke and Emanuelke

The lovers and the pleasant ones that did not part each other in their life and in their death. They excelled in painting and writing songs. Chaimke's poems were printed in the journal "Davar liyladim."

* * *

There, in the land of Judah, on one of the lovely hills, four people are sleeping under the branches of a thick tree.

They slept that way undisturbed. And even when the morning came, the sleeping ones did not wake up from their sleep, they enjoy their rest.

The wind blew slowly and shook the tree's branches, birds sang to the Creator

And when the darkness arrived, I came quietly to the trees, sat down, listened to the sound of the howling of the mournful wind.

And I waited and waited…

Will the sleeping ones wake up?

Miriam Maharshak

by S. B.

Translated by Mira Eckhaus

Edited by Jane S. Gabin

Miriam Maharshak, the butcher's wife and philosopher, the mother of a deep-rooted and extensive family, the religious and Zionist activist, who did countless deeds and was an object of admiration, has passed away.

She was born 84 years ago in Slutsk, in White Russia, to Reb Zachariah, a "regular" merchant, who was known in the city for knowing the Shas by heart.

Together with her husband, Reb Shmuel Maharshak, the author of "Shmuel's meditations," who was one of the Zionist leaders, she established in her home in Slutsk, the center of the Zionist underground in the years 1920-1923.

On a winter night in 1923, she left Slutsk with her family on her way to the United States, and two of her children left behind. That night a trial was held in Slutsk against five Zionists, among whom was her daughter. In the United States, she was active in the Rochester community and the "Mizrahi wives" movement, and as in Soviet Russia, her home was open to all Zionists and pioneers. After her husband died and most of her children immigrated to Israel, she uprooted from her comfortable home in the diaspora and immigrated to the Land of Israel.

She lived her last ten years in Tel Aviv, in the Bitzaron neighborhood, she was full of love, activity and zest for life. She acted for the building of the synagogue in the neighborhood and for bringing the hearts of its residents closer together.

[Page 259]

Baruch Lifshitz
(Died on 18th of Iyar 5721, 4.5.1961)

by C. H.

Translated by Mira Eckhaus

Edited by Jane S. Gabin

Apparently, this is so strange: a man lives his best years. He is in his full power, multi-tasking, full of energy, active in public life, he doesn't know what a disease is. And suddenly – he falls ill, he is confined to his bed for several weeks, and dies.

* * *

Baruch had been lively since his youth and dedicated himself to political life. He studied in high school and reached the higher classes. He did not get carried away by the current of careerism, he did not take the easy way, and helped those who swim against the current, who hold the flag of Zionism.

He excelled in the clarity of thought, in the gift of speech. He was well versed in what was happening in the wider world. In the school, there were circles, whose members would submit reviews from the newspapers, each about a different country. In that period, there were wide discussions on the question of the Ruhr region and the Saar region and the annexation of the Allies who defeated Germany in the First World War. Baruch was familiar with this question, he knew it from the bottom up and lectured in the circle on this topic.

He worked with all his zeal in the Zionist youth Histadrut "Kadima," which operated underground. He was among its active members, and held responsible positions. When he and four other members printed the movement's newspaper, they were banned by the G.P.O. A trial was conducted against these five members and he was released due to his young age, along with three other members.

In 1924, Zionists' arrests were held all over Russia. Many were banned in Slutsk, among them, of course, Baruch. The members were imprisoned in the prison in Minsk for about four months and finally the verdict was given: exile to the Urals for three years, or deportation to Israel.

On September 2, 1924, the deportees from Minsk and Slutsk arrived in Israel on the Italian ship "Milano." They were divided into two groups. The left part was associated with the "Ahdut HaAvoda" party (not to be confused with the "Ahdut HaAvoda" party nowadays) and was accepted into Kibbutz Ein Harod to the Ein Tivon company (Ktar Yehezkel). Among those who came from Slutsk that were sent to this company were: Baruch, Ratner, Hazanovitz and Maharshak.

A short time later they started sending the members to different companies of the kibbutz. Baruch was sent to Yagur. He acclimatized very quickly in Israel and wanted to be called by a Hebrew name, therefore he chose the name Amnon.

At first, the members from Slutsk were very close to each other and exchanged letters. Their interest in the fate of the members who remained in Russia was great. There was an urgent need to send money to Russia to support members who remained there and were languishing in prisons and exiled countries. Accordingly, an idea arose to organize a group made up of various members of Kibbutz Ein Harod companies, who would work in Tel Aviv as a construction contractor group and the money they would earn would be sent to Russia. The kibbutz management agreed and the idea began to take shape. The group was called "Help for Russia."

Baruch was enthusiastic about this idea; he invested a lot of energy in the organization of the group and was its center. However, the group did not last long. There was a crisis in Israel at the time, and a great lack of work. The group broke up and left debts. Baruch stayed in Tel Aviv to cover the deficit and pay the debts.

It should be noted that even in the first year of his arrival in Israel he took care of the immigration to Israel of his family from Slutsk, despite the crisis in Israel, and he really succeeded in this.

In 1925, after the union between the right wing of Poalei Zion and S.Z., there was a faction in the "Ahdut HaAvoda" party called "Avuka," whose members were mostly from the right wing of Poalei Zion.

Baruch and several other members from Slutsk were among this group, and he even participated in the magazine *Avuka* that was published by this faction.

In 1926 he went to France, studied chemistry at a university and graduated as a chemical engineer. After completing his studies, he returned to Israel. He worked in various jobs, related to his profession. In 1940 he was the secretary of the student union, members of the Histadrut, at Beit Brenner.

In 1936, he married a woman and had two daughters.

From 1950, he started working in the "Mashbir" as a senior official and continued

working there until his last day.

Apart from his day-to-day work, he carried the burden of public action: he was active in the Engineers' Association, he was a secretary in the Hapoel Secretariat, in the Central Parents' Committee, in the Tenants' Association.

On September 2, 1944, on the 20th anniversary of the arrival of the first group from Minsk and Slutsk to Israel, a meeting was held between the members. On September 2, 1954, a meeting was held again, dedicated to celebrating 30 years in Israel. Baruch was the main initiator of these gatherings; he took the trouble and traveled from place to place and organized them.

Soon it will be 40 years since the group came to Israel, but the place of the main initiator of these gatherings will be taken and he will no longer be with us.

In those days, when he was full of energy and desire for action, after his silver wedding was celebrated, he was overtaken by the evil hand of fate, he fell silent forever.

[Page 260]

The History of the Book

by The Editors

Translated by Mira Eckhaus

Edited by Jane S. Gabin

The idea of commemorating Slutsk and its surroundings was conceived by Slutsk expatriates in Israel, even before the existence of the state. In the beginning, the trend was to dedicate a book of remembrance to this. Later, with the visit to Israel of the representatives of the Slutsk expatriate organizations in New York (Dr. Bunin, Harry Lafrak and his wife and Israel Schwedelson) the trend changed. It was decided to establish Yad Vashem for Slutsk in the form of a public institution, to be named after Slutsk.

After negotiations and discussions, "Beit Slutsk" was established in Magdiel, a pulmonary hospital on behalf of the health maintenance organization. The funds were donated by Slutsk expatriates in New York.

However, we, the initiators of the book, were not satisfied with the establishment of the aforementioned institution and continued to look for ways and handle the publication of the book, which historically is important, in our opinion, more than a public institution. Our tendency was to reflect in the book the nature of the city and the surrounding towns, their way of life and their history over hundreds of years and to bring up characters and memories.

During our work in searching and collecting material, we learned that some time before, this was also dealt with by the late Prof. Rabbi S. Assaf, who received a certain amount of money for it from the pioneer of heavy industry in Israel, the late Mr. Michael Polyak. As is known, he came from the Sialki mansion in the suburbs of Slutsk, where the brothers Michael, Shevah, Nahum and their sisters were born.

For this reason Michael Polyak sought to commemorate his homeland. From the estate of the late Rabbi Assaf, only collections about the Slutsk rabbis and the like came to us.

We turned again to the chairman of the organization of the Slutsk expatriates in New York, and asked for his help in our mission, but he did not believe that this enterprise might come true and therefore refrained from participating with us. In the meantime, Mr. Reichman and his wife visited in Israel, and they responded to our request and promised to devote their time and energy to this matter. And indeed, they kept their promise. When our friends Avraham Meisel and his wife Haike from the Ravitz family, visited in Israel, the idea began to take shape. Upon their return to New York, they founded a group of activists and a committee for the publication of the book was established. This committee was joined by Rabbi Reb Nissan Waxman of Starovin and the member Eliyahu Altman. It is worth noting that upon the request of the member Nachmani from his relative David Ozdan, the latter donated all the paper needed to print the book, in memory of Arozova, his hometown. And in this we express our deep gratitude to him.

The material has been collected and gathered for years: in Israel by Nachum Hinitz and in America by Rabbi Reb Nissan Waxman.

We thank our townsman, the writer Y.D. Berkowitz, who went over the material in large part and guided us with his instructive advice. Our friends, who are active in the New York book committee, who joined the effort and made it possible to publish the book of remembrance, will also be blessed. Especially Rabbi Reb Nissan Waxman, Rabbi Avraham Meisel and Eliyahu Altman.

Zvi Assaf, Nahum Hinitz, Shimshon Nachmani, Zvi Givati

NAME INDEX

www.ingramcontent.com/pod-product-compliance
Lightning Source LLC
Chambersburg PA
CBHW062019090426

42811CB00005B/896